TWENTIETH-CENTURY AMERICA:
Recent Interpretations

Under the General Editorship of
JOHN MORTON BLUM
Yale University

HARCOURT, BRACE & WORLD, INC.
New York Chicago San Francisco Atlanta

TWENTIETH-CENTURY AMERICA:
Recent Interpretations

edited by

BARTON J. BERNSTEIN
Stanford University

and

ALLEN J. MATUSOW
Rice University

TO DAVID M. POTTER

Preface

Although the actuality of the past does not change, perception of the past alters at least once a generation. After the Second World War, scholars challenged many earlier conceptions of events in American history and in so doing shaped interpretations that, until recently, dominated historical inquiry. Even now a new generation of scholars is challenging these accepted interpretations. This volume of essays is designed to introduce students to postwar research on four periods of American history in the twentieth century —the Progressive Era, the Twenties, the New Deal and the Coming of War, and the Era of the Cold War. In selecting the essays for this collection we have chosen to emphasize four themes that are particularly relevant to our time as well as important for understanding the past: business-government relations, race relations, poverty, and the sources and consequences of war.

The relations of big business and government have been a central problem of domestic politics throughout the twentieth century. Reformers, lamenting the subservience of the government to

v

the interests of concentrated capital, have periodically called on the state to bring corporate power to heel. Race relations did not become a major concern of the American people until after the Second World War, but the manner in which previous generations treated the problem illuminates both the present crisis and the limits of earlier social understanding. As for the enduring problem of poverty, Americans have sometimes ignored, sometimes acknowledged, its reality, the response of each generation revealing in large measure its perception of the whole social order. The fourth theme, the sources and consequences of war, has only recently taken on a crucial relevance for domestic society. Until the rise of fascism in the 1930's, American participation in international wars was regarded as exceptional. Since the Second World War, however, war and preparation for war have become a permanent condition of American life. As the Cold War lingers on, critics who fear its effects on domestic society are investigating the consequences of past wars on dissent, distribution of power, and relations among social groups. The essays we have selected are not confined to these four themes; nor do they reflect a single point of view. Wherever possible and desirable, we have established a historical dialogue by presenting differing interpretations of important events or movements.

Each of the four parts of the book is introduced by a brief discussion of the period covered and the problems of historical interpretation it presents. In addition, we have introduced each essay with background information and some critical reflections. Following each introduction to a part and each essay we have appended an annotated bibliography to assist students in their reading and research. The scholarly literature on the period since 1945 will, we hope, be of service to those professors and students interested in the postwar years as a subject for historical inquiry.

The titles in the bibliographies available in paperback are marked by an asterisk. We have generally not included in the bibliography for an essay a title that had previously been mentioned in the bibliography for the part, in the introduction, or in the essay itself.

We gratefully acknowledge the wise counsel of John M. Blum, Otis L. Graham, Jr., and Otis A. Pease, who assisted us in refining this project. Judith A. Ryerson and Silke-Malia Garrels typed the manuscript with unfailing good humor, and Theodore E. Skowronski and Frank Eisenberg aided us in completing the research and checking citations. To Oscar Handlin, director of the Charles Warren Center at Harvard University, where one of us was a Fellow during the year, we owe a debt of gratitude for providing the personnel and facilities that speeded the completion of this project.

BARTON J. BERNSTEIN and ALLEN J. MATUSOW

Contents

PART IV. THE ERA OF THE COLD WAR 345

The Progressive Era

At the turn of the century, a vague disquiet had begun to pervade America. The preceding generation had witnessed the stunning triumphs of industrialism, the near-transformation of America into an urban society, and periodic eruptions of bitter class warfare. As the twentieth century began, the Jeffersonian self-image so long cherished by Americans seemed suddenly obsolete and the individualistic ethic shaped in the rural past, obviously untenable. Historians call the complex, confused, and often contradictory responses to this crisis the progressive movement.

The progressive movement has been most often regarded as a popular revolt against the consequences of the new organization of American life. Traditional accounts emphasize that progressivism was a rebellion against the unfettered power of large corporations and against the political machines that corrupted public institutions and negated democracy. It was also an expression of concern for the innocent victims of the new order: the workers and immigrants confined to slums and exploited by corporations and politicians. Historians customarily note that before 1900 Populists, labor leaders, and fringe intellectuals had failed in their attempt to convert middle-class America to the task of reform. But after 1900 the urban middle classes, especially small businessmen and independent professionals, joined the reform army and gave progressivism its distinctive character.

Particularly since World War II, many historians (most notably Richard Hofstadter in his influential *The Age of Reform* [Knopf, 1955]) have sought to add a new dimension to the traditional interpretation: The progressive movement, they point out, has a paucity of real achievement to show for its passionate rhetoric and energetic activity. Economically secure and essentially optimistic in their social views, middle-class progressives enacted only mild measures that never really threatened existing power relationships. When rural progressives like Wisconsin's great Senator Robert M. La Follette attempted to enact programs to smash corporate power, they found few who would follow them. To democratize the political order, the progressives designed mechanical reforms like the direct primary, which achieved only indifferent success in countering boss rule. As for social justice, the movement on the state level did cause child labor to be outlawed, some protection of women workers to be extended, and programs of workmen's compensation to be initiated, but the United States remained far behind Europe in the field of social welfare. At the end of the progressive era, unskilled workers were still unorganized, poverty was still the lot of the majority of Americans, and, in spite of the income tax amendment, inequalities in the distribution of the national wealth remained essentially uncorrected. Recognizing how limited the progressive accomplishments were, many historians in the last twenty years have judged the movement as essentially conservative.

Some recent writers, such as Robert Wiebe, Gabriel Kolko, Samuel Hays, and James Weinstein, find the progressive movement "conservative" not because it seemed to offer only mild opposition to big businessmen, but because big business itself played a major role in shaping so-called progressive legislation. This new research successfully challenges the old notion of progressive politics as a simple dualistic struggle between middle-class reformers and major business interests. Thus in the great battle to regulate railroads, shippers fought for governmental authority to lower rates, and in time the railroads themselves saw in federal regulation a way to curb harmful competition within the industry. Because they desired efficiency, businessmen participated in other areas of reform such as conservation of natural resources and municipal reform movements. Gabriel Kolko has even argued that progressivism was dominated by big businessmen who sought escape from competition and instability through federal regulation of their industries. In Kolko's view progressivism was not conservative because it did so little to curb business; rather, it was conservative because it did so much to assist the corporate order in achieving its present dominance. In attempting to erect a new framework to accommodate the events of the progressive era, Kolko and Weinstein have been criticized for not adequately explaining the complexity of social forces operating in that period, but their work has gained recognition for casting discredit on the traditional interpretation. As a result, at this stage of historical inquiry many scholars of progressivism are faced by confusion and seem far away from finding a satisfying new synthesis.

The foreign policy of the progressive years was marked by continued commercial expansion abroad and repeated intervention in Latin America. Adhering to his Big Stick policy, President Theodore Roosevelt "liberated" the Panamanian isthmus and intervened elsewhere in the Caribbean with marines. In many ways the conduct of foreign policy in these years supports those historians who now argue that governments in the progressive era actually best served the interests of big business. Although Roosevelt usually emphasized the nation's mission and duty while embarking on his imperialist ventures, President Taft proudly labeled his own policy "Dollar Diplomacy" and openly linked his efforts to the needs and desires of financiers and industrialists who wanted markets and stability. Though most Americans, including many progressives, were not deeply interested in foreign policy during the years before World War I, a few, like Senators Robert La Follette and William Borah, opposed Taft's policies because they objected to American imperialism. The State Department, the Wisconsin progressive charged, was becoming "a trading post for Wall Street interests" (*La Follette's Weekly,* June 29, 1912). Repudiating "Dollar Diplomacy" and explicitly denying that "a gunboat goes with each bond," Wilson promised that the United States would be more successful in expanding trade if it did not seek special favors or resort to coercion. Nevertheless, to establish the stability essential for an expanding trade and to protect American security in the hemisphere, the Wilson Administration in practice continued to intervene in Latin America. Paul Birdsall's article in this section makes an interesting case for the contention that concern for markets played an important role in Wilson's European diplomacy before World War I.

SUGGESTED READING

Richard Hofstadter's *The Age of Reform* * (Knopf, 1955) is a sensitive, speculative, and important interpretation of progressivism. His concept of the "status revolution," based in part on George Mowry's "The California Progressive and His Rationale; A Study in Middle-Class Politics," *Mississippi Valley Historical Review,* XXXVI (Sept., 1949), 239–50, has been criticized by many historians, including Norman Wilensky in *Conservatives in the Progressive Era: The Taft Republicans of 1912* (Univ. of Florida Press, 1965).

Eric Goldman in *Rendezvous with Destiny* * (Knopf, 1952) understands progressivism as part of the healthy liberal reform movement. Samuel Hays' *The Response to Industrialism* * (Univ. of Chicago Press, 1957) and Robert Wiebe's *The Search for Order* * (Hill & Wang, 1967) are ambitious efforts to place the reform movement in a broader context of responses to instability.

John M. Blum's *The Republican Roosevelt* * (Harvard Univ. Press, 1954) is a perceptive analysis of Roosevelt's conservatism and is an outgrowth of his work with Elting Morison *et al.,* eds., *The Letters of Theodore Roosevelt* (Harvard Univ. Press, 1951–58, 8 vols.), an indispensable source for understanding Roosevelt. George Mowry's *The Era of Theodore Roosevelt, 1900–1912* * (Harper & Row, 1958) remains the best volume on

Roosevelt's presidency and can be supplemented for the later years by Mowry's *Theodore Roosevelt and the Progressive Movement* * (Univ. of Wisconsin Press, 1946), which reveals more of an agrarian bias. Carleton Putnam is writing a multivolume study of the Roosevelt Administration; the first volume, *Theodore Roosevelt: The Formative Years* (Houghton Mifflin, 1958), a detailed study, is available.

Arthur Link's *Woodrow Wilson and the Progressive Era, 1910–1917* * (Harper & Row, 1954) is the best single volume on Wilson's early presidency and is more critical than Link's authoritative multivolume series, *Wilson* (Princeton Univ. Press, 1947–, 5 vols.). John M. Blum's *Woodrow Wilson and the Politics of Morality* * (Little, Brown, 1956) is a brief, critical interpretation.

Arthur Mann, ed., *The Progressive Era* * (Holt, Rinehart & Winston, 1963) provides a useful collection on the period. Midwestern politics are surveyed in Russell B. Nye's *Midwestern Progressive Politics* * (Michigan State Univ. Press, 1959), which traces the reform movement back to the agrarian unrest of the nineties. James Holt in *Congressional Insurgents and the Party System, 1909–1916* (Harvard Univ. Press, 1967) gives a perceptive analysis of the insurgents in the Senate; Holt concludes that most of them were not involved in the protests of the nineties.

The best general interpretations of Southern progressivism are C. Vann Woodward's *The Origins of the New South* * (Louisiana State Univ. Press, 1951), a splendid study, and George B. Tindall's *The Emergence of the New South* (Louisiana State Univ. Press, 1967), a fine synthesis of the period from 1913 to 1948.

Attitudes toward poverty are well described by Robert Bremner in *From the Depths* * (New York Univ. Press, 1956), and social workers are studied in Allen F. Davis' *Spearheads for Reform* (Oxford Univ. Press, 1967). David Shannon's *The Socialist Party* * (Macmillan, 1950); Ira Kipnis' *The American Socialist Movement, 1897–1912* (Columbia Univ. Press, 1952); and Daniel Bell's "The Background and Development of Marxism Socialism in the United States," in Donald Egbert and Stow Persons, eds., *Socialism and American Life* (Princeton Univ. Press, 1952); and Bell's "Socialism: The Dream and the Reality," *Antioch Review*, XII (March, 1952), 3–17, are criticized severely by James Weinstein, who argues in "The American Socialist Party, Its Roots and Strength," *Studies on the Left*, I (Fall, 1960), 89–108, and in the *Decline of Socialism in America, 1912–1925* (Monthly Review Press, 1967) that socialism was strong even during the war and was weakened not by official suppression but by the split over bolshevism. Kenneth McNaught in "American Progressives and the Great Society," *Journal of American History*, LIII (Dec., 1966), 504–20, contends that socialism failed because the American liberal tradition lacks a tolerance for political deviations.

The intellectual history of these years has been interpreted by many writers. Morton White's *Social Thought in America: The Revolt Against Formalism* * (Beacon, 1949) is a bold and pioneering volume that concentrates on five men. Henry May in *The End of American Innocence* * (Knopf, 1959) finds in the years before Versailles many of the ideas attributed to intellectuals in the twenties, an interpretation sketched by May in "Rebellion of the Intellectuals, 1912–1917," *American Quarterly,* VIII (Summer, 1956), 114–26. William Hutchison in "Liberal Protestantism and 'The End of Innocence,' " *ibid.,* XV (Summer, 1963), 126–39, finds some similar themes among liberal theologians in the three decades before the Depression. Charles Forcey's *The Crossroads of Liberalism: Croly, Weyl, Lippmann, and the Progressive Era* * (Oxford Univ. Press, 1961) focuses on the intellectuals of the *New Republic.* David Noble's *The Paradox of Progressive Thought* (Minnesota Univ. Press, 1958) is an often convoluted analysis of reform thought partly summarized in his essay by the same title in *American Quarterly,* V (Fall, 1953), 201–12. Daniel Levine in *The Varieties of Reform Thought* (State Historical Society of Wisconsin, 1940) emphasizes the diversity among such reformers as Jane Addams and Samuel Gompers and concludes by questioning the concept of progressivism. Christopher Lasch in *The New Radicalism in America: The Intellectual as a Social Type* * (Knopf, 1965) argues that "modern radicalism or liberalism can best be understood as a phase of the social history of the intellectuals" and examines, among others, Jane Addams, Randolph Bourne, Mabel Dodge Luhan, and Lincoln Steffens.

Howard K. Beale's *Theodore Roosevelt and the Rise of America to World Power* * (Johns Hopkins Press, 1956) remains the best volume that considers Roosevelt's foreign policy, but it should be supplemented by Charles Neu's *An Uncertain Friendship; Theodore Roosevelt and Japan, 1906–1909* (Harvard Univ. Press, 1967). William E. Leuchtenburg in "Progressivism and Imperialism: The Progressive Movement and American Foreign Policy, 1898–1916," *Mississippi Valley Historical Review,* XXXIX (Dec., 1952), 483–504, argues that the progressives were usually imperialists, supporters of an aggressive policy that often included military intervention. He is supported in part by William Appleman Williams, who in *The Tragedy of American Diplomacy,* * rev. ed. (World, 1962), places progressive foreign policy in a larger framework of political capitalism and emphasizes the widespread support for economic expansion. Leuchtenburg's analysis is criticized by Barton J. Bernstein and Franklin A. Leib in "Progressive Republican Senators and American Imperialism, 1898–1916: A Reappraisal," *Mid-America,* L (July, 1968), 163–205, which finds that an important part of the progressive community moved to oppose Caribbean adventurism. Charles Vevier in "American Continentalism: An Idea of Expansion, 1845–1910," *American Historical Review,* LXV (Jan., 1960), 323–35, contends that continentalism and subsequent overseas expansion were closely linked and often shaped by similar impulses. Dana Munro in *Intervention and Dollar Diplomacy in the Caribbean, 1900–1921* (Princeton Univ. Press, 1965) denies that the government's interventionist policies were inspired largely by economic considerations, and he emphasizes the humanitarian and moralistic impulses behind American efforts in Latin America.

GABRIEL KOLKO

The Triumph of Conservatism

INTRODUCTION

As he has made clear in two books (*Railroads and Regulation, 1877–1916* and *The Triumph of Conservatism*), Gabriel Kolko believes that government regulation in the progressive era was inspired by big businessmen primarily to escape the harsh consequences of competition. For example, railroad leaders in need of binding pooling agreements and noncompetitive freight rates sought rescue through establishment of the Interstate Commerce Commission (ICC) and passage of such legislation as the Hepburn and Elkins acts. Big meat packers, interested in expanding export markets and bringing their unregulated small competitors under tough inspection

FROM Gabriel Kolko, *The Triumph of Conservatism*, pp. 1–10, 279–87. © by The Free Press of Glencoe, a Division of The Macmillan Company, 1963. Reprinted with permission of The Macmillan Company. Part [I] represents the "Introduction" and part [II] "Conclusion: The Lost Democracy."

laws, supported the greater part of the Meat Inspection Act of 1906.

Unlike Robert Wiebe, who in *Businessmen and Reform* (Harvard Univ. Press, 1962) stresses the disunity of the American business community (for example, eastern versus western businessmen, shippers versus railroads, big versus small), Kolko believes that the big businesses were united by common goals and values and that they wielded sufficient power to realize their aims. Kolko argues not only that progressivism was the tool of big business, but also that progressivism set the pattern for later business-government relations and was largely responsible for giving the American corporate order its permanent form. Using progressivism as a test case of twentieth-century American liberalism, he has found that liberal political leaders were recruited from the same social class as big businessmen and shared the same values. Liberals were, in fact, the handmaidens of corporate enterprise.

Kolko's books, however arresting their thesis, have been subjected to certain criticisms. By concentrating exclusively on business-government relations, he has neglected other aspects of the progressive movement, such as social-justice legislation, which may not in fact be triumphs of conservativism. He has ignored the powerful popular agitation and the efforts of progressive senators like Robert La Follette and William Borah to obtain regulatory legislation. And the evidence presented in *The Triumph of Conservatism* fails to prove either that most big businessmen had a clear conception of "political capitalism" or that they succeeded in passing legislation equal to their alleged conception. While it may be argued that railroad regulation and the Federal Reserve System rationalized the transportation and financial sectors of the economy, the industrial sector was not seriously affected by such measures as the Federal Trade Commission. Moreover, scholars have questioned Kolko's analysis of particular episodes. Thus, in *Change and Continuity in Twentieth-Century America* (Ohio State Univ. Press, 1964), John Braeman disputes Kolko on the forces behind the Meat Inspection Act of 1906 and the role played in its passage by the big meat packers, finding that they opposed any regulation not controlled by themselves. Robert U. Harbeson, reviewing Kolko's book on railroads (*"Railroads and Regulation, 1877–1916, Conspiracy or Public Interest?" Journal of Economic History*, XXVII [June, 1967], 230–42), argues that the ICC did *not* favor the railroads at the expense of shippers and consumers. (Edwin A. Purcell, Jr., in "Ideas and Interests: Businessmen and the Interstate Commerce Act," *Journal of American History*, LIV [Dec., 1967], 561–78, finds "widespread and vocal opposition to the Interstate Commerce Act on the part of many railroad executives," but concludes that there was also widespread support among businessmen for regulation because they sought "federal intervention as a means of protecting their own individual interests.")

Despite these criticisms, Kolko's important work has com-

pelled historians to reconsider the nature of liberal reform, has focused attention on the analysis of power and the role of the state,
has promoted a reconsideration of the nature and "ideology" of
big business, and has emphasized the need for reinvestigating the
sources and actual effects of progressive legislation.

[I]

*T*his [study] is motivated by a concern with the seemingly non-aca-
demic question of "what might have been." All men speculate or dream as
they choose, but the value of the speculation depends on the questions asked
and on the way they are answered. Speculation of the type prompting this
[study] has its value only if it leads to the reexamination of what happened—
what *really* happened—in the past.

The political or economic history of a single nation, especially during a
specific, critical period which has a determining influence on the decades
that follow, should be examined with provocative questions in mind. And
there is no more provocative question than: Could the American political experience in the twentieth century, and the nature of our economic institutions, have been radically different? Every society has its Pangloss who will
reply in the negative. But to suggest that such a reply is mere apologetics
would be a fruitless, inaccurate oversimplification. Predominantly, the great
political and sociological theorists of this century have pessimistically described and predicted an inexorable trend toward centralization, conformity, bureaucracy—toward a variety of totalitarianism—and yet they
have frequently been personally repelled by such a future.

Unless one believes in an invisible, transcendent destiny in American
history, the study of men and institutions becomes the prerequisite for dis-
covering how one's question should be answered. The nature of the questions in this study demands that history be more than a reinterpretation of
what is already known, in large part because what is known is insufficient,
but also because histories of America from the turn of the century onwards
have all too frequently been obsessed by effects rather than causes. Theories
and generalizations based on such an approach have ignored concrete actions and intentions, and for this reason the study of consequences and effects has also been deficient.

Assuming that the burden of proof is ultimately on the writer, I contend
that the period from approximately 1900 until the United States' intervention
in the war, labeled the "progressive" era by virtually all historians, was really
an era of conservatism. Moreover, the triumph of conservatism . . . was the
result not of any impersonal, mechanistic necessity but of the conscious
needs and decisions of specific men and institutions.

There were any number of options involving government and economics abstractly available to national political leaders during the period 1900–1916, and in virtually every case they chose those solutions to problems advocated by the representatives of concerned business and financial interests. Such proposals were usually motivated by the needs of the interested businesses, and political intervention into the economy was frequently merely a response to the demands of particular businessmen. In brief, conservative solutions to the emerging problems of an industrial society were almost uniformly applied. The result was a conservative triumph in the sense that there was an effort to preserve the basic social and economic relations essential to a capitalist society, an effort that was frequently consciously as well as functionally conservative.

I use the attempt to preserve existing power and social relationships as the criterion for conservatism because none other has any practical meaning. Only if we mechanistically assume that government intervention in the economy, and a departure from orthodox laissez faire, automatically benefits the general welfare can we say that government economic regulation by its very nature is also progressive in the common meaning of that term. Each measure must be investigated for its intentions and consequences in altering the existing power arrangements, a task historians have largely neglected.

I shall state my basic proposition as baldly as possible so that my essential theme can be kept in mind. . . . For the sake of communication I will use the terms *progressive* and *progressivism*, but not, as have most historians, in their commonsense meanings.

Progressivism was initially a movement for the political rationalization of business and industrial conditions, a movement that operated on the assumption that the general welfare of the community could be best served by satisfying the concrete needs of business. But the regulation itself was invariably controlled by leaders of the regulated industry, and directed toward ends they deemed acceptable or desirable. In part this came about because the regulatory movements were usually initiated by the dominant businesses to be regulated, but it also resulted from the nearly universal belief among political leaders in the basic justice of private property relations as they essentially existed, a belief that set the ultimate limits on the leaders' possible actions.

It is business control over politics (and by "business" I mean the major economic interests) rather than political regulation of the economy that is the significant phenomenon of the Progressive Era. Such domination was direct and indirect, but significant only insofar as it provided means for achieving a greater end—political capitalism. *Political capitalism* is the utilization of political outlets to attain conditions of stability, predictability, and security—to attain rationalization—in the economy. *Stability* is the elimination of internecine competition and erratic fluctuations in the economy. *Predictability* is the ability, on the basis of politically stabilized and secured means, to plan future economic action on the basis of fairly calculable expectations. By *security* I mean protection from the political attacks latent in any formally democratic political structure. I do not give to *rationalization* its frequent definition as the iimprovement of efficiency, output, or internal organization of a company; I mean by the term, rather, the organization of the economy and the larger political and social spheres in a manner that will allow corporations to function in a predictable and secure environment permitting reasonable profits over the long run. My contention . . . is not that all of these objectives were attained by World War I, but that important and significant legislative steps in these directions were taken, and that these steps include most of the distinctive legislative measures of what has commonly been called the Progressive Period.

Political capitalism, as I have defined it, was a term unheard of in the Progressive Period. Big business did not always have a coherent theory of economic goals and their relationship to immediate actions, although certain individuals did think through explicit ideas in this connection. The advocacy of specific measures was frequently opportunistic, but many individuals with similar interests tended to prescribe roughly the same solution to each concrete problem, and to operationally construct an economic program. It was never a question of regulation or no regulation, of state control or laissez faire; there were, rather, the questions of what kind of regulation and by whom. The fundamental proposition that political solutions were to be applied freely, if not for some other industry's problems then at least for one's own, was never seriously questioned in practice. My focus is on the dominant trends, and on the assumptions behind these trends as to the desirable distribution of power and the type of social relations one wished to create or preserve. And I am concerned with the implementation and administration of a political capitalism, and with the political and economic context in which it flourished.

Why did economic interests require and demand political intervention by the *federal* government and a reincarnation of the Hamiltonian unity of politics and economics?

In part the answer is that the federal government was *always* involved in the economy in various crucial ways, and that laissez faire never existed in an economy where local and federal governments financed the construction of a significant part of the railroad system, and provided lucrative means of obtaining fortunes. This has been known to historians for decades, and need not be belabored. But the significant reason for many businessmen welcoming and working to increase federal intervention into their affairs has been virtually ignored by historians and economists. This oversight was due to the illusion that American industry was centralized and monopolized to such an extent that it could rationalize the activity in its various branches voluntarily. Quite the opposite was true.

Despite the large number of mergers, and the growth in the absolute size of many corporations, the dominant tendency in the American economy at the beginning of this century was toward growing competition. Competition was unacceptable to many key business and financial interests, and the merger movement was to a large extent a reflection of voluntary, unsuccessful business efforts to bring irresistible competitive trends under control. Although profit was always a consideration, rationalization of the market was frequently a necessary prerequisite for maintaining long-term profits. As new competitors sprang up, and as economic power was diffused throughout an expanding nation, it became apparent to many important businessmen that only the national government could rationalize the economy. Although specific conditions varied from industry to industry, internal problems that could be solved only by political means were the common denominator in those industries whose leaders advocated greater federal regulation. Ironically, contrary to the consensus of historians, it was not the existence of monopoly that caused the federal government to intervene in the economy, but the lack of it.

There are really two methods, both valid, of examining the political control of the economy during the period 1900–1916. One way would be to examine the effects of legislation insofar as it aided or hurt industries irrespective of those industries' attitude toward a measure when it was first proposed. The other approach is to examine the extent to which business advocated some measure before it was enacted, and the nature of the final law. Both procedures will be used in this study. The second is the more significant, however, since it points up the needs and nature of the economy, and focuses more clearly on the disparity between the conventional interpretation of progressivism and the informal realities. Moreover, it illustrates the fact that many key businessmen articulated a conscious policy favoring the intervention of the national government into the economy. Because of such a policy there was a consensus on key legislation regulating business that has been overlooked by historians. Important businessmen did not, on the whole, regard politics as a necessary evil, but as an important part of their larger position in society. Because of their positive theory of the state, key business elements managed to define the basic form and content of the major federal legislation that was enacted. They provided direction to existing opinion for regulation, but in a number of crucial cases they were the first to initiate that sentiment. They were able to define such sentiment because, in the last analysis, the major political leaders of the Progressive Era—Roosevelt, Taft, and Wilson—were sufficiently conservative to respond to their initiatives.

Although the main view in the business community was for a rationalization of the conditions of the economy through political means, advocates of such intervention, the J. P. Morgan interests being the most notable, were occasionally prepared to exploit the government in an irregular manner that was advantageous as well. The desire for a larger industrial stability did not exclude an occasional foray into government property, or the utilization of the government to sanction a business arrangement of questionable legality. Such side actions, however, did not alter the basic pattern. In addition, business advocacy of *federal* regulation was motivated by more than a desire to stabilize industries that had moved beyond state boundaries. The needs of the economy were such, of course, as to demand federal as opposed to random state economic regulation. But a crucial factor was the bulwark which essentially conservative national regulation provided against state regulations that were either haphazard or, what is more important, far more responsible to more radical, genuinely progressive local communities. National progressivism, then, becomes the defense of business against the democratic ferment that was nascent in the states.

Federal economic regulation took two crucial forms. The first was a series of informal détentes and agreements between various businesses and the federal government, a means especially favored by Theodore Roosevelt. The second and more significant approach was outright regulation and the creation of administrative commissions intended to maintain continuous supervision over phases of the economy. We shall examine both forms from the viewpoint of their origins, intent, and consequences; we shall examine, too, a number of movements for regulation that failed to find legislative fulfilment of any sort but that provide insight into the problems and needs of the economy in the Progressive Era.

If business did not always obtain its legislative ends in the precise shape it wanted them, its goals and means were nevertheless clear. In the long run, key business leaders realized, they had no vested interest in a chaotic industry and economy in which not only their profits but their very existence might be challenged.

The questions of whether industrialism imposes narrow limits on the economic and political organization of a society, or on the freedom of men to alter the status quo in some decisive way, have been relatively settled ones for the large majority of social scientists. Max Weber, perhaps more than any social theorist of the past century, articulated a comprehensive framework which has profoundly influenced Western social science to answer such questions in the positive. The bureaucratic nature of the modern state and of modern industry, to Weber, restricted all possibilities for changing the basic structure of modern society. The tendency toward centralization in politics and industry, toward a mechanical impersonality designed to maximize efficiency, seemed to Weber to be the dominant theme in Western society, and the Weberian analysis has sunk deep roots into academic discussions of the problem. The systematic economics of Karl Marx—as opposed to that of "Marxists"—also sustained the argument that the basic trend in capitalist development was toward the centralization of industry. Indeed, such centralization was an indispensable aspect of Western industrialism, and could not be circumvented. Both Marx and Weber, one an opponent of capitalism and the other indifferent to it, suggested that industrialism and capitalism, as they saw both develop, were part of the unalterable march of history.

The relevance of the American experience to the systematic theories of both Weber and Marx will be explored in greater detail in the conclusion, my argument being that neither of the two men, for all their sensitivity and insight, offered much that is of value to understanding the development of capitalism and industrialism in the United States. Indeed, the American experience, I shall try to contend, offers much to disprove the formal theories of probably the two greatest social theorists of the past century. It is perhaps unfair to Marx, who based his case on the conditions existing in England and Western Europe in the mid-nineteenth century, to burden him with American history at the beginning of the twentieth, but he was not terribly modest about its applicability, and any respectable theory should have the predictive value its author ascribes to it. Weber, on the other hand, frequently stated that the United States was the prime example of modern capitalism in the twentieth century, if not the best proof of his theory.

American historians, with some notable exceptions, have tended, without relying on comprehensive theoretical systems of the Weberian or Marxist variety, also to regard the development of the economy as largely an impersonal, inevitable phenomenon. All too frequently they have assumed that concentration and the elimination of competition—business giantism or monopoly—was the dominant tendency in the economy. The relationship between the growth of new competition and new centers of economic power and the legislative enactments of the Progressive Era has been virtually ignored. On the contrary, federal legislation to most historians has appeared to be a reaction against the power of the giant monopoly, or a negative response to the very process of industrialism itself by a threatened middle-class being uprooted from its secure world by corporate capitalism. A centralized economy, historians have asserted, required a centralized federal power to prevent it from damaging the public interest, and the conventional political image of the Progressive Era is of the federal government as a neutral, if not humane, shield between the public and the Morgans, Rockefellers, and Harrimans. Progressivism has been portrayed as essentially a middle-class defense against the status pretensions of the new industrialists, a defense of human values against acquisitive habits, a reassertion of the older tradition of rural individualism.

Recent historians have, for the most part, assumed monopoly was an economic reality concomitant with maximum efficiency even where . . . it was little more than a political slogan. For it is one thing to say that there was a growth of vast accumulations of corporate power, quite another to claim that there existed a largely monopolistic control over the various economic sectors. Power may be concentrated, as it was, but the extent of that concentration is crucial. Historians of the period have too often confused the power of corporate concentration with total monopoly. The distinction is not merely important to American economic history, it is vital for the understanding of the political history of the period. And to the extent that historians have accepted the consensus among contemporaries as to the inevitable growth of monopoly at the turn of the century, they have failed to appreciate the dynamic interrelationship between politics and economics in the Progressive Era.

I shall be accused of oversimplifying what historians have written about the Progressive Era, and with some justice. But I believe it can be stated that although there are important and significant monographic works or histories of specific phases of progressivism which provide evidence to disprove aspects of such a comprehensive interpretation, no other theory of the nature of the Progressive Era has, in fact, yet been offered. And even most of the critical historians have accepted the traditional view of progressivism as a whole. No synthesis of the specific studies disproving what is, for better or worse, the conventionally accepted interpretation among historians of the Progressive Period, has been attempted. Nor has there really been a serious effort to re-examine the structural conditions and problems of the economy during the period and to relate them to the political and especially the detailed legislative history of the era. And it is here, more than any other place, that a new synthesis and a new interpretation is required.

Yet the exceptional historical works that have raised doubts about specific phases of the larger image of progressivism are suggestive in that they indicate that the time for reinterpreting the Progressive Era and the nature, character, and purpose of progressivism, is opportune. The work of the Handlins, Louis Hartz, and Carter Goodrich, to name only a few, in showing the *dependence* of business on politics for government aid and support until the Civil War, suggests that the unity of business and politics was still a relatively fresh memory by the end of the nineteenth century. Sidney Fine has pointed out how many businessmen treated laissez faire and Social Darwinian doctrine gingerly when it was to their interest to have the government aid them. William Miller has shown that the background and origins, and hence the status, of the triumphant industrialists was respectable and at least well-to-do, implicitly raising questions about the status conflict between the allegedly old elite and the new. John Morton Blum has expressed doubts as to the radicalism of Theodore Roosevelt, whom he has portrayed as a progressive conservative, but ultimately a conservative. And, perhaps more than anyone else, Arthur S. Link has critically dissected the history of the Wilson Administration in a manner that forces the historian to doubt whether the conventional usage of the term "progressive" really describes the New Freedom.

Although other monographs and studies can be cited, there are still too many loose ends in the traditional view of the Progressive Period, and no synthesis. More important, there has been no effort to study the entire period as an integrated whole. The very best work, such as Link's, deals with presidential periods, but the movements for legislative enactments ran through nearly all the administrations, and can only be really understood in that context. For without such a comprehensive view, the origins and motives behind the legislative components of the Progressive Period cannot be fully comprehended, assuming that there is some correlation between intentions or purposes and results. And although historians have increasingly been puzzled by the growing incompatibility of the specific studies with the larger interpretation, they have not been able to reconcile or explain the disparities. The Progressive Era has been treated as a series of episodes, unrelated to one another in some integrated manner, with growing enigmas as the quantity of new research into the period increases. The Progressive Party was one incident, the Food and Drug Act another, the conservation movement yet one more event.

In this study I shall attempt to treat the Progressive Era as an interrelated and, I hope, explicable whole, set in the context of the nature and tendencies of the economy. Ultimately, the analysis that follows is of interest only if it throws light on the broader theoretical issues concerning the extent to which a larger industrial necessity imposed limits on the political structure, and the manner in which politics shaped the economic system.

[II]

The American political experience during the Progressive Era was conservative, and this conservatism profoundly influenced American society's response to the problems of industrialism. The nature of the economic process in the United States, and the peculiar cast within which industrialism was molded, can only be understood by examining the political structure. Progressive politics is complex when studied in all of its aspects, but its dominant tendency on the federal level was to functionally create, in a piecemeal and haphazard way that was later made more comprehensive, the synthesis of politics and economics I have labeled "political capitalism."

The varieties of rhetoric associated with progressivism were as diverse as its followers, and one form of this rhetoric involved attacks on businessmen —attacks that were often framed in a fashion that has been misunderstood by historians as being radical. But at no point did any major political tendency dealing with the problem of big business in modern society ever try to go beyond the level of high generalization and translate theory into concrete economic programs that would conflict in a fundamental way with business supremacy over the control of wealth. It was not a coincidence that the results of progressivism were precisely what many major business interests desired.

Ultimately businessmen defined the limits of political intervention, and specified its major form and thrust. They were able to do so not merely because they were among the major initiators of federal intervention in the economy, but primarily because no politically significant group during the Progressive Era really challenged their conception of political intervention. The basic fact of the Progressive Era was the large area of consensus and unity among key business leaders and most political factions on the role of the federal government in the economy. There were disagreements, of course, but not on fundamentals. The overwhelming majorities on votes for basic progressive legislation is testimony to the near unanimity in Congress on basic issues.

Indeed, an evaluation of the Progressive Era must concede a much larger importance to the role of Congress than has hitherto been granted by historians who have focused primarily on the more dramatic Presidents. Congress was the pivot of agitation for banking reform while Roosevelt tried to evade the issue, and it was considering trade commissions well before Wilson was elected. Meat and pure foot agitation concentrated on Congress, and most of the various reform proposals originated there. More often than not, the various Presidents evaded a serious consideration of issues until Congressional initiatives forced them to articulate a position. And businessmen seeking reforms often found a sympathetic response among the members of the House and Senate long before Presidents would listen to them. This was particularly true of Roosevelt, who would have done much less than he did were it not for the prodding of Congress. Presidents are preoccupied with patronage to an extent unappreciated by anyone who has not read their letters.

The Presidents, considered—as they must be—as actors rather than ideologists, hardly threatened to undermine the existing controllers of economic power. With the possible exception of Taft's Wickersham, none of the major appointees to key executive posts dealing with economic affairs were men likely to frustrate business in its desire to use the federal government to strengthen its economic position. Garfield, Root, Knox, Straus—these men were important and sympathetic pipelines to the President, and gave additional security to businessmen who did not misread what Roosevelt was trying to say in his public utterances. Taft, of course, broke the continuity between the Roosevelt and Wilson Administrations because of political decisions that had nothing to do with his acceptance of the same economic theory that Roosevelt believed in. The elaborate relationship between business and the Executive created under Roosevelt was unintentionally destroyed because of Taft's desire to control the Republican Party. Wilson's appointees were quite as satisfactory as Roosevelt's, so far as big business was concerned, and in his concrete implementation of the fruits of their political agitation—the Federal Reserve Act and the Federal Trade Commission Act— Wilson proved himself to be perhaps the most responsive and desirable to business of the three Presidents. Certainly it must be concluded that historians have overemphasized the basic differences between the Presidents of the

Progressive Era, and ignored their much more important similarities. In 1912 the specific utterances and programs of all three were identical on fundamentals, and party platforms reflected this common agreement.

This essential unanimity extended to the area of ideologies and values, where differences between the Presidents were largely of the sort contrived by politicians in search of votes, or seeking to create useful images. None of the Presidents had a distinct consciousness of any fundamental conflict between their political goals and those of business. Roosevelt and Wilson especially appreciated the significant support business gave to their reforms, but it was left to Wilson to culminate the decade or more of agitation by providing precise direction to the administration of political capitalism's most important consequences in the Progressive Era. Wilson had a small but articulate band of followers who seriously desired to reverse the process of industrial centralization—Bryan and the Midwestern agrarians reflected this tradition more than any other group. Yet ultimately he relegated such dissidents to a secondary position—indeed, Wilson himself represented the triumph of Eastern Democracy over Bryanism—and they were able to influence only a clause or amendment, here and there, in the basic legislative structure of political capitalism.

But even had they been more powerful, it is debatable how different Bryanism would have been. Bryan saw the incompatibility between giant corporate capitalism and political democracy, but he sought to save democracy by saving, or restoring, a sort of idealized competitive capitalist economy which was by this time incapable of realization or restoration, and was in any event not advocated by capitalists or political leaders with more power than the agrarians could marshal. Brandeis, for his part, was bound by enigmas in this period. Big business, to him, was something to be ultimately rejected or justified on the basis of efficiency rather than power accumulation. He tried to apply such technical criteria where none was really relevant, and he overlooked the fact that even where efficient or competitive, business could still pose irreconcilable challenges to the political and social fabric of a democratic community. Indeed, he failed to appreciate the extent to which it was competition that was leading to business agitation for federal regulation, and finally he was unable to do much more than sanction Wilson's actions as they were defined and directed by others.

There was no conspiracy during the Progressive Era. It is, of course, a fact that people and agencies acted out of public sight, and that official statements frequently had little to do with operational realities. But the imputation of a conspiracy would sidetrack a serious consideration of progressivism. There was a basic consensus among political and business leaders as to what was the public good, and no one had to be cajoled in a sinister manner. If détentes, private understandings, and the like were not publicly proclaimed it was merely because such agreements were exceptional and, generally known, could not have been denied to other business interests also desiring the security they provided. Such activities required a delicate sense of public relations, since there was always a public ready to oppose preferential treatment for special businesses, if not the basic assumptions behind such arrangements.

Certainly there was nothing surreptitious about the desire of certain businessmen for reforms, a desire that was frequently and publicly proclaimed, although the motives behind it were not appreciated by historians and although most contemporaries were unaware of how reforms were implemented after they were enacted. The fact that federal regulation of the economy was conservative in its effect in preserving existing power and economic relations in society should not obscure the fact that federal intervention in the economy was conservative in purpose as well. This ambition was publicly proclaimed by the interested business forces, and was hardly conspiratorial.

It is the intent of crucial business groups, and the structural circumstances within the economy that motivated them, that were the truly significant and unique aspects of the Progressive Era. The effects of the legislation were only the logical conclusion of the intentions behind it. The ideological consensus among key business and political leaders fed into a stream of common action, action that was sometimes stimulated by different specific goals but which nevertheless achieved the same results. Political leaders, such as Roosevelt, Wilson, and their key appointees, held that it was proper for an industry to have a decisive voice or veto over the regulatory process within its sphere of interest, and such assumptions filled many key businessmen with confidence in the essential reliability of the federal political mechanism, especially when it was contrasted to the unpredictability of state legislatures.

Business opposition to various federal legislative proposals and measures did exist, of course, especially if one focuses on opposition to particular clauses in specific bills. Such opposition, as in the case of the Federal Reserve Bill, was frequently designed to obtain special concessions. It should not be allowed to obscure the more important fact that the essential purpose and goal of any measure of importance in the Progressive Era was not merely endorsed by key representatives of businesses involved; rather such bills were first proposed by them.

One can always find some businessman, of course, who opposed federal regulation at any point, including within his own industry. Historians have relished in detailing such opposition, and, indeed, their larger analysis of the period has encouraged such revelations. But the finding of division in the ranks of business can be significant only if one makes the false assumption of a monolithic common interest among all capitalists, but, worse yet, assumes that there is no power center among capitalists, and that small-town bankers or hardware dealers can be equated with the leaders of the top industrial, financial, and railroad corporations. They can be equated, of course, if all one studies is the bulk of printed words. But in the political as well as in the economic competition between small and big business, the larger interests always managed to prevail in any specific contest. The rise of National Association of Manufacturers in the Progressive Era is due to its antilabor position, and not to its opposition to federal regulation, which it voiced only after the First World War. In fact, crucial big business support could be found for every major federal regulatory movement, and frequent small business support could be found for any variety of proposals to their benefit, such as price-fixing and legalized trade associations. Progressivism was not the triumph of small business over the trusts, as has often been suggested but the victory of big businesses in achieving the rationalization of the economy that only the federal government could provide.

Still, the rise of the N.A.M. among businessmen in both pro- and anti-regulation camps only reinforces the fact that the relationship of capitalists to the remainder of society was essentially unaltered by their divisions on federal intervention in the economy. In terms of the basic class structure, and the conditions of interclass relationships, big and small business alike were hostile to a labor movement interested in something more than paternalism and inequality. In this respect, and in their opposition or indifference to the very minimal social welfare reforms of the Progressive Era (nearly all of which were enacted in the states), American capitalism in the Progressive Era acted in the conservative fashion traditionally ascribed to it. The result was federal regulation in the context of a class society. Indeed, because the national political leadership of the Progressive Period shared this *noblesse oblige* and conservatism toward workers and farmers, it can be really said that there was federal regulation because there *was* a class society, and political leaders identified with the values and supremacy of business.

This identification of political and key business leaders with the same set of social values—ultimately class values—was hardly accidental, for had such a consensus not existed the creation of political capitalism would have been most unlikely. Political capitalism was based on the functional unity of major political and business leaders. The business and political elites knew each other, went to the same schools, belonged to the same clubs, married into the same families, shared the same values—in reality, formed that phenomenon which has lately been dubbed The Establishment. Garfield and Stetson met at Williams alumni functions, Rockefeller, Jr. married Aldrich's daughter, the Harvard clubmen always found the White House door open to them when Roosevelt was there, and so on. Indeed, no one who reads Jonathan Daniels' remarkable autobiography, *The End of Innocence,* can fail to realize the significance of an interlocking social, economic, and political elite in American history in this century.

The existence of an Establishment during the Progressive Era was convenient, even essential, to the functional attainment of political capitalism, but it certainly was not altogether new in American history, and certainly had antecedents in the 1890's. The basic causal factor behind national progressivism was the needs of business and financial elements. To some extent, however, the more benign character of many leading business leaders, especially those with safe fortunes, was due to the more secure, mellowed characteristics and paternalism frequently associated with the social elite. Any number of successful capitalists had long family traditions of social graces and refinement which they privately doubted were fully compatible with their role as capitalists. The desire for a stabilized, rationalized political capitalism was fed by this current in big business ideology, and gave many businessmen that air of responsibility and conservatism so admired by Roosevelt and Wilson. And, from a practical viewpoint, the cruder economic conditions could also lead to substantial losses. Men who were making fortunes with existing shares of the market preferred holding on to what they had rather than establishing control over an industry, or risking much of what they already possessed. Political stabilization seemed proper for this reason as well. It allowed men to relax, to hope that crises might be avoided, to enjoy the bountiful fortunes they had already made.

Not only were economic losses possible in an unregulated capitalism, but political destruction also appeared quite possible. There were disturbing gropings ever since the end of the Civil War: agrarian discontent, violence and strikes, a Populist movement, the rise of a Socialist Party that seemed, for a time, to have an unlimited growth potential. Above all, there was a labor movement seriously divided as to its proper course, and threatening to follow in the seemingly radical footsteps of European labor. The political capitalism of the Progressive Era was designed to meet these potential threats, as well as the immediate expressions of democratic discontent in the states. National progressivism was able to short-circuit state progressivism, to hold nascent radicalism in check by feeding the illusions of its leaders—leaders who could not tell the difference between federal regulation *of* business and federal regulation *for* business.

Political capitalism in America redirected the radical potential of mass grievances and aspirations—of genuine progressivism—and to a limited extent colored much of the intellectual ferment of the period, even though the amorphous nature of mass aspirations frequently made the goals of business and the rest of the public nearly synonymous. Many well-intentioned writers and academicians worked for the same legislative goals as businessmen, but their innocence did not alter the fact that such measures were frequently designed by businessmen to serve business ends, and that business ultimately reaped the harvest of positive results. Such innocence was possible because of a naive, axiomatic view that government economic regulation, per se, was desirable, and also because many ignored crucial business support for such measures by focusing on the less important business opposition that existed. The fetish of government regulation of the economy as a positive social good was one that sidetracked a substantial portion of European socialism as well, and was not unique to the American experience. Such axiomatic and simplistic assumptions of what federal regulation would bring did not take into account problems of democratic control and participation, and in effect assumed that the power of government was neutral and socially beneficent. Yet many of the leading muckrakers and academics of the period were more than naive but ultimately conservative in their intentions as well. They sought the paternalism and stability which they expected political capitalism to bring, since only in this way could the basic virtues of capitalism be maintained. The betrayal of liberalism that has preoccupied some intellectual historians did not result from irrelevant utopianism or philosophical pragmatism, but from the lack of a truly radical, articulated alternative economic and political program capable of synthesizing political democracy with industrial reality. Such a program was never formulated in this period either in America or Europe.

Historians have continually tried to explain the seemingly sudden collapse of progressivism after the First World War, and have offered reasons that varied from moral exhaustion to the repression of nonconformity. On the whole, all explanations suffer because they really fail to examine progressivism beyond the favorable conventional interpretation. Progressive goals, on the concrete, legislative level, were articulated by various business interests. These goals were, for the most part, achieved, and no one formulated others that big business was also interested in attaining. Yet a synthesis of business and politics on the federal level was created during the war, in various administrative and emergency agencies, that continued throughout the following decade. Indeed, the war period represents the triumph of business in the most emphatic manner possible. With the exception of a brief interlude in the history of the Federal Trade Commission, big business gained total support from the various regulatory agencies and the Executive. It was during the war that effective, working oligopoly and price and market agreements became operational in the dominant sectors of the American economy. The rapid diffusion of power in the economy and relatively easy entry virtually ceased. Despite the cessation of important new legislative enactments, the unity of business and the federal government continued throughout the 1920's and thereafter, using the foundations laid in the Progressive Era to stabilize and consolidate conditions within various industries. And, on the same progressive foundations and exploiting the experience with the war agencies, Herbert Hoover and Franklin Roosevelt later formulated programs for saving American capitalism. The principle of utilizing the federal government to stabilize the economy, established in the context of modern industrialism during the Progressive Era, became the basis of political capitalism in its many later ramifications.

In this sense progressivism did not die in the 1920's, but became a part of the basic fabric of American society. The different shapes political capitalism has taken since 1916 deserve a separate treatment, but suffice it to say that even Calvin Coolidge did not mind evoking the heritage of Theodore Roosevelt, and Hoover was, if anything, deeply devoted to the Wilsonian tradition in which Franklin Roosevelt gained his first political experience.

SUGGESTED READING

Though Kolko's *The Triumph of Conservatism* ° was the subject for a session at the American Historical Association annual meeting (1966), the criticisms by Gerald Nash, J. Joseph Huthmacher, and Richard Abrams have not been published. John Braeman, in a review essay, "Seven Progressives," *Business History Review,* XXXV (Winter, 1961), 581–92, follows the usual analysis of progressivism, breaking the political reformers into two groups—"moderns" (Perkins, Stimson, Croly, Roosevelt), who championed regulation of corporations and meeting the nation's responsibilities abroad, and "traditionalists" (La Follette and Borah), who became isolationists and also hoped to recapture rural America.

G. Cullom Davis in "The Transformation of the Federal Trade Commission, 1914–1929," *Mississippi Historical Review,* XLIX (Dec. 1962), 437–55, disagrees with Kolko's interpretation of the FTC. Support of Kolko's thesis is found in James Weinstein's *The Corporate Ideal in the Liberal State, 1900–1918* (Beacon, 1968), which includes "Big Business and the Origins of Workmen's Compensation," originally appearing in *Labor History,* VIII (Spring, 1967), 156–74; and Martin Sklar's "Woodrow Wilson and the Political Economy of United States Liberalism," *Studies on the Left,* I (Fall, 1960), 17–47. Weinstein argues that some of the social-justice legislation was part of the conservative movement and views these reforms as a part of corporate liberalism.

Paul A. C. Koistinen's "The 'Industrial-Military Complex' in Historical Perspective: World War I," and Robert Cuff's "A Dollar-a-Year Man in Government: George N. Peek and the War Industries Board," *Business History Review,* XLI (Winter, 1967), 378–403, are important for a study of business-government relations during the war. They disagree with Robert Himmelberg ("The War Industries Board and the Antitrust Question," *Journal of American History,* LII [June, 1965], 59–74) and Daniel Beaver (*Newton D. Baker and the American War Effort, 1917–1919* [University of Nebraska Press, 1966]), who minimize or neglect the efforts of big businessmen serving in the Government to use their influence to assist major corporations and to protect the corporate order they dominated. K. Austin Kerr's *American Railroad Politics 1914–1920: Rates, Wages, and Efficiency* (Univ. of Pittsburgh Press, 1968) focuses on the relationship between interest groups and federal policy toward the railroads.

J. JOSEPH HUTHMACHER

Urban Liberalism
and the Age of Reform

INTRODUCTION

Though one segment of the progressive movement was located in
the agrarian West and sent to the Congress men like William Borah
of Idaho and George Norris of Nebraska, another segment was
rooted largely in the cities of the industrial East. By 1910, cities and
towns already contained almost half of America's population and
were beginning to dominate American culture. Confronted with
social problems different from those of rural America, cities developed their own styles of progressivism and produced reformers
like Jane Addams of Chicago's Hull House, Robert Wagner of New
York, and Louis Brandeis of Boston—men and women sympathetic to the plight of industrial workers.

FROM J. Joseph Huthmacher, "Urban Liberalism and the Age of Reform," *Mississippi Valley Historical Review*, XLIX (September, 1962), pp. 231–41. Reprinted by permission.

It is the role of urban reform and its sources of support that concern J. Joseph Huthmacher, the author of the following essay. Focusing on political activities and legislative efforts, he concludes that the progressive era, contrary to the analyses of Richard Hofstadter and George Mowry, cannot be understood "exclusively" as a manifestation of the middle-class Yankee ethos. Lower-class workers, he contends, contributed much of the support for reform legislation, and without their endorsement some important liberal reforms would have failed. Unlike some of the middle-class reformers, workers were unconcerned about maintaining individualism and laissez faire, but they did ally with reformers to support bread-and-butter issues beneficial to themselves.

Huthmacher's interpretation can be questioned on both empirical and conceptual grounds. His case rests on scanty evidence from two states, New York and Massachusetts, and Richard Abrams, in *Conservatism in the Progressive Era* (Harvard Univ. Press, 1964), disputes Huthmacher's finding for Massachusetts, noting, to cite just one point, that progressives in that state generally feared the non-Yankee wage-earning classes and were reluctant to ally with them. As for his conception, Huthmacher's analysis does not carefully distinguish between the actions of legislators and the wishes of their constituents. His interpretation rests on the assumption that the decisions of legislators automatically reflect their constituents' demands; on this basis he then proceeds to offer some hypotheses regarding the nature of lower-class liberalism and the aspirations and political consciousness of immigrants and their children. Moreover, his generalizations lump together Italians, Irish, and Jews, assuming without proof that they held similar views and that generational distinctions were unimportant.

Finally, his analysis does not measure the comparative importance of workers and their representatives in the reform movement. While Huthmacher is probably correct in stating that workers *sometimes* provided important support for reform, it is still possible logically to accept the view that many workers often were an obstacle to some types of reform and that other workers constituted the majority of the socialist movement in the East. Even so, Huthmacher's focus on urban workers as supporters of certain liberal reforms is useful in correcting some earlier interpretations that denied this group any place in the progressive coalition.

*M*ost historians of twentieth-century America would agree that the effective beginnings of the present-day "people's capitalism"—the present-day liberalism—can be traced back to the Progressive Era. And most of them would agree that the essential ingredient which made possible the practical achievement of reforms at that time was the support given by city dwellers who, at the turn of the century, swung behind reform movements in large numbers for the first time since America's rush into industrialism following the Civil War. True, the Populists and other agrarian radicals had done spadework on behalf of various proposals in the late nineteenth century, such as trust regulation, the income tax, and direct election of senators. But their efforts had gone unrewarded, or had been frustrated by enactment of half-way measures. Not until the reform spirit had seized large numbers of urbanites could there be hope of achieving meaningful political, economic, and social adjustments to the demands of the new industrial civilization.

Between 1900 and 1920 American statute books became studded with the results of urban-oriented reform drives. The direct primary, the initiative, the Seventeenth Amendment; the Clayton Act, a revived Interstate Commerce Commission, and the Federal Trade Commission; workmen's compensation, child labor laws, and Prohibition—these and many other achievements testified to the intensity of Progressivism. It is admitted, of course, that not everything done in the name of reform was desirable. Some measures, notably Prohibition, are counted today as being wrong-headed, while some political panaceas like the direct primary elicited an undue degree of optimism on the part of their exponents. Nevertheless, the Progressive Era did witness America's first modern reform upsurge, and much of substantial worth was accomplished. Moreover, it established patterns and precedents for the further evolution of American liberalism, an evolution whose later milestones would bear the markings "New Deal" and "New Frontier."

In accounting for the genesis and success of urban liberalism in the Progressive Era, however, the historians who have dominated its study thus far have concentrated on one population element, the urban middle class, and its Yankee-Protestant system of values. "The great majority of the reformers came from the 'solid middle class,'" Professor George E. Mowry tells us. "If names mean anything, an overwhelming proportion of this reform group came from old American stock with British origins consistently indicated." Professor Richard Hofstadter adds that "the key words of Progressivism were terms like *patriotism, citizen, democracy, law, character, conscience* . . . terms redolent of the sturdy Protestant Anglo-Saxon moral and intellectual roots of the Progressive uprising." [1] The component parts of this amorphous middle class, and the reasons for their new interest in reform at the turn of the century, have been described by various scholars.[2] We have been told about the "white collar" group which saw, in the increasing bu-

[1] George E. Mowry, *The Era of Theodore Roosevelt, 1900–1912* (New York, 1958), 86; Richard Hofstadter, *The Age of Reform* (New York, 1955), 318.

[2] Mowry, *Era of Theodore Roosevelt;* Hofstadter, *Age of Reform;* C. Wright Mills, *White Collar* (New York, 1951); Eric Goldman, *Rendezvous with Destiny* (New York, 1952); Samuel P. Hays, *The Response to Industrialism, 1885–1914* (Chicago, 1957).

reaucratization of big business, the blotting out of its traditional belief in the American "rags to riches" legend. Some writers have dwelt upon the middle-class intellectuals—writers, publicists, ministers, college women, professors—who, in response to changing patterns of social thought represented by the rise of "realism" in literature, religion, and the social sciences, determined to uplift the living conditions of their less fortunate brothers. Others have examined the "Old Aristocracy" threatened by a "status revolution," and fighting to maintain the degree of deference that had been theirs before the rise of the newly rich moguls of business and finance.

Imbued with this mixture of selfish and altruistic motives, reinforced by the pocketbook-pinching price inflation that got under way in 1897, the urban middle-class reformers set out to right the wrongs of their society. They introduced a variety of new democratic techniques into our political mechanics, in an attempt to break the grip of the corrupt bosses who manipulated irresponsible immigrant voters and unscrupulous businessmen in ways that subverted good government. They augmented the government's role as watchdog over the economy, either to maintain the traditional "small business" regime of competitive free enterprise, or at least to make sure that oligopolists passed on to consumers the benefits of large-scale operation. Through the activities of their philanthropic organizations, coupled with support of paternalistic labor and social welfare legislation, the middle-class reformers also sought to uplift the standards of the alien, slum-dwelling, urban working class to something more closely approximating the Yankee-Protestant ideal. So runs the "middle-class" interpretation of Progressivism, an interpretation which has set the fashion, by and large, for scholarly work on the subject.

There is no doubt, of course, that discontented elements among the urban middle class contributed much to Progressivism, or that the historians who have explored their contributions and their motives deserve the plaudits of the profession. Nevertheless, it may be pertinent to ask whether these historians have not overstressed the role of middle-class reformers, to the neglect or exclusion of other elements—such as organized labor—who have had something to do with the course of modern American liberalism.[3] More particularly, a number of circumstances call into question the assertion that "In politics . . . the immigrant was usually at odds with the reform aspirations of the American Progressive."[4] If such were the case, how does one

---

[3] The suggestions made in this and the following paragraphs stem primarily from the author's research for *Massachusetts People and Politics, 1919–1933* (Cambridge, Mass., 1959), and for a projected biography of Senator Robert F. Wagner of New York. Senator Wagner's papers are deposited at Georgetown University, Washington, D.C.

[4] Hofstadter, *Age of Reform,* 180–81. It is clear, of course, that Professor Hofstadter is referring not only to the first-generation immigrants themselves, but to the whole society which they, their offspring, and their culture were creating within our industrial, urban maze.

explain the drive and success of Progressive Era reform movements in places like New York and Massachusetts—states that were heavily populated with non-Protestant, non-Anglo-Saxon immigrants and sons of immigrants? How could reformers succeed at the polls or in the legislatures in such states if, "Together with the native conservative and the politically indifferent, the immigrants formed a potent mass that limited the range and the achievements of Progressivism"?[5] Moreover, how does one explain the support which individuals like Al Smith, Robert F. Wagner, James A. Foley, James Michael Curley, and David I. Walsh gave to a large variety of so-called Progressive measures in their respective office-holding capacities?[6] Surely these men do not conform to the middle-class, Yankee-Protestant "Progressive Profile" as etched by Professor Mowry.[7]

If the Progressive Era is to be considered a manifestation of the Yankee-Protestant ethos almost exclusively, how does one explain the fact that in the legislatures of New York and Massachusetts many reform bills received more uniform and consistent support from respresentatives of the urban lower class than they received from the urban middle-class or rural representatives? Some of the most effective middle-class reformers, such as social worker Frances Perkins, realized this fact at the time and charted their legislative strategy accordingly.[8] It may be pointed out also that, even when submitted to popular referendums, typically Progressive measures sometimes received more overwhelming support in the melting-pot wards than they received in the middle-class or rural constituencies. This was the case, for example, in Massachusetts when, in 1918, the voters passed upon a proposed initiative and referendum amendment to the state constitution. Such circumstances become especially compelling when we remember that reform measures, no matter how well formulated and publicized by intellectuals, cannot become effective in a democracy without skillful political generalship and—even more important—votes.

---

[5] *Ibid.*, 181.

[6] Oscar Handlin, *Al Smith and His America* (Boston, 1958); Joseph F. Dinneen, *The Purple Shamrock: The Honorable James Michael Curley of Boston* (New York, 1949); Dorothy G. Wayman, *David I. Walsh: Citizen Patriot* (Milwaukee, 1952). See also Arthur Mann, *La Guardia: A Fighter against His Times* (Philadelphia, 1959). Among the measures which Robert F. Wagner introduced as a New York state senator between 1909 and 1918 were the following: a bill to provide for direct election of United States senators; a bill to authorize a twenty million dollar bond issue for conservation and public development of state water power; a direct primary bill; a short-ballot bill; a resolution to ratify the federal income tax amendment; a bill establishing the Factory Investigating Commission; a civil rights bill; a woman suffrage amendment to the state constitution; numerous bills for child labor regulation; a bill to extend home rule to municipalities; a bill to establish a minimum wage commission for women; a bill limiting the issuance of labor injunctions; a bill to authorize municipal ownership of power plants; and a corrupt practices bill.

[7] Mowry, *Era of Theodore Roosevelt*, chap. 5.

[8] Frances Perkins, *The Roosevelt I Knew* (New York, 1946), 12–26.

Marshaled together, then, the foregoing evidence suggests that the triumphs of modern liberalism in the Progressive Era, and in subsequent reform eras, were owed to something more than a strictly middle-class dynamism. It indicates that the urban lower class provided an active, numerically strong, and politically necessary force for reform—and that this class was perhaps as important in determining the course of American liberalism as the urban middle class, about which so much has been written.

Today's liberals look to the "northern" Democrats and the "eastern" Republicans—those whose elections are due largely to the votes of the urban working class—for support of their proposals. If, as is contended, this phenomenon of urban lower-class liberalism can be traced back beyond the election of 1960, beyond the New Deal, and to the Progressive Era, then the probing of its chronological origins and the operational details of its emergence present wide fields for fruitful research. In the process of such studies, many other questions will present themselves to the investigator. What were the sources of lower-class interest in reform? How did its sources affect its nature, specific content, and practical effects? How, if at all, did urban lower-class liberalism differ in these respects from urban middle-class liberalism? At the risk of premature generalization, tentative suggestions, indicated by research thus far conducted, may be set forth regarding these matters.

The great source of urban working-class liberalism was experience. Unlike the middle-class reformers, who generally relied on muckrakers, Social Gospelers, and social scientists to delineate the ills of society, the urban working class knew at first hand the conditions of life on "the other side of the tracks." Its members and spokesmen grew to manhood "in the midst of alternately shivering and sweltering humanity in ancient rat-infested rookeries in the swarming, anonymous, polyglot East Side, an international center before the U.N. was dreamed of," where "souls and bodies were saved by the parish priest, the family doctor, and the local political saloonkeeper and boss who knew everyone and was the link between the exploited immigrant and the incomprehensible, distant law." [9] Such people were less imbued than the middle class with the "old American creed" which expounded individualism, competition, and laissez-faire free enterprise as the means of advance from "rags to riches." Their felt needs, largely of the bread and butter type, were of the here and now, and not of the middle-class variety which fastened upon further advancement to a higher station from one already fairly comfortable. Moreover, their constant immersion in the depths of human misery and frailty, and the semi-pessimistic nature of their religious psychology, limited their hopes for environmental improvement within the bounds of reasonable expectation. Their outlook tended to be more practical and "possibilistic" than that of some middle-class Progressives who allowed their reform aspira-

---

[9] Robert Moses, "Salute to an East Side Boy Named Smith," *New York Times Magazine* (October 8, 1961), 113.

tions to soar to Utopian heights, envisaging a "Kingdom of God on Earth" or a perfect society to be achieved by means of sociological test tubes. Finally, the previous political experience of the immigrant workers, centering about their security-oriented relations with a paternalistic ward boss, conditioned them to transfer the same functional conception to the city, state, and national governments as they became progressively aware of their ability, through their voting power, to make those governing bodies serve their needs. Consequently, their view of government was much less permeated with fears of paternalism and centralization than that of traditionally individualistic middle-class reformers, many of whom abated their attachment to the laissez-faire principle with only the greatest trepidation.[10]

The influence of these conditioning factors seems clearly discernible in the specific types of reform programs to which the urban lower class and its spokesmen lent greatest support. It is commonplace to say, for example, that the immigrants were not interested in political machinery reforms simply as reforms. Unlike the remaining middle-class "genteel reformers," they did not look upon political tinkering as the be-all and end-all of reform. Yet it is an injustice to imply that the immigrants' attitude on this matter was due to an inherent inability to comprehend the Yankee-Protestant concept of political behavior, and that they were therefore immune to all proposals for political reform. These lower-class voters seemed willing enough to support specific proposals which would enable them to secure the voice necessary to satisfy their economic and social needs, recognizing, quite properly, that the latter were the real sources of society's maladjustment. Since the rural areas of Massachusetts generally controlled the Bay State legislature, the urban working class supported the initiative and referendum amendment which might enable them to by-pass tight-fisted rural solons. Since the same situation prevailed in the New York legislature, the New York City delegation was glad to secure popular election of United States senators. In brief, it would seem that the line-up on such questions depended more upon local conditions of practical politics than upon the workings of a Yankee-Protestant ethos.

In the realm of economic reform, pertaining particularly to the problem of "big business," indications are that the urban lower class tended—unwittingly, of course—to favor the "New Nationalism" approach of Herbert Croly and Theodore Roosevelt over the "New Freedom" of Wilson and the trust-busters. Its members had seldom experienced the white collar group's "office boy to bank president" phenomenon themselves. They had never been part of the "Old Aristocracy," and hence had not suffered a downward revision in status at the hands of big business moguls. They shared few of the aspirations of the industrial "small businessman" and, indeed, recognized that the latter was all too frequently identified with sweatshop conditions.

---

[10] See Hofstadter, *Age of Reform*, chap. 6.

Consequently, the urban lower class was little stirred by Wilsonian cries to give the "pygmies" a chance. To workers the relative size of the employer's establishment was quite immaterial so long as he provided job security and adequate wages and working conditions, and passed some of the benefits of large-scale production on to consumers in the form of lower prices. Governmental stabilization of the economy and regulation of big business might well prove more successful in guaranteeing these conditions than would government antitrust drives. As a result, we find urban lower-class representatives introducing a large variety of business regulatory measures on the local and state levels during the Progressive Era. And it is symbolic, perhaps, to find Senator Robert F. Wagner introducing the National Industrial Recovery Act in 1933, while Senator David I. Walsh of Massachusetts had sponsored somewhat similar, forerunner, measures in Congress during the 1920's.

What has been said above indicates the basis for urban lower-class interest in the many types of social welfare and labor measures which became novelties, and then commonplace enactments, during the Progressive Era. If the middle class faced the fear of insecurity of status, then the working class faced an equally compelling fear of insecurity of livelihood and living conditions. The precarious condition of the lower class had now become known even to those on the better side of the tracks and, partly for humanitarian reasons and partly to defend their own civilization against a "revolution from below," middle-class reformers had become interested in social justice movements—which involved "doing things for others." But the recipients of this benevolence might surely be expected to show at least an equal interest in such movements—which involved doing something for themselves. That such was the case is clearly indicated by study of the legislative history of measures like workmen's compensation, widows' pensions, wages and hours legislation, factory safety legislation, and tenement laws in the legislatures of New York and Massachusetts during the Progressive years. The representatives of lower-class constituencies were the most active legislative sponsors and backers of such bills and, in collaboration with middle-class propagandists and lobbyists, they achieved a record of enactments which embraced much of the best and most enduring part of the Progressive Era's heritage.

The operations of the New York State Factory Investigating Commission are a case in point. Established by the legislature following the tragic Triangle Shirtwaist Company fire in 1911, the Commission recommended and secured passage of over fifty labor laws during the next four years, providing a model factory code that was widely copied in other states. The Commission's most active legislative members were State Senator Robert F. Wagner and Assemblyman Alfred E. Smith, two products of the East Side, while its most effective investigator and lobbyist was Miss Frances Perkins, a middle-class, college trained social worker. (It should be noted also that the Commission received notable assistance from Samuel Gompers and other leaders of organized labor.) Again it is rather striking to observe that the Social Security Act of 1935, which began the transfer of industrial security matters from the state to the national level, was introduced by Senator Wagner, to be administered by a federal Department of Labor headed by Miss Perkins.

Effective social reform during the Progressive Era, and in later periods, seems thus to have depended upon constructive collaboration, on specific issues, between reformers from both the urban lower class and the urban middle class (with the further co-operation, at times, of organized labor). Of course, such co-operation could not be attained on all proposals that went under the name of social "reform." When, during the Progressive Era, certain old-stock, Protestant, middle-class reformers decided that the cure for social evils lay not only in environmental reforms, but necessitated also a forcible "uplifting" of the lower-class immigrants' cultural and behavior standards to "100 per cent American" levels, the parting of the ways came. Lower-class reform spokesmen had no use for compulsory "Americanization" through Prohibition, the closing of parochial schools, or the enforcement of puritanical "blue laws." Nor had they any use for immigration restriction laws which were based upon invidious, quasi-racist distinctions between allegedly "superior" and "inferior" nationality stocks.[11] To them reform, in so far as the use of government compulsion was concerned, was a matter of environment. The fundamentals of a man's cultural luggage—his religion, his emotional attachment to his "old country" and its customs, his habits and personal behavior—were of concern to himself and his God, and to them alone. The lower-class reformers were products of the melting pot, and most of them took seriously the inscription on the base of the famous statue in New York harbor. True, there were many religious and ethnic differences among the component elements of the lower class, which often resulted in prejudice and violence. But each of these elements resented the Old Stock's contention that all of them were equally inferior to the "real Americans" of Yankee-Protestant heritage, and they resisted the attempts, which grew as the Progressive Era wore on, to enforce conformity to a single cultural norm.

In so far as conformity-seeking "cultural" reforms were enacted in the Progressive years, then, the responsibility must be assigned to urban middle-class reformers, joined in this instance by their rural "bible belt" brethren. The lower class can share no part of the "credit" for reforms like Prohibition. But in resisting such movements, were they not waging an early fight on behalf of what we today call "cultural pluralism"—acceptance of which has

---

[11] "If the literacy test was not applied to the Irish and the German, why should it now be applied to the Jew, the Italian or the Slav of the new immigration? Like our ancestors, they are now flying from persecution, from ignorance, from inequality; like our ancestors they expect to find here freedom and equal opportunity. Are we going to deny them an equal opportunity? Are we going to withhold from them the equality and opportunities which our fathers enjoyed?" (Excerpt from a speech by Robert F. Wagner in the New York State Senate, on a resolution which he introduced in 1917 petitioning Congress not to pass the literacy test bill. Wagner Papers).

become a cardinal tenet in the standard definition of "liberalism" in the modern world? Indeed, it may not be too much to say that in all three fields of reform—the political and economic, as well as the social—indications are that the urban lower-class approach was more uniformly "advanced" than that of the middle class, in the sense of being more in line with what has become the predominant liberal faith in modern America. After all, does not the lower-class reform impulse, as outlined above, resemble the "hard-headed," realistic, and pluralistic liberalism for which spokesmen like Reinhold Niebuhr and Arthur Schlesinger, Jr., plead today, so that the "Children of Light" might not fall easy prey to the "Children of Darkness"? [12]

It is not contended, of course, that all members of the urban working class became interested in reform during the Progressive Era, any more than it can be contended that all members of the urban middle class did so. The same "sidewalks of New York" that produced Al Smith and Robert Wagner continued to produce their share of "unreconstructed" machine politicians, whose vision never rose above their own pockets. Nor is it argued that the nature and zeal of lower-class attachment to liberalism remained constant throughout the twentieth century, or that the degree of co-operation attained with other reform minded elements remained unchanging. In the 1920's, for example, mutual suspicion and distrust, based largely on ethnic or "cultural" differences, seem to have displaced the former mood of limited collaboration between lower- and middle-class spokesmen, and in these changed circumstances Progressive-type measures found little chance of enactment. It is also possible that the high level of general prosperity prevailing since 1941 has vitiated urban working-class devotion to economic reform, and that the increasing degree of acceptance enjoyed by ethnic elements formerly discriminated against is causing their members to forget the lessons of cultural pluralism. All of these matters deserve further study.

The last-mentioned problems, dealing with the contemporary scene, may lie more properly within the realm of the political scientist and sociologist. But surely the evolution of America's twentieth-century liberal society, from the Progressive Era through the New Deal, is a province for historical inquiry. It is suggested that the historians who enter it might do better if they modify the "middle-class" emphasis which has come to dominate the field and devote more attention to exploring hitherto neglected elements of the American social structure. Such exploration necessitates tedious research, focusing at first on the local and state levels, in unalluring source materials such as local and foreign-language newspapers, out-of-the-way manuscript collections, and the correlations between the make-up and voting records of small-scale election districts. In the course of this research, however, our conception of the Progressive Era, and of recent American history as a whole,

---

[12] See, for example, Reinhold Niebuhr, *The Children of Light and the Children of Darkness* (New York, 1945); Arthur M. Schlesinger, Jr., *The Vital Center* (Boston, 1949).

may undergo change. In fact, it may even begin to appear that "old fashioned" political historians, if they inform their work with up-to-date statistical and social science skills, still have as much to contribute to our knowledge of ourselves as do the intellectual and social historians, who are, perhaps, sometimes prone to over-generalize on the basis of historical psychoanalysis.

SUGGESTED READING

For support of Huthmacher's analysis, see his "Charles Evans Hughes and Charles F. Murphy: The Metamorphosis of Progressivism," *New York History*, XLVI (Jan., 1965), 25–40, and his *Senator Robert F. Wagner and the Rise of Urban Liberalism* (Atheneum, 1968); see also Robert Wesser's "Charles Evans Hughes and the Urban Sources of Political Progressivism," *New York History*, L (Oct., 1966), 365–400, and his *Charles Evans Hughes: Politics and Reform in New York* (Cornell Univ. Press, 1967); and Philip Gleason's "An Immigrant Group's Interest in Progressive Reform: The Case of the German-American Catholics," *American Historical Review*, LXXIII (Dec., 1967), 367–79.

None of these studies adequately assesses the comparative importance of the urban workers in the progressive coalition, but M. Rogin in "Progressives and the California Electorate," *Journal of American History*, LV (Sept., 1968), 297–314, relying heavily on an analysis of voting statistics, finds that the progressive Hiram Johnson "depended on immigrant, working-class votes" and suggests that the "New Deal coalition had roots in the progressive period." There is little support for Huthmacher's thesis in two recent monographs: Irwin Yellowitz's *Labor and the Progressive Movement in New York State* (Cornell Univ. Press, 1965); and Jeremy P. Felt's *Hostages of Fortune: Child Labor Reform in New York State* (Syracuse Univ. Press, 1965). Huthmacher's analysis represents a disagreement with the views of his teacher, Oscar Handlin, author of *The Uprooted* ° (Little, Brown, 1951) and *Al Smith and his America* ° (Little, Brown, 1959), who views the immigrants as bulwarks of conservatism and opponents of reform.

SAMUEL P. HAYS

The Politics of Reform in Municipal Government in the Progressive Era

INTRODUCTION

In the developing reassessment of progressivism, Samuel P. Hays has played an important role. He argues in *Conservation and the Gospel of Efficiency* (Harvard Univ. Press, 1959) that the struggle for conservation did not pit the people against corporate business, but was primarily the achievement of scientists and businessmen who were committed to the rational and planned use of natural resources. In the article reprinted below, Hays examines the progressive agitation for good municipal government and finds that it cannot be understood as a polar struggle between business and the masses, or between corrupt bosses and righteous middle-class Yankee reformers, or between status-conscious professionals and

FROM Samuel P. Hays, "The Politics of Reform in Municipal Government in the Progressive Era," *Pacific Northwest Quarterly*, LV (October, 1964), pp. 157–69. Reprinted by permission of the author.

the corporations that usurped their authority. Ignoring rhetoric and distinguishing between political ideology and practice, Hays contends that the main seekers of reformed city government were those business, professional, and upper-class groups interested in developing political institutions susceptible to their control.

Hays not only does not find the progressive impulse in the middle class; he deftly reveals the methodological errors committed by those historians who have tried to explain middle-class reform activity in psychological terms—for example, as an irrational response to the fear that status is being threatened or lost. In addition, Hays argues that corruption, after all, might serve a social function.

Unfortunately, Hays does not clearly distinguish between the upper and middle classes, and he fails to explain satisfactorily how a minority committed to undemocratic reforms could be so successful. Nevertheless, his important article has significance far beyond the particular cases studied, for Hays has effectively emphasized the value of examining political behavior and not rhetoric, has suggested the need to explore the nature of political and social power, and has explained municipal reform as part of the larger movement of business rationalization. Contributing to the recent renaissance in local history, Hays makes it clear that research on communities can avoid antiquarianism and local pride and can focus on the central themes that disclose the nature of the political and economic structure.

*I*n order to achieve a more complete understanding of social change in the Progressive Era, historians must now undertake a deeper analysis of the practices of economic, political, and social groups. Political ideology alone is no longer satisfactory evidence to describe social patterns because generalizations based upon it, which tend to divide political groups into the moral and the immoral, the rational and the irrational, the efficient and the inefficient, do not square with political practice. Behind this contemporary rhetoric concerning the nature of reform lay patterns of political behavior which were at variance with it. Since an extensive gap separated ideology and practice, we can no longer take the former as an accurate description of the latter, but must reconstruct social behavior from other types of evidence.

Reform in urban government provides one of the most striking examples of this problem of analysis. The demand for change in municipal affairs, whether in terms of over-all reform, such as the commission and city-manager plans, or of more piecemeal modifications, such as the development of city-wide school boards, deeply involved reform ideology. Reformers loudly proclaimed a new structure of municipal government as more moral, more rational, and more efficient and, because it was so, self-evidently more desirable. But precisely because of this emphasis, there seemed to be no need to analyze the political forces behind change. Because the goals of reform were good, its causes were obvious; rather than being the product of particular people and particular ideas in particular situations, they were deeply imbedded in the universal impulses and truths of "progress." Consequently, historians have rarely tried to determine precisely who the municipal reformers were or what they did, but instead have relied on reform ideology as an accurate description of reform practice.

The reform ideology which became the basis of historical analysis is well known. It appears in classic form in Lincoln Steffens' *Shame of the Cities*. The urban political struggle of the Progressive Era, so the argument goes, involved a conflict between public impulses for "good government" against a corrupt alliance of "machine politicians" and "special interests."

During the rapid urbanization of the late 19th century, the latter had been free to aggrandize themselves, especially through franchise grants, at the expense of the public. Their power lay primarily in their ability to manipulate the political process, by bribery and corruption, for their own ends. Against such arrangements there gradually arose a public protest, a demand by the public for honest government, for officials who would act for the public rather than for themselves. To accomplish their goals, reformers sought basic modifications in the political system, both in the structure of government and in the manner of selecting public officials. These changes, successful in city after city, enabled the "public interest" to triumph.[1]

Recently, George Mowry, Alfred Chandler, Jr., and Richard Hofstadter have modified this analysis by emphasizing the fact that the impulse for reform did not come from the working class.[2] This might have been suspected from the rather strained efforts of National Municipal League writers in the "Era of Reform" to go out of their way to demonstrate working-class support for commission and city-manager governments.[3] We now know that they clutched at straws, and often erroneously, in order to prove to themselves as well as to the public that municipal reform was a mass movement.

The Mowry-Chandler-Hofstadter writings have further modified older

---

[1] See, for example, Clifford W. Patton, *Battle for Municipal Reform* (Washington, D.C., 1940), and Frank Mann Stewart, *A Half-Century of Municipal Reform* (Berkeley, 1950).

[2] George E. Mowry, *The California Progressives* (Berkeley and Los Angeles, 1951), 86–104; Richard Hofstadter, *The Age of Reform* (New York, 1955), 131–269; Alfred D. Chandler, Jr., "The Origins of Progressive Leadership," in Elting Morrison *et al.*, ed., *Letters of Theodore Roosevelt* (Cambridge, 1951–54), VIII, Appendix III, 1462–64.

[3] Harry A. Toulmin, *The City Manager* (New York, 1915), 156–68; Clinton R. Woodruff, *City Government by Commission* (New York, 1911), 243–53.

views by asserting that reform in general and municipal reform in particular sprang from a distinctively middle-class movement. This has now become the prevailing view. Its popularity is surprising not only because it is based upon faulty logic and extremely limited evidence, but also because it, too, emphasizes the analysis of ideology rather than practice and fails to contribute much to the understanding of who distinctively were involved in reform and why.

Ostensibly, the "middle-class" theory of reform is based upon a new type of behavioral evidence, the collective biography, in studies by Mowry of California Progressive party leaders, by Chandler of a nationwide group of that party's leading figures, and by Hofstadter of four professions—ministers, lawyers, teachers, editors. These studies demonstrate the middle-class nature of reform, but they fail to determine if reformers were distinctively middle class, specifically if they differed from their opponents. One study of 300 political leaders in the state of Iowa, for example, discovered that Progressive party, Old Guard, and Cummins Republicans were all substantially alike, the Progressives differing only in that they were slightly younger than the others and had less political experience.[4] If its opponents were also middle class, then one cannot describe Progressive reform as a phenomenon, the special nature of which can be explained in terms of middle-class characteristics. One cannot explain the distinctive behavior of people in terms of characteristics which are not distinctive to them.

Hofstadter's evidence concerning professional men fails in yet another way to determine the peculiar characteristics of reformers. For he describes ministers, lawyers, teachers, and editors without determining who within these professions became reformers and who did not. Two analytical distinctions might be made. Ministers involved in municipal reform, it appears, came not from all segments of religion, but peculiarly from upper-class churches. They enjoyed the highest prestige and salaries in the religious community and had no reason to feel a loss of "status," as Hofstadter argues. Their role in reform arose from the class character of their religious organizations rather than from the mere fact of their occupation as ministers.[5] Professional men involved in reform (many of whom—engineers, architects, and doctors—Hofstadter did not examine at all) seem to have come especially from the more advanced segments of their professions, from those who

---

[4] Eli Daniel Potts, "A Comparative Study of the Leadership of Republican Factions in Iowa, 1904–1914," M.A. thesis (State University of Iowa, 1956). Another satisfactory comparative analysis is contained in William T. Kerr, Jr., "The Progressives of Washington, 1910–12," *PNQ*, Vol. 55 (1964), 16–27.

[5] Based upon a study of eleven ministers involved in municipal reform in Pittsburgh, who represented exclusively the upper-class Presbyterian and Episcopal churches.

sought to apply their specialized knowledge to a wider range of public affairs.[6] Their role in reform is related not to their attempt to defend earlier patterns of culture, but to the working out of the inner dynamics of professionalization in modern society.

The weakness of the "middle-class" theory of reform stems from the fact that it rests primarily upon ideological evidence, not on a thoroughgoing description of political practice. Although the studies of Mowry, Chandler, and Hofstadter ostensibly derive from behavioral evidence, they actually derive largely from the extensive expressions of middle-ground ideological position, of the reformers' own descriptions of their contemporary society, and of their expressed fears of both the lower and the upper classes, of the fright of being ground between the millstones of labor and capital.[7]

Such evidence, though it accurately portrays what people thought, does not accurately describe what they did. The great majority of Americans look upon themselves as "middle class" and subscribe to a middle-ground ideology, even though in practice they belong to a great variety of distinct social classes. Such ideologies are not rationalizations or deliberate attempts to deceive. They are natural phenomena of human behavior. But the historian should be especially sensitive to their role so that he will not take evidence of political ideology as an accurate representation of political practice.

In the following account I will summarize evidence in both secondary and primary works concerning the political practices in which municipal reformers were involved. Such an analysis logically can be broken down into three parts, each one corresponding to a step in the traditional argument. First, what was the source of reform? Did it lie in the general public rather than in particular groups? Was it middle class, working class, or perhaps of other composition? Second, what was the reform target of attack? Were reformers primarily interested in ousting the corrupt individual, the political or business leader who made private arrangements at the expense of the public, or were they interested in something else? Third, what political innovations did reformers bring about? Did they seek to expand popular participation in the governmental process?

There is now sufficient evidence to determine the validity of these specific elements of the more general argument. Some of it has been available for several decades; some has appeared more recently; some is presented here for the first time. All of it adds up to the conclusion that reform in municipal government involved a political development far different from what we have assumed in the past.

---

[6] Based upon a study of professional men involved in municipal reform in Pittsburgh, comprising eighty-three doctors, twelve architects, twenty-five educators, and thirteen engineers.

[7] See especially Mowry, *The California Progressives.*

Available evidence indicates that the source of support for reform in municipal government did not come from the lower or middle classes, but from the upper class. The leading business groups in each city and professional men closely allied with them initiated and dominated municipal movements. Leonard White, in his study of the city manager published in 1927, wrote:

> The opposition to bad government usually comes to a head in the local chamber of commerce. Business men finally acquire the conviction that the growth of their city is being seriously impaired by the failures of city officials to perform their duties efficiently. Looking about for a remedy, they are captivated by the resemblance of the city-manager plan to their corporate form of business organization.[8]

In the 1930's White directed a number of studies of the origin of city-manager government. The resulting reports invariably begin with such statements as, "the Chamber of Commerce spearheaded the movement," or commission government in this city was a "businessmen's government." [9] Of thirty-two cases of city-manager government in Oklahoma examined by Jewell C. Phillips, twenty-nine were initiated either by chambers of commerce or by community committees dominated by businessmen.[10] More recently James Weinstein has presented almost irrefutable evidence that the business community, represented largely by chambers of commerce, was the overwhelming force behind both commission and city-manager movements.[11]

Dominant elements of the business community played a prominent role in another crucial aspect of municipal reform: the Municipal Research Bureau movement.[12] Especially in the larger cities, where they had less success in shaping the structure of government, reformers established centers to conduct research in municipal affairs as a springboard for influence.

The first such organization, the Bureau of Municipal Research of New York City, was founded in 1906; it was financed largely through the efforts of

---

[8] Leonard White, *The City Manager* (Chicago, 1927), ix–x.

[9] Harold A. Stone *et al.*, *City Manager Government in Nine Cities* (Chicago, 1940); Frederick C. Mosher *et al.*, *City Manager Government in Seven Cities* (Chicago, 1940); Harold A. Stone *et al.*, *City Manager Government in the United States* (Chicago, 1940). Cities covered by these studies include: Austin, Texas; Charlotte, North Carolina; Dallas, Texas; Dayton, Ohio; Fredericksburg, Virginia; Jackson, Michigan; Janesville, Wisconsin; Kingsport, Tennessee; Lynchburg, Virginia; Rochester, New York; San Diego, California.

[10] Jewell Cass Phillips, *Operation of the Council-Manager Plan of Government in Oklahoma Cities* (Philadelphia, 1935), 31–39.

[11] James Weinstein, "Organized Business and the City Commission and Manager Movements," *Journal of Southern History*, XXVIII (1962), 166–82.

[12] Norman N. Gill, *Municipal Research Bureaus* (Washington, 1944).

Andrew Carnegie and John D. Rockefeller. An investment banker provided the crucial support in Philadelphia, where a Bureau was founded in 1908. A group of wealthy Chicagoans in 1910 established the Bureau of Public Efficiency, a research agency. John H. Patterson of the National Cash Register Company, the leading figure in Dayton municipal reform, financed the Dayton Bureau, founded in 1912. And George Eastman was the driving force behind both the Bureau of Municipal Research and city-manager government in Rochester. In smaller cities data about city government was collected by interested individuals in a more informal way or by chambers of commerce, but in larger cities the task required special support, and prominent businessmen supplied it.

The character of muncipal reform is demonstrated more precisely by a brief examination of the movements in Des Moines and Pittsburgh. The Des Moines Commercial Club inaugurated and carefully controlled the drive for the commission form of government.[13] In January, 1906, the Club held a so-called "mass meeting" of business and professional men to secure an enabling act from the state legislature. P. C. Kenyon, president of the Club, selected a Committee of 300, composed principally of business and professional men, to draw up a specific proposal. After the legislature approved their plan, the same committee managed the campaign which persuaded the electorate to accept the commission form of government by a narrow margin in June, 1907.

In this election the lower-income wards of the city opposed the change, the upper-income wards supported it strongly, and the middle-income wards were more evenly divided. In order to control the new government, the Commitee of 300, now expanded to 530, sought to determine the nomination and election of the five new commissioners, and to this end they selected an avowedly businessman's slate. Their plans backfired when the voters swept into office a slate of anticommission candidates who now controlled the new commission government.

Proponents of the commission form of government in Des Moines spoke frequently in the name of the "people." But their more explicit statements emphasized their intent that the new plan be a "business system" of government, run by businessmen. The slate of candidates for commissioner endorsed by advocates of the plan was known as the "businessman's ticket." J. W. Hill, president of the committees of 300 and 530, bluntly declared: "The professional politician must be ousted and in his place capable business men chosen to conduct the affairs of the city." I. M. Earle, general counsel of the Bankers Life Association and a prominent figure in the movement, put the point more precisely: "When the plan was adopted it was the intention to get businessmen to run it."

---

[13] This account of the movement for commission government in Des Moines is derived from items in the Des Moines *Register* during the years from 1905 through 1908.

Although reformers used the ideology of popular government, they in no sense meant that all segments of society should be involved equally in municipal decision-making. They meant that their concept of the city's welfare would be best achieved if the business community controlled city government. As one businessman told a labor audience, the businessman's slate represented labor "better than you do yourself."

The composition of the municipal reform movement in Pittsburgh demonstrates its upper-class and professional as well as its business sources.[14] Here the two principal reform organizations were the Civic Club and the Voters' League. The 745 members of these two organizations came primarily from the upper class. Sixty-five per cent appeared in upper-class directories which contained the names of only 2 per cent of the city's families. Furthermore, many who were not listed in these directories lived in upper-class areas. These reformers, it should be stressed, comprised not an old but a new upper class. Few came from earlier industrial and mercantile families. Most of them had risen to social position from wealth created after 1870 in the iron, steel, electrical equipment, and other industries, and they lived in the newer rather than the older fashionable areas.

Almost half (48 per cent) of the reformers were professional men: doctors, lawyers, ministers, directors of libraries and museums, engineers, architects, private and public school teachers, and college professors. Some of these belonged to the upper class as well, especially the lawyers, ministers, and private school teachers. But for the most part their interest in reform stemmed from the inherent dynamics of their professions rather than from their class connections. They came from the more advanced segments of their organizations, from those in the forefront of the acquisition and application of knowledge. They were not the older professional men, seeking to preserve the past against change; they were in the vanguard of professional life, actively seeking to apply expertise more widely to public affairs.

Pittsburgh reformers included a large segment of businessmen; 52 per cent were bankers and corporation officials or their wives. Among them were the presidents of fourteen large banks and officials of Westinghouse, Pittsburgh Plate Glass, U.S. Steel and its component parts (such as Carnegie Steel, American Bridge, and National Tube), Jones and Laughlin, lesser steel companies (such as Crucible, Pittsburgh, Superior, Lockhart, and H. K. Porter), and H. J. Heinz Company, and the Pittsburgh Coal Company, as well as officials of the Pennsylvania Railroad and the Pittsburgh and Lake Erie. These men were not small businessmen; they directed the most powerful banking and industrial organizations of the city. They represented not the

[14] Biographical data constitutes the main source of evidence for this study of Pittsburgh reform leaders. It was found in city directories, social registers, directories of corporate directors, biographical compilations, reports of boards of education, settlement houses, welfare organizations, and similar types of material. Especially valuable was the clipping file maintained at the Carnegie Library of Pittsburgh.

old business community, but industries which had developed and grown primarily within the past fifty years and which had come to dominate the city's economic life.

These business, professional, and upper-class groups who dominated municipal reform movements were all involved in the rationalization and systematization of modern life; they wished a form of government which would be more consistent with the objectives inherent in those developments. The most important single feature of their perspective was the rapid expansion of the geographical scope of affairs which they wished to influence and manipulate, a scope which was no longer limited and narrow, no longer within the confines of pedestrian communities, but was now broad and citywide, covering the whole range of activities of the metropolitan area.

The migration of the upper class from central to outlying areas created a geographical distance between its residential communities and its economic institutions. To protect the latter required involvement both in local ward affairs and in the larger city government as well. Moreover, upper-class cultural institutions, such as museums, libraries, and symphony orchestras, required an active interest in the larger municipal context from which these institutions drew much of their clientele.

Professional groups, broadening the scope of affairs which they sought to study, measure, or manipulate, also sought to influence the public health, the educational system, or the physical arrangements of the entire city. Their concerns were limitless, not bounded by geography, but as expansive as the professional imagination. Finally, the new industrial community greatly broadened its perspective in governmental affairs because of its new recognition of the way in which factors throughout the city affected business growth. The increasing size and scope of industry, the greater stake in more varied and geographically dispersed facets of city life, the effect of floods on many business concerns, the need to promote traffic flows to and from work for both blue-collar and managerial employees—all contributed to this larger interest. The geographically larger private perspectives of upper-class, professional, and business groups gave rise to a geographically larger public perspective.

These reformers were dissatisfied with existing systems of muncipal government. They did not oppose corruption per se—although there was plenty of that. They objected to the structure of government which enabled local and particularistic interests to dominate. Prior to the reforms of the Progressive Era, city government consisted primarily of confederations of local wards, each of which was represented on the city's legislative body. Each ward frequently had its own elementary schools and ward-elected school boards which administered them.

These particularistic interests were the focus of a decentralized political life. City councilmen were local leaders. They spoke for their local areas, the economic interests of their inhabitants, their residential concerns, their educational, recreational, and religious interests—i.e., for those aspects of community life which mattered most to those they represented. They rolled logs in the city council to provide streets, sewers, and other public works for their local areas. They defended the community's cultural practices, its distinctive languages or national customs, its liberal attitude toward liquor, and its saloons and dance halls which served as centers of community life. One observer described this process of representation in Seattle:

> The residents of the hill-tops and the suburbs may not fully appreciate the faithfulness of certain downtown ward councilmen to the interests of their constituents. . . . The people of a state would rise in arms against a senator or representative in Congress who deliberately misrepresented their wishes and imperilled their interests, though he might plead a higher regard for national good. Yet people in other parts of the city seem to forget that under the old system the ward elected councilmen with the idea of procuring service of special benefit to that ward.[15]

In short, pre-reform officials spoke for their constituencies, inevitably their own wards which had elected them, rather than for other sections or groups of the city.

The ward system of government especially gave representation in city affairs to lower- and middle-class groups. Most elected ward officials were from these groups, and they, in turn, constituted the major opposition to reforms in municipal government. In Pittsburgh, for example, immediately prior to the changes in both the city council and the school board in 1911 in which city-wide representation replaced ward representation, only 24 per cent of the 387 members of those bodies represented the same managerial, professional, and banker occupations which dominated the membership of the Civic Club and the Voters' League. The great majority (67 per cent) were small businessmen—grocers, saloonkeepers, livery-stable proprietors, owners of small hotels, druggists—white-collar workers such as clerks and bookkeepers, and skilled and unskilled workmen.[16]

This decentralized system of urban growth and the institutions which arose from it reformers now opposed. Social, professional, and economic life had developed not only in the local wards in a small community context, but also on a larger scale had become highly integrated and organized, giving rise to a superstructure of social organization which lay far above that of ward life and which was sharply divorced from it in both personal contacts and perspective.

By the late 19th century, those involved in these larger institutions

---

[15] *Town Crier* (Seattle), Feb. 18, 1911, p. 13.

[16] Information derived from same sources as cited in footnote 14.

found that the decentralized system of political life limited their larger objectives. The movement for reform in municipal government, therefore, constituted an attempt by upper-class, advanced professional, and large business groups to take formal political power from the previously dominant lower- and middle-class elements so that they might advance their own conceptions of desirable public policy. These two groups came from entirely different urban worlds, and the political system fashioned by one was no longer acceptable to the other.

Lower- and middle-class groups not only dominated the pre-reform governments, but vigorously opposed reform. It is significant that none of the occupational groups among them, for example, small businessmen or white-collar workers, skilled or unskilled artisans, had important representation in reform organizations thus far examined. The case studies of city-manager government undertaken in the 1930's under the direction of Leonard White detailed in city after city the particular opposition of labor. In their analysis of Jackson, Michigan, the authors of these studies wrote:

> The *Square Deal*, oldest Labor paper in the state, has been consistently against manager government, perhaps largely because labor has felt that with a decentralized government elected on a ward basis it was more likely to have some voice and to receive its share of privileges.[17]

In Janesville, Wisconsin, the small shopkeepers and workingmen on the west and south sides, heavily Catholic and often Irish, opposed the commission plan in 1911 and in 1912 and the city-manager plan when adopted in 1923.[18] "In Dallas there is hardly a trace of class consciousness in the Marxian sense," one investigator declared, "yet in city elections the division has been to a great extent along class lines." [19] The commission and city-manager elections were no exceptions. To these authors it seemed a logical reaction, rather than an embarrassing fact that had to be swept away, that working-men should have opposed municipal reform.[20]

In Des Moines working-class representatives, who in previous years might have been council members, were conspicuously absent from the "businessman's slate." Workingmen acceptable to reformers could not be found. A workingman's slate of candidates, therefore, appeared to challenge the reform slate. Organized labor, and especially the mineworkers, took the lead; one of their number, Wesley Ash, a deputy sheriff and union member,

---

[17] Stone *et al.*, *Nine Cities*, 212.

[18] *Ibid.*, 3–13.

[19] *Ibid.*, 329.

[20] Stone *et al.*, *City Manager Government*, 26, 237–41, for analysis of opposition to city-manager government.

made "an astonishing run" in the primary, coming in second among a field of more than twenty candidates.[21] In fact, the strength of anticommission candidates in the primary so alarmed reformers that they frantically sought to appease labor.

The day before the final election they modified their platform to pledge both an eight-hour day and an "American standard of wages." They attempted to persuade the voters that their slate consisted of men who represented labor because they had "begun at the bottom of the ladder and made a good climb toward success by their own unaided efforts." [22] But their tactics failed. In the election on March 30, 1908, voters swept into office the entire "opposition" slate. The business and professional community had succeeded in changing the form of government, but not in securing its control. A cartoon in the leading reform newspaper illustrated their disappointment; John Q. Public sat dejectedly and muttered, "Aw, What's the Use?"

The most visible opposition to reform and the most readily available target of reform attack was the so-called "machine," for through the "machine" many different ward communities as well as lower- and middle-income groups joined effectively to influence the central city government. Their private occupational and social life did not naturally involve these groups in larger city-wide activities in the same way as the upper class was involved; hence they lacked access to privately organized economic and social power on which they could construct political power. The "machine" filled this organizational gap.

Yet it should never be forgotten that the social and economic institutions in the wards themselves provided the "machine's" sustaining support and gave it larger significance. When reformers attacked the "machine" as the most visible institutional element of the ward system, they attacked the entire ward form of political organization and the political power of lower- and middle-income groups which lay behind it.

Reformers often gave the impression that they opposed merely the corrupt politician and his "machine." But in a more fundamental way they looked upon the deficiencies of pre-reform political leaders in terms not of their personal shortcomings, but of the limitations inherent in their occupational, institutional, and class positions. In 1911 the Voters' League of Pittsburgh wrote in its pamphlet analyzing the qualifications of candidates that "a man's occupation ought to give a strong indication of his qualifications for membership on a school board." [23] Certain occupations inherently disqualified a man from serving:

---

[21] Des Moines *Register and Leader*, March 17, 1908.

[22] *Ibid.*, March 30, March 28, 1908.

[23] Voters' Civic League of Allegheny County, "Bulletin of the Voters' Civic League of Allegheny County Concerning the Public School System of Pittsburgh," Feb. 14, 1911, pp. 2–3.

> Employment as ordinary laborer and in the lowest class of mill work would
> naturally lead to the conclusion that such men did not have sufficient educa-
> tion or business training to act as school directors. . . . Objection might also
> be made to small shopkeepers, clerks, workmen at many trades, who by lack of
> educational advantages and business training, could not, no matter how hon-
> est, be expected to administer properly the affairs of an educational system,
> requiring special knowledge, and where millions are spent each year.

These, of course, were precisely the groups which did dominate Pittsburgh
government prior to reform. The League deplored the fact that school boards
contained only a small number of "men prominent throughout the city in
business life . . . in professional occupations . . . holding positions as
managers, secretaries, auditors, superintendents and foremen" and exhorted
these classes to participate more actively as candidates for office.

Reformers, therefore, wished not simply to replace bad men with good;
they proposed to change the occupational and class origins of decision-
makers. Toward this end they sought innovations in the formal machinery of
government which would concentrate political power by sharply centraliz-
ing the processes of decision-making rather than distribute it through more
popular participation in public affairs. According to the liberal view of the
Progressive Era, the major political innovations of reform involved the equalization of political power through the primary, the direct election of public
officials, and the initiative, referendum, and recall. These measures played a
large role in the political ideology of the time and were frequently incorporated into new municipal charters. But they provided at best only an occasional and often incidental process of decision-making. Far more important
in continuous, sustained, day-to-day processes of government were those innovations which centralized decision-making in the hands of fewer and
fewer people.

The systematization of municipal government took place on both the
executive and the legislative levels. The strong-mayor and city-manager
types became the most widely used examples of the former. In the first decade of the 20th century, the commission plan had considerable appeal, but
its distribution of administrative responsibility among five people gave rise
to a demand for a form with more centralized executive power; consequently,
the city-manager or the commission-manager variant often replaced it.[24]

A far more pervasive and significant change, however, lay in the centralization of the system of representation, the shift from ward to city-wide

[24] In the decade 1911 to 1920, 43 per cent of the municipal charters adopted in eleven
home rule states involved the commission form and 35 per cent the city-manager form; in
the following decade the figures stood at 6 per cent and 71 per cent respectively. The
adoption of city-manager charters reached a peak in the years 1918 through 1923 and
declined sharply after 1933. See Leonard D. White, "The Future of Public Administration," *Public Management,* XV (1933), 12.

election of councils and school boards. Governing bodies so selected, reformers argued, would give less attention to local and particularistic matters and more to affairs of city-wide scope. This shift, an invariable feature of both commission and city-manager plans, was often adopted by itself. In Pittsburgh, for example, the new charter of 1911 provided as the major innovation that a council of twenty-seven, each member elected from a separate ward, be replaced by a council of nine, each elected by the city as a whole.

Cities displayed wide variations in this innovation. Some regrouped wards into larger units but kept the principle of areas of representation smaller than the entire city. Some combined a majority of councilmen elected by wards with additional ones elected at large. All such innovations, however, constituted steps toward the centralization of the system of representation.

Liberal historians have not appreciated the extent to which municipal reform in the Progressive Era involved a debate over the system of representation. The ward form of representation was universally condemned on the grounds that it gave too much influence to the separate units and not enough attention to the larger problems of the city. Harry A. Toulmin, whose book, *The City Manager*, was published by the National Municipal League, stated the case:

> The spirit of sectionalism had dominated the political life of every city. Ward pitted against ward, alderman against alderman, and legislation only effected by "log-rolling" extravagant measures into operation, mulcting the city, but gratifying the greed of constituents, has too long stung the conscience of decent citizenship. This constant treaty-making of factionalism has been no less than a curse. The city manager plan proposes the commendable thing of abolishing wards. The plan is not unique in this for it has been common to many forms of commission government. . . .[25]

Such a system should be supplanted, the argument usually went, with city-wide representation in which elected officials could consider the city "as a unit." "The new officers are elected," wrote Toulmin, "each to represent all the people. Their duties are so defined that they must administer the corporate business in its entirety, not as a hodge-podge of associated localities."

Behind the debate over the method of representation, however, lay a debate over who should be represented, over whose views of public policy should prevail. Many reform leaders often explicitly, if not implicitly, expressed fear that lower- and middle-income groups had too much influence in decision-making. One Galveston leader, for example, complained about the movement for initiative, referendum, and recall:

---

[25] Toulmin, *The City Manager*, 42.

We have in our city a very large number of negroes employed on the docks; we also have a very large number of unskilled white laborers; this city also has more barrooms, according to its population, than any other city in Texas. Under these circumstances it would be extremely difficult to maintain a satisfactory city government where all ordinances must be submitted back to the voters of the city for their ratification and approval.[26]

At the National Municipal League convention of 1907, Rear Admiral F. E. Chadwick (USN Ret.), a leader in the Newport, Rhode Island, movement for municipal reform, spoke to this question even more directly:

Our present system has excluded in large degree the representation of those who have the city's well-being most at heart. It has brought, in municipalities . . . a government established by the least educated, the least interested class of citizens.

It stands to reason that a man paying $5,000 taxes in a town is more interested in the well-being and development of his town than the man who pays no taxes. . . . It equally stands to reason that the man of the $5,000 tax should be assured a representation in the committee which lays the tax and spends the money which he contributes. . . . Shall we be truly democratic and give the property owner a fair show or shall we develop a tyranny of ignorance which shall crush him.[27]

Municipal reformers thus debated frequently the question of who should be represented as well as the question of what method of representation should be employed.

That these two questions were intimately connected was revealed in other reform proposals for representation, proposals which were rarely taken seriously. One suggestion was that a class system of representation be substituted for ward representation. For example, in 1908 one of the prominent candidates for commissioner in Des Moines proposed that the city council be composed of representatives of five classes: educational and ministerial organizations, manufacturers and jobbers, public utility corporations, retail merchants including liquor men, and the Des Moines Trades and Labor Assembly. Such a system would have greatly reduced the influence in the council of both middle- and lower-class groups. The proposal revealed the basic problem confronting business and professional leaders: how to reduce

---

[26] Woodruff, *City Government*, 315. The Galveston commission plan did not contain provisions for the initiative, referendum, or recall, and Galveston commercial groups which had fathered the commission plan opposed movements to include them. In 1911 Governor Colquitt of Texas vetoed a charter bill for Texarkana because it contained such provisions; he maintained that they were "undemocratic" and unnecessary to the success of commission government. *Ibid.*, 314–15.

[27] *Ibid.*, 207–208.

the influence in government of the majority of voters among middle- and lower-income groups.[28]

A growing imbalance between population and representation sharpened the desire of reformers to change from ward to city-wide elections. Despite shifts in population within most cities, neither ward district lines nor the apportionment of city council and school board seats changed frequently. Consequently, older areas of the city, with wards that were small in geographical size and held declining populations (usually lower and middle class in composition), continued to be overrepresented, and newer upper-class areas, where population was growing, became increasingly underrepresented. This intensified the reformers' conviction that the structure of government must be changed to give them the voice they needed to make their views on public policy prevail.[29]

It is not insignificant that in some cities (by no means a majority) municipal reform came about outside of the urban electoral process. The original commission government in Galveston was appointed rather than elected. "The failure of previous attempts to secure an efficient city government through the local electorate made the business men of Galveston willing to put the conduct of the city's affairs in the hands of a commission dominated by state-appointed officials." [30] Only in 1903 did the courts force Galveston to elect the members of the commission, an innovation which one writer described as "an abandonment of the commission idea," and which led to the decline of the influence of the business community in the commission government.[31]

In 1911 Pittsburgh voters were not permitted to approve either the new city charter or the new school board plan, both of which provided for city-wide representation; they were a result of state legislative enactment. The governor appointed the first members of the new city council, but thereafter they were elected. The judges of the court of common pleas, however, and not the voters, selected members of the new school board.

The composition of the new city council and new school board in Pittsburgh, both of which were inaugurated in 1911, revealed the degree to which the shift from ward to city-wide representation produced a change in group representation.[32] Members of the upper class, the advanced professional men, and the large business groups dominated both. Of the fifteen members

---

[28] Des Moines *Register and Leader*, Jan. 15, 1908.

[29] Voters' Civic League of Allegheny County, "Report on the Voters' League in the Redistricting of the Wards of the City of Pittsburgh" (Pittsburgh, n.d.).

[30] Horace E. Deming, "The Government of American Cities," in Woodruff, *City Government*, 167.

[31] *Ibid.*, 168.

[32] Information derived from same sources as cited in footnote 14.

of the Pittsburgh Board of Education appointed in 1911 and the nine members of the new city council, none were small businessmen or white-collar workers. Each body contained only one person who could remotely be classified as a blue-collar worker; each of these men filled a position specifically but unofficially designed as reserved for a "representative of labor," and each was an official of the Amalgamated Association of Iron, Steel, and Tin Workers. Six of the nine members of the new city council were prominent businessmen, and all six were listed in upper-class directories. Two others were doctors closely associated with the upper class in both professional and social life. The fifteen members of the Board of Education included ten businessmen with city-wide interests, one doctor associated with the upper class, and three women previously active in upper-class public welfare.

Lower- and middle-class elements felt that the new city governments did not represent them.[33] The studies carried out under the direction of Leonard White contain numerous expressions of the way in which the change in the structure of government produced not only a change in the geographical scope of representation, but also in the groups represented. "It is not the policies of the manager or the council they oppose," one researcher declared, "as much as the lack of representation for their economic level and social groups." [34] And another wrote:

> There had been nothing unapproachable about the old ward aldermen. Every voter had a neighbor on the common council who was interested in serving him. The new councilmen, however, made an unfavorable impression on the less well-to-do voters. . . . Election at large made a change that, however desirable in other ways, left the voters in the poorer wards with a feeling that they had been deprived of their share of political importance.[35]

The success of the drive for centralization of administration and representation varied with the size of the city. In the smaller cities, business, professional, and elite groups could easily exercise a dominant influence. Their close ties readily enabled them to shape informal political power which they could transform into formal political power. After the mid-1890's the widespread organization of chambers of commerce provided a base for political action to reform municipal government, resulting in a host of small-city commission and city-manager innovations. In the larger, more heterogeneous

---

[33] W. R. Hopkins, city manager of Cleveland, indicated the degree to which the new type of government was more responsive to the business community: "It is undoubtedly easier for a city manager to insist upon acting in accordance with the business interests of the city than it is for a mayor to do the same thing." Quoted in White, *The City Manager*, 13.

[34] Stone *et al.*, *Nine Cities*, 20.

[35] *Ibid.*, 225.

cities, whose subcommunities were more dispersed, such community-wide action was extremely difficult. Few commission or city-manager proposals materialized here. Mayors became stronger, and steps were taken toward centralization of representation, but the ward system or some modified version usually persisted. Reformers in large cities often had to rest content with their Municipal Research Bureaus through which they could exert political influence from outside the municipal government.

A central element in the analysis of municipal reform in the Progressive Era is governmental corruption. Should it be understood in moral or political terms? Was it a product of evil men or of particular socio-political circumstances? Reform historians have adopted the former view. Selfish and evil men arose to take advantage of a political arrangement whereby unsystematic government offered many opportunities for personal gain at public expense. The system thrived until the "better elements," "men of intelligence and civic responsibility," or "right-thinking people" ousted the culprits and fashioned a political force which produced decisions in the "public interest." In this scheme of things, corruption in public affairs grew out of individual personal failings and a deficient governmental structure which could not hold those predispositions in check, rather than from the peculiar nature of social forces. The contestants involved were morally defined: evil men who must be driven from power, and good men who must be activated politically to secure control of municipal affairs.

Public corruption, however, involves political even more than moral considerations. It arises more out of the particular distribution of political power than of personal morality. For corruption is a device to exercise control and influence outside the legal channels of decision-making when those channels are not readily responsive. Most generally, corruption stems from an inconsistency between control of the instruments of formal governmental power and the exercise of informal influence in the community. If powerful groups are denied access to formal power in legitimate ways, they seek access through procedures which the community considers illegitimate. Corrupt government, therefore, does not reflect the genius of evil men, but rather the lack of acceptable means for those who exercise power in the private community to wield the same influence in governmental affairs. It can be understood in the Progressive Era not simply by the preponderance of evil men over good, but by the peculiar nature of the distribution of political power.

The political corruption of the "Era of Reform" arose from the inaccessibility of municipal government to those who were rising in power and influence. Municipal government in the United States developed in the 19th century within a context of universal manhood suffrage which decentralized political control. Because all men, whatever their economic, social, or cultural conditions, could vote, leaders who reflected a wide variety of community interests and who represented the views of people of every circumstance arose to guide and direct municipal affairs. Since the majority of urban voters were workingmen or immigrants, the views of those groups carried great and often decisive weight in governmental affairs. Thus, as Herbert Gutman has shown, during strikes in the 1870's city officials were usually friendly to workingmen and refused to use police power to protect strikebreakers.[36]

Ward representation on city councils was an integral part of grass-roots influence, for it enabled diverse urban communities, invariably identified with particular geographical areas of the city, to express their views more clearly through councilmen peculiarly receptive to their concerns. There was a direct, reciprocal flow of power between wards and the center of city affairs in which voters felt a relatively close connection with public matters and city leaders gave special attention to their needs.

Within this political system the community's business leaders grew in influence and power as industrialism advanced, only to find that their economic position did not readily admit them to the formal machinery of government. Thus, during strikes, they had to rely on either their own private police, Pinkertons, or the state militia to enforce their use of strikebreakers. They frequently found that city officials did not accept their views of what was best for the city and what direction municipal policies should take. They had developed a common outlook, closely related to their economic activities, that the city's economic expansion should become the prime concern of municipal government, and yet they found that this view had to compete with even more influential views of public policy. They found that political tendencies which arose from universal manhood suffrage and ward representation were not always friendly to their political conceptions and goals and had produced a political system over which they had little control, despite the fact that their economic ventures were the core of the city's prosperity and the hope for future urban growth.

Under such circumstances, businessmen sought other methods of influencing municipal affairs. They did not restrict themselves to the channels of popular election and representation, but frequently applied direct influence —if not verbal persuasion, then bribery and corruption. Thereby arose the graft which Lincoln Steffens recounted in his *Shame of the Cities*. Utilities were only the largest of those business groups and individuals who requested special favors, and the franchises they sought were only the most sensational of the prizes which included such items as favorable tax assessments and rates, the vacating of streets wanted for factory expansion, or permission to operate amid antiliquor and other laws regulating personal behavior. The relationships between business and formal government became a maze of ac-

---

[36] Herbert Gutman, "An Iron Workers' Strike in the Ohio Valley, 1873–74," *Ohio Historical Quarterly*, LXVIII (1959), 353–70; "Trouble on the Railroads, 1873–1874: Prelude to the 1877 Crisis," *Labor History*, II (Spring, 1961), 215–36.

commodations, a set of political arrangements which grew up because effective power had few legitimate means of accomplishing its ends.

Steffens and subsequent liberal historians, however, misread the significance of these arrangements, emphasizing their personal rather than their more fundamental institutional elements. To them corruption involved personal arrangements between powerful business leaders and powerful "machine" politicians. Just as they did not fully appreciate the significance of the search for political influence by the rising business community as a whole, so they did not see fully the role of the "ward politician." They stressed the argument that the political leader manipulated voters to his own personal ends, that he used constituents rather than reflected their views.

A different approach is now taking root, namely, that the urban political organization was an integral part of community life, expressing its needs and its goals. As Oscar Handlin has said, for example, the "machine" not only fulfilled specific wants, but provided one of the few avenues to success and public recognition available to the immigrant.[37] The political leader's arrangements with businessmen, therefore, were not simply personal agreements between conniving individuals; they were far-reaching accommodations between powerful sets of institutions in industrial America.

These accommodations, however, proved to be burdensome and unsatisfactory to the business community and to the upper third of socio-economic groups in general. They were expensive; they were wasteful; they were uncertain. Toward the end of the 19th century, therefore, business and professional men sought more direct control over municipal government in order to exercise political influence more effectively. They realized their goals in the early 20th century in the new commission and city-manager forms of government and in the shift from ward to city-wide representation.

These innovations did not always accomplish the objectives that the business community desired because other forces could and often did adjust to the change in governmental structure and reëstablish their influence. But businessmen hoped that reform would enable them to increase their political power, and most frequently it did. In most cases the innovations which were introduced between 1901, when Galveston adopted a commission form of government, and the Great Depression, and especially the city-manager form which reached a height of popularity in the mid-1920's, served as vehicles whereby business and professional leaders moved directly into the inner circles of government, brought into one political system their own power and the formal machinery of government, and dominated municipal affairs for two decades.

Municipal reform in the early 20th century involves a paradox: the ideology of an extension of political control and the practice of its concentra-

---

[37] Oscar Handlin, *The Uprooted* (Boston, 1951), 209–17.

tion. While reformers maintained that their movement rested on a wave of popular demands, called their gatherings of business and professional leaders "mass meetings," described their reforms as "part of a world-wide trend toward popular government," and proclaimed an ideology of a popular upheaval against a selfish few, they were in practice shaping the structure of municipal government so that political power would no longer be broadly distributed, but would in fact be more centralized in the hands of a relatively small segment of the population. The paradox became even sharper when new city charters included provisions for the initiative, referendum, and recall. How does the historian cope with this paradox? Does it represent deliberate deception or simply political strategy? Or does it reflect a phenomenon which should be understood rather than explained away?

The expansion of popular involvement in decision-making was frequently a political tactic, not a political system to be established permanently, but a device to secure immediate political victory. The prohibitionist advocacy of the referendum, one of the most extensive sources of support for such a measure, came from the belief that the referendum would provide the opportunity to outlaw liquor more rapidly. The Anti-Saloon League, therefore, urged local option. But the League was not consistent. Towns which were wet, when faced with a county-wide local-option decision to outlaw liquor, demanded town or township local option to reinstate it. The League objected to this as not the proper application of the referendum idea.

Again, "Progressive" reformers often espoused the direct primary when fighting for nominations for their candidates within the party, but once in control they often became cool to it because it might result in their own defeat. By the same token, many municipal reformers attached the initiative, referendum, and recall to municipal charters often as a device to appease voters who opposed the centralization of representation and executive authority. But, by requiring a high percentage of voters to sign petitions— often 25 to 30 per cent—these innovations could be and were rendered relatively harmless.

More fundamentally, however, the distinction between ideology and practice in municipal reform arose from the different roles which each played. The ideology of democratization of decision-making was negative rather than positive; it served as an instrument of attack against the existing political system rather than as a guide to alternative action. Those who wished to destroy the "machine" and to eliminate party competition in local government widely utilized the theory that these political instruments thwarted public impulses, and thereby shaped the tone of their attack.

But there is little evidence that the ideology represented a faith in a purely democratic system of decision-making or that reformers actually wished, in practice, to substitute direct democracy as a continuing system of sustained decision-making in place of the old. It was used to destroy the political institutions of the lower and middle classes and the political power which those institutions gave rise to, rather than to provide a clear-cut guide for alternative action.[38]

The guide to alternative action lay in the model of the business enterprise. In describing new conditions which they wished to create, reformers drew on the analogy of the "efficient business enterprise," criticizing current practices with the argument that "no business could conduct its affairs that way and remain in business," and calling upon business practices as the guides to improvement. As one student remarked:

> The folklore of the business elite came by gradual transition to be the symbols of governmental reformers. Efficiency, system, orderliness, budgets, economy, saving, were all injected into the efforts of reformers who sought to remodel municipal government in terms of the great impersonality of corporate enterprise.[39]

Clinton Rodgers Woodruff of the National Municipal League explained that the commission form was "a simple, direct, businesslike way of administering the business affairs of the city . . . an application to city administration of that type of business organization which has been so common and so successful in the field of commerce and industry." [40] The centralization of decision-making which developed in the business corporation was now applied in municipal reform.

The model of the efficient business enterprise, then, rather than the New England town meeting, provided the positive inspiration for the municipal reformer. In giving concrete shape to this model in the strong-mayor, commission, and city-manager plans, reformers engaged in the elaboration of the processes of rationalization and systematization inherent in modern science and technology. For in many areas of society, industrialization brought a gradual shift upward in the location of decision-making and the geographical extension of the scope of the area affected by decisions.

Experts in business, in government, and in the professions measured, studied, analyzed, and manipulated ever wider realms of human life, and devices which they used to control such affairs constituted the most fundamental and far-reaching innovations in decision-making in modern America,

---

[38] Clinton Rodgers Woodruff of the National Municipal League even argued that the initiative, referendum, and recall were rarely used. "Their value lies in their existence rather than in their use." Woodruff, *City Government*, 314. It seems apparent that the most widely used of these devices, the referendum, was popularized by legislative bodies when they could not agree or did not want to take responsibility for a decision and sought to pass that responsibility to the general public, rather than because of a faith in the wisdom of popular will.

[39] J. B. Shannon, "County Consolidation," *Annals of the American Academy of Political and Social Science*, Vol. 207 (January, 1940), 168.

[40] Woodruff, *City Government*, 29–30.

whether in formal government or in the informal exercise of power in private life. Reformers in the Progressive Era played a major role in shaping this new system. While they expressed an ideology of restoring a previous order, they in fact helped to bring forth a system drastically new.[41]

The drama of reform lay in the competition for supremacy between two systems of decision-making. One system, based upon ward representation and growing out of the practices and ideas of representative government, involved wide latitude for the expression of grass-roots impulses and their involvement in the political process. The other grew out of the rationalization of life which came with science and technology, in which decisions arose from expert analysis and flowed from fewer and smaller centers outward to the rest of society. Those who espoused the former looked with fear upon the loss of influence which the latter involved, and those who espoused the latter looked only with disdain upon the wastefulness and inefficiency of the former.

The Progressive Era witnessed rapid strides toward a more centralized system and a relative decline for a more decentralized system. This development constituted an accommodation of forces outside the business community to the political trends within business and professional life rather than vice versa. It involved a tendency for the decision-making processes inherent in science and technology to prevail over those inherent in representative government.

Reformers in the Progressive Era and liberal historians since then misread the nature of the movement to change municipal government because they concentrated upon dramatic and sensational episodes and ignored the analysis of more fundamental political structure, of the persistent relationships of influence and power which grew out of the community's social, ideological, economic, and cultural activities. The reconstruction of these patterns of human relationships and of the changes in them is the historian's most crucial task, for they constitute the central context of historical development. History consists not of erratic and spasmodic fluctuations, of a series of random thoughts and actions, but of patterns of activity and change in which people hold thoughts and actions in common and in which there are close connections between sequences of events. These contexts give rise to a structure of human relationships which pervade all areas of life; for the political historian the most important of these is the structure of the distribution of power and influence.

---

[41] Several recent studies emphasize various aspects of this movement. See, for example, Loren Baritz, *Servants of Power* (Middletown, 1960); Raymond E. Callahan, *Education and the Cult of Efficiency* (Chicago, 1962); Samuel P. Hays, *Conservation and the Gospel of Efficiency* (Cambridge, 1959); Dwight Waldo, *The Administrative State* (New York, 1948), 3–61.

The structure of political relationships, however, cannot be adequately understood if we concentrate on evidence concerning ideology rather than practice. For it is becoming increasingly clear that ideological evidence is no safe guide to the understanding of practice, that what people thought and said about their society is not necessarily an accurate representation of what they did. The current task of the historian of the Progressive Era is to quit taking the reformers' own description of political practice at its face value and to utilize a wide variety of new types of evidence to reconstruct political practice in its own terms. This is not to argue that ideology is either important or unimportant. It is merely to state that ideological evidence is not appropriate to the discovery of the nature of political practice.

Only by maintaining this clear distinction can the historian successfully investigate the structure of political life in the Progressive Era. And only then can he begin to cope with the most fundamental problem of all: the relationship between political ideology and political practice. For each of these facets of political life must be understood in its own terms, through its own historical record. Each involves a distinct set of historical phenomena. The relationship between them for the Progressive Era is not now clear; it has not been investigated. But it cannot be explored until the conceptual distinction is made clear and evidence tapped which is pertinent to each. Because the nature of political practice has so long been distorted by the use of ideological evidence, the most pressing task is for its investigation through new types of evidence appropriate to it. The reconstruction of the movement for municipal reform can constitute a major step forward toward that goal.

SUGGESTED READING

Among the recent studies of cities and politics during the progressive period are Zane Miller's *Urbanization in the Progressive Era* (Oxford Univ. Press, 1968), a study of Cincinnati; James Crooks' *Politics and Progress: The Rise of Urban Progressivism in Baltimore, 1895–1911* (Louisiana State Univ. Press, 1968); and Robert Fogelson's *The Fragmented Metropolis: Los Angeles, 1850–1930* (Harvard Univ. Press, 1967), especially Chapter X.

Unfortunately, historians have generally neglected Hays' very important article on municipal reform, though his earlier volume on conservation has influenced Samuel Haber in *Efficiency and Uplift: Scientific Management in the Progressive Era, 1890–1920* (Univ. of Chicago Press, 1964) and Roy Lubove in *The Progressives and the Slums* (Univ. of Pittsburgh Press, 1963). Hays has more fully developed his ideas in "The Social Analysis of American Political History, 1880–1920," *Political Science Quarterly*, LXXX (Sept., 1965), 373–94.

Among the studies other than Hays' that criticize the "status revolution" (the theory that status anxiety greatly contributed to, or produced, progressivism) are Richard B. Sherman's "The Status Revolution and Massachusetts Progressive Leadership," *Political Science Quarterly*, LXXVIII (March, 1963), 59–65; E. Daniel Potts' "The Progressive Profile in Iowa," *Mid-America*, XLVII (Oct., 1965), 257–68; and Jack Tager's "Progressives, Conservatives and the Theory of the Status Revolution," *Mid-America*, XLVIII (July, 1966), 162–75. These writers generally conclude that state progressive political leaders did not differ significantly in social profile from Republican leaders. The theory of the "status revolution," however, might be partly redeemed if status is defined by the individual reformer's *own* perception; but then there is still a need to explain why such perceptions were so different from those of others in the *same objective* positions. What is needed to test the interpretation that a "status revolution" contributed to the making of progressives is a collective biography of progressive and nonprogressive leaders that will delve beyond objective criteria of social position (such as education, religion, occupation) to examine through diaries, reports, and other sources, the views that these men held of their own position, and whether they thought they were rising or falling on the social scale.

DEWEY W. GRANTHAM, JR.

The Progressive Movement
and the Negro

INTRODUCTION

It is one of the ironies of American history, concludes Dewey Grantham, a historian of the South, that the first significant reform movement in the twentieth century neglected the plight of the Negro and that one progressive President, Woodrow Wilson, even advanced the spread of racial segregation within the federal government. Many progressives outside the South, Grantham explains, were too involved in the pressing problems of restraining business abuses, assailing the boss system, and correcting other social injustices to act on behalf of the Negro. Most did not even seem to notice the growth of Negro ghettos, although a few social workers created settlement houses for the black man.

FROM Dewey W. Grantham, Jr., "The Progressive Movement and the Negro," *South Atlantic Quarterly*, LIV (October, 1955), pp. 461–77. Reprinted by permission of Duke University Press and the author.

To most Americans the plight of the Negro was primarily a Southern and not a national problem, for in 1910 nearly 90 percent of the black citizens lived in the South. In the South itself, political reformers often relied on "Negro-phobes" for support, and even those Southern liberals who were somewhat sympathetic to the Negro refused to oppose actively the hardening patterns of segregation. Among the few progressive political leaders troubled by the nation's abandonment of the Negro were Senators Robert La Follette of Wisconsin, Moses Clapp of Minnesota, and Albert Cummins of Iowa. President Theodore Roosevelt and other reformers clearly understood that the Fifteenth Amendment was being violated, but they saw little chance of enforcing the Constitution in the South.

Thus the middle-class reformers, whom historians have characterized as respectful of law and order, generally tolerated intimidation and violence as long as it was visited only on the black man, and they shared with their fellow countrymen varying degrees of racism. The answer in the first decade of this century to Ray Stannard Baker's question: "Does democracy really include Negroes as well as white men?" was a resounding "No."

In 1905 a small group of Negro intellectuals decided to fight racial injustice and oppose the policy of black acquiescence promoted publicly by Booker T. Washington. Led by the historian-sociologist W. E. B. Du Bois, they met at Niagara Falls to announce their demands for economic and political equality and equal treatment in public accommodations. They declared, "We refuse to allow the impression to remain that the Negro-American assents to inferiority, is submissive under oppression and apologetic before insults." In their public challenge to white America, the members of the Niagara Movement complained of the curtailment of political rights for Negroes, their exclusion from juries in many courts, and the increased difficulties they faced in making a decent living. Asserting that their race had been "ravished and degraded," they proclaimed, "This nation will never stand justified before God until things are changed."

Not until three years later, after an anti-Negro riot in Springfield, Illinois, did a handful of Northern whites become greatly distressed by the Negro's worsening situation. In 1909 a group of white nonpolitical progressives, led by William English Walling and Oswald Garrison Villard and including Lillian Wald, Jane Addams, John Haynes Holmes, Moorfield Storey, Lincoln Steffens, and Clarence Darrow, founded the National Association for the Advancement of Colored People. Most of the Niagara movement members joined the new bi-racial movement, which was largely white. Clearly a fringe group among progressives, the NAACP never attracted many reformers to its ranks. Nevertheless, a study of progressivism and the Negro, based on Grantham's survey, might well address itself to analyzing the reasons why reformers in the NAACP did not share the dominant attitudes toward America's black citizens.

*T*he progressive movement in the United States affected the whole of American life during the two decades before World War I. Walter E. Weyl noted that "Men in the Middle West, in the Far West, in the East and South; men in the factory and on the farm; men, and also women . . . are looking at America with new eyes, as though it were the morning of the first day." William Allen White, himself one of the Progressives, remembered that reform was everywhere:

> A sudden new interest in the under dog was manifest in the land. . . . Some way, into the hearts of the dominant middle class of this country, had come a sense that their civilization needed recasting, that their government had fallen into the hands of self-seekers, that a new relation should be established between the haves and the have-nots . . . because we felt that to bathe and feed the under dog would release the burden of injustice on our conscience.

Yet, despite the comprehensive nature of their proposed reforms, American liberals of the Progressive era gave little attention to the status of the Negro, which all agreed represented one of the nation's social and political problems. This omission in the Progressive program poses the provocative question of why. By such indices as ownership of property, rate of literacy, entry into new occupations, and development of social and cultural institutions American Negroes made substantial advances during the four decades following Appomattox. The material progress and industrial leadership epitomized by the Atlanta Compromise and the efforts of Booker T. Washington won increasing endorsement of whites both North and South and apparently improved the relations between the two races. But the progress, particularly after 1877, was exasperatingly slow and painful, and Negroes remained in large part landless, uneducated, and diseased—the downtrodden bottom rail.

As the new century opened, the difficulty of reconciling the American ideals of democracy and legal processes with the prejudices of the dominant groups was outlined in sharp relief. The heavy lynching tolls of the 1890's continued into the twentieth century, and Negroes were often victims of antiquated convict leasing and chain-gang practices, of peonage, and of inferior accommodations on public carriers and in public places. Furthermore, the process of legal disfranchisement by the Southern states was well on the way to completion, and even where the Negro retained the right to vote, he could not participate in the Democratic primaries that really controlled Southern elections. In many ways the thirty-year period after 1877 was an era of retrogression for the Negro. Walter Hines Page wrote of the Southern Negro in 1907, "I'm afraid he's a 'goner.'" To liberals the Negro problem posed a challenge, but a challenge that might be rationalized and explained away or evaded.

Generalization about the nature of Progressivism is not without hazards. The Progressives were reformers, but reform could mean "all sorts of things"; Ralph H. Gabriel has called it "a potpourri of social theories and beliefs." A writer in 1912 observed that Progressivism was "inchoate and speaks with many voices. To many men it means many things." Whatever the regional and individual variations among Progressives, they were optimists who held fast to the idea of progress. The evils and imperfections that had come with the powerful economic tides of a changing America could be removed through the agency of the state. The rules must be changed somewhat, but not radically; economic power must be responsible to the government, and "new weapons of democracy" must make the government responsible to the people. There must be legislation to improve the lot of the working man, to restrain monopoly and abolish special privilege, to widen the electoral franchise and institute direct democracy. Man was fundamentally good and rational; if dealt with fairly he would deal justly with his fellow men. The Progressives believed, as William Allen White wrote, that if the underdog were given "a decent kennel, wholesome food, regular baths, properly directed exercise, [and if someone would] cure his mange and abolish his fleas, and put him in the blue-ribbon class, all would be well."

If Progressives were convinced of the possibility of progress, if they advocated the abandonment of laissez faire and the use of positive government to promote that progress, if they desired to help the depressed elements in the nation's population and to answer "the simple demand for fair dealing, [and] for exact justice between man and man," it is pertinent to ask what they did about the nation's major minority problem. As individuals and as members of philanthropic groups many Progressives considered the Negro question at some length and made significant contributions to the amelioration of the conditions that created the problem. To answer the question What did American liberals do about the Negro in a political way? requires a longer examination.

Progressive reformers appeared first on the municipal level; their attention was largely focused on breaking the control of the political machines, on effecting tax reforms, and on establishing a more wholesome relationship between public utilities and city governments. Mark Fagan and George L. Record, for instance, strove to improve the educational, health, and recreational facilities of Jersey City, but they fought their most vigorous battles for tax reform and control of public utilities. Tom Johnson made Cleveland "the best governed city in America," but his major efforts were to secure municipal ownership of street railways and to equalize the city's taxes. Joseph W. Folk flashed into the national limelight because of his sensational exposures of the corrupt alliance between business and government in St. Louis. In California the Los Angeles nonpartisan movement aimed at breaking the control of the Southern Pacific machine. Negroes as well as whites might benefit from reduced street railway fares, from tax reassessment, and from better school facilities, but the most spectacular municipal reforms did not occur in the South, where most Negroes were concentrated, and when good government movements did reach Southern cities, Negroes seldom shared equally in such reforms. At any rate, the Negro question was incidental to other reforms supported on the city level during the Progressive period.

Much the same was true of Progressivism on the state level. Robert M. La Follette, of Wisconsin, was a democrat in the best sense of the word; he possessed a genuine concern for the rights and dignity of the individual and a keen desire to promote the welfare of the depressed man. La Follette, like most Progressives, felt that most political issues had a moral answer, but he saw that economic power was the keystone in the arch of American society. Therefore it was necessary to solve in some fashion the problem of the misuse of economic power, whether by aggregations of powerful business corporations, as in Wisconsin, or by strong organizations of labor, as in California. For this reason Progressives across the land concentrated their efforts toward handling the problem of the monopolization of economic forces; their belief in democracy led them to sponsor numerous democratic devices in an effort to make economic power responsible to political authority. There were state and regional variations, but in all states where Progressivism was strong Progressive leaders concentrated on the problem of dealing with powerful organizations of capital or labor and widening the base of a political democracy to nourish the state government.

The concern of political reformers on the state and local levels with the regulation of privilege and monopoly and their efforts to forge new "weapons of democracy" did not prevent them from attacking many specific problems involving social welfare. There were laws to abolish child labor, to regulate the working conditions of women, to provide for workmen's compensation, to increase the appropriations for public education, and to establish more adequate institutions for the care of unfortunates. Negroes might benefit from all of these reforms, but the fact was there were relatively few Negroes outside of the South before the World War, and the Progressive movement was most effective in other regions. The Negro question for such non-Southern Progressives was thus a theoretical question or at most a national problem. Meanwhile, state and local Progressives focused their attention on their own pressing concerns.

There were reform governors and liberal leaders in the South during the Progressive period. Attempts were made there to regulate more effectively railroads and other corporations, to provide tax reforms, to abolish free passes and corrupt lobbying practices. Primary elections came into wide-spread use, and corrupt-practices legislation was enacted. The convict-leasing system was abolished, beginnings were made in the regulation of child labor, legislation to control the liquor traffic was adopted, and in-creased appropriations were made for public education and health facilities, agricultural services, and state care of unfortunates. Negroes undoutedly profited from much of this reform program despite the fact that most of its political sponsors were aiming at "Progressivism for whites only." But while the Negro might benefit from such reforms, their passage often cost his race a heavy price. This was true because the strongest group of Southern Progres-sives—those who sponsored the major reforms—were insurgent politicians who came to power not only because they denounced the corporations and sponsored a program of neo-Populism but also because many of them made the race issue their chief stock-in-trade and led such anti-Negro movements as that of disfranchisement. The strongest supporters of these political lead-ers were the most rabid Negro-phobes. The Vardamans and Hoke Smiths might have represented "a genuine movement for a more democratic gov-ernment in the South," as Ray Stannard Baker contended, but their democ-racy was for whites only and did great harm to the cause of the Negro and to good relations between blacks and whites.

Among another group of Southern liberals during the Progressive era were such men and women as Charles B. Aycock, Edwin A. Alderman, Wal-ter Hines Page, Edgar Gardner Murphy, and Julia Tutwiler: men and women who worked for education, good government, the regulation of child labor, prohibition, and help for the Negroes. Believing that the South's hope lay in industrial and educational progress, they were more conciliatory to-ward the corporations than were the agrarian Progressives and less enthusi-astic about vigorous government, although in their humanitarianism and middle-class approach they were similar to Progressives in other regions. Clearly, their restraint in dealing with the race question, their constructive work for education, and their espousal of such reforms as the abolition of child labor and of the convict-leasing system made a greater contribution to the progress of Negroes than did the work of the more radical agrarian lead-ers. But they were unwilling and unable to sponsor reforms for the Negro that would drastically change the relationship of the two races in the South. Furthermore, while their concern for social justice might be real, most of them were not in politics, and they were often opposed to the agrarian Pro-gressives who were in power. Their interest in the advancement of the Negro might be genuine, but it was also paternalistic and philanthropic; their solu-tion lay within the framework of white supremacy.

Thousands of people in the South wished the Negro well, but, as a con-temporary Progressive noted, "The South is psychologically cramped." The ideology of white supremacy was all pervasive, and few were the Southerners who would answer in the affirmative Ray Stannard Baker's question, "Does democracy really include Negroes as well as white men?" Baker himself spoke of "a vigorous minority point of view," which he labeled the "broadest and freest thought" of the South: "a party of ideas, force, convictions, with a definite constructive programme." Yet the philosophy of this group rested on the maintenance of "racial integrity," the "gospel of industrial education," and disfranchisement. Charles H. Brough, professor of Economics and Sociology at the University of Arkansas, spoke for them when he declared: "As the sons of proud Anglo-Saxon sires, we of the South doubt seriously the wisdom of the enfranchisement of an inferior race." These "liberals" expressed their belief in progress for the Negroes, but, as Brough said: "I believe that by the recognition of the fact that in the Negro are to be found the essential elements of human nature, capable of conscious evolution through education and economic and religious betterment, we will be led at last to a conception of a world of unity, whose Author and Finisher is God." Even Edgar Gardner Murphy, one of the Southerners most concerned with social justice, held Negroes to be a "backward and essentially unassimilable people," whom the "consciousness of kind" would forever set apart from the whites, whatever the race's advancement.

If the race problem was a national concern, as some people said it was, what were the attitudes of the national parties and political leaders as the twentieth century ushered in the Progressive period? Party pronouncements avoided the Negro question or at most had little to say on the subject. The Populist platform of 1896 condemned "the wholesale system of disfranchisement adopted in some States as unrepublican and undemocratic." The Socialist Labor platform in 1896 called for the equal right of suffrage without regard to color. The Republicans condemned lynching and termed "revolutionary" certain devices designed to overthrow the Fifteenth Amendment. In 1904 they called for a Congressional investigation to determine whether the vote had been unconstitutionally limited in any state and threatened proportionate reductions in representation if such restrictions were found to exist. In 1908 they asked for the enforcement of the Civil War amendments while reminding Negroes that the Republican party had been their "constant friend" for fifty years. These promises, it soon developed, were about as far as the party was willing to go on the Negro problem. The truth was that the Republicans had all but deserted the Negro. The Democratic position was well stated in the party's platform in 1904. While criticizing Republican imperialism for following one set of laws "at home" and another "in the colonies," the Democrats declared: "To revive the dead and hateful race and sectional animosities . . . means confusion, distraction of business, and the reopening of wounds now happily healed."

The literature of the muckrakers gave attention to the position of the Negro. Disfranchisement, sharecropping, peonage, racial segregation, the Negro's failure to obtain justice in the courts, lynchings, and race riots were seized upon as worthy materials by such writers as Richard Barry, Benjamin

O. Flower, and William English Walling. Ray Stannard Baker's articles in the *American Magazine*, though perhaps not muckraking in the strict sense of the term, were widely read and were published in book form in 1908 under the title *Following the Color Line*. But Americans failed, somehow, to get very excited about muckraking materials on the Negro, and the Negro question proved a poor second to such topics as corporation evils and political corruption.

If the muckrakers failed to arouse widespread interest in the status of the American Negro, the same could not be said of President Theodore Roosevelt. Roosevelt expressed a deep concern for the Negroes, and his actions and his utterances stimulated avalanches of editorial copy. The President's closeness to Booker T. Washington, his denunciation of lynching and disfranchisement, and his announced determination to see that the Negro received his due generated a wave of hope among liberals on the race question and among the Negroes themselves. But what could Roosevelt do? As he wrote Albion W. Tourgée in the fall of 1901, "I have not been able to think out any solution of the terrible problem offered by the presence of the negro on this continent. . . ." He had decided, however, that "the only wise and honorable and Christian thing to do is to treat each black man and each white man strictly on his merits as a man." His objective for the Negro came to be "cautiously, temperately, and sanely, to raise him up."

In practice even this modest goal was beset with difficulties. Roosevelt might appoint only "reputable and upright colored men to office," as was his constant claim, but by doing so he alienated the whites in the South who were otherwise attracted to the Republican party. He was interested in building up the Republican party in the South and therefore anxious "not to shock southern sentiment," although, as he wrote Lyman Abbott, it would be a serious mistake to let Southerners "think that they were blameless, or to let them cast the blame on anyone else." The mounting pressure on the part of white Republicans in the South for a lily-white party led Roosevelt to seek middle ground. His philosophy was well stated in a letter to Booker T. Washington in June, 1904: "The safety for the colored man in Louisiana is to have a white man's party which shall be responsible and honest, in which the colored man shall have representation but in which he shall not be the dominant force—a party in which, as is now the case in the Federal service under me, he shall hold a percentage of the offices but in which a majority of the offices shall be given to white men of high character who will protect the negro before the law." This was to remain essentially Roosevelt's position. He contended that his administration through the federal courts had accomplished a good deal to break up Negro peonage in the South and to secure equal facilities for Negroes on interstate carriers, but he saw little hope of federal action to enforce the Fifteenth Amendment, and in 1908 opposed including such a threat in the Republican platform. The principal hope of the Negro, he declared, must lie in the sense of justice and good will of Southerners, for the Northern people could do little for him. But Southerners, he found, continued to show a "wrong-headedness and folly" about the race question. while men like Oswald Garrison Villard and Charles Francis Adams, who had a genuine interest in promoting the Negro cause, had in the President's opinion "frittered away their influence" until they had no weight with either party.

Theodore Roosevelt's correspondence reveals the enigmatic quality of the Negro problem in his mind during the first dozen years of the century. Like his contemporaries, he never found an adequate solution, although he probably gave more thought to it than most other political leaders on the national scene. The "condition of violent chronic hysteria" on the subject in the South baffled him, and at times he felt that the region never made any progress on the race problem unless forced by outside pressure. Yet in the end he was not sure that his own efforts, which were certainly interpreted in the South as outside pressure, had been of much avail. He agreed with Owen Wister that the Negroes as a race and in the mass were "altogether inferior to the whites," and that the progress of the race would be slow and painful, but he did believe that progress was possible. After his action in the Brownsville affair, he became increasingly suspicious of the more radical Negro leaders and of what he called "shortsighted white sentimentalists." By the middle of his second administration, many Negroes and their white supporters had become convinced that they could expect little in the way of positive aid from Roosevelt. Nevertheless, the President was right when he wrote in 1908: ". . . I have stood as valiantly for the rights of the Negro as any president since Lincoln. . . ."

The election of William Howard Taft promised small encouragement for a positive program to advance the cause of Negroes. Taft was a peaceful man and refused to ruffle the political waters by making anything of the race question.

But, as the strong tides of Progressivism began to roll through the major parties on the national level, advocates of Negro progress began to experience a new optimism and a faith that Progressive ideals might also include the Negro. For a time the greatest expectations centered in the Progressive revolt in the Republican party and in Theodore Roosevelt's embryonic Progressive party with its liberal promises of positive federal action to promote the social welfare. Here, such leaders as W. E. Burghardt Du Bois felt, was "a splendid chance for a third party movement, on a broad platform of votes for Negroes and the democratization of industry." But when Roosevelt decided to endorse the organization of the new party on a lily-white basis in the South, in the hope that a strong, permanent party might thus be established in that region, he lost the support of many Negroes, including such leaders as Du Bois. The former President attempted to straddle the perplexing issue by advocating one policy for the North, where it was possible "to bring the best colored men into the movement on the same terms as the white men," and another for the South, where "actual conditions and actual needs and feelings" dictated a traditionally Southern approach. Roosevelt still believed that the Negro's best hope lay with the "intelligent and benevolent" whites of the South. "We have made the Progressive issue a moral, not a racial issue," he declared.

With their hopes thus dashed, where could Progressive Negro leaders turn? The Republicans under Taft provided no hope for a Progressive era. With some misgivings, many of the more militant Negro leaders accepted the New Freedom of Woodrow Wilson, aware of the danger posed by the South's part in the Wilson movement and of Wilson's own background, but encouraged by the liberalism that he represented and by certain promises he was understood to have made. One Negro reminded Wilson in the summer of 1913, "We enlisted with the delight of children at play under your standard and fought a good fight. . . ." Having helped elect the new President, Negroes turned to his administration for a share of the patronage and for additional evidences of justice to their race. The editor of the New York *Age* expressed the attitude of many Negroes when he wrote: "The race, as a whole, is not so deeply concerned in the question of the appointment of Negroes to office as it is [in] the attitude President Wilson will assume—whether he will give a helping hand to a struggling people or whether he will co-operate with those who believe that it is humane and American to do all in their power to keep the Negro down, thereby hindering the progress of the Nation."

Negro leaders were soon disappointed by Woodrow Wilson's course. The new President's attitude toward the Negro, as Arthur S. Link has said, was characteristically Southern. While he abhorred Southern demagogues who made the race issue a bête noire, his feeling toward the Negro was at best one of tolerance and kindliness, strongly paternalistic. He soon found that it was difficult enough to carry the South with him in the enactment of his major program and that to make an issue of the race question would jeopardize measures which he considered much more important than a frontal attack on a difficult minority problem. Thus it was that he allowed racial segregation among federal employees in certain of the federal departments, refused to make many Negro appointments, and failed to appoint a federal commission to investigate the Negro situation as some people urged. Southerners in Washington, led by James K. Vardaman, were vociferous in their demands that no Negroes be appointed to federal positions. When the news of one Negro appointment spread, Thomas Dixon wrote to Wilson to say, "I am heartsick over the announcement that you have appointed a Negro to boss white girls as Register of the Treasury." The President's reply was reassuring to white Southerners: "We are handling the force of colored people who are now in the departments in just the way they ought to be handled. We are trying—and by degrees succeeding—a plan of concentration which will put them all together and will not in any one bureau mix the two races." Wilson explained his dilemma to Oswald Garrison Villard in August, 1913:

"It would be hard to make any one understand the delicacy and difficulty of the situation I find existing here with regard to the colored people." Emphasizing such matters as the tariff and antitrust legislation, Wilson viewed the Negro problem as a peripheral issue and one that was increasingly irritating. He desired to avoid "a bitter agitation" and to hold things "at a just and cool equipoise."

The disillusionment on the part of Negro leaders was rapid and eventually complete. Booker T. Washington wrote in late summer, 1913: "I have recently spent several days in Washington, and I have never seen the colored people so discouraged and bitter. . . ." The Negro press, Negro leaders, and men like Villard protested, but the President remained aloof. By 1916 Du Bois felt that the political situation was hopeless.

Still, many of the more moderate Negro leaders, such as Robert R. Moton of Tuskegee, admired Wilson for his accomplishments and for the idealism that permeated his addresses. Moton wrote Wilson late in 1916, "I realize that it was embarrassing and perhaps unwise for you to make any reference to the race question as it might perhaps hazard in some way the other important policies of your administration, but now that your election is assured and your policies are pretty definitely established and accepted by the nation as a whole, I am wondering if you could refer in some way to the ten or eleven millions of Negroes in our country." The President promised to do his best, but he was not optimistic. ". . . the truth is," he wrote, "that I have not been able to form a confident judgment as to what would be effective and influential." Nor did he form such a judgment.

The East St. Louis riot of July, 1917, brought heated demands to the Wilson administration for action against such "unchecked savagery." The lynchings in 1918 and the discriminations against Negroes in the armed forces brought further protests, while the President's course on the race question at the Paris Peace Conference was also criticized by some Negro spokesmen. Wilson publicly announced his abhorrence of lynching and commended the valor of Negro soldiers, but he gave no indication that he considered the Negro problem of primary importance. It seems fair to say that he never conceived of the Negro question in a broad sense as a federal problem. At any rate, the more extreme Negro leaders would have echoed the statement of a Philadelphia Negro, James S. Stemons, who wrote Woodrow Wilson in November, 1920: "The verdict of the masses, regardless of race or creed or clan, has long been that while you were vigorously preaching one thing you were, when expediency demanded it, as vigorously practicing the direct opposite."

If sectionalism and racial prejudice frustrated any possibilities of direct action on the Negro question by Woodrow Wilson's New Freedom and Theodore Roosevelt's New Nationalism, the same was true even of the Socialist party in its consideration of the problem. Socialists in the South proved no more tolerant on the race question than non-Socialists, and this prejudice was not restricted to the South. Victor Berger, for instance, declared in 1902: "There can be no doubt that the negroes and mulattoes constitute a lower race—that the Caucasians and indeed even the Mongolians have the start on them in civilization by many thôusand years—so that negroes will find it difficult ever to overtake them." About the best the Socialists could do was to advertise Socialism as exclusively an economic movement, having nothing to do with social equality. Indeed, moderate Socialists contended that the races did not want to live together and that capitalism was at fault, since it forced them to do so. Eugene Debs opposed all discrimination, and the left-wing Socialists urged that racial prejudice be wiped out. But the Socialist party in the period before World War I made no real opposition to Negro discriminations as such.

It will be helpful at this point to differentiate between certain practical considerations that entered into the failure of Progressives to deal with the race question and the more fundamental philosophical background that conditioned their attitudes toward the Negro. As for the practical considerations, the fact was that the Negro problem prior to the World War was still essentially seçtional. A great majority of the Negroes were still concentrated in the South, and the leading Progressives, such as Robert M. La Follette, Hiram W. Johnson, and Albert B. Cummins, operated in other regions. They never really came in contact with the Negro question, at least in a situation where they could make a direct contribution to its solution. They could adopt academically a liberal position on the question, and they sometimes took an incidental stand in Congress, but that was all. Such matters as suffrage and the whole broad question of social legislation were still considered the primary responsibility of state and local governments, although the Progressives generally emphasized a more vigorous central government. Many of the Progressives, however, were averse to centralized power, as was true of supporters of Wilson's original program. Another consideration was the inability of Negro leaders and their most zealous white supporters to agree upon a positive program or upon the means necessary to advance their cause.

To explain the philosophical limitations of the Progressive movement in facing the Negro question in American democracy is more difficult. It would appear paradoxical that a philosophy which emphasized the worth and the dignity of man and which laid stress on the democratic process should reveal this blind spot in regard to what was really a complete refutation of its most sacred premises.

One of the keys to this apparent enigma is to be found in the attitude of Americans during the period between 1898 and 1918 toward imperialism and the so-called "backward" races that were the subjects of imperialism. Progressives were no more willing to accord equal civil and social rights to the people recently subjugated by the American republic than were the majority of Americans. Most of them agreed with the imperialistic views of Theodore

Roosevelt and Albert J. Beveridge, although many of them were probably influenced in their views on the subject by the mastery Roosevelt held over them. Roosevelt was emphatic in stating his position: ". . . I have the impatient contempt that I suppose all practical men must have for the ridiculous theorists who decline to face facts and who wish to give even to the most utterly undeveloped races of mankind a degree of self-government which only the very highest races have been able to exercise with any advantage." If the Filipinos were inferior and entitled to the privileges of American democracy only after a long apprenticeship, was not the same true of Orientals on the West Coast and of Negroes in the South? There was, moreover, what Southerners described as the "dreadful episode of Reconstruction" to provide apparent documentation of the Negro's backwardness supplemented by the widely circulated accounts of his continued degradation in the post-Reconstruction years. Once having accepted the ideology of the new imperialism, it was difficult to escape the logic of the Southerners' position. As Benjamin R. Tillman said, chiding the Republicans for their imperialism: "Your slogans of the past—brotherhood of man and fatherhood of God—have gone glimmering down through the ages." The conquered, it seemed, had overcome the conquerors.

Fortunately for Republican and Progressive theoreticians, the new sciences or pseudo-sciences, with their theories of the multiple origin of the races and the notion of retarded races, seemed to provide a scientific explanation that would justify imperialism, while history itself seemed to prove the superiority of Western culture. As for the democratic concept that governmental authority rested on the consent of the governed, Senator Beveridge pointed out that this was true only where the governed were capable of self-government. Lyman Abbott said the important thing was not government by the "consent of the governed" but government for the "benefit of the governed." Thus American imperialism could be viewed as a crusade to free backward people from their antiquated overlords and to set them on the road of progress under the tutelage of a benign and liberal government.

At home there was powerful evidence that Negroes, retarded as was their race, were making headway. This evidence was particularly apparent in the Booker T. Washington School, the material gains of which could not be doubted. Here was progress, tangible and capable of being measured; more important perhaps, progress based on a philosophy that received the whole-hearted endorsement of the middle-class heart of America—and of Progressives. It emphasized philanthropy and practical education, and it sought to avoid conflict between employer and employee, between class and class, and between race and race. It eschewed politics and worked within a framework that received the enthusiastic approval of the Southern whites. Thus it provided an opening for the powerful Northern philanthropic organizations, which were eager to help the Negro and to work with the more moderate Southern white leaders. So pervasive was the Washington philosophy that it received widespread support throughout the country. A non-Southerner such as Bourke Cockran could appeal for justice for the Negro in one breath and advocate the repeal of the Fifteenth Amendment in the next, while Ray Stannard Baker could say some years later that the North, "wrongly or rightly, is today more than half convinced that the South is right in imposing some measure of limitation upon the franchise." In 1909, in the words of Hilary A. Herbert, "Intelligent public opinion at the north is at this writing so thoroughly with us that there is now no longer any danger of interference with us from Washington, either legislative or executive, so long as we do not, by harsh or unjust treatment of the negro, now at our mercy, alienate the sympathies of the majority section of our union." The Progressive *New Republic's* solution followed the course charted by Booker T. Washington. "The greatest service which can be rendered the Negro to-day," declared its editors in 1916, "is to be dispassionate about it. It is, after all, only a problem like any other. There is no need to keep alight the old fire upon the abolition altar, or to blow into flames smouldering embers upon the ruined hearth of the old South."

Another element in the Booker T. Washington philosophy was the idea of self-advancement, the belief that the Negro must make his own way and demonstrate his own abilities to get ahead in the contest of life. This idea found easy lodgement in the Progressive rationale. It was implicit in much of Theodore Roosevelt's writing. Even such a zealous believer in Negro rights as Moorfield Storey counseled "patience, courage, and faith." "The prejudice against you today," asserted Storey, "is no stronger than the prejudice which Jews and Irish have overcome." "You are all soldiers in a great army fighting for the future of your race. . . ." Negroes must now work out their own destiny, declared Charles Francis Adams in 1908. "It is for the Afro-Americans, as for the American descendant of the Celt, the Slav, or the Let, to shape his own future, accepting the common lot of mankind."

This was not as inconsistent with the Progressive philosophy as might appear at first glance. Despite its humanitarian outlook and its interest in moral issues, the Progressive movement aimed at "the equalizing of opportunity" by an approach that was essentially negative. As Herbert Croly wrote in *The Progressive Democracy* (1914): ". . . the expectation was that if the concentrated economic system could be checked and disintegrated, small local producers, both agricultural and industrial, would have a much better chance of prosperity." The Progressives, then, hoped to produce a condition in which men might be free to prove their merit. If the Negro could make his way on the economic front, political and civil rights would take care of themselves.

Such were the main philosophical components that influenced the attitude of Progressives toward the Negro problem. To this explanation might be added what Herbert Croly described as the "Promise of American Life," an apt phrase with which he summed up the American faith in progress and in the peculiar destiny of America. That is, Americans believed their nation to be progressive regardless of its shortcomings.

In *The New Democracy* (1912) Walter Weyl called the Negro question "the mortal spot of the new democracy." But he noted that Americans wanted to avoid the issue; to illustrate his point he discussed Negro suffrage: "To-day, millions of men, discouraged by the dwindling but still large residuum of Negro ignorance, discouraged by the passion which seeps like a torrid wind over every phase of the question, seek to avoid the question of Negro suffrage. . . ." In reality Northerners and Republicans—and Progressives as well—had adopted attitudes toward Negroes and other colored races not unlike those of the South. What George W. Cable had written about the Negro question a generation before still seemed apropos. "The popular mind in the old free States," he had written, "weary of strife at arm's length, bewildered by its complications, vexed by many a blunder, eager to turn to the cure of other evils, and even tinctured by that race feeling whose grosser excesses it would so gladly see suppressed, has retreated from its uncomfortable dictatorial attitude and thrown the whole matter over to the States of the South."

The Progressive movement had certainly touched a responsive chord in the ranks of American Negroes, although it was true, as Walter Weyl said, that "The race is too poor, weak, ignorant, and disunited to make effective protest." Negro leaders, however, did protest, and many of them were inspired to believe that the Progressives really intended to battle abuses and to urge democracy on all fronts. Negro leaders themselves were divided and uncertain. As Du Bois wrote, "We all believed in thrift, we all wanted the Negro to vote, we all wanted to abolish lynching, we all wanted assertion of our essential manhood; but how to get these things—there, of course, must be wide divergence of opinion."

The Progressive movement came to be associated by the more militant Negro leaders with the Booker T. Washington school of thought. The failure of Roosevelt and then of Wilson to include the Negroes in their agendas for progress, the death of Washington, and the frustration of Negro aspirations in the World War precipitated a new unity among Negro leaders and an acceptance of the philosophy of the National Association for the Advancement of Colored People. In conclusion it may be said that the Progressive movement, or perhaps it would be more accurate to say the climate of Progressivism, did bring some advances for American Negroes. There were the indirect benefits of Progressive legislation and gains deriving from humanitarian agencies. But in a larger sense the Progressive movement passed over the Negro question and, ironically, by doing so helped to promote the militant approach to the problem that most Progressives would have abhorred.

SUGGESTED READING

Dewey W. Grantham, Jr., in *Hoke Smith and the Politics of the New South* ° (Louisiana State Univ. Press, 1958) and Albert D. Kirwan in *Revolt of the Rednecks: Mississippi Politics, 1876–1925* ° (Univ. of Kentucky Press, 1951) provide fine studies of state politics and include important information on the race issue. For information on Roosevelt's and Wilson's handling of the Negro problem see Seth Scheiner, "President Roosevelt and the Negro, 1901–1908," *Journal of Negro History,* XLVII (July, 1962), 169–82; James Tinsley, "Roosevelt, Foraker, and the Brownsville Affair," *ibid.,* XLI (Jan., 1956), 43–65; Kathleen Wogelmuth, "Woodrow Wilson and Federal Segregation," *ibid.,* XLIV (Jan., 1959), 158–73; and Henry Blumenthal, "Woodrow Wilson and the Race Question," *ibid.,* XLVIII (Jan., 1963), 1–21.

The early history of the NAACP is treated in Charles Kellogg's *NAACP, A History of the National Association for the Advancement of Colored People* (Johns Hopkins Univ. Press, 1967). August Meier's perceptive analysis, *Negro Thought in America, 1880–1915* ° (Univ. of Michigan Press, 1963), notes the divergence between Booker T. Washington's public counsel and private actions. Francis Broderick in *W. E. B. DuBois: Negro Leader in Time of Crisis* ° (Stanford Univ. Press, 1959) and Elliot Rudwick in *W. E. B. DuBois: A Study in Minority Group Leadership* ° (Univ. of Pennsylvania Press, 1960) examine Washington's chief challenger. Harvey Wish's "Negro Education and the Progressive Movement," *Journal of Negro History,* XLIX (July, 1964), 151–68, is thin but useful on this neglected subject

Robert Bannister's *Ray Stannard Baker, the Mind and Thought of a Progressive* (Yale Univ. Press, 1966) is a good biography of the author of *Following the Color Line.* David Southern studies progressive attitudes in *Yankee Progressives and the Negro Question, 1901–1914* (Loyola Univ. Press, 1968).

Allen Davis' *Spearheads of Reform* (Oxford Univ. Press, 1967) contains a chapter on social workers and the Negro. Gilbert Osofsky in "Progressivism and the Negro: New York, 1900–1915," *American Quarterly,* XVI (Summer, 1964), 153–68, concludes that industrial and municipal reformers as well as social workers expressed "a serious, positive and hopeful interest . . . in the Negro's welfare." This article was later adapted as a chapter for his volume, *Harlem: The Making of a Ghetto* (Harper & Row, 1966), which along with Allan H. Spear's *Black Chicago: The Making of a Negro Ghetto, 1890–1920* (Univ. of Chicago Press, 1967) and Seth Scheiner's, *Negro Mecca* (New York Univ. Press, 1965), a study of Harlem, is among the best recent studies on Northern Negro communities during the progressive years.

PAUL BIRDSALL

Neutrality and Economic Pressures, 1914–1917

INTRODUCTION

Aside from a few individuals like the diplomat Lewis Einstein, who argued from the beginning of World War I that the American national interest was at stake, and Theodore Roosevelt, who mixed this perception with a lust for combat, American citizens and politicians hoped during the early years of the war that their nation could remain uninvolved in the conflict. Woodrow Wilson, despite his own Anglophilia, exhorted the nation to act and speak in "the spirit of neutrality and friendship," and in 1916 the Democratic party re-elected Wilson on the slogan, "He kept us out of war." Yet in the spring of 1917, a reluctant America found herself a belligerent power enmeshed in the tragedy of the war in Europe. Scholars

FROM Paul Birdsall, "Neutrality and Economic Pressures, 1914–1917," *Science and Society*, III (Spring, 1939), pp. 217–28. Reprinted by permission.

have since engaged in often fierce controversies as to why the seemingly pacific Wilson decided finally to intervene.

Among other issues, historians have disputed the role of idealism in Wilson's decision for war. In the years of disillusionment that followed the peace settlement, many scholars came to regard World War I as a great mistake and cynically discounted Wilson's ideals as a mere cloak for dark purposes. More recently, in the early years of the Cold War, George Kennan and other realists have affirmed the sincerity of Wilson's ideals but have judged his adherence to them as regrettable. The realists argue that a proper foreign policy would have rested not on moralism but on the necessity to preserve the balance of power and thereby American security. In this view, Wilson's decision to fight was made too late and for the wrong reasons. In defense of Wilson, Arthur Link in *Wilson: The Diplomatist* (Johns Hopkins Univ. Press, 1957) comes close to accepting the realists' criteria for an appropriate policy, but he goes on to assert that Wilson had actually performed realistically: In acting in response to Germany's declaration of unlimited submarine warfare in February, 1917, Wilson clearly saw that a "German victory imperiled the balance of power and all his hopes for the future reconstruction of the world community."

Another perennial subject of controversy is the role of economic considerations in American foreign policy. During the Depression some scholars concluded that munition manufacturers and bankers pushed the Administration into war for the purpose of protecting their loans to the Allies and creating wider markets for war supplies. That crude theory has been discredited, but it does not necessarily invalidate other economic interpretations.

In a sophisticated and dispassionate economic analysis written on the eve of World War II, Paul Birdsall argues that fears of a depression forced the Administration to back away in 1915 from its earlier prohibition on private loans to the Allies and that those loans financed the trade that Germany could halt only by resorting to submarine warfare. Birdsall marshals impressive evidence that Wilson's advisers understood the necessity for credit to revive American trade. Wilson, however, was the crucial decision-maker, and his motivations still seem open to doubt. Though Birdsall believes that Wilson's motivations in 1915 were economic, he cites no direct evidence.

Two recent studies of Wilson's diplomacy—Link's *Wilson: The Struggle for Neutrality, 1914–1915* (Princeton Univ. Press, 1960) and Ernest May's *The World War and American Isolation, 1914–1917* (Harvard Univ. Press, 1959)—agree with Birdsall, but their conclusions are also unsupported by direct evidence concerning Wilson. A final verdict on the matter, therefore, cannot yet be rendered.

*T*wenty years of debate have not yet produced a satisfactory or even a coherent neutrality policy for the United States, nor have they yet offered any real understanding of the problem of neutrality in the modern world to serve as a basis for policy making. Until we have some adequate analysis of the forces which destroyed President Wilson's neutrality policy between 1914 and 1917 no government is likely to be more successful than his in future efforts to master such forces. Nor will the neutrality legislation of the past years help very much if it simply ignores these forces.

The trouble with much of the writing on the World War period is that it deals with separate aspects of the problem in watertight compartments with complete disregard of the complex interrelations between economic and political phenomena. Thus Charles Seymour deals almost exclusively with the diplomatic record of our relations with Imperial Germany and from that record draws the only possible conclusion, that "It was the German submarine warfare and nothing else that forced him [Wilson] to lead America into war." [1] The late Newton D. Baker arrives by the same route at the same conclusion: "Certainly the occasion of the United States entering the World War was the resumption of submarine warfare." That Baker had a glimpse of more remote and subtle causation is indicated by his choice of the word "occasion" and by his admission that critics may with some justification charge him with oversimplification by confusing "occasion" with "cause." "This," he says, "I may to some extent have done." [2] Each of these authors is content with a surface record of diplomacy and politics without reference to the fundamental context of economic and social phenomena which alone can give it significance for analysis of the large problem of neutrality.

Nor does it advance the investigation to turn one's back completely on the diplomatic record and resort to a narrow economic determinism, as does Senator Nye. Ignoring the inescapable evidence that German submarine warfare was the immediate "occasion" for American entry into the war, he argues the simple thesis that American bankers first forced the American Government to authorize large loans to France and Great Britain, and when those countries were faced with defeat, then forced the American Government into the war to protect the bankers' investments. I have heard Senator Nye publicly express embarrassment at the lack of any direct evidence to

[1] *American Diplomacy during the World War* (Baltimore, The Johns Hopkins Press, 1934), p. 210. See also *American Neutrality, 1914–1917* (New Haven, Yale University Press, 1935).

[2] *Foreign Affairs*, xv (Oct., 1936), p. 85.

support the second, and for his purposes the essential, part of his thesis, but what he lacks in evidence he makes up in faith.[3]

What is most needed is careful synthesis of the accurate and valid parts of the diplomatic and economics theses. Senator Nye's committee has given us invaluable data on the development of close economic ties with the Entente Powers in the face of a government policy of neutrality designed to prevent just that development, even if the committee failed to analyze the precise forces at work.[4] We have accurate and scholarly studies explaining the *immediate* cause of American intervention as due to the German decision to wage unrestricted submarine warfare. But no one has yet demonstrated the connection between American economic ties with Germany's enemies and Germany's submarine campaign which provoked American intervention. It is precisely this connection which reveals the true significance of the economic relationship, namely that it makes neutrality in modern war impossible—unless the economic relationships with belligerents can somehow be prevented. And that must be the first subject of investigation.

If Senator Nye is right in contending that it was primarily the intrigues of the banking interests which prevented a genuine neutrality policy, then the present legislation to curb such activity in the future should prove adequate. But careful study of the evidence he has himself unearthed does not bear him out.

The Wilson administration attempted to enforce a neutrality policy identical with that now prescribed by statute in respect to loans to belligerents. To be sure there was no effort to prevent the sale of munitions to belligerents, and Secretary of State Bryan explained why in a letter of January 20, 1915 to Senator Stone of the Senate Committee on Foreign Relations. He said that "the duty of a neutral to restrict trade in munitions of war has never been imposed by international law or municipal statute. . . . [It] has never been the policy of this government to prevent the shipment of arms or ammunition into belligerent territory, except in the case of the American Republics, and then only when civil strife prevailed." [5] Moreover the German government admitted the legality of the munitions traffic as late as December 15, 1914 even while they complained of its disadvantage to their cause.

Very different was the official attitude toward loans to belligerent governments. The State Department recognized no greater legal obligation to prevent them from the sale of munitions. Lansing, Bryan's subordinate and

---

[3] C. C. Tansill, *America Goes to War* (Boston, 1938), p. 133.

[4] *Hearings before the Special Senate Committee on the Investigation of the Munitions Industry.* United States Senate. 74th Cong., 2nd sess. (Washington, 1937). Many of the same documents were published in the New York *Times* (Jan. 8–12, 1936). Many are to be found in R. S. Baker, *Woodrow Wilson* (Garden City, 1935), v.

[5] Baker, *Wilson*, v, p. 179–184 and 189.

successor, said he knew of no legal objection but agreed with Bryan in urging that the United States government refuse to approve loans to belligerents. Bryan said that "money is the worst of all contrabands," and on August 15, 1914, wrote J. P. Morgan, who wished to finance a French loan, "There is no reason why loans should not be made to the governments of neutral nations, but in the judgment of this government, *loans by American bankers to any foreign nation which is at war are inconsistent with the spirit of true neutrality.*" [6] Our State Department has never received the credit it deserves for its realistic appraisal of the issues of neutrality and its refusal to take refuge in the technicalities of international law. It is scarcely the fault of the State Department that powerful economic forces almost at once began to undermine its policy and within the year forced its abandonment. Nor can it be denied that the German government itself helped destroy the policy by sinking the *Lusitania.*

The first efforts to modify the State Department's policy came from the bankers, specifically the house of J. P. Morgan. Lamont testifies that Morgan's firm accepted the State Department ruling but asked permission at least to extend credits to foreign governments to facilitate purchases in the United States, on the theory that this was purely a bookkeeping arrangement very different from the sale of belligerent bonds on the open market. On October 23, 1914 Lansing recorded a conversation he had with President Wilson dealing with this request, in which Wilson accepted the distinction as valid. "There is a decided difference between an issue of government bonds, sold in the open market to investors, and an arrangement for easy exchange in meeting debts incurred between the government and American merchants." The latter was merely a means of facilitating trade. Accordingly Straight of the firm of Morgan was authorized to open credits of this character for belligerent governments, particularly the French. On March 31, 1915 the State Department issued a public statement of its policy in the following press release. "While loans to belligerents have been disapproved, this government has not felt that it was justified in interposing objections to the credit arrangements which have been brought to its attention. It has neither approved these nor disapproved—it has simply taken no action and expressed no opinion." [7]

The destruction of the *Lusitania* by a German submarine undermined the State Department's neutrality policy in two ways, by causing the resignation of Bryan (who refused to take responsibility for Wilson's stiff notes of protest to Germany), and by establishing in the post of Secretary of State his former subordinate Lansing. Lansing says in his memoirs that after the *Lusitania* there was always in his mind the "conviction that we would ultimately

---

[6] New York *Times*, Jan. 8, 1936; Baker, *Wilson*, v, p. 175 f.

[7] New York *Times*, Jan. 8, 1936. Also Baker, *op. cit.*, p. 186 f.

become the ally of Britain." [8] He was therefore less disposed to maintain the rigid standards of neutrality set by Bryan. Yet in the event it was economic pressures that overwhelmed the policy.

In August of 1915 the British pound sterling began to sag in the exchange market under the pressure of war finance, and the first note of warning of threat to American export business appears in a letter of August 14 from Governor Strong of the New York Federal Reserve Bank to Col. House. Strong said that the drop of sterling to below $4.71 had already led to cancellation of many foreign contracts for the purchase of American grain. He predicted more to follow and feared for the drastic curtailment of all American exports. On August 21 Secretary of the Treasury McAdoo wrote to President Wilson, "Great Britain is and always has been our best customer. . . . The high prices for food products have brought great prosperity to the farmers, while the purchasers of war munitions have stimulated industry and have set factories going to full capacity. . . . Great prosperity is coming. It is, in large measure, already here. It will be tremendously increased if we can extend reasonable credits to our customers." It was therefore imperative, he said, that Great Britain be permitted to float a loan of $500,000,000 at once. "To maintain our prosperity we must finance it." Unfortunately, according to him, the way was barred by the State Department ban on foreign loans, and by the pro-German attitude of two members of the Federal Reserve Board, Miller and Warburg. [9]

Wilson's reply was an evasion. On August 26, he wrote Lansing, "My opinion is that we should say that 'parties would take no action either for or against such a transaction,' but that this should be orally conveyed, and not put in writing. Yrs. W. W." But Lansing wanted something more definite and wrote a long letter rehearsing all McAdoo's arguments. "Doubtless Sec'y McAdoo has discussed with you the necessity of floating government loans for the belligerent nations, which are purchasing such great quantities of goods in this country, in order to avoid a serious financial situation which will not only affect them but this country as well." He estimated excess of American exports over imports for the entire year at $2,500,000,000 and alleged that the figure from December 1, 1914 to June 30, 1915 was only slightly less than $1,000,000,000. "If the European countries cannot find the means to pay for the excess of goods sold them over those purchased from them, they will have to stop buying and our present export trade will shrink proportionately. The result would be restriction of output, industrial depression, idle capital, idle labor, numerous failures, financial demoralization, and general unrest and suffering among the laboring classes. . . . Can we afford to let a declaration as to our conception of the 'true spirit of neutrality,' made in the early days of

---

[8] *War Memoirs of Robert Lansing* (Indianapolis, 1935), p. 128.

[9] New York *Times*, Jan. 10, 1936. *Cf.* Baker, *op. cit.*, p. 380 f.

the war, stand in the way of our national interests which seem to be seriously threatened?" McAdoo had stressed the opportunity for national prosperity; Lansing threatened the horrors of national depression. Wilson replied two days later, on September 8, "I have no doubt that our oral discussion of this letter suffices. If it does not, will you let me know that you would like a written reply? W. W." Shortly after this the house of Morgan floated a loan of $500,000,000 on behalf of the British and French governments.[10]

What of Senator Nye's contention that the bankers got us into the war by exerting direct pressure on Washington to protect their "investment"? It remains to be proved that the investment did get us into the war, and it is perfectly clear that direct pressure on Washington ceased when their desire to float loans for belligerent governments was granted. It is likewise clear that the government did not relinquish its ban on such loans out of any tender concern for the bankers as a group. What McAdoo, Lansing, and Wilson feared was a national economic depression. The bankers were in the happy position of being able to serve both God and Mammon. The situation is summarized in a single paragraph of Lansing's letter of September 6: "I believe that Secretary McAdoo is convinced, and I agree with him, that there is only one means of avoiding this situation which would so seriously affect economic conditions in this country, and that is the flotation of large bond issues by the belligerent governments. Our financial institutions have the money to loan and wish to do so." [11]

At this point the conclusions of Seymour and Baker seem irresistible. They conclusively demonstrate from the diplomatic record that German resort to unrestricted submarine warfare was the immediate cause of American participation in the war. Yet they are strangely incurious about the reasons for the German decision, which have a very direct connection with the American departure from its own deliberately adopted policy of forbidding loans to belligerents. The fact that the German decision was made with full realization that it would force the United States into the war is certainly something that needs to be explained and the search for an explanation is revealing.

There were two forces struggling for control within Germany, the civilian government of Chancellor Bethmann-Hollweg, and the naval-military element. The latter favored extreme military policies without regard to diplomatic consequences, while Bethmann waged a losing fight on behalf of elementary political common-sense. In regard to the specific issue of submarine warfare the military group were uncompromising advocates of its unrestricted use as against Bethmann's warnings that such a policy was certain to bring the United States into the war in the ranks of Germany's enemies. After

---

[10] New York *Times*, Jan. 10 and 11, 1936. Baker, *op. cit.*, p. 381–383.

[11] *Ibid.*

the sinking of the *Sussex* in March 1916 Bethmann was able to dominate the situation for the rest of the year. On May 4, 1916 the German Government gave to the United States a pledge to abide by the rules of cruiser warfare, abandoning the attacks on passenger ships, and promising to obey the rules of visit and search as they applied to merchant vessels. That the pledge was conditional on American enforcement of international law on Great Britain was a clear indication that Bethmann's victory was not decisive. The military element opposed the pledge from the beginning and fought for its abrogation from May throughout the rest of the year, with ultimate success.[12]

They did not in the least contest the civilian thesis that unrestricted submarine warfare would force the United States into the war. They blithely admitted it—and said it did not matter! Here is the reasoning. On May 4, the very day of the *Sussex* pledge, General Falkenhayn wrote Bethmann: "I consider unrestricted U-boat warfare not only one, but the *only* effective instrument of war at our disposal capable of bringing England to consider peace negotiations. . . . So far as this situation is concerned [the probable entry of the United States into the war] *America's step from secret war in which it has long been engaged against us, to an openly declared hostility can effect no real change.*" [13] Hindenburg and Ludendorff grew more and more impatient of the civilians' incurable timidity about war with the United States. They renewed their attack at the end of August, and Holtzendorff of the Admiralty Staff carried their complaints to Bethmann. "The objections to this mode of warfare are not considered mainly from the standpoint of the effect upon England, but from that of the reaction upon the United States. . . . *The United States can scarcely engage in more hostile activities than she has already done up to this time.*" [14] On August 31 at Pless, the civilian and military elements fought it out, with Jagow, Helferrich, and Bethmann standing firmly together against the generals. All three warned that war with the United States must inevitably follow resumption of submarine warfare, and that active American participation would be fatal to Germany. For the time being they again won their point, and it was agreed that final decision might await the outcome of the Rumanian campaign.[15] Even after that Bethmann was permitted to try his hand at peace negotiations in December, but their complete failure, coupled with Wilson's inability to mediate, inevitably brought renewed pressure from the military. Ludendorff on December 22 told the Foreign Office again that formal American participation in the war

---

[12] Carnegie Endowment, *Official German Documents Relating to the World War* (New York, Oxford University Press, 1923), II, p. 1151, no. 155.

[13] *Ibid.*, p. 1151 f., no. 156.

[14] *Ibid.*, p. 1153, no. 157.

[15] *Ibid.*, p. 1154–1163, no. 158.

would alter nothing, and on the same day Holtzendorff brought in an Admiralty report to much the same effect. It dismissed the danger of American troops by showing how much time was needed for their training and transport; it calculated that the American supply of munitions—already at capacity—would be less rather than more available to Germany's enemies because they would be reserved for American use. Positive advantage would accrue to Germany from restored freedom of action in sinking even passenger ships which carried munitions. The only disadvantage conceded by the report was the possible increase in American loans to the belligerents, but the amount of these was already so tremendous a factor in the economic strength of the hostile coalition that little additional danger from that source was to be anticipated.[16] Bethmann had for some time been yielding to the arguments and the importunities of the military, and the conference at Pless on January 9, 1917 sealed his defeat by the decision to renew unrestricted submarine warfare. Hindenburg's final words were, "It simply must be. We are counting on the possibility of war with the United States, and have made all preparations to meet it. *Things cannot be worse than they now are.* The war must be brought to an end by the use of all means as soon as possible." [17] The United States declared war on April 6, 1917.

The civilians were right and the military were wrong in their calculations as to the ultimate importance of a formal declaration of war by the United States. But the arguments of the military were plausible and they carried the day. Their promise to reduce England speedily to prostration was tempting, but it was essentially a gamble, and it is hard to see how they could have overborne civilian opposition if they had not had so plausible an answer to the one serious argument that the civilians presented. The answer was always that formal participation of the United States in the war would bring no change in the fundamental situation of American economic support to the Allies. The major influence in shaping the decision which brought the United States into the war is to be found in American policy in the economic sphere, specifically the decision of the Wilson administration in August, 1915 to abandon a policy deliberately adopted in the interest of neutrality early in the war. It was government permission to bankers to float loans for belligerent governments in order to finance American export trade that provided the Allies with resources which Germany could not obtain. That in turn weighted the scales in favor of the extremists and against the moderates in Germany, and provoked the decision which forced the United States into the war.

It is equally clear that the administration yielded to pressures which no

---

[16] *Ibid.*, p. 1200 f., no. 177 and p. 1218 f., no. 190.

[17] *Ibid.*, p. 1317–1319, no. 212.

administration is likely to withstand. The alternative policy of strict adherence to its earlier standards of neutrality meant economic depression on a national scale. It is scarcely drawing the long bow to say that the fundamental cause of the failure of American neutrality policy was economic nor is it unreasonable to suppose that the same economic factors will again in the future make a genuine and strict policy of neutrality unworkable, no matter what laws may be written on the statute books to enforce it. The only sensible course is to renounce our illusions and to face the world of reality where there is no longer any such thing as neutrality. In the face of a possible collapse of the collective security system as an alternative to ostrich isolationism and "neutrality" the area of choice is tragically narrowed. It would seem to involve a choice between deciding whether we should now affirm our decision publicly that we will align ourselves with the democracies of the world in the event of war on the long chance of preventing the war, or follow that policy of drift which will sooner or later involve us in inevitable war without our having any very clear cut program of war aims to achieve.

Is such realism conceivable in the present state of confusion of mind? Probably not, because of the tenacity of outworn but hallowed concepts and policies. Neutrality has a long history and its own particular folklore. Two of its high priests, Borchard and Lage, treat it as an all-sufficient decalogue when rightly interpreted and strictly adhered to. ". . . Neutral rights were as clear in 1914 as was any other branch of public law, and while the law was grossly violated during the war, it has not thereby been ended or modified." [18] The real difficulty they discover in Wilson's repudiation of "the very basis of American tradition in foreign policy." The submarine controversy with Germany is made to turn on Wilson's "insistence as a matter of National Honor that American citizens were privileged to travel unmolested on belligerent vessels." [19] It follows that there was no adequate excuse for the United States to break "with its fundamental principles by the unprecedented decision to participate in a European war. . . ." [20] Consequently there is no need to explore the economic background against which the drama of neutrality was played out, unless indeed there was no such drama at all, but only a skillful bit of play acting. Borchard and Lage devote exactly one page out of a total of three hundred and fifty to the administration's retreat from its original prohibition of loans to belligerent governments, with the remark that "No more than casual reference needs to be made to one of the more egregious lurches into unneutrality, whereby the United States and its people were led into financing the munitions supply of one set of the bel-

---

[18] *Neutrality for the United States* (New Haven, Yale University Press, 1937), p. 345.

[19] *Ibid.*, p. 346.

[20] *Ibid.*, p. 344.

ligerents, the Allies." [21] In their account this appears as but a minor detail in a general policy of partisanship of the Allies' cause. And so at the end they reject the argument that the conditions of the modern world make American neutrality impossible as "humiliating to American independence." [22] Denying the efficacy of any improvised formula, they recommend "an honest intention to remain aloof from foreign conflict, a refusal to be stampeded by unneutral propaganda, *a knowledge of the law and capacity to stand upon it*, meeting emergencies and problems not romantically but wisely." [23] It can be argued plausibly that President Wilson fought against overwhelming odds to realize exactly that program.

At least historians should not become victims of the legal exegesis that obscures the unreality of the neutrality concept. But the latest and most comprehensive account of American intervention in the World War, Tansill's *America Goes to War*, is almost totally lacking in interpretative treatment and completely lacking in synthesis. His very full chapters on the events leading to abandonment of the administration's loan policy are written largely in terms of "War Profits Beckon to 'Big Business,'" [24] with very little reference to the administration's concern with the economic condition of the country as a whole. Moreover he fails completely to show the political and diplomatic implications of the economic ties in his concluding paragraph that deals with them. "The real reasons why America went to war cannot be found in any single set of circumstances. There was no clear-cut road to war that the President followed with certain steps that knew no hesitation. There were many dim trails of doubtful promise, and one along which he travelled with early misgivings and reluctant tread was that which led to American economic solidarity with the Allies." [25] Tansill leaves it at that without any attempt to pursue the profound effect of this economic solidarity on the equilibrium of political forces in Germany which I have been at pains to trace in the central portion of this essay. This is all the more remarkable because Tansill is the only writer on the subject who has conscientiously studied that unstable equilibrium extensively in the German official documents. He has used most if not all of the documents I have cited to prove the decisive effect of the economic argument on the submarine decision—and many more— without ever apparently noting the presence of that argument at all. In his quotations from the documents he simply does not quote the passages where the argument appears. Despite his failure to see relationships, and his avoid-

---

[21] *Ibid.*, p. 40. The authors say, p. 41, that ". . . only public lending could meet the need, and that meant war." They do not explain why.

[22] *Ibid.*, p. 345.

[23] *Ibid.*, p. 350. (The italics are mine.)

[24] Title of chapter 3, p. 67–89.

[25] C. C. Tansill, *America Goes to War*, p. 134.

ance of interpretation, his account is still the fullest treatment available of all the complex phenomena, economic, political, psychological, inherent in the neutrality problem. But it is a compendium devoid of significance for an intelligent understanding of the neutrality problem.

The definitive study at once analytical and interpretative as well as comprehensive has yet to appear, and until it does appear there is small hope of enlightenment.[26]

SUGGESTED READING

The studies of the American entry into World War I and the struggle over the peace treaty are already legion. Good surveys of the historiographical controversy on entry into the war include Richard Leopold's "The Problem of American Intervention, 1917: An Historical Retrospect," *World Politics*, II (April, 1950), 405–25; Ernest May's *American Intervention: 1917 and 1941* ° (Service Center for Teachers of History, No. 30, 1960); and Daniel Smith's "National Interest and American Intervention, 1917: An Historiographical Appraisal," *Journal of American History*, LII (June, 1965), 5–24. In "Robert Lansing and the Formulation of American Neutrality Policies," *Mississippi Valley Historical Review*, XLIII (June, 1956), 59–81, Smith examines the period that Birdsall studies. Smith's general interpretation is available in his *The Great Departure* ° (Wiley, 1965). The early "revisionists" are analyzed in Warren I. Cohen's *The American Revisionists* (Univ. of Chicago Press, 1967).

The best statements of the realist criticism of Wilson are found in George Kennan's *American Diplomacy* ° (Univ. of Chicago, 1950); in Robert Osgood's *Ideals and Self-interest in America's Foreign Relations* ° (Univ. of Chicago Press, 1953) and his "Woodrow Wilson, Collective Security, and the Lessons of History," *Confluence*, V (Winter, 1957), 341–54; and in Hans Morgenthau's *In Defense of the National Interest* (Univ. of Chicago Press, 1951). Edward Buehrig in *Woodrow Wilson and the Balance of Power* (Indiana Univ. Press, 1955) argues, as Link does, that Wilson understood that American security depended on maintaining the balance of power. Much of his argument is summarized in his "Wilson's Neutrality Re-Examined," *World Politics*, III (Oct., 1950), 1–19. N. Gordon Levin in *Woodrow Wilson and World Politics* (Oxford Univ. Press, 1968) explains Wilson's responses within the larger framework of the effort to establish a world order that would al-

---

[26] I have deliberately omitted from consideration in these pages one of the most colorful of the historical accounts, Walter Millis's *Road to War* (Cambridge, 1935). It is journalistic and dramatic with little pretense at analysis. There is recognition that economic relations with the Allies were dangerous to neutrality, but no attempt to show precisely how. For example, p. 336, ". . . the United States was enmeshed more deeply than ever in the cause of Allied victory." But there is no effort to explain the submarine decision in these terms (p. 372 f.).

low free trade and advance democratic values within a liberal capitalistic system. A similar theory is developed in Arno J. Mayer's *The Political Origins of the New Diplomacy, 1917–1918* ° (Yale Univ. Press, 1959), and he has extended this conception to emphasize in *Politics and Diplomacy of Peacemaking* (Knopf, 1968) the importance of the fear of bolshevism at the Versailles conference.

The attitudes of the business community to neutrality and the war have never been systematically studied, but Harold Syrett's "The Business Press and American Neutrality, 1914–1917," *Mississippi Valley Historical Review*, XXXII (Sept., 1945), 215–30, is useful.

The response of progressives to the war has been dealt with by Walter Trattner in "Progressivism and World War I: A Re-Appraisal," *Mid-America*, XLIV (July, 1962), 131–45; Trattner finds a mixed pattern, contrary to William E. Leuchtenburg's conclusion (in "Progressivism and Imperialism") that the progressives were generally strong supporters of imperialism. Howard W. Allen's "Republican Reformers and Foreign Policy, 1913–1917," *Mid-America*, XLIV (Oct., 1962), 222–29; and Warren Sutton's "Progressive Republican Senators and the Submarine Crisis, 1915–1916," *ibid.*, LVII (April, 1965), 75–88, also dissent from Leuchtenburg's thesis.

STANLEY COBEN

A Study in Nativism:
The American
Red Scare of 1919–1920

INTRODUCTION

The idealism so characteristic of the middle classes during the
progressive era reached its climax in the crusade to make the
world safe for democracy. But inevitably the moral zeal of World
War I became the servant of an aroused nationalism, and the result
in the United States was an authoritarian campaign to enforce one
hundred percent Americanism, especially on the more than two
million foreign-born Germans and their children. A widespread
campaign against German culture led not only to occasional violence directed against the German community but also to the elim-

FROM Stanley Coben, "A Study in Nativism: The American Red Scare of 1919–1920,"
Political Science Quarterly, LXXIX (March, 1964), pp. 52–75. Reprinted by permission.

I am grateful to Robert D. Cross and Clyde C. Griffen for their critical reading of this
article, and to Anthony F. C. Wallace and Abram Kardiner for their helpful comments on
my use of anthropological and psychological material.

ination of the German language from many high schools, the disappearance of German music from concert halls, and the transformation of "sauerkraut" into "liberty cabbage."

Manifesting the desire for a disciplined, unified society in wartime, the movement for one hundred percent Americanism opposed not just German culture but any deviation from the American norm—especially "un-American" ideas. Because many socialists and such radicals as the Wobblies opposed the war, anti-radicalism became an especially virulent component of the drive for conformity to American standards.

As Stanley Coben makes clear in the article that follows, the end of World War I did not extinguish repressive nationalism. Social tensions actually increased in 1919, and the patriotic societies spawned during the war directed their energies exclusively against the radicals, whom they now viewed as the sole source of the nation's problems. The fantasies of the patriots were nourished in 1919 by the outbreak of Red revolutions in Bavaria and Hungary, the formation of American Communist parties, and numerous attempts to kill prominent Americans with bombs.

At first the Wilson Administration resisted the mounting hysteria and demands for action to save the Republic. But in October, 1919, the Senate unanimously passed a resolution asking Attorney General A. Mitchell Palmer how he intended to meet the threat of radicalism. Although Palmer bears the ultimate responsibility for the excesses of the government crackdown that followed, Coben makes clear in his excellent biography of the Attorney General (*A. Mitchell Palmer: Politician* [Columbia Univ. Press, 1963]) that the real mastermind of the Palmer raids was J. Edgar Hoover, the twenty-four-year-old head of the Justice Department's General Intelligence Division, whose job it was to collect information on radical activity.

The Immigration Act of 1917, as amended, provided that aliens who were anarchists or who advocated violent overthrow of the government or belonged to groups espousing such beliefs could be deported on warrants signed by the Secretary of Labor. With this statute as his authority, Hoover obtained warrants, rounded up some radicals in November, 1919, and then on January 2, 1920, sent his agents into thirty-three cities to make more than six thousand arrests—the most massive single violation of civil liberties in American history.

In the next months Hoover became convinced that May Day, 1920, would see the uprising of the Reds in America; consequently, Palmer began issuing daily warnings. When May Day passed without incident, Palmer became the object of general ridicule, and the hysteria that had sustained the Red Scare rapidly subsided. In the meantime, Assistant Secretary of Labor Louis Post cancelled warrants of doubtful legality; when he had finished, only some six-hundred aliens were still deportable.

As historians have been doing with increasing frequency, Coben resorts in this article to other social sciences for enlightenment. Drawing on the findings of some social psychologists and anthropologists, he concludes that the Red Scare and the nativist movement represented the efforts of Americans to defend themselves "against severe inner turmoil by enforcing order in [their] external life." To explain the increased need for order, he focuses on "severe social and economic dislocations"—runaway prices, a brief depression, foreign revolutions, bombings at home, the increased flow of radical literature—"which threatened the national equilibrium." These dislocations, rather than establishment of the accuracy of the theory that he has borrowed, constitute the major subject of his essay. Yet, unless there is a systematic linkage of inner stress and nativism among particular people and groups, Coben's analysis remains unproven, though still useful and plausible.

At a victory loan pageant in the District of Columbia on May 6, 1919, a man refused to rise for the playing of "The Star-Spangled Banner." As soon as the national anthem was completed an enraged sailor fired three shots into the unpatriotic spectator's back. When the man fell, the *Washington Post* reported, "the crowd burst into cheering and handclapping." In February of the same year, a jury in Hammond, Indiana, took two minutes to acquit the assassin of an alien who yelled, "To Hell with the United States." Early in 1920, a clothing store salesman in Waterbury, Connecticut, was sentenced to six months in jail for having remarked to a customer that Lenin was "the brainiest," or "one of the brainiest" of the world's political leaders.[1] Dramatic episodes like these, or the better known Centralia Massacre, Palmer Raids, or May Day riots, were not everyday occurrences, even at the height of the Red Scare. But the fanatical one hundred per cent Americanism reflected by the Washington crowd, the Hammond jury, and the Waterbury judge pervaded a large part of our society between early 1919 and mid-1920.

Recently, social scientists have produced illuminating evidence about

---

[1] *Washington Post*, May 7, 1919; Mark Sullivan, *Our Times, The United States 1900– 1925* (New York, 1935), VI, 169; *The Nation*, CX (April 17, 1920), 510–11. The most complete account of the Red Scare is Robert K. Murray, *Red Scare, A Study in National Hysteria* (Minneapolis, 1955). But see the critical review of Murray's book by John M. Blum in *Mississippi Valley Historical Review*, XLII (1955), 145. Blum comments that Murray failed to explain "the susceptibility of the American people and of their elite to the 'national hysteria.' . . . About hysteria, after all, psychology and social psychology in particular have had considerable to say." John Higham places the postwar movement in historical perspective in his superb *Strangers in the Land, Patterns of American Nativism, 1860–1925* (New Brunswick, 1955), especially Chaps. 8 and 9.

the causes of eruptions like that of 1919–20. They have attempted to identify experimentally the individuals most responsive to nativistic appeals, to explain their susceptibility, and to propose general theories of nativistic and related movements. These studies suggest a fuller, more coherent picture of nativistic upheavals and their causes than we now possess, and they provide the framework for this attempt to reinterpret the Red Scare.

Psychological experiments indicate that a great many Americans—at least several million—are always ready to participate in a "red scare." These people permanently hold attitudes which characterized the nativists of 1919–20: hostility toward certain minority groups, especially radicals and recent immigrants, fanatical patriotism, and a belief that internal enemies seriously threaten national security.[2]

In one of the most comprehensive of these experiments, psychologists Nancy C. Morse and Floyd H. Allport tested seven hypotheses about the causes of prejudice and found that one, national involvement or patriotism, proved to be "by far the most important factor" associated with prejudice. Other widely held theories about prejudice—status rivalry, frustration-aggression, and scapegoat hypotheses, for example—were found to be of only secondary importance.[3] Summarizing the results of this and a number of other psychological experiments, Gordon W. Allport, a pioneer in the scientific study of prejudice, concluded that in a large proportion of cases the prejudiced person is attempting to defend himself against severe inner turmoil by enforcing order in his external life. Any disturbance in the social *status quo* threatens the precarious psychic equilibrium of this type of individual, who, according to Allport, seeks "an island of institutional safety and security. The nation is the island he selects. . . . It has the definiteness he needs."

Allport pointed out that many apprehensive and frustrated people are not especially prejudiced. What is important, he found,

---

[2] On the incidence of prejudice against minorities in the United States, see Gordon W. Allport and Bernard M. Kramer, "Some Roots of Prejudice," *Journal of Psychology*, XXII (1946), 9–39; Morris Janowitz and Dwaine Marvick, "Authoritarianism and Political Behavior," *Public Opinion Quarterly*, XVII (1953), 185–201; Bruno Bettelheim and Morris Janowitz, *Dynamics of Prejudice, A Psychological and Sociological Study of Veterans* (New York, 1950), 16, 26, and *passim*.

[3] Nancy C. Morse and F. H. Allport, "The Causation of Anti-Semitism: An Investigation of Seven Hypotheses," *Journal of Psychology*, XXXIV (1952), 197–233. For further experimental evidence indicating that prejudiced individuals are no more anxious, neurotic, or intolerant of ambiguity than those with more "liberal" attitudes, Anthony Davids, "Some Personality and Intellectual Correlates to Intolerance of Ambiguity," *Journal of Abnormal and Social Psychology*, LI (1955), 415–20; Ross Stagner and Clyde S. Congdon, "Another Failure to Demonstrate Displacement of Aggression," *Journal of Abormal and Social Psychology*, LI (1955), 695–96; Dean Peabody, "Attitude Content and Agreement Set in Scales of Authoritarianism, Dogmatism, Anti-Semitism and Economic Conservatism," *Journal of Abnormal and Social Psychology*, LXIII (1961), 1–11.

is the way fear and frustration are handled. The institutionalistic way—especially the nationalistic—seems to be the nub of the matter. What happens is that the prejudiced person defines 'nation' to fit his needs. The nation is first of all a protection (the chief protection) of him as an individual. It is his ingroup. He sees no contradiction in ruling out of its beneficent orbit those whom he regards as threatening intruders and enemies (namely, American minorities). What is more, the nation stands for the status quo. It is a conservative agent; within it are all the devices for safe living that he approves. His nationalism is a form of conservatism.[4]

Substantial evidence, then, suggests that millions of Americans are both extraordinarily fearful of social change and prejudiced against those minority groups which they perceive as "threatening intruders." Societal disruption, especially if it can easily be connected with the "intruders," not only will intensify the hostility of highly prejudiced individuals, but also will provoke many others, whose antagonism in more stable times had been mild or incipient, into the extreme group.

A number of anthropologists have come to conclusions about the roots of nativism which complement these psychological studies. Since the late nineteenth century, anthropologists have been studying the religious and nativistic cults of American Indian tribes and of Melanesian and Papuan groups in the South Pacific. Recently, several anthropologists have attempted to synthesize their findings and have shown striking parallels in the cultural conditions out of which these movements arose.[5] In every case, severe societal disruption preceded the outbreak of widespread nativistic cult behavior. According to Anthony F. C. Wallace, who has gone farthest toward

---

[4] Gordon W. Allport, *The Nature of Prejudice* (Cambridge, 1955), 406; see Boyd C. Shafer, *Nationalism, Myth and Reality* (New York, 1955), 181.

[5] See, especially, the works of Anthony F. C. Wallace: "Revitalization Movements," *American Anthropologist*, LVIII (1956), 264–81; "Handsome Lake and the Great Revival in the West," *American Quarterly*, IV (1952), 149–65; "Stress and Rapid Personality Change," *International Record of Medicine and General Practice Clinics*, CLXIX (1956), 761–73; "New Religions Among the Delaware Indians, 1600–1900," *Southwest Journal of Anthropology*, XII (1956), 1–21. Also, Michael M. Ames, "Reaction to Stress: A Comparative Study of Nativism," *Davidson Journal of Anthropology*, III (1957), 16–30; C. S. Belshaw, "The Significance of Modern Cults in Melanesian Development," *Australian Outlook*, IV (1950), 116–25; Raymond Firth, "The Theory of 'Cargo' Cults: A Note on Tikopia," *Man*, LV (1955), 130–32; Lawrence Krader, "A Nativistic Movement in Western Siberia," *American Anthropologist*, LVIII (1956), 282–92; Ralph Linton, "Nativistic Movements," *American Anthropologist*, XLV (1943), 220–43; Margaret Mead, *New Lives for Old* (New York, 1956); Peter Worsley, *The Trumpet Shall Sound* (London, 1957). Several sociologists and psychologists have come to conclusions about the causes of these movements that are similar in important respects to Wallace's, although less comprehensive. See Leon Festinger, *A Theory of Cognitive Dissonance* (New York, 1957); Hadley Cantril, *The Psychology of Social Movements* (New York, 1941), especially pp. 3–4, Chaps. 5, 8, and 9; Hans H. Toch, "Crisis Situations and Ideological Revaluation," *Public Opinion Quarterly*, XIX (1955), 53–67.

constructing a general theory of cult formation, when the disruption has proceeded so far that many members of a society find it difficult or impossible to fulfill their physical and psychological needs, or to relieve severe anxiety through the ordinary culturally approved methods, the society will be susceptible to what Wallace has termed a "revitalization movement." This is a convulsive attempt to change or revivify important cultural beliefs and values, and frequently to eliminate alien influences. Such movements promise and often provide participants with better means of dealing with their changed circumstances, thus reducing their very high level of internal stress.[6]

American Indian tribes, for example, experienced a series of such convulsions as the tide of white settlers rolled west. The Indians were pushed onto reservations and provided with Indian agents, missionaries, and physicians, who took over many of the functions hitherto assumed by chiefs and medicine men. Indian craftsmen (and craftswomen) were replaced by dealers in the white man's implements. Most hunters and warriors also lost their vocations and consequently their self-respect. What an anthropologist wrote of one tribe was true of many others: "From cultural maturity as Pawnees they were reduced to cultural infancy as civilized men." [7]

One of the last major religious upheavals among the Indians was the Ghost Dance cult which spread from Nevada through Oregon and northern California in the eighteen-seventies, and a similar movement among the Rocky Mountain and western plains Indians about 1890. Although cult beliefs varied somewhat from tribe to tribe, converts generally were persuaded that if they followed certain prescribed rituals, including the dance, they would soon return to their old ways of living. Even their dead relatives would be restored to life. Most Indians were too conscious of their military weakness to challenge their white masters directly. Ghost Dancers among the Dakota Sioux, however, influenced by the militant proselyter Sitting Bull, became convinced that true believers could not be harmed by the white man's bullets and that Sioux warriors would drive the intruders from Indian

[6] Wallace, "Revitalization Movements." For a recent verification of Wallace's theories see Thomas Rhys Williams, "The Form of a North Borneo Nativistic Behavior," *American Anthropologist*, LXV (1963), 543–51. On the psychological results of socially caused stress, Wallace, "Stress and Rapid Personality Change"; William Caudill, *Effects of Social and Cultural Systems in Reactions to Stress*, Social Science Research Council Pamphlet No. 14 (New York, 1958); Caudill, "Cultural Perspectives on Stress," Army Medical Service Graduate School, *Symposium on Stress* (Washington, D.C., 1953); Hans Selye, *The Stress of Life* (New York, 1956); Roland Fischer and Neil Agnew, "A Hierarchy of Stressors," *Journal of Mental Science*, CI (1955), 383–86; Daniel H. Funkenstein, Stanley H. King, and Margaret E. Drolette, *Mastery of Stress* (Cambridge, 1957); M. Basowitz *et al.*, *Anxiety and Stress: An Interdisciplinary Study of a Life Situation* (New York, 1955).

[7] Alexander Lesser, *The Pawnee Ghost Dance Hand Game. A Study of Cultural Change* (New York, 1933), 44.

lands. Their dreams were rudely smashed at the massacre of Wounded Knee Creek in December 1890.[8]

The Boxer movement in China, 1898 to 1900, resembled in many respects the Indian Ghost Dance cults; however, the Boxers, more numerous and perhaps less demoralized than the Indians, aimed more directly at removing foreign influences from their land. The movement erupted first in Shantung province where foreigners, especially Japanese, British, and Germans, were most aggressive. A flood of the Yellow River had recently deprived about a million people in the province of food and shelter. Banditry was rampant, organized government ineffective. The Boxer movement, based on the belief that these tragic conditions were due almost entirely to the "foreign devils" and their agents, determined to drive the enemy out of China. Boxers went into action carrying charms and chanting incantations supposed to make them invulnerable to the foreigners' bullets. The first object of the Boxers' nativistic fury were Chinese who had converted to Christianity, the intruders' religion. The patriots then attacked railroad and telegraph lines, leading symbols of foreign influence. Finally, the Boxers turned against the foreigners themselves, slaughtering many. Not until after the Boxers carried on a two-month siege of the foreign community in Peking did American, European, and Japanese armies crush the movement.[9]

Other revitalization attempts proved more successful than the Boxers or Ghost Dancers. The Gaiwiio movement, for example, helped the Iroquois Indians of western New York State to retain their identity as a culture while adjusting successfully to an encroaching white civilization during the first decade of the nineteenth century. The movement implanted a new moral code among the Indians, enjoining sobriety and family stability and encouraging acceptance of Western technology, while revivifying cohesive Indian traditions.[10]

---

[8] Cora DuBois, The 1870 Ghost Dance, Anthropological Records, III (Berkeley, 1946); Leslie Spier, The Ghost Dance of 1870 Among the Klamath of Oregon, University of Washington Publications in Anthropology, II (Seattle, 1927); Lesser, Ghost Dance; A. L. Kroeber, Handbook of the Indians of California, Bureau of American Ethnology Bulletin 78 (Washington, D.C., 1925). Anthropologists recently have argued about the origins of the Ghost Dance cults. Both sides agree, however, that whatever their origins, the cults took the form they did because of intolerable cultural conditions caused largely by white encroachments. David F. Aberle, "The Prophet Dance and Reactions to White Contact," Southwest Journal of Anthropology, XV (1959), 74–83; Leslie Spier, Wayne Suttles, and Melville Herskovits, "Comment on Aberle's Thesis of Deprivation," Southwest Journal of Anthropology, XV (1959), 84–88.

[9] The best account of the Boxer movement is Chester C. Tan, The Boxer Catastrophe (New York, 1955). Also, George N. Steiger, China and the Occident, the Origin and Development of the Boxer Movement (New Haven, 1927); Peter Fleming, The Siege at Peking (New York, 1959).

[10] Wallace, "Handsome Lake." Wallace compared the Gaiwiio with a Chinese attempt to accommodate their society to Western civilization in "Stress and Rapid Personality Change." For a successful movement in the South Pacific see Mead, New Lives for Old.

Dominant as well as conquered peoples, Ralph Linton has pointed out, undergo nativistic movements. Dominant groups, he observed, are sometimes threatened "not only by foreign invasion or domestic revolt but also by the invidious process of assimilation which might, in the long run, destroy their distinctive powers and privileges." Under such circumstances, Linton concluded, "the frustrations which motivate nativistic movements in inferior or dominated groups" are "replaced by anxieties which produce very much the same [nativistic] result" in dominant groups.[11]

Communist "brainwashers" have consciously attempted to achieve results comparable to those obtained by prophets of movements like the Ghost Dance cult and the Boxers. They create intolerable stress within individuals, not through rapid societal change, but by intentional physical debilitation and continual accusations, cross-examinations, and use of other anxiety-provoking techniques. Then they offer their prisoners an escape from the induced psychological torment: conversion to the new gospel.[12]

The similarity in the mental processes involved in "brainwashing" and in the formation of nativistic movements becomes even clearer upon examination of the Chinese Communist attempt to establish their doctrines in mainland China. Again, the Communists intentionally have created conditions like those out of which nativistic cults have arisen more spontaneously in other societies. In addition to the stress which ordinarily would accompany rapid industrialization of an economically backward society, the Chinese leaders have provoked additional anxiety through the systematic use of group confessions and denunciations and have intentionally disrupted family life. Hostility toward the American enemy has been purposely aroused and used to unify the masses, as well as to justify the repression of millions of alleged internal enemies. The whole population has been continually urged to repent their sins and to adopt wholeheartedly the Communist gospel, which has a strong nativistic component. As a psychologist has remarked, to a large extent the Chinese Communists provide both the disease and the cure.[13]

The ferocious outbreak of nativism in the United States after World War I was not consciously planned or provoked by any individual or group,

---

[11] Linton, 237. Also, Carroll L. Riley and John Hobgood, "A Recent Nativistic Movement Among the Southern Tepehuan Indians," *Southwest Journal of Anthropology*, XV (1959), 355–60.

[12] Robert J. Lifton, "Thought Reform in Western Civilians in Chinese Communist Prisons," *Psychiatry*, XIX (1956), 173–95; Edgar H. Schein, "The Chinese Indoctrination Program for Prisoners of War, A Study of Attempted Brainwashing," *Psychiatry*, XIX (1956), 149–72.

[13] Edgar H. Schein, with Inge Schneier and Curtis H. Bark, *Coercive Persuasion* (New York, 1961); William Sargent, *Battle for the Mind* (New York, 1957), 150–65; Robert J. Lifton, *Thought Reform and the Psychology of Totalism* (New York, 1961); R. L. Walker, *China Under Communism* (London, 1946).

although some Americans took advantage of the movement once it started. Rather, the Red Scare, like the Gaiwiio and Boxer movements described above, was brought on largely by a number of severe social and economic dislocations which threatened the national equilibrium. The full extent and the shocking effects of these disturbances of 1919 have not yet been adequately described. Runaway prices, a brief but sharp stock market crash and business depression, revolutions throughout Europe, widespread fear of domestic revolt, bomb explosions, and an outpouring of radical literature were distressing enough. These sudden difficulties, moreover, served to exaggerate the disruptive effects already produced by the social and intellectual ravages of the World War and the preceding reform era, and by the arrival, before the war, of millions of new immigrants. This added stress intensified the hostility of Americans strongly antagonistic to minority groups, and brought new converts to blatant nativism from among those who ordinarily were not overtly hostile toward radicals or recent immigrants.

Citizens who joined the crusade for one hundred per cent Americanism sought, primarily, a unifying force which would halt the apparent disintegration of their culture. The movement, they felt, would eliminate those foreign influences which the one hundred per centers believed were the major cause of their anxiety.

Many of the postwar sources of stress were also present during World War I, and the Red Scare, as John Higham has observed, was partly an exaggeration of wartime passions.[14] In 1917–18 German-Americans served as the object of almost all our nativistic fervor; they were the threatening intruders who refused to become good citizens. "They used America," a patriotic author declared in 1918 of two million German-Americans, "they never loved her. They clung to their old language, their old customs, and cared nothing for ours. . . . As a class they were clannish beyond all other races coming here." [15] Fear of subversion by German agents was almost as extravagant in 1917–18 as anxiety about "reds" in the postwar period. Attorney General Thomas Watt Gregory reported to a friend in May 1918 that "we not infrequently receive as many as fifteen hundred letters in a single day suggesting disloyalty and the making of investigations." [16]

Opposition to the war by radical groups helped smooth the transition among American nativists from hatred of everything German to fear of radical revolution. The two groups of enemies were associated also for other reasons. High government officials declared after the war that German leaders

---

[14] Higham, 222.

[15] Emerson Hough, *The Web* (Chicago, 1919), 23. Hough was a rabid one hundred per center during the Red Scare also.

[16] T. W. Gregory to R. E. Vinson, May 13, 1918, Papers of Thomas Watt Gregory (Library of Congress, Washington, D. C.).

planned and subsidized the Bolshevik Revolution.[17] When bombs blasted homes and public buildings in nine cities in June 1919, the director of the Justice Department's Bureau of Investigation asserted that the bombers were "connected with Russian bolshevism, aided by Hun money."[18] In November 1919, a year after the armistice, a popular magazine warned of "the Russo-German movement that is now trying to dominate America. . . ."[19]

Even the wartime hostility toward German-Americans, however, is more understandable when seen in the light of recent anthropological and psychological studies. World War I disturbed Americans not only because of the real threat posed by enemy armies and a foreign ideology. For many citizens it had the further effect of shattering an already weakened intellectual tradition. When the European governments decided to fight, they provided shocking evidence that man was not, as most educated members of Western society had believed, a rational creature progressing steadily, if slowly, toward control of his environment. When the great powers declared war in 1914, many Americans as well as many Europeans were stunned. The *New York Times* proclaimed a common theme—European civilization had collapsed: The supposedly advanced nations, declared the *Times,* "have reverted to the condition of savage tribes roaming the forests and falling upon each other in a fury of blood and carnage to achieve the ambitious designs of chieftains clad in skins and drunk with mead."[20] Franz Alexander, director for twenty-five years of the Chicago Institute of Psychoanalysis, recently recalled his response to the outbreak of the World War:

> The first impact of this news is [*sic*] unforgettable. It was the sudden intuitive realization that a chapter of history had ended. . . . Since then, I have discussed this matter with some of my contemporaries and heard about it a great deal in my early postwar psychoanalytic treatments of patients. To my amazement, the others who went through the same events had quite a similar

---

[17] Subcommittee of Senate Committee on the Judiciary, *Hearings, Brewing and Liquor Interests and German and Bolshevik Propaganda,* 66th Congress, 1st Session, 1919, 2669 ff.; *The New York Times,* July 7, August 11 and 29, September 15–21, 1918.

[18] *Washington Post,* July 3, 1919. Bureau Director William J. Flynn produced no evidence to back this assertion. Later he claimed to have conclusive proof that the bombers were Italian anarchists. Flynn to Attorney General Harry Daugherty, April 4, 1922, Department of Justice Records, File 202600, Sect. 5 (National Archives, Washington, D. C.).

[19] *Saturday Evening Post,* CXCII (November 1, 1919), 28. For similar assertions in other publications, Meno Lovenstein, *American Opinion of Soviet Russia* (Washington, D. C., 1941), Chap. 1, *passsim.*

[20] Quoted in William E. Leuchtenburg, *The Perils of Prosperity, 1914–32* (Chicago, 1958), 13. There is no comprehensive study of the effects of the war on the American mind. For brief treatments, Henry F. May, *The End of American Innocence* (New York, 1959), 361–67; Merle Curti, *The Growth of American Thought* (New York, 1951), 687–705; Ralph Henry Gabriel, *The Course of American Democratic Thought* (New York, 1956), 387, 404; André Siegfried, *America Comes of Age* (New York, 1927), 3; Walter Lord, *The Good Years, From 1900 to the First World War* (New York, 1960), 339–41.

reaction. . . . It was an immediate vivid and prophetic realization that
something irrevocable of immense importance had happened in history.[21]

Americans were jolted by new blows to their equilibrium after entering
the war. Four million men were drafted away from familiar surroundings and
some of them experienced the terrible carnage of trench warfare. Great numbers of women left home to work in war industries or to replace men in other
jobs. Negroes flocked to Northern industrial areas by the hundreds of thousands, and their first mass migration from the South created violent racial
antagonism in Northern cities.

During the war, also, Americans sanctioned a degree of government
control over the economy which deviated sharply from traditional economic
individualism. Again, fears aroused before the war were aggravated, for the
reform legislation of the Progressive era had tended to increase government
intervention, and many citizens were further perturbed by demands that the
federal government enforce even higher standards of economic and social
morality. By 1919, therefore, some prewar progressives as well as conservatives feared the gradual disappearance of highly valued individual opportunity and responsibility. Their fears were fed by strong postwar calls for continued large-scale government controls—extension of federal operation of
railroads and of the Food Administration, for example.

The prime threat to these long-held individualistic values, however,
and the most powerful immediate stimulus to the revitalistic response, came
from Russia. There the Bolshevik conquerors proclaimed their intention of exporting Marxist ideology. If millions of Americans were disturbed in 1919 by
the specter of communism, the underlying reason was not fear of foreign invasion—Russia, after all, was still a backward nation recently badly defeated
by German armies. The real threat was the potential spread of communist
ideas. These, the one hundred per centers realized with horror, possessed
a genuine appeal for reformers and for the economically underprivileged,
and if accepted they would complete the transformation of America.

A clear picture of the Bolshevik tyranny was not yet available; therefore, as after the French Revolution, those who feared the newly successful
ideology turned to fight the revolutionary ideals. So the *Saturday Evening
Post* declared editorially in November 1919 that "History will see our present
state of mind as one with that preceding the burning of witches, the children's crusade, the great tulip craze and other examples of softening of the
world brain." The *Post* referred not to the Red Scare or the impending Palmer Raids, but to the spread of communist ideology. Its editorial concluded:
"The need of the country is not more idealism, but more pragmatism; not

---

[21] Franz Alexander, *The Western Mind in Transition* (New York, 1960), 73–74. Also see
William Barrett, *Irrational Man* (Garden City, N. Y., 1961), 32–33.

communism, but common sense." [22] One of the most powerful patriotic groups, the National Security League, called upon members early in 1919 to "teach 'Americanism.' This means the fighting of Bolshevism . . . by the creation of well defined National Ideals." Members "must preach Americanism and instil the idealism of America's Wars, and that American spirit of service which believes in giving as well as getting." [23] New York attorney, author, and educator Henry Waters Taft warned a Carnegie Hall audience late in 1919 that Americans must battle "a propaganda which is tending to undermine our most cherished social and political institutions and is having the effect of producing widespread unrest among the poor and the ignorant, especially those of foreign birth." [24]

When the war ended Americans also confronted the disturbing possibility, pointed up in 1919 by the struggle over the League of Nations, that Europe's struggles would continue to be their own. These factors combined to make the First World War a traumatic experience for millions of citizens. As Senator James Reed of Missouri observed in August 1919, "This country is still suffering from shell shock. Hardly anyone is in a normal state of mind. . . . A great storm has swept over the intellectual world and its ravages and disturbances still exist." [25]

The wartime "shell shock" left many Americans extraordinarily susceptible to psychological stress caused by postwar social and economic turbulence. Most important for the course of the Red Scare, many of these disturbances had their greatest effect on individuals already antagonistic toward minorities. First of all, there was some real evidence of danger to the nation in 1919, and the nation provided the chief emotional support for many Americans who responded easily to charges of an alien radical menace. Violence flared throughout Europe after the war and revolt lifted radicals to power in several Eastern and Central European nations. Combined with the earlier Bolshevik triumph in Russia these revolutions made Americans look more anxiously at radicals here. Domestic radicals encouraged these fears; they became unduly optimistic about their own chances of success and boasted openly of their coming triumph. Scores of new foreign language anarchist and communist journals, most of them written by and for Southern and Eastern European immigrants, commenced publication, and the established radical press became more exuberant. These periodicals never tired of assuring readers in 1919 that "the United States seems to be on the verge of a revo-

---

[22] *Saturday Evening Post,* CXCII (November 1, 1919), 28.

[23] National Security League, *Future Work* (New York, 1919), 6.

[24] Henry Waters Taft, *Aspects of Bolshevism and Americanism, Address before the League for Political Education at Carnegie Hall, New York, December 6, 1919* (New York, 1919), 21.

[25] U. S., *Congressional Record,* 66th Congress, 1st Session, August 15, 1919, 3892.

lutionary crisis." [26] American newspapers and magazines reprinted selections from radical speeches, pamphlets, and periodicals so their readers could see what dangerous ideas were abroad in the land.[27] Several mysterious bomb explosions and bombing attempts, reported in bold front page headlines in newspapers across the country, frightened the public in 1919. To many citizens these seemed part of an organized campaign of terror carried on by alien radicals intending to bring down the federal government. The great strikes of 1919 and early 1920 aroused similar fears.[28]

Actually American radical organizations in 1919 were disorganized and poverty-stricken. The Communists were inept, almost without contact with American workers and not yet dominated or subsidized by Moscow. The IWW [International Workers of the World] was shorn of its effective leaders, distrusted by labor, and generally declining in influence and power. Violent anarchists were isolated in a handful of tiny, unconnected local organizations.[29] One or two of these anarchist groups probably carried out the "bomb conspiracy" of 1919; but the extent of the "conspiracy" can be judged from the fact that the bombs killed a total of two men during the year, a night watchman and one of the bomb throwers, and seriously wounded one person, a maid in the home of a Georgia senator.[30]

Nevertheless, prophecies of national disaster abounded in 1919, even among high government officials. Secretary of State Robert Lansing confided to his diary that we were in real peril of social revolution. Attorney General

---

[26] Robert E. Park, *The Immigrant Press and Its Control* (New York, 1922), 214, 230–38, 241–45; R. E. Park and Herbert A. Miller, *Old World Traits Transplanted* (New York, 1921), 99–101; Daniel Bell, "The Background and Development of Marxian Socialism in the United States," in Donald Drew Egbert and Stow Persons, *Socialism in American Life* (Princeton, 1952), I, 334; Lovenstein, 7–50; Leuchtenburg, 67–68; Murray, 33–36.

[27] The Justice Department distributed pamphlets containing such material to all American newspapers and magazines; *Red Radicalism, as Described by Its Own Leaders* (Washington, D. C., 1920); National Popular Government League, *To the American People, Report Upon the Illegal Practices of the Department of Justice* (Washington, D. C., 1920), 64–66. The staunchly antiradical *New York Times* published translations from a large sample of foreign language radical newspapers on June 8, 1919.

[28] Murray, Chaps. 5, 7–10. Asked by a congressional committee a few weeks after the spate of bombings in June 1919 whether there was real evidence of an organized effort to destroy the federal government, Assistant Attorney General Francis P. Garvan replied, "Certainly." Garvan was in charge of federal prosecution of radicals. *Washington Post,* June 27, 1919.

[29] Theodore Draper, *The Roots of American Communism* (New York, 1957), 198–200, 302, 312–14; David J. Saposs, *Left Wing Unionism, A Study in Policies and Tactics* (New York, 1926), 49–50, 152–57; Selig Perlman and Philip Taft (eds.), *Labor Movements* in John R. Commons (ed.), *History of Labour in the United States 1896–1932,* IV (New York, 1935), 621, 431–32; Jerome Davis, *The Russian Immigrant* (New York, 1922), 114–-18; Kate Holladay Claghorn, *The Immigrant's Day in Court* (New York, 1923), 363–73; John S. Gambs, *The Decline of the I.W.W.* (New York, 1932), 133; Murray, 107–10.

[30] *The New York Times,* May 1, June 3, 4, 1919.

A. Mitchell Palmer advised the House Appropriations Committee that "on a certain day, which we have been advised of," radicals would attempt "to rise up and destroy the Government at one fell swoop." Senator Charles Thomas of Colorado warned that "the country is on the verge of a volcanic upheaval." And Senator Miles Poindexter of Washington declared, "There is real danger that the government will fall." [31] A West Virginia wholesaler, with offices throughout the state, informed the Justice Department in October 1919 that "there is hardly a respectable citizen of my acquaintance who does not believe that we are on the verge of armed conflict in this country." William G. McAdoo was told by a trusted friend that "Chicago, which has always been a very liberal minded place, seems to me to have gone mad on the question of the 'Reds.'" Delegates to the Farmers National Congress in November 1919 pledged that farmers would assist the government in meeting the threat of revolution.[32]

The slight evidence of danger from radical organizations aroused such wild fear only because Americans had already encountered other threats to cultural stability. However, the dislocations caused by the war and the menace of communism alone would not have produced such a vehement nativistic response. Other postwar challenges to the social and economic order made the crucial difference.

Of considerable importance was the skyrocketing cost of living. Retail prices more than doubled between 1915 and 1920, and the price rise began gathering momentum in the spring of 1919.[33] During the summer of 1919 the dominant political issue in America was not the League of Nations; not even the "red menace" or the threat of a series of major strikes disturbed the public as much as did the climbing cost of living. The *Washington Post* early in August 1919 called rising prices, "the burning domestic issue. . . ." Democratic National Chairman Homer Cummings, after a trip around the country, told President Woodrow Wilson that more Americans were worried about prices than about any other public issue and that they demanded govern-

---

[31] "The Spread of Bolshevism in the United States," private memorandum, dated July 26, 1919, Papers of Robert Lansing (Library of Congress, Washington, D. C.); "One Point of View of the Murders at Centralia, Washington," private memorandum, dated November 13, 1919, Lansing Papers; U. S., *Congressional Record*, 66th Congress, 1st Session, October 14, 1919, 6869; *Washington Post*, February 16, 1919; New York *World*, June 19, 1919.

[32] Henry Barham to Palmer, October 27, 1919, Justice Department Records, File 202600; unidentified correspondent to McAdoo, February 10, 1920, McAdoo Papers (Library of Congress, Washington, D. C.); A. P. Sanders to Palmer, November 12, 1919, Justice Department Records, File 202600; *The New York Times*, October 31, 1919.

[33] U. S. Bureau of the Census, *Historical Statistics of the United States, Colonial Times to 1952, A Statistical Abstract Supplement* (Washington, D. C., 1960), 91, 92, 126; U. S. Department of Labor, Bureau of Labor Statistics, Bulletin Number 300, *Retail Prices 1913 to December, 1920* (Washington, D. C., 1922), 4; Daniel J. Ahearn, Jr., *The Wages of Farm and Factory Laborers 1914–1944* (New York, 1945), 227.

ment action. When Wilson decided to address Congress on the question the Philadelphia *Public Ledger* observed that the administration had "come rather tardily to a realization of what is uppermost in the minds of the American people." [34]

Then the wave of postwar strikes—there were 3,600 of them in 1919 involving over 4,000,000 workers [35]—reached a climax in the fall of 1919. A national steel strike began in September and nationwide coal and rail walkouts were scheduled for November 1. Unions gained in membership and power during the war, and in 1919 labor leaders were under strong pressure to help workers catch up to or go ahead of mounting living costs. Nevertheless, influential government officials attributed the walkouts to radical activities. Early in 1919, Secretary of Labor William B. Wilson declared in a public speech that recent major strikes in Seattle, Butte, Montana, and Lawrence, Massachusetts, had been instituted by the Bolsheviks and the IWW for the sole purpose of bringing about a nationwide revolution in the United States.[36] During the steel strike of early fall, 1919, a Senate investigating committee reported that "behind this strike there is massed a considerable element of I.W.W.'s, anarchists, revolutionists, and Russian soviets. . . ." [37] In April 1920 the head of the Justice Department's General Intelligence Division, J. Edgar Hoover, declared in a public hearing that at least fifty per cent of the influence behind the recent series of strikes was traceable directly to communist agents.[38]

Furthermore, the nation suffered a sharp economic depression in late 1918 and early 1919, caused largely by sudden cancellations of war orders. Returning servicemen found it difficult to obtain jobs during this period, which coincided with the beginning of the Red Scare. The former soldiers had been uprooted from their homes and told that they were engaged in a patriotic crusade. Now they came back to find "reds" criticizing their country and threatening the government with violence, Negroes holding good jobs in the big cities, prices terribly high, and workers who had not served in

---

[34] *Washington Post*, August 1, 4, 1919; *The New York Times*, July 30, August 1, 1919; Philadelphia *Public Ledger*, August 5, 1919.

[35] Florence Peterson, *Strikes in the United States, 1880–1936*, U. S. Department of Labor Bulletin Number 651 (Washington, D. C., 1938), 21. More employees engaged in strikes in 1919 than the total over the ten-year period 1923–32.

[36] *Washington Post*, February 21, 1919. As late as April 1920, Secretary Wilson agreed with Palmer during a Cabinet meeting that the nationwide rail walkout had been caused by Communists and the IWW. Entry in Josephus Daniels' Diary for April 14, 1920, Papers of Josephus Daniels (Library of Congress, Washington, D. C.).

[37] U. S. Senate, Committee on Education and Labor, *Report, Investigation of Strike in Steel Industry*, 66th Congress, 1st Session, 1919, 14.

[38] *The New York Times*, April 25, 1920, 23.

the armed forces striking for higher wages.[39] A delegate won prolonged applause from the 1919 American Legion Convention when he denounced radical aliens, exclaiming, "Now that the war is over and they are in lucrative positions while our boys haven't a job, we've got to send those scamps to hell." The major part of the mobs which invaded meeting halls of immigrant organizations and broke up radical parades, especially during the first half of 1919, was comprised of men in uniform.[40]

A variety of other circumstances combined to add even more force to the postwar nativistic movement. Long before the new immigrants were seen as potential revolutionists they became the objects of widespread hostility. The peak of immigration from Southern and Eastern Europe occurred in the fifteen years before the war; during that period almost ten million immigrants from those areas entered the country. Before the anxious eyes of members of all classes of Americans, the newcomers crowded the cities and began to disturb the economic and social order.[41] Even without other postwar disturbances a nativistic movement of some strength could have been predicted when the wartime solidarity against the German enemy began to wear off in 1919.

In addition, not only were the European revolutions most successful in Eastern and to a lesser extent in Southern Europe, but aliens from these areas predominated in American radical organizations. At least ninety per cent of the members of the two American Communist parties formed in 1919 were born in Eastern Europe. The anarchist groups whose literature and bombs captured the imagination of the American public in 1919 were composed almost entirely of Italian, Spanish, and Slavic aliens. Justice Department announcements and statements by politicians and the press stressed the predominance of recent immigrants in radical organizations.[42] Smoldering prejudice against new immigrants and identification of these immigrants with European as well as American radical movements, combined with

---

[39] George Soule, *Prosperity Decade, From War to Depression: 1917–1929* (New York, 1947), 81–84; Murray, 125, 182–83.

[40] *Proceedings and Committees, Caucus of the American Legion* (St. Louis, 1919), 117; *The New York Times,* May 2, 1919; *Washington Post,* May 2, 1919. Ex-servicemen also played major roles in the great Negro-white race riots of mid-1919. *Washington Post,* July 20–23, 28–31.

[41] *Historical Statistics of the United States,* 56. On the causes of American hostility to recent immigrants see John Higham's probing and provocative essay "Another Look at Nativism," *Catholic Historical Review,* XLIV (1958), 147–58. Higham stresses status conflicts, but does not explain why some competitors on the crowded social ladder were much more antagonistic to the new immigrants than were others.

[42] Draper, 189–90; *Annual Report of the Attorney General for 1920* (Washington, D.C., 1920), 177; Higham, *Strangers in the Land,* 226–27.

other sources of postwar stress to create one of the most frenzied and one of the most widespread nativistic movements in the nation's history.

The result, akin to the movements incited by the Chinese Boxers or the Indian Ghost Dancers, was called Americanism or one hundred per cent Americanism.[43] Its objective was to end the apparent erosion of American values and the disintegration of American culture. By reaffirming those beliefs, customs, symbols, and traditions felt to be the foundation of our way of life, by enforcing conformity among the population, and by purging the nation of dangerous foreigners, the one hundred per centers expected to heal societal divisions and to tighten defenses against cultural change.

Panegyrics celebrating our history and institutions were delivered regularly in almost every American school, church, and public hall in 1919 and 1920. Many of these fervent addresses went far beyond the usual patriotic declarations. Audiences were usually urged to join a crusade to protect our hallowed institutions. Typical of the more moderate statements was Columbia University President Nicholas Murray Butler's insistence in April 1919 that "America will be saved, not by those who have only contempt and despite for her founders and her history, but by those who look with respect and reverence upon the great series of happenings extending from the voyage of the Mayflower. . . ."[44]

What one historian has called "a riot of biographies of American heroes —statesmen, cowboys, and pioneers"[45] appeared in this brief period. Immigrants as well as citizens produced many autobiographical testimonials to the superiority of American institutions. These patriotic tendencies in our literature were as short-lived as the Red Scare, and have been concealed by "debunking" biographies of folk heroes and skeptical autobiographies so common later in the nineteen-twenties. An unusual number of motion pictures about our early history were turned out immediately after the war and the reconstruction of colonial Williamsburg and of Longfellow's Wayside Inn was begun. With great fanfare, Secretary of State Lansing placed the original documents of the Constitution and the Declaration of Independence on display in January 1920, and the State Department distributed movies of

---

[43] The word "Americanism" was used by the nativists of the eighteen-forties and eighteen-fifties. During World War I, the stronger phrase "100 per cent Americanism" was invented to suit the belligerent drive for universal conformity.

[44] Horace M. Kallen, *Culture and Democracy in the United States* (New York, 1924), Chap. 3, 154–55; Edward G. Hartman, *The Movement to Americanize the Immigrant* (New York, 1948), Chap. 9; Nicholas Murray Butler, *Is America Worth Saving? An Address Delivered Before the Commercial Club of Cincinnati, Ohio, April 19, 1919* (New York, 1919), 20.

[45] Emerson Hunsberger Loucks, *The Ku Klux Klan in Pennsylvania* (New York, 1936), 163.

this ceremony to almost every town and city in the United States.[46] Organizations like the National Security League, the Association for Constitutional Government, the Sons and the Daughters of the American Revolution, the Colonial Dames of America, with the cooperation of the American Bar Association and many state Bar Associations, organized Constitution Day celebrations and distributed huge numbers of pamphlets on the subject throughout the country.

The American flag became a sacred symbol. Legionaires demanded that citizens "Run the Reds out from the land whose flag they sully." [47] Men suspected of radical leanings were forced to kiss the stars and stripes. A Brooklyn truck driver decided in June 1919 that it was unpatriotic to obey a New York City law obliging him to fly a red cloth on lumber which projected from his vehicle. Instead he used as a danger signal a small American flag. A policeman, infuriated at the sight of the stars and stripes flying from a lumber pile, arrested the driver on a charge of disorderly conduct. Despite the Brooklyn patriot's insistence that he meant no offense to the flag, he was reprimanded and fined by the court.[48]

Recent immigrants, especially, were called to show evidence of real conversion. Great pressure was brought to bear upon the foreign-born to learn English and to forget their native tongues. As Senator William S. Kenyon of Iowa declared in October 1919, "The time has come to make this a one-language nation." [49] An editorial in the *American Legion Weekly* took a further step and insisted that the one language must be called "American. Why even in Mexico they do not stand for calling the language the Spanish language." [50]

Immigrants were also expected to adopt our customs and to snuff out remnants of Old World cultures. Genteel prewar and wartime movements to speed up assimilation took on a "frightened and feverish aspect." [51] Welcoming members of an Americanization conference called by his department, Secretary of the Interior Franklin K. Lane exclaimed in May 1919, "You have been gathered together as crusaders in a great cause. . . . There is no other question of such importance before the American people as the solidifying and strengthening of true American sentiment." A Harvard University offi-

---

[46] Kallen, Chap. 3, 154–55; Division of Foreign Intelligence, "Memorandum about Constitution Ceremonies," January 19, 1920, Lansing Papers; *The New York Times*, January 18, 1920.

[47] *American Legion Weekly*, I (November 14, 1919), 12.

[48] Sullivan, VI, 118; New York *World*, June 22, 1919.

[49] *The New York Times*, October 14, 1919.

[50] *American Legion Weekly*, I (November 14, 1919), 12.

[51] Higham, *Strangers in the Land*, 225.

cial told the conference that "The Americanization movement . . . gives men a new and holy religion. . . . It challenges each one of us to a renewed consecration and devotion to the welfare of the nation." [52] The National Security League boasted, in 1919, of establishing one thousand study groups to teach teachers how to inculcate "Americanism" in their foreign-born students.[53] A critic of the prevailing mood protested against "one of our best advertised American mottoes, 'One country, one language, one flag,' " which, he complained, had become the basis for a fervent nationwide program.[54]

As the postwar movement for one hundred per cent Americanism gathered momentum, the deportation of alien nonconformists became increasingly its most compelling objective. Asked to suggest a remedy for the nationwide upsurge in radical activity, the Mayor of Gary, Indiana, replied, "Deportation is the answer, deportation of these leaders who talk treason in America and deportation of those who agree with them and work with them." "We must remake America," a popular author averred, "We must purify the source of America's population and keep it pure. . . . We must insist that there shall be an American loyalty, brooking no amendment or qualification." [55] As Higham noted, "in 1919, the clamor of 100 per centers for applying deportation as a purgative arose to an hysterical howl. . . . Through repression and deportation on the one hand and speedy total assimilation on the other, 100 per centers hoped to eradicate discontent and purify the nation." [56]

Politicians quickly sensed the possibilities of the popular frenzy for Americanism. Mayor Ole Hanson of Seattle, Governor Calvin Coolidge of Massachusetts, and General Leonard Wood became the early heroes of the movement.[57] The man in the best political position to take advantage of the

---

[52] United States Department of the Interior, Bureau of Education, *Organization Conference, Proceedings* (Washington, D. C., 1919), 293, 345–50.

[53] National Security League, 4.

[54] *Addresses and Proceedings of the Knights of Columbus Educational Convention* (New Haven, 1919), 71. Again note the family resemblance between the attempt to protect America through absolute conformity in 1919–20 and the more drastic, centrally-planned Chinese Communist efforts at national indoctrination. A student of Chinese "coercive persuasion" described the "elaborate unanimity rituals like parades, . . . 'spontaneous' mass demonstrations and society-wide campaigns, the extensive proselytizing among the 'heretics' or the 'infidels,' the purges, programs of re-education, and other repressive measures aimed at deviants." In China, also, past national glory is invoked as evidence of present and future greatness. Schein *et al.*, 62; Lifton, *Thought Reform and the Psychology of Totalism;* Walker, *China Under Communism.*

[55] Emerson Hough, "Round Our Town," *Saturday Evening Post,* CXCII (February 21, 1920), 102; Hough, *The Web,* 456.

[56] Higham, *Strangers in the Land,* 227, 255.

[57] Murray, 62–65, 147–48, 159–60.

popular feeling, however, was Attorney General A. Mitchell Palmer.[58] In 1919, especially after the President's physical collapse, only Palmer had the authority, staff, and money necessary to arrest and deport huge numbers of radical aliens. The most virulent phase of the movement for one hundred per cent Americanism came early in 1920, when Palmer's agents rounded up for deportation over six thousand aliens and prepared to arrest thousands more suspected of membership in radical organizations. Most of these aliens were taken without warrants, many were detained for unjustifiably long periods of time, and some suffered incredible hardships. Almost all, however, were eventually released.[59]

After Palmer decided that he could ride the postwar fears into the presidency, he set out calculatingly to become the symbol of one hundred per cent Americanism. The Palmer raids, his anti-labor activities, and his frequent pious professions of patriotism during the campaign were all part of this effort. Palmer was introduced by a political associate to the Democratic party's annual Jackson Day dinner in January 1920 as "an American whose Americanism cannot be misunderstood." In a speech delivered in Georgia shortly before the primary election (in which Palmer won control of the state's delegation to the Democratic National Convention), the Attorney General asserted: "I am myself an American and I love to preach my doctrine before undiluted one hundred per cent Americans, because my platform is, in a word, undiluted Americanism and undying loyalty to the republic." The same theme dominated the address made by Palmer's old friend, John H. Bigelow of Hazleton, Pennsylvania, when he placed Palmer's name in nomination at the 1920 National Convention. Proclaimed Bigelow: "No party could survive today that did not write into its platform the magic word 'Americanism.' . . . The Attorney-General of the United States has not merely professed, but he has proved his true Americanism. . . . Behind him I see a solid phalanx of true Americanism that knows no divided allegiance." [60]

Unfortunately for political candidates like Palmer and Wood, most of the social and economic disturbances which had activated the movement they sought to lead gradually disappeared during the first half of 1920. The European revolutions were put down; by 1920 communism seemed to have

---

[58] For a full discussion of Palmer's role, Stanley Coben, *A. Mitchell Palmer: Politician* (New York, 1963).

[59] Coben, *Palmer*, Chaps. 11, 12; Claghorn, Chap. 10; Constantine Panunzio, *The Deportation Cases of 1919–1920* (New York, 1920); Zechariah Chafee, Jr., *Free Speech in the United States* (Cambridge, 1941), 204–17; Murray, Chap. 13.

[60] Coben, *Palmer*, Chap. 13; *The New York Times*, January 9, 1920; Atlanta *Constitution*, April 7, 1920; *Official Report of the Proceedings of the Democratic National Convention, 1920* (Indianapolis, 1920), 113–14. Palmer also launched a highly publicized campaign to hold down soaring prices in 1919–20, by fixing retail prices and bringing suits against profiteers and hoarders.

been isolated in Russia. Bombings ceased abruptly after June 1919, and fear of new outrages gradually abated. Prices of food and clothing began to recede during the spring. Labor strife almost vanished from our major industries after a brief railroad walkout in April. Prosperity returned after mid-1919 and by early 1920 business activity and employment levels exceeded their wartime peaks.[61] At the same time, it became clear that the Senate would not pass Wilson's peace treaty and that America was free to turn its back on the responsibilities of world leadership. The problems associated with the new immigrants remained; so did the disillusionment with Europe and with many old intellectual ideals. Nativism did not disappear from the American scene; but the frenzied attempt to revitalize the culture did peter out in 1920. The handful of unintimidated men, especially Assistant Secretary of Labor Louis F. Post, who had used the safeguards provided by American law to protect many victims of the Red Scare, found increasing public support. On the other hand, politicians like Palmer, Wood, and Hanson were left high and dry, proclaiming the need for one hundred per cent Americanism to an audience which no longer urgently cared.

It is ironic that in 1920 the Russian leaders of the Comintern finally took charge of the American Communist movement, provided funds and leadership, and ordered the Communist factions to unite and participate actively in labor organizations and strikes. These facts were reported in the American press.[62] Thus a potentially serious foreign threat to national security appeared just as the Red Scare evaporated, providing a final illustration of the fact that the frenzied one hundred per centers of 1919–20 were affected less by the "red menace" than by a series of social and economic dislocations.

Although the Red Scare died out in 1920, its effects lingered. Hostility toward immigrants, mobilized in 1919–20, remained strong enough to force congressional passage of restrictive immigration laws. Some of the die-hard one hundred per centers found a temporary home in the Ku Klux Klan until that organization withered away during the mid-twenties. As its most lasting accomplishments, the movement for one hundred per cent Americanism fostered a spirit of conformity in the country, a satisfaction with the status quo, and the equation of reform ideologies with foreign enemies. Revitalization movements have helped many societies adapt successfully to new conditions. The movement associated with the American Red Scare, however, had no such effect. True, it unified the culture against the threats faced in 1919–20; but the basic problems—a damaged value system, an unrestrained business cycle, a hostile Russia, and communism—were left for future generations of Americans to deal with in their own fashion.

---

[61] Bell, 334; Soule, 83–88; *Seventh Annual Report of the Federal Reserve Board for the Year 1920* (Washington, D. C., 1920), 7.

[62] Draper, 244, 267–68; New York *World*, March 29, 1920.

SUGGESTED READING

John M. Blum's "Nativism, Anti-Radicalism, and the Foreign Scare, 1917–1920," *Midwest Journal,* III (Winter, 1950–51) does not openly rely on the same social-science theories that Coben stresses, but the analysis is similar.

Paul Murphy in "Sources and Nature of Intolerance in the 1920's," *Journal of American History,* LI (June, 1964), 60–76; and Oscar Handlin in *The American People in the Twentieth Century* ° (Harvard Univ. Press, 1954) extend the investigation of nativism into the twenties. William Preston, *Aliens and Dissenters; Federal Supression of Radicals, 1903–33* ° (Harvard Univ. Press, 1963) offers a broad perspective.

Kenneth O'Brien, Jr., in "Education, Americanization and the Supreme Court: The 1920's," *American Scholar,* XIII (Summer, 1961), 161–71, notes that "a conservative court in a conservative decade" declared legislation designed to combat foreign ideas unconstitutional.

II

The Twenties

The 1920's has seemed to many historians an aberrant decade, a kind of vacuum between the progressive period and the crisis of the Depression. Warren
G. Harding contributed the most famous phrase of the era in his campaign for
the presidency in 1920: He urged "not heroism but healing, not nostrums but
normalcy"; and thereby delivered both an obituary and a manifesto.

In the twenties, doubts about big business that prevailed in the first two
decades of the century evaporated, and in their place occurred a near-
universal celebration of America's business civilization. The heroes of this
civilization were not crusading politicians or morally outraged journalists, but
tycoons like Henry Ford, the high priest of mass production and inventor of
the conveyor belt. When this unlettered mechanic pronounced an aphorism
like "Machinery is the new Messiah," his views received reverent attention.

Many intellectuals once critical of business power came in the twenties
to proclaim its beneficence. Lincoln Steffens wrote, "Big business in America
is producing what the Socialists held up as their goal: food, shelter, and clothing for all. You will see it during the Hoover administration." The greatest of
the so-called progressive historians, Charles A. Beard, concluded his monu-

mental book *The Rise of American Civilization* by observing that the period of the twenties was "the dawn, not the dusk, of the gods." Only the literary intellectuals rejected the values of business culture, but they rejected politics and reform as well. Retreating into personal and esthetic experience, writers like Ernest Hemingway and Ezra Pound expressed their dissent by taking up residence abroad.

In the realm of politics the issues and coalitions of the twenties bore scant resemblance to those of progressivism. The Republican party found that its open commitment to single-interest government did not bar it from national supremacy. Social conflict rather than concern with trusts or civic corruption now dominated politics. In 1916 Woodrow Wilson had assembled the classic progressive coalition: Southern and Western agrarians aligned with laborers, social workers, and the concerned middle classes of the cities. But in the 1920's rural America made its last stand against the values cultivated by the metropolis, and the unity of the old progressive coalition was shattered.

The small towns of the West and South provided millions of recruits for the crusade of the Ku Klux Klan against Negroes, Catholics, Jews, and new immigrants who had crowded into the big cities. In 1921 and in 1924 congressmen from the South and West passed immigration acts that discriminated against Southern and Eastern Europeans. Those scientific concepts that were opposed to their religious beliefs and that threatened to spread from the city into the American village caused the rural fundamentalists to rally around the campaign of William Jennings Bryan to expel Darwinism from the public schools. Small-town Americans also provided a sympathetic public for the prosecution at the *Tennessee v. John Thomas Scopes* trial. And of course the Eighteenth Amendment, which outlawed the manufacture and sale of alcoholic beverages, tellingly revealed the diverging morality of dry Protestants in the American countryside and thirsty sophisticates and immigrants in the city.

The Democratic party was nearly destroyed by the conflict between its urban and rural wings. In 1924 at its national convention in Madison Square Garden, the party had to endure more than one hundred deadlocked ballots, with Governor Al Smith of New York City's Irish slums and William Gibbs McAdoo, a former Georgian, each refusing to defer to the other. As testimony to the party's impotence as a counter to business domination, the Democrats chose as their compromise nominee John W. Davis, a Wall Street lawyer with impeccable conservative credentials.

But it would be a mistake to stress only the differences between progressivism and the attitudes of the twenties, for many historians have come to see the decade as continuous with the preceding years. For instance, Arthur Link's article, reprinted in this part, describes the persistence of progressivism among the Western and Southern congressmen, who passed farm-relief legislation and fought for public power, and among the labor leaders and social workers, who were somewhat successful at the state level. Robert M. La Follette, running in 1924 on a third-party progressive ticket without funds or organization, polled at least 16.6 percent of the vote, although some historians argue that much of his support came from groups who were grateful for his antiwar stand in 1917 rather than for his progressivism. Even the ugliest aspects of the twenties—Prohibition, the racism of the movement for immigration restriction, and the perverted idealism of the Ku Klux Klan—have been ascribed to the progressive mood that had gone sour.

The continuities between the progressive years and the twenties have seemed most obvious for those who have argued that progressivism sealed the alliance between big business and the Government. Dedicated to laissez faire only in theory, Republican politicians lavished government favors on businessmen. With the antitrust laws suspended, the Government smiled on a flourishing merger movement and actually encouraged the formation of trade associations in which firms of the same industry devised various forms of co-operation. Secretary of the Treasury Andrew Mellon promoted tax policies designed to favor wealthy individuals and business corporations. Against the best advice of professional economists, Republican administrations sponsored the highest tariffs in American history. And under Herbert Hoover, the Commerce Department sought ways to maximize business efficiency and assiduously cultivated foreign markets.

Beyond this cooperation between business and government, the twenties shared still another characteristic with the progressive years: the refusal to come seriously to grips with widespread poverty and inequality of wealth. While labor productivity rose 32 percent and corporate profits soared 62 percent from 1923 to 1929, real wages increased only 8 percent. Farmers were mired in depression, and their share of the national income fell from 17 percent in the good year of 1919 to 8 percent in 1929. Sixteen million of America's twenty-seven million families in the 1920's lived on an income of less than $2,000, which was then regarded as the minimum for maintaining health and decency. In the end, the nation paid a penalty for the structural weaknesses in the economy, for they contributed to the Great Depression of 1929, which brought the twenties to a sad conclusion.

SUGGESTED READING

William Leuchtenburg's *The Perils of Prosperity, 1914–1932* * (Univ. of Chicago Press, 1958) remains the finest volume interpreting the twenties. For a perceptive journalistic account, see Frederick Lewis Allen's *Only Yesterday* * (Harper & Row, 1931). Eric Goldman in *Rendezvous with Destiny* * (Knopf, 1952) analyzes the decade as "the shame of the Babbitts." Paul Carter's *The Twenties in America* * (Crowell, 1968) is a breezy survey of the culture.

John Hicks' *Republican Ascendancy, 1921–1933* * (Harper & Row, 1960) is seldom more than a superficial analysis. A better study is found in Arthur Schlesinger, Jr.'s *The Crisis of the Old Order* * (Houghton Mifflin, 1957), the first volume of *The Age of Roosevelt;* Schlesinger, however, emphasizes Republican mistakes from a New Deal perspective. Karl Schriftgiesser's *This Was Normalcy* (Little, Brown, 1948) is very critical of Republican policies, but it is disappointing for it seldom penetrates below the surface. Malcolm Moos in *The Republicans* (Random House, 1956) treats Republican policies more favorably. Donald McCoy's *Calvin Coolidge* (Macmillan, 1967) is a solid political study that demolishes old myths.

Frank Freidel's *Franklin D. Roosevelt, II, The Ordeal* (Little, Brown, 1954) is an excellent book on Democratic politics during the decade. It should be supplemented by J. Joseph Huthmacher's *Massachusetts People and Politics, 1919–1933* (Harvard Univ. Press, 1959); David Burner's *The Politics of Provincialism: The Democratic Party in Transition, 1918–1932* (Knopf, 1968); and Samuel Lubell's *The Future of American Politics* * (Doubleday, 1952), all of which stress the shift of the city populations toward the Democratic party. This thesis was first developed by Samuel Eldersveld in "The Influence of Metropolitan Party Pluralities in Presidential Elections Since 1920," *American Political Science Review*, XLIII (Dec., 1949), 1189–1206.

John Higham in *Strangers in the Land: Patterns of American Nativism, 1860–1925* * (Rutgers Univ. Press, 1954) and Oscar Handlin in *The American People in the Twentieth Century* * (Harvard Univ. Press, 1954) present probing studies of the social history of the era. John W. Ward in "The Meaning of Lindbergh's Flight," *American Quarterly* X (Spring, 1958), 3–16, emphasizes the nostalgia for the past and for lost values. This theme is also examined in Charles Anderson's "The Metamorphosis of American Agrarian Idealism in the 1920's and 1930's," *Agricultural History*, XXXV (Oct., 1961), 182–88. Lawrence W. Levine's *Defender of the Faith: William Jennings Bryan* * (Oxford Univ. Press, 1965) is an excellent examination of the later Bryan and the ideas he represented. David Chalmers' *Hooded Americanism* * (Doubleday, 1965) and Kenneth Jackson's *The Ku Klux Klan in the City, 1915–1930* (Oxford Univ. Press, 1968) replace John Mecklin's earlier volume, *The Ku Klux Klan: A Study of the American Mind* (Harcourt, Brace & World, 1924), though Jackson's book seems to exaggerate the urban strength of the Klan. Clarke Chambers' *Seedtime of Reform: American Social Service and Social Action, 1918–1933* * (Univ. of Minnesota Press, 1963) finds a strong social-welfare movement in the decade.

Arthur Link's article in this section and Burl Noggle's "The Twenties: A New Historiographical Frontier," *Journal of American History*, LIII (Sept., 1966), 299–314, are fine introductions to the historical literature on the decade. *Change and Continuity in Twentieth-Century America: The 1920's*, edited by John Braeman, *et al.* (Ohio State Univ. Press, 1968), is a collection of useful essays. Robert Burke in *The 1920's* (forthcoming from Holt, Rinehart & Winston) and Milton Plesur in *The 1920's* (Allyn & Bacon, 1969), have collected earlier published interpretations of the twenties.

ARTHUR S. LINK

What Happened
to the Progressive Movement
in the 1920's?

INTRODUCTION

Arthur S. Link, who has devoted most of his scholarly life to a multivolume biography of Woodrow Wilson, attempts in the following
essay to define progressivism, account for its deterioration after
1918, and demonstrate its partial survival in the 1920's. Complex
and subtle, Link's important article has done much to discredit the
old notion of fundamental discontinuity between progressivism
and the ideology of the twenties. But however bold, his efforts are
not entirely convincing.

FROM Arthur S. Link, "What Happened to the Progressive Movement in the 1920's?,"
American Historical Review, LXIV (July, 1959), pp. 833–51. Reprinted by permission of
the author.

This paper was read in a slightly different form before a joint meeting of the American
Historical Association and the Mississippi Valley Historical Association in New York City
on December 28, 1957.

Link himself would concede that the prewar reform ethos did not survive into the 1920's and that democratic idealism was scarcely in evidence. Furthermore, he slides over the problem of the apparently contradictory character of progressivism by simply including all unresolved contradictions within his conception of it. Thus he asserts that prewar progressivism embraced both democratic idealists and special interest groups, both middle-class citizens disturbed by business power and businessmen committed to the "strengthening instead of the shackling of the business community." Link's overly inclusive conception of progressivism allows him to claim a strange assortment of activities in the 1920's as evidence of progressivism's survival: the fight for public power and government encouragement of private monopoly, special-interest legislation for farmers and racist immigration laws, prohibition, and tariff protectionism.

In short, working with an inadequate notion of progressivism, Link has necessarily presented a flawed case, for until historians form a convincing conception of what progressivism was before the war, they will find it nearly impossible to trace its course afterward.

*I*f the day has not yet arrived when we can make a definite synthesis of political developments between the Armistice and the Great Depression, it is surely high time for historians to begin to clear away the accumulated heap of mistaken and half-mistaken hypotheses about this important transitional period. Writing often without fear or much research (to paraphrase Carl Becker's remark), we recent American historians have gone on indefatigably to perpetuate hypotheses that either reflected the disillusionment and despair of contemporaries, or once served their purpose in exposing the alleged hiatus in the great continuum of twentieth-century reform.

Stated briefly, the following are what might be called the governing hypotheses of the period under discussion: The 1920's were a period made almost unique by an extraordinary reaction against idealism and reform. They were a time when the political representatives of big business and Wall Street executed a relentless and successful campaign in state and nation to subvert the regulatory structure that had been built at the cost of so much toil and sweat since the 1870's, and to restore a Hanna-like reign of special privilege to benefit business, industry, and finance. The surging tides of nationalism and mass hatreds generated by World War I continued to engulf the land and were manifested, among other things, in fear of communism, suppression of civil liberties, revival of nativism and anti-Semitism most crudely exemplified by the Ku Klux Klan, and in the triumph of racism and prejudice in immigration legislation. The 1920's were an era when great traditions and ideals were repudiated or forgotten, when the American people, propelled by a crass materialism in their scramble for wealth, uttered a curse on twenty-five years of reform endeavor. As a result, progressives were stunned and everywhere in retreat along the entire political front, their forces disorganized and leaderless, their movement shattered, their dreams of a new America turned into agonizing nightmares.

To be sure, the total picture that emerges from these generalizations is overdrawn. Yet it seems fair to say that leading historians have advanced each of these generalizations, that the total picture is the one that most of us younger historians saw during the years of our training, and that these hypotheses to a greater or lesser degree still control the way in which we write and teach about the 1920's, as a reading of textbooks and general works will quickly show.

This paper has not been written, however, to quarrel with anyone or to make an indictment. Its purposes are, first, to attempt to determine the degree to which the governing hypotheses, as stated, are adequate or inadequate to explain the political phenomena of the period, and, second, to discover whether any new and sounder hypotheses might be suggested. Such an effort, of course, must be tentative and above all imperfect in view of the absence of sufficient foundations for a synthesis.

Happily, however, we do not have to proceed entirely in the dark. Historians young and old, but mostly young, have already discovered that the period of the 1920's is the exciting new frontier of American historical research and that its opportunities are almost limitless in view of the mass of manuscript materials that are becoming available. Thus we have (the following examples are mentioned only at random) excellent recent studies of agrarian discontent and farm movements by Theodore Saloutos, John D. Hicks, Gilbert C. Fite, Robert L. Morlan, and James H. Shideler; of nativism and problems of immigration and assimilation by John Higham, Oscar Handlin, Robert A. Devine, and Edmund D. Cronon; of intellectual currents, the social gospel, and religious controversies by Henry F. May, Paul A. Carter, Robert M. Miller, and Norman F. Furniss; of left-wing politics and labor developments by Theodore Draper, David A. Shannon, David Bell, Paul M. Angle, and Matthew Josephson; of the campaign of 1928 by Edmund A. Moore; and of political and judicial leaders by Alpheus T. Mason, Frank Freidel, Arthur M. Schlesinger, Jr., Merlo J. Pusey, and Joel F. Paschal.[1]

---

[1] Theodore Saloutos and John D. Hicks, *Agrarian Discontent in the Middle West, 1900–1939* (Madison, Wis., 1951); Gilbert C. Fite, *Peter Norbeck: Prairie Statesman* (Columbia, Mo., 1948), and *George N. Peek and the Fight for Farm Parity* (Norman, Okla., 1954); Robert L. Morlan, *Political Prairie Fire: The Nonpartisan League, 1915–1922* (Minneapolis, Minn., 1955); James H. Shideler, *Farm Crisis, 1919–1923* (Berkeley, Calif., 1957); John Higham, *Strangers in the Land: Patterns of American Nativism, 1860–1925* (New

Moreover, we can look forward to the early publication of studies that will be equally illuminating for the period, like the biographies of George W. Norris, Thomas J. Walsh, and Albert B. Fall now being prepared by Richard Lowitt, Leonard Bates, and David Stratton, respectively, and the recently completed study of the campaign and election of 1920 by Wesley M. Bagby.[2]

Obviously, we are not only at a point in the progress of our research into the political history of the 1920's when we can begin to generalize, but we have reached the time when we should attempt to find some consensus, however tentative it must now be, concerning the larger political dimensions and meanings of the period.

In answering the question of what happened to the progressive movement in the 1920's, we should begin by looking briefly at some fundamental facts about the movement before 1918, facts that in large measure predetermined its fate in the 1920's, given the political climate and circumstances that prevailed.

The first of these was the elementary fact that the progressive movement never really existed as a recognizable organization with common goals and a political machinery geared to achieve them. Generally speaking (and for the purposes of this paper), progressivism might be defined as the popular effort, which began convulsively in the 1890's and waxed and waned afterward to our own time, to insure the survival of democracy in the United States by the enlargement of governmental power to control and offset the power of private economic groups over the nation's institutions and life.

Brunswick, N. J., 1955); Oscar Handlin, *The American People in the Twentieth Century* (Cambridge, Mass., 1954); Robert A. Devine, *American Immigration Policy, 1924–1952* (New Haven, Conn., 1957); Edmund D. Cronon, *Black Moses: The Story of Marcus Garvey and the Universal Negro Improvement Association* (Madison, Wis., 1955); Henry F. May, "Shifting Perspectives on the 1920's," *Mississippi Valley Historical Review*, XLIII (Dec., 1956), 405–27; Paul A. Carter, *The Decline and Revival of the Social Gospel* (Ithaca, N. Y., 1956); Robert M. Miller, "An Inquiry into the Social Attitudes of American Protestantism, 1919–1939," doctoral dissertation, Northwestern University, 1955; Norman F. Furniss, *The Fundamentalist Controversy, 1918–1931* (New Haven, Conn., 1954); Theodore Draper, *The Roots of American Communism* (New York, 1957); David A. Shannon, *The Socialist Party of America: A History* (New York, 1955); Daniel Bell, "The Background and Development of Marxian Socialism in the United States," *Socialism and American Life*, ed. Donald D. Egbert and Stow Persons (2 vols., Princeton, N. J., 1952), I, 215–405; Paul M. Angle, *Bloody Williamson* (New York, 1952); Matthew Josephson, *Sidney Hillman: Statesman of American Labor* (New York, 1952); Edmund A. Moore, *A Catholic Runs for President: The Campaign of 1928* (New York, 1956); Alpheus Thomas Mason, *Brandeis: A Free Man's Life* (New York, 1946), and *Harlan Fiske Stone: Pillar of the Law* (New York, 1956); Frank Freidel, *Franklin D. Roosevelt: The Ordeal* (Boston, 1954); Arthur M. Schlesinger, Jr., *The Age of Roosevelt: The Crisis of the Old Order* (Boston, 1957); Merlo J. Pusey, *Charles Evans Hughes* (2 vols., New York, 1951); Joel Francis Paschal, *Mr. Justice Sutherland: A Man against the State* (Princeton, N J., 1951).

[2] Wesley M. Bagby, "Woodrow Wilson and the Great Debacle of 1920," MS in the possession of Professor Bagby; see also his "The 'Smoked-Filled Room' and the Nomination of Warren G. Harding," *Mississippi Valley Historical Review*, XLI (Mar., 1955), 657–74, and "Woodrow Wilson, a Third Term, and the Solemn Referendum," *American Historical Review*, LX (Apr., 1955), 567–75.

Actually, of course, from the 1890's on there were many "progressive" movements on many levels seeking sometimes contradictory objectives. Not all,
but most of these campaigns were the work of special interest groups or
classes seeking greater political status and economic security. This was true
from the beginning of the progressive movement in the 1890's; by 1913 it was
that movement's most important characteristic.

The second fundamental fact—that the progressive movements were
often largely middle class in constituency and orientation—is of course well
known, but an important corollary has often been ignored. It was that several
of the most important reform movements were inspired, staffed, and led by
businessmen with very specific or special-interest objectives in view. Because
they hated waste, mismanagement, and high taxes, they, together with their
friends in the legal profession, often furnished the leadership of good government campaigns. Because they feared industrial monopoly, abuse of
power by railroads, and the growth of financial oligarchy, they were the
backbone of the movements that culminated in the adoption of the Hepburn
and later acts for railroad regulation, the Federal Reserve Act, and the Federal Trade Commission Act. Among the many consequences of their participation in the progressive movement, two should be mentioned because of
their significance for developments in the 1920's: First, the strong identification of businessmen with good government and economic reforms for which
the general public also had a lively concern helped preserve the good reputation of the middle-class business community (as opposed to its alleged natural enemies, monopolists, malefactors of great wealth, and railroad barons)
and helped to direct the energies of the progressive movement toward the
strengthening instead of the shackling of the business community. Second,
their activities and influence served to intensify the tensions within the
broad reform movement, because they often opposed the demands of farm
groups, labor unions, and advocates of social justice.

The third remark to be made about the progressive movement before
1918 is that despite its actual diversity and inner tensions it did seem to have
unity; that is, it seemed to share common ideals and objectives. This was true
in part because much of the motivation even of the special-interest groups
was altruistic (at least they succeeded in convincing themselves that they
sought the welfare of society rather than their own interests primarily); in
part because political leadership generally succeeded in subordinating inner
tensions. It was true, above all, because there were in fact important idealistic elements in the progressive ranks—social gospel leaders, social justice
elements, and intellectuals and philosophers—who worked hard at the task
of defining and elevating common principles and goals.

Fourth and finally, the substantial progressive achievements before
1918 had been gained, at least on the federal level, only because of the temporary dislocations of the national political structure caused by successive
popular uprisings, not because progressives had found or created a viable

organization for perpetuating their control. Or, to put the matter another way, before 1918 the various progressive elements had failed to destroy the existing party structure by organizing a national party of their own that could survive. They, or at least many of them, tried in 1912; and it seemed for a time in 1916 that Woodrow Wilson had succeeded in drawing the important progressive groups permanently into the Democratic party. But Wilson's accomplishment did not survive even to the end of the war, and by 1920 traditional partisan loyalties were reasserting themselves with extraordinary vigor.

With this introduction, we can now ask what happened to the progressive movement or movements in the 1920's. Surely no one would contend that after 1916 the political scene did not change significantly, both on the state and national levels. There was the seemingly obvious fact that the Wilsonian coalition had been wrecked by the election of 1920, and that the progressive elements were divided and afterward unable to agree upon a program or to control the national government. There was the even more "obvious" fact that conservative Republican presidents and their cabinets controlled the executive branch throughout the period. There was Congress, as Eric F. Goldman had said, allegedly whooping through procorporation legislation, and the Supreme Court interpreting the New Freedom laws in a way that harassed unions and encouraged trusts.[3] There were, to outraged idealists and intellectuals, the more disgusting spectacles of Red hunts, mass arrests and deportations, the survival deep into the 1920's of arrogant nationalism, crusades against the teaching of evolution, the attempted suppression of the right to drink, and myriad other manifestations of what would now be called a repressive reaction.[4]

Like the hypotheses suggested at the beginning, this picture is overdrawn in some particulars. But it is accurate in part, for progressivism was certainly on the downgrade if not in decay after 1918. This is an obvious fact that needs explanation and understanding rather than elaborate proof. We can go a long way toward answering our question if we can explain, at least partially, the extraordinary complex developments that converge to produce the "obvious" result.

For this explanation we must begin by looking at the several progressive elements and their relation to each other and to the two major parties after 1916. Since national progressivism was never an organized or independent movement (except imperfectly and then only temporarily in 1912), it could succeed only when its constituent elements formed a coalition strong

---

[3] Eric F. Goldman, *Rendezvous with Destiny* (New York, 1953), 284. The "allegedly" in this sentence is mine, not Professor Goldman's.

[4] H. C. Peterson and Gilbert C. Fite, *Opponents of War, 1917–1918* (Norman, Okla., 1957); Robert K. Murray, *Red Scare: A Study in National Hysteria, 1919–1920* (Minneapolis, Minn., 1955).

enough to control one of the major parties. This had happened in 1916, when southern and western farmers, organized labor, the social justice elements, and a large part of the independent radicals who had heretofore voted the Socialist ticket coalesced to continue the control of Wilson and the Democratic party.

The important fact about the progressive coalition of 1916, however, was not its strength but its weakness. It was not a new party but a temporary alliance, welded in the heat of the most extraordinary domestic and external events. To be sure, it functioned for the most part successfully during the war, in providing the necessary support for a program of heavy taxation, relatively stringent controls over business and industry, and extensive new benefits to labor. Surviving in a crippled way even in the months following the Armistice, it put across a program that constituted a sizable triumph for the progressive movement—continued heavy taxation, the Transportation Act of 1920, the culmination of the long fight for railroad regulation, a new child labor act, amendments for prohibition and woman suffrage, immigration restriction, and water power and conservation legislation.

Even so, the progressive coalition of 1916 was inherently unstable. Indeed, it was so wracked by inner tensions that it could not survive, and destruction came inexorably, it seemed systematically, from 1917 to 1920. Why was this true?

First, the independent radicals and antiwar agrarians were alienated by the war declaration and the government's suppression of dissent and civil liberties during the war and the Red scare. Organized labor was disaffected by the administration's coercion of the coal miners in 1919, its lukewarm if not hostile attitude during the great strikes of 1919 and 1920, and its failure to support the Plumb Plan for nationalization of the railroads. Isolationists and idealists were outraged by what they thought was the President's betrayal of American traditions or the liberal peace program at Paris. These tensions were strong enough to disrupt the coalition, but a final one would have been fatal even if the others had never existed. This was the alienation of farmers in the Plains and western states produced by the administration's refusal to impose price controls on cotton while it maintained ceilings on the prices of other agricultural commodities,[5] and especially by the administration's failure to do anything decisive to stem the downward plunge of farm prices that began in the summer of 1920.[6] Under the impact of all these stresses, the Wilsonian coalition gradually disintegrated from 1917 to 1920 and disappeared entirely during the campaign of 1920.

---

[5] On this point, see Seward W. Livermore, "The Sectional Issue in the 1918 Congressional Elections," *Mississippi Valley Historical Review*, XXXV (June, 1948), 29–60.

[6] Arthur S. Link, "The Federal Reserve Policy and the Agricultural Depression of 1920–1921," *Agricultural History*, XX (July, 1946), 166–75; and Herbert F. Margulies, "The Election of 1920 in Wisconsin: The Return to 'Normalcy' Reappraised," *Wisconsin Magazine of History*, XXXVIII (Autumn, 1954), 15–22.

The progressive coalition was thus destroyed, but the components of a potential movement remained. As we will see, these elements were neither inactive nor entirely unsuccessful in the 1920's. But they obviously failed to find common principles and a program, much less to unite effectively for political action on a national scale. I suggest that this was true, in part at least, for the following reasons:

First, the progressive elements could never create or gain control of a political organization capable of carrying them into national office. The Republican party was patently an impossible instrument because control of the GOP was too much in the hands of the eastern and midwestern industrial, oil, and financial interests, as it had been since about 1910. There was always the hope of a third party. Several progressive groups—insurgent midwestern Republicans, the railroad brotherhoods, a segment of the AF of L, and the moderate Socialists under Robert M. La Follette—tried to realize this goal in 1924, only to discover that third party movements in the United States are doomed to failure except in periods of enormous national turmoil, and that the 1920's were not such a time. Thus the Democratic party remained the only vehicle that conceivably could have been used by a new progressive coalition. But that party was simply not capable of such service in the 1920's. It was so torn by conflicts between its eastern, big city wing and its southern and western rural majority that it literally ceased to be a national party. It remained strong in its sectional and metropolitan components, but it was so divided that it barely succeeded in nominating a presidential candidate at all in 1924 and nominated one in 1928 only at the cost of temporary disruption.[7]

Progressivism declined in the 1920's, in the second place, because, as has been suggested, the tensions that had wrecked the coalition of 1916 not only persisted but actually grew in number and intensity. The two most numerous progressive elements, the southern and western farmers, strongly supported the Eighteenth Amendment, were heavily tinged with nativism and therefore supported immigration restriction, were either members of, friendly to, or politically afraid of the Ku Klux Klan, and demanded as the principal plank in their platform legislation to guarantee them a larger share of the national income. On all these points and issues the lower and lower middle classes in the large cities stood in direct and often violent opposition to their potential allies in the rural areas. Moreover, the liaison between the farm groups and organized labor, which had been productive of much significant legislation during the Wilson period, virtually ceased to exist in the 1920's. There were many reasons for this development, and I mention only

---

[7] For a highly partisan account of these events see Karl Schriftgiesser, *This Was Normalcy* (Boston, 1948). More balanced are the already cited Freidel, *Franklin D. Roosevelt: The Ordeal*, and Schlesinger, *The Age of Roosevelt: The Crisis of the Old Order*.

one—the fact that the preeminent spokesmen of farmers in the 1920's, the new Farm Bureau Federation, represented the larger commercial farmers who (in contrast to the members of the leading farm organization in Wilson's day, the National Farmers' Union) were often employers themselves and felt no identification with the rank and file of labor.

It was little wonder, therefore (and this is a third reason for the weakness of progressivism in the 1920's), that the tension-ridden progressive groups were never able to agree upon a program that, like the Democratic platform of 1916, could provide the basis for a revived coalition. So long as progressive groups fought one another more fiercely than they fought their natural opponents, such agreement was impossible; and so long as common goals were impossible to achieve, a national progressive movement could not take effective form. Nothing illustrates this better than the failure of the Democratic conventions of 1924 and 1928 to adopt platforms that could rally and unite the discontented elements. One result, among others, was that southern farmers voted as Democrats and western farmers as Republicans. And, as Professor Frank Freidel once commented to the author, much of the failure of progressivism in the 1920's can be explained by this elementary fact.

A deeper reason for the failure of progressives to unite ideologically in the 1920's was what might be called a substantial paralysis of the progressive mind. This was partly the result of the repudiation of progressive ideals by many intellectuals and the defection from the progressive movement of the urban middle classes and professional groups, as will be demonstrated. It was the result, even more importantly, of the fact that progressivism as an organized body of political thought found itself at a crossroads in the 1920's, like progressivism today, and did not know which way to turn. The major objectives of the progressive movement of the prewar years had in fact been largely achieved by 1920. In what direction should progressivism now move? Should it remain in the channels already deeply cut by its own traditions, and, while giving sincere allegiance to the ideal of democratic capitalism, work for more comprehensive programs of business regulation and assistance to disadvantaged classes like farmers and submerged industrial workers? Should it abandon these traditions and, like most similar European movements, take the road toward a moderate socialism with a predominantly labor orientation? Should it attempt merely to revive the goals of more democracy through changes in the political machinery? Or should it become mainly an agrarian movement with purely agrarian goals?

These were real dilemmas, not academic ones, and one can see numerous examples of how they confused and almost paralyzed progressives in the 1920's. The platform of La Follette's Progressive party of 1924 offers one revealing illustration. It embodied much that was old and meaningless by this time (the direct election of the president and a national referendum before the adoption of a war resolution, for example) and little that had any real significance for the future.[8] And yet it was the best that a vigorous and idealistic movement could offer. A second example was the plight of the agrarians and insurgents in Congress who fought so hard all through the 1920's against Andrew Mellon's proposals to abolish the inheritance tax and to make drastic reductions in the taxes on large incomes. In view of the rapid reduction of the federal debt, the progressives were hard pressed to justify the continuation of nearly confiscatory tax levels, simply because few of them realized the wide social and economic uses to which the income tax could be put. Lacking any programs for the redistribution of the national income (except to farmers), they were plagued and overwhelmed by the surpluses in the federal Treasury until, for want of any good arguments, they finally gave Secretary Andrew Mellon the legislation he had been demanding.[9] A third and final example of this virtual paralysis of the progressive mind was perhaps the most revealing of all. It was the attempt that Woodrow Wilson, Louis D. Brandeis, and other Democratic leaders made from 1921 to 1924 to draft a new charter for progressivism. Except for its inevitable proposals for an idealistic world leadership, the document that emerged from this interchange included little or nothing that would have sounded new to a western progressive in 1912.

A fourth reason for the disintegration and decline of the progressive movement in the 1920's was the lack of any effective leadership. Given the political temper and circumstances of the 1920's, it is possible that such leadership could not have operated successfully in any event. Perhaps the various progressive elements were so mutually hostile and so self-centered in interests and objectives that even a Theodore Roosevelt or a Woodrow Wilson, had they been at the zenith of their powers in the 1920's, could not have drawn them together in a common front. We will never know what a strong national leader might have done because by a trick of fate no such leader emerged before Franklin D. Roosevelt.

Four factors, then, contributed to the failure of the progressive components to unite successfully after 1918 and, as things turned out, before 1932: the lack of a suitable political vehicle, the severity of the tensions that kept progressives apart, the failure of progressives to agree upon a common program, and the absence of a national leadership, without which a united movement could never be created and sustained. These were all weaknesses that stemmed to a large degree from the instability and failures of the progressive movement itself.

---

[8] For a different picture see Belle C. La Follette and Fola La Follette, *Robert M. La Follette* (2 vols., New York, 1953); and Russel B. Nye, *Midwestern Progressive Politics, 1870–1950* (East Lansing, Mich., 1951). Both works contribute to an understanding of progressive politics in the 1920's.

[9] Here indebtedness is acknowledged to Sidney Ratner, *American Taxation: Its History as a Social Force in Democracy* (New York, 1942).

There were, besides, a number of what might be called external causes for the movement's decline. In considering them one must begin with what was seemingly the most important—the alleged fact that the 1920's were a very unpropitious time for any new progressive revolt because of the ever-increasing level of economic prosperity, the materialism, and the general contentment of the decade 1919 to 1929. Part of this generalization is valid when applied to specific elements in the population. For example, the rapid rise in the real wages of industrial workers, coupled with generally full employment and the spread of so-called welfare practices among management, certainly did much to weaken and avert the further spread of organized labor, and thus to debilitate one of the important progressive components. But to say that it was prosperity per se that created a climate unfriendly to progressive ideals would be inaccurate. There was little prosperity and much depression during the 1920's for the single largest economic group, the farmers, as well as for numerous other groups. Progressivism, moreover, can flourish as much during periods of prosperity as during periods of discontent, as the history of the development of the progressive movement from 1901 to 1917 and of its triumph from 1945 to 1956 prove.

Vastly more important among the external factors in the decline of progressivism was the widespread, almost wholesale, defection from its ranks of the middle classes—the middling businessmen, bankers, and manufacturers, and the professional people closely associated with them in ideals and habits—in American cities large and small. For an understanding of this phenomenon no simple explanations like "prosperity" or the "temper of the times" will suffice, although they give some insight. The important fact was that these groups found a new economic and social status as a consequence of the flowering of American enterprise under the impact of the technological, financial, and other revolutions of the 1920's. If, as Professor Richard Hofstadter had claimed,[10] the urban middle classes were progressive (that is, they demanded governmental relief from various anxieties) in the early 1900's because they resented their loss of social prestige to the *nouveaux riches* and feared being ground under by monopolists in industry, banking, and labor—if this is true, then the urban middle classes were not progressive in the 1920's for inverse reasons. Their temper was dynamic, expansive, and supremely confident. They knew that they were building a new America, a business civilization based not upon monopoly and restriction but upon a whole new set of business values—mass production and consumption, short hours and high wages, full employment, welfare capitalism. And what was more important, virtually the entire country (at least the journalists, writers in popular magazines, and many preachers and professors) acknowledged that the nation's destiny was in good hands. It was little wonder, therefore,

---

[10] Richard Hofstadter, *The Age of Reform: From Bryan to F.D.R.* (New York, 1955), 131 ff.

that the whole complex of groups constituting the urban middle classes, whether in New York, Zenith, or Middletown, had little interest in rebellion or even in mild reform proposals that seemed to imperil their leadership and control.

Other important factors, of course, contributed to the contentment of the urban middle classes. The professionalization of business and the full-blown emergence of a large managerial class had a profound impact upon social and political ideals. The acceleration of mass advertising played its role, as did also the beginning disintegration of the great cities with the spread of middle- and upper-middle-class suburbs, a factor that diffused the remaining reform energies among the urban leaders.

A second external factor in the decline of the progressive movement after 1918 was the desertion from its ranks of a good part of the intellectual leadership of the country. Indeed, more than simple desertion was involved here; it was often a matter of a cynical repudiation of the ideals from which progressivism derived its strength. I do not mean to imply too much by this generalization. I know that what has been called intellectual progressivism not only survived in the 1920's but actually flourished in many fields.[11] I know that the intellectual foundations of our present quasi-welfare state were either being laid or reinforced during the decade. Even so, one cannot evade the conclusion that the intellectual-political climate of the 1920's was vastly different from the one that had prevailed in the preceding two decades.

During the years of the great progressive revolt, intellectuals—novelists, journalists, political thinkers, social scientists, historians, and the like—had made a deeply personal commitment to the cause of democracy, first in domestic and then in foreign affairs. Their leadership in and impact on many phases of the progressive movement had been profound. By contrast, in the 1920's a large body of this intellectual phalanx turned against the very ideals they had once deified. One could cite, for example, the reaction of the idealists against the Versailles settlement; the disenchantment of the intellectuals with the extension of government authority when it could be used to justify the Eighteenth Amendment or the suppression of free speech; or the inevitable loss of faith in the "people" when en masse they hounded so-called radicals, joined Bryan's crusade against evolution, or regaled themselves as Knights of the Ku Klux Klan. Whatever the cause, many alienated intellectuals simply withdrew or repudiated any identification with the groups they had once helped to lead. The result was not fatal to progressivism, but it was serious. The spark plugs had been removed from the engine of reform.

The progressive movement, then, unquestionably declined, but was it

---

[11] *Ibid.*, 5, 131, 135 ff. For a recent excellent survey, previously cited, see Henry F. May, "Shifting Perspectives on the 1920's." Schlesinger's previously cited *Age of Roosevelt* sheds much new light on the economic thought of the 1920's.

defunct in the 1920's? Much, of course, depends upon the definition of terms. If we accept the usual definition for "defunct" as "dead" or "ceasing to have any life or strength," we must recognize that the progressive movement was certainly not defunct in the 1920's; that on the contrary at least important parts of it were very much alive; and that it is just as important to know how and why progressivism survived as it is to know how and why it declined.

To state the matter briefly, progressivism survived in the 1920's because several important elements of the movement remained either in full vigor or in only slightly diminished strength. These were the farmers, after 1918 better organized and more powerful than during the high tide of the progressive revolt; and politically conscious elements among organized labor, particularly the railroad brotherhoods, who wielded a power all out of proportion to their numbers; the Democratic organizations in the large cities, usually vitally concerned with the welfare of the so-called lower classes; a remnant of independent radicals, social workers, and social gospel writers and preachers; and finally, an emerging new vocal element, the champions of public power and regional developments.

Although they never united effectively enough to capture a major party and the national government before 1932, these progressive elements controlled Congress from 1921 to about 1927 and continued to exercise a near control during the period of their greatest weakness in the legislative branch, from 1927 to about 1930.

Indeed, the single most powerful and consistently successful group in Congress during the entire decade from 1919 to 1929 were the spokesmen of the farmers. Spurred by an unrest in the country areas more intense than at any time since the 1890's,[12] in 1920 and 1921 southern Democrats and midwestern and western insurgents, nominally Republican, joined forces in an alliance called the Farm Bloc. By maintaining a common front from 1921 to 1924 they succeeded in enacting the most advanced agricultural legislation to that date, legislation that completed the program begun under Wilsonian auspices. It included measures for high tariffs on agricultural products, thoroughgoing federal regulation of stockyards, packing houses, and grain exchanges, the exemption of agricultural cooperatives from the application of the antitrust laws, stimulation of the export of agricultural commodities, and the establishment of an entirely new federal system of intermediate rural credit.

When prosperity failed to return to the countryside, rural leaders in Congress espoused a new and bolder plan for relief—the proposal made by George N. Peek and Hugh S. Johnson in 1922 to use the federal power to obtain "fair exchange" or "parity" prices for farm products. Embodied in the

---

[12] It derived from the fact that farm prices plummeted in 1920 and 1921, and remained so low that farmers, generally speaking, operated at a net capital loss throughout the balance of the decade.

McNary-Haugen bill in 1924, this measure was approved by Congress in 1927 and 1928, only to encounter vetoes by President Calvin Coolidge.

In spite of its momentary failure, the McNary-Haugen bill had a momentous significance for the American progressive movement. Its wholesale espousal by the great mass of farm leaders and spokesmen meant that the politically most powerful class in the country had come full scale to the conviction that the taxing power should be used directly and specifically for the purpose of underwriting (some persons called it subsidizing) agriculture. It was a milestone in the development of a comprehensive political doctrine that it was government's duty to protect the economic security of all classes and particularly depressed ones. McNary-Haugenism can be seen in its proper perspective if it is remembered that it would have been considered almost absurd in the Wilson period, that it was regarded as radical by non-farm elements in the 1920's, and that it, or at any rate its fundamental objective, was incorporated almost as a matter of course into basic federal policy in the 1930's.

A second significant manifestation of the survival of progressivism in the 1920's came during the long controversy over public ownership or regulation of the burgeoning electric power industry. In this, as in most of the conflicts that eventually culminated on Capitol Hill, the agrarian element constituted the core of progressive strength. At the same time a sizable and well-organized independent movement developed that emanated from urban centers and was vigorous on the municipal and state levels. Throughout the decade this relatively new progressive group fought with mounting success to expose the propaganda of the private utilities, to strengthen state and federal regulatory agencies, and to win municipal ownership for distributive facilities. Like the advocates of railroad regulation in an earlier period, these proponents of regulation or ownership of a great new natural monopoly failed almost as much as they had succeeded in the 1920's. But their activities and exposures (the Federal Trade Commission's devastating investigation of the electric power industry in the late 1920's and early 1930's was the prime example) laid secure foundations for movements that in the 1930's would reach various culminations.

Even more significant for the future of American progressivism was the emergence in the 1920's of a new objective, that of committing the federal government to plans for large hydroelectric projects in the Tennessee Valley, the Columbia River watershed, the Southwest, and the St. Lawrence Valley for the purpose, some progressives said, of establishing "yardsticks" for rates, or for the further purpose, as other progressives declared, of beginning a movement for the eventual nationalization of the entire electric power industry. The development of this movement in its emerging stages affords a good case study in the natural history of American progressivism. It began when the Harding and Coolidge administrations attempted to dispose of the government's hydroelectric and nitrate facilities at Muscle Shoals, Alabama, to private interests. In the first stage of the controversy, the progressive objective was merely federal operation of these facilities for the production of cheap fertilizer—a reflection of its exclusive special-interest orientation. Then, as new groups joined the fight to save Muscle Shoals, the objective of public production of cheap electric power came to the fore. Finally, by the end of the 1920's, the objective of a muultipurpose regional development in the Tennessee Valley and in other areas as well had taken firm shape.

In addition, by 1928 the agrarians in Congress led by Senator George W. Norris had found enough allies in the two houses and enough support in the country at large to adopt a bill for limited federal development of the Tennessee Valley. Thwarted by President Coolidge's pocket veto, the progressives tried again in 1931, only to meet a second rebuff at the hands of President Herbert Hoover.

All this might be regarded as another milestone in the maturing of American progressivism. It signified a deviation from the older traditions of mere regulation, as President Hoover had said in his veto of the second Muscle Shoals bill, and the triumph of new concepts of direct federal leadership in large-scale development of resources. If progressives had not won their goal by the end of the 1920's, they had at least succeeded in writing what would become perhaps the most important plank in their program for the future.

The maturing of an advanced farm program and the formulation of plans for public power and regional developments may be termed the two most significant progressive achievements on the national level in the 1920's. Others merit only brief consideration. One was the final winning of the old progressive goal of immigration restriction through limited and selective admission. The fact that this movement was motivated in part by racism, nativism, and anti-Semitism (with which, incidentally, a great many if not a majority of progressives were imbued in the 1920's) should not blind us to the fact that it was also progressive. It sought to substitute a so-called scientific and a planned policy for a policy of laissez faire. Its purpose was admittedly to disturb the free operation of the international labor market. Organized labor and social workers had long supported it against the opposition of large employers. And there was prohibition, the most ambitious and revealing progressive experiment of the twentieth century. Even the contemned anti-evolution crusade of Bryan and the fundamentalists and the surging drives for conformity of thought and action in other fields should be mentioned. All these movements stemmed from the conviction that organized public power could and should be used purposefully to achieve fundamental social and so-called moral change. The fact that they were potentially or actively repressive does not mean that they were not progressive. On the contrary, they superbly illustrated the repressive tendencies that inhered in progressivism precisely because it was grounded so much upon majoritarian principles.

Three other developments on the national level that have often been cited as evidences of the failure of progressivism in the 1920's appear in a somewhat different light at second glance. The first was the reversal of the tariff-for-revenue-only tendencies of the Underwood Act with the enactment of the Emergency Tariff Act of 1921 and the Fordney-McCumber Act of 1922. Actually, the adoption of these measures signified, on the whole, not a repudiation but a revival of progressive principles in the realm of federal fiscal policy. A revenue tariff had never been an authentic progressive objective. Indeed, at least by 1913, many progressives, except for some southern agrarians, had concluded that it was retrogressive and had agreed that the tariff laws should be used deliberately to achieve certain national objectives—for example, the crippling of noncompetitive big business by the free admission of articles manufactured by so-called trusts, or benefits to farmers by the free entry of farm implements. Wilson himself had been at least partially converted to these principles by 1916, as his insistence upon the creation of the Federal Tariff Commission and his promise of protection to the domestic chemical industry revealed. As for the tariff legislation of the early 1920's, its only important changes were increased protection for aluminum, chemical products, and agricultural commodities. It left the Underwood rates on the great mass of raw materials and manufactured goods largely undisturbed. It may have been economically shortsighted and a bad example for the rest of the world, but for the most part it was progressive in principle and was the handiwork of the progressive coalition in Congress.

Another development that has often been misunderstood in its relation to the progressive movement was the policies of consistent support that the Harding and Coolidge administrations adopted for business enterprise, particularly the policy of the Federal Trade Commission in encouraging the formation of trade associations and the diminution of certain traditional competitive practices. The significance of all this can easily be overrated. Such policies as these two administrations executed had substantial justification in progressive theory and in precedents clearly established by the Wilson administration.

A third challenge to usual interpretations concerns implications to be drawn from the election of Harding and Coolidge in 1920 and 1924. These elections seem to indicate the triumph of reaction among the mass of American voters. Yet one could argue that both Harding and Coolidge were political accidents, the beneficiaries of grave defects in the American political and constitutional systems. The rank and file of Republican voters demonstrated during the preconvention campaign that they wanted vigorous leadership and a moderately progressive candidate in 1920. They got Harding instead, not because they wanted him, but because unusual circumstances permitted a small clique to thwart the will of the majority.[13] They took Coolidge as their

---

[13] Much that is new on the Republican preconvention campaign and convention of 1920 may be found in William T. Hutchinson, *Lowden of Illinois: The Life of Frank O. Lowden* (2 vols., Chicago, 1957).

candidate in 1924 simply because Harding died in the middle of his term and there seemed to be no alternative to nominating the man who had succeeded him in the White House. Further, an analysis of the election returns in 1920 and 1924 will show that the really decisive factor in the victories of Harding and Coolidge was the fragmentation of the progressive movement and the fact that an opposition strong enough to rally and unite the progressive majority simply did not exist.

There remains, finally, a vast area of progressive activity about which we yet know very little. One could mention the continuation of old reform movements and the development of new ones in the cities and states during the years following the Armistice: For example, the steady spread of the city manager form of government, the beginning of zoning and planning movements, and the efforts of the great cities to keep abreast of the transportation revolution then in full swing. Throughout the country the educational and welfare activities of the cities and states steadily increased. Factory legislation matured, while social insurance had its experimental beginnings. Whether such reform impulses were generally weak or strong, one cannot say; but what we do know about developments in cities like Cincinnati and states like New York, Wisconsin, and Louisiana[14] justifies a challenge to the assumption that municipal and state reform energies were dead after 1918 and, incidentally, a plea to young scholars to plow this unworked field of recent American history.

Let us, then, suggest a tentative synthesis as an explanation of what happened to the progressive movement after 1918:

First, the national progressive movement, which had found its most effective embodiment in the coalition of forces that reelected Woodrow Wilson in 1916, was shattered by certain policies that the administration pursued from 1917 to 1920, and by some developments over which the administration had no or only slight control. The collapse that occurred in 1920 was not inevitable and cannot be explained by merely saying that "the war killed the progressive movement."

Second, large and aggressive components of a potential new progressive coalition remained after 1920. These elements never succeeded in uniting effectively before the end of the decade, not because they did not exist, but because they were divided by conflicts among themselves. National leadership, which in any event did not emerge in the 1920's, perhaps could not have succeeded in subduing these tensions and in creating a new common front.

Third, as a result of the foregoing, progressivism as an organized national force suffered a serious decline in the 1920's. This decline was heightened by the defection of large elements among the urban middle classes and the intellectuals, a desertion induced by technological, economic, and demo-

---

[14] See e.g., Allan P. Sindler, *Huey Long's Louisiana: State Politics, 1920–1952* (Baltimore, Md., 1956).

graphic changes, and by the outcropping of certain repressive tendencies in progressivism after 1917.

Fourth, in spite of reversals and failures, important components of the national progressive movement survived in considerable vigor and succeeded to a varying degree, not merely in keeping the movement alive, but even in broadening its horizons. This was true particularly of the farm groups and of the coalition concerned with public regulation or ownership of electric power resources. These two groups laid the groundwork in the 1920's for significant new programs in the 1930's and beyond.

Fifth, various progressive coalitions controlled Congress for the greater part of the 1920's and were always a serious threat to the conservative administrations that controlled the executive branch. Because this was true, most of the legislation adopted by Congress during this period, including many measures that historians have inaccurately called reactionary, was progressive in character.

Sixth, the progressive movement in the cities and states was far from dead in the 1920's, although we do not have sufficient evidence to justify any generalizations about the degree of its vigor.

If this tentative and imperfect synthesis has any value, perhaps it is high time that we discard the sweeping generalizations, false hypotheses, and clichés that we have so often used in explaining and characterizing political developments from 1918 to 1929. Perhaps we should try to see these developments for what they were—the normal and ordinary political behavior of groups and classes caught up in a swirl of social and economic change. When we do this we will no longer ask whether the progressive movement was defunct in the 1920's. We will ask only what happened to it and why.

SUGGESTED READING

Historians have generally contended that Link overstated his case for the continuation of progressivism in the twenties. Herbert Margulies in "Recent Opinion on the Decline of the Progressive Movement," *Mid-America,* XL (Oct., 1963), 250–68, summarizes the various positions. Among those who modify Link's analysis are Paul Glad in "Progressives and the Business Culture of the 1920's," *Journal of American History,* LIII (June, 1966), 75–89; and George Tindall in "Business Progressivism: Southern Politics in the Twenties," *South Atlantic Quarterly,* LXII (Winter, 1963), 92–106.

Louis Galambos' *Competition and Cooperation: The Emergence of a National Trade Association* (Johns Hopkins Univ. Press, 1966) and his earlier article, "The Cotton-Textile Institute and the Government: A Case Study in Interacting Values Systems," *Business History Review,* XXXVIII (Summer, 1964), 186–213, are fine studies of one trade association and its efforts to restrain competition and seek federal assistance;

in part they correct the analysis of James Prothro's *The Dollar Decade: Business Ideas in the 1920's* (Louisiana State Univ. Press, 1954), which focuses largely on the public statements of laissez faire by the National Association of Manufacturers and the Chamber of Commerce. Morrell Heald in "Business Thought in the Twenties: Social Responsibility," *American Quarterly*, XIII (Summer, 1961), 126–39, cites instances of social responsibility in the decade. Otis Pease in *The Responsibilities of American Advertising: Private Control and Public Influence, 1920– 1940* (Yale Univ. Press, 1958) is an important and penetrating volume on the neglected subject of advertising in American history and is informative on business and public values between the two world wars.

HENRY F. MAY

Shifting Perspectives on the 1920's

INTRODUCTION

In the following article, Henry F. May has written the best introduction to the problem of interpreting the 1920's, a period that has so
far defied all efforts to categorize adequately its development. After tracing the contradictory analyses offered over nearly four
decades, May concludes that fragmenting values and disintegrating traditions are at once the crucial developments of the 1920's and
the cause of conflicting judgments about the period. Because that
decade has offered no common standards for those who have studied it, they have necessarily rendered conflicting evaluations.

In an article entitled "The Rebellion of the Intellectuals"
(*American Quarterly*, VIII [Summer, 1956], 114–26), May finds the
origins of the cultural fragmentation in the progressive era. Until

FROM Henry F. May, "Shifting Perspectives on the 1920's," *Mississippi Valley Historical Review*, XLIII (December, 1956), pp. 405–27. Reprinted by permission.

the twilight of progressivism, American civilization rested on the confidence that moral values were universal and self-evident and that by the application of reason men could achieve progress in their social and political order. But after 1912, a small group of young intellectuals (such as Ezra Pound, Walter Lippmann, and H. L. Mencken) became bored with this attitude and found prophets whose teachings corroded the old faith. Henri Bergson, the French philosopher, denied both certainty and reason and found that only change perceived by intuition is real. The naive rationalism underlying the American democratic faith seemed discredited by the insight of Sigmund Freud and the brilliant scorn of Frederich Nietzsche. William James' fascination with the irrational, mysticism, and inner experience attracted a generation tired of preoccupation with pious politics.

The young intellectuals in revolt before World War I craved experience, novelty, and action for their own sakes, and so they romanticized the Wobblies and wrote poems emancipated from established forms. Until the war the rebels were exuberant and optimistic, but afterward their reflections assumed a somber cast; by the 1920's many of the precocious intellectuals of the prewar years had become (in May's words) "despairing nihilists." Undiminished, however, were their attacks on conventional morality, democracy, and rationalism, and their boredom with American materialism.

But, as May makes clear in the following essay, the ideas of the literary intellectuals were by no means the only ideas produced in the 1920's. It should not be forgotten that some intellectuals in fields other than the literary realm, such as Wesley C. Mitchell and Charles A. Beard, actually endorsed many of the values of their time and looked forward to the future with optimism.

To comment on the 1920's today is to put oneself in the position of a Civil War historian writing in the 1890's. The period is over and major changes have taken place. The younger historian himself belongs to a generation which barely remembers the great days. From the point of view of the veterans, still full of heroic memories, such a historian obviously has no right to talk—he was not there. Yet historians are led by their training to hope that one kind of truth—not the only kind and perhaps not always the most important kind—emerges from the calm study of the records.

Calm study of this decade is not easy. Like the Civil War itself, the cultural battles of the twenties have been fought again and again. Successive writers have found it necessary either to condemn or to praise the decade, though what they have seen in it to condemn or praise has differed. Perhaps this fact offers us our best starting point. If we can trace the shifting and changing picture of the decade through the last thirty years, and still better, if we can understand the emotions that have attached themselves to one version or another, we may be closer to knowing what the decade really meant. In the process, we can hardly help learning something of the intellectual history of the intervening period.

It is immediately apparent, as one turns through the literature about the twenties, that most of the striking contributions have not come from men we usually think of as historians, but rather from journalists, literary critics, and social scientists. This is perhaps not surprising, since most of the excitement has centered in areas outside the historian's traditional domain. Historians today, of course, claim a territory stretching far beyond past politics; but this is a recent expansion, and all of us enter such fields as literature and science only with caution. Caution is necessary, but it must not prevent exploration. If the best insights into a period come from economists, or anthropologists, or literary critics, we must try to understand and even to assess them, hoping that our inevitable mistakes will be made in a good cause.

At least three pictures of the twenties had formed before the decade was over. For different reasons, spokesmen of business, social science, and literary revolt all wanted to get clear away from the past, to discard history. For this reason, all three groups were constantly discussing their own historical role. Perhaps the dominant current version was that proclaimed by the businessmen, the picture of the period usually conveyed by the phrase New Era itself. Out of the postwar upheaval was emerging, in this view, a new civilization. Its origin was technology, its efficient causes high wages and diffusion of ownership, its leadership enlightened private management. This picture of the period was far more than a matter of political speeches and *Saturday Evening Post* editorials. It was buttressed by academic argument and attested by foreign observers. To its believers, we must remember, it was not a picture of conservatism but of innovation, even, as Thomas Nixon Carver strikingly asserted, of revolution.[1]

It is not surprising that this interpretation of the period gained the allegiance of many of its first historians. Preston W. Slosson, surveying his own time for the *History of American Life* series, came to a typical New Era conclusion on the basis of a typical New Era criterion: "Often in history the acid test of wealth has been applied to a favored class; alone in all nations and all ages the United States of the 1920's was beginning to apply that test to a whole people."[2] James C. Malin found, with no apparent anguish, that political democracy was being replaced by self-government in industry.[3] No seri-

---

[1] Thomas N. Carver, *The Present Economic Revolution in the United States* (Boston, 1926), is perhaps the most effective single presentation of this common version of the period.

[2] Preston W. Slosson, *The Great Crusade and After* (New York, 1930), 729.

[3] James C. Malin, *The United States after the World War* (Boston, 1930), 530–43. Like some of the social scientists discussed below, Malin thought that "It is possible that in the long run the changes even extended effective governmental regulative powers, although critics of the new policies held the opposite view" (p. 540).

ous dissent was expressed in Charles A. Beard's great synthesis, published in 1927. Beard deplored the politics and other obsolete folkways surviving in the postwar era. But he found the center of current development, and the climax of his whole vast story, in the achievements of the machine age. Continuous invention was the hope of the future. Standardization had made possible not only better living for all but a more generous support for the life of the mind. Those who feared the machine were lumped together by Beard as "artists of a classical bent and . . . spectators of a soulful temper." [4] Lesser and more conventional historians usually struck the same note; and the textbooks of the period, if they ventured beyond Versailles, emerged into a few pages of peace and prosperity.[5]

Sociologists of the period, full of the élan of their new subject, exultant over the apparent defeat of religious obscurantism, were as optimistic as the businessmen and the historians, though for different reasons. Their New Era lay in the future rather than the present; its motivating force was not technology alone but the guiding social intelligence. This picture of the decade as a transitional age emerges most clearly from the sociological periodicals of the early twenties, where one finds at least four important assumptions. First, the scientific study of society is just coming into its own. Second, social scientists are now able to abandon sentiment, impressionism, and introspection and seek accurate information, especially quantitative information. Third, this new knowledge should be, and increasingly will be, the guide for practical statesmanship, replacing custom and tradition. Fourth, Utopia is consequently just around the corner. The present may look chaotic, but the new élite will be able to lead us fairly quickly out of the fog of dissolving tradition and toward the end of controversy and the reign of universal efficiency.[6]

To condense is always unfair, and it would be incorrect to assume that all social scientists in the twenties saw their role or their period this simply. Yet it is easy enough to find all these beliefs stated very positively in textbooks and even learned articles, with both the behaviorist dogmatism and

---

[4] Charles A. and Mary R. Beard, *The Rise of American Civilization* (2 vols., New York, 1927), II, 729.

[5] Paul L. Haworth, *The United States in Our Own Times, 1865–1920* (New York, 1920), called his last chapter "A Golden Age in History," and left both title and contents nearly unchanged in his editions of 1924, 1925, and 1931. More temperately, Samuel E. Forman, *Our Republic* (Rev. ed., New York, 1929), 881, balanced "stupendous productivity" against such blemishes as technological unemployment and concluded that the country was "sound at the core."

[6] for optimism about the prospects of social science, see for instance Emory S. Bogardus' preface to Elmer S. Nelson, Charles E. Martin, and William H. George, *Outlines of the Social Sciences* (Los Angeles, 1923), xvii–xx. For a strong statement about the role of social scientists in correcting all existing abuses, see John Candler Cobb, "The Social Sciences," *American Journal of Sociology* (Chicago), XXXI (May, 1926), 721. An unusually strong statement of the necessity for the well-informed to control society is that by the historian of the social sciences, Harry Elmer Barnes, "History and Social Intelligence," *Journal of Social Forces* (Chapel Hill), II (November, 1923), 151–64.

the authoritarian implications full-blown. Part of the confidence of these prophets rested on real and important achievement by social scientists in the period, but those who had actually contributed the most new knowledge were sometimes less dogmatic than their colleagues. In *Middletown*, for instance, the social science interpretation of the twenties is buried in a mass of scrupulously collected facts, but it is there. At certain points in describing the decline of labor unionism or the standardization of leisure the authors seem to be deploring changes that have taken place since 1890. Yet in their conclusion they trace the tensions of Middletown to the lag of habits and institutions behind technological progress. Individual child-training, religion, and the use of patriotic symbols represent the past, while the future is represented by whatever is thoroughly secular and collective, particularly in the community's work life. The town has tended to meet its crises by invoking tradition in defense of established institutions. Their whole investigation, the Lynds conclude, suggests instead "the possible utility of a deeper-cutting procedure that would involve a re-examination of the institutions themselves." [7]

The typical economic thought of the twenties, while it avoided Utopian extremes, shared with the other social sciences an unlimited confidence in the present possibilities of fact-finding and saw in the collection and use of statistics much of the promise and meaning of the era. In his brilliant concluding summary of *Recent Economic Trends*, Professor Wesley C. Mitchell, for instance, found the main explanation for the progress of 1922–1928 in the new application of intelligence to business, government, and trade-union administration.[8]

The third contemporary interpretation of the period, that offered by its literary intellectuals, differed sharply from the other two. Completely repudiating the optimism of the businessmen, it agreed with the social scientists only in its occasional praise of the liberated intelligence. For the most part, as we are all continually reminded, the writers and artists of the twenties saw their age as one of decline.

The most publicized group of pessimists was that typified by Harold Stearns and his colleagues of 1922, who, with their many successors, left an enduring picture of a barren, neurotic, Babbitt-ridden society. These critics have drawn a lot of patriotic fire, and indeed some of them are sitting ducks. They were often, though not always, facile, unoriginal, and ignorant. They seldom made clear the standards by which they found American society so lacking. Yet their lament is never altogether absurd or capricious. If one studies the civilization they saw around them through its press, one hardly finds it a model of ripeness or serenity. The fact remains, for historians to deal

---

[7] Robert S. and Helen M. Lynd, *Middletown* (New York, 1929), 502.

[8] President's Conference on Unemployment, *Recent Economic Changes* (New York, 1929), 862.

with, that American civilization in the twenties presented to many of its most sensitive and some of its gifted members only an ugly and hostile face.

A more thoughtful and sadder group of writers than most of the young Babbitt-beaters traced their own real malaise not to the inadequacies of America but to the breakdown of the entire Western civilization. The New Humanists had long been deploring the decline of literary and moral discipline. At the opposite extreme in taste the up-to-date followers of Spengler agreed that decay impended. Joseph Wood Krutch in 1929 described the failure first of religion and then of the religion of science to give life meaning: "Both our practical morality and our emotional lives are adjusted to a world which no longer exists. . . . There impends for the human spirit either extinction or a readjustment more stupendous than any made before." [9]

Many accepted this statement of the alternatives, and chose according to their natures. Walter Lippmann, who had played some part in the confident prewar attack on tradition and custom, chose the duty of reconstruction and published, in 1929, his earnest attempt to find a naturalist basis for traditional moral standards.[10] On the other hand, T. S. Eliot painted a savage and devastating picture of present civilization and left it to live in the world which Krutch thought no longer existent. As Eliot assumed the stature of a contemporary classic, his description of the Waste Land, the world of Sweeney and Prufrock, and also his path away from it, seriously influenced later conceptions of the period.

With the depression, the twenties shot into the past with extraordinary suddenness. The conflicting pictures of the decade, rosy and deep black, changed sharply, though none disappeared. Of them all, it was the New Era point of view, the interpretation of the decade as the birth of a new and humane capitalism, that understandably suffered most. Ironically, the most plausible and heavily documented version of this description, and one of the most influential later, appeared only in 1932 when Adolf A. Berle, Jr., and Gardiner C. Means described the separation of management from ownership.[11] At the time, however, the economic order of the twenties was collapsing, and its harassed defenders retreated temporarily into the Republican last ditch.

The other optimistic vision of the decade, that of the social scientists, depended less directly on prosperity and in the thirties survived somewhat better, though it became difficult to see the preceding period as the triumphant application of social intelligence. It is a startling example of the prestige of the social science point of view in 1929 that a president should commission a group of social scientists to make a complete and semi-official

---

[9] Joseph W. Krutch, *The Modern Temper* (New York, 1929), 26.

[10] Walter Lippmann, *A Preface to Morals* (New York, 1929).

[11] Adolf A. Berle, Jr., and Gardiner C. Means, *The Modern Corporation and Private Property* (New York, 1932).

portrait of a whole civilization. The fact that *Recent Social Trends* was not completed and published until 1932 probably accounts in part for its excellence; it is the most informative document of the twenties which we have and also a monument of the chastened social science of the thirties. The committee that wrote this survey still believed, as its chairman, Wesley Mitchell, had earlier, that much of the meaning of the twenties lay in the harnessing of social intelligence to collective tasks. Consciously and subtly, the various authors documented the contradiction between the period's individualistic slogans and its actual movement toward social and even governmental control.[12] Yet they were conscious throughout that all this had ended in depression.

Like the authors of *Middletown*, the committee found its synthetic principle in the doctrine that change proceeds at different rates in different areas. Again like the Lynds, it assumed that society's principal objective should be "the attainment of a situation in which economic, governmental, moral and cultural arrangements should not lag too far behind the advance of basic changes," and basic here means primarily technological.[13] Occasionally *Recent Social Trends* displays, as for instance in its chapters on the child and on education, a surviving trace of the easy authoritarianism of the preceding decade's social theorists, and occasional chapters refer in the early optimistic manner to the hope of solving all social problems through the new psychological knowledge.[14] But in most of this great work, and particularly in its brilliant introduction, the authors left behind the social-science utopianism of the early twenties. It would take an increasingly powerful effort of social intelligence to bring us into equilibrium. Moreover, this effort must be a subtle one; the committee took pains to state that it was "not unmindful of the fact that there are important elements in human life not easily stated in terms of efficiency, mechanization, institutions, rates of change or adaptations to change." [15] Therefore, what was called for was not a ruthless rejection of tradition but a re-examination leading to a restatement in terms of modern life. *Recent Social Trends* is in places a work of art as well as of social science, and it is one of the few books about the twenties that point the way toward a comprehensive understanding of the period.

The view of the previous decade presented in the thirties by most historians was far less subtle and complete. Instead of either a New Era, a liberation, or a slow scientific adaptation, the twenties became a deplorable interlude of reaction. This view, stated sometimes with qualifications and

---

[12] President's Research Committee on Social Trends, *Recent Social Trends* (2 vols., New York, 1933). This is a main theme of Chapters 23 to 29, II, 1168–1541.

[13] *Ibid.*, I, lxxiv.

[14] *Ibid* II, 1185

[15] *Ibid.*, I, lxxv.

sometimes very baldly, has continued to dominate academic historical writing from the thirties almost until the present.

Most of the historians who were publishing in the thirties had received their training in the Progressive Era. Many had been deeply influenced by Frederick Jackson Turner, and had tended to look for their synthesis not to the decline of Europe but to the expansion of America. Though the Turner doctrine can be turned to pessimistic uses, Turner himself in the twenties prophesied that social intelligence would find a substitute for the disappearing force of free land.[16] As this suggests, the outlook of John Dewey pervaded much of historical writing as it did the work of social scientists. Yet historians still tended to give most of their attention to politics. For these reasons, and because they shared the opinion of their readers, historians usually found the meaning of American history in the nineteenth-century growth of political and social democracy and the twentieth-century effort to adapt it to new conditions.

As we have seen, many of the historians actually writing in the twenties had not found their own period an interruption of this beneficent adaptation. The interruption had come in 1929 and then, after an interval of confusion and paralysis, Franklin D. Roosevelt had appealed for support partly in terms of the progressive view of history. Roosevelt himself justified his program by pointing to the end of free land [17] and claimed the progressive succession from Theodore Roosevelt and Woodrow Wilson, his cousin and his former chief. Few historians were disposed to deny his claim, and accepting it made the twenties an unfortunate interregnum, sometimes covered by a chapter called "The Age of the Golden Calf," or "Political Decadence," or even "A Mad Decade." [18]

This does not mean that an emphasis on the political conservatism of the decade, or a hostile criticism of the Harding-Coolidge policies, is in itself a distortion. Yet stubborn standpattism was only one ingredient in a varied picture. It is not history to make the twenties, as some of the briefer historical treatments do, merely a contrasting background for the New Deal. Some-

---

[16] See his statement of 1924, quoted in Henry Nash Smith, *Virgin Land* (Cambridge, 1950), 258–59.

[17] See his famous Commonwealth Club Address, Samuel I. Rosenman (ed.), *The Public Papers and Addresses of Franklin D. Roosevelt* (13 vols., New York, 1938–1950), I, 742–56.

[18] The first two of these occur in Dwight L. Dumond, *Roosevelt to Roosevelt* (New York, 1937), the general title of which indicates its outspoken loyalties; the last in James Truslow Adams, *The March of Democracy* (2 vols., New York, 1933). Adams' best-selling *Epic of America* (Boston, 1931) contains one of the most complete indictments of all aspects of the culture of the twenties. The above generalizations about American historians do not, however, apply fully to Adams, whose ideas are somewhat atypical. His dislike of the decade's culture was expressed early in his *Our Business Civilization* (New York, 1929), which repeats many of the criticisms made by the literary anti-conformists.

times even prosperity—an important fact despite the exceptions—is belittled almost out of existence, the prophets of abundance are denied credit for good intentions, the approach of the depression becomes something that nearly anybody could have foreseen, and the decade's many advances in science, social science, medicine, and even government are left out.[19]

While they deplored the businessmen and politicians of the twenties, the progressive historians of the thirties and later tended also to belittle the period's literary achievement. This negative judgment was sustained by a powerful writer, Vernon L. Parrington, himself a thorough and fervent exponent of the progressive interpretation of American history. In Parrington's last, fragmentary volume, published in 1930, he read the younger authors of the twenties out of the American tradition as "a group of youthful poseurs at the mercy of undigested reactions to Nietzsche, Butler, Dadaism, Vorticism, Socialism; overbalanced by changes in American critical and creative standards, and in love with copious vocabularies and callow emotions." "With the cynicism that came with postwar days," said Professor Parrington, "the democratic liberalism of 1917 was thrown away like an empty whiskey-flask." [20]

Though Parrington did not live to explain this rejection or treat it at length, he obviously believed that the liberal whisky was still there and still potent, and so, in the thirties and often since, have many of his readers. Some historians, understandably impressed by Parrington's great architectural achievement, willingly and specifically took over his literary judgments; others doubtless arrived at similar opinions independently.[21] For whatever reason, by the thirties the most widespread historical picture of the twenties was that of a sudden and temporary repudiation of the progressive tradition by reactionary politicians and also by frivolous or decadent littérateurs.

Some of the historians writing in the thirties, and far more of the literary critics, found their historical principle not in American progressivism but in Marxism. John Chamberlain demonstrated to his own temporary satisfaction the futility of the preceding Progressive Era, and Lewis Corey and oth-

---

[19] Fred A. Shannon, *America's Economic Growth* (Rev. ed., New York, 1940), describes the economic policies of the period thus: "It was in this atmosphere of rapacity and high-pressured seduction that governments reverted to *laissez faire* policy, contorted to mean government assistance to business" (p. 585), and refers to the "fools' paradise" and the "years of paper prosperity" of the period (pp. 701, 727). A later judgment is that of Henry B. Parkes, *Recent America* (New York, 1946), that "There was probably more materialism, more illiberality, and more cynicism than ever before in American history" (p. 464). One can think at least of close contenders to some of these titles.

[20] Vernon L. Parrington, *Main Currents in American Thought* (3 vols., New York, 1927–1930), Vol. III, *The Beginning of Critical Realism in America*, 385–86, 412.

[21] An example is Louis M. Hacker, *American Problems of Today* (New York, 1938), which quotes and cites Parrington's judgments liberally (e.g., p. 165). A historian who states his admiration of Parrington very strongly in our own time is Henry Steele Commager, *The American Mind* (New Haven, 1950), 445.

ers depicted the resultant triumph of monopoly capitalism, characterized by
a false prosperity and leading inevitably to the depression and (before 1935)
the disguised fascism of the New Deal.[22] At their worst, and in most of their
specifically historical writing, the Marxist writers seem now unbelievably
crude and schematic. But the Marxist version of the twenties came not only
from the pamphleteers but also from gifted literary artists. For many of the
generation that grew up in the thirties the concept of the previous decade
was strongly influenced by the work of John Dos Passos. His brilliant
sketches of Woodrow Wilson, Henry Ford, Thorstein Veblen, and other
giants, the post-war violence, the defeat of hopes, and the gradual inevitable
corruption of the "big money" from a picture that is hard to forget—that Dos
Passos himself in sackcloth and ashes is entirely unable to wipe out. Among
the many critics and literary historians who were then Marxists, most of them
dull and fashion-ridden, were a few writers of insight. It is still suggestive to
see the literary rebellion of the twenties, through the 1935 eyes of Granville
Hicks, as a reflection of the insecurity of the middle class.[23] Most of the rebellious writers *had* come from this class, and even from a particular segment of
it that had lost prestige, and many of them had been self-conscious and worried about this origin.

Sometimes, despite their basic differences, the Marxist writers agreed
in part in the thirties with the progressive historians. Often, however, the
literary Marxists made a different combination. Starting in the twenties as
rebels in the name of art, they had found their esthetic distaste for capitalism
confirmed by prophecies of its inevitable doom. The resultant mixture of individualist rebellion and socialist revolution was unstable and short-lived,
but in the thirties powerful. Edmund Wilson describes the representative
mood, and the resultant attitude toward the twenties: "To the writers and
artists of my generation who had grown up in the shadow of the Big Business
era and had always resented its barbarism, its crowding-out of everything
they cared about, these depression years were not depressing but stimulating. One couldn't help being exhilarated at the sudden unexpected collapse
of that stupid gigantic fraud." [24]

One other and opposite group of writers in the thirties contributed to
the previous decade's bad press. This was the varied group stemming from
T. S. Eliot's neo-classical essays and I. A. Richards' effort at a scientific criticism that came to be known as "the New Critics." This school of writers could
almost be defined as a counterrevolution against the individualist rebellion

---

[22] Lewis Corey, *The Decline of American Capitalism* (New York, 1934), and *The Crisis of
the Middle Class* (New York, 1935). An example of Marxist interpretation at its simplest is
Bruce Minton and John Stewart, *The Fat Years and the Lean* (New York, 1940).

[23] Granville Hicks, *The Great Tradition* (New York, 1935), 215.

[24] Edmund Wilson, "The Literary Consequences of the Crash" (first published in 1932), in
Wilson, *The Shores of Light* (New York, 1952), 409.

of the twenties, in which some of them, not surprisingly, had themselves played a part. Some of the New Critics called for a revival of the Catholic, or Anglo-Catholic, or humanist, or southern tradition; others hoped to find a new credo in literature itself. They agreed only in valuing such qualities as complexity, tension, and intellectual strictness. In the thirties, despite the noise made by opposite groups, it was the New Critics who were moving quietly toward a position of dominance in criticism and in the college teaching of literature; a position they clearly hold today.

Like their enemies, the Marxists and progressives, the New Critics found little to praise in the twenties. To begin with, they stoutly rejected any tendency to measure the progress of civilization in terms of technology or standard of living. Thus they saw both the business civilization of the New Era and the opposing humanitarian progressivism as two variants of the same shallow materialism.[25] To them the social science Utopias forecast in the twenties were merely a repulsive climax to current tendencies. Allen Tate, for instance, associated social science not only with innocent barbarism but with the current triumph of the total state: "What we thought was to be a conditioning process in favor of a state planned by Teachers College of Columbia University will be a conditioning equally useful for Plato's tyrant state. . . . The point of view that I am sketching here looks upon the rise of the social sciences and their influence in education, from Comtism to Deweyism, as a powerful aid to the coming of the slave society." Looking back at the previous period, Tate remembered sadly "How many young innocent men— myself among them—thought, in 1924, that laboratory jargon meant laboratory demonstration." [26]

Most of the New Critics rejected the rebellious literature of the twenties as completely as they did the business civilizations of the era. Exceptions had to be made, of course, for the more careful and rigorous poets—Marianne Moore, Eliot, sometimes Ezra Pound. The abler of the New Critics realized, as some moralists did not, that the writers of the twenties expressed, rather than caused, the disintegration of tradition which they deplored. Some of them were able to admire men like Ernest Hemingway and Hart Crane who bravely tried to give literary form to moral and intellectual disorder. But the general direction of the literature of the decade was, they agreed, disintegration.[27]

---

[25] This radical separation of material and spiritual values may be found in Eliot's essays in the early twenties and is strongly stated in John Crowe Ransom, "Flux and Blur in Contemporary Art," *Sewanee Review* (Sewanee, Tenn.), XXXVII (July, 1929), 353–66. It was in the thirties, however, that the New Critic movement drew together as a school. As early as 1931, Max Eastman acutely pointed out that this radical dualism was a curious attitude in those who wanted to restore the unity of Western cultural tradition. Eastman, *The Literary Mind* (New York, 1931).

[26] Allen Tate, *Reason in Madness* (New York, 1935), 7, 11.

[27] A good sample of the attitude of the New Critics toward the twenties, conveying both the acuteness and the dogmatism of the movement, is Richard P. Blackmur, "Notes on

Progressives, Marxists, and neo-classicists all found the twenties deplorable, yet in writers from all these camps, and in others who wrote in the thirties, a note of nostalgia often broke through the sermon. Frivolous, antisocial, and decadent as the literature of the twenties seemed, it had to be conceded the somewhat contradictory qualities of freshness and excitement. And nostalgia, in the thirties, extended beyond the previous decade's literature to its manners and customs. In 1931 Frederick L. Allen performed a remarkable feat of impressionist recall of the period just over, and in 1935 Mark Sullivan brought back vividly its clothes and songs and sensations.[28] Already in the work of these two excellent reporters, and later in the versions of a number of minor and more sentimental merchants of nostalgia, the twenties appeared strange, fantastic, and appealing. They appealed with particular strength to those who did not remember them; it was the peculiar feat of these reporters to fill the new generation with nostalgia for scenes they had not seen. For the college student of the next decade, if the twenties was one half the betrayal of progress, the other half was the jazz age. Irresponsibility, to the solemn and uneasy thirties, was both deplorable and attractive.

This paradoxical attitude toward the twenties continued and the paradox sharpened in the next period. In the dramatic and tragic days of World War II, few found much to admire in the age of Ford and Coolidge. James Burnham, combining Berle and Means's data on the separation of ownership and control with an apocalyptic vision of the rise of the total state, made the New Era into the beginning of the "Managerial Revolution." [29] To the F. D. R. liberals, who already blamed the twenties for abandoning progressivism, the period's major crime was now its rejection of the Wilsonian international program. Teachers worried whether the earlier postwar disillusion, which they had helped to propagate, would make it impossible to

---

E. E. Cummings' Language," published in *Hound and Horn* (Portland, Me.), in 1931, and reprinted in Morton D. Zabel's very helpful anthology, *Literary Opinion in America* (New York, 1937; rev. ed., 1951), 296–314. A typical verdict from an atypical critic is that of Yvor Winters: "During the second and third decades of the twentieth century, the chief poetic talent of the United States took certain new directions, directions that appear to me in the main regrettable. The writers between Robinson and Frost, on the one hand, and Allen Tate and Howard Baker on the other, who remained relatively traditional in manner were with few exceptions minor or negligible; the more interesting writers . . . were misguided." Winters, *Primitivism and Decadence* (New York, 1937), 15. A little later Randall Jarrell acutely suggested, from a New Critic point of view, the similarity between the period's rebels and its dominant tendencies: "How much the modernist poets disliked their society, and how much they resembled it! How often they contradicted its letter and duplicated its spirit! They rushed, side by side with their society, to the limits of all tendencies." Jarrell, "The End of the Line" (first published in 1942), in Zabel, *Literary Opinion in America* (rev. ed.), 742–48.

[28] Frederick L. Allen, *Only Yesterday* (New York, 1931); Mark Sullivan, *Our Times: The United States, 1900–1925* (6 vols., New York, 1926–1935), Vol. VI, *The Twenties*. A later sensational and amusing treatment of some aspects of the decade is Laurence Greene, *The Era of Wonderful Nonsense* (Indianapolis, 1939).

[29] James Burnham, *The Managerial Revolution* (New York, 1941).

revive a fighting spirit—a worry which proved unnecessary and perhaps a little conceited. Editorial writers wondered whether the country would again fail in its responsibilities after the war. Above all, those who responded most generously to the call for the defense of Western culture feared that the literary rebels of the twenties had done great, even disastrous, damage to the nation's morale.

Even before the war broke out, Walter Lippmann was concerned about the lack of fighting convictions among civilized men and blamed, in part, the rejection of tradition in which he had long ago taken part. Archibald Mac-Leish blamed both the artists and the scholars of the previous period for their different kinds of detachment. Van Wyck Brooks, looking back at the writers who had answered his own summons for a new literature, found that they differed from all previous writers in one striking way: they had ceased to be "voices of the people." [30] "How could a world," he wondered, "that was sapped by these negative feelings resist the triumphant advance of evil." [31]

This high estimate of the power and responsibility of literature seemed to be shared by Bernard DeVoto, though he took writers to task for making literature the measure of life. Writers of the "Age of Ignominy" had condemned their period partly out of sheer ignorance. In his eagerness to demonstrate this DeVoto revived, earlier than many, some of the New Era interpretation of the twenties. "What truly was bankrupt was not American civilization but the literary way of thinking about it." Actually, "The nation that came out of the war into the 1920's was . . . the most cheerful and energetic society in the world." [32] A true picture of it would have emphasized its achievements in education, medicine, humanitarian improvement, and the writing of local history.

MacLeish, Brooks, DeVoto, and others condemned the writers of the twenties for damaging the nation's fighting morale, and strangely enough, Charles and Mary Beard, writing in 1942 of the American Spirit, made the same charges from an isolationist point of view. For the Beards, American cynicism had come from Europe: "In the tempers and moods fostered by foreign criticisms and by American weakness displayed in reactions to the im-

---

[30] Walter Lippmann, *The Good Society* (New York, 1937); Archibald MacLeish, *The Irresponsibles* (New York, 1940); Van Wyck Brooks, *The Opinions of Oliver Allston* (New York, 1941). "Allston" condemns the rebellious poets and novelists of the twenties and, even more vigorously, their opponents the New Critics (as "coterie writers," pp. 241 ff.). He rejects the "excuses" characteristic of the postwar authors and insists that the trouble is not relativity, mechanization, etc., but the emotional inadequacy of the writers themselves (pp. 249–50).

[31] Brooks, *Opinions of Allston*, 205. The opinions quoted are those of "Allston," Brooks's thinly disguised fictional counterpart.

[32] Bernard DeVoto, *The Literary Fallacy* (Boston, 1944), 123, 162.

pacts, multitudes of young men and women were brought to such a plight that they derided the whole American scene." [33]

All these works, including in part that of the Beards (which was not one of the major productions of these great historians), were wartime pamphlets rather than history. None of them offered a halfway satisfactory explanation of the alienation they discussed, which was certainly a more important phenomenon than the inadequacy of a few individuals. Yet one thing the wartime writers said was true and worth saying, that in the twenties a deep chasm had opened between the views of life of most writers and their fellow citizens. Perhaps the importance of this fact could not be emotionally grasped until the years when DeVoto heard Ezra Pound on the Italian radio.

Yet, even in wartime, and for some perhaps especially in wartime, the freedom and creativity and even the irresponsibility of the previous generation of writers had a paradoxical attraction. Alfred Kazin's admirable and by no means uncritical chapters on the period, which appeared in 1942, were called "The Great Liberation (1918–1929)." [34] And the paradox seemed to reach its most acute form in DeVoto himself. In the same short volume the literature of the twenties was "debilitated, capricious, querulous, and irrelevant" and yet the decade was "one of the great periods of American literature, and probably the most colorful, vigorous, and exciting period." It was a literature that was "not . . . functional in American life," but "idle, dilettante, flippant, and intellectually sterile," and yet one which had "achieved something like a charter of liberties for American writers." [35]

In the nineteen-fifties, as in other periods, it is dangerous to equate the latest insights with truth. Yet it is hard not to conclude that now, in the second postwar period, some writers are converging from various directions toward a better understanding of the twenties. For one thing, the decade is longer past and it is no longer acutely necessary to break with its viewpoint. Fairly recently the twenties have come to be a fair field for the dissertation and the monograph, which bring at least a different kind of knowledge. One survivor of the period says that instead of being revived, it is being excavated like a ruin, and another complains that he and his friends are already being preserved in complete bibliographies while yet, as far as they can tell, alive.[36]

Disapproval and nostalgia, of course, remain. Editorials worry about

---

[33] Charles A. and Mary R. Beard, *The American Spirit* (New York, 1942), 474. For the Beards, as for many other cultural historians, "The American Philosophy" is that of John Dewey (p. 665). This version of American intellectual history seems to need considerable qualification.

[34] Alfred Kazin, *On Native Grounds* (New York, 1942), 187.

[35] DeVoto, *Literary Fallacy*, 13, 15, 165–66, 169.

[36] Malcolm Cowley, *The Literary Situation* (New York, 1954), 3; Edmund Wilson, "Thoughts on Being Bibliographed," *Princeton University Library Chronicle* (Princeton), V (February, 1944), 51–61.

the effect on Europe of the vogue there of the literature of the twenties. Professor Howard Mumford Jones has continued something like DeVoto's charges in more analytic tones, accusing the postwar writers both of brilliance and of detachment amounting to solipsism.[37] The choice of Scott Fitzgerald for revival and in some quarters canonization indicates the perverse attraction which self-destruction seems to hold for our period. Budd Schulberg's novel specifically contrasts a romantic and defeated alcoholic writer of the twenties with a crass, earnest young radical of the thirties to the latter's obvious disadvantage.[38]

In general, however, literary opinion seems to have gone beyond both nostalgia and reproof into a more mature and solidly based appreciation of the achievements of this era now so safely in the past. To many, the apparent sterility of the present literary scene furnishes a depressing contrast. Whatever else they rejected, writers of the twenties took their writing seriously, and, as Cowley has pointed out, publishers made it possible for them to do so.[39] Professor Frederick J. Hoffman in the most thorough of many recent accounts finds the period's literature full of daring, variety, and technical brilliance. This estimate by now represents more than a cult; it is an accepted consensus.[40]

One achievement of the twenties which has received only a little specific comment is nevertheless widely recognized today. The period of alienation and exile gave rise, curiously enough, to a thorough, rich, and continuing inquiry into the whole American past. The sources of this inward turn are as complicated as the decade itself. Many of the major historians who wrote then, including Parrington, Beard, Carl Becker, and Arthur M. Schlesinger, Sr., belong to the group that always found its major synthesis in the course of democratic progress. But others turned to the past with Van Wyck Brooks, partly in a spirit of cultural nationalism, to destroy the English and Anglophile genteel tradition and replace it with something native. Still others

---

[37] Howard M. Jones, *The Bright Medusa* (Urbana, Ill., 1952). Jones analyzes with considerable success both the attraction of the twenties and what he sees as their characteristic fault.

[38] Budd Schulberg, *The Disenchanted* (New York, 1950). As some reviewers pointed out, Schulberg is not sure whether he more admires or pities his major character, clearly modeled on Fitzgerald. The Fitzgerald revival reached its greatest extent with the discussions arising out of Arthur Mizener's biography, *The Far Side of Paradise* (New York, 1950).

[39] Malcolm Cowley, "How Writers Lived," Robert E. Spiller *et al.*, *Literary History of the United States* (Rev. ed., New York, 1953), 1263–72.

[40] Frederick J. Hoffman, *The Twenties: American Writing in the Postwar Decade* (New York, 1955). Another estimate that emphasizes the same qualities is John K. Hutchens in his preface to his anthology, *The Twenties* (Philadelphia, 1952), 11–34.
     A critical but high estimate from the point of view of a present-day novelist is that of James A. Michener, "The Conscience of the Contemporary Novel," Lewis Mumford *et al.*, *The Arts in Renewal* (Philadelphia, 1951), 107–40.

went first through a phase of violent rejection of American culture and then, finding Europe essentially unavailable as a substitute, returned to look desperately for roots at home. By the forties and fifties it was possible to see the lines converging in a cultural history which, at its best, could be critical, conscious of irony and failure, and yet, in a meaningful and necessary way, patriotic.[41]

With the literature and historical research of the twenties, its economic achievement, once overvalued and then rated too low, has again turned the corner into a rising market. In the years of the Marshall Plan, when American capitalism was called on to shoulder an immense burden, it was hard to think of it as a failure and a mistake. And in the still rising prosperity of the Eisenhower period, far more widespread and soundly based than that under Coolidge but inevitably reminiscent, a reassessment of the earlier period was natural enough.

Part of the reassessment arose from the increasing complexity of economics and the development of a new economic history. Beginning about 1940, a number of economists and historians had demanded that American economic history separate itself from the political framework and give more attention to such matters as real wages and volume of production, and somewhat less to labor organization and the political struggles between farmers and merchants.[42] Even earlier, the business historians had been asking for a more analytic and less emotional approach to the history of management.[43] By the forties, it was impossible for an informed historian to duplicate the sweeping judgments about the boom and crash that had been easy ten years earlier. In 1947 George Soule, in his detailed economic history of the twenties, concluded perhaps rather to his own surprise that the rich grew richer

---

[41] For a helpful analysis of the development of American literary studies, see Howard M. Jones, *The Theory of American Literature* (Ithaca, 1948). A contemporary document which brings out the various approaches of the twenties to the American past is Norman Foerster (ed.), *The Reinterpretation of American Literature* (New York, 1928). An extreme example of the tendency today to credit the twenties with a major accomplishment in this respect is Malcolm Cowley's dictum that "Perhaps the greatest creative work of the last three decades in this country has not been any novel or poem or drama of our time . . . perhaps it has been the critical rediscovery and reinterpretation of Melville's *Moby Dick* and its promotion step by step to the position of national epic." Cowley, "The Literary Situation: 1953," *Perspectives USA* (New York), No. 5 (Fall, 1953), 5–13. This promotion began in the twenties and owes much to the outlook of that decade.

[42] A most valuable account of the beginnings of this movement is Herbert Heaton, "Recent Developments in Economic History," *American Historical Review* (New York), XLVII (July, 1942), 727–46. But note that the results seem barely yet apparent to Mr. Heaton in a review of four economic histories in *Mississippi Valley Historical Review* (Cedar Rapids), XXXVIII (December, 1951), 556–61.

[43] Norman S. B. Gras, *Business and Capitalism* (New York, 1939), states the point of view of the business historians. The genesis and progress of the movement are excellently described in Henrietta M. Larson's introduction to her *Guide to Business History* (Cambridge, 1948), 3–37.

without the poor growing poorer, that new amenities became available on a scale impossible to ignore, and that no measures then available would certainly have prevented the crash.[44] Most of the more recent economic history textbooks seem either to suggest a similar assessment or to avoid passing judgment altogether. Even the economic foreign policy of the twenties, long a favorite target of liberal historians, has been presented by Herbert Feis as a well-intentioned though ineffective forerunner of Point Four.[45] In 1955 John K. Galbraith, even in a book on the "Great Crash," took historians mildly to task for underrating what was good in the Coolidge era, and unfairly blaming Coolidge himself for a failure of prophecy.[46]

Such opposite kinds of writers as Peter Drucker, Frederick L. Allen, and the editors of *Fortune* have argued, without special reference to the twenties, that American capitalism since about the turn of the century has been evolving into a new kind of democratic and humane economic order.[47] Most recently David M. Potter concludes that we have always been the "People of Plenty" and that this fact, more than the frontier or political freedom, has shaped our mores.[48] Professor Potter, more sophisticated than earlier prophets of abundance, has learned from the social scientists that a country has to pay for production in competitive strain, and perhaps later for security in loss of mobility. Yet his perspective, like that deriving from our whole political and economic climate, shifts the meaning of the earlier prosperity era. If productivity holds much of the meaning of American history, it is the depression and not the twenties that marks the interruption in a steady development. The New Era represents at worst a promising try at a new economy, a chapter in a book with a happy ending.

There is much in this reassessment that is invigorating, especially in a period when the leftist clichés are the tiredest of all. Yet several cautions are in order. Historians must remember, first, that the early 1880's and the 1920's

---

[44] George Soule, *Prosperity Decade* (New York, 1947), especially p. 335.

[45] Herbert Feis, *The Diplomacy of the Dollar: First Era, 1919–1932* (Baltimore, 1950). I have not mentioned among the recent optimistic historians of the twenties Professor Frederic L. Paxson, whose detailed volume on the period is, by the author's design, as lacking in interpretative comment as it is possible for a book to be. Paxson's occasional generalizations, however, indicate that he did not regard the twenties as an interruption in the readjustment of the federal government to the facts of a changing life, "and even that a new pattern was developing in American society, a pattern which meant for many Americans a more open future." Frederic L. Paxson, *American Democracy and the World War* (3 vols., Boston and Berkeley, 1936–1948), Vol. III, *Postwar Years: Normalcy, 1918–1923*, introduction, 2.

[46] John K. Galbraith, *The Great Crash, 1929* (Boston, 1955), 608.

[47] Peter F. Drucker, *The New Society* (New York, 1949); The Editors of *Fortune*, *U. S. A.: The Permanent Revolution* (New York, 1951); Frederick L. Allen, *The Big Change* (New York, 1952). In the last two of these it is not altogether clear whether the twenties are a part of the fortunate development or a break in it.

[48] David M. Potter, *People of Plenty* (Chicago, 1954).

and the 1950's are different and separated periods of prosperity, no matter
how similar; second, that the depressions, even if in the long run temporary
interruptions, did not look that way to their victims; and third, that even
complete economic success does not, either now or for the twenties, refute all
criticisms of American culture.

There is little danger that we will altogether forget this last caution.
While some contemporary writers present a view of our recent history that
emphasizes economic success, to another group such success is not so much
false as irrelevant. The anti-optimists today are not rebels but traditionalists,
a group that can be lumped together as anti-materialist conservatives. Some
of these derive from and continue the new criticism, others reflect the revival
of theology, and still others rely partly on new scientific theory. All have been
led or forced, during the recent era of world catastrophe, to place their trust
not in secular progress but primarily in moral and religious tradition, and
from this standpoint the twenties are difficult to rehabilitate.

Joseph Wood Krutch has devoted a volume to repudiating the mechanistic determinism he voiced so powerfully in 1930, and Walter Lippmann
has even more specifically repudiated his early relativism. In 1955 Lippmann
concluded that the whole debacle in international politics, starting in 1917
and continuing through and after Versailles, resulted primarily from "the
growing incapacity of the large majority of the democratic peoples to believe
in intangible realities," specifically in a transcendent, universally valid, natural law.[49]

Many powerful contemporary writers agree with Lippmann not only in
his diagnosis of the trouble but in his fixing the responsibility for breakdown
in the 1920's. Some of these, however, find in the decade enough just men to
save it from complete condemnation. Russell Kirk, for instance, resurrects
the New Humanists and marvels that "these years of vulgarity and presump-
tion" produced the coming of an age of American conservatism in a group of
thinkers who struggled against "the vertiginous social current of the Harding and Coolidge and Hoover years." [50] (It marks perhaps the high point in
this reassessment to make Coolidge, rather than Freud or Einstein, a symbol
of vertigo.) A more subtle conservative and antimaterialist finds in the literary rebels the saving remnant. In his curious, dogmatic, but occasionally
suggestive *Yankees and God,* Chard Powers Smith suggests that the young
iconoclasts of the twenties were really the last, or next-to-the-last, wave of
Puritanism, despite their use of the term Puritan as the ultimate of abuse.[51]
This apparently bizarre thesis is really neither absurd nor entirely original.

---

[49] Joseph W. Krutch, *The Measure of Man* (New York, 1953); Walter Lippmann, *The
Public Philosophy* (Boston, 1955), 55.

[50] Russell Kirk, *The Conservative Mind* (Chicago, 1953), 362–63.

[51] Chard Powers Smith, *Yankees and God* (New York, 1954), 451–59.

Perry Miller in 1950 gave the rebels of the twenties a similarly respectable pedigree when he compared them to the transcendentalists. Both of these movements spoke for the spirit against the rule of things, and both, said Professor Miller, belonged in a series of "revolts by the youth of America against American philistinism." [52] One can go a very little further and agree with Mr. Smith that both are basically Protestant; it is not hard to recognize in the young intellectuals of the twenties together with their iconoclasm a tortured uneasiness, a conscious responsibility for the faults of the era that are suggestive of a long heritage.

In the 1950's, then, the familiar division continued. Spokesmen of the New Era rehabilitated the twenties by using one set of standards while antimaterialists blamed or praised them according to another. At the same time, however, a number of scholars of varying views were reaching toward an understanding of such paradoxes by treating the twenties as a period of profound social change. Most of these students derived their insights to some extent from the sociologists, and it is interesting that some of the gloomiest insights stem today from this once exuberant science. David Riesman's strikingly influential vision of the shift from inner-direction to other-direction is not strictly dated by its creator, but it often seems to be a description of the end of the genteel tradition and the birth of the New Era, the defeat of Wilsonian moralism and the victory of the Babbitts.[53] In different terms and with a more clearly stated value judgment, C. Wright Mills has documented the rise of a regimented, rootless, and docile new middle class to the arbitral position in American society.[54] The increase of the white-collar salariat and its implications extended before and after the twenties but went especially fast in that period, as the authors of *Recent Social Trends*, among others, pointed out. Samuel Lubell and others have seen another social change in the twenties, the beginning of the coming-of-age of the new immigration.[55] Drawing together Lubell's interpretation and Mills', Richard Hofstadter emphasizes the "Status Revolution" as a main event of the period about the turn of the century.[56] The Protestant upper middle class, long a semi-aristocracy with a monopoly on advanced education, had declined, and so had the independent farmers. In their places other groups had grown and gained some power —the new middle class, the ethnic minorities, and labor. All these processes of change had, by the twenties, proceeded a long way, and all were continuing and accelerating, with the partial exception of the rise of labor. Surely

---

[52] Perry Miller, *The Transcendentalists* (Cambridge, 1950), 8, 14–15.

[53] David Riesman, *The Lonely Crowd* (New Haven, 1950).

[54] C. Wright Mills, *White Collar* (New York, 1951).

[55] Samuel Lubell, *The Future of American Politics* (New York, 1953), 34–41.

[56] Richard Hofstadter, *The Age of Reform* (New York, 1955), 131–72.

this social upheaval, impossible to see clearly until our own time, has considerable meaning for the intellectual history of the twenties as for its politics, for the collapse, that is, of a long-frayed moral and literary tradition.

The nearest we can come to summarizing or explaining the shifting opinions of the twenties may well be to see the period in some such terms as these, and to see it as a disintegration. There is certainly nothing original about such a conclusion, but perhaps we are now in a position to give disintegration a fuller and more various meaning. The twenties were a period in which common values and common beliefs were replaced by separate and conflicting loyalties. One or another of the standards arising from the age itself has been used by each of its historians ever since. This is what has made their judgments so conflicting, so emotional, so severally valid and collectively confusing. It is equally true and equally partial to talk about the rising standard of living and the falling standard of political morality, the freshness and individuality of literature and the menace of conformity, the exuberance of manufacturers or social scientists and the despair of traditional philosophers. Somehow, we must learn to write history that includes all these, and the first step is to understand the decade when the fragmentation first became deep and obvious.

At least two recent writers are useful to those who want to look at the twenties from this point of view. One is Lionel Trilling, who deplores and analyzes the split between liberalism and the imagination, between the values we take for granted as socially desirable and those that have now the power to move us in art, between collective welfare and individual dignity.[57] What is lacking, says Trilling, and what has been lacking specifically since the twenties, is a view of the world, in his word a faith through not necessarily a religion, that will give meaning both to society and to art, to progress and to tragedy. Professor Henry Nash Smith in a recent address has sketched, somewhat similarly, two diametrically opposite points of view which, he says, have divided our culture since 1910.[58] One he calls the realistic-progressive view and the other the counter-enlightenment; one takes for its standards measurable welfare and humanitarian progress and equality; the other values only the individual imagination, nourished on tradition, holding out desperately against a mechanized culture, and accepting if necessary alienation and despair as the price of its survival.

The conflict of values that culminated, for it certainly did not begin, in the twenties was more than two-sided, and neither of these two critics has completely explored it. But they have indicated the right starting point. The

---

[57] Lionel Trilling, *The Liberal Imagination* (Pocket ed., New York, 1950 [first published, 1948]), especially pp. 97–106, 245–87.

[58] Henry Nash Smith, "The Reconstruction of Literary Values in the United States, 1900–1950" (unpublished manuscript, 1952).

way to understand our recent cultural history is to understand why and how
its exponents fail to agree.

How can historians proceed further along this path? First, it hardly
needs saying that to understand the twenties better we must make use of
techniques drawn from various fields. The most important developments in
the decade did not take place in the realms of politics, or economics, or literature, or science alone, but in all these areas and the relation, or lack of relation, among them. If one uses one kind of sources one will inevitably emerge
with one point of view, which will be inadequate to understand the others.

Second, it seems clear that one cannot say much about the twenties as a
disintegration or revolution without giving more attention to the old regime,
the presumed prewar agreement. There seems to have been a greater degree
of unity in American culture before 1917 or perhaps 1910, but a description of
it is not easy and a casual reference to the genteel tradition or the cultural
inheritance will not suffice. Immediately prewar America must be newly explored. We must look not so much at its articulate political or philosophical
beliefs and more at its inarticulate assumptions—assumptions in such areas
as morality, politics, class and race relations, popular art and literature, and
family life. In short, we must concentrate on what Tocqueville would have
called its manners. We are now, perhaps, in a position at least to undertake
this recapture in an impartial mood. In 1956 we do not need to lament or
rejoice at the destruction of the America of 1914; it is nearly as far off as
Greece or Rome, and as inevitably a part of us.

Third, we must try to look at the succeeding disintegration, the revolution of the twenties, with a similar absence of passion. The literary scoffers
who have been so thoroughly scolded were not, after all, the only rebels. The
prophets of mechanization and welfare, the Fords and Edisons who scorned
history and tradition, were equally revolutionary. Most revolutionary of all,
perhaps, were the prophets of psychology and social science, with their
brand new societies full of brand new human beings.

Finally, if we can really look back on this revolutionary decade from a
perspective which has the advantage of thirty years of continuing revolution,
we may be able to see which of the separate movements of the twenties has
lasted best, and whether any of them are beginning to come together. Are
there really in this decade of novelty beginnings as well as ends? Is it possible
by now really to glimpse what so many have announced: the beginnings of a
new period of American history and even of a new civilization?

SUGGESTED READING

Because historians are still struggling to gain a clear focus on the twenties, much of the intellectual history of the period is limited to particular
intellectuals or narrow movements. Among the most revealing studies

are Lucille Birnbaum's "Behaviorism in the 1920's," *American Quarterly*, VII (Spring, 1955), 15–30, a study first prepared in May's graduate seminar; Arthur Mizener's "The Novel in America: 1920–1940," *Perspectives USA*, XV (Spring, 1956), 134–47; Clarke A. Chambers' "The Belief in Progress in Twentieth-Century America," *Journal of the History of Ideas*, XIX (April, 1958), 198–224; and Warren Susman's "The Useless Past: American Intellectuals and the Frontier Image, 1910–1930," *Bucknell Review*, XI (March, 1963), 1–20. Alfred Kazin includes a fine analysis of the literature during the decade in *On Native Grounds* ° (Doubleday, 1942). Freud's early influence is briefly discussed in Celia Stendler's "New Ideas for Old: How Freudianism Was Received in the United States from 1900 to 1925," *Journal of Educational Psychology*, XXXVII (April, 1947), 193–206.

John Bradbury in *The Fugitives: A Critical Account* ° (Univ. of North Carolina Press, 1958) and Louise Cowan in *The Fugitive Group: A Literary History* ° (Louisiana State Univ. Press, 1959) analyze the Southern agrarians who opposed technology and the business culture. Paul Carter's *The Decline and Revival of the Social Gospel* (Cornell Univ. Press, 1956) should be supplemented by Robert M. Miller's *American Protestantism and Social Issues, 1919–1939* (Univ. of North Carolina Press, 1958) and Donald B. Meyer's *The Protestant Search for Political Realism, 1919–1940* (Univ. of California Press, 1960).

Carl Degler in "The Sociologist as Historian: Riesman's *The Lonely Crowd*," *American Quarterly*, XV (Winter, 1963), 483–97, argues, contrary to May's assumptions, that Riesman viewed "other-direction" as dominant long before the twenties. Cushing Strout in "A Note on Degler, Riesman and Tocqueville," *ibid.* (Spring, 1964), 100–02, disagrees, finding the twenties a likely "seed-bed for those emphases of style which *The Lonely Crowd* has identified so vividly."

Richard Hofstadter's *The Progressive Historians* (Knopf, 1968) is a study of Beard, Becker, and Turner. Other good sources on history in the twenties are Howard K. Beale, ed., *Charles A. Beard: A Critical Appraisal* (Univ. of Kentucky Press, 1955); John Higham *et al.*, *History: The Development of Historical Studies in the United States* ° (Prentice-Hall, 1965); and Cushing Strout, *The Pragmatic Revolt in American History: Carl Becker and Charles Beard* ° (Yale Univ. Press, 1958).

IRVING BERNSTEIN

The Worker in an
Unbalanced Society

INTRODUCTION

The American labor movement, after a burst of growth in World
War I, suffered an unexpected decline in the twenties. Membership
dropped from 5 million in 1920 to 3.6 million in 1923 and hovered
near that level for the rest of the decade. Effective unionization was
concentrated in a few industries—coal, railroads, construction,
and clothing. Labor organizations were largely or totally absent
from such newer and bitterly anti-union industries as rubber, electrical equipment, and automobiles and were ineffectual in such

FROM Irving Bernstein, *The Lean Years: Workers in an Unbalanced Society*, pp. 47–51,
53–67, 69–72, 75–76, 80–82. Copyright © 1960 by Irving Bernstein. Reprinted by
permission of the publisher, Houghton Mifflin Company, and the author. Song excerpt on
page 159 from *American Ballads and Folk Songs*, collected, adapted, and arranged by
John A. and Alan Lomax, copyright 1934 by John A. and Alan Lomax. Reprinted by permission of Alan Lomax. Song excerpt on pages 163–64 from *American Folksongs of
Protest* by John Greenway. Reprinted by permission of the University of Pennsylvania
Press.

older industries as steel and oil. Strikebreaking, crusades against the union shop, and welfare unionism all helped cut membership rolls. Divisions within the working class, the hostility of the courts to unions, improved technology, and unemployment also explain what once seemed to economists a paradox—the decline of unionism during a period of apparently general prosperity.

But as Irving Bernstein, historian of the twentieth-century American worker, makes clear in the essay reprinted below, the history of American labor is actually far broader than the history of the labor movement. Only recently, after freeing themselves from the long domination of John R. Commons and his associates, who concentrated on the labor movement, have American historians come to analyze the life, institutions, and conditions of the workingman.

The data are often fragmentary and the difficulties of analysis and historical reconstruction formidable in this undertaking. Ordinary workers leave little documentation; they are often simply names on tax lists and in census records. Despite the historical research of the past three decades on the life of the immigrant and the recent studies in urban history, scholars still know very little about the life—much less the aspirations and expectations—of workers at the broad base of American city populations. In spite of these difficulties, Bernstein is able to sketch the facts of poverty and unemployment among workers in the twenties and to reach certain conclusions about the absence of working-class consciousness.

The symbol of the twenties is gold. This was the age of the gold standard, a time when people with money slept with confidence: their banknotes were redeemable in the precious metal. Small boys received gold watches on ceremonial occasions, and little girls were given gold pieces as birthday gifts. The noted Philadelphia banking family, the Stotesburys, equipped their bathroom with gold fixtures ("You don't have to polish them you know"). Writing in gloomy 1932, the economist Frederick C. Mills spoke of the economy of the twenties as having "the aspects of a golden age." The historians Charles and Mary Beard titled the introductory chapter on the twenties of *America in Midpassage* "The Golden Glow." To a contemporary reader the title seemed just right.

Yet hindsight finds the image unfitting. The twenties were, indeed, golden, but only for a privileged segment of the American population. For the great mass of people whose welfare is the concern of this study—workers and their families—the appropriate metallic symbol may be nickel or copper or perhaps even tin, but certainly not gold. Although on the surface American workers appeared to share in the material advantages of the time, the serious maladjustments within the economic system fell upon them with disproportionate weight. This interplay between illusion and reality is a key to the period. In fact, this was a society in imbalance and workers enjoyed few of its benefits.

In the twenties two population changes occurred that were to prove profoundly significant to labor: the shift from farm to city speeded up and immigration from abroad slowed down. The American farmer's venerable propensity to move to town reached a climax. During the ten years from 1920 to 1929, according to the Department of Agriculture, 19,436,000 people made the trek; in every year except 1920 and 1921 over 2 million left the land, though many returned. The farm population, despite a higher fertility rate, declined by 3.7 per cent between 1920 and 1930 (31.6 to 30.4 million), while the nonfarm population rose by 24.6 per cent (74.1 to 92.3 million). Not only did these displaced husbandmen go to town; they appear to have gone to the big towns. Communities with over 100,000 grew by 32.4 per cent from 1920 to 1930, while those with 2500 to 5000 increased by only 7.6 per cent. Never before had the United States experienced such an immense flow from farm to city.

. . . . .

The impact of this movement upon labor can hardly be exaggerated. Employers, despite the drop in immigration from abroad, had at their disposal a great pool of workmen, particularly the unskilled and semiskilled. This large labor supply, inured to the low level of farm income, relieved an upward pressure on wage rates that might have occurred. Workers drawn from a rural background were accustomed to intermittency and so did not insist on regularity of employment. Although they adapted readily to machinery, they were without skills in the industrial sense. The fact that the price of skilled labor was high and of unskilled low induced management to substitute machines for craftsmen. The displaced farmers carried into industry the agricultural tradition of mobility, especially geographic and to a lesser extent occupational. They brought with them, as well, the conservative outlook and individualistic accent of the rural mind. Since they were predominantly of older stocks, their entry into the urban labor force had an Americanizing influence, reversing the tendency to ethnic diversity produced by the wave of immigration that preceded World War I. There was, however, one divisive element in this trend to homogeneity: the Negro's emergence on a large scale in the urban working class.

The unskilled rural Negro of the South won his foothold in northern industry during the war, particularly in the metalworking, auto, and meat industries. By 1923, for example, Ford had 5000 colored employees. In the early twenties the demand for this class of labor was brisk, but slacked off after 1924, when industry in the North achieved a labor supply equilibrium.

Some 1,200,000 Negroes migrated from South to North between 1915 and 1928. At this time the Negro took a long stride in the direction of integration with the dominant urban industrial society in America. Folklorists at the end of the twenties, for example, found a Negro cook in Houston singing:

> Niggers gittin' mo' like white folks,
> Mo' like white folks every day.
> Niggers learnin' Greek and Latin,
> Niggers wearin' silk and satin—
> Niggers gittin' mo' like white folks every day.

To the employer the agricultural influx was a blessing. The resulting surplus of labor gave him little cause to fear turnover; money wage rates were stable; and unionism was in the doldrums. To the labor movement the migration was a short-term disaster. In the economic and political context of the twenties this accretion to the urban labor force was unorganizable. For the economy as a whole the movement was, of course, both inevitable and desirable, but it carried a danger. With a larger number of people now wholly dependent upon wages and salaries, President Hoover's Committee on Social Trends noted, "any considerable and sustained interruption in their money income exposes them to hardships which they were in a better position to mitigate when they were members of an agricultural or rural community." [1]

. . . .

During the twenties declining immigration joined a falling birth rate to slow population growth, with the obvious implication for the labor force. As significant as the gross change was its selective character; the entry of unskilled labor from abroad was virtually halted, while the inflow of skilled workmen, for whom there was a considerable demand, was little impaired. The old American custom of employing the most recent immigrants to do the heaviest and dirtiest work had produced constant upward occupational mobility. Now it would be harder for the worker to rise and, by the same token, easier for him to develop class consciousness. Further, as Sumner H. Slichter pointed out, restriction required management to reverse its policy "to adapt jobs to men rather than men to jobs." Hence employers sought to use labor

---

[1] The basic data appear in *Historical Statistics*, 29, 31; National Resources Committee, *The Problems of a Changing Population* (Washington: 1938), 88; Harry Jerome, *Mechanization in Industry* (New York: National Bureau of Economic Research, 1934), 122–25; Edward E. Lewis, *The Mobility of the Negro* (New York: Columbia University Press, 1931), 131–32; National Urban League, *Negro Membership in American Labor Unions* (New York: National Urban League, 1930), 8; John A. and Alan Lomax, comps., *American Ballads and Folk Songs* (New York: Macmillan, 1934), xxx, *Recent Social Trends*, vol. 2, p. 806.

more efficiently. A key solution, of course, was mechanization, helping to explain the high rate of technological advance during the decade.[2]

. . . .

The conditions for mechanization were almost ideal: wages were high in relation to the price of machinery, immigration was limited, and the capital market was abundant and easy. These factors created—as the current phrase had it—the Machine Age. Eugene O'Neill wrote a play about it, *Dynamo*, as did Elmer Rice with *The Adding Machine*. The term "robot," exported from Czechoslovakia, became part of the American language.[3]

The march of machinery in the twenties affected almost every segment of the economy, and a few dramatic illustrations suggest its impact. In 1927 the introduction of continuous strip-sheet rolling opened a new era in sheet-steel and tin-plate production; a continuous mill had the capacity of forty to fifty hand mills. The Danner machine for glass tubing, first offered in 1917, completely replaced the hand process by 1925. The Ross carrier for handling lumber came into general use. The first successful machine to produce a complete cigar was patented in 1917; by 1930, 47 per cent of the 6.5 billion cigars turned out were made by machine. Mechanical coal-loading devices were widely accepted, while mine locomotives displaced the horse and the mule for haulage. Heavy construction was revolutionized by the power shovel, the belt and bucket conveyor, pneumatic tools, the concrete mixer, the dump truck, and the highway finishing machine. The street-railway industry converted to the one-man trolley. Several communication devices won general acceptance: the automatic switchboard and dial telephone, the teletype, and the market-quotation ticker. The motion picture industry entered a new phase with production of the first "talkie" in 1926. More important in the aggregate than these spectacular innovations, however, were the countless small changes which produced, for example, extraordinary increases in output in blast furnaces, in pulp and paper manufacture, in the automobile and rubber tire industries, and in beet sugar mills. Between 1919 and 1929, horsepower per wage earner in manufacturing shot up 50 per cent, in mines and quarries 60 per cent, and in steam railroads 74 per cent.[4]

---

[2] Preston William Slosson, *The Great Crusade and After, 1914–1928* (New York: Macmillan, 1930), 299–301; *Historical Statistics*, 33; "The U.S. Steel Corporation: III," *Fortune*, 13 (May 1936), 136; H. B. Butler, *Industrial Relations in the United States* (Geneva: International Labor Office, 1927), 14; Sumner H. Slichter, "The Current Labor Policies of American Industries," *QJE*, 43 (May 1929), 393.

[3] *The Daily Mail Trade Union Mission to the United States* (London: Daily Mail, [1927]), 81, 84. See also Parliament of the Commonwealth of Australia, *Report of the Industrial Delegation . . .* (Canberra: 1927), 16–17, and André Siegfried, *America Comes of Age* (New York: Harcourt, Brace, 1927), 149; Edward Bliss Reed, ed., *The Commonwealth Fund Fellows and Their Impressions of America* (New York: Commonwealth Fund, 1932), 90. The American employer is quoted in D. D. Lescohier, *What Is the Effect and Extent of Technical Changes on Employment Security?* (American Management Association, Personnel Series No. 1, 1930), 12.

[4] Jerome, *Mechanization, passim*.

Advancing technology was the principal cause of the extraordinary increase in productivity that occurred during the twenties. Between 1919 and 1929, output per man-hour rose 72 per cent in manufacturing, 33 per cent in railroads, and 41 per cent in mining. Put somewhat differently by David Weintraub, unit labor requirements (the number of man-hours required per unit of output) declined between 1920 and 1929 by 30 per cent in manufacturing, 20 per cent in railroads, 21 per cent in mining, and 14 per cent in telephone communications. Mills estimated that the physical volume of production for agriculture, raw materials, manufacturing, and construction climbed 34 per cent from 1922 to 1929, an average annual increment of 4.1 per cent. It was his impression that services, if they had been measurable, would have shown an even faster rate of growth. In fact, Americans generally were inclined to explain their economic society largely in terms of its mounting fruitfulness. When W. Wareing, an official of the British Amalgamated Engineering Union, asked John W. Lieb, vice-president of the Edison Company of New York, the secret of high wages, the reply came back promptly: "Productivity."

Rising output was the central force in the steady growth of national income during the twenties. Measured in current prices, which fluctuated narrowly, Simon Kuznets found that national income moved from $60.7 billion in 1922 to $87.2 billion in 1929, a gain of 43.7 per cent, or an average increment of 6.2 per cent per year. The share going to wages and salaries mounted from $36.4 billion to $51.5 billion, an increase of 41.5 per cent. The wage and salary proportion remained unusually constant at about 59 per cent of national income. The share of dividends rose more sharply from $3 billion in 1922 to $6.3 billion in 1929, up 110 per cent. This resulted in a relative increase in dividends from 5 per cent to 7.2 per cent of national income. Wage earners, in other words, did not enjoy as great a rise in income as did those in the higher brackets. A noted study by the Brookings Institution confirms this with respect to the wage and salary share, concluding that "since the war salaries have expanded much more rapidly than wages." [5]

The labor force that shared this national income entered a new phase in the twenties, a slowing rate of growth accompanied by a shift from manual to nonmanual employment. Immigration restriction joined with a falling birth rate to retard population advance. In contrast to a gain of 24 per cent in the first decade of the century, between 1920 and 1930 the number of people ten years old and over rose only 19 per cent.

---

[5] *Historical Statistics*, 71–72; David Weintraub, "Unemployment and Increasing Productivity," in National Resources Committee, *Technological Trends and National Policy* (Washington: 1937), 77; Frederick C. Mills, *Economic Tendencies in the United States* (New York: National Bureau of Economic Research, 1932), 243–51; *Daily Mail*, 21; Simon Kuznets, *National Income and Its Composition, 1919–1938* (New York: National Bureau of Economic Research, 1941), vol. 1, pp. 216–17; Maurice Leven, Harold G. Moulton, and Clark Warburton, *America's Capacity to Consume* (Washington: Brookings, 1934), 28.

More dramatic than slowing over-all growth was the marked movement from blue-collar to white-collar work, from physically productive to
overhead employment. The total number of gainful workers advanced from
41.6 to 48.8 million between 1920 and 1930, a gain of 17.4 per cent. Despite
this, the extractive industries—agriculture, forestry and fisheries, and mining—suffered a loss of 3.4 per cent, from 12.2 to 11.9 million persons. Similarly, the manufacturing labor force remained almost stationary, rising only
0.9 per cent from 10,890,000 in 1920 to 10,990,000 in 1930. By contrast, the
predominantly white-collar and service industries rose sharply. Trade,
finance and real estate, education, the other professions, domestic and personal service, and government employment climbed 45.7 per cent from 11.5
to 16.7 million.

The same pattern emerges when the analysis is transferred from industry to occupation. Between 1920 and 1930, the number of manual workers in
the labor force (farmers, farm laborers, skilled workers and foremen, semiskilled workers, and laborers) rose only 7.9 per cent from 28.5 to 30.7 million.
Nonmanual workers (professionals, wholesale and retail dealers, other proprietors, and clerks and kindred workers) advanced 38.1 per cent from 10.5 to
14.5 million. During the twenties, that is, the American worker on an increasing scale took off his overalls and put on a white shirt and necktie.

Or, put on an elegant frock, silk stockings, and high-heeled shoes, for
women entered the labor force at an accelerated pace at this time. The number of females fifteen and over gainfully occupied rose 27.4 per cent between
1920 and 1930, from 8.3 to 10.6 million. By the latter date, in fact, almost one
of every four persons in the labor force was a woman. In Middletown the
Lynds found that 89 per cent of the high school girls expected to work after
graduation, only 3 per cent indicating they definitely would not. This female
employment came as a jolt to foreigners, especially the British.

> It was a remarkable sight to see rows of bobbed, gum-chewing, spruce females
> seated on each side of a rapidly moving conveyor and so busily engaged with
> their work that not one of them had time to cast a passing glance upon the
> group of stalwart Britishers, who had considerable difficulty in following the
> movements of their nimble fingers.

Even more impressive was the 28.9 per cent increase between 1920 and 1930
in the number of employed married women, a rise from 1.9 to 3.1 million. In
Middletown the old rule that a girl quit her job with marriage broke down
under economic necessity in the twenties. A jobless husband or a need to
support a child's education forced working-class mothers into the factories,
shops, and offices. The female influx was another bar to organization. Even
women who intended to work permanently carried over a vestigial attitude
of impermanency that made them hesitant to take out union cards.

The decade of the twenties by contrast witnessed a decline in the employment of children. While in 1910 about one fourth of the boys aged ten to fifteen and one eighth of the girls of the same ages were employed, by 1930 the proportion of boys dropped to 6 per cent and of girls to 3 per cent. The Lynds found an almost total absence of child labor in Middletown. This great social advance was accompanied by a sharp rise in school attendance. The total increase at all levels of education exceeded 6 million between 1919 and 1928. The percentage of those between 14 and 17 enrolled in high school rose from 32 per cent in 1920 to 51 per cent in 1930. "If education is oftentimes taken for granted by the business class," wrote the Lynds, ". . . it evokes the fervor of a religion, a means of salvation, among a large section of the working class." There were many reasons for the decline in child labor: laws in most states fixing a minimum age for employment and compelling school attendance, the pressure of reform groups and organized labor, advancing mechanization, an adequate adult labor supply, and rising personnel standards in industry.

. . . .

The worker was seldom afforded the opportunity to rise in the social scale. He lacked the qualifications for the professions and the capital for business. His main hope for upward mobility was within the hierarchy of the firm that employed him. Even here, however, the opportunities were limited. In twenty-one months in 1923–24, plants employing 4240 workers in Middletown had only ten vacancies for foremen—one chance in 424. A businessman, the Lynds found, looked forward to the steady improvement of his lot. But, "once established in a particular job, the limitations fixing the possible range of advancement seem to be narrower for an industrial worker." His position, of course, was more dismal if he happened to be a member of a minority group. In greater or lesser degree, the Irish, the Italians, the Jews, the Mexicans, and the Negroes suffered in the labor market. To dwell only upon the last, the ones who probably enjoyed the doubtful distinction of sustaining the most severe discrimination: Negroes were the last to be hired and the first to be fired, were seldom allowed to do skilled work and almost never given supervisory jobs, were assigned the older, dirtier, and less pleasant work places, were paid less for the same work, and were often denied membership in labor unions. A Negro song of protest went this way:

Trouble, trouble, had it all mah day.
. . . .
Cain't pawn no diamonds,
Can't pawn no clo'
An' boss man told me,
Can't use me no mo'.

Rather get me a job, like white folks do.
Rather get me a job, like white folks do.

Trampin' 'round all day,
Say, "Nigger, nothin' fo' you." [6]

This complaint could have been voiced as well by white members of the labor force, since the prosperity of the twenties was accompanied by heavy unemployment. Foreign observers reported more men than jobs in each locality they visited. The absence of government statistics, disgraceful in itself, makes it impossible to report the actual volume of joblessness. Evidence that severe unemployment existed, however, is beyond dispute. The noted Brookings Institution study, *America's Capacity to Produce*, estimated that the economy in 1929 operated at only 80 per cent of its practical capacity. Weintraub calculated that the jobless constituted 13 per cent of the labor force in 1924 and 1925, 11 per cent in 1926, 12 per cent in 1927, 13 per cent in 1928, and 10 per cent in 1929. Woodlief Thomas made minimum unemployment estimates for nonagricultural industries of 7.7 per cent in 1924, 5.7 per cent in 1925, 5.2 per cent in 1926, and 6.3 per cent in 1927.

．　．　．　．

So severe, in fact, was unemployment during the decade that social workers, burdened with the misery that followed in its wake, became alarmed. The International Conference of Settlements, meeting at Amsterdam in 1928, heard the Belgian economist Henri de Man claim that industrialism produced both more goods and more permanently unemployed. The National Federation of Settlements, convening in Boston that same year, found that unemployment was the prime enemy of the American family. Nor were all employers as callous as those in Middletown. It was on December 17, 1928, that President Daniel Willard of the Baltimore & Ohio made his famous statement before the Couzens Committee:

> It is a dangerous thing to have a large number of unemployed men and women—dangerous to society as a whole—dangerous to the individuals who constitute society. When men who are willing and able to work and want to work are unable to obtain work, we need not be surprised if they steal before they starve. Certainly I do not approve of stealing, but if I had to make a choice between stealing and starving, I would surely not choose to starve— and in that respect I do not think I am unlike the average individual.

The least onerous form of unemployment—seasonal—worsened during the twenties. Mild government pressure to regularize production in those trades noted for intermittency—construction, garments, maritime, and entertainment—had no noticeable effect. In addition, the great new automo-

---

[6] Lynds, *Middletown*, 48, 68; Herman Feldman, *Racial Factors in American Industry* (New York: Harper, 1931), ch. 2; John Greenway, *American Folksongs of Protest* (Philadelphia: University of Pennsylvania Press, 1953), 113.

tive industry and its suppliers contributed heavily to seasonality. "Because of the ease with which labour can be obtained and discarded," an Australian observed, "there is little necessity for the employer to stabilize his rate of production over the year."

Far more serious was technological unemployment, the price paid for progress. A paradox of the American economy in the twenties was that its glittering technical achievement gave birth to a dismal social failure. At the top of the boom in 1929 Wesley Mitchell wrote that technological unemployment "is a matter of the gravest concern in view of the millions of families affected or threatened . . . and in view of their slender resources." Weintraub estimated that between 1920 and 1929 in manufacturing, railways, and coal mining, machines displaced 3,272,000 men, of whom 2,269,000 were reabsorbed and 1,003,000 remained unemployed. There were, naturally, sharp variations in employment impact among industries. This is evident from Jerome's figure on labor time saved by particular machines: talkies saved 50 per cent, cigar machines 50 to 60 per cent, the Banbury mixer 50 per cent, the highway finishing machine 40 to 60 per cent, and various coal loaders 25 to 50 per cent.

. . . Jerome found that mechanization had a differential impact in various segments of the industrial process: in material handling it displaced the unskilled; in systematizing the flow of production it reduced the skilled; in displacing manual by machine processing it usually diluted skills; in improving already mechanized operations it cut down on the semiskilled; in stimulating machine construction and repair it increased the demand for the skilled. A workman taking a job in the twenties had little way of knowing whether his skills would improve or decline; he could be reasonably certain, however, that a machine would soon change the content of his job.

.   .   .   .   .

Labor's burden in this period of prosperity was not limited to unemployment; workers faced as well an unequal distribution of income. There were in 1929, the Brookings Institution found, 27,474,000 families of two or more persons. Nearly 6 million families, over 21 per cent, received less than $1000 per year; about 12 million, more than 42 per cent (including those below $1000), had incomes under $1500; nearly 20 million, 71 per cent (including those under $1500), took in less than $2500. The combined incomes of 0.1 per cent of the families at the top of the scale were as great as those of the 42 per cent at the bottom. The number who received over $1 million per year rose from 65 in 1919 to 513 in 1929. The distorted distribution of savings was even more striking. The 21,546,000 families at the low end, 78.4 per cent, had no aggregate savings at all, while the 24,000 families at the high end, 0.9 per cent, provided 34 per cent of total savings. The authors of *America's Capacity to Consume* went further:

It appears . . . that . . . income was being distributed with increasing inequality, particularly in the later years of the period. While the proportion of
high incomes was incréasing . . . there is evidence that the income of those
at the very top was increasing still more rapidly. That is to say, in the late
twenties a larger percentage of the total income was received by the portion of
the population having very high incomes than had been the case a decade
earlier.

Inequality in distribution exerted a constant pressure upon those at the
bottom of the scale to supplement the head of family's job earnings. A study
of federal workers in five cities in 1928 with salaries not in excess of $2500
showed that 15 to 33 per cent of the husbands took outside work, 15 to 32 per
cent of the wives got jobs, and many children contributed to family income.
Only 2 to 10 per cent of the families lived within the husband's government
salary.

Even in the relatively prosperous year 1929 a majority of workers' families failed to enjoy an "American standard of living." This conclusion cannot
be substantiated precisely, because the government made no survey of workers' budgets between 1919 and the mid-thirties, another illustration of the
sorry state of labor statistics. The most careful contemporary student of the
problem, Paul Douglas, made estimates for larger cities that can be keyed in
roughly with the family income distribution published in *America's Capacity to Consume.* Though Douglas' work, *Wages and the Family,* appeared in
1925 it is not inapplicable to 1929, because retail prices fluctuated fairly narrowly.

Douglas set out four standards of living: poverty, minimum subsistence, minimum health and decency, and minimum comfort ("the American
standard"). At the poverty level the family would have an inadequate diet,
overcrowding, and no resources for unexpected expenses. This would cost a
family of five $1000 to $1100. In 1929 there were 5,899,000 families of two or
more with incomes of less than $1000. The minimum subsistence level was
sufficient to meet physical needs with nothing left over for emergencies or
pleasures. To reach it a family of five needed $1100 to $1400. There were
11,653,000 families of two or more who received less than $1500. The mini-
mum health and decency level supplied adequate food, housing, and clothing as well as a modest balance for recreation. It cost $1500 to $1800. There
were 16,354,000 families with incomes under $2000. Since "the American
standard" required an income of $2000 to $2400, it seems safe to conclude
that the majority of wage earners' families failed to reach this level.

Income inequality and the relatively low standard of living of American workers, however, did not arouse social protest. There were two principal reasons for this silence. The first, doubtless the more important, was that
the material well-being of the employed sector of the labor force was improving. Lincoln Steffens wrote in 1929: "Big business in America is producing
what the Socialists held up as their goal: food, shelter and clothing for all."

Douglas estimated that the average annual earnings of employed workers in all industries, including agriculture, advanced from $1288 in 1923 to $1405 in 1928, a gain of 9.1 per cent. Their real annual earnings improved slightly more, 10.9 per cent. The movement of wages, money and real, actually understates the impact of the rising standard of life because it fails to account for either the diversity of items on which income was spent or the benefits available free. In the twenties consumption broadened markedly to encompass goods and services that made life easier and more diverting—automobiles, telephones, radios, movies, washing machines, vacuum cleaners, and electric iceboxes, as well as improved medicine, hospitalization, and life insurance. The growth of installment buying made the consumer durables available to many with small cash resources. To a limited extent workers were able to share in this advance; ownership of a Model T, even if shared with the finance company, was more than entertaining: it inclined one to accept things as they were. In addition, all segments of the population benefited from the sharp improvement in free social services, most notably education, but including also public libraries, playgrounds and parks, and public health facilities.

The other reason for the failure of social protest to emerge was that the standard of living of American workmen, regardless of its deficiencies, was among the highest in the world, a consideration of no mean importance to urban masses who were largely immigrants themselves or the children of immigrants. Foreign observers visiting this country were, on the whole, impressed with the differential in living standards between the United States and their own nations. "Taken all in all," André Siegfried remarked, "the American worker is in a unique position." [7]

The uniqueness of the American worker's position in the late twenties with respect to wages, hours, and conditions of employment deserves examination. In so far as wages are concerned, it is necessary to note again the

---

[7] Leven, *et al.*, *America's Capacity*, 54–56, 93, 103–4; "Cost of Living of Federal Employees in Five Cities," MLR, 29 (Aug. 1929), 315; Paul H. Douglas, *Wages and the Family* (Chicago: University of Chicago Press, 1925), 5–6; Steffens to Jo Davidson, Feb. 18, 1929, in *Letters of Lincoln Steffens*, Ella Winter and Granville Hicks, eds. (New York: Harcourt, Brace, 1938), vol. 2, p. 830; Paul H. Douglas, *Real Wages in the United States, 1890–1926* (Boston: Houghton Mifflin, 1930), 391; Paul H. Douglas and Florence Tye Jennison, *The Movement of Money and Real Earnings in the United States, 1926–28* (Chicago: University of Chicago Press, 1930), 27. Wages in 1929 differed little from 1928 figures. Annual earnings in manufacturing rose to $1341 in 1929 from $1325 in 1928. Since the cost of living also advanced, by one point, real wages rose by a fraction of 1 per cent. Paul H. Douglas and Charles J. Coe, "Earnings," *American Journal of Sociology*, 35 (May, 1930), 935–39; *Recent Economic Changes*, vol. 1, pp. 60–67, 325; *Recent Social Trends*, vol. 2, pp. 827, 858–89, 915–26; Siegfried, *America Comes of Age*, 159. See also *Daily Mail*, 23. Some of the British made the admission more cautiously, while an Australian stated flatly that real wages were higher in his country. *Report of the Delegation Appointed to Study Industrial Conditions in . . . the United States*, Cmd. 2833 (Mar. 1927), 33; Adam, *An Australian*, 46.

inadequacy of the statistics. Though they are superior to those for employment, the data leave much to be desired. Those who doubt this statement are referred to the preface of Douglas' *Real Wages in the United States, 1890–1926* for an account of the extraordinary expenditure of energy demanded of the serious student of wages at that time. To this must be added some reluctance by employers, the prime source, to reveal how much they paid their workers.

During the prosperity of the twenties wages, money and real, moved gently upward. Unlike the two preceding periods of good times, the turn of the century and the first war, there was no sharp rise. In fact, wages in the era 1923–29 were characteristically stable, reflecting the surplus of labor and weak unions.

Average hourly earnings in all industries, according to Douglas, advanced from 66.2¢ in 1923 to 71¢ in 1928. A survey of 1500 manufacturing plants by the National Industrial Conference Board revealed that their average hourly earnings moved from 54¢ in 1923 to 58.1¢ in 1929. Hourly earnings in bituminous coal fell from 84.5¢ in 1923 to 68.1¢ in 1929. Railroad earnings moved from 56.5¢ in 1923 to 62.5¢ in 1929. The average hourly earnings of common laborers in the basic steel industry were 41.7¢ in 1923 and 41.4¢ in 1929. The average daily wages without board of farm laborers were $2.25 in both years.

Weekly earnings, according to the same sources, were cut from a similar pattern. The Douglas figures for all industries were $30.39 in 1923 and $33.32 in 1928. The NICB series for manufacturing advanced from $26.54 in 1923 to $28.24 in 1929. Weekly earnings in bituminous coal were virtually unchanged, $25.60 in 1923 and $25.72 in 1929. On the railroads there was a rise from $26.65 in 1923 to $28.49 in 1929. Farm wages without board per month were $48.25 in 1923 and $51.22 in 1929.

The movement in real wages was little different since the Bureau of Labor Statistics Cost of Living Index showed virtually no change in the terminal years. Real hourly earnings in all industries, Douglas found, rose 7.2 per cent between 1923 and 1928, while real weekly earnings, reflecting some drop in hours, advanced only 2.5 per cent. The NICB, covering real earnings in manufacturing at the end of the period, found that hourly rose 2.1 per cent and weekly 0.7 per cent between the opening quarter of 1928 and final quarter of 1929.

. . . .

[A] differential of note in the twenties was that between union and nonunion rates. Although it is not possible to measure this spread statistically, its existence is beyond question. Douglas, for example, calculated average hourly earnings in 1926 for the following predominantly organized industries: building trades $1.313, granite and stone $1.301, newspaper printing $1.150, book and job printing $1.037, planing mills $1.027, metal trades 96.1¢, baking 92.5¢, and bituminous coal 71.9¢. By contrast, earnings in the following mainly nonunion manufacturing industries in 1926 were: steel 63.7¢, shoes 52.8¢, meat packing 49.4¢, woolens 49.1¢, sawmills 36.1¢, and cotton 32.8¢. An Australian delegation which visited the United States in 1927 concluded that unions had a substantial effect in keeping nonunion rates from falling, since employers feared that wage cuts would lead to organization. This differential, like the others, widened during the twenties. That is, some unions, particularly in the building trades, pushed wages up more rapidly than did the employers of unorganized workers. A study by Frederick C. Mills of the annual rate of advance in nine wage series between 1922 and 1929 planned union wages in the lead. Trade unions, though on the defensive at this time, succeeded in maintaining and even improving wage differentials over unorganized workers, another illustration of the inequity of income distribution inasmuch as union membership was heavily weighted by the skilled.

· · · ·

The stickiness of money and real wages between 1923 and 1929, at a time when productivity was rising dramatically, had an unhealthy effect upon the economy as a whole. As Douglas observed, "This failure of real wages to advance was at least one cause of the rising profits during this period, and was consequently an appreciable factor in the extraordinary increase of stock market values which occurred." Between 1923 and 1929, according to Simon Kuznets, the dividend component of national income rose 64.1 per cent while wages and salaries advanced only 20.6 per cent. The cases of U.S. Steel and Toledo-Edison are instructive. While hourly earnings in Big Steel rose modestly and weekly earnings fell, profits almost doubled between 1923 and 1929. Toledo-Edison's net earnings advanced from $2.8 million in 1925 to $4.5 million in 1929; no general wage increase was granted during this period. Noting the sharp rise in profit margins, Mills commented, "An ultimate explanation of the economic collapse which was precipitated in 1929 must give full weight to this striking fact." [8]

· · · ·

Although there was a good deal of talk in the twenties about shortening the work week, almost no one did anything about it. The steel industry, in the face of public condemnation of the twelve-hour day during the 1919 strike, improved hours early in the decade. Yet in 1929 average full-time weekly hours were still 54.6, and 14 per cent of steel employees customarily worked in excess of sixty hours. The AFL endorsed the five-day week in 1926 but made no effort to achieve it. In January 1928 the Clothing Workers sought the forty-hour week in the Chicago and Rochester markets without success. The railway unions, disturbed over technological unemployment, came out

---

[8] NICB, *Wages . . . 1914–1929*, 201; Butler, *Industrial Relations*, 37; Douglas, *Real Wages*, 590; Kuznets, *National Income*, 332–33, 352–53; U.S. Steel Corp., *Annual Report, 1955*, 30–31; Charles P. Taft, 2d, to Martin Egan, June 7, 1934, Record Group No. 25, National Archives; Mills, *Economic Tendencies*, 404.

for the eight-hour day and the five-day week in April 1929, but accomplished nothing. The notable gains were made by the decade's most prominent anti-Semite, Henry Ford, and the Jewish Sabbath Alliance. Ford inaugurated the five-day week in his plants in 1926, and the Alliance persuaded a matzoth factory to institute this schedule shortly afterward. A survey in 1928 uncovered only 216,000 workers on five days, many of them working as many hours as they had on the six-day week. The only general improvement that occurred was the five-and-one-half-day week; the Lynds found that the Saturday half holiday prevailed in Middletown.

Unions, excepting the case of Ford, were mainly responsible for these modest gains. Further, organized workers enjoyed a marked superiority in hours of work. Douglas found that in 1926 average weekly hours in six primarily union manufacturing industries were 45.9 in contrast with 52.2 in the eight predominantly nonunion industries he studied.

The economic significance of stability of hours at a high level in the face of rising productivity is much the same as that for wages. Advancing technology permitted a sharp reduction in the work week; with spotty exceptions, no gains were made. Nor is there any evidence that American workers, as distinguished from unions, sought shorter hours. As an Australian observer remarked:

> I think that the most striking thing about labor in America is that it has become the slave of the paymaster. In Australia men value their hours of leisure too highly to sell them for any wages. In America men can be got to work . . . for almost any hours if it means extra pay.[9]

. . . . .

The urban worker without effective means of voicing his grievances within the shop began to express them haltingly by indirection in his vote. The inadequacy of the statistics measuring the economic lot of labor in the twenties is compounded in an attempt to assess political behavior, for the election results afford no precise way of separating voters who were workers from those who were not. Nor did the 1928 presidential election, the basis of the present analysis of workers' political attitudes, provide evidence of a labor vote as such.

The presidential race in which Herbert Hoover decisively defeated Alfred Smith has been conventionally regarded as a triumph for the *status quo*,

---

[9] Douglas, *Real Wages*, 112–16, 208; Solomon Fabricant, *Employment in Manufacturing, 1899–1939* (New York: National Bureau of Economic Research, 1942), 234; Lazare Teper, *Hours of Labor* (Baltimore: Johns Hopkins University Press, 1932), 35; BLS, Bull. No. 513, *Wages and Hours*, 4; "Hours of Labor and the 7-Day Week in the Iron and Steel Industry," *MLR*, 30 (June 1930), 184–85; Marion Cotter Cahill, *Shorter Hours: A Study of the Movement Since the Civil War* (New York: Columbia University Press, 1932), *passim;* "Extent of the Five-Day Week in Manufacturing," *MLR*, 30 (Feb. 1930), 368; Lynds, *Middletown*, 54; Adam, *An Australian*, 117–18.

an election in which the voters of the nation reaffirmed their approval of the happy marriage between the Republican Party and Coolidge prosperity. As a Hoover campaign card put it:

HARD TIMES
Always come when Democrats try to run the nation.
ASK DAD—HE KNOWS!
Take No Chances!
Vote a Straight Republican Ticket!!

To be sure, domestic bliss was ruffled by two seemingly extraneous issues: prohibition and Al Smith's Catholicism. According to the usual view of the election, the "real" issues of the day—the fragility of prosperity, the sorry plight of coal and textiles, the farm depression, and the inequities in income distribution—were largely ignored.

Reassessment of the 1928 election against the backdrop of political developments in the thirties has placed it not at the close of an old era but rather at the onset of a new one. There can be no doubt of the soundness of this approach and its relevance to the present study.

The central emerging force in American political society at this time was what Samuel Lubell has called the revolt of the city. The 1920 census was the first to show that a majority of the people in the United States lived in urban areas. The immense movement of population to the cities came primarily from immigration and secondarily from agrarian regions, largely the Appalachian area and the South. Both streams flowed into the urban working class and contributed to its growth by a much higher birth rate than that characteristic of the older stocks that formed the backbone of the middle class and the Republican Party. Between 1920 and 1928 some 17 million potential voters reached the age of twenty-one, mainly the children of poor immigrants and migrants to the cities. To them, Lubell has observed, "the loyalties of Appomattox and the Homestead Act were details in history books"; nor did they owe allegiance to the individualistic tradition of the farm and the small town.

The 1928 presidential election was the first in which this emergent force became evident, but it was not as sharply defined as it was to become later, reflecting the crosscurrents of a transition phase. In part the conflict was between city and farm, in part between the ethnic strains of the "new" immigration pressing for status against the older Anglo-Saxon and northern European stocks, in part between Catholics and to a lesser extent Jews pushing into a dominantly Protestant society, and in part between the working and middle classes. Where the new forces joined, as in Boston, the Democrats made sweeping gains by virtue of the coincidence of urbanism, Irish Catholicism, and the working class. Where they were blurred, as in Los Angeles, the Democrats made only slight advances because urbanism was diluted by transplanted midwestern farmers who were mainly old stock Protestants and were without a working-class outlook.

. . . .

In conclusion, city workers and coal miners, their numbers growing prodigiously, began in the twenties that great movement into the Democratic Party that was to become so critical a feature of American politics in the following decade. In large part this voting shift spoke with the voice of protest. But the grievances of labor in 1928 were primarily related to status, ethnic and religious minorities yearning for equality. In lesser part the complaints were economic. With the crash and the Great Depression that followed, economic protest became the cutting edge of politics; at that time American labor was simply to reaffirm in larger measure the political choice it had already made.

By way of postscript for 1928 it is necessary to chart the dismal labor showing of the Marxist parties. Norman Thomas on the Socialist ticket polled only 268,000 votes, more than a third of them in New York. He ran far behind Debs's 902,000 in 1920. The Communists, led by William Z. Foster, did much worse, winning only 48,000 adherents. American labor, obviously, showed little inclination to choose either of these parties as the vehicle of protest.[10]

Although the 1928 election was a portent for the future, its contemporary significance for labor lay in the fact that Hoover and the Republican Party scored a signal victory. This could not have occurred unless many workers had voted for Hoover, and their willingness to do so is suggestive of their social outlook at the end of the twenties.

Observers were struck with the materialism that permeated all levels of American society, including labor; workers shared with their bosses a devout reverence for the almighty dollar. In Middletown workmen derived little satisfaction from their work. "There isn't twenty-five per cent of me paying attention to the job," a bench molder stated. Since this frustration was linked to a dim prospect for advancement as workers, the more energetic strove to enter the middle class. The acquisition of money was the main objective of life, and people were measured by the externals money bought—where they lived, how they lived, the make of car they drove. In the shops, workers were more concerned with maximizing income than with learning skills or gaining leisure by shorter hours.

Inasmuch as this materialism was joined to a vestigial rural tradition of individualism as well as a heterogeneous labor force, trade unionism found the social climate forbidding. As Lewis L. Lorwin pointed out, "The desire for steady employment and higher earnings became more dominant in the minds of the workers than the feeling for industrial freedom and independence."

---

[10] Peel and Donnelly, *1928 Campaign,* 171.

Among the workers who benefited economically the mood was conservative. "The American workman," a French visitor observed, "when he realizes that society assures him a comfortable income, is ready to accept the existing organization of industry. He has made an excellent place for himself . . . so he has no wish to destroy it by stirring up a revolution." From the standpoint of social outlook Douglas emphasized the direction rather than the amount of change in real wages. The fact that the lot of the workers was improving rather than deteriorating made them "more satisfied with the social and political system." "Arise ye wretched of the earth," the appeal of the "Internationale," he found "curiously unreal to the better-paid American workers who, with few exceptions, are not afflicted with starvation, and the more skilled of whom own automobiles, radio sets, small homes, and bank books, as well as chains." [11]

This comment by Douglas raises a question: Did a working "class" emerge? Manipulations of census data are not significant because the problem is in the realm of ideas rather than of statistics. The answer is two-headed and, in a sense, internally contradictory. On the one hand, a growing proportion of the labor force found itself in an employee rather than a self-employed status, a fact of immense importance in the daily lives of the people involved. On the other hand, they failed to develop class consciousness—self-realization as a proletariat—in the Marxist sense.

This dichotomy formed the central finding of *Middletown:*

> It is . . . this division into working class and business class that constitutes the outstanding cleavage in Middletown. The mere fact of being born upon one or the other side of the watershed roughly formed by these two groups is the most significant single cultural factor tending to influence what one does all day long throughout one's life; whom one marries; when one gets up in the morning; whether one belongs to the Holy Roller or Presbyterian church; or drives a Ford or a Buick; whether or not one's daughter makes the desirable high school Violet Club; or one's wife meets with the Sew We Do Club or with the Art Students' League; whether one belongs to the Odd Fellows or to the Masonic Shrine; whether one sits about evenings with one's necktie off; and so on indefinitely throughout the daily comings and goings of a Middletown man, woman, or child.

Yet, search as they did, the Lynds failed to find evidence of working-class consciousness. Radical movements had no influence; left-wing publications were virtually unknown; and even the relatively conservative AFL struggled merely to survive. Though the great majority of workers were destined to remain workers for the duration of their productive lives, many were sus-

---

[11] Lynds, *Middletown*, 75; Lewis L. Lorwin, *The American Federation of Labor* (Washington: Brookings, 1933), 239; Siegfried, *America Comes of Age*, 165; Douglas, *Real Wages*, 572–74.

tained by the hope of rising to a higher class. Large majorities of high school boys and girls, for example, could find nothing upsetting in the fact that some people were rich. If the collectivity of workers constituted a "class," it was an inert body with little dynamism or direction.[12] The labor movement reflected this inertia.

SUGGESTED READING

Aside from the reminiscences of workers, the records of scattered social organizations, and such studies as the Lynds' *Middletown*,° (Harcourt, Brace & World, 1967), historians have little basis for conclusions about class consciousness and social aspirations of workers in the twenties. Even reliance on content analysis of popular literature cannot definitively answer such questions as whether the Horatio Alger myth constituted part of the worker's system of beliefs or whether it was simply a symbolic source of escape. Leo Lowenthal's study, "Biographies in Popular Magazines," reprinted without much change in his *Literature, Popular Culture, and Society* (Prentice-Hall, 1961), suggests the possibilities of content analysis.

The literature on the economy of the twenties is ample. George Soule's *Prosperity Decade; From War to Depression: 1917–1929* (Holt, Rinehart & Winston, 1947) is an adequate survey of the decade. Joseph Schumpeter's "The American Economy in the Interwar Period: The Decade of the Twenties," *American Economic Review*, XXXVI (May, 1946), 1–10, provides useful commentary.

Philip Taft's *The A. F. of L. in the Time of Gompers* (Harper & Row, 1957) and *The A. F. of L. from the Death of Gompers to the Merger* (Harper & Row, 1959) are still the best volumes on the federation in this period. David Brody's *Labor in Crisis: The Steel Strike of 1919* (Lippincott, 1962), though dealing with a slightly earlier period, is a better source on labor history and the workingman. Henry Pelling's *American Labor* (Univ. of Chicago Press, 1960) has a brief chapter on organized labor entitled "Suffering from Prosperity."

Valuable contemporary essays include Sumner Slichter's "The Current Labor Policies of American Industries," *Quarterly Journal of Economics*, XLIII (May, 1929), 393–435; David Saposs' "The American Labor Movement Since the War," *ibid.* (Feb., 1935), 236–54; and Lyle Cooper's "The American Labor Movement in Prosperity and Depression," *American Economic Review*, XXII (Dec., 1932), 641–59.

---

[12] See Tillman M. Sogge, "Industrial Classes in the United States in 1930," *JASA*, 28 (June 1933), 199–203; Lynds, *Middletown*, 23–24.

EDMUND DAVID CRONON

Black Moses:
Marcus Garvey and Garveyism

INTRODUCTION

Until the 1960's, when Malcolm X and Martin Luther King sought to lead them to the "promised land," no Negro leader had been more successful among the nation's black citizens than Marcus Garvey. A Jamaican-born Negro, he came to the United States in 1916 at age twenty-eight to establish branches of his Universal Negro Improvement Association. Within a few years his fame was worldwide and his popularity among Negroes unmatched. Though the records are scanty and his organization's claims of membership obviously inflated, the UNIA probably had more than 75,000 members, and his admirers undoubtedly numbered above a million.

FROM Edmund David Cronon, *Black Moses: The Story of Marcus Garvey and the Universal Negro Improvement Association*, the University of Wisconsin Press, 1955, pp. 170–201. Reprinted by permission of the copyright owners, the Regents of the University of Wisconsin.

Garvey's followers were probably ghetto blacks who had been lured north by the promise of better jobs. Finding bitter discrimination, violence, squalor, and injustice, these Negroes turned to Garvey for some dignity and purpose and for a sense of participation in achievements that had seemed beyond them. His Black Star shipping line and other commercial ventures symbolized the new power and potential of black men. His call for a return to Africa renewed their pride in their own past. "Up you mighty race, you can accomplish what you will," he declared to his fellow black men. Garvey counseled as desirable what was then a fact of American life—Negro segregation; in this respect his program coincided to some extent with that of Booker T. Washington, who had publicly accepted racial segregation and stressed self-help.

Garvey's values and program, however, directly conflicted with the integrationist aims of the middle-class NAACP and of men like W. E. B. DuBois and A. Philip Randolph. Prodded by Randolph and other of Garvey's opponents, the Justice Department prosecuted him for mail fraud. He served two years of a five-year sentence before Calvin Coolidge commuted his sentence in 1927. When he was released from prison, deportation (on the grounds that he was not an American citizen and had been convicted of a felony) cut him off from his American base. Quarrels with associates split the UNIA, already weakened by Garvey's bad business practices and his jail term. In the Depression decade he struggled to rebuild the shattered movement, but he found less enthusiasm outside the United States than he had among America's black citizens. After meeting rebuffs in his native Jamaica, he moved to London, where he died in 1940 after trying unsuccessfully to revive the movement.

The appeal of Garveyism has not yet been adequately investigated by historians. Garvey's successes and failures have been sketched, but the dynamics of his movement and the favorable responses it evoked remain largely unexamined. In *From Plantation to Ghetto* (Hill & Wang, 1966), August Meier and Elliot Rudwick suggest that Garvey's movement "provided a compensatory escape for Negroes to whom the urban promised land had turned out to be a hopeless ghetto." And they further point out that "the peaks of interest in African colonization among Negroes since the Civil War coincided with the peaks of domestic migration—in the late 1870's, around 1890, and again on the eve of the First World War."

Perhaps, as Oscar Handlin has suggested, Garveyism should be understood as part of the larger movement in which hyphenated Americans, finding their sense of identity upset by the nationalisms provoked by war abroad and the one-hundred percent Americanism at home, formed organizations to reestablish their identity and affirm their pride. Perhaps, also, if Garveyism is viewed as an "internal migration" (of the mind), a study of the impulses behind it would reveal that it continued in transmuted and perverted form in the storefront churches and movements in the thirties that gave to Negroes a sense of purpose in a nation that disregarded them.

Before the civil rights revolution of the 1960's, American historians had generally disregarded Negro history. Only in recent years have they sought to move beyond the study of race relations to examine the American Negro's life, communities, institutions, and values. And only in the mid-1960's did historians more generally come to focus on earlier movements of black nationalism and black separatism, which are in important ways linked to the Black Power movement and the questioning by some disaffected blacks of whether racial integration in America is possible or desirable.

In the year after *Brown v. Board of Education* (1954), when the vision of racial integration was unchallenged among American white liberals and Negro organizations, E. David Cronon published his *Black Moses: The Study of Marcus Garvey and the Universal Negro Improvement Association.* The following selection from that book is his analysis of Garvey's philosophy of black nationalism.

Each race should be proud and stick to its own,
And the best of what they are should be shown;
This is no shallow song of hate to sing,
But over Blacks there should be no white king.

Every man on his own foothold should stand,
Claiming a nation and a fatherland!
White, Yellow, and Black should make their own laws,
And force no one-sided justice with flaws.
—Marcus Garvey [1]

Be as proud of your race today as our fathers were in the days of yore. We have a beautiful history, and we shall create another in the future that will astonish the world.

—Marcus Garvey [2]

*A*lthough Marcus Garvey never set foot on African soil, the basis for his race philosophy was Africa, the Negro homeland. For out of the moist green depths of the African jungle had come the endless files of hapless

[1] Marcus Garvey, *The Tragedy of White Injustice* (N.Y.: Amy Jacques Garvey, 1927), p. 7.

[2] Garvey, *Philosophy and Opinions of Marcus Garvey,* I (N.Y.: Universal Publishing House, 1923), p. 7.

Negro slaves, a seemingly inexhaustible labor force to be devoured by the hungry plantations of the Americas. And in spite of the substantial but largely unrecognized contribution of these black slaves to the building of a New World civilization, their life of servitude under white masters had tended to destroy their African culture and to tear down their national and personal self-respect. To Garvey it seemed axiomatic that a redemption of the Negroes of the world must come only through a rebuilding of their shattered racial pride and a restoration of a truly Negro culture. Race pride and African nationalism were inextricably woven together in the Garvey philosophy, therefore, and the program of the Universal Negro Improvement Association centered around these two complementary objectives.

To understand Marcus Garvey and his extraordinary movement, it is necessary to consider in detail this strong emphasis on racism and African nationalism. Such a study helps not only to illumine the ideas of the man but also to show the basis for his wide appeal. Garvey's unparalleled success in capturing the imagination of masses of Negroes throughout the world can be explained only by recognizing that he put into words—and what magnificent inspiring words they were—what large numbers of his people were thinking. Garveyism as a social movement, reflecting as it did the hopes and aspirations of a substantial section of the Negro world, may best be studied by considering the ideas of its founder and leader, since these contain the key to Garvey's remarkable success.

In trying to establish a philosophy of Garveyism, however, it is important to place the movement in the context of general Negro thought in the period immediately following World War I. This was the era of the New Negro reaction to the race riots and frustrated hopes of the war years, and it was an age distinguished by the great artistic and literary activity that has been justly called the Negro Renaissance. Garveyism was for the most part decisively repudiated by the Negro intellectuals and it is thus difficult to give Garvey any credit for the flowering of the Negro Renaissance. Certainly his unceasing efforts to restore a strong sense of pride in things Negro was a march down the same path as that trod by the New Negroes, however, and the same forces that stimulated the Negro Renaissance helped to create an audience for Garveyism. Garvey's bombastic efforts to whip up an intense black nationalism were a logical counterpart to the more subtle but equally militant contemporary verse of such Negro poets as Claude McKay, Langston Hughes, and Countee Cullen.

The significance of Garveyism lies in its appeal to the dreams of millions of Negroes throughout the world. The amazingly loyal support given Marcus Garvey by the Negro masses, particularly in the United States and the West Indies, was forthcoming because he told his followers what they most wanted to hear, or, as E. Franklin Frazier has said, he made them "feel like somebody among white people who have said they were nobody." [3] Two

---

[3] E. Franklin Frazier, "The Garvey Movement," *Opportunity*, IV (November, 1926), 347.

decades after Garvey's inglorious departure for Atlanta penitentiary a new Harlem generation still remembered him as the man who "brought to the Negro people for the first time a sense of pride in being black." [4] This is the core of Marcus Garvey's philosophy; around this ideal he centered his life.

Coming at a time when Negroes generally had so little of which to be proud, Garvey's appeal to race pride quite naturally stirred a powerful response in the hearts of his eager black listeners. "I am the equal of any white man," Garvey told his followers. "I want you to feel the same way." [5] "We have come now to the turning point of the Negro," he declared with calm assurance, "where we have changed from the old cringing weakling, and transformed into full-grown men, demanding our portion as MEN." [6] One of the delegates to the first U.N.I.A. convention in Harlem in 1920 served notice that "it takes 1,000 white men to lick one Negro" and gave an illuminating preview of the type of Negro leadership needed in the future. "The Uncle Tom nigger has got to go, and his place must be taken by the new leader of the Negro race," he asserted. "That man will not be a white man with a black heart, nor a black man with a white heart, but a black man with a black heart." [7]

Garvey felt strongly that only through concerted action could Negroes achieve any betterment of their lowly status. "The world ought to know that it could not keep 400,000,000 Negroes down forever," [8] he once remarked, and he constantly spoke optimistically of the Negroes of the world "standing together as one man." [9] The black man could hope to better himself, Garvey believed, only by joining his own actions with those of others of his race. "It has been said that the Negro has never yet found cause to engage himself in anything in common with his brother," the U.N.I.A. founder admitted, "but the dawn of a new day is upon us and we see things differently. We see now, not as individuals, but as a collective whole, having one common interest." [10] One of his followers put it a little more strongly:

> Men and women of the Negro race, rouse ye in the name of your posterity, summon your every sense, collect your every faculty, thrust the scales from your eyes and be converted to the cause of Negro advancement and dignity;

---

[4] Adam Clayton Powell, Jr., *Marching Blacks* (N.Y.: Dial, 1945), p. 50.

[5] Quoted in Rollin Lynde Hartt, "The Negro Moses and His Campaign to Lead the Black Millions into Their Promised Land," *Independent*, CV (February 26, 1921), 206.

[6] Garvey, *Philosophy and Opinions*, I, 9.

[7] New York *World*, August 7, 1920.

[8] Garvey, *Philosophy and Opinions*, I, 9.

[9] *Ibid.*, II, 15.

[10] Quoted by Hartt in *Independent*, CV, 219.

Negro power and Sovereignty; Negro freedom and integrity; thereby becoming the giants of your own destiny! Your posterity is crying out to you.[11]

This plea for racial solidarity was one in which Negroes of widely varying political persuasions could join.[12]

"It is obvious, according to the commonest principles of human action," Garvey told his followers, "that no man will do as much for you as you will do for yourself." [13] Accordingly, he counseled Negroes to work for a strong and united black nation able to demand justice instead of sympathy from the ruling powers of the world. "If we must have justice, we must be strong," he explained; "if we must be strong, we must come together; if we must come together, we can only do so through the system of organization." "Let us not waste time in breathless appeals to the strong while we are weak," he advised, "but lend our time, energy, and effort to the accumulation of strength among ourselves by which we will voluntarily attract the attention of others." [14] Create a strong Negro nation, Garvey said in essence, and never more will you fear oppression at the hands of other races.

This spirit of race confidence and solidarity pervaded all of the many activities of the Garvey movement. The Black Star Line and its successor, the Black Cross Navigation and Trading Company, the Negro Factories Corporation, and indeed the African Legion, the Black Cross Nurses, and the other components of the U.N.I.A. itself were all a part of the general plan to weld the Negro people into a racially conscious, united group for effective mass action. Outsiders might laugh or scoff at some of the antics of the various Garvey organizations, their serious members ludicrous with high-toned titles and elaborate uniforms, but the importance of this aspect of the movement in restoring the all but shattered Negro self-confidence should not be overlooked.

Garvey exalted everything black and exhorted Negroes to be proud of their distinctive features and color. Negroid characteristics were not shameful marks of inferiority to be camouflaged and altered; they were rather symbols of beauty and grace. In his poem, "The Black Woman," Garvey voiced his love of pure Negro beauty:

Black queen of beauty, thou hast given color to the world!
Among other women thou art royal and the fairest!
Like the brightest jewels in the regal diadem,
Shin'st thou, Goddess of Africa, Nature's purest emblem!

---

[11] Branstan S. Clark, *Is It the Color of Our Skin that Is Responsible for Our Down-Trodden Condition All over the World?* (Pittsburgh, Pa.: Branstan S. Clark, 1921), p. 20.

[12] See, for example, T.S. Boone, *Paramount Facts in Race Development* (Chicago: Hume, 1921), pp. 20–21.

[13] Quoted by Hartt in *Independent*, CV, 218.

[14] Garvey, *Philosophy and Opinions*, II, 12.

Black men worship at thy virginal shrine of purest love,
Because in thine eyes are virtue's steady and holy mark,
As we see no other, clothed in silk or fine linen,
From ancient Venus, the Goddess, to mythical Helen.[15]

These sentiments were, after all, not very different from those expressed by other, perhaps more lyric poets of the Negro Renaissance, and they reflected the growing sense of race pride developing in the Negro world.

It is perhaps significant that from this period of intensified race consciousness dates the first large-scale production of Negro dolls. Whether or not Negro children had any instinctive preference for dolls of their own color, their parents now came to believe in increasing numbers that their children should play with colored dolls.[16] In 1919 the Harlem firm of Berry and Ross started the profitable production of dolls of a dusky hue designed to satisfy the most discriminating young mistress—or parent.[17] The Universal Negro Improvement Association encouraged this revolutionary toy development, and Garvey's *Negro World* plugged the sale of black dolls. "Little Thelma Miller, eight years old, is very fond of her little colored doll," ran the caption under a U.N.I.A. photograph of a happy young mother proudly holding her very black toy baby. "She has never had the opportunity and pleasure of playing with no other doll except a colored doll. She is a real Garveyite." [18] The fact that most of these Negro dolls were advertised as "light-brown," "high-brown," or "mulatto," however, seems to indicate that Negroes continued to look upon lightness of color as a desirable characteristic.

One of the methods used by Garvey to build up a sense of pride in the Negro heritage was his constant reference to the exploits of Negro heroes and to the land from which the race had come. He angrily accused white scholars of distorting Negro history to make it unfavorable to colored people. "Every student of history, of impartial mind," Garvey taught, "knows that the Negro once ruled the world, when white men were savages and barbarians living in caves; that thousands of Negro professors . . . taught in the universities in Alexandria." [19] The intent Negro audiences in Liberty Hall delighted in

---

[15] Garvey, *Selections from the Poetic Meditations of Marcus Garvey* (N.Y.: Amy Jacques Garvey, 1927), pp. 22–23; *Negro World*, October 13, 1928.

[16] See James H. A. Brazelton, *Self-Determination: The Salvation of the Race* (Oklahoma City, Okla.: The Educator, 1918), p. 65; W. D. Weatherford, *The Negro from Africa to America* (N.Y.: Doran, 1924), pp. 427–28.

[17] Hodge Kirnon, New York, to the author, March 28, 1949; Roi Ottley, *"New World A-Coming": Inside Black America* (Boston: Houghton Mifflin, 1943), p. 75; advertisements in *Negro World*, August 21, 1920, and February 2, 1924, and New York *Amsterdam News*, December 21, 1927.

[18] Cincinnati Division No. 146, U.N.I.A., *Sixth Anniversary Drive, May 8th to 18th, 1927*, pp. 9–10.

[19] Garvey, *Philosophy and Opinions*, II, 19. See also p. 82.

Garvey's vivid recollections of a creative black civilization at a time when white men were nothing:

> When Europe was inhabited by a race of cannibals, a race of savages, naked men, heathens and pagans, Africa was peopled with a race of cultured black men, who were masters in art, science and literature; men who were cultured and refined; men, who, it was said, were like the gods. Even the great poets of old sang in beautiful sonnets of the delight it afforded the gods to be in companionship with the Ethiopians. Why, then, should we lose hope? Black men, you were once great; you shall be great again. Lose not courage, lose not faith, go forward. The thing to do is to get organized.[20]

This was in fact a subject upon which Garvey could wax angrily poetic:

> *Out of cold old Europe these white men came,*
> *From caves, dens and holes, without any fame,*
> *Eating their dead's flesh and sucking their blood,*
> *Relics of the Mediterranean flood.*[21]

Not only were white men of a low breed, far below their darker brothers, but the time had come to tell the world about the great heroes of Negro history. "Negroes, teach your children they are direct descendants of the greatest and proudest race who ever peopled the earth," Garvey preached with earnest intensity.[22] Wherever Negroes had lived they had produced eminent men and accomplished notable achievement. "Sojurner Truth is worthy of the place of sainthood alongside of Joan of Arc; Crispus Attucks and George William Gordon are entitled to the halo of martyrdom with no less glory than that of the martyrs of any other race," Garvey cried. "Toussaint L'Ouverture's brilliancy as a soldier and statesman outshone that of a Cromwell, Napoleon, and Washington; hence he is entitled to the highest place as a hero among men." [23] Turn back the pages of Negro history as far as you like and ever the result would be to the lasting glory of the proud Negro people:

> *So down the line of history we come,*
> *Black, courtly, courageous and handsome.*
> *No fear have we today of any great man*
> *From Napoleon back to Genghis Khan.*[24]

---

[20] *Ibid.*, I, 77.

[21] Garvey, *Tragedy of White Injustice*, p. 3.

[22] Garvey, *Philosophy and Opinions*, II, 82.

[23] *Ibid.*, p. 415.

[24] Garvey, *Tragedy of White Injustice*, p. 6.

The Garvey historical examination might not be as critical as more objective scholars would desire, but it did act as a massive dose of adrenalin to the nationalism now beginning to throb in Negro breasts.

Along with the reborn Negro pride in the glorious past and distinctive color of the race went a reorientation in religion as well. Garvey believed that Negroes should end their subserviency to the white man through the worship of his white God. This rejection of an alien deity embodying Caucasian features was not original with Garvey and was in fact a logical part of any intensely race-conscious movement of this nature. Religious workers in Africa had long noted the tendency of their converts to think of the deity in terms of Negro pigmentation and to reject the concept of a white God.[25] Indeed, many religious cults and sects among American Negroes had projected the idea of a black God long before Garvey arrived in the United States.[26] Even some whites had suggested that Negro ministers should think in black terms, one fastidious southerner going so far as to assert that the Negro's Bible "ought to teach him that he will become a black angel and go home at death to a black God." [27] Garvey's extreme racial nationalism demanded fulfillment in a truly Negro religion, for, as his widow explains, "It is really logical that although we all know God is a spirit, yet all religions more or less visualize Him in a likeness akin to their own race. . . . Hence it was most vital that pictures of God should be in the likeness of the [Negro] Race." [28]

To implement the black religion, Garvey called upon the Reverend George Alexander McGuire, a prominent Episcopal clergyman who left his Boston pulpit in 1920 to become Chaplain General of the Universal Negro Improvement Association. On September 28, 1921, in a service conducted by dignitaries of the Greek Orthodox Church, McGuire was ordained a bishop and consecrated as head of the new African Orthodox Church.[29] Probably because Garvey had been brought up a Roman Catholic and Bishop McGuire had formerly been associated with the Episcopalian Church, the ritual of the new black religion followed much the same pattern as the liturgy of those two churches.

From the first, however, Bishop McGuire urged the Garveyites to "for-

---

[25] Everett V. Stonequist, *The Marginal Man: A Study in Personality and Culture Conflict* (N.Y.: Scribners, 1937), p. 21.

[26] Joel A. Rogers, *Sex and Race: Negro-Caucasian Mixing in All Ages and All Lands* (N.Y.: J. A. Rogers, 1940), I, 254–71; James M. Webb, *A Black Man Will Be the Coming Universal King: Proven by Biblical History* (Chicago: Author [1918]), p. 12; Brazelton, *Self-Determination*, pp. 248–49.

[27] Kelsey Blanton, *Color-Blind and Skin-Deep Democracy* ([Tampa, Fla.:] Kelsey Blanton, 1924), p. 60.

[28] Amy Jacques Garvey, Kingston, Jamaica, to the author, July 5, 1949.

[29] *Negro Churchman*, I (March, 1923), 1.

get the white gods." "Erase the white gods from your hearts," he told his
congregation. "We must go back to the native church, to our own true God." [30]
The new Negro religion would seek to be true to the principles of Christianity without the shameful hypocrisy of the white churches.[31] Garvey
himself urged Negroes to adopt their own religion, "with God as a Being, not
as a Creature," a religion that would show Him "made in our own image—
black." [32] When queried by a white reporter as to his reputed belief in the
Negro ancestry of Christ, Garvey hedged a bit and replied that he believed
"simply that Christ's ancestry included all races, so that He was Divinity in-
carnate in the broadest sense of the word." [33] In spite of strong opposition
from the regular Negro clergy, Garvey's African Orthodox Church was able
to report in its monthly magazine, the *Negro Churchman,* that "in its first
year" it had "extended its missions through several states, into Canada,
Cuba, and Hayti." Bishop McGuire reported that he had already recruited
"10 Priests, 4 Deacons, 2 Sub-deacons and several Deaconesses, Catechists
and Seminiarians in training." [34]

By the time the Fourth International Convention of the Negro Peoples
of the World met in 1924, moreover, the leaders of the black religion were
openly demanding that Negroes worship a Negro Christ. During the opening parade through the streets of Harlem, U.N.I.A. members marched under
a large portrait of a black Madonna and Child.[35] The convention session of
August 5, 1924, drew the attention of the white press when Bishop McGuire
advised Negroes to name the day when all members of the race would tear
down and burn any pictures of the white Madonna and the white Christ
found in their homes. "Then let us start our Negro painters getting busy,"
the Bishop declared, "and supply a black Madonna and a black Christ for
the training of our children." Bishop McGuire gave added weight to his
words by speaking under a large oil painting that clearly portrayed the type
of Madonna and Child he had in mind.[36]

Bishop McGuire told of an aged Negro woman who had gratefully of-

---

[30] Quoted in Claude McKay, *Harlem: Negro Metropolis* (N.Y.: Dutton, 1940), p. 166; Ottley, *"New World A-Coming,"* p. 73.

[31] See, for instance, Garvey, *Tragedy of White Injustice,* pp. 4–5; Garvey, *Philosophy
and Opinions,* I 27; Marcus Garvey, "The White, Sinful Church," (*Black Man,* I (July,
1935), 8.

[32] Quoted in Truman Hughes Talley, "Marcus Garvey: the Negro Moses?" *World's Work,*
XLI (December, 1920), 165; "A Black Moses and His Dream of a Promised Land," *Current Opinion,* LXX (March, 1921), 330.

[33] Quoted by Hartt in *Independent,* CV, 205.

[34] *Negro Churchman,* I (March, 1923), 1.

[35] "Garvey," *Opportunity,* II (September, 1924), 284–85; *Negro World,* August 16,
1924.

[36] *New York Times,* August 6, 1924.

fered her African Orthodox pastor five dollars for telling her of the black Christ, because she knew that "no white man would ever die on the cross for me." Speaking emphatically so that none of his listeners might fail to catch the import of his message, the Bishop declared that Christ had actually been a reddish brown in color, and he predicted that if the Saviour were to visit New York He would not be able to live on fashionable Riverside Drive but would have to go to Harlem, "because all the darker people live here in Harlem." Bishop McGuire complained that the western Negro was the only Negro in the world who accepted the white man's characterization of the devil as being black, and he announced that henceforth the Negro's devil would be white. Another speaker at the same meeting, the Reverend J. D. Barber of Ethiopia, prophesied that the Negro would soon have his own illustrated Bible, complete with inspiring pictures of Negro saints and angels. Reverend Barber recalled St. John's description of Christ as "a black man, with feet that shone as polished brass, hair of lamb's wool and eyes with flames of fire," a rather elastic reference to the account in the prologue of the Book of Revelation.[37]

Garvey clung to the concept of a Negro Deity until his death. To him the sufferings of Christ typified the age-old sorrows of the Negro race:

> White men the Saviour did crucify,
> For eyes not blue, but blood of Negro tie.[38]

At the Seventh U.N.I.A. Convention held at Kingston, Jamaica, in August, 1934, the delegates passed a resolution endorsing the principles of Christianity but urging Negroes to "conceive their Deity unforeign to their own creation but akin to it." Negroes were advised to worship a God whose physical form, image, and likeness would be "dramatized in the physical beauty and characteristics of the Negro himself." [39] Garvey could not conceive of a God who would differentiate between any of the children He had made to live on His earth:

> Thou art made to be so white
> That no black man has a claim:
> Could'st this, God, be ever right
> That you made us ill of fame?
> Thou art God in every way,
> Caring not for black nor white.[40]

---

[37] Ibid.

[38] Garvey, Tragedy of White Injustice, p. 12.

[39] Black Man, I (November, 1934), quoted in Ralph J. Bunche, "The Programs, Ideologies, Tactics, and Achievements of Negro Betterment and Interracial Organizations" (unpublished monograph prepared for the Carnegie-Myrdal Study, 1940; Schomburg Collection, N.Y. Public Library), p. 417.

[40] Garvey, "A Black Man's Prayer," Black Man, I (July, 1935), 18.

An impartial God meant also a multiracial heaven and Garvey therefore offered for sale one of his devotional poems as a "picture motto with the design of a Negro Angel." [41]

Garvey's efforts to deny the Jewish ancestry of Christ recalled the earlier attempt of Houston Stewart Chamberlain, that pathetic Englishman turned German, to bring the Saviour into the Aryan fold. "Whoever makes the assertion that Christ was a Jew is either ignorant or insincere," the worried prophet of Nordic supremacy had written around the turn of the century. "The probability that Christ was no Jew, that He had not a drop of genuinely Jewish blood in His veins, is so great that it is almost equivalent to a certainty." [42] Like the shocked reaction to Chamberlain's ludicrous bigotry, the response to Garvey's call for an all-black religion was mostly negative. The Negro press generally shared the sentiments of George Harris, the anti-Garvey editor of the New York *News,* who indignantly declared that Garvey had installed "a black God as the deity colored folks must worship for the sake of attracting the limelight." [43] Humorist George S. Schuyler saw only the ironical aspect of Garvey's racial God and tied the black religion to the collapse of the various U.N.I.A. enterprises. "Last summer Marcus accused the Deity of being a Negro," Schuyler chuckled. "No wonder luck went against him!" [44] Kelly Miller was even more hostile in his denunciation of the new creed. "Marcus Garvey some little while ago shocked the spiritual sensibilities of the religious world by suggesting that the Negro should paint God black," he complained, adding that "the idea was revolting even to the Negro." [45]

Except for an insignificant handful of converts to the African Orthodox Church, the regular Negro clergy firmly rejected the new black religion, and it has been estimated—"guess-timated" is doubtless a more precise term—that as many as four out of five American Negro preachers were opposed to the concept of a black God.[46] William Pickens suggests that this rejection of Garvey's spiritual leadership may have amounted more to a distrust of his

[41] Cover advertisements, *ibid.,* II (December, 1937), and III (March, July, and November, 1938).

[42] Houston Stewart Chamberlain, *Foundations of the Nineteenth Century* (London: Lane, 1912), I, 211–12.

[43] New York *News,* August 16, 1924. Called to my attention by Mr. Hodge Kirnon of New York City.

[44] George S. Schuyler and Theophilus Lewis, "Shafts and Darts," *Messenger,* VII (March, 1925), 129.

[45] New York *Amsterdam News,* February 16, 1927. Called to my attention by Mr. Hodge Kirnon of New York City.

[46] Talley in *World's Work,* XLI, 165; "Black Moses and His Dream," *Current Opinion,* LXX, 330; Harold E. Zickfoose, "The Garvey Movement" (unpublished Master of Arts thesis, Iowa State University, 1931), p. 62.

political aims and business methods than to any indication of convictions on the subject of color.[47] More convincing is A. Philip Randolph's explanation that Negro preachers opposed the African Orthodox Church out of fear they would lose their following, since their congregations had been conditioned in a white civilization and had thus grown up believing in a white God and in a Christian religion that had been fashioned and proselytized by white men.[48] Garvey's widow believes that the antipathy resulted largely from economic considerations, since the consolidation of Negroes into one denomination would mean the end of individual power and prestige for the preachers leading the innumerable small sects and independent churches.[49] Another consideration might be the need to retain white support in areas such as the American South where the Negro preacher has traditionally looked to white leaders for his cue in matters of politics and social action.

Unwittingly Garvey demonstrated a keen awareness of social psychology when he used a black God of Israel to stimulate racial nationalism among the Negro masses. And in spite of the loud outcries from Negro intellectuals and the horrified regular clergy when he first launched the campaign for the new religion, Garvey had the satisfaction before he died of seeing a decided shift in favor of a Negro-oriented spiritualism among certain elements of the Negro intelligentsia.[50] An eminent Negro sociologist has summed up perhaps better than anyone else Garvey's shrewd awareness of the spiritual needs of his followers. "The intellectual can laugh, if he will," wrote E. Franklin Frazier of the black God, "but let him not forget the pragmatic value of such a symbol among the type of people Garvey was dealing with." [51]

Much more important in the stimulation of black nationalism was the U.N.I.A. program to lead Negroes back to their African homeland. With customary flamboyance Garvey assured his followers that a few years would see Africa as completely dominated by Negroes as Europe was by whites. "No one knows when the hour of Africa's Redemption cometh," he warned mysteriously. "It is in the wind. It is coming. One day, like a storm, it will be here." [52] To his Liberty Hall supporters Garvey exclaimed, "Let Africa be our guiding star—our star of destiny," [53] while to the dark motherland he

---

[47] William Pickens, Washington, to the author, May 27, 1949.

[48] A. Philip Randolph, New York, to the author, June 24, 1949.

[49] Amy Jacques Garvey, Kingston, Jamaica, to the author, July 5, 1949.

[50] See, for example, Benjamin E. Mays, *The Negro's God as Reflected in His Literature* (Boston: Chapman and Grimes, 1938), pp. 184–85.

[51] Frazier in *Opportunity*, IV, 347.

[52] Garvey, *Philosophy and Opinions*, I, 10.

[53] *Ibid.*, p. 6.

called, "Wake up Ethiopia! Wake up Africa! Let us work towards the one glorious end of a free, redeemed and mighty nation. Let Africa be a bright star among the constellation of nations." [54]

A great independent African nation was the essential ingredient in the Garvey recipe for race redemption and he was earnestly convinced that Negroes needed the dark continent to achieve their destiny as a great people. Like another ardent disciple of racial nationalism, Garvey demanded *Lebensraum* for his people. It fell to the U.N.I.A. to lead the struggle to regain Africa and in the fight Garvey foresaw divine intervention. "At this moment methinks I see Ethiopia stretching forth her hands unto God," he declared fervently, "and methinks I see the angel of God taking up the standard of the Red, the Black, and the Green, and saying, 'Men of the Negro race, Men of Ethiopia, follow me!' It falls to our lot to tear off the shackles that bind Mother Africa." "Climb ye the heights of liberty," Garvey exhorted the U.N.I.A. legions, "and cease not in well-doing until you have planted the banner of the Red, the Black, and the Green upon the hilltops of Africa." [55]

But what of the powerful European nations that had carved up the African continent and now controlled the homeland? Garvey frequently disclaimed any animus against the white race,[56] but at the same time he pointedly told his followers: "We shall not ask England or France or Italy or Belgium, 'Why are you here?' We shall only command them, 'Get out of here.' " [57] The barrier to a free Africa was the white man, and Garvey warned ominously: "We say to the white man who now dominates Africa that it is to his interest to clear out of Africa now, because we are coming . . . 400,-000,000 strong." [58] Garvey loved to speculate on the tremendous power that would belong to the Negro people once they discovered what their numerical strength could do for them.[59] "We are going home after a long vacation," he told the U.N.I.A., "and are giving notice to the tenant to get out. If he doesn't there is such a thing as forcible ejection." [60] "You will find ten years from now, or 100 years from now," he warned a white audience, "Garvey was

---

[54] *Ibid.*, p. 5.

[55] Quoted in Mary White Ovington, *Portraits in Color* (N.Y.: Viking, 1927), p. 18.

[56] See Garvey, *Philosophy and Opinions*, I, 13; Garvey, *Speech at Madison Square Garden* (N.Y.: 1924); Garvey, *Speech at Royal Albert Hall* (London: U.N.I.A., 1928), pp. 26–27; "Black Moses and His Dream," *Current Opinion*, LXX, 331; Worth M. Tuttle, "A New Nation in Harlem," *World Tomorrow*, IV (September, 1921), 279–81; Benjamin G. Brawley, *A Short History of the American Negro* (N.Y.: Macmillan, 1927, 1931, and 1939), p. 266.

[57] New York *World*, August 3, 1920. See also Garvey, *Philosophy and Opinions*, I, 40–41.

[58] Quoted in James Weidon Johnson, *Black Manhattan* (N.Y.: Knopf, 1930), p. 254; *Revolutionary Radicalism: A Report of the Joint Legislative Committee of New York Investigating Seditious Activities*, II (N.Y.: J. B. Lyon, 1920), p. 1513.

[59] Garvey, *Philosophy and Opinions*, I, 39.

[60] New York *World*, August 5, 1920.

not an idle buffoon but was representing the new vision of the Negro who was looking forward to great accomplishments in the future." [61]

It was never Garvey's intention that all Negroes in the New World would return to Africa and in this sense it is misleading to call his scheme a Back to Africa movement. Rather he believed like many Zionists that once a strong African nation was established Negroes everywhere would automatically gain needed prestige and strength and could look to it for protection if necessary.[62] "At no time did he visualize all American Negroes returning to Africa," says his widow.[63] "We do not want all the Negroes in Africa," Garvey informed a U.N.I.A. audience in Madison Square Garden in 1924. "Some are no good here, and naturally will be no good there." [64] Those particularly needed for the work in Africa would be engineers, artisans, and willing workers of all sorts—in short, the pioneering elements upon which all civilizations are built.

Garvey's address at his inauguration as Provisional President of Africa in 1920 demonstrated his strong belief in a personal destiny as the liberator of Africa. "The signal honor of being Provisional President of Africa is mine," he exulted. "It is a political calling for me to redeem Africa. It is like asking Napoleon to take the world. . . . He failed and died at St. Helena. But may I not say that the lessons of Napoleon are but stepping stones by which we shall guide ourselves to African liberation?" [65] The possibility of going down in history as the father of his country fascinated Garvey, and after a visit to the grave of George Washington he described "a new thought, a new inspiration" that had come to him at Mount Vernon. "It was the vision of a day— near, probably—when hundreds of other men and women will be worshipping at a shrine. This time the vision leads me to the shrine of some black man, the father of African independence." [66] Garvey continued the comparison with his poem "Hail! United States of Africa!" in which he managed to mention all of the twenty-six possible African states:

> Hail! United States of Africa—free!
> Country of the brave black man's liberty;
> State of greater nationhood thou hast won,
> A new life for the race has just begun.[67]

---

[61] Garvey, *Minutes of a Speech at Century Theatre, London, 1928* (London: Vail, 1928), p. 29.

[62] Hartt in *Independent*, CV, 206.

[63] Amy Jacques Garvey, Kingston, Jamaica, to the author, February 19, 1949, and February 14, 1951.

[64] Garvey, *Speech at Madison Square Garden.*

[65] Quoted by W. E. B. DuBois in "Marcus Garvey," *Crisis*, XXI (January, 1921), 114.

[66] Quoted by Hartt in *Independent*, CV, 218.

[67] Garvey, *Tragedy of White Injustice*, pp. 20–21.

Most American Negro editors scoffed at the Back to Africa talk and loudly proclaimed the desire of Negroes to remain in the United States. The Chicago *Defender*, which generally avoided use of the word Negro in its columns, announced proudly, "The Race considers itself African no more than white Americans consider themselves European." The *Defender* went on to suggest pointedly that "in the United States lunacy commissions still have legal standing." [68] An anti-Garvey cartoon showed a strong manly Negro holding a small nondescript "Back to Africa fanatic" and advising, "The best thing you can do is stay right *here* and fight out your salvation." [69] Even the white press, when it deigned to notice Garvey, was hostile to the idea of a redemption of Africa.[70] Negro intellectuals generally opposed Garvey's methods if not his interest in Africa. Booker T. Washington had preached against any idea of a return to Africa and doubtless his philosophy still carried great weight with many American Negroes.[71] Sometimes, however, even Garvey's critics saw fascinating possibilities in the awakened interest in the ancestral homeland. Writing after Garvey's confinement in Atlanta, Professor Alain Locke declared, "Garveyism may be a transient, if spectacular, phenomenon, but the possible role of the American Negro in the future development of Africa is one of the most constructive and universally helpful missions that any modern people can lay claim to." [72]

It is interesting to note that the idea of setting up an independent African state remained a part of Garvey's program to the end of his life. One of the last issues of his monthly magazine, the *Black Man*, contained an earnest plea for support of U.S. Senator Theodore G. Bilbo's bill for the repatriation of American Negroes to Africa. Garvey admitted that the motives of this bigoted southern racist might "not be as idealistic as Negroes may want," but he gave the Bilbo bill his endorsement because "independent nationality is the greatest guarantee of the ability of any people to stand up in our present civilization." He therefore asked all divisions of the Universal Negro Improvement Association in the United States "to give their undivided and whole-hearted support to Senator Bilbo's Bill." [73]

Garvey's passionate interest in Africa was a logical development of his firm conviction that Negroes could expect no permanent progress in a land

---

[68] Chicago *Defender*, September 13, 1924.

[69] *Ibid.*, September 2, 1922.

[70] *New York Times*, August 4, 1920.

[71] See Victoria Earle Matthews, *Black Belt Diamonds: Gems from the Speeches, Addresses, and Talks to Students of Booker T. Washington* (N.Y.: Fortune and Scott, 1898), pp. 9, 19, 27, and 58–59.

[72] Alain Locke, "Enter the New Negro," *Survey*, LIII (March, 1925), 634; Locke (ed.), *The New Negro: An Interpretation* (N.Y.: Boni, 1925), p. 15.

[73] *Black Man*, III (November, 1938), 19. See also Chicago *Defender*, June 15, 1940.

dominated by white men.[74] No doubt he would have agreed completely with Mr. Dooley's shrewd analysis of the American race problem: "Th' throuble is that th' naygurs iv th' North have lived too long among th' white people, an' th' white people iv th' South have lived too long among th' naygurs." [75] Garvey said essentially the same thing when he told Negroes to develop "a government, a nation of our own, strong enough to lend protection to the members of our race scattered all over the world, and to compel the respect of the nations and the races of the earth." [76] When Garvey spoke of discrimination, he touched a subject painfully familiar to every Negro: "If you cannot live alongside the white man in peace, if you cannot get the same chance and opportunity alongside the white man, even though you are his fellow citizen; if he claims that you are not entitled to this chance or opportunity because the country is his by force of numbers, then find a country of your own and rise to the highest position within that country." [77] The Garvey solution for Negro ills was to make the race "so strong as to strike fear" into the hearts of the oppressor white race.[78] Only when Negroes could compel respect and justice through their connection with a strong Negro government would the position of the race be secure.

Garvey had no illusions about the white man's Christian love and believed that it would be used only when conveniently suitable. The U.N.I.A. therefore conceded the right of whites to do as they pleased in their own lands provided that Negroes were allowed to develop a nation of their own in Africa.[79] "Political, social and industrial America," Garvey cautioned, "will never become so converted as to be willing to share up equitably between black and white." [80] Though Negroes might live as useful citizens in the United States for thousands of years, Garvey believed that as long as the white population was numerically superior to them the blacks could never hope for political justice or social equality.[81]

Garvey's plain abdication of Negro rights in America quickly brought him the open support of such white supremacy groups as the Ku Klux Klan and the Anglo-Saxon Clubs, both flourishing mightily in the postwar years. Garvey's major book, the second volume of his *Philosophy and Opinions*, carried an advertisement for Major Earnest Sevier Cox's *White America*, a polemical work strongly preaching the separation of the races. Major Cox some-

---

[74] Garvey, *Philosophy and Opinions*, II, 3, 40, 46, 49, and 97.

[75] [Finley P. Dunne] *Dissertations by Mr. Dooley* (N.Y.: Harper, 1906), p. 190.

[76] Quoted in Ovington, *Portraits in Color*, p. 30.

[77] Quoted by Hartt in *Independent*, CV, 206.

[78] *Ibid.*, p. 218.

[79] Garvey, *Philosophy and Opinions*, II, 46.

[80] *Ibid.*, p. 49.

[81] *Ibid.*, pp. 97–98.

times spoke to U.N.I.A. audiences at Liberty Hall in New York, and he even dedicated a pamphlet on racial purity to Garvey, whom he called "a martyr for the independence and integrity of the Negro race." [82] Another white supporter was John Powell, the fanatical organizer of the Anglo-Saxon Clubs of America. Garvey expressed great admiration for men like Cox and Powell because of "their honesty and lack of hypocrisy" in openly working to maintain the power of the white race.[83] Speaking at Liberty Hall late in 1925, Powell congratulated the U.N.I.A. on its racial improvement program and reaffirmed the mutual desire of blacks and whites to preserve the purity of their respective races.[84] Garvey also received support from some southern whites who looked upon his movement with favor because it was likely to attract Negroes who might otherwise be resentful of their subordinate caste position in the United States.[85] After he was deported, some of Garvey's white friends were active in a campaign to permit the return of the exiled U.N.I.A. leader.[86]

"Lynchings and race riots," said Garvey with reference to the grim postwar period of racial strife and violence, "all work to our advantage by teaching the Negro that he must build a civilization of his own or forever remain the white man's victim." [87] Bishop McGuire, the religious leader of the U.N.I.A. and spiritual head of the African Orthodox Church, declared frankly that the Ku Klux Klan's campaign of intimidation and violence would benefit the movement by driving harassed Negroes into the Garvey organization.[88] In 1922 Garvey indicated his tacit support of the dread Klan, an alliance his opponents had suspected for some time. "The Ku Klux Klan is going to make this a white man's country," Garvey asserted in stating his belief that the K.K.K. was the invisible government of America. "They are perfectly honest and frank about it. Fighting them is not going to get you anywhere." [89]

Early in 1922 Garvey went to Atlanta, Georgia, for a conference with

---

[82] Earnest Sevier Cox, *Let My People Go* (Richmond, Va.: William Byrd Press, 1938), p. 4. See also Cox, *The South's Part in Mongrelizing the Nation* (Richmond, Va.: White America Society, 1926), pp. 8–9, 93–94, 103, 108.

[83] Garvey, *Philosophy and Opinions*, II, 338.

[84] *Ibid.*, p. 347.

[85] Blanton, *Color-Blind and Skin-Deep Democracy*, pp. 61–62.

[86] Earnest Sevier Cox, *Lincoln's Negro Policy* (Richmond, Va.: William Byrd Press, 1938), pp. 29–32; Cox, *South's Part in Mongrelizing*, pp. 93–94.

[87] Quoted by Hartt in *Independent*, CV, 219.

[88] Chicago *Defender*, August 16, 1924.

[89] *New York Times*, July 10, 1922.

Edward Young Clarke, Imperial Giant of the Klan.[90] The purpose of the meeting was apparently to see how strong the Klan was and whether or not Garvey could hope for its support for the Back to Africa program of the U.N.I.A. Garvey's widow explains that far from approving of the Klan's violent actions against Negroes, her husband merely believed "that the prejudice exhibited by the Klan in hysteria, hate, cruelty, and mob violence was the prejudice common to most white Americans, which deep in their hearts they felt, but culture and refinement prevented many from showing any trace of it." [91] The meeting was one of expediency, then, rather than of mutual admiration, but it was nonetheless a serious tactical blunder.

Although details of the Atlanta conference were withheld, the mere thought that a responsible Negro leader would collaborate with the leading avowed enemy of his race brought down a storm of criticism upon Garvey's head. Alderman George Harris, editor of the New York *News*, denounced Garvey as "misrepresenting the attitude of 100 per cent of our native-born Americans and 75 per cent of the foreign-born group" when he surrendered to Clarke. "When Garvey agrees with the Klan's theory that this is a white man's country," Harris complained angrily, "he sadly misrepresents our people." [92] William Pickens, who had at one time very nearly accepted a high U.N.I.A. post, now spurned with contempt a Garvey title of nobility because of this rumored alliance with the Ku Klux Klan.[93] W. E. B. DuBois let go a powerful blast against the U.N.I.A. president in *Crisis*, the organ of the National Association for the Advancement of Colored People. "Marcus Garvey is, without doubt, the most dangerous enemy of the Negro race in America and the world," sputtered the indignant editor of *Crisis*. "He is either a lunatic or a traitor." [94] Unperturbed by this barrage of Negro criticism, Garvey countered with a candid appraisal of white America. "I regard the Klan, the Anglo-Saxon Clubs and White American Societies," he maintained, "as better friends of the race than all other groups of hypocritical whites put together. I like honesty and fair play. You may call me a Klansman if you will, but, potentially every white man is a Klansman, as far as the Negro in competition with whites socially, economically and politically is concerned, and there is no use lying about it." [95]

The main reason that Garvey and his organization were acceptable to

---

[90] Chicago *Defender*, July 8, 1922; *New York Times*, February 8, 1923; W. E. B. DuBois, "Back to Africa," *Century*, CV (February, 1923), 547; Burgit Aron, "The Garvey Movement" (unpublished Master of Arts thesis, Columbia University, 1947), p. 117.

[91] Amy Jacques Garvey, Kingston, Jamaica, to the author, February 19, 1949.

[92] Quoted in Chicago *Defender*, July 22, 1922.

[93] *Ibid.*, July 29, 1922.

[94] "A Lunatic or a Traitor," *Crisis*, XXVIII (May, 1924), 8–9.

[95] Garvey, *Philosophy and Opinions*, II, 71; Ottley, *"New World A-Coming,"* p. 74.

the Ku Klux Klan and other white supremacy groups was that the U.N.I.A. leader preached race purity to his followers. He thundered that racial amalgamation must cease forthwith and warned that any member of the Universal Negro Improvement Association who married a white would be summarily expelled.[96] Not only did Garvey advocate race purity, but as a Jamaican black he attempted to transfer the West Indian three-way color caste system to the United States by attacking mulatto leaders. He laughed at the light-skinned mulattoes, who, he said, were always seeking "excuses to get out of the Negro Race," [97] and he scornfully accused his mulatto opponents of being "time-serving, boot-licking agencies of subserviency to the whites." [98] The average Negro leader, Garvey said, sought to establish himself as "the pet of some philanthropist of another race," thereby selling out the interests of his own people.[99]

The U.N.I.A. catered to the darker Negroes; in fact, Garvey's definition of Negro seemed to require a purity of racial origin. At first the anti-mulatto propaganda helped to inflate the egos of darker Negroes, but it was doomed to failure in the United States where neither whites nor Negroes make any appreciable distinction between Negroes of different shades of color.[100] American blacks lacked the fierce resentment toward the favored position of mulattoes that had been a part of Garvey's Jamaican conditioning. The U.N.I.A. continued to preach racial purity, however, and its founder maintained his attack on his light-skinned critics by asserting that they favored racial amalgamation. "I believe in racial purity, and in maintaining the standard of racial purity," he asserted. "I am proud I am a Negro. It is only the so-called 'colored' man who talks of social equality." [101] "We are not seeking social equality," Garvey told whites. "We do not seek intermarriage, nor do we hanker after the impossible. We want the right to have a country of our own, and there foster and re-establish a culture and civilization exclusively ours." [102] Garvey's advocacy of racial purity was noticed even in Germany, where the so-called German Emergency League against the Black Horror sought to enlist his aid in securing the removal of French Negro occupation troops from the Rhineland.[103]

---

[96] Hartt in *Independent*, CV, 219.

[97] Garvey, *Philosophy and Opinions*, I, 6.

[98] Quoted by Talley in *World's Work*, XLI, 163; "Black Moses and His Dream," *Current Opinion*, LXX, 330.

[99] Garvey, *Philosophy and Opinions*, I, 29–30.

[100] Ottley, *"New World A-Coming,"* p. 74; DuBois in *Century*, CV, 542; Johnson, *Black Manhattan*, p. 257.

[101] New York *World*, June 29, 1923.

[102] Garvey, *Speech at Madison Square Garden*.

[103] *Münchener neueste Nachrichten*, November 25, 1921, in *Nation*, CXIII (December 28, 1921), 769.

In Garvey's vocabulary, as in that of most southern whites, social equality meant "the social intermingling of both races, intermarriages, and general social co-relationship." [104] Believing that such intermingling would inevitably lead to "an American race, that will neither be white nor black." [105] Garvey directed a constant stream of criticism against Dr. W. E. B. DuBois of the N.A.A.C.P. for his efforts on behalf of Negro social and political equality.[106] At least part of this animosity was doubtless due to DuBois' own dignified attacks on the U.N.I.A. and to the fact that the cultured editor of *Crisis* possessed an excellent formal education of the sort Garvey had always desired but had never been able to obtain. E. Franklin Frazier suggests that "Garvey constantly directed the animosity of his followers against the intellectuals because of his own lack of formal education." [107] Though the *Negro World* in 1922 listed DuBois as one of the "twelve greatest living Negroes" (Garvey was of course also on the list),[108] the 1924 convention of the U.N.I.A. resolved to ostracize DuBois "from the Negro race, so far as the U.N.I.A. is concerned," declaring him "an enemy of the black people of the world." [109]

Garvey denounced other Negro leaders as being bent on cultural assimilation, cravenly seeking white support, and miserably compromising between accommodation and protest.[110] The National Association for the Advancement of Colored People was the worst offender in Garvey's mind, because, he said, it "wants us all to become white by amalgamation, but they are not honest enough to come out with the truth." "To be a Negro is no disgrace, but an honor," Garvey indignantly affirmed, "and we of the U.N.I.A. do not want to become white." [111] He warned both whites and blacks that the purity of the two races was endangered by the false prophets of amalgamation. "It is the duty of the virtuous and morally pure of both the white and black races," he announced, "to thoughtfully and actively protect the future of the two peoples, by vigorously opposing the destructive propaganda and vile efforts of the miscegenationists of the white race, and their associates, the hybrids of the Negro race." [112] "I believe in a pure black race," Garvey proclaimed loudly, "just as how all self-respecting whites believe in a

---

[104] Garvey, *Philosophy and Opinions*, II, 3.

[105] *Ibid.*, p. 2.

[106] See *ibid.*, pp. 39, 57, 86, and 324–25; Garvey, "A Barefaced Coloured Leader," *Black Man*, I (July, 1935), 5–8; New York *World*, August 4, 1920.

[107] Frazier in *Opportunity*, IV, 346.

[108] *Negro World*, August 26, 1922.

[109] Chicago *Defender*, September 6, 1924.

[110] Garvey, *Philosophy and Opinions*, I, 29–30; Gunnar Myrdal, *An American Dilemma: The Negro Problem and Modern Democracy* (N.Y.: Harper, 1945), p. 746.

[111] Garvey, *Philosophy and Opinions*, II, 325–26; John Hope Franklin, *From Slavery to Freedom: A History of American Negroes* (N.Y.: Knopf, 1947), p. 482.

[112] Garvey, *Philosophy and Opinions*, II, 62; Ottley, *"New World A-Coming,"* p. 73.

pure white race, as far as that can be." [113] The U.N.I.A. chief felt constrained
to warn the white world of the dangers inherent in social equality. "Some
Negroes believe in social equality," he cautioned. "They want to intermarry
with the white women of this country, and it is going to cause trouble later
on. Some Negroes want the same jobs you have. They want to be Presidents
of the nation." [114]

On the other hand, white Americans need have no fears of the aims of
the Universal Negro Improvement Association, which Garvey declared was
stoutly opposed to "miscegenation and race suicide" and believed strongly
"in the purity of the Negro race and the purity of the white race." [115] So intent was Garvey on the goal of complete racial compartmentalization that he
even went so far as to warn individual whites of the danger of allowing Negroes to become elected officials, artisans, or skilled laborers while white
workers were unemployed. Such ill-considered opportunities for blacks, he believed, would only lead to "bloody . . . wholesale mob violence." [116] This
abandonment of Negro economic rights was too much for former sympathizer
William Pickens, who exploded wrathfully, "This squat, energetic, gorilla-
jawed black man is one of the worst enemies of his own Race." [117] Garvey
intended, of course, that Negroes should create their own economic opportunities through such race enterprises as the Black Star Line and the Negro
Factories Corporation. In this connection it is of interest to note, however,
that at least five of the important operational posts in the Black Star Line
were at one time or another filled by white men, including three ship cap-
tains, a first assistant engineer, and a marine superintendent. Apparently,
suitably skilled Negroes were not easy to find, even for service with a Negro
steamship company.

In October, 1921, President Warren G. Harding made a controversial
speech on race relations while visiting Birmingham, Alabama. Quoting from
Lothrop Stoddard's alarmist book, *The Rising Tide of Color against White
World Supremacy,* Harding asserted his belief in the old Booker T. Washington ideal of the social separation of the two races. "There shall be recognition
of the absolute divergence in things social and racial," the President declared. "Men of both races may well stand uncompromisingly against every
suggestion of social equality. . . . Racial amalgamation there cannot be," [118]
Though southern Negroes may have agreed with the Washington *Bee's*

---

[113] Garvey, *Philosophy and Opinions,* I, 37.

[114] Quoted in Len S. Nembhard, *Trials and Triumphs of Marcus Garvey* (Kingston, Jamaica: Gleaner, 1940), p. 84.

[115] Garvey, *Philosophy and Opinions,* II, 81.

[116] Chicago *Defender,* March 29, 1924.

[117] *Ibid.,* April 26, 1924.

[118] *New York Times,* October 27, 1921.

appraisal of the Harding speech as "a brave, courageous, fearless, heroic deed," [119] the more militant Negro leadership in the North indicated its stunned dismay at the President's apparently unfriendly attitude. Garvey, however, immediately telegraphed his congratulations to President Harding and expressed "the heartfelt thanks of four hundred million Negroes of the world for the splendid interpretation you have given the race problem." "All true Negroes are against social equality," the U.N.I.A. president asserted, "believing that all races should develop on their own social lines." [120] Harding's Birmingham address, Garvey later wrote, "was one that revealed his depth of thought for the Negro." [121] Those Negroes with an eye for the *double-entendre* could find a wry bit of humor in the assertion. Others might criticize both Harding and his predecessor, Woodrow Wilson, for their lack of sympathetic activity on behalf of colored citizens, but to Garvey they "came nearest to playing the Christ in the leadership of the American people." [122]

How well Garvey's aggressive philosophy of racial purity and social separation permeated the lowest echelons of the Universal Negro Improvement Association may be shown by a letter to the mayor of New Orleans from the women's auxiliary of the local division of the organization:

> We like your "Jim Crow" laws, in that they defend the purity of races and any person married to any but a Negro cannot become a member of our organization. We are not members . . . of that class who are spending their time imitating the rich whites . . . studying Spanish so as to be able to pass for anything but a Negro, thereby getting a chance to associate with you. We are not ashamed of the Race to which we belong and we feel sure that God made black skin and kinky hair because He desired to express Himself in that type.[123]

It is not hard to see from the foregoing why Garvey was opposed so vigorously by the militant Negro rights organizations like the N.A.A.C.P., and conversely, why he received open encouragement from such white supremacy groups as the Ku Klux Klan.

Garvey had a strong distaste for any alliance with white labor organizations, a skepticism that probably stemmed in part from his early failure as a strike leader in Jamaica. This distrust of the labor movement also reflected a

---

[119] Washington *Bee*, November 5, 1921.

[120] *New York Times*, October 27, 1921.

[121] Garvey, *Philosophy and Opinions*, II, 51.

[122] *Ibid.*, p. 52.

[123] Chicago *Defender*, March 31, 1923.

feeling that the white worker was the Negro's greatest competitor and most dangerous rival.[124] Rather than seek an alliance with white workers, Garvey told Negroes that the white employer was their best friend until such time as the race had achieved economic independence.[125] The Negro Factories Corporation and the Black Star Line were direct moves to set up Negro-owned business enterprises so that Negroes would not have to beg for employment from whites. It seemed self-evident to Garvey that "the only convenient friend" of the American Negro worker was "the white capitalist," who "being selfish—seeking only the largest profit out of labor—is willing and glad to use Negro labor wherever possible on a scale 'reasonably' below the standard white union wage." The white employer would "tolerate the Negro" only if he accepted "a lower standard of wage than the white union man." Garvey's solution for the black worker, therefore, was to "keep his scale of wage a little lower than the whites" and thereby "keep the goodwill of the white employer," all the time husbanding Negro resources so that the race could ultimately become economically free.[126] Needless to say, this cheerful rejection of trade unionism did little to endear Garvey to Negro labor leaders, and it early won for him the bitter hostility of men like Chandler Owen and A. Philip Randolph, who were currently engaged in a successful campaign to establish a union of Negro sleeping car porters.

Similarly, Garvey refused to have anything to do with socialism and communism, despite the alarmist attempts of the Lusk Committee and the Department of Justice to portray him as a dangerous radical agitator. He felt that these movements of the left, although they made a pretense of helping the Negro, were inherently prejudiced against the black race, since they were dominated by whites. "Fundamentally what racial difference is there between a white Communist, Republican or Democrat?" Garvey demanded to know. "On the appeal of race interest the Communist is as ready as either to show his racial . . . superiority over the Negro." [127] The U.N.I.A. leader suspected that for all his fine talk the Communist would just as quickly join a lynch mob as would the less radical white citizen, and consequently he believed that communism must first prove itself as a really new reform movement before the Negro could safely accept it.[128] The Communists were not initially opposed to Garvey's Universal Negro Improvement Association, though they deplored his emphasis on African Zionism. Party members in-

---

[124] Abram L. Harris and Sterling D. Spero, "Negro Problem," *Encyclopaedia of the Social Sciences*, XI (1937), 350.

[125] Bunche, "Programs, Ideologies, Tactics, and Achievements," p. 412; Harry Haywood, *Negro Liberation* (N.Y.: International Publishers, 1948), p. 202.

[126] Garvey, *Philosophy and Opinions*, II, 69–70.

[127] *Ibid.*; Garvey, "The Future," *Black Man*, II (July-August, 1936), 8–9.

[128] Garvey, *Philosophy and Opinions*, II, 70.

side the U.N.I.A. were ordered to push the fight for Negro equality within the United States, but they were so few in number that they were never able either to "capture" the association or to challenge successfully Garvey's leadership.[129] The Communist Party was greatly impressed with the amazing lower-class appeal of the U.N.I.A., however, and after the organization had begun to disintegrate in 1926 Robert Minor wrote disconsolately: "A breaking up of this Negro association would be a calamity to the Negro people and to the working class as a whole. . . . It is composed very largely, if not almost entirely, of Negro workers and impoverished farmers, although there is a sprinkling of small business men." [130]

In spite of Garvey's announced opposition to communism as a reform movement, he publicly mourned the death of Nikolai Lenin, the founder of the Soviet Union, in 1924. In a *Negro World* editorial he called Lenin "probably the world's greatest man between 1917 and . . . 1924," and announced that the U.N.I.A. had dispatched a cablegram to Moscow "expressing the sorrow and condolence of the 400,000,000 Negroes of the world." [131] This action need not be seen as a startling reversal of Garvey's earlier views, but merely as an example of his unexcelled flair for the dramatic and his egotistical desire to be associated with the important men of the day.

Although Garvey had once defined "radical" as "a label that is always applied to people who are endeavoring to get freedom," [132] he never hesitated to use the confusing term to discredit his opponents. In January, 1923, for example, after the "Committee of Eight" had written the Department of Justice protesting the delay in the trial of the four Black Star officials, Garvey wired the United States Attorney General to assure him of the patriotic loyalty of the U.N.I.A. In his telegram Garvey sought to smear his Negro critics. The National Association for the Advancement of Colored People was dominated by Socialists, Garvey declared, and he called the Friends of Negro Freedom "a red Socialistic organization." He accused the African Blood Brotherhood, another hostile group, of being composed of "representatives of the Bolsheviki of Russia." [133] This was a shady dodge as old as the game of politics itself: discredit your opponents by fair means or foul and perhaps they will stop asking embarrassing questions. There was just enough truth in Garvey's allegations, however, to warrant making the charges in this period of general reaction against leftist movements.

---

[129] Wilson Record, *The Negro and the Communist Party* (Chapel Hill: Univ. of North Carolina Press, 1951), pp. 40–41.

[130] Robert Minor, "Death or a Program," *Workers Monthly*, V (April, 1926), 270, quoted in *ibid.*, p. 41. Cf. I. Amter, *The World Liberative Movement of the Negroes* (Moscow: Soviet State Publishing House, 1925).

[131] *Negro World*, February 2, 1924.

[132] Garvey, *Philosophy and Opinions*, I, 18–19.

[133] *New York Times*, January 21, 1923.

The Universal Negro Improvement Association, far from being oriented to the left, may be classified as a movement of the extreme right. Its intense nationalism and narrow racial outlook had little in common with liberal groups that were seeking to tear down these barriers between men and nations. In 1937, after Italy's legions had overrun Ethiopia, Garvey boasted that he had been the first prophet of fascism. "We were the first Fascists," he told a friend. "We had disciplined men, women, and children in training for the liberation of Africa. The black masses saw that in this extreme nationalism lay their only hope and readily supported it. Mussolini copied Fascism from me but the Negro reactionaries sabotaged it." [134]

One may question whether Garvey was aware of all the connotations of either fascism or communism, but certainly his U.N.I.A., with its fierce chauvinistic nationalism and strongly centralized leadership, had fascist characteristics. Garvey talked of a democratic African republic but it is a little hard to imagine him in such a government. Much more likely would have been a black empire with Garvey upon its throne. "Liberty and true Democracy means," he once said, "that if one man can be the President, King, Premier or Chancellor of a country then the other fellow can be the same also." [135] There never was much doubt in the mind of this supremely confident black man as to just what his personal role in the "democratic" shift of power would be.

In many respects Garveyism resembled another movement of minority group nationalism, the Jewish Zionism of Theodor Herzl. Arnold Rose has pointed out the interesting similarity in background and outlook shared by Herzl and Garvey. Neither was exposed to strong anti-minority feelings in his formative years and later each reacted against prejudice in terms of escape to a land free of discrimination. Both adopted a chauvinistic, even religious nationalism, and both sought support from those groups most hostile to their own minority group.[136] Both movements took on elements of fanaticism in their belligerent determination to secure a new life for their oppressed peoples. There is nothing to suggest that Garvey was familiar with Herzl's *Judenstaat,* published some twenty years before Garvey launched his own program of black Zionism, though he once described his followers as "Zionists" (Case A, 1699). However similar the aims and origin of the two movements, Zionism proved to be by far the stronger and more successful, perhaps because it managed to secure heavy financial and intellectual support from the Jews of the world. Garveyism, on the other hand, was greatly handicapped by the fact that it always remained the personal crusade of a single leader whose autocratic methods and slipshod financial practices alienated

---

[134] Quoted in Joel Rogers, *World's Great Men of Color,* II (N.Y.: J. A. Rogers, 1946), 602.

[135] U.N.I.A. circular, January, 1920, quoted in Case A, 2667.

[136] Arnold M. Rose, *The Negro's Morale: Group Identification and Protest* (Minneapolis: Univ. of Minnesota Press, 1949), pp. 43–44.

much of the support the movement might otherwise have received. And regardless of the similarity between Jewish Zionism and Garveyism, the U.N.I.A. leader entertained strong prejudices against Jews in general.[137]

Marcus Garvey's philosophy of race relations was inextricably bound up in his staunch belief that it was useless for the Negro to attempt to better his condition in a country dominated by another, inherently hostile race. Firmly convinced that the United States would always be a white man's country, and concerned lest the Negro should forget his racial and cultural background, Garvey willingly relinquished Negro rights in America for the dubious right to establish a black nation in Africa. His zeal in securing this Negro state led him to co-operate with the most reactionary and anti-Negro groups in the United States. It is both a mistake and an injustice to assume, however, as some careless writers have done, that Garvey was merely an opportunistic demagogue anxious to build up a powerful following for personal gain.[138] Demagogue he most certainly was, but his motives, mistaken as they often seemed to many Negro Americans eager to win full status as citizens of the only country they had ever known, were much more complex than that. Garvey was determined to help his suffering people and his devotion often led him to act in a way that was incomprehensible to American-born Negroes.

In 1919, the year Garvey first began to be noticed in the United States, Walter Lippmann concluded that Americans would have to work out a civilization where "no Negro need dream of a white heaven and of bleached angels." "Pride of race will come to the Negro when a dark skin is no longer associated with poverty, ignorance, misery, terror and insult," Lippmann declared. "When this pride arises every white man in America will be the happier for it. He will be able then, as he is not now, to enjoy the finest quality of civilized living—the fellowship of different men." [139] The creation of a powerful feeling of race pride is perhaps Garvey's greatest and most lasting contribution to the American race scene. Marcus Garvey is gone and with him many of the more spectacular yet ephemeral aspects of his colorful movement, but the awakened spirit of Negro pride that he so ardently championed remains an important legacy to the Negro people.

---

[137] See, for example, Garvey, "The Jews in Palestine," *Black Man*, II (July-August, 1936), 3.

[138] A good example of this sort of writing is to be found in William J. Slocum, "Sucker Traps: Plain and Fancy," *Collier's*, CXXV (January 28, 1950), 49–50.

[139] Walter Lippmann's Introduction in Carl Sandburg, *The Chicago Race Riots* (N.Y.: Harcourt, Brace & World, 1919), p. iv.

SUGGESTED READING

The literature on Negro protest movements before the sit-ins is still very limited, and the Garvey movement—its sources of support and the activities of its former members in the thirties—has never been adequately explored. Robert Brisbane's "Some New Light on the Garvey Movement," *Journal of Negro History*, XXXVI (Jan., 1951), 53–62, is superficial. Oscar Handlin's *The American People in the Twentieth Century* ° (Harvard Univ. Press, 1954) briefly discusses Garvey. *Negro Protest Thought in the Twentieth Century*,° edited by Francis Broderick and August Meier (Bobbs-Merrill, 1965), includes two items by Garvey, sandwiched between materials by A. Philip Randolph and Langston Hughes.

Arna Bontemps and Jack Conroy's *Anyplace But Here* ° (Hill & Wang, 1966) is a good survey of Negro migration to the North. Thomas Woofter's *Negro Migration* (Gray,1920), is a valuable contemporary account. The report by the Chicago Commission on Race Relations, *The Negro in Chicago* (1922), remains the best source on the postwar riot in Chicago, and Elliot Rudwick's *Race Riot at East St. Louis, July 2, 1917* ° (Southern Illinois Univ. Press, 1964) is a thoughtful analysis by a sociologist. Arthur Waskow, *From Race Riot to Sit-In* ° (Doubleday, 1966) surveys the period from the riots to the early sixties but focuses on the riots. E. U. Essien-Udom's *Black Nationalism: A Search for an Identity in America* ° (Harvard Univ. Press, 1962) and "The Nationalist Movements of Harlem," *Freedomways*, III (Summer, 1963), 335–42, offer some intelligent comments about the movement.

An excellent introduction to the Harlem Renaissance is *The New Negro* ° (Boni, 1925), edited by Alain Locke. This should be supplemented by Langston Hughes' autobiography, *The Big Sea*° (Knopf, 1945).

WILLIAM APPLEMAN WILLIAMS

The Legend of Isolationism
in the 1920's

INTRODUCTION

For years historians characterized American foreign policy in the
1920's as isolationist and attributed to policy makers and ordinary
citizens a desire to remain uninvolved with the rest of the world.
There is still some doubt about the attitudes of the citizens toward
foreign policy, but it is clear that the concept of isolationism, if extended to mean more than opposition to collective security, poorly
fits the actual policies of the twenties. In reconsidering the foreign
policy of that decade, William Appleman Williams asserts that
American businessmen and policy makers were actively engaged
in expanding American economic power abroad and in seeking to

FROM William Appleman Williams, "The Legend of Isolationism in the 1920's," *Science
and Society*, XVIII (Winter, 1954), pp. 1–20. Reprinted by permission.

This paper was read before the December, 1953, meeting of the Pacific Historical Association, held at Davis College, California.

impose on the world a system that would curb revolutions and maintain equal access for all nations to markets and outlets for investments (the Open Door policy).

The Treaty of Versailles, he notes, was shaped with the specter of Bolshevik Russia hovering over the meetings, and the final version expressed Wilson's eagerness to use American power to maintain the status quo in the world. The American debate over the League of Nations, Williams contends, was not for the most part a controversy between isolationists and internationalists but a dispute over the appropriate tactics for extending American power and advancing the national interest.

Williams' treatment of the twenties is exemplary of his general theory about American foreign policy from the 1890's to the Cold War: the desire for economic expansion has provided the force behind American foreign involvement. According to his conception, policy makers and other groups (most notably big businessmen) considered economic expansion abroad as a necessary method of maintaining domestic prosperity. Depression at home, they feared, could entail turmoil, class division, and the destruction of democracy. International trade and investments required international stability and depended on law and order; consequently, revolutions (particularly left-wing movements) were contrary to American interests.

The Williams analysis, based on the earlier work of Charles A. Beard, interprets American policy as an effort to protect and advance a world order in which liberal capitalism can flourish. ("Our investments and trade relations are such," declared Calvin Coolidge, "that it is almost impossible to conceive of any conflict anywhere on earth which would not affect us injuriously.") In effect, Williams argues that American foreign policy is based on a particular conception of political economy (an ideology), and in so doing he questions the traditional analysis of events that separates the categories of politics and economics.

At the University of Wisconsin, Williams has trained some of the more prominent young historians of American foreign policy, and his books, particularly *The Tragedy of American Diplomacy,* rev. ed. (World, 1962), have in recent years captured the imagination of many younger historians. Despite his impact on the reinterpretation of American history, there have been no published general criticisms of his framework and no careful re-examination of his premises. Judging from reviews and occasional comments about his interpretation, it seems that the most common criticism is that he has imposed on policy makers and others a centrality of vision and concern with the political economy of capitalism that the evidence does not adequately support. In addition, his own work often seems ambiguous about whether the Open Door policy is a tactic or a preeminent value, and his concept of ideology sometimes seems too loose, evading any analysis of a hierarchy of values. (At times Williams has been wrongly interpreted as being an economic determinist or as arguing that foreign policy is governed by economics; actually he links economics and politics within an ideology of political economy.)

In the following essay (which appears in expanded form in *The Tragedy of American Diplomacy*) his analysis curiously fails to consider the pressure within America in the twenties for a high tariff. Such short-sighted economic nationalism, even if not interpreted as isolationism (though some historians so label it), brings into doubt his conception of a sophisticated policy-making élite, which believed that American and world prosperity depended on a relaxation of trade barriers and an expansion of trade.

The widely accepted assumption that the United States was isolationist from 1920 through 1932 is no more than a legend. Sir Francis Bacon might have classed this myth of isolation as one of his Idols of the Market-Place. An "ill and unfit choice of words," he cautioned, "leads men away into innumerable and inane controversies and fancies." [1] And certainly the application of the terms *isolation* and *isolationism* to a period and a policy that were characterized by vigorous involvement in the affairs of the world with consciousness of purpose qualifies as an "ill and unfit choice of words." Thus the purpose of this essay: on the basis of an investigation of the record to suggest that, far from isolation, the foreign relations of the United States from 1920 through 1932 were marked by express and extended involvement with—and intervention in the affairs of—other nations of the world.

It is both more accurate and more helpful to consider the twenties as contiguous with the present instead of viewing those years as a quixotic interlude of low-down jazz and lower-grade gin, fluttering flappers and Faulkner's fiction, and bootlegging millionaires and millionaire bootleggers. For in foreign policy there is far less of a sharp break between 1923 and 1953 than generally is acknowledged. A closer examination of the so-called isolationists of the twenties reveals that many of them were in fact busily engaged in extending American power. Those individuals and groups have not dramatically changed their outlook on foreign affairs. Their policies and objectives may differ with those of others (including professors), but they have never sought to isolate the United States.

This interpretation runs counter to the folklore of American foreign relations. Harvard places isolationism "in the saddle." Columbia sees "Ameri-

---

[1] F. Bacon, *Novum Organum*, Headlam's translation as revised by C. P. Curtis and F. Greenslet, *The Practical Cogitator* (Boston, Houghton Mifflin Co., 1945), p. 14–16.

cans retiring within their own shell." Yale judges that policy "degenerated" into isolation—among other things.[2] Others, less picturesque but equally positive, refer to a "marked increase of isolationist sentiment" and to "those years of isolationism." Another group diagnoses the populace as having "ingrained isolationism," analyzes it as "sullen and selfish" in consequence, and characterizes it as doing "its best to forget international subjects." Related verdicts describe the Republican party as "predominantly isolationist" and as an organization that "fostered a policy of deliberate isolation." [3]

Most pointed of these specifications is a terse two-word summary of the diplomacy of the period: "Isolation Perfected." [4] Popularizers have transcribed this theme into a burlesque. Their articles and books convey the impression that the Secretaries of State were in semi-retirement and that the citizenry wished to do away with the Department itself.[5] Columnists and commentators have made the concept an eerie example of George Orwell's double-think. They label as isolationists the most vigorous interventionists.

The case would seem to be closed and judgment given if it were not for the ambivalence of some observers and the brief dissents filed by a few others. The scholar who used the phrase "those years of isolationism," for example, remarks elsewhere in the same book that "expansionism . . . really was long a major expression of isolationism." Another writes of the "return to an earlier policy of isolation," and on the next page notes a "shift in policy dur-

---

[2] A. M. Schlesinger, *Paths to the Present* (New York, The Macmillan Co., 1949), p. 69, 201; L. M. Hacker, "American International Relations," in *The United States and Its Place in World Affairs, 1918–1943*, ed. by A. Nevins and L. M. Hacker, (Boston, D. C. Heath and Co., 1943), p. 166; S. F. Bemis, "The Shifting Strategy of American Defense and Diplomacy," in *Essays in History and International Relations in Honor of George Hubbard Blakeslee*, ed. by D. E. Lee and G. E. McReynolds (Worcester, Clark University, 1949), p. 9.

[3] In sequence, these quotations come from S. Adler, "The War-Guilt Question and American Disillusionment, 1919–1928," *The Journal of Modern History*, XXIII, NO. 1 (March, 1951), p. 27; A. K. Weinberg, *Manifest Destiny. A Study of Nationalist Expansion in American History* (Baltimore, Johns Hopkins Press, 1935), p. 473; L. M. Hacker and H. S. Zahler, *The United States in the 20th Century* (New York, Appleton-Century-Crofts, Inc., 1952), p. 278, 302; W. Wilson, quoted in Weinberg, *Manifest Destiny*, p. 473; F. D. Roosevelt, *Foreign Affairs*, VI, NO. 4 (July, 1928), p. 577; W. Johnson, *The Battle Against Isolation* (Chicago, Chicago University Press, 1944), p. 132. For similar expressions see S. F. Bemis, *A Diplomatic History of the United States* (3rd ed., New York, Henry Holt and Co., 1950), p. 705; J. D. Hicks, *The American Nation* (Boston, Houghton Mifflin Co., 1949), p. 565; D. Perkins, *The Evolution of American Foreign Policy* (New York, Oxford University Press, 1949), p. 110; and A. Nevins, *America in World Affairs* (London, Oxford University Press, 1941), p. 80.

[4] D. F. Fleming, *The United States and World Organization, 1920–1933* (New York, Columbia University Press, 1938), title of Chapter VI.

[5] This literature is far too vast to cite, but even a perusal of *The Reader's Guide to Periodical Literature* will indicate the great volume of such material. It is vital to note, however, that the so-called disillusionment writers did not make this mistake—whatever their other errors. They criticized the policies of the time, but documented, in such journals as *The Nation*, the active character of the diplomacy.

ing the twenties amounting almost to a 'diplomatic revolution.'" A recent biographer states that Henry Cabot Lodge "did not propose . . . an isolationist attitude," but then proceeds to characterize the Monroe Doctrine— upon which Lodge stood in his fight against the League of Nations treaty— as a philosophy of "isolation." And in the last volume of his trilogy, the late Professor Frederick L. Paxton summed up a long review of the many diplomatic activities of the years 1919–1923 with the remark that this was a foreign policy of "avoidance rather than of action." [6]

But a few scholars, toying with the Idol of the Market-Place, have made bold to rock the image. Yet Professor Richard Van Alstyne was doing more than playing the iconoclast when he observed that the "militant manifest destiny men were the isolationists of the nineteenth century." For with this insight we can translate those who maintain that Lodge "led the movement to perpetuate the traditional policy of isolation." Perhaps William G. Carleton was even more forthright. In 1946 he pointed out that the fight over the League treaty was not between isolationists and internationalists, and added that many of the mislabeled isolationists were actually "nationalists and imperialists." Equally discerning was Charles Beard's comment in 1933 that the twenties were marked by a "return to the more aggressive ways . . . [used] to protect and advance the claims of American business enterprise." All these interpretations were based on facts that prompted another scholar to change his earlier conclusion and declare in 1953 that "the thought was all of keeping American freedom of action." [7]

---

[6] Quotations, in order, from Weinberg, *Manifest Destiny*, p. 473, 454; H. U. Faulkner, *American Political and Social History* (6th ed., New York, Appleton-Century-Crofts, Inc., 1952), p. 700, 701; J. A. Garraty, *Henry Cabot Lodge. A Biography* (New York, Alfred A. Knopf, 1953), p. 348, 364–65; F. L. Paxton, *American Democracy and the World War. Postwar Years. Normalcy, 1918–1923* (Berkeley, University of California Press, 1948), p. 367. For other examples of this ambiguity see D. Perkins, *The American Approach to Foreign Policy* (Cambridge, Harvard University Press, 1952), p. 26; T. A. Bailey, *A Diplomatic History of the American People* (4th ed., New York, Appleton-Century-Crofts, Inc., 1950), p. 682—where he says that the Harding Administration "retreated into what ex-President Wilson described as 'sullen and selfish isolation'"; H. J. Carman and H. C. Syrett, *A History of the American People* (New York, Alfred A. Knopf, 1952), p. 264–65, and title of Chapter XII; S. E. Morison and H. S. Commager, *The Growth of the American Republic* (4th ed., New York, Oxford University Press, 1950), Volume II, p. 497; and H. B. Parkes, *The United States of America* (New York, Alfred A. Knopf, 1953).

[7] R. W. Van Alstyne, "The Significance of the Mississippi Valley in American Diplomatic History, 1686–1890," *Mississippi Valley Historical Review*, xxxvi, no. 2 (September, 1949), p. 238; L. L. Leonard, *Elements of American Foreign Policy* (New York, McGraw-Hill Book Co., Inc., 1953), p. 220; among the many others who characterize Lodge in this manner is S. Adler in his recent article on isolation, "Isolationism Since 1914," *The American Scholar*, xxi, no. 3 (Summer, 1952), p. 340; W. G. Carleton, "Isolationism and the Middle West," *Mississippi Valley Historical Review*, xxxiii, no. 3 (December, 1946), p. 381–82; C. A. and M. R. Beard, *The Rise of American Civilization* (New Edition. Two Volumes in One. Revised and Enlarged. New York, The Macmillan Co., 1933), p. 681–83; and compare D. Perkins, *The American Approach to Foreign Policy*, p. 26, with D. Perkins, "The Department of State and Public Opinion," Chapter IX in *The Diplomats 1919–*

These are perceptive comments. Additional help has recently been supplied by two other students of the period. One of these is Robert E.
Osgood, who approached the problem in terms of *Ideals and Self-Interest in American Foreign Relations*.[8] Though primarily concerned with the argument that
Americans should cease being naive, Osgood suggests that certain stereotypes are misleading. One might differ with his analysis of the struggle over
the Treaty of Versailles, but not with his insistence that there were fundamental differences between Senators Lodge and William E. Borah—as well
as between those two and President Woodrow Wilson. Osgood likewise
raises questions about the reputed withdrawal of the American public. Over
a thousand organizations for the study of international relations existed in
1926, to say nothing of the groups that sought constantly to make or modify
foreign policy.

Osgood gives little attention to this latter aspect of foreign relations, a
surprising omission on the part of a realist.[9] But the underlying assumption of
his inquiry cannot be challenged. The foreign policy issue of the twenties was
never isolationism. The controversy and competition were waged between
those who entertained different concepts of the national interest and disagreed over the means to be employed to secure that objective. Secretary of
State Charles Evans Hughes was merely more eloquent, not less explicit.

1939, ed. by G. A. Graig and F. Gilbert (Princeton, Princeton University Press, 1953),
p. 308. Interestingly enough, both Carleton and Van Alstyne addressed their remarks to
meetings of the Mississippi Valley Historical Association, and their articles later appeared
as lead articles in the *Review*. On the same program with Van Alstyne, furthermore, was
Professor Richard Leopold, whose comments were of a similar nature and whose paper
was also printed. This professional audience seems to have ignored their keen suggestions.
Professor Weinberg's article, "The Historical Meaning of the American Doctrine of Isolation," *The American Political Science Review*, xxxiv (1940), p. 539–47, offers certain
concepts that would go far to resolve the contradictions in his earlier *Manifest Destiny*,
but he did not apply the ideas to any later period. H. Feis writes of America's active
foreign economic policy in *The Diplomacy of the Dollar, First Era, 1919–1932* (Baltimore, Johns Hopkins Press, 1950), but fails to note that these facts contradict the idea of
isolation. The same approach is taken by G. Soule, *Prosperity Decade. From War to Depression: 1917–1929* (New York, Rinehart and Co., Inc., 1947), p. 252–74. Far
more stimulating than either Feis or Soule is S. Kuznets, "Foreign Economic Relations of
the United States and Their Impact Upon the Domestic Economy," Chapter 11 in his
Economic Change (New York, W. W. Norton and Co., 1953), p. 296–333. See also the
neglected work of A. D. Gayer and C. T. Schmidt, *American Economic Foreign Policy.
Postwar History, Analysis, and Interpretation* (New York, no publisher given, 1939), especially p. 11–17.

[8] R. E. Osgood, *Ideals and Self-Interest in America's Foreign Relations. The Great Transformation of the Twentieth Century* (Chicago, University of Chicago Press, 1953).

[9] This is strange for a realist trained in the school of Professor Hans J. Morgenthau's *Realpolitik*. For the realists emphasize the fact that the relationship between power and ideals
is reciprocal. Not only do ideas fail to have consequences without power, but the sources
and the nature of the power have some correlation with the character of the ideals. Thus it
would seem doubly unrealistic to slight the sources of power and at the same time discuss
the ideas without reference to the private as well as the public record of the groups and
individuals in question.

"Foreign policies," he explained in 1923, "are not built upon abstractions. They are the result of practical conceptions of national interest arising from some immediate exigency or standing out vividly in historical perspective." [10]

Historian George L. Grassmuck used this old-fashioned premise of the politician as a tool with which to probe the *Sectional Biases in Congress on Foreign Policy*. Disciplining himself more rigorously in the search for primary facts than did Osgood, Grassmuck's findings prompted him to conclude that "the 'sheep and goats' technique" of historical research is eminently unproductive. From 1921 to 1933, for example, the Republicans in both houses of Congress were "more favorable to both Army and Navy measures than . . . Democrats." Eighty-five percent of the same Republicans supported international economic measures and agreements. As for the Middle West, that much condemned section did not reveal any "extraordinary indication of a . . . tendency to withdraw." Nor was there "an intense 'isolationism' on the part of [its] legislators with regard to membership in a world organization." [11] And what opposition there was seems to have been as much the consequence of dust bowls and depression as the product of disillusioned scholars in ivory towers.

These investigations and correlations have two implications. First, the United States was neither isolated nor did it pursue a policy of isolationism from 1920 to 1933. Second, if the policy of that era, so generally accepted as the product of traditional isolationist sentiment, proves non-isolationist, then the validity and usefulness of the concept when applied to earlier or later periods may seriously be challenged.

Indeed, it would seem more probable that the central theme of American foreign relations has been the expansion of the United States. Alexander Hamilton made astute use of the phrase "no entangling alliances" during the negotiation of Jay's Treaty in 1794, but his object was a *de facto* affiliation with the British Fleet—not isolation.[12] Nor was Thomas Jefferson seeking to withdraw when he made of Monticello a counselling center for those seeking to emulate the success of the American Revolution. A century later Senator Lodge sought to revise the Treaty of Versailles and the Covenant of the League of Nations with reservations that seemed no more than a restatement of Hamilton's remarks. Yet the maneuvers of Lodge were no more isolationist in character and purpose than Hamilton's earlier action. And while surely no

---

[10] C. E. Hughes, "The Centenary of the Monroe Doctrine," *The Annals of the American Academy of Political and Social Science*, Supplement to Volume CXI (January, 1923), p. 7.

[11] G. L. Grassmuck, *Sectional Biases in Congress on Foreign Policy* (Baltimore, Johns Hopkins Press, 1951), p. 32, 93, 162, 49.

[12] Hamilton to the British Minister, as quoted by S. F. Bemis, *Jay's Treaty. A Study in Commerce and Diplomacy* (New York, Macmillan and Co., 1924), p. 246.

latter-day Jefferson, Senator Borah was anything but an isolationist in his concept of the power of economics and ideas. Borah not only favored the recognition of the Soviet Union in order to influence the development of the Bolshevik Revolution and as a check against Japanese expansion in Asia, but also argued that American economic policies were intimately connected with foreign political crises. All those men were concerned with the extension of one or more aspects of American influence, power, and authority.

Approached in this manner, the record of American foreign policy in the twenties verifies the judgments of two remarkably dissimilar students: historian Richard W. Leopold and Senator Lodge. The professor warns that the era was "more complex than most glib generalizations . . . would suggest"; and the scholastic politician concludes that, excepting wars, there "never [was] a period when the United States [was] more active and its influence more felt internationally than between 1921 and 1924." [13] The admonition about perplexity was offered as helpful advice, not as an invitation to anti-intellectualism. For, as the remarks of the Senator implied, recognition that a problem is involved does not mean that it cannot be resolved.

Paradox and complexity can often be clarified by rearranging the data around a new focal point that is common to all aspects of the apparent contradiction. The confusion of certainty and ambiguity that characterizes most accounts of American foreign policy in the twenties stems from the fact that they are centered on the issue of membership in the League of Nations. Those Americans who wanted to join are called internationalists. Opponents of that move became isolationists. But the subsequent action of most of those who fought participation in the League belies this simple classification. And the later policies of many who favored adherence to the League casts serious doubts upon the assumption that they were willing to negotiate or arbitrate questions that they defined as involving the national interest. More pertinent is an examination of why certain groups and individuals favored or disapproved of the League, coupled with a review of the programs they supported after that question was decided.

Yet such a re-study of the League fight is in itself insufficient. Equally important is a close analysis of the American reaction to the Bolshevik Revolution. Both the League Covenant and the Treaty of Versailles were written on a table shaken by that upheaval. The argument over the ratification of the combined documents was waged in a context determined as much by Nikolai Lenin's *Appeal to the Toiling, Oppressed, and Exhausted Peoples of Europe*

---

[13] R. W. Leopold, "The Mississippi Valley and American Foreign Policy, 1890–1941: an Assessment and an Appeal," *Mississippi Valley Historical Review*, xxxvii, no. 4 (March, 1951), p. 635; H. C. Lodge, "Foreign Relations of the United States, 1921–1924," *Foreign Affairs*, ii, no. 4 (June, 1924), p. 526.

and the Soviet *Declaration to the Chinese People* as by George Washington's Farewell Address.[14]

Considered within the setting of the Bolshevik Revolution, the basic question was far greater than whether or not to enter the League. At issue was what response was to be made to the domestic and international division of labor that had accompanied the Industrial Revolution. Challenges from organized urban labor, dissatisfied farmers, frightened men of property, searching intellectual critics, and colonial peoples rudely interrupted almost every meeting of the Big Four in Paris and were echoed in many Senate debates over the treaty. And those who determined American policy through the decade of the twenties were consciously concerned with the same problem.

An inquiry into this controversy over the broad question of how to end the war reveals certain divisions within American society. These groupings were composed of individuals and organizations whose position on the League of Nations was coincident with and part of their response to the Bolsheviks; or, in a wider sense, with their answer to that general unrest, described by Woodrow Wilson as a "feeling of revolt against the large vested interests which influenced the world both in the economic and the political sphere." [15] Once this breakdown has been made it is then possible to follow the ideas and actions of these various associations of influence and power through the years 1920 to 1933.

At the core of the American reaction to the League and the Bolshevik Revolution was the quandary between fidelity to ideals and the urge to power. Jefferson faced a less acute version of the same predicament in terms of whether to force citizenship on settlers west of the Mississippi who were reluctant to be absorbed in the Louisiana Purchase. A century later the anti-imperialists posed the same issue in the more sharply defined circumstances of the Spanish-American War. The League and the Bolsheviks raised the question in its most dramatic context and in unavoidable terms.

There were four broad responses to this reopening of the age-old di-

---

[14] None of the authors cited above makes this association of events central to their discussion of the League issue. Few of them even connect the two. The integration has, of course, been made: most notably by E. H. Carr, *The Soviet Impact on the Western World* (New York, The Macmillan Co., 1947); M. Dobb, *Political Economy and Capitalism. Some Essays in Economic Tradition* (New York, International Publishers, 1945), Chapter VII, and *Studies in the Development of Capitalism* (New York, International Publishers, 1947), Chapter VIII; H. J. Laski, *Reflections on the Revolution of Our Time* (New York, 1947); Sir L. Namier, *Conflicts. Studies in Contemporary History* (London, The Macmillan Co., 1942), Chapter I; and, of especial significance, H. Hoover, *American Individualism* (Garden City, Doubleday, Page and Co., 1923).

[15] W. Wilson, remarks to the Council of Ten, January 16, 1919, *Papers Relating to the Foreign Relations of the United States. Paris Peace Conference* (13 vols., Washington, D. C.), III, p. 583.

lemma. At one pole stood the pure idealists and pacifists, led by William Jennings Bryan. A tiny minority in themselves, they were joined, in terms of general consequences if not in action, by those Americans who were preoccupied with their own solutions to the problem. Many American business men, for example, were concerned primarily with the expansion of trade and were apathetic toward or impatient with the hullabaloo over the League.[16] Diametrically opposed to the idealists were the vigorous expansionists. All these exponents of the main chance did not insist upon an overt crusade to run the world, but they were united on Senator Lodge's proposition that the United States should dominate world politics. Association with other nations they accepted, but not equality of membership or mutuality of decision.

Caught in the middle were those Americans who declined to support either extreme. A large number of these people clustered around Woodrow Wilson, and can be called the Wilsonites. Though aware of the dangers and temptations involved, Wilson declared his intention to extend American power for the purpose of strengthening the ideals. However noble that effort, it failed for two reasons. Wilson delegated power and initiative to men and organizations that did not share his objectives, and on his own part the president ultimately "cast in his lot" with the defenders of the status quo.[17]

Led by the Sons of the Wild Jackass, the remaining group usually followed Senator Borah in foreign relations. These men had few illusions about the importance of power in human affairs or concerning the authority of the United States in international politics. Prior to the world war they supported —either positively or passively—such vigorous expansionists as Theodore Roosevelt, who led their Progressive Party. But the war and the Bolshevik Revolution jarred some of these Progressives into a closer examination of their assumptions. These reflections and new conclusions widened the breach with those of their old comrades who had moved toward a conservative position on domestic issues. Some of those earlier allies, like Senator Albert J. Beveridge, continued to agitate for an American century. Others, such as Bainbridge Colby, sided with Wilson in 1916 and went along with the president on foreign policy.

But a handful had become firm anti-expansionists by 1919.[18] No at-

---

[16] See the excellent essay by J. H. Foote, "American Industrialists and Foreign Policy, 1919–1922. A Study in Attitudes," Master's Thesis, University of Wisconsin, Madison, 1947; for a typical expression see the remarks of Senator Walter E. Edge—"we wasted, practically wasted, two years of the opportunity presented to us at that time, unequaled, as I say, in the history of the world"—in National Foreign Trade Council, *Official Report of the Eighth National Foreign Trade Convention, 1921* (New York, 1921), p. 553.

[17] W. Wilson, remarks to the Big Five, February 14, 1919, *Foreign Relations. Russia, 1919* (Washington, D. C., 1937), p. 59.

[18] C. Vevier reviewed these early expansionist sympathies of the Progressives in "The Progressives and Dollar Diplomacy," Master's Thesis, University of Wisconsin, Madison,

tempt was made by these men to deny the power of the United States. Nor did they think that the nation could become self-sufficient and impregnable in its strength. Borah, for example, insisted that America must stand with Russia if Japan and Germany were to be checked. And Johnson constantly pointed out that the question was not whether to withdraw, but at what time and under what circumstances to use the country's influence. What these men did maintain was that any effort to run the world by establishing an American system comparable to the British Empire was both futile and un-American.

In this they agreed with Henry Adams, who debated the same issue with his brother Brooks Adams, Theodore Roosevelt, and Henry Cabot Lodge in the years after 1898. "I incline now to anti-imperialism, and very strongly to anti-militarism," Henry warned. "If we try to rule politically, we take the chances against us." By the end of the first world war another generation of expansionists tended to agree with Henry Adams about ruling politically, but planned to build and maintain a similar pattern of control through the use of America's economic might. Replying to these later expansionists, Borah and other anti-expansionists of the nineteen-twenties argued that if Washington's influence was to be effective it would have to be used to support the movements of reform and colonial nationalism rather than deployed in an effort to dam up and dominate those forces.

For these reasons they opposed Wilson's reorganization of the international banking consortium, fearing that the financiers would either influence strongly or veto—as they did—American foreign policies. With Senator Albert B. Cummins of Iowa they voted against the Wilson-approved Webb-Pomerene Act, which repealed the anti-trust laws for export associations. In the same vein they tried to prevent passage of the Edge Act, an amendment to the Federal Reserve Act that authorized foreign banking corporations.[19] Led by Borah, they bitterly attacked the Versailles Treaty because, in their view, it committed the United States to oppose colonial movements for self-government and to support an unjust and indefensible status quo. From the

1949. W. E. Leuchtenburg later published a summary of his own study of the same question as "Progressivism and Imperialism: The Progressive Movement and American Foreign Policy, 1898–1916," *Mississippi Valley Historical Review*, xxxix, no. 3 (December, 1952), p. 483–504. It would seem, however, that Leuchtenburg missed the split within the Progressives over Wilson's foreign policy. For in note 38, page 493, he considers it "remarkable" that the Progressives fought Wilson in view of the degree to which the president "was involved with American imperialist aspirations." This writer's information on the division comes from the manuscript papers of Calvin Coolidge, William E. Borah, William Judson, Samuel N. Harper, Theodore Roosevelt, Alexander Gumberg, Raymond Robins, and Woodrow Wilson; from the materials in the National Archives; and the *Congressional Record*.

[19] See, for example, the debates on the Webb-Pomerene Act in *Congressional Record*, Volume 56, Part 1, p. 69–71; and the votes on the same legislation, p. 168, 186.

same perspective they criticized and fought to end intervention in Russia and the suppression of civil liberties at home.[20]

Contrary to the standard criticism of their actions, however, these anti-expansionists were not just negative die-hards. Senator Cummins maintained from the first that American loans to the allies should be considered gifts. Borah spoke out on the same issue, hammered away against armed intervention in Latin America, played a key role in securing the appointment of Dwight Morrow as Ambassador to Mexico, and sought to align the United States with, instead of against, the Chinese Revolution. On these and other issues the anti-expansionists were not always of one mind, but as in the case of the Washington Conference Treaties the majority of them were far more positive in their actions than has been acknowledged.[21]

Within this framework the key to the defeat of the League treaty was the defection from the Wilsonites of a group who declined to accept the restrictions that Article X of the League Covenant threatened to impose upon the United States. A morally binding guarantee of the "territorial integrity and existing political integrity of all members of the League" was too much for these men. First they tried to modify that limitation. Failing there, they followed Elihu Root and William Howard Taft, both old time expansionists, to a new position behind Senator Lodge. Among those who abandoned Wilson on this issue were Herbert Hoover, Calvin Coolidge, Charles Evans Hughes, and Henry L. Stimson.

Not all these men were at ease with the vigorous expansionists. Stimson, for one, thought the Lodge reservations "harsh and unpleasant," and later adjusted other of his views.[22] Hoover and Hughes tried to revive their version of the League after the Republicans returned to power in 1920. But at

---

[20] Especially pertinent are the remarks of Borah, *Congressional Record*, V54:1:636; V57:1:190; V58:3143–44; and his letter to F. Lynch, August 1, 1919, *Papers of William E. Borah*, Library of Congress, Manuscript Division, Washington, D. C. Also important are the comments of Senator Hiram Johnson, *Congressional Record*, V53:1:503, 505. Eric Goldman's penetrating study of the Progressives, *Rendezvous With Destiny. A History of Modern American Reform* (New York, Alfred A. Knopf, 1952), completely misses this development. On p. 273–74, Goldman remarks that the "most striking deviation of American progressivism in foreign affairs from its attitudes in domestic affairs was the enthusiasm for international order in the form of the League of Nations." He proceeds, then, to argue that if the progressives had applied the same criticism to the League as they had to its laissez faire counterpart in domestic affairs "they could hardly have emerged with a favorable attitude." But the key point is that the hard core of the Progressives did exactly this and came out in opposition to the League.

[21] This paragraph is based on much the same material cited in note 18. But see, as representative, Cummins' remarks on the loans, *Congressional Record*, V55:1:757, 762; Borah on economic factors, V64:1:930–31; and the parliamentary maneuvers over the Liberian Loan, V63:1:287–88.

[22] Stimson, Diary entry of December 3, 1919, quoted in H. L. Stimson and McGeorge Bundy, *On Active Service in Peace and War* (New York, Harper and Brothers, 1948), p. 104.

the time all of them were more uneasy about what one writer has termed Wilson's "moral imperialism." [23] They were not eager to identify themselves with the memories of that blatant imperialism of the years 1895 to 1905, but neither did they like Article X. That proviso caught them from both sides, it illegalized changes initiated by the United States, and obligated America to restore a status quo to some aspects of which they were either indifferent or antagonistic. But least of all were they anxious to run the risk that the Wilsonian rhetoric of freedom and liberty might be taken seriously in an age of revolution. Either by choice or default they supported the idea of a community of interest among the industrialized powers of the world led by an American-British entente as against the colonial areas and the Soviet Union.

This postwar concept of the community of interest was the first generation intellectual off-spring of Herbert Croly's *Promise of American Life* and Herbert Hoover's *American Individualism*. Croly's opportunistic nationalism provided direction for Hoover's "greater mutuality of interest." The latter was to be expressed in an alliance between the government and the "great trade associations and the powerful corporations." [24] Pushed by the Croly-Hoover wing of the old Progressive Party, the idea enjoyed great prestige during the twenties. Among its most ardent exponents were Samuel Gompers and Matthew Woll of the labor movement, Owen D. Young of management, and Bernard Baruch of finance.

What emerged was an American corporatism. The avowed goals were order, stability, and social peace. The means to those objectives were labor-management co-operation, arbitration, and the elimination of waste and inefficiency by closing out unrestrained competition. State intervention was to be firm, but moderated through the cultivation and legalization of trade associations which would, in turn, advise the national government and supply leaders for the federal bureaucracy. The ideal was union in place of diversity and conflict.[25]

---

[23] H. F. Cline, *The United States and ·Mexico* (Cambridge, Harvard University Press, 1953), p. 141.

[24] H. Croly, *The Promise of American Life* (New York, The Macmillan Co., 1909); H. Hoover, *American Individualism*, p. 43; and Hoover, quoted in Goldman, *Rendezvous With Destiny*, p. 309. Goldman makes this identification between Croly and Hoover, but does not develop it, either as corporatism or in foreign affairs. Other Americans had spoken the language of the community of interest. J. P. Morgan used it to describe his ideal in the economic realm. Brooks Adams warned Theodore Roosevelt that such coordination at the national level was necessary to insure American supremacy in the world. The Adams argument emphasized the need for an intellectual and political elite chosen from the upper classes to supervise the community of interest through control of the national government.

[25] American corporatism is a neglected field. This writer is greatly indebted to Professor Paul Farmer, University of Wisconsin, for many long discussions of the question. Farmer brought to these conversations his intimate and extended knowledge of French corporative theory and practice as it developed to and culminated in the Vichy Government. His insights into the American scene were equally penetrating. At a later date M. H. Elbow,

Other than Hoover, the chief spokesmen of this new community of interest as applied to foreign affairs were Secretaries of State Hughes and Stimson. In the late months of 1931 Stimson was to shift his ground, but until that time he supported the principle. All three men agreed that American economic power should be used to build, strengthen, and maintain the cooperation they sought. As a condition for his entry into the cabinet, Hoover demanded—and received—a major voice in "all important economic policies of the administration." [26] With the energetic assistance of Julius Klein, lauded by the National Foreign Trade Council as the "international business go-getter of Uncle Sam," Hoover changed the Department of Commerce from an agency primarily concerned with interstate commerce to one that concentrated on foreign markets and loans, and control of import sources.[27] Hughes and Stimson handled the political aspects of establishing a "community of ideals, interests and purposes." [28]

These men were not imperialists in the traditional sense of that much abused term. All agreed with Klein that the object was to eliminate "the old imperialistic trappings of politico-economic exploitation." They sought instead the "internationalization of business." [29] Through the use of economic power they wanted to establish a common bond, forged of similar assumptions and purposes, with both the industrialized nations and the native business community in the colonial areas of the world. Their deployment of

---

French Corporative Theory, 1789–1948. A Chapter in the History of Ideas (New York, Columbia University Press, 1953), was helpful in review. Of other published material, the following were most helpful: S. D. Alinsky, *Reveille For Radicals* (Chicago, University of Chicago Press, 1946); G. A. Almond, "The Political Attitudes of Wealth," *Journal of Politics*, vii, no. 3 (August, 1945); R. A. Brady, *Business as a System of Power* (New York, Columbia University Press, 1938); R. Bendix, "Bureaucracy and the Problem of Power," *Public Administration Review*, v, no. 3 (Summer, 1945); J. A. C. Grant, "The Guild Returns to America," *Journal of Politics*, iv, nos. 3 AND 4 (August, November, 1942); W. E. Henry, "The Business Executive: the Psycho-Dynamics of a Social Role," *American Journal of Sociology*, liv, no. 1 (January, 1949); E. J. Howenstine, "Public Works Policy in the Twenties," *Social Research*, xii (December, 1946); F. Hunter, *Community Power Structure. A Study of Decision Makers* (Chapel Hill, University of North Carolina Press, 1953); R. S. Lynd, "Power Politics and the Post War World," in *The Postwar World. The Merrick Lectures for 1944* (New York, Abingdon-Cokesbury Press, 1945); and M. Weber, *The Theory of Social and Economic Organization*, trans. by A. M. Henderson and T. Parsons, ed. by T. Parsons (New York, Oxford University Press, 1947). For a revealing glimpse of the later bi-partisan movement toward corporatism, and the consequences thereof, see *The Welfare State and the National Welfare. A Symposium on Some of the Threatening Tendencies of Our Times*, ed. by S. Glueck (Cambridge, Addison-Wesley Press, Inc., 1952); and the last chapter in Goldman, *Rendezvous With Destiny*.

[26] *The Memoirs of Herbert Hoover. The Cabinet and the Presidency, 1920–1933* (New York, The Macmillan Co., 1952), p. 36.

[27] *Official Report of the 18th Foreign Trade Convention, 1931* (New York, 1931), p. 287.

[28] C. E. Hughes, remarks concerning a substitute for Article X of the League Covenant, Union League Club Speech, New York, March 26, 1919.

[29] J. Klein, *Frontiers of Trade* (New York, The Century Co., 1929), p. 40, 46.

America's material strength is unquestioned. President Calvin Coolidge reviewed their success, and indicated the political implications thereof, on Memorial Day, 1928. "Our investments and trade relations are such," he summarized, "that it is almost impossible to conceive of any conflict anywhere on earth which would not affect us injuriously." [30]

Internationalization through the avoidance of conflict was the key objective. This did not mean a negative foreign policy. Positive action was the basic theme. The transposition of corporatist principles to the area of foreign relations produced a parallel policy. American leadership and intervention would build a world community regulated by agreement among the industrialized nations. The prevention of revolution and the preservation of the sanctity of private property were vital objectives. Hughes was very clear when he formulated the idea for Latin America. "We are seeking to establish a *Pax Americana* maintained not by arms but by mutual respect and good will and the tranquillizing processes of reason." There would be, he admitted, "interpositions of a temporary character"—the Secretary did not like the connotations of the word intervention—but only to facilitate the establishment of the United States as the "exemplar of justice." [31]

Extension to the world of this pattern developed in Latin America was more involved. There were five main difficulties, four in the realm of foreign relations and one in domestic affairs. The internal problem was to establish and integrate a concert of decision between the government and private economic groups. Abroad the objectives were more sharply defined: circumscribe the impact of the Soviet Union, forestall and control potential resistance of colonial areas, pamper and cajole Germany and Japan into acceptance of the basic proposition, and secure from Great Britain practical recognition of the fact that Washington had become the center of Anglo-Saxon collaboration. Several examples will serve to illustrate the general outline of this diplomacy, and to indicate the friction between the office holders and the office dwellers.

Wilson's Administration left the incoming Republicans a plurality of tools designed for the purpose of extending American power. The Webb-Pomerene Law, the Edge Act, and the banking consortium were but three of the more obvious and important of these. Certain polishing and sharpening remained to be done, as exemplified by Hoover's generous interpretation of the Webb-Pomerene legislation, but this was a minor problem. Hoover and Hughes added to these implements with such laws as the one designed to give American customs officials diplomatic immunity so that they could do cost accounting surveys of foreign firms. This procedure was part of the plan to provide equal opportunity abroad, under which circumstances Secretary

---

[30] C. Coolidge, Address of May 30, 1928, *Congressional Record*, V69:10:10729.

[31] C. E. Hughes, "Centenary of the Monroe Doctrine," *Annals*, p. 17; and Hughes, remarks to the Havana Conference, 1928.

Hughes was confident that "American business men would take care of themselves." [32]

It was harder to deal with the British, who persisted in annoying indications that they considered themselves equal partners in the enterprise. Bainbridge Colby, Wilson's last Secretary of State, ran into the same trouble. Unless England came "to our way of thinking," Colby feared that "agreement [would] be impossible." A bit later Hughes told the British Ambassador that the time had come for London's expressions of cordial sentiment to be "translated into something definite." After many harangues about oil, access to mandated areas, and trade with Russia, it was with great relief that Stimson spoke of the United States and Great Britain "working together like two old shoes." [33]

Deep concern over revolutionary ferment produced great anxiety. Hughes quite agreed with Colby that the problem was to prevent revolutions without making martyrs of the leaders of colonial or other dissident movements. The despatches of the period are filled with such expressions as "very grave concern," "further depressed," and "deeply regret," in connection with revolutionary activity in China, Latin America, and Europe.[34] American foreign service personnel abroad were constantly reminded to report all indications of such unrest. This sensitivity reached a high point when one representative telegraphed as "an example of the failure to assure public safety . . . the throwing of a rock yesterday into the state hospital here." Quite in keeping with this pattern was Washington's conclusion that it would support "any provisional government which gave satisfactory evidence of an intention to re-establish constitutional order." [35]

Central to American diplomacy of the twenties was the issue of Germany and Japan. And it was in this area that the government ran into trouble with its partners, the large associations of capital. The snag was to convince the bankers of the validity of the long range view. Hoover, Hughes and Stimson all agreed that it was vital to integrate Germany and Japan into the American community. Thus Hughes opposed the French diplomacy of force

---

[32] The story of the fight over diplomatic immunity for consular officers can be followed in *Foreign Relations, 1925*, p. 211–54; the quote from Hughes is by J. Butler Wright, in *Official Report of the 12th National Foreign Trade Convention, 1925* (New York, 1925), p. 165.

[33] Colby to Wright, November 5, 1920, *National Archives of the United States* (hereafter cited as *NA*), 574.D1/240b; Hughes, Memorandum of conversation with Geddes, September 20, 1921, *NA*, 500.A 4/190.5; Stimson, Memorandum of July 20, 1931, *NA*, 462.00 R 296/4594.5.

[34] Colby to Russell, August 13, 1920, *NA*, 333.3921 L 96/3; Hughes to Cottrell, April 9, 1923, *NA*, 824.51/174; Hughes to Morales, June 30, 1923, *NA*, 815.00/2609; same to same, May 15, 1923, *NA*, 815.00/2574.

[35] Kodding to Hughes, October 10, 1924, *NA*, 375.1123 Coleman and Delong/89; Hughes to Welles, April 10, 1924, *NA*, 815.00/3077 a supplement.

on the Rhine, and for his own part initiated the Dawes Plan. But the delegation of so much authority to the financiers backfired in 1931. The depression scared the House of Morgan and it refused to extend further credits to Germany. Stimson "blew up." He angrily told the Morgan representative in Paris that this strengthened France and thereby undercut the American program. Interrupted in the midst of this argument by a trans-Atlantic phone call from Hoover, Stimson explained to the president that "if you want to help the cause you are speaking of you will not do it by calling me up, but by calling Tom Lamont." Stimson then turned back to Lamont's agent in Europe and, using "unregulated language," told the man to abandon his "narrow banking axioms." [36]

Similar difficulties faced the government in dealing with Japan and China. The main problem was to convince Japan, by persuasion, concession, and the delicate use of diplomatic force, to join the United States in an application of its Latin American policy to China. Washington argued that the era of the crude exploitation of, and the exercise of direct political sovereignty over, backward peoples was past. Instead, the interested powers should agree to develop and exercise a system of absentee authority while increasing the productive capacity and administrative efficiency of China. Japan seemed amenable to the proposal, and at the Washington Conference, Secretary Hughes went a great distance to convince Tokyo of American sincerity. Some writers, such as George Frost Kennan and Adolf A. Berle, claim that the United States did not go far enough.[37] This is something of a mystery. For in his efforts to establish "cooperation in the Far East," as Hughes termed it, the Secretary consciously gave Japan "an extraordinarily favorable position." [38]

Perhaps what Kennan and Berle have in mind is the attitude of Thomas Lamont. In contrast to their perspective on Europe, the bankers took an extremely long range view of Asia. Accepting the implications of the Four and Nine Power Treaties, Lamont began to finance Japan's penetration of the mainland. Hughes and Stimson were trapped. They continued to think in terms of American business men taking care of themselves if given an opportunity, and thus strengthening Washington's position in the world community. Hughes wrote Morgan that he hoped the consortium would become an

---

[36] Stimson, Memorandum of talks with representatives of J. P. Morgan and Co., Paris, July 17, 1931, NA, 462.00 R 296/4587.5.

[37] G. F. Kennan, *American Diplomacy, 1900–1950* (Chicago, University of Chicago Press, 1951), p. 82; A. A. Berle, Jr., review of H. Feis, *The China Tangle*, in the *New York Times*, Book Review Section, October 4, 1953.

[38] Hughes to Judge Hiscock, April 24, 1924, quoted in M. J. Pusey, *Charles Evans Hughes* (2 vols., New York, The Macmillan Co., 1951), II, p. 516; Hughes to Bell, October 22, 1924, NA, 893.51/4699; Hughes, Memorandum of conversations with Kato and Balfour, December 2, 1921, NA, 500.A4b/547.5.

"important instrumentality of our 'open door' policy." [39] But the American members of the banking group refused to antagonize their Japanese and British colleagues, and so vetoed Washington's hope to finance the Chinese Eastern Railway and its efforts to support the Federal Telegraph Company in China.

In this context it is easy to sympathize with Stimson's discomfort when the Japanese Army roared across Manchuria. As he constantly reiterated to the Japanese Ambassador in Washington, Tokyo had come far along the road "of bringing itself into alignment with the methods and opinion of the Western World." [40] Stimson not only wanted to, but did in fact give Japan every chance to continue along that path. So too did President Hoover, whose concern with revolution was so great that he was inclined to view Japanese sovereignty in Manchuria as the best solution. Key men in the State Department shared the president's conclusion.[41]

Stimson's insight was not so limited. He realized that his predecessor, Secretary of State Frank B. Kellogg, had been right: the community of interest that America should seek was with the Chinese. The Secretary acknowledged his error to Senator Borah, who had argued just such a thesis since 1917. Stimson's letter to Borah of February 23, 1932, did not say that America should abandon her isolationism, but rather that she had gone too far with the wrong friends. The long and painful process of America's great awakening had begun. But in the meantime President Hoover's insistence that no move should be made toward the Soviet Union, and that the non-recognition of Manchukuo should be considered as a formula looking toward conciliation, had opened the door to appeasement.

SUGGESTED READING

Williams' analysis, while leading some historians to greater caution in their use of the concept of "isolationism," has been generally disregarded in interpreting American foreign policy in the twenties. Selig Adler in *The Isolationist Impulse: The Twentieth-Century Reaction* (Abelard-Schuman, 1957) often broadens his concept of isolationism to mean far more than opposition to entangling alliances or collective security, and he attributes to the average citizen in the twenties a desire

[39] Hughes to Morgan, August 8, 1921, NA, 861.77/2184.

[40] Stimson, Memorandum of November 21, 1931, NA, 793.94/2865; and see Stimson, Memorandum of February 27, 1933, NA, 793.94/5953, for a clear review of his changing attitudes.

[41] This writer is greatly indebted to Professor Richard N. Current, University of Illinois, for sharing his extended knowledge of the Manchurian Crisis. Professor Current's study will be published in the spring of 1954 by Rutgers University Press.

to withdraw from foreign (usually European) affairs. He disagrees with Williams but never cites his work.

Efforts to explain popular American attitudes toward isolationism have often failed to define the concept meaningfully and clearly. Most historians have focused on the Midwest, where there was considerable political opposition to intervention in both world wars. Samuel Lubell in *The Future of American Politics* ° (Doubleday, 1952) explains isolationism in terms of ethnic influences and emphasizes the concentration of German immigrants and their descendants in the Midwest. Ray Allen Billington in "The Origins of Middle Western Isolationism," *Political Science Quarterly*, LX (March, 1945), 44–64, also acknowledges the influence of the immigrants, arguing unpersuasively that the Midwest's allegiance to the Republican party and its anti-Eastern biases also shaped attitudes toward foreign policy. William Carleton in "Isolationism and the Middle West," *Mississippi Valley Historical Review*, XXXIII (Dec., 1946), 377–90, has dissented from this analysis. Ralph Smuckler's "The Region of Isolationism," *American Political Science Review*, XLVII (June, 1953), 386–401, though focusing on the years after 1934, raises doubts about the intimate relationship between isolationism and ethnic background.

George Grassmuck's *Sectional Biases in Congress on Foreign Policy* (Johns Hopkins Univ. Press, 1950) is a useful analysis of regional voting patterns. Richard Leopold in "The Mississippi Valley and American Foreign Policy, 1890–1941: An Assessment and an Appeal," *American Historical Review*, XXXVII (March, 1951), 625–42, surveys much of the literature on the attitudes within the Valley to foreign policy. Bernard Fensterwald, Jr., "The Anatomy of American 'Isolationism' and Expansion," *Journal of Conflict Resolution*, II (June, 1958), 111–39 (Dec., 1958), 280–309, makes an uneven attempt to survey events and to offer a psychological theory about the American attitudes toward foreign policy.

Robert F. Smith, a former student of Williams, offers an essay, "American Foreign Relations, 1920–1942," in Barton J. Bernstein, ed., *Towards A New Past* ° (Pantheon, 1968) that builds on Williams' analysis in *The Tragedy of American Diplomacy*. Another Williams student, Carl Parrini, in *Heir to Empire: United States Economic Diplomacy, 1916–1923* (Univ. of Pittsburgh Press, 1969), presents a detailed study of wartime and postwar American policy. Joseph Brandes in *Herbert Hoover and Economic Diplomacy: Department of Commerce Policy* (Univ. of Pittsburgh Press, 1962) and Joan Wilson in *American Business and Foreign Policy, 1920–1933* (Univ. of Kentucky Press, 1969) provide support for Williams' emphasis on economic expansion.

Christopher Lasch in *The American Liberals and the Russian Revolution* (Columbia Univ. Press, 1967) and Peter Filene in *Americans and the Soviet Experiment, 1917–1933* (Harvard Univ. Press, 1967) stress the interest of Americans in the Soviet Union and the fear that bolshevism evoked. Betty Miller Unterberger has edited a collection of previously published materials in *American Intervention in the Russian Civil War* ° (Heath, 1969). Soviet analyses of American actions and intentions are harshly criticized in George Kennan's "Soviet Historiography and America's Role in the Intervention," *American Historical Review* LXV (June, 1960), 302–22.

CARL N. DEGLER

The Ordeal of Herbert Hoover

INTRODUCTION

Though the nation would later repudiate him and turn elsewhere for leadership, few men in American political life during the 1920's seemed by training and experience better prepared than Herbert Hoover to deal with the Great Depression. His successful directorship of European relief won the admiration of businessmen and the nation's respect, and his achievements as Secretary of Commerce seemed to confirm their judgment. In that position he sought to continue the wartime cooperation among businessmen, and he sponsored trade associations so that industries might escape from some of the perils of competition.

Opposed to laissez faire, Hoover was not an uncritical observer of American society in the twenties. In 1922, in his book

FROM Carl N. Degler, "The Ordeal of Herbert Hoover," *The Yale Review*, LII (Summer, 1963), pp. 563–83. Copyright © 1963 by Yale University. Reprinted by permission.

American Individualism, he acknowledged "the faulty results of our system":

> the spirit of lawlessness; the uncertainty of employment in some call-ings; the deadening effect of certain repetitive processes of manufac-ture; the 12-hour day in a few industries; unequal voice in bargaining for wage in some employment; arrogant domination by some employers and some labor leaders; child labor in some states; inadequate instruc-tion in some areas; unfair competition in some industries; some for-tunes excessive far beyond the needs of stimulation to initiative; sur-vivals of religious intolerance.

Hoover's suggestions for correcting these faults were sometimes obscure and often ambiguous; the book evidences a tension be-tween affirming the spirit of voluntarism and relying on the govern-ment to maintain equality of opportunity. Although Hoover's preference for cooperation rather than economic conflict led him to favor unions for workers, trade associations for industry, market-ing cooperatives for farmers, and even collective bargaining to avoid strife between classes, he sought to keep government above these interests and out of the control of any particular one. "It is where dominant private property is assembled in the hands of the groups who control the state that the individual begins to feel capi-tal as an oppressor," he warned.

Historians, including Carl Degler, the author of the following essay, have found in *American Individualism* clues to explain Hoover's responses to the Depression. Degler sees continuities with progressivism in Hoover's bold efforts to deal with the De-pression, but he notes also the restrictions imposed by Hoover's ideology that barred truly effective action: his fears of public relief eroding the human spirit, his often dogged reliance on voluntarism and local initiative, his opposition to the idea of allowing the gov-ernment to compete with private enterprise, his concern for budget balancing.

Yet Degler believes, as did Walter Lippmann during the early years of Roosevelt's Administration, that Hoover was not the last of the old Presidents. But whereas Lippmann found Hoover the first of the new Presidents, Degler concludes that he was a "transitional figure in the development of government as an active force in the economy in times of depression."

*I*n 1958 Herbert Hoover published a book about his old chief entitled *The Ordeal of Woodrow Wilson.* Wilson's struggle for the League was short and his part in it has gained lustre with passing years. Not so with the ordeal of Herbert Hoover. The Great Depression was considerably longer and his reputation has never been free from the memory of that ordeal. Today, in fact, there are two Hoovers. The first is the living man, the former President who has unstintingly and very capably served Democratic and Republican Administrations alike. He is the Hoover of nation-wide birthday celebrations, of rhapsodic editorials, of admiring Republican national conventions. That conception bears almost no relation to the second, the historical Hoover. In the history books his Administration is usually depicted as cold-hearted, when not pictured as totally devoid of heart, inept, or actionless in the face of the Great Depression. Simply because of the wide gulf between the two Hoovers it is time to try to answer the question William Allen White posed over thirty years ago. Writing an evaluation of Hoover's Administration in the *Saturday Evening Post* of March 4, 1933, White closed his piece with the following words: "So history stands hesitant waiting for time to tell whether Herbert Hoover . . . by pointing the way to social recovery . . . is the first of the new Presidents . . . or whether . . . he is the last of the old."

The notion of two Hoovers should never have grown up; his life and views were too consistent for that. During Hoover's tenure of office, Theodore Joslin, his press secretary, undertook to examine closely all the President's utterances and writings of the preceding ten or eleven years. "In all of those million-odd words, dealing with every important subject," Joslin reported in 1934, "the number of times he reversed himself or modified an important position could be counted on the fingers of one hand." And so it has remained even after March 4, 1933.

Nor were those principles, to which Hoover held so consistently, simply conservative ones, as has so often been assumed. In 1920, for example, when Hoover's political career began, he was the darling of the progressives who still clustered about the figure of the fallen Wilson. College and university faculties were calling upon Hoover to run for president that year—on either ticket. Indeed, his silence as to which party he belonged to, for a time caused his name to figure as prominently in Democratic primaries as in Republican. For example, he received the most votes by far in the Michigan Democratic primary that year. That year, too, Franklin Roosevelt, who was also a member of Woodrow Wilson's Administration, wrote Josephus Daniels that Herbert Hoover "is certainly a wonder, and I wish we could make him President of the United States. There could not be a better one." (Nor did Roosevelt's enthusiasm cool until much later. In 1928 he refused to write an article against Hoover's candidacy because Hoover was "an old personal friend.")

Hoover's principles were distinctly and publicly progressive. In 1920, for example, he defended the principle of collective bargaining and the right to strike—two very unpopular principles at that date—before a frosty Chamber of Commerce in Boston. As Secretary of Commerce in the Harding Administration he opposed the sweeping federal injunction against the railroad strikers and worked with Harding to have the steel industry abandon the twelve-hour day. In his book of guiding principles, *American Individualism,* which he published in 1922, he was careful to distinguish his views from laissez-faire capitalism. The American way, he insisted, "is not capitalism, or socialism, or syndicalism, nor a cross breed of them." It did include, though, government regulation in order to preserve equality of opportunity and individual rights. "This regulation is itself," he pointed out, "proof that we have gone a long way toward the abandonment of the 'capitalism' of Adam Smith. . . ." While Secretary of Commerce in the 1920's he instituted much needed regulations for the burgeoning radio and airplane industries. It was Herbert Hoover who said in 1922 at the first conference on radio that "the ether is a public medium and its use must be for the public benefit. The use of radio channels is justified only if there is public benefit. The dominant element of consideration in the radio field is, and always will be, the great body of the listening public, millions in number, country-wide in distribution." In the same address, he said, "It is inconceivable that we should allow so great a possibility for service to be drowned in advertising chatter." In 1928 he was recommending that a three billion dollar reserve of public works be built up to serve as an economic stabilizer in times of recession.

In short, though he served both Harding and Coolidge, Herbert Hoover was not of their stripe. As he himself said later in his memoirs, "Mr. Coolidge was a real conservative, probably the equal of Benjamin Harrison. . . . He was a fundamentalist in religion, in the economic and social order, and in fishing." (The last because Coolidge, the fishing tyro, used worms for bait.) Moreover, unlike Coolidge, Hoover did not publicly ignore the scandals that rocked the Harding Administration. In June 1931, while dedicating the Harding Memorial at Marion, Ohio, Hoover went out of his way to speak of the tragedy of Warren Harding and of the enormity of the betrayal of a public trust by Harding's friends.

Hoover's record as president contains a number of truly progressive achievements. Although he cannot take credit for initiating the Norris-La Guardia Act of 1932, the fact remains that one of the most important prolabor acts in the whole history of American labor was signed by Herbert Hoover. Like other progressives, he sponsored legislation for conservation like the giant Boulder Dam project and the St. Lawrence Seaway.

But perhaps the most striking example of Hoover's willingness to recognize the new role of government in dealing with the complexities of an industrial economy was his breaking precedent to grapple directly with the Depression. From the outset Hoover rejected the advice of his Secretary of the Treasury, Andrew Mellon, who, as Hoover himself said, was a country-banker of narrow social vision. Mellon believed the crash should be permitted to run its course unmolested. His simple formula in a depression, as he told Hoover, was "Liquidate labor, liquidate stocks, liquidate farms, liquidate real estate." A panic, he told the President, was not so bad. "It will purge the rottenness out of the system. High costs of living and high living will come down. People will work harder, live more moral lives. Values will be adjusted, and enterprising people will pick up the wrecks from less competent people."

In contrast, Hoover's anti-depression action was swift in coming. Within a matter of weeks after the great crash of the stock market at the end of October, Hoover called a meeting of prominent business, labor, and farm leaders to work out plans for preventing the market crash from adversely affecting the rest of the economy. A week later he met for the same purpose with railway presidents. The economic leaders agreed to his plan of holding the line on wages and encouraging industrial expansion. In his annual message to Congress in December 1929, Hoover proudly told of these and other efforts his Administration had made to stem the economic decline. These efforts, he said, "must be vigorously pursued until normal conditions are restored." In January he continued to expand public works on Boulder Dam and on highway construction. By the end of July 1930, the Administration had got underway $800 million in public works, and the President called upon the states and local units of government to follow the national government's example in order to provide as much employment as possible.

The President was well aware of the unprecedented character of his swift anti-depression action. He said as much in his message to Congress in December 1929; he made the same point more explicitly at the Gridiron dinner in April 1930. The country, he said, had avoided the dole and other unsatisfactory devices to meet unemployment by "voluntary cooperation of industry with the Government in maintaining wages against reductions, and the intensification of construction work. Thereby we have inaugurated one of the greatest economic experiments in history on a basis of nation-wide cooperation not charity."

At first Hoover was optimistic about the effects of his program. Several times during the first year he compared the economic decline with that of 1921–22, usually with the observation that the earlier one was the more difficult. As he told the Chamber of Commerce in May 1930, the amount of public works contracted for was already three times the amount in the corresponding period of the previous "great depression."

Yet his optimism did not keep him from action. One thing he emphasized was the necessity of learning from this Depression about the prevention of future ones. He advocated better statistical measures and reform of the banking structure to prevent the drain of credit from productive to speculative enterprise, such as had led to the stock market boom and crash. Moreover, although he emphasized from the beginning that the Depression was "worldwide" and that its "causes and its effects lie only partly in the United States," he did not use this as an excuse for inactivity. There was no need simply to wait for the rest of the world to recover, he said. "We can make a very large degree of recovery independently of what may happen else-

where." In October 1930 he told the American Bankers Association that depressions were not simply to be borne uncomplainingly. "The economic fatal-
ist believes that these crises are inevitable and bound to be recurrent. I
would remind these pessimists that exactly the same thing was once said of
typhoid, cholera, and smallpox." But instead of being pessimistic, medical
science went to work and conquered those diseases. "That should be our attitude toward these economic pestilences. They are not dispensations of Prov-
idence. I am confident in the faith that their control, so far as the cause lies
within our own boundaries, is within the genius of modern business."

Hoover also told the bankers that he could not condone the argument
which had been reported from some of them that the people would have to
accept a lower standard of living in order to get through the Depression.
Such a suggestion, he said, could not be countenanced either on idealistic or
on practical grounds. To accept it would mean a "retreat into perpetual unemployment and the acceptance of a cesspool of poverty for some large part
of our people." Several times during the Depression Hoover made it clear
that the government had a responsibility to employ as many as possible as its
contribution to the mitigation of the unemployment which was growing
alarmingly.

The failure of the economy to respond to treatment and the loss of many
Republican seats in the elections of 1930 caused Hoover for a while to place
new emphasis upon the foreign sources of the Depression. At the end of 1930
he told the Congress that the "major forces of the depression now lie outside
of the United States." In fact, though, the real collapse of the European economy was still almost six months away. Hoover was most fearful that the growing Congressional demands for new expenditures would throw the budget
out of balance. His concern about the budget and his hostility toward the
Congress were both measured in his tactless remark at a press conference in
May 1931 that "I know of nothing that would so disturb the healing process
now undoubtedly going on in the economic situation" as a special session of
Congress. "We cannot legislate ourselves out of a world economic depression; we can and will work ourselves out."

The last sentence, because it was obviously too sweeping to be accurate, was to plague him for years. More important, he quite clearly did not
believe it himself, since he later advocated legislation for just the purposes he
said it could not serve. In the very next month, for example, he explained at
some length to a group of Republican editors just how much the Administration had been doing to extricate the country from the Depression. "For the
first time in history the Federal Government has taken an extensive and positive part in mitigating the effects of depression and expediting recovery. I
have conceived that if we would preserve our democracy this leadership
must take the part not of attempted dictatorship but of organizing cooperation in the constructive forces of the community and of stimulating every element of initiative and self-reliance in the country. There is no sudden stroke

of either governmental or private action which can dissolve these world difficulties; patient, constructive action in a multitude of directions is the strategy of success. This battle is upon a thousand fronts." Unlike previous
administrations, he continued, his had expanded, instead of curtailing, public works during a depression. Public works expenditures, both by the federal
and state governments, he said, continued to increase. Some two billion dollars were being spent, and a million men were employed on these projects.
Aid was also being given to farmers in the drought areas of the South and the
Middle West.

That Hoover truly favored action over patient waiting for the storm to
lift was further shown in his elaborate twelve-point program for recovery
presented in his annual message in December 1931. Among his recommendations was the Reconstruction Finance Corporation, which would become one
of the major agencies of his Administration and of the New Deal for stabilizing banks and aiding recovery. At a press conference the same month he
emphasized anew the desirability of domestic action. "The major steps we
must take are domestic. The action needed is in the home field and it is
urgent. While reestablishment of stability abroad is helpful to us and to the
world, and I am convinced that it is in progress, yet we must depend upon
ourselves. If we devote ourselves to these urgent domestic questions we can
make a very large measure of recovery irrespective of foreign influences." By
early February 1932 the Reconstruction Finance Corporation was in operation. That same month he persuaded the Congress to enact the Glass-Steagall
banking bill, which increased the bases for Federal Reserve bank reserves
and thus expanded credit and conserved gold. The purpose of the RFC was
to shore up failing banks and other financial institutions caught in runs upon
their deposits. With the permission of the Interstate Commerce Commission,
the RFC could also extend financial aid to railroads.

Beyond these operations, though, the President would not let the lending agency go. Especially did he resist federal aid to the unemployed, although the demands for it were growing monthly. He even opposed Congressional appropriations to the Red Cross on the ground that they would
dry up private sources of relief funds. A dole, he said in 1931, must be avoided
at all costs because "the net results of governmental doles are to lower wages
toward the bare subsistence level and to endow the slackers." He did urge
the citizenry generously to support, as he did himself, private charities, like
the Red Cross, which were carrying so much of the burden of unemployment
relief. At no time, of course, did Hoover object to helping the unemployed; he
was no Social Darwinist arguing for the survival of only the fittest. Again and
again, using the most idealistic language, he called upon Americans to extend a hand to those fellow citizens in need. But as much as he publicly and
privately deplored the suffering which the economic crisis brought, he feared
and deplored even more the effects which would be sure to follow if the federal government provided relief to the unemployed. Nowhere was the rigid-

ity of Hoover's highly trained, agile, and well-stocked intellect more apparent than in this matter. Throughout his years as president, despite the cruelest of sarcastic barbs in the press and from the public platform, he held to his position.

Yet surprising as it may seem today, for a long time the country was with him. This was true even during 1931 and early 1932 when it was becoming increasingly evident that private charities, municipal relief funds, and even the resources of the states were inadequate to meet the costs of providing for ten or eleven million unemployed. Already in August 1931 Governor Franklin Roosevelt had told the New York legislature that unemployment relief "must be extended by government—not as a matter of charity but as a matter of social duty." Yet, as late as February 1932 the country was still following Hoover's view of relief and not Roosevelt's. This was shown by the fate of a bill sponsored by liberal Senators Robert M. La Follette, Jr. of Wisconsin and Edward F. Costigan of Colorado to provide federal money to the states for relief. The bill was defeated by a vote of 48 to 35. Democratic Senators made up some forty percent of the votes which killed the measure.

By May 1932, though, the pressure for some federal assistance in relief matters was building up fast. The National Conference of Social Workers, which in the previous year had refused to endorse the principle of federal relief, now switched to supporting it. More important from Hoover's standpoint was the announcement by Senator Joseph Robinson, the conservative Democratic leader in the Senate, that he was joining the liberals in favoring federal relief. Within two days the President announced, after consultation with Robinson, that the RFC would hereafter lend money to the states if their resources for relief were exhausted. The next day the President defended the extraordinary powers of the RFC as necessitated by the economic emergency. In words which sound in retrospect like those of his successor, he said, "We used such emergency powers to win the war; we can use them to fight the depression, the misery and suffering from which are equally great."

Soon thereafter, though, the President demonstrated that he would not take another step toward putting the federal government into the relief field. Two bills by Democrats which went beyond his limits were successfully vetoed. After Congress had adjourned in July 1932, he issued a nine-point program for economic recovery, but most of the items on it were old and the rest were only recommendations for exploratory conferences. By the summer of 1932, then, the Hoover program for recovery had been completed; his principles would permit him to go no further.

As one reviews the actions which Hoover took it is impossible to describe him as a do-nothing president. He was unquestionably one of the truly activist presidents of our history. But he was an activist within a very rigid framework of ideology. Of all American presidents, Herbert Hoover was probably the most singlemindedly committed to a system of beliefs. His pragmatism was well hidden and what there was of it emerged only after great prodding from events. To a remarkable degree, one can observe in his acts as president those principles of individualism which he set forth so simply in his book ten years before. The very same principle, for example, which prevented his sanctioning federal relief to the unemployed, dictated the tone and content of his veto of the bill to create a government corporation to operate Muscle Shoals. The government, he said, should not compete with private enterprise. Moreover, such a project, by being run by the federal government, abrogated the basic principle that all such enterprises should be "administrated by the people upon the ground, responsible to their own communities, directing them solely for the benefit of their communities and not for the purposes of social theories or national politics. Any other course deprives them of liberty." It was this same belief in individual freedom and cooperation which kept him from accepting a governmental system of old age and unemployment insurance. He advocated such measures only when undertaken voluntarily and through private insurance companies.

Even the Reconstruction Finance Corporation, perhaps his most enduring anti-depression agency, was created to assist private business, not to supplant it. True, it was a credit agency in competition with private enterprise, but it was designed to perform tasks which no private institution dared risk; the competition was therefore minimal if not nonexistent. Moreover, although it has been frequently alleged that the RFC lent money to corporations while the Administration denied relief to the unemployed, in Hoover's mind the distinction was crucial and real. The RFC was making loans which would be repaid—and most were—when the banks got back on their feet; it was not making grants. Even when Hoover did permit the RFC to lend money to the states for relief purposes he still insisted that no grants of federal funds be made.

But there was an even more important social justification for agencies like the RFC and the Federal Home Loan Board, which Congress created in July 1932 at the President's request. Hoover recognized as no president had before that the welfare of society was dependent upon business and that government, therefore, must step in. He did this, not because, as some critics said, he favored business over the common people, but because he recognized that if the banks failed the economy would collapse, savings would be lost, and jobs destroyed. The RFC and the Federal Home Loan Board, in effect, socialized the losses of financial institutions by using government to spread their obligations through society. Hoover was not prepared, though, to socialize the losses of the unemployed. That step in ameliorating the impact of the Depression was undertaken by the New Deal through the WPA and other relief agencies. In this respect Hoover was a transitional figure in the development of the government as an active force in the economy in times of depression. He was the first to smash the old shibboleth of government unconcern and impotence.

Perhaps his long-term role was even greater. In the face of great oppo-

sition and much outright hostility, he made a determined and even courageous effort to give the business community and voluntary private agencies a
chance to show whether they could bring the nation out of a depression.
Their failure to do so gave a moral as well as a political impetus to the New
Deal. Just as after Munich no one could say the West had not done its utmost
to meet Hitler halfway, so after Hoover's Administration no one could say
that government had rushed in before other social or economic agencies had
been given a try. That this was so goes a long way toward explaining the
remarkable consensus among Americans ever since the 1930's that government has the prime responsibility for averting or cushioning the effects of a
depression.

A second principle which stopped Hoover from permitting the federal
government to provide relief was his conviction that the budget must not be
unbalanced. As early as February 1930 he warned the Congress against extravagance and told of his own efforts to economize. Economy was essential,
he emphasized, in order to avoid increasing taxes. But as decreasing revenues began to fall behind expenditures, Hoover's concern to keep the budget
in balance overcame his reluctance to increase taxes. On July 1, 1931 the deficit was almost $500 million—an astronomical figure in those days when the
total federal budget was less than $4 billion. In December of that same year
Hoover recommended an increase in taxes. When Congress proved dilatory
he told a press conference in March 1932 that a balanced budget "is the very
keystone of recovery. It must be done." Anything less would undo all the
recovery measures. "The Government," he warned, "no more than individual families can continue to expend more than it receives without inviting
serious consequences."

Hoover recommended a manufacturers' sales tax as the chief new revenue device, in which suggestion he was joined by the new Democratic
Speaker of the House, John Nance Garner of Texas. Garner enjoyed a reputation for being hostile to business and something of a radical in the old Populist tradition, but in the matter of bringing the budget into balance he stood
foursquare with the President. Congress did not pass the sales tax, but it did
pass one of the largest peacetime tax increases in American history.

Today it seems incredible that in a time of economic slump when consumer purchasing power was the principal requirement for recovery, the nation should elect to take money out of the hands of consumers. Yet this was
precisely what the bill, recommended and signed by the Republican President and passed by the Democratic House, entailed. In fact, when in the
course of the debate the House seemed hesitant about increasing taxes, the
Democratic Speaker, John Garner, could not contain his anxiety. Conspicuously forsaking the Speaker's chair, Garner advanced to the well of the
House to make an earnest plea for more taxes. At the conclusion of his speech,
he asked "every man and every woman in this House who . . . is willing to
try to balance the budget to rise in their seats." Almost the whole House,

with its majority of Democrats, rose to its feet, to a growing round of applause. When he asked those who did not want to balance the budget to rise, no one did. The overwhelming majority of the newspapers of the country strongly commended the Congress in June 1932 for its efforts to balance the budget through increased taxes.

During the campaign of 1932 the Democrats continued to equal or even outdo Hoover in their slavish adherence to the ideal of a balanced budget. Franklin Roosevelt, for example, unmercifully attacked the Administration for its extravagance and its unbalanced budget, calling the fifty percent increase in expenditures since 1927 "the most reckless and extravagant past that I have been able to discover in the statistical record of any peacetime government anywhere, any time." He promised a cut of 25 percent in the budget if he were elected. Nor was this simply campaign oratory. As Frank Freidel has observed in his biography, Roosevelt was perfectly sincere in his dismay at the Hoover deficit and he would continue to be regretful about deficits until well after 1933.

From the record, then, it is evident that Democrats were in no better theoretical position to deal with the Depression than Hoover. Leaders of both parties thought of the government as a large household whose accounts must be balanced if national bankruptcy were to be avoided. Neither party could conceive of the central role which government must play in the economy in an industrial society in time of depression. It would take the whole decade of the New Deal and the continuance of the Depression before that fact would be learned by leaders and people alike.

Despite his fixation on the question of the budget, Hoover's conception of the Depression was sophisticated, rational, and coherent; the remedies he suggested were equally so, given his assumptions. In trying to find a way out, Hoover placed most reliance on what modern economists would call the "expectations" of businessmen. If businessmen feel that times are good or at least that they are getting better, they will invest in new plant and equipment, which in turn will employ men and create purchasing power. In substance, the remedies Hoover offered were designed to raise the expectations of businessmen and to maintain purchasing power until the economy picked up again. His first step was securing agreement among businessmen to hold the line on wages in order to keep purchasing power from falling. (And, by and large, as a result of his efforts, wage rates did not fall until the middle of 1931, but employment did, with, unfortunately, the same effect.) A second step in his program was to use government to help out with public work projects and, when private agencies proved inadequate, to provide credit through agencies like the RFC and the Home Loan Board. Finally, as a third arrow in his anti-depression quiver, Hoover sought, through the prestige of his office, to create that sense of confidence and approaching good times which would encourage businessmen to invest. As it turned out, though, he gambled and lost. For with each successive ineffectual statement, the value of his words dropped, until, like the worthless coins of a profligate monarch who debases his own coinage, they were hurled back at his head by a disenchanted press and people.

The Hoover recovery program failed, but probably no government program then thought permissible could have been any more successful. Certainly the New Deal with its more massive injection of government money into the economy succeeded little better. It ended the decade with 9.5 million still unemployed, and industrial production remained below the 1929 level throughout the 1930's except for a brief period in late 1936 and early 1937. On the other hand, most of the countries of Western and Central Europe regained the 1929 level of production by early 1935.

Part of Hoover's ordeal during the Great Depression undoubtedly derived from his personality, which, for a president, was unusual. Indeed, until he became President he had rarely been connected with government other than in an office which was nonpartisan or which he soon made so. Outwardly, at least, he was far removed from the stereotype of the politician; he could not slap a back or utter a guffaw. He appeared shy in public, though stolid was a more accurate description. A bulky man of over 200 pounds, standing almost six feet when he entered the White House, he gave a paradoxical impression of conservative solidity and beaming youth at the same time. His public speech, like his writing, was formal, often stiff, and sometimes bordered on the pedantic. Early in Hoover's Administration, soon after the stock market crash, William Allen White, a Hoover supporter, spotted the new President's weakness. "The President has great capacity to convince intellectuals," he wrote. "He has small capacity to stir people emotionally and through the emotions one gets to the will, not through the intellect." Even Hoover's press secretary recognized that he "experienced the greatest difficulty in interpreting himself and his acts to the public." Indeed, it was characteristic of Hoover that though he found speech writing one of the most laborious of his tasks, he insisted upon writing all his own speeches. The compulsion could be at least enervating, and at worst dangerous to his health. Often he traded sleep for time to work on his speeches and at least once, at St. Paul in the campaign of 1932, he was on the verge of collapse from fatigue. His method of writing was tedious and incredibly time-consuming, involving innumerable drafts, meticulously gone over by himself, only to have still further proofs run off for more rewriting. Yet, after all this effort, his final draft usually was dry, too long, and ponderous.

In view of his poor public image, it is not surprising that for most of his presidency, Hoover's relations with the press were strained when not downright painful. Although he continued the press conferences which Wilson had begun, they were formal affairs with written questions; many reporters were convinced that the President concealed more than he revealed in the meetings. But it was probably Hoover's sensitivity to criticism that worked the real damage. His annual addresses to newspapermen at the Gridiron

Club, which, as was customary, mercilessly lampooned his administration, often carried an edge, betraying his sensitivity to the press corps' jibes. Only occasionally did his private wit break through in public. At the Gridiron Club dinner in December 1932, after his defeat for reelection, he puckishly said, "You will expect me to discuss the late election. Well, as nearly as I can learn, we did not have enough votes on our side. During the campaign I remarked that this Administration had been fighting on a thousand fronts; I learned since the campaign that we were fighting on 21 million fronts." (The size of the Democratic vote.) This was one of the rare times that Hoover poked fun at himself in public.

Yet, despite his difficulties as a public figure, in private Hoover was neither phlegmatic nor shy. In fact he was extremely convivial, seeking constant company, whether at the White House or at his retreat on the Rapidan in the Blue Ridge Mountains. His wife told Joslin that the President could not be happy without numbers of people around him. His friends cherished his constant flow of stories and he delighted in his cigars and pipe. He was an outdoor type of man, reveling in fishing and hiking. Although he liked a joke, he rarely laughed out loud, though his friends knew well his soft chuckle. His own brand of humor could be heavy-handed. Thus in January 1931, when addressing the National Automobile Chamber of Commerce, he observed, with a smile, that 3.5 million cars had been sold in the first year of the depression and that consumption of gasoline was up five percent. "This certainly means," he twitted, "that we have been cheerful in the use of automobiles; I do not assume they are being used for transportation to the poorhouse. While I am aware that many people are using the old automobile a little longer it is obvious that they are still using it and it is being worn out. Altogether the future for the industry does not warrant any despondency." Will Rogers was not so sure. Some months later in a radio broadcast, he drawled, "We are the first nation in the history of the world to go to the poorhouse in an automobile."

Part of the reason Hoover resented the barbed comments of the press was that he worked so hard. It was as characteristic of Herbert Hoover that he was the first president to have a telephone on his desk as it was characteristic of Calvin Coolidge that he refused to have one. Hoover rose at 6 a.m. each morning, joined a group of his friends for a brisk half-hour session with a five pound medicine ball on an improvised court on the White House grounds, then went in to breakfast. He was at his desk by 8:30. He worked steadily all day, smoking incessantly, and usually well into the night. Often he would wake up in the middle of the night and pore over papers or write for an hour or two before going back to sleep. Nevertheless, he rose at the same early hour. Subordinates were not always able to keep up with his pace; some had to be dispatched to rest, but Hoover, miraculously, never succumbed to his self-imposed regimen. His secretary reports that he was not sick a single day of the four years he spent in the White House. A few days at the camp on the Rapidan or a short trip usually sufficed to restore his energies and his will to work. But toward the end of his tenure, even the optimism and strength of a Hoover faltered, at least once. He told his secretary, "All the money in the world could not induce me to live over the last nine months. The conditions we have experienced make this office a compound hell."

Aside from the circumstances in which he found himself as President, one of the reasons the office was "hell" was that Hoover was a poor politician. Often it is said that he did not like politics, or even that he was above politics. Both statements describe the image he held of himself, but many of Hoover's actions while in office are clearly partisan and political. If, for example, he could objectively recognize the weaknesses of the Harding Administration once he was elected president, he could also say during the campaign of 1928 that "the record of the seven and one years" of Coolidge and Harding "constitutes a period of rare courage in leadership and constructive action. Never has a political party been able to look back upon a similar period with more satisfaction." In December 1931, when some voices were calling for a coalition government to deal with the worsening depression, Hoover made it clear that he would have nothing to do with Democrats. "The day that we begin coalition government you may know that our democracy has broken down," he told newspapermen at a Gridiron Club dinner. On the other hand, he could appoint Democrats to office, as he did former Senator Atlee Pomerene to head the RFC when he wanted that office to win support from Democrats. Nor was he devoid of political dramatics. In September 1931 he made a quick descent upon the American Legion Convention in Detroit in a successful effort to stop the Legion from going on record in favor of a bonus for veterans. By going all the way to Detroit, speaking for eleven minutes, and then immediately leaving for Washington again, he demonstrated the importance of his message and the weight of the schedule of work he pursued in Washington. Moreover, as the account written by his Press Secretary Joslin makes clear, he was no more above benefiting from parliamentary trickery in Congress than the next politically-minded president. As Joslin wrote, "It was characteristic of the President to hit back when attacked." Hoover suffered deeply when attacked, and he did not turn the other cheek. As William Allen White, who supported and admired the President, wrote in 1933, "he was no plaster saint politically. He had, during his three years, rather consistently and with a nice instinct chosen to honor in public office men of a conservative type of mind." Moreover, the behind-the-scenes circumstances of his nomination in 1928 and his renomination in 1932, both of which were steam-roller operations, should remove any doubts about his willingness and ability to use devices and tactics quite customary in politics.

No, it was not that he was above politics or that he really despised the operations of politicians. His difficulty was that he was temperamentally incapable of doing what a politican has to do—namely, to admit he could be wrong and to compromise. In the whole volume of his memoirs devoted to the Depression there is not a single mention of a major error on his part, though his opponents are taxed with errors in every chapter. Over a hundred pages of the volume are devoted to the answering of every charge of Franklin Roosevelt in 1932. Nowhere, though, does he notice that in 1932, he himself in his speech at Detroit incorrectly quoted Roosevelt and then proceeded to criticize at length his opponent for something he never said. This inability to admit error, to compromise, William Allen White recognized in 1931 as Hoover's undoing. After all, White wrote, "Politics . . . is one of the minor branches of harlotry, and Hoover's frigid desire to live a virtuous life and not follow the Pauline maxim and be all things to all men, is one of the things that has reduced the oil in his machinery and shot a bearing. . . ." Hoover's inability to admit error and the seriousness with which he viewed himself are both illustrated in another incident during the campaign of 1932. One of the Democrats' favorite sports that year was recalling, with appropriate sounds of derision, Hoover's remarks in 1928 to the effect that the United States was well on the way to abolishing poverty. Hoover, instead of admitting he had been somewhat optimistic, once again donned his hair shirt and stolidly endorsed the earlier statement because, as he said, it expressed the ideals for which Americans stood. Yet this was in the middle of the Depression and he was running for reelection.

In good times, Herbert Hoover's humble birth might have been an asset, but in the Great Depression it was not. Left an almost penniless orphan at nine, Hoover became a world figure and a millionaire before he was forty-five. With such spectacular success behind him it was understandable that he should think, albeit mistakenly, that anyone could achieve at least half as much as he. Undoubtedly his own experience fostered his insistence, throughout his life, that individual initiative was the prime motive force in a good society. What to other men appear as obstacles or handicaps, to the self-made man appear, at least in retrospect, as goads or incentives. Like most such men, Hoover attributed his success to will. When Theodore Joslin once asked him what had been his boyhood ambition, he replied without hesitation, "to be able to earn my own living without the help of anybody, anywhere." To such a man individual effort seems capable of moving mountains unaided; he is loath to see it shunted aside by collective action even in times of economic dislocation. The self-made man can indeed be the wrong man at such times.

Nor was it an accident that the other prominent self-made politician of the time, Alfred E. Smith, was also doubtful about the virtues of government aid to the unemployed, that he should attack Franklin Roosevelt for accusing the Hoover Administration of aiding the corporations and ignoring the poor. "I will take off my coat and vest," Smith vowed in the spring of 1932, "and fight to the end against any candidate who persists in any demagogic appeal to the masses of the working people of this country to destroy themselves by setting class against class and rich against poor." In a short time, Smith's views, like Hoover's, would bring him to outright opposition to the New Deal. It is not without significance in this respect that Roosevelt, who came to represent government benevolence toward the unemployed, was no self-made man, but lived securely and unadventurously on inherited wealth.

The differences in social origins of Roosevelt and Hoover, of course, are only one facet of the divergence between the Hoover Administration and the New Deal. Indeed, since the 1930's it has become commonplace to see Hoover and Roosevelt as opposites. Certainly there are differences—and important ones—between the administrations of the two Presidents, but we are now far enough removed from both to recognize also the real continuity between them that William Allen White was prescient enough to foresee dimly. When the two administrations are seen against the backdrop of previous administrations and earlier social attitudes, the gulf between them shrinks appreciably. Both men, it is worth recalling, were protégés of Woodrow Wilson; both of them, therefore, accepted a role for government in the economy which added up to a sharp departure from laissez-faire. Both, in the course of their respective administrations, drew upon their experiences in the First World War, where they had seen government intervening in the economy. Hoover's RFC, for example, was frankly modeled, as he said, after the War Finance Corporation. Both saw big business standing in need of controls, and, for a while, both believed that cooperation between business and government was the best way to achieve that control. Hoover, for instance, cited the Federal Reserve System as the ideal kind of business and government cooperation for purposes of regulating the economy; Roosevelt in the NRA also placed his trust in controls worked out through business and government cooperation. Moreover, both Roosevelt and Hoover took the view that it was government's responsibility to do something about a depression; neither man was willing to subscribe to the view which prevailed before 1929—namely, that economic declines were simply natural phenomena through which the nation struggled as best it could and that government could not be expected to do much about them.

Finally, it is also worth noticing that the temperament of the two men, their conceptions of America and of its future are much closer than the conventional picture paints them. (It was Roosevelt, during the campaign of 1932, who created the erroneous image of Hoover as the man without faith or hope in the future.) All through the Depression, Hoover's unvarying theme was that all this would pass and the essential vigor of the American economy would reassert itself. Undoubtedly he counted too heavily on the influence of his words to overcome the lack of business confidence, but there is no question of his optimistic outlook. One measure of it was the shock he received when he read Roosevelt's address to the Commonwealth Club in San Francisco. That was the speech in which Roosevelt talked about the frontier being ended and opportunities for economic growth being limited. Hoover took up the challenge, denying "the whole idea that we have ended the advance of

America, that this country has reached the zenith of its power, the height of its development. That is the counsel of despair for the future of America. That is not the spirit by which we shall emerge from this depression." The important point is that such pessimism was really not expressive of Roosevelt's thought, either. Although historians have frequently referred to the Commonwealth Club address as the one clear indication during the campaign of 1932 of the philosophy behind the New Deal, we now know that the speech was neither written by Roosevelt, nor read by him before he appeared before his audience. As Rexford Tugwell has pointed out, the Commonwealth Club address, which Berle and he wrote, did not reflect Roosevelt's true attitude toward the American economic future. Indeed, its very singularity among Roosevelt's campaign speeches demonstrates how foreign it was to Roosevelt's feelings and convictions. The speech belied his abundant enthusiasm for the future, and his deep faith in the country and its capacities. Moreover, he soon contradicted its import in his Inaugural Address, when he electrified the country with the cry, "All we have to fear is fear itself."

How ironical that these words of Roosevelt should be so well known, when it was Herbert Hoover who all along had been saying the same thing— in less graphic and less credible language, to be sure—but saying it nonetheless. That fact, too, contributed to the ordeal of Herbert Hoover.

SUGGESTED READING

Richard Hofstadter in *The American Political Tradition* ° (Knopf, 1948), on the basis of much the same evidence that Degler uses, is harshly critical of Hoover and calls him a utopian capitalist. In addition to emphasizing the limitations of his ideology, Hofstadter notes the contradiction between Hoover's concern with expanding foreign trade and his failure to understand that the high tariff made it impossible for prospective buyers to sell in the American market. William Appleman Williams in *The Contours of American History* ° (World, 1961) argues that Hoover's responses to the Depression were limited by his ideological fear of placing the control of government in the major organized blocs (labor, business and agriculture), a situation that Hoover described as "a syndicalist nation on a gigantic scale."

Hoover in his *Memoirs* (Macmillan, 1951–52, 3 vols.) discusses his political experience in the Great Depression and offers a spirited defense of his policies. Favorable studies of the Administration are provided by W. S. Myers and W. H. Newton in *The Hoover Administration: A Documented Narrative* (Scribner, 1936), and by Ray Lyman Wilbur and Arthur Hyde in *The Hoover Policies* (Scribner, 1937).

Albert Romasco's *The Poverty of Abundance: Hoover, the Nation, the Depression* ° (Oxford Univ. Press, 1965), published shortly before Hoover's presidential papers became available to scholars, describes the President's efforts to halt the economic downturn. Harris G. Warren's *Herbert Hoover and the Great Depression* ° (Oxford Univ. Press, 1959) is also worth consulting. Walter Lippmann in "The Permanent New Deal," *Yale Review*, XXIV (June, 1935), 649–67, stresses the continuities between Hoover's efforts and the early New Deal.

Gerald D. Nash in "Herbert Hoover and the Origins of the Reconstruction Finance Corporation," *Mississippi Valley Historical Review*, XLVI (Dec., 1959), 455–68, notes, unlike Degler, Hoover's reluctance to accept the legislation for the RFC. In "Herbert Hoover and the Federal Farm Board Project," *Mississippi Valley Historical Review*, XLII (March, 1956), 710–29, James H. Shideler discusses a pre-Depression agency.

The significance of Al Smith's Catholicism in Hoover's election is discounted by Richard Hofstadter in "Could a Protestant Have Beaten Hoover in 1928?" *Reporter*, XXII (March 17, 1960), 31–33, and by Paul Carter, in "The Other Catholic Candidate: The 1928 Presidential Bid of Thomas J. Walsh," *Pacific Northwest Quarterly*, LV (Jan., 1964), 1–8.

III

The New Deal and the Coming of War

As a problem for historical interpretation, the New Deal presents fewer difficulties than either progressivism, a movement that continues to defy definition, or the 1920's, whose complex contradictions still are unresolved. Unlike the preceding periods, the New Deal was dominated by a single political figure—Franklin D. Roosevelt; and from the beginning the New Deal had a clearly defined task: to repair the breakdown in the economic order. Historians have thus focused their attention on the New Deal's efforts to revive and re-order the economy and have asked the same questions about the period: To what extent was the New Deal a break with the American past? Did it effect significant changes in the social and economic structure of American society? Was it revolutionary or conservative?

Perhaps the debate can be clarified by phrasing the question at issue in such a way that the task of analysis can be made more precise: To what extent did the New Deal redistribute wealth and power in America? This formulation relegates to secondary importance inquiries into the Progressive roots of the New Deal or the extent of Roosevelt's break with America's laissez-faire past. The major subject for investigation instead becomes the ways in which New

Deal measures in operation affected various interests and classes, and a new series of questions presents itself: Did the lower classes gain from the New Deal a significant measure of security from the excesses of the business cycle? Did labor increase its power in dealing with capital? Was the autonomy of large corporations diminished by the expansion of state power? Did New Deal tax measures correct the maldistribution of wealth in America?

The New Deal's social-welfare program for the lower classes, for example, illustrates the ambiguity of its accomplishment and the difficulty of passing simple judgment. In initiating social security, public housing, minimum wages, and unemployment insurance, New Dealers unquestionably made a contribution to many of the nation's economically vulnerable citizens. Yet scholars who argue that the New Deal was conservative have not been impressed. They point out that only in the United States are government pensions partially financed from the current earnings of workers, that the social-security tax on wages is regressive, and that the Social Security Act originally exempted millions who were most in need of coverage.

As for public housing, the Government built only 180,000 units during the New Deal, and, as is now well known, the concept of slum clearance too often meant removal rather than improvement of the poor. At a time when twelve million workers in interstate commerce were earning less than forty cents an hour, Congress set the minimum wage at twenty-five cents an hour and extended coverage to only half a million workers. As for unemployment insurance, it was administered by the states, lacked federal standards, and was marred by widely varying benefits. Emphasizing the limits of this legislation, critics of the New Deal find its welfare program designed to appease popular discontent with the least cost to the nation's wealthier classes.

Roosevelt's belated support of the labor movement in the 1930's was certainly his most important contribution to redistributing power in the economic order. In 1933 only 2.8 million workers, mostly in the AFL, were in unions; however, partly because of the Administration's vigorous implementation of the Wagner Act (1935), which granted labor the legal right to bargain collectively, a period of unprecedented growth ensued. Led by John L. Lewis, a group of rebels bolted the AFL in 1935 and established the rival CIO, which organized workers by industry rather than craft and so at last offered unskilled workers a place in the American union movement. By the beginning of World War II the AFL had 4.5 million members, and the CIO claimed 5 million.

The dark age of the company union was over. But critics have argued that the positive effects of the union movement of the 1930's have been overrated. Unions have generally abandoned their earlier idealism for the pursuit of narrow self-interest and are conservative bulwarks of the existing order. Moreover, the growth of unions after 1935 has not increased labor's overall share of the national income, but has merely meant disproportionate wage gains for union workers at the expense of the nonunionized half of the labor force. Thus one of the major effects of unionization has been to increase inequalities within the working class.

As for the power of big business, the New Deal did expand the scope of government regulation, thereby diminishing in some measure the autonomy of businessmen. As a result of New Deal legislation, the Securities and Exchange Commission began policing the stock market, the Federal Reserve Board enjoyed wider powers, and the Federal Power Commission and Interstate Commerce Commission were granted greater authority to stabilize power and transportation rates. Congress created a Maritime Commission to subsidize the merchant marine and a Civil Aeronautics Authority (later, Board) to regulate the airlines. It passed the Robinson-Patman Act to prevent wholesalers and manufacturers from discriminating on behalf of chain stores to the disadvantage of small retailers, and it passed bills to permit the coal and oil industries to stabilize production. In one of their most controversial efforts, New Dealers in 1935 pushed through an act that loosened the grip of giant holding companies on the electric-power industry.

But those who argue the conservative meaning of the New Deal have pointed out that regulation may be on behalf of the interests to be regulated, and indeed New Deal legislation helped certain businesses by imposing order on chaotic industries (for example, coal) and by restraining competition harmful to industrial stability. Though forced to permit the government to participate in making crucial regulatory decisions, businessmen in the affected industries suffered neither declines in their profits nor real threats to the existing structure of the corporate order. Whether because of the New Deal or in spite of it, big business remained in command of the American economy.

The available evidence yields a more certain conclusion on the effect of tax measures on wealth distribution. Some redistribution of wealth occurred during the New Deal, but not much. Figures in Herman Miller's *Income Distribution in the United States* (Government Printing Office, 1966) indicate that from 1935–36 through 1941 (that is, from the year of the New Deal tax reform until the beginning of World War II) the personal income share of the highest fifth fell from 52 to 49 percent. The result was a gain of 1 percent for each of the middle three income fifths but no change in the share (4 percent) received by the lowest fifth. The most significant innovation in government taxation in Roosevelt's Administration occurred not during the Depression, but at the time of World War II when the need to pay for the war forced the Government to reduce income-tax exemptions until the number of Americans paying income taxes rose from 4 million in 1939 to 42.4 million in 1944. For the first time middle- and lower-class Americans were ensnared in the income-tax system, where most remained thereafter.

This analysis of alterations in the structure of the economy and society admittedly has ignored changes in ideology and ethos. Certainly such changes during the New Deal were real. But the ultimate test of how significant new ideas are is their success or failure in affecting the social system —and the changes in ideology and ethos were not far reaching or greatly influential during the New Deal in changing the structure of American society or in redistributing power.

SUGGESTED READING

Though some of the larger questions about the New Deal remain unexamined, the literature on the period and its President is already voluminous.

Frank Freidel is writing the authoritative multivolume biography (*Franklin D. Roosevelt* [Little, Brown, 1952–56, 3 vols.]); the latest volume has reached the election of 1932. William E. Leuchtenburg's *Franklin D. Roosevelt and the New Deal* * (Harper & Row, 1963) is the best one-volume synthesis of the period. Arthur Schlesinger, Jr., has completed three impressive volumes of his generally admiring study in *The Age of Roosevelt;* the last two volumes, *The Coming of the New Deal* * (Houghton Mifflin, 1958) and *The Politics of Upheaval* * (Houghton Mifflin, 1960) are on the early New Deal years.

James MacGregor Burns' *Roosevelt: The Lion and the Fox* * (Harcourt, Brace & World, 1956) is often critical of Roosevelt and his departures from reformism and Keynesianism. In *The Democratic Roosevelt* (Doubleday, 1957), Rexford Tugwell, one of Roosevelt's early advisers, applauds the efforts of the so-called First New Deal but is disturbed by later policies, particularly by the shift to antitrust activities. His interpretation appeared earlier in a series of articles in *Western Political Quarterly* (June, 1948), *Political Quarterly* (July–Sept., 1950), *Antioch Review* (Dec., 1953), and *Ethics* (1953–54).

*Franklin D. Roosevelt: A Profile,** edited by Leuchtenburg (Hill & Wang, 1967), is a fine collection of previously published materials on Roosevelt and includes Clarke Chambers' "FDR: Pragmatist-Idealist," *Pacific Northwest Quarterly,* LII (April, 1961), 50–55; Richard Hofstadter's essay on Roosevelt, from *The American Political Tradition* * (Knopf, 1948); and Morton Frisch's "Roosevelt the Conservator: A Rejoinder to Hofstadter," *Journal of Politics,* XV (May, 1962), 361–72. Other useful collections are Morton Keller, ed., *The New Deal: What Was It?* * (Holt, Rinehart & Winston, 1963), which contains mostly excerpts from books but also includes Arthur Schlesinger, Jr., "Sources of the New Deal: Reflections on the Temper of a Time," *Columbia University Forum,* II (Fall, 1959), 4–12; Bernard Sternsher, ed., *The New Deal: Doctrines and Democracy* * (Allyn & Bacon, 1966), which includes Heinz Eulau's "Neither Ideology nor Utopia: The New Deal in Retrospect," *Antioch Review,* XIX (Winter, 1959–60); and Edwin Rozwenc, ed., *The New Deal, Revolution or Evolution* * (Heath, 1949).

Paul Conklin in *The New Deal* * (Crowell, 1967); Barton J. Bernstein, in Bernstein, ed., *Towards a New Past* (Pantheon, 1968); and Howard Zinn, in Zinn, ed., *New Deal Social Thought* * (Bobbs-Merrill, 1966) all emphasize the limitations of the ideology and accomplishments of the New Deal. In an angry response to these writers, who are sometimes lumped together as "New Left" historians, Jerold Auerbach, in "New Deal, Old Deal, or Raw Deal: Some Thoughts on New Left Historiography," *Journal of Southern History,* XXXV (Feb., 1969), 18–30, assesses their work as intemperate, ahistorical, and moralistic. Eric Goldman's *Rendezvous with Destiny* * (Knopf, 1952) is an earlier and important study of the movement of the American polity away from laissez-faire and toward the benificent liberalism that he finds in the New Deal. Richard Hofstadter's *The Age of Reform* * (Knopf, 1955), departing from his earlier more critical analysis of the New Deal in *The American Political Tradition* * (Knopf, 1948), emphasizes the "revolutionary" aspects of the New Deal, stresses its discontinuity with the moralism and cautious reforms of the progressive years, and finds much to praise in the response of the New Deal to the need for reform and the challenge of depression.

The best surveys of New Deal scholarship are Richard Kirkendall's "The Great Depression: Another Watershed in American History?" in John Braeman et al., eds., *Change and Continuity in Twentieth-Century America* * (Ohio State Univ. Press, 1964), and Kirkendall's "The New Deal as Watershed: The Recent Literature," *Journal of American History*, LIV (March, 1968), 839–52. Leuchtenburg's "The New Deal and the Analogue of War," in Braeman's book cited above, is an important essay. Daniel Aaron's *Writers on the Left* * (Harcourt, Brace & World, 1961); James B. Gilbert's *Writers and Partisans* (Wiley, 1968); and Otis L. Graham, Jr.'s *An Encore for Reform: The Old Progressives in the New Deal* * (Oxford Univ. Press, 1967) are valuable for understanding the intellectual history of these years.

James Patterson's *Congressional Conservatism and the New Deal* (Univ. of Kentucky Press, 1967) is a fine study of the actions of the conservative coalition and should be supplemented by his "The Failure of Party Realignment in the South, 1937–1939," *Journal of Politics*, XXVII (Aug., 1965), 602–17. *Labor and the New Deal* (Univ. of Wisconsin Press, 1957), edited by Milton Derber and Edwin Young, provides a useful summary of events. Samuel Lubell's *The Future of American Politics* * (Doubleday, 1951) remains the best general analysis of the New Deal coalition.

The New Deal: A Documentary History * (Harper & Row, 1968), edited by William Leuchtenburg, and *The New Deal and the American People* * (Prentice-Hall, 1964), edited by Frank Freidel, are fine collections of materials gathered for students by two of the outstanding scholars of the New Deal. *The Public Papers and Addresses of Franklin D. Roosevelt* (Harper & Row, 1938–50, 13 vols.), edited by Samuel Rosenman, an important speechwriter of the President, provides the texts of press conferences, speeches, state papers, and other important public announcements. Elliott Roosevelt has edited *F.D.R.: His Personal Letters* (Harper & Row, 1947–50, 4 vols.), an uneven collection of materials. Among the other important primary sources on the New Deal are Harold L. Ickes' *The Secret Diary of Harold L. Ickes* (Simon & Schuster, 1953–54, 3 vols.), which expresses the self-righteousness of its author; *Roosevelt and Frankfurter: Their Correspondence, 1928–1945* (Little, Brown, 1968), edited by Max Freedman; and Eleanor Roosevelt's *This I Remember* (Harper & Row, 1949), the very selective memoirs by the former first lady. Frances Perkins' *The Roosevelt I Knew* (Viking, 1946) is a friendly but not uncritical memoir by Roosevelt's former Secretary of Labor. Raymond Moley's *After Seven Years* (Harper & Row, 1939) is sharply critical of the President whom he had briefly served, and in *The First New Deal* (Harper & Row, 1967), Moley returned to similar themes.

FRANK FREIDEL

The New Deal
in Historical Perspective

INTRODUCTION

Writing after the New Deal had lapsed as an issue in contemporary politics, Frank Freidel, author of a multivolume biography of Franklin D. Roosevelt, offers a cautious appraisal of the New Deal. It was bolder and more humane than Hoover's program, he concludes, but it was still conservative in a fundamental sense: "Roosevelt and . . . his contemporaries . . . unquestioningly believed in the American free enterprise system [and] were suspicious of strong government." So conservative was Roosevelt in the early years of his Presidency, Freidel stresses, that he reopened the banks in 1933 after imposing only slight modifications in banking practices; furthermore, these revisions had been formulated by Hoover's Treasury officials. Freidel also notes that Roosevelt at

FROM Frank Freidel, *The New Deal in Historical Perspective*, revised edition, Washington, D. C., Service Center for Teachers of History, 1965. Reprinted by permission.

this time frequently sought the counsel of Wall Streeters, and even in the later years of his Administration in the so-called second New Deal he tried to avoid offending powerful business interests.

Rather than representing a striking departure from the past —a "third American Revolution" as Carl Degler argues—the New Deal, Freidel emphasizes, was heavily indebted to the practices and assumptions of progressivism and the World War I experience of business-government collaboration. In turn, the place of the New Deal is secure in the American consensus, for citizens take for granted many of the changes established by the reforms of the 1930's.

In less than a generation, the New Deal has passed into both popular legend and serious history. The exigencies of American politics long demanded that its partisans and opponents paint a picture of it either in the most glamorous whites or sinister blacks. Long after the New Deal was over, politicians of both major parties tried at each election to reap a harvest of votes from its issues.

Gradually a new generation of voters has risen which does not remember the New Deal and takes for granted the changes that it wrought. Gradually too, politicians have had to recognize that the nation faces new, quite different problems since the second World War, and that campaigning on the New Deal has become as outmoded as did the "bloody shirt" issue as decades passed after the Civil War. At the same time, most of the important manuscript collections relating to the New Deal have been opened to scholars so rapidly that careful historical research has been possible decades sooner than was true for earlier periods of United States history. (The Franklin D. Roosevelt papers and the Abraham Lincoln papers became available for research at about the same time, just after the second World War.)

It has been the task of the historians not only to analyze heretofore hidden aspects of the New Deal on the basis of the manuscripts, but also to remind readers of what was once commonplace and is now widely forgotten. A new generation has no firsthand experience of the depths of despair into which the depression had thrust the nation, and the excitement and eagerness with which people greeted the new program. Critics not only have denied that anything constructive could have come from the New Deal but they have even succeeded in creating the impression in the prosperous years since 1945 that the depression really did not amount to much. How bad it was is worth remembering, since this is a means of gauging the enormous pressure for change.

Estimates of the number of unemployed ranged up to thirteen million out of a labor force of fifty-two million, which would mean that one wage-earner out of four was without means of support for himself or his family. Yet of these thirteen million unemployed, only about a quarter were receiving any kind of assistance. States and municipalities were running out of relief funds; private agencies were long since at the end of their resources. And those who were receiving aid often obtained only a pittance. The Toledo commissary could allow for relief only 2.14 cents per person per meal, and the Red Cross in southern Illinois in 1931 was able to provide families with only seventy-five cents a week for food. It was in this crisis that one of the most flamboyant members of the Hoover administration suggested a means of providing sustenance for the unemployed: restaurants should dump left-overs and plate scrapings into special sanitary cans to be given to worthy unemployed people willing to work for the food. It was a superfluous suggestion, for in 1932 an observer in Chicago reported:

> Around the truck which was unloading garbage and other refuse were about thirty-five men, women, and children. As soon as the truck pulled away from the pile, all of them started digging with sticks, some with their hands, grabbing bits of food and vegetables.

The employed in some instances were not a great deal better off. In December 1932 wages in a wide range of industries from textiles to iron and steel, averaged from a low of 20 cents to a high of only 30 cents an hour. A quarter of the women working in Chicago were receiving less than 10 cents an hour. In farming areas, conditions were equally grim. In bitter weather on the Great Plains, travelers occasionally encountered a light blue haze that smelled like roasting coffee. The "old corn" held over from the crop of a year earlier would sell for only $1.40 per ton, while coal cost $4 per ton, so many farmers burned corn to keep warm. When Aubrey Williams went into farm cellars in the Dakotas in the early spring of 1933 farm wives showed him shelves and shelves of jars for fruits and vegetables—but they were all empty. Even farmers who could avoid hunger had trouble meeting payments on their mortgages. As a result a fourth of all farmers in the United States lost their farms during these years.

Despairing people in these pre-New Deal years feared President Herbert Hoover had forgotten them or did not recognize the seriousness of their plight. As a matter of fact he had, more than any other depression president in American history, taken steps to try to bring recovery. But he had functioned largely through giving aid at the top to prevent the further collapse of banks and industries, and the concentric rings of further collapses and unemployment which would then ensue. Also he had continued to pin his faith upon voluntary action. He felt that too great federal intervention would undermine the self-reliance, destroy the "rugged individualism" of the American people, and that it would create federal centralization, thus paving the way for socialism.

President Hoover was consistent in his thinking, and he was humane.

But it would have been hard to explain to people like those grubbing on the Chicago garbage heap, why, when the Reconstruction Finance Corporation was loaning $90,000,000 to a single Chicago bank, the President would veto a bill to provide federal relief for the unemployed, asserting, "never before has so dangerous a suggestion been seriously made in this country." It was not until June 1932 that he approved a measure permitting the RFC to loan $300,000,000 for relief purposes.

It seems shocking in retrospect that such conditions should have existed in this country, and that any president of either major party should so long have refused to approve federal funds to alleviate them. It adds to the shock when one notes that many public figures of the period were well to the right of the President—for instance, Secretary of the Treasury Andrew Mellon—and that almost no one who was likely to be in a position to act, including Governor Roosevelt of New York, was ready at that time to go very far to the left of Hoover.

Roosevelt, who was perhaps the most advanced of the forty-eight governors in developing a program to meet the depression, had shown little faith in public works spending. When he had established the first state relief agency in the United States in the fall of 1931, he had tried to finance it through higher taxes, and only later, reluctantly, abandoned the pay-as-you-go basis. He was, and he always remained, a staunch believer in a balanced budget. He was never more sincere than when, during the campaign of 1932, he accused the Hoover administration of having run up a deficit of three and three-quarters billions of dollars in the previous two years. This, he charged, was "the most reckless and extravagant past that I have been able to discover in the statistical record of any peacetime Government anywhere, any time."

Governor Roosevelt's own cautious record did not exempt him from attack. In April 1932, seeking the presidential nomination, he proclaimed himself the champion of the "forgotten man," and talked vaguely about raising the purchasing power of the masses, in part through directing Reconstruction Finance Corporation loans their way. This little was sufficient to lead many political leaders and publicists, including his Democratic rival, Al Smith, to accuse Roosevelt of being a demagogue, ready to set class against class.

Smith and most other public figures, including Roosevelt, favored public works programs. A few men like Senators Robert F. Wagner of New York and Robert M. La Follette of Wisconsin visualized really large-scale spending on public construction, but most leaders also wanted to accompany the spending with very high taxes which would have been deflationary and thus have defeated the program. None of the important political leaders, and none of the economists who had access to them, seemed as yet to visualize the decisive intervention of the government into the economy of the sort that is considered commonplace today. The term "built-in stabilizers" had yet to be coined.

The fact was that Roosevelt and most of his contemporaries, who like him were products of the Progressive Era, were basically conservative men who unquestioningly believed in the American free enterprise system. On the whole, they were suspicious of strong government, and would indulge in it only as a last resort to try to save the system. This was their limitation in trying to bring about economic recovery. On the other hand, part of their Progressive legacy was also a humanitarian belief in social justice. This belief would lead them to espouse reforms to improve the lot of the common man, even though those reforms might also take them in the direction of additional government regulation. Roosevelt as governor had repeatedly demonstrated this inconsistency in his public statements and recommendations. He had ardently endorsed states rights and small government in a truly Jeffersonian way. Then in quite contrary fashion (but still in keeping with Jeffersonian spirit applied to twentieth century society) he had pointed out one or another area, such as old age security, in which he believed the government must intervene to protect the individual.

At this time, what distinguished Governor Roosevelt from his fellows were two remarkable characteristics. The first was his brilliant political skill, which won to him an overwhelming proportion of the Democratic politicians and the general public. The second was his willingness to experiment, to try one or another improvisation to stop the slow economic drift downward toward ruin. During the campaign of 1932, many a man who had observed Roosevelt felt as did Harry Hopkins that he would make a better president than Hoover, "chiefly because he is not afraid of a new idea."

Roosevelt's sublime self-confidence and his willingness to try new expedients stood him in good stead when he took over the presidency. On that grim March day in 1933 when he took his oath of office, the American economic system was half-paralyzed. Many of the banks were closed; the remainder he quickly shut down through presidential proclamation. Industrial production was down to 56 per cent of the 1923–25 level. Yet somehow, Roosevelt's self-confidence was infectious. People were ready to believe, to follow, when he said in words that were not particularly new, "The only thing we have to fear is fear itself." He offered "leadership of frankness and vigor," and almost the whole of the American public and press—even papers like the Chicago *Tribune* which soon became bitter critics—for the moment accepted that leadership with enthusiasm.

For a short period of time, about one hundred days, Roosevelt had behind him such overwhelming public support that he was able to push through Congress a wide array of legislation which in total established the New Deal. It came in helter-skelter fashion and seemed to go in all directions, even at times directions that conflicted with each other. There was mildly corrective legislation to get the banks open again, a slashing of government costs to balance the budget, legalization of 3.2 beer, establishment of the Civilian Conservation Corps, of the Tennessee Valley Authority, and of a wide variety of other agencies in the areas of relief, reform, and, above all in those first months, of recovery.

What pattern emerged in all of this legislation? How sharply did it break with earlier American political traditions? The answer was that it represented Roosevelt's efforts to be president to all the American people, to present something to every group in need. And it was based squarely on American objectives and experience in the Progressive Era and during the first World War. It went beyond the Hoover program in that while the word "voluntary" remained in many of the laws, they now had behind them the force of the government or at least strong economic incentives.

It has been forgotten how basically conservative Roosevelt's attitudes remained during the early period of the New Deal. He had closed the banks, but reopened them with relatively little change. Indeed, the emergency banking measure had been drafted by Hoover's Treasury officials. What banking reform there was came later. His slashing of the regular government costs was something he had promised during his campaign, and in which he sincerely believed and continued to believe. He kept the regular budget of the government low until the late thirties. While he spent billions through the parallel emergency budget, he did that reluctantly, and only because he felt it was necessary to keep people from starving. He was proud that he was keeping the credit of the government good, and never ceased to look forward to the day when he could balance the budget. For the first several years of the New Deal he consulted frequently with Wall Streeters and other economic conservatives. His first Director of the Budget, Lewis Douglas, parted ways with him, but late in 1934 was exhorting: "I hope, and hope most fervently, that you will evidence a real determination to bring the budget into actual balance, for upon this, I think, hangs not only your place in history but conceivably the immediate fate of western civilization." (Douglas to FDR, November 28, 1934)

Remarks like this struck home with Roosevelt. Douglas's successors as Director of the Budget held much the same views, and Henry Morgenthau, Jr., who became Secretary of the Treasury at the beginning of 1934, never failed to prod Roosevelt to slash governmental expenditures.

We should add parenthetically that Roosevelt always keenly resented the untrue newspaper stories that his parents had been unwilling to entrust him with money. As a matter of fact he was personally so thrifty when he was in the White House that he used to send away for bargain mail-order shirts, and when he wished summer suits, switched from an expensive New York tailor to a cheaper one in Washington. This he did despite the warning of the New York tailor that he might thus lose his standing as one of the nation's best-dressed men.

Financial caution in governmental affairs rather typifies Roosevelt's economic thinking throughout the entire New Deal. He was ready to go much further than Hoover in construction of public works, but he preferred the kind which would pay for themselves, and did not think there were many possibilities for them in the country. His estimate before he became president was only one billion dollars worth. In 1934, he once proposed that the government buy the buildings of foundered banks throughout the nation and use them for post-offices rather than to construct new buildings. This is how far he was from visualizing huge public works expenditures as a means of boosting the country out of the depression. His course in this area was the middle road. He wished to bring about recovery without upsetting the budget any further than absolutely necessary. He did not launch the nation on a program of deliberate deficit financing.

When Roosevelt explained his program in a fireside chat at the end of July 1933, he declared:

> It may seem inconsistent for a government to cut down its regular expenses and at the same time to borrow and to spend billions for an emergency. But it is not inconsistent because a large portion of the emergency money has been paid out in the form of sound loans . . . ; and to cover the rest . . . we have imposed taxes. . . .
>
> So you will see that we have kept our credit good. We have built a granite foundation in a period of confusion.

It followed from this that aside from limited public works expenditures, Roosevelt wanted a recovery program which would not be a drain on governmental finances. Neither the Agricultural Adjustment Administration nor the National Recovery Administration were. He had promised in the major farm speech of his 1932 campaign that his plan for agricultural relief would be self-financing; this was achieved through the processing tax on certain farm products. The NRA involved no governmental expenditures except for administration.

Both of these programs reflected not the progressivism of the first years of the century, but the means through which Progressives had regulated production during the first World War. This had meant regulation which would as far as possible protect both producers and consumers, both employers and employees. Here the parallel was direct. The rest of Roosevelt's program did not parallel the Progressives' wartime experience, for during the war, in terms of production regulation had meant channeling both factories and farms into the maximum output of what was needed to win the war. Now the problem in the thirties was one of reducing output in most areas rather than raising it, and of getting prices back up rather than trying to hold them down.

Certainly the nation badly needed this sort of a program in 1933. The products of the fields and mines and of highly competitive consumers' goods industries like textiles were being sold so cheaply that producers and their employees alike were close to starvation. The overproduction was also wasteful of natural resources. In an oilfield near Houston, one grocer advertised when 3.2 beer first became legal that he would exchange one bottle of beer for one barrel of oil. They were worth about the same. In other heavy industries like automobiles or farm machinery, production had been cut drastically while prices remained high. One need was to bring prices throughout industry and agriculture into a more equitable relationship with each other, and with the debt structure.

The NRA scheme in theory would help do this. Its antecedents were in the regulatory War Industries Board of the first World War, and indeed it was run by some of the same men. The War Industries Board had functioned through industrial committees; in the twenties these committees had evolved into self-regulatory trade associations. Unfortunately, as Roosevelt had found when he headed the association created to discipline one of the largest and most chaotic of industries, the American Construction Council, self-regulation without the force of law behind it, had a tendency to break down. When the depression had hit, some businessmen themselves had advocated the NRA scheme, but Hoover would have none of it. Roosevelt was receptive.

The theory was that committees in a few major fields like steel, textiles, bituminous coal and the like, would draw up codes of fair practice for the industry. These would not only stabilize the price structure, but also protect the wages and working conditions of labor. Even consumers would benefit, presumably through receiving more wages or profits, and thus enjoying larger purchasing power with which to buy goods at somewhat higher prices.

In practice, the NRA program went awry. Too many committees drew up too many codes embodying many sorts of unenforceable provisions. There was a code even for the mopstick industry. What was more important, some manufacturers rushed to turn out quantities of goods at the old wage and raw material level before the code went into effect, hoping then to sell these goods at new higher prices. Consequently during the summer of 1933 there was a short NRA boom when industrial production jumped to 101 per cent of the 1923–25 level, and wholesale prices rose from an index figure of 60.2 in March to 71.2 by October. The crop reduction program of the AAA led to a corresponding rise in agricultural prices.

Had consumers at the same time enjoyed a correspondingly higher purchasing power, the recovery scheme might well have worked. Some of its designers had visualized pouring the additional dollars into consumers' pockets through a heavy public works spending program. Indeed the bill which created the NRA also set up a Public Works Administration with $3,300,000,000 to spend. This money could have been poured here and there into the economy where it was most needed to "prime the pump." But Roosevelt and his most influential advisers did not want to give such an enormous spending power to the administrator of the NRA, nor had they really accepted the deficit spending school of thought. Hence while some of the money being spent by the New Deal went for immediate relief of one form or another, it went to people so close to starvation that they were forced to spend what they received on bare necessities. This was of little aid in priming the pump. The public works fund, which could have served that purpose, went to that sturdy old Progressive, "Honest Harold" Ickes. He slowly went about the process of allocating it in such a way that the government and the public would get a return of one hundred cents (or preferably more) on every dollar spent. Raymond Moley has suggested that if only the cautious Ickes had headed the NRA and the impetuous Johnson the Public Works Administration the scheme might have worked.

Without a huge transfusion of dollars into the economy, the industrial and agricultural recovery programs sagged in the fall of 1933. Roosevelt turned to currency manipulation to try to get prices up. He explained to a critical Congressman, "I have always favored sound money, and do now, but it is 'too darned sound' when it takes so much of farm products to buy a dollar." Roosevelt also accepted a makeshift work relief program, the Civil Works Administration, to carry the destitute through the winter.

Already the New Deal honeymoon was over, and in 1934 and 1935 a sharp political struggle between Roosevelt and the right began to take form. To conservatives, Roosevelt was shattering the constitution with his economic legislation. Al Smith was attacking the devaluated currency as "baloney dollars," and was writing articles with such titles as "Is the Constitution Still There?" and "Does the Star-Spangled Banner Still Wave?" Former President Hoover published his powerful jeremiad, *The Challenge to Liberty*.

Many businessmen complained against the NRA restrictions, the favoritism allegedly being shown to organized labor, and the higher taxes. Although some of them had advocated the NRA, the significant fact was that the thinking of most businessmen seems to have remained about what it had been in the 1920's. They were eager for aid from the government, as long as it involved no obligations on their part or restrictions against them. They wanted a government which could protect their domestic markets with a high tariff wall, and at the same time seek out foreign markets for them, a court system which could discipline organized labor with injunctions, and a tax structure which (as under Secretary of the Treasury Mellon) would take no enormous bite of large profits, and yet retain disciplinary levies on the lower-middle income groups. All these policies they could understand and condone. The New Deal, which would confer other benefits upon them, but require corresponding obligations, they could not.

This hostile thinking which began to develop among the business community was sincere. Businessmen genuinely believed that under the New Deal program too large a share of their income had to go to organized labor, and too much to the government. They freely predicted federal bankruptcy as the deficit began to mount. If they had capital to commit, they refused to expend it on new plants and facilities (except for some introduction of labor-saving machinery). They were too unsure of the future, they complained, because they could not tell what that man in the White House might propose next. Business needed a "breathing spell," Roy Howard wrote Roosevelt, and the President promised one. Nevertheless, the legislative requests continued unabated.

All this, important though it is in delineating the ideology of business-men, is not the whole story. The fact is that during the long bleak years after October 1929 they had slipped into a depression way of thinking. They re-garded American industry as being over-built; they looked upon the Ameri-can market as being permanently contracted. By 1937 when industrial production and stock dividends were up to within ten percent of the 1929 peak, capital expenditures continued to drag along the depression floor. In-dustrialists did not engage in the large-scale spending for expansion which has been a significant factor in the boom since 1945. As late as 1940 to 1941, many of them were loathe to take the large defense orders which required construction of new plants. Unquestionably the pessimism of businessmen during the thirties, whether or not linked to their hatred of Roosevelt and fear of the New Deal, was as significant a factor in perpetuating the depres-sion, as their optimism since the war has been in perpetuating the boom.

The paradox is that some of the New Deal measures against which the businessmen fought helped introduce into the economy some of the stabiliz-ers which today help give businessmen confidence in the continuation of prosperity. These came despite, not because of, the businessmen. Roosevelt long continued to try to co-operate with the leaders of industry and banking. Their anger toward him, and frequently-expressed statements that he had betrayed his class, at times bewildered and even upset him. For the most part he laughed them off. He hung in his bedroom a favorite cartoon. It showed a little girl at the door of a fine suburban home, apparently tattling to her mother, "Johnny wrote a dirty word on the sidewalk." And the word, of course, was "Roosevelt."

To some of his old friends who complained to him, he would reply with patience and humor. Forever he was trying to point out to them the human side of the problem of the depression. Perhaps the best illustration is a witty interchange with a famous doctor for whom he had deep affection. The doc-tor wired him in March 1935:

Pediatricians have long been perplexed by difficulty of weaning infant from breast or bottle to teaspoon or cup. The shift often establishes permanent neu-rosis in subsequent adult. According to report in evening paper twenty-two million citizen infants now hang on federal breasts. Can you wean them doc-tor and prevent national neurosis?

Roosevelt promptly replied:

As a young interne you doubtless realize that the interesting transitional process, which you describe in your telegram, presupposes that the bottle, teaspoon, or cup is not empty. Such vehicles of feeding, if empty, produce flatulence and the patient dies from a lack of nutrition.
    The next question on your examination paper is, therefore, the following:
    Assuming that the transitional period has arrived, where is the Doctor to get the food from to put in the new container?

As time went on, and the attacks became virulent from some quarters, at times even passing the bounds of decency, Roosevelt struck back vigorously. During his campaign in 1936 he excoriated the "economic royalists." When he wound up the campaign in Madison Square Garden, he declared:

> We had to struggle with the old enemies of peace—business and financial monopoly, speculation, reckless banking, class antagonism, sectionalism, war profiteering. They had begun to consider the Government of the United States as a mere appendage to their own affairs. And we know now that Government by organized money is just as dangerous as Government by organized mob.
>
> Never before in all our history have these forces been so united against one candidate as they stand today. They are unanimous in their hate for me—and I welcome their hatred.

To these sharp words Roosevelt had come from his position early in the New Deal as the impartial arbiter of American economic forces. He had come to them less because of what he considered as betrayal from the right than through pressure from the left. How had this pressure applied between 1934 and the campaign of 1936?

Back in 1934, while the economic temperature chart of the near frozen depression victim had fluctuated up and down, still dangerously below normal, the dispossessed millions began to look at the New Deal with despair or even disillusion. Those workers going on strike to obtain the twenty-five or thirty-five cents an hour minimum wage or the collective bargaining privileges promised by the NRA began to wisecrack that NRA stood for the National Run-Around. Some of them and of the unemployed millions in northern cities still dependent upon meager relief handouts, began to listen to the stirring radio addresses of Father Charles Coughlin. Old people began to pay five cents a week dues to Dr. Francis Townsend's clubs, which promised them fantastically large benefits. Throughout the South (and even in parts of the North) the dispossessed small farmers listened with enthusiasm to the exhortations of the Louisiana Kingfish, Huey Long, that he would share the wealth to make every man a king.

Many Democratic politicians were surprisingly oblivious to these rumblings and mutterings. Much of the private conversation of men like Vice President John Nance Garner sounded like the public demands of the Liberty Leaguers: cut relief and balance the budget. Garner, who spent the 1934 campaign hunting and fishing in Texas, predicted the usual mid-term loss of a few congressional seats back to the Republicans. Instead the Democrats picked up a startling number of new seats in both houses of Congress. The dispossessed had continued to vote with the Democratic party—but perhaps because there was no alternative but the Republicans who offered only retrenchment. Charles Beard commented that the 1934 election was "thunder on the left."

President Roosevelt, who was brilliantly sensitive to political forces, sensed fully the threat from the left. At the beginning of that crisis year 1935 he proposed in his annual message to Congress the enactment of a program to reinforce "the security of the men, women, and children of the nation" in their livelihood, to protect them against the major hazards and vicissitudes of life, and to enable them to obtain decent homes. In this increased emphasis upon security and reform, Professor Basil Rauch sees the beginnings of a second New Deal.

Certainly the pattern as it emerged in the next year was a brilliant one. Roosevelt neutralized Huey Long with the "soak the rich" tax, the "holding company death sentence," and with various measures directly of benefit to the poorer farmers of the South. Before an assassin's bullet felled Long, his political strength was already undercut. Similarly Roosevelt undermined the Townsend movement by pressing passage of the Social Security Act, which provided at least small benefits for the aged, at the same time that a congressional investigation disclosed how men around Townsend were fattening themselves on the nickels of millions of the aged. As for Father Coughlin, the Treasury announced that money from his coffers had gone into silver speculation at a time he had been loudly advocating that the government buy more silver at higher prices. More important, Coughlin had less appeal to employed workers after the new National Labor Relations Act raised a benign federal umbrella over collective bargaining. For the unemployed, a huge and substantial work relief program, the Works Progress Administration, came into existence.

Partly all this involved incisive political counterthrusts; partly it was a program Roosevelt had favored anyway. In any event, combined with Roosevelt's direct and effective appeal in radio fireside chats, it caused the dispossessed to look to him rather than to demagogues as their champion. Millions of them or their relations received some direct aid from the New Deal, whether a small crop payment or a WPA check. Millions more received wage boosts for which they were more grateful to Roosevelt than to their employers. Others through New Deal mortgage legislation had held onto their farms or homes. All these people, benefitting directly or indirectly, looked to Roosevelt as the source of their improved economic condition, and they were ready to vote accordingly. Roosevelt, who had been nominated in 1932 as the candidate of the South and the West, the champion of the farmer and the middle-class "forgotten man," after 1936 became increasingly the leader of the urban masses and the beneficiary of the growing power of organized labor.

What happened seems sharper and clearer in retrospect than it did at the time. Secretary Ickes, recording repeatedly in his diary during the early months of 1935 that the President was losing his grip, was echoing what many New Dealers and part of the public felt. They did not see a sharp shift into a second New Deal, and that is understandable. Roosevelt ever since he had become president had been talking about reform and from time to time recommending reform measures to Congress. He seems to have thought at the outset in two categories, about immediate or short-range emergency recovery measures to bring about a quick economic upswing, and also in terms of long-range reform legislation to make a recurrence of the depression less likely. Some of these reform measures like TVA had been ready for immediate enactment; others, like a revision of banking legislation and the social security legislation, he had planned from the beginning but were several years in the making. Frances Perkins has vividly described in her memoirs the lengthy task she and her associates undertook of drafting and selling to Congress and the public what became the Social Security Act of 1935.

Then Roosevelt had to face the additional factor that the emergency legislation had not succeeded in bringing rapid recovery. He had to think in terms of more permanent legislation with which to aim toward the same objectives. That meant he ceased trying to save money with a temporary program of cheaper direct relief, and switched instead to work relief (in which he had always believed) to try to stop some of the moral and physical erosion of those unfortunates who had been without employment for years.

In part the Supreme Court forced the recasting of some of his legislation. It gave a mercy killing in effect to the rickety, unwieldy NRA code structure when it handed down the Schechter or "sick chicken" decision of May 1935. On the whole the NRA had been unworkable, but it had achieved some outstanding results—in abolishing child labor, in bringing some order in the chaotic bituminous coal industry, and the like. Roosevelt was furious with the court, since the decision threatened to undermine all New Deal economic regulation. He charged that the justices were taking a horse and buggy view of the economic powers of the government. There followed six months later the court invalidation of the Triple-A processing tax, which for the moment threw out of gear the agricultural program.

The answer to these and similar Supreme Court decisions was Roosevelt's bold onslaught against the court after he had been reelected in the great landslide of 1936. He had carried every state but Maine and Vermont; he considered himself as having a great mandate from the people to continue his program. Nor had he any reason to doubt his ability to push a court reform program through Congress, since the already bulging New Deal majorities had become still bigger. He was wrong; he failed. His failure came as much as anything through a great tactical error. He disguised his program as one to bring about a speedier handling of cases, when he should have presented it frankly as a means of ending the court obstruction of the New Deal. This obstruction was real. Many corporations openly flaunted the National Labor Relations Act, for example, they were so confident that the Supreme Court would invalidate it.

However laudable the end, to many a well-educated member of the middle class who had supported Roosevelt even through the campaign of

1936, Roosevelt's resort to subterfuge smacked of the devious ways of dictators. In 1937, Americans were all too aware of the way in which Hitler and Mussolini had gained power. It was not that any thinking man expected Roosevelt to follow their example, but rather that many objected to any threat, real or potential, to the constitutional system including the separation of powers. After Roosevelt, they argued, the potential dictator might appear. It may be too that times had improved sufficiently since March 1933 so that constitutional considerations could again overweigh economic exigencies. In any event, Roosevelt lost his battle—and won his war.

While the struggle was rocking the nation, the justices began exercising the judicial self-restraint which one of their number, Harlan F. Stone, had urged upon them the previous year. They surprised the nation by upholding the constitutionality of the National Labor Relations Act and the Social Security Act. In large part this eliminated the necessity for the New Dealers to make any change in the personnel of the court, and thus helped contribute to Roosevelt's defeat in Congress. Further, the fight had helped bring into existence a conservative coalition in Congress which from this time on gave Roosevelt a rough ride. Many old-line Democratic congressmen now dared proclaim in public what they had previously whispered in private. All this added up to a spectacular setback for Roosevelt—so spectacular that it is easy to overlook the enormous and permanent changes that had come about.

In the next few years the Supreme Court in effect rewrote a large part of constitutional law. The federal and state governments were now able to engage in extensive economic regulation with little or no court restraint upon them. The limits upon regulation must be set for the most part by the legislative branch of the government, not the judiciary. Not only were the National Labor Relations Act and Social Security constitutional, but a bulging portfolio of other legislation.

These laws were not as spectacular as the measures of the Hundred Days, but in the bulk they were far more significant, for they brought about lasting changes in the economic role of the federal government. There was the continued subsidy to agriculture in order to maintain crop control—based upon soil conservation rather than a processing tax. There were all the agricultural relief measures which came to be centralized in the Farm Security Administration. Although that agency has disappeared, most of its functions have continued in one way or another. There was a beginning of slum clearance and public housing, and a continuation of TVA, held constitutional even before the court fight. There was a stiffening of securities regulation. There was a continuation of much that Roosevelt had considered beneficial in the NRA through a group of new laws usually referred to as the "little NRA." These perpetuated the coal and liquor codes, helped regulate oil production, tried to prevent wholesale price discriminations and legalized the establishment of "fair trade" prices by manufacturers. Most important of all, the Fair Labor Standards Act of 1937 set a national minimum of

wages and maximum of hours of work, and prohibited the shipping in interstate commerce of goods made by child labor. These are lasting contributions
of the New Deal, either substantial laws in themselves or the seeds for later
legislation.

What then, is to be said of the recession and the anti-monopoly program? A Keynesian point of view is that public works spending, the other
New Deal spending programs, and the payment of the bonus to veterans of
the first World War (over Roosevelt's veto, incidentally), all these together
had poured so much money into the economy that they brought about a substantial degree of recovery, except in employment, by the spring of 1937. At
this point Roosevelt tried to balance the budget, especially by cutting public
works and work relief expenditures. The result was a sharp recession. Roosevelt was forced to resort to renewed pump-priming, and in a few months the
recession was over.

Even this recession experience did not convert Roosevelt to Keynesianism. Keynes once called upon Roosevelt at the White House and apparently
tried to dazzle him with complex mathematical talk. Each was disappointed
in the other. In 1939, after the recession when a protégé of Mrs. Roosevelt's
proposed additional welfare spending, Roosevelt replied by listing worth-
while projects in which the government could usefully spend an additional
five billions a year. Then he pointed out that the deficit was already three
billions, which could not go on forever. How, he inquired, could an eight billion dollar deficit be financed.

As for economists, many of them saw the answer in the enormous
spending power which would be unleashed if the government poured out
billions in time of depression. To most of them the lesson from the recession
was that the only way to right the economy in time of upset was through
spending.

As for businessmen, they could see in the recession only the logical outcome of Roosevelt's iniquitous tinkering with the economy. They had been
especially angered by the protection the Wagner act had given to protective
bargaining with the resulting militant expansion of organized labor. Roosevelt reciprocated the businessmen's feelings and blamed the recession upon
their failure to co-operate. To a considerable degree he went along with a
powerful handful of Progressive Republicans and Western Democrats in the
Senate, like William E. Borah of Idaho and Joseph O'Mahoney of Wyoming,
in attacking corporate monopoly as the villain. There are some indications,
however, that the anti-monopoly program that he launched in the Department of Justice through the urbane Thurman Arnold was intended less to
bust the trusts than to forestall too drastic legislation in the Congress. Roosevelt gave his strong backing to Arnold's anti-trust division only for the first
year or two, and Arnold functioned for the most part through consent de-
crees. These in many instances allowed industries to function much as they
had in the NRA days. The new program was in some respects more like a
negative NRA than the antithesis of the NRA.

Thus from the beginning of the New Deal to the end, Roosevelt functioned with a fair degree of consistency. He heartily favored humanitarian welfare legislation and government policing of the economy, so long as these did not dangerously unbalance the budget. He preferred government cooperation with business to warfare with it.

Many of the New Dealers went far beyond Roosevelt in their views, and sometimes saw in his reluctance to support them, betrayal rather than a greater degree of conservatism. They had valid grievances some of the time when Roosevelt stuck to a middle course and seemed to them to be compromising away everything for which they thought he stood, in order to hold his motley political coalitions together. It is a serious moral question whether he compromised more than necessary, and whether at times he compromised his principles. It has been charged that his second four years in the White House represented a failure in political leadership.

In terms of gaining immediate political objectives, like the fiasco of the court fight, and the abortive "purge" in the 1938 primaries, this is undoubtedly true. In terms of the long-range New Deal program, I think the reverse is the case. These were years of piecemeal unspectacular consolidation of the earlier spectacular changes. It was many years before historians could say with certainty that these changes were permanent. By 1948 various public opinion samplings indicated that an overwhelming majority of those queried, even though Republican in voting habits, favored such things as social security and the TVA. The election of a Republican president in 1952 did not signify a popular repudiation of these programs. In the years after 1952 they were accepted, and in some instances even expanded, by the Republican administration. The only serious debate over them concerned degree, in which the Republicans were more cautious than the Democrats. The New Deal changes have even come for the most part to be accepted by the business community, although the United States Chamber of Commerce now issues manifestoes against federal aid to education with all the fervor it once directed against Roosevelt's proposals. The fact is that the business community in part bases its plans for the future upon some things that began as New Deal reforms. It takes for granted such factors as the "built-in stabilizers" in the social security system—something, incidentally, that Roosevelt pointed out at the time the legislation went into effect.

In January 1939 Roosevelt, concerned about the threat of world war, called a halt to his domestic reform program. What he said then, concerning the world crisis of 1939, is remarkably applicable to the United States more than two decades later:

We have now passed the period of internal conflict in the launching of our program of social reform. Our full energies may now be released to invigorate the processes of recovery in order to preserve our reforms, and to give every man and woman who wants to work a real job at a living wage.

But time is of paramount importance. The deadline of danger from within and from without is not within our control. The hour-glass may be in the hands of other nations. Our own hour-glass tells us that we are off on a race to make democracy work, so that we may be efficient in peace and therefore secure in national defense.

SUGGESTED READING

Broadus Mitchell's, *Depression Decade, From New Era Through New Deal* (Holt, Rinehart & Winston, 1947) is an economic history critical of the New Deal; it affirms the conservatism of Roosevelt's policies. This view also receives support in Philip Selznick's, *TVA and the Grass Roots, A Study in the Sociology of Formal Organization* ° (Univ. of California Press, 1949); in R. G. Tugwell and E. C. Banfield's, "Grass Roots Democracy—Myth or Reality?," *Public Administration Review*, X (Winter, 1950), 47–55; and in William Appleman Williams' *The Contours of American History* ° (World, 1961). Gabriel Kolko in *Wealth and Power in America* ° (Praeger, 1962) concludes that there was no redistribution of income during the New Deal.

CARL N. DEGLER

The Third American Revolution

INTRODUCTION

In *Out of Our Past: The Forces that Shaped Modern America,* Carl
Degler entitled his section on the New Deal "The Third American
Revolution." In that essay, reprinted below, Degler stresses the
enduring bold changes effected during the New Deal era and emphasizes in particular the shift in popular attitudes toward accepting the concept of federal responsibility for the economy.

Yet, many historians who argue for the continuity of the New
Deal with earlier decades conclude that the reforms that Degler focuses on—aid to agriculture, the Tennessee Valley Authority and
regional development, social security and unemployment compensation, and separation of commercial and investment banking—

FROM Carl N. Degler, "The Third American Revolution," in *Out of Our Past,* pp. 379–94,
397–99, 402, 404–06, 410–16. Copyright © 1959 by Carl N. Degler. Reprinted by permission of Harper & Row, Publishers, Incorporated.

were not generally bold accomplishments nor ideas new to the 1930's. Indeed, in the preceding decade such concerns as regulation of business and federal assistance to agriculture had received substantial political support, and businessmen in some prominent industries had even sought legislation to restrain competition.

Although in this essay Degler is concerned with the novelty of the New Deal, and thus differs from the analysis of Frank Freidel, who affirms the conservatism and continuity of the Roosevelt reforms (see pp. 246–62), in his later essay on Hoover (see pp. 223–39) Degler seems to revise his judgment. Rather than characterizing Hoover's program as a "fatalistic and defeatist course" and viewing the New Deal as an abrupt change, Degler acknowledged in 1963 that "we are now far enough removed from both [Hoover and Roosevelt] to recognize . . . the real continuity between them. . . ."

Twice since the founding of the Republic, cataclysmic events have sliced through the fabric of American life, snapping many of the threads which ordinarily bind the past to the future. The War for the Union was one such event, the Great Depression of the 1930's the other. And, as the Civil War was precipitated from the political and moral tensions of the preceding era, so the Great Depression was a culmination of the social and economic forces of industrialization and urbanization which had been transforming America since 1865. A depression of such pervasiveness as that of the thirties could happen only to a people already tightly interlaced by the multitudinous cords of a machine civilization and embedded in the matrix of an urban society.

In all our history no other economic collapse brought so many Americans to near starvation, endured so long, or came so close to overturning the basic institutions of American life. It is understandable, therefore, that from that experience should issue a new conception of the good society.

The economic dimensions of the Great Depression are quickly sketched —too quickly perhaps to permit a full appreciation of the abyss into which the economy slid between 1929 and 1933. The value of stocks on the New York Exchange, for example, slumped from a high of $87 billion in 1929 to a mere $19 billion in 1933. Wholesale prices dropped 38 per cent by 1933 and farm prices seemed almost to have ceased to exist: they were 60 per cent below the low level of 1929. Within less than three years, realized national income plummeted to almost half of what it had been in the last boom year; and the same was true of industrial production. The human cost of this catastrophic breakdown in the complicated industrial machine, *Fortune* magazine estimated in September, 1932, was 10 million totally unemployed or 25 million people without any source of income.

To worsen matters, the industrial stagnation was accompanied by a spreading fever of bank failures. First here and there, then all over the country, the banks began to close their doors in the faces of their depositors. By the beginning of 1933, the financial self-confidence of the nation reached a dangerously low level, requiring the new administration of Franklin Roosevelt, as its first official act, to order the closing of all banks. In all, more than 10,000 deposit banks failed in the five years after 1929. If the banks, the custodians of the measure of value, proved to be unsound, men might well wonder what was left to cling to as the winds of disaster gained in fury.

Unnerving as the failure of the banks undoubtedly was, for most people the Great Depression became starkly real only when unemployment struck. No one knew whom it would hit next; the jobless were everywhere—in the cities, in the towns, on the farms. Their helplessness, their bewilderment, were often written in their faces, reflected in their discouraged gaits, and mirrored in their run-down dwellings. John Dos Passos reported seeing the unemployed of Detroit in 1932 living in caves scooped out of giant abandoned sand piles. Though it was said that no one would be allowed to starve, *Fortune,* in September, 1932, suggested that some had already. The magazine counted the millions of the unemployed and told of families subsisting on a single loaf of bread for over a week or of going without food for two or three days on end. Discarded and spoiled vegetables or wild dandelions were the substance of meals for some families. Other reports in 1933 told of at least twenty-nine persons who died of starvation in New York City. Moreover, thousands must have died from diseases which gained an easy foothold in weakened and underfed bodies; but these unfortunates were never counted. Food, casually consumed in good times, suddenly became the focus of existence for thousands. In their desperation some urban folk actually tried to wring their food from the barren soil of the city. In Gary, Indiana, for example, 20,000 families were raising food on lots lent by the city; Robert and Helen Lynd reported that in Middletown in 1933, 2,500 of the town's 48,000 people eked out their food budgets with relief gardens.

The spreading unemployment generated new and deep-seated fears. When the unkempt veterans of the First World War camped in Washington in 1932, demanding a bonus to tide them over their joblessness, a fearful and unsure President had them dispersed by troops armed with tear gas. And when Congress in that same year voted a 10 per cent cut in government salaries, President Hoover sent a secret message urging that the enlisted men of the Army and the Navy be excluded from such decreases so that in case of domestic troubles the federal government would not be compelled to rely upon disgruntled troops.

Nor was it only the federal government that felt uneasy in the presence of the specter which was stalking the land. Malcolm Cowley, in an eyewitness account, described how the trucks bearing the disillusioned veterans out of Washington were quickly sped through town after town, the local authorities fearing that some of the unemployed veterans would jump off and become burdens on already overtaxed communities. Cowley tells of one citizen in Washington, not a marcher at all, who was hurriedly bundled into a truck by mistake and could not get off until he reached Indianapolis!

Driven by their desperation, some Americans began to talk of violence. Mutterings of revolution and threats to return with rifles were heard among the bonus marchers as they left Washington. Out on the farms, the dissatisfaction of the veterans was matched by sullen farmers who closed the courts and disrupted mortgage auctions to save their homes. The ugly turn which the discontent could take was revealed by the arrest of a man in Wisconsin in 1932 on suspicion of having removed a spike from the railroad track over which President Hoover's train was to pass. In that bleak year it was not uncommon for the President of the United States to be booed and hooted as he doggedly pursued his ill-starred campaign for re-election. To Theodore Dreiser, as the cold night of the depression settled over the land, it seemed that Karl Marx's prediction "that Capitalism would eventually evolve into failure . . . has come true."

Even for the Lords of Creation, as Frederick Lewis Allen was to call them, the Great Depression was an unsettling and confusing experience. "I'm afraid, every man is afraid," confessed Charles M. Schwab of United States Steel. "I don't know, we don't know, whether the values we have are going to be real next month or not." And in the very early months of the Roosevelt administration, Harold Ickes, attending a dinner of the Chamber of Commerce of the United States, could sense the pitiable impotence to which the nation's industrial leaders had sunk. "The great and the mighty in the business world were there in force," he rather gleefully noted in his diary, "and I couldn't help thinking how so many of these great and mighty were crawling to Washington on their hands and knees these days to beg the Government to run their businesses for them."

But it was the unspectacular, the everyday dreariness of unemployment that must have cut the deepest and endured the longest as far as the ordinary American was concerned. The simplest things of life, once taken for granted, now became points of irritation. "I forget how to cook good since I have nothing to cook with," remarked one housewife. Children lost their appetites upon seeing the milk and mush "that they have seen so often." Even the rare treat of fresh meat could not awaken an appetite long accustomed to disappointment and pallid food.

The routine entertainments of the poor were casualties to unemployment. "Suppose you go to a friend's house and she gives you a cup of tea and something," the wife of an unemployed worker told a social worker. "You feel ashamed. You think, now I got to do the same when she comes to my house. You know you can't so you stay home." Shifts in entertainment patterns among the unemployed were revealed in a study made of some 200 families in New Haven. Before the breadwinner lost his job, some 55 per cent went to the movies; once unemployment hit, however, only 16 per cent did. In the days when work was to be had, only 13 per cent found recreation in "sitting around the house," but now 25 per cent did so. With the loss of their jobs, 12 per cent of the men admitted they "chatted and gossiped" for recreation, although none of them did when they had work.

Unemployment's effect upon the family was often more profound and far-reaching. In recounting the case history of the Raparka family, one sociologist wrote that when Mr. Raparka "lost his job in the fall of 1933, he dominated the family. Two years later it was Mrs. Raparka who was the center of authority." Again and again social workers chronicled the alteration in the father's position in the family during a period of unemployment. Humiliation settled over many a father no longer able to fulfill his accustomed role in the family. "I would rather turn on the gas and put an end to the whole family than let my wife support me," was the way one unemployed father put it. One investigator found that one fifth of her sample of fifty-nine families exhibited a breakdown in the father's authority, particularly in the eyes of the wife. For example, one wife said, "When your husband cannot provide for the family and makes you worry so, you lose your love for him."

Fathers discovered that without the usual financial power to buy bikes or bestow nickels, their control and authority over children were seriously weakened and sometimes completely undermined. In one family where the father was unemployed for a long time, his role was almost completely taken over by the eldest son. The father himself admitted: "The son of twenty-two is just like a father around the house. He tries to settle any little brother-and-sister fights and even encourages me and my wife." In the same family, a younger son who was working summed up his relationship to his parents in a few words. "I remind them," he said, "who makes the money. They don't say much. They just take it, that's all. I'm not the one on relief." In such circumstances, it is no exaggeration to say that the massive weight of the depression was grinding away at the bedrock of American institutions.

The ties of a home struck by unemployment were weak and the opportunities for fruitful and satisfying work were almost totally absent in 1932–33. *Fortune* reported in February, 1933, that something like 200,000 young men and boys were traveling around the country on railroad trains for lack of anything better to do. Tolerated by the railroads because of their obvious poverty and lack of jobs, the boys were often suffering from disease and malnutrition. The authorities in Los Angeles asserted, for example, that 25 per cent of those coming into the city needed clinical attention and 5 per cent required hospitalization. During a single season, one railroad announced, fifty such footloose boys were killed and one hundred injured. From Kansas City it was reported that girl wanderers, dressed in boy's clothing, were on the increase. To many such young people, now grown, the Great Depression must still seem the most purposeless, the most enervating period of their lives.

What Robert and Helen Lynd concluded for their study of Middletown in 1935 can be applied to America as a whole: ". . . the great knife of the depression had cut down impartially through the entire population cleaving open lives and hopes of rich as well as poor. The experience has been more nearly universal than any prolonged recent emotional experience in the city's history; it has approached in its elemental shock the primary experiences of birth and death."

Perhaps the most striking alteration in American thought which the depression fostered concerned the role of the government in the economy. Buffeted and bewildered by the economic debacle, the American people in the course of the 1930's abandoned, once and for all, the doctrine of laissez faire. This beau ideal of the nineteenth-century economists had become, ever since the days of Jackson, an increasingly cherished shibboleth of Americans. But now it was almost casually discarded. It is true, of course, that the rejection of laissez faire had a long history; certainly the Populists worked to undermine it. But with the depression the nation at large accepted the government as a permanent influence in the economy.[1]

Almost every one of the best-known measures of the federal government during the depression era made inroads into the hitherto private preserves of business and the individual. Furthermore, most of these new measures survived the period, taking their places as fundamental elements in the structure of American life. For modern Americans living under a federal government of transcendent influence and control in the economy, this is the historic meaning of the great depression.

Much of what is taken for granted today as the legitimate function of government and the social responsibility of business began only with the legislation of these turbulent years. Out of the investigation of banking and bankers in 1933, for example, issued legislation which separated commercial banking from the stock and bond markets, and insured the bank deposits of ordinary citizens. The stock market, like the banks, was placed under new controls and a higher sense of responsibility to the public imposed upon it by the new Securities and Exchange Commission. The lesson of Black Tuesday in 1929 had not been forgotten; the classic free market itself—the Exchange —was hereafter to be under continuous governmental scrutiny.

---

[1] A complementary and highly suggestive way of viewing this trend away from laissez faire, of which the events of the 1930's are a culmination, is that taken in K. William Kapp, *The Social Costs of Private Enterprise* (Cambridge, Mass., 1950). Kapp observes that for a long time private enterprise had shifted the social costs of production—like industrially polluted water, industrial injuries, smoke nuisances and hazards, unemployment, and the like—onto society. The decline of laissez faire has, in this view, actually been a movement to compel industry to pay for those social costs of production which it has hitherto shirked.

The three Agricultural Adjustment Acts of 1933, 1936, and 1938, while somewhat diverse in detail, laid down the basic lines of what is still today the American approach to the agricultural problem. Ever since the collapse of the boom after the First World War, American agriculture had suffered from the low prices born of the tremendous surpluses. Unable to devise a method for expanding markets to absorb the excess, the government turned to restriction of output as the only feasible alternative. But because restriction of output meant curtailment of income for the farmer, it became necessary, if farm income was to be sustained, that farmers be compensated for their cut in production. Thus was inaugurated the singular phenomenon, which is still a part of the American answer to the agricultural surplus, of paying farmers for *not* growing crops. The other device introduced for raising farm prices, and still the mainstay of our farm policy, came with the 1938 act, which provided that the government would purchase and store excess farm goods, thus supporting the price level by withdrawing the surplus from the competitive market. Both methods constitute a subsidy for the farmer from society at large.[2]

Though the Eisenhower administration in the 1950's called for a return to a free market in farm products—that is, the removal of government supports from prices—very few steps have been taken in that direction, and probably very few ever will. A free market was actually in operation during the twenties, but it succeeded only in making farmers the stepchildren of the golden prosperity of that decade. Today the farm bloc is too powerful politically to be treated so cavalierly. Moreover, the depression has taught most Americans that a free market is not only a rarity in the modern world but sometimes inimical to a stable and lasting prosperity.

Perhaps the most imaginative and fruitful of these innovations was the Tennessee Valley Authority, which transformed the heart of the South. "It was and is literally a down to earth experiment," native Tennesseean Broadus Mitchell has written, "with all that we know from test tube and logarithm tables called on to help. It was a union of heart and mind to restore what had been wasted. It was a social resurrection." For the TVA was much more than flood and erosion control or even hydroelectric power—though its gleaming white dams are perhaps its most striking and best-known monuments. It was social planning of the most humane sort, where even the dead were carefully removed from cemeteries before the waters backed up behind the dams. It brought new ideas, new wealth, new skills, new hope into a wasted, tired, and discouraged region.

---

[2] On the day that the first AAA was declared unconstitutional, a Gallup poll revealed that, although the nation as a whole did not like the AAA, the farmers of the South and Midwest did. As a result, invalidation of the act by the Court did not mean the end of such a policy, but only the beginning of a search to find a new way of accomplishing the same end. Hence there were successive AAA's, whereas, when NRA was declared unconstitutional in 1935, it was dropped, primarily because neither business nor labor, for whose interests it had been organized, found much merit in its approach to their problems.

At the time of the inception of the TVA, it was scarcely believable that the "backward" South would ever utilize all the power the great dams would create. But in its report of 1956, the Authority declared that the Valley's consumption of electricity far exceeded that produced from water sites: almost three quarters of TVA's power is now generated from steam power, not from waterfall. In large part it was the TVA which taught the Valley how to use more power to expand its industries and to lighten the people's burdens. Back in 1935, Drew and Leon Pearson saw this creation of consumer demand in action. "Uncle Sam is a drummer with a commercial line to sell," they wrote in *Harper's Magazine.* "He sold liberty bonds before, but never refrigerators."

Measured against textbook definitions, the TVA is unquestionably socialism. The government owns the means of production and, moreover, it competes with private producers of electricity.[3] But pragmatic Americans— and particularly those living in the Valley—have had few sleepless nights as a consequence of this fact. The TVA does its appointed job and, as the recent fight over the Dixon and Yates contract seemed to show, it is here to stay. It, too, with all the talk of "creeping socialism," has been absorbed into that new American Way fashioned by the experimentalism of the American people from the wreckage of the Great Depression.

Undoubtedly social security deserves the appellation "revolutionary" quite as much as the TVA; it brought government into the lives of people as nothing had since the draft and the income tax. Social security legislation actually comprises two systems: insurance against old age and insurance in the event of loss of work. The first system was completely organized and operated by the federal government; the second was shared with the states— but the national government set the standards; both were clear acknowledgment of the changes which had taken place in the family and in the business of making a living in America. No longer in urban America could the old folks, whose proportion in the society was steadily increasing, count on being taken in by their offspring as had been customary in a more agrarian world. Besides, such a makeshift arrangement was scarcely satisfying to the self-respect of the oldsters. With the transformation of the economy by industrialization, most Americans had become helpless before the vagaries of the business cycle. As a consequence of the social forces which were steadily

---

[3] The extent of the intellectual change which the depression measures introduced can be appreciated by a quotation from President Hoover's veto in 1931 of a bill to develop a public power project in what was later to be the TVA area. "I am firmly opposed to the Government entering into any business the major purpose of which is competition with our citizens." Emergency measures of such a character might be tolerated, he said. "But for the Federal government deliberately to go out to build up and expand such an occasion to the major purpose of a power and manufacturing business is to break down the initiative and enterprise of the American people; it is destruction of equality of opportunity amongst our people; it is the negation of the ideals upon which our civilization has been based."

augmenting social insecurity, only collective action by the government could arrest the drift.

To have the government concerned about the security of the individual was a new thing. Keenly aware of the novelty of this aim in individualistic America,[4] Roosevelt was careful to deny any serious departure from traditional paths. "These three great objectives—the security of the home, the security of livelihood, and the security of social insurance," he said in 1934, constitute "a minimum of the promise that we can offer to the American people." But this, he quickly added, "does not indicate a change in values."

Whether the American people thought their values had changed is not nearly as important as the fact that they accepted social security. And the proof that they did is shown in the steady increase in the proportion of the population covered by the old-age benefit program since 1935; today about 80 per cent of nonfarm workers are included in the system. Apart from being a minimum protection for the individual and society against the dry rot of industrial idleness, unemployment insurance is now recognized as one of the major devices for warding off another depression.

It is true, as proponents of the agrarian life have been quick to point out, that an industrialized people, stripped as they are of their economic self-reliance, have felt the need for social insurance more than people in other types of society. But it is perhaps just as important to recognize that it is only in such a highly productive society that people can even dare to dream of social security. Men in other ages have felt the biting pains of economic crisis, but few preindustrial people have ever enjoyed that surfeit of goods which permits the fat years to fill out the lean ones. But like so much else concerning industrialism, it is not always easy to calculate whether the boons it offers exceed in value the burdens which it imposes.

For the average man, the scourge of unemployment was the essence of the depression. Widespread unemployment, permeating all ranks and stations in society, drove the American people and their government into some of their most determined and deliberate departures from the hallowed policy of "hands off." But despite the determination, as late as 1938 the workless still numbered almost ten million—two thirds as great as in 1932 under President Hoover. The governmental policies of the 1930's never appreciably diminished the horde of unemployed—only the war prosperity of 1940 and after did that—but the providing of jobs by the federal government was a reflection of the people's new conviction that the government had a responsibility to alleviate economic disaster. Such bold action on the part of

---

[4] Characteristically enough, as his memoirs show, President Hoover had long been interested in both old-age and unemployment insurance, but always such schemes were to be worked out through private insurance companies, or at best with the states—never under the auspices of the federal government. "It required a great depression," he has written somewhat ruefully, "to awaken interest in the idea" of unemployment insurance.

government, after the inconclusive, bewildered approach of the Hoover administration, was a tonic for the dragging spirits of the people.[5]

A whole range of agencies, from the Civil Works Administration (CWA) to the Works Progress Administration (WPA), were created to carry the attack against unemployment. It is true that the vast program of relief which was organized was not "permanent" in the sense that it is still in being, but for two reasons it deserves to be discussed here. First, since these agencies constituted America's principal weapon against unemployment, some form of them will surely be utilized if a depression should occur again. Second, the various relief agencies of the period afford the best examples of the new welfare outlook, which was then in the process of formation.

Though in the beginning relief programs were premised on little more than Harry Hopkins' celebrated dictum, "Hunger is not debatable," much more complex solutions to unemployment were soon worked out. The relief program of the WPA, which after 1935 was the major relief agency, was a case in point. In 1937, *Fortune* magazine commented on "the evolution of unemployment relief from tool to institution"—a recognition of the importance and duration of relief in America. "In 1936, the federal government was so deeply involved in the relief of the unemployed," *Fortune* contended, "that it was not only keeping them alive, but it was also giving them an opportunity to work; and not only giving them an opportunity to work but giving them an opportunity to work at jobs for which they were peculiarly fitted; and not only giving them an opportunity to work at jobs for which they were peculiarly fitted, but creating for them jobs of an interest and usefulness which they could not have expected to find in private employment." The statement somewhat distorts the work of the WPA, but it sums up the main outlines of the evolution of the relief program.

The various artistic and cultural employment programs of the WPA are excellent examples of how relief provided more than employment, though any of the youth agencies like the Civilian Conservation Corps or the Na-

---

[5] It was the misfortune of Herbert Hoover to have been President at a time when his considerable administrative and intellectual gifts were hamstrung by his basic political philosophy, which, instead of being a guide to action, served as an obstacle. Much more of an old-fashioned liberal than a reactionary, and deeply attached to the Jeffersonian dogma of the limited powers of the federal government, Hoover was psychologically and philosophically unable to use the immense powers and resources of his office in attacking the urgent threat of unemployment. Back in 1860–61, another President—James Buchanan —had been paralyzed in the midst of a national crisis by his limited conception of the federal power, but in that instance his inaction was palliated by the fact that his successor was to take office within less than three months. Hoover, however, wrestled with the depression for three years, and all during that trying period he stoutly held to his rigid intellectual position that federally supplied and administered relief would destroy the foundations of the nation. Never has an American President, including the two Adamses, defied overwhelming popular opinion for so long for the sake of his own ideals as Herbert Hoover did then; and never has a President since Buchanan fallen so quickly into obscurity as Hoover did after March 4, 1933.

tional Youth Administration (it subsidized student work) would serve equally well. At its peak, the Federal Writers' Project employed some 6,000 journalists, poets, novelists, and Ph. D.'s of one sort or another; unknowns worked on the same payroll, if not side by side, with John Steinbeck, Vardis Fisher, and Conrad Aiken. The $46 million expended on art—that is, painting and sculpture—by the WPA in 1936–37 exceeded the artistic budget of any country outside the totalitarian orbit—and there art was frankly propagandistic. *Fortune*, in May, 1937, found the American government's sponsorship of art singularly free of censorship or propaganda. The magazine concluded that "by and large the Arts Projects have been given a freedom no one would have thought possible in a government run undertaking. And by and large that freedom has not been abused." During the first fifteen months of the Federal Music Project, some fifty million people heard live concerts; in the first year of the WPA Theater, sixty million people in thirty states saw performances, with weekly attendance running to half a million. T. S. Eliot's *Murder in the Cathedral*, too risky for a commercial producer, was presented in New York by the Federal Theater to 40,000 people at a top price of 55 cents.

"What the government's experiments in music, painting, and the theater actually did," concluded *Fortune* in May, 1937, "even in their first year, was to work a sort of cultural revolution in America." For the first time the American audience and the American artist were brought face to face for their mutual benefit. 'Art in America is being given its chance," said the British writer Ford Madox Ford, "and there has been nothing like it since before the Reformation. . . ."

Instead of being ignored on the superficially plausible grounds of the exigencies of the depression, the precious skills of thousands of painters, writers, and musicians were utilized. By this timely rescue of skills, tastes, and talents from the deadening hand of unemployment, the American people, through their government, showed their humanity and social imagination. Important for the future was the foresight displayed in the conserving of artistic talents and creations for the enrichment of generations to come.

The entrance of the federal government into a vast program of relief work was an abrupt departure from all previous practice, but it proved enduring. "When President Roosevelt laid it down that government had a social responsibility to care for the victims of the business cycle," *Fortune* remarked prophetically in 1937, "he set in motion an irreversible process." The burden of unemployment relief was too heavy to be carried by local government or private charities in an industrialized society; from now on, the national government would be expected to shoulder the responsibility. "Those who are on relief and in close contact otherwise with public matters realize that what has happened to the country is a bloodless revolution," wrote an anonymous relief recipient in *Harper's* in 1936. The government, he said, has assumed a new role in depressions, and only the rich might still be oblivious to it. But they too "will know it by 1940. And in time," they will "come to approve the idea of everyone having enough to eat." [6] Few people escaped the wide net of the depression: "Anybody sinks after a while," the anonymous reliefer pointed out. "Even you would have if God hadn't preserved, without apparent rhyme or reason, your job and your income." That the depression was a threat to all was perhaps the first lesson gained from the 1930's.

The second was that only through collective defense could such a threat be met. By virtue of the vigorous attack made upon the economic problems of the thirties by the government, the age-old conviction that dips in the business cycle were either the will of God or the consequence of unalterable economic laws was effectively demolished. As recently as 1931, President Hoover had told an audience that some people "have indomitable confidence that by some legerdemain we can legislate ourselves out of a world-wide depression. Such views are as accurate as the belief that we can exorcise a Caribbean hurricane." From the experience of the depression era, the American people learned that something could and ought to be done when economic disaster strikes. No party and no politician with a future will ever again dare to take the fatalistic and defeatist course of Herbert Hoover in 1929—33.

As the enactment of the Employment Act of 1946 showed, the prevention of depression now occupies top listing among the social anxieties of the American people. The act created a permanent Council of Economic Advisers to the President, to keep him continuously informed on the state of the economy and to advise him on the measures necessary to avoid an economic decline. And the Joint Committee on the Economic Report does the same for Congress.

Today political figures who indignantly repudiate any "left-wing" philosophy of any sort readily accept this inheritance from the depression. "Never again shall we allow a depression in the United States," vowed Republican candidate Eisenhower in 1952. As soon as we "foresee the signs of any recession and depression," he promised, ". . . the full power of private industry, of municipal government, of state government, of the Federal Government will be mobilized to see that that does not happen." Ignoring the fact that as a prospective federal official he had promised more than he could deliver, he innocently and accurately added, "I cannot pledge you more than that." Sensing the tremendous importance of the matter to the American people, Eisenhower made substantially the same statement three other times—at Yonkers, Peoria, and Pittsburgh. At Yonkers he said that he had "repeated this particular pledge over and over again in the

---

[6] The providing of work relief instead of the dole did more than fill hungry stomachs; it reestablished faith in America and in one's fellow man. "I'm proud of our United States," said one relief recipient. "There ain't no other nation in the world that would have sense enough to think of WPA and all the other A's." The wife of one WPA worker was quoted as saying, "We aren't on relief any more—my man is working for the government."

United States" and that he and his associates were "dedicated to this proposition. . . ."

In the White House, Eisenhower continued to reflect this underlying and persistent fear that a depression would once again stride through the land. According to the account in Robert Donovan's semiofficial *Eisenhower: The Inside Story*, at session after session of the Cabinet during the recession of 1953–54, it was the President who stressed the urgency of the economic situation. It was he who constantly prodded Arthur F. Burns of the Council of Economic Advisers to prepare plans with which to forestall a serious drop in the economic indicators. Indeed as late as June, 1954, just after Burns had delivered an optimistic report on the condition and future of the economy, as Donovan tells it, "The President . . . was still concerned about whether the administration was doing enough. Even though it jarred the logic of some members of the Cabinet, he insisted, everything possible must be done to restore vigor to the economy. It was important, the President said, to produce results and to err on the side of doing too much rather than too little."

In the midst of the recession of 1957–58, Vice-President Nixon, speaking on April 24, 1958, specifically repudiated the Hoover approach of permitting the economy to right itself without government intervention. "Let us recognize once and for all," he told his audience, "that the time is past in the United States when the Federal Government can stand by and allow a recession to be prolonged or to deepen into depression without decisive Government action." Though Eisenhower was obviously worried that hasty measures might bring on further inflation, on May 20, in a public address, he agreed with the Vice-President that the government had "a continuing responsibility . . . to help counteract recession." In the same speech the President enumerated concrete measures already taken, such as extension of unemployment benefits, speeding up of defense and civilian procurement, acceleration of government construction projects, and the easing of credit by the Federal Reserve.

The Republican administration's evident acceptance of the new obligations of government in the economy is strikingly suggestive of the shock which the depression dealt conventional economic thought in America.

In passing through the dark valley of the depression, Americans discarded more than conventional economics; they also revised their political preferences. Like downswings in other times, the depression of the thirties spawned a number of ephemeral political aberrations like the Share the Wealth of Huey Long, the oldsters' rebellion led by Dr. Francis E. Townsend, and the soured Populism of Father Coughlin's crusade for Social Justice. But the most portentous shift in popular political thought was the Roosevelt Revolution—the raising of the Democratic party to the predominant position in American political life. What the War for the Union did for Republicans, the Great Depression achieved for the Democrats; and ever since, they have been making as steady use of the tattered shirt as the Republicans did of the bloody shirt. It has worked, too; even in the mid-fifties, as the election of 1956 demonstrates, there are more Democrats than Republicans in the country. For despite the re-election of Eisenhower, the Republicans lost both houses of Congress, an unprecedented failure for a party with a winning President. The grip of the depression on the American psyche has barely loosened a full generation after 1933.

This massive shift in popular opinion from the Republican to the Democratic party was a direct result of the wide range of social groups to which the Democratic administration offered succor and recognition. Midwestern farmers, for example, had always been deemed safe within the Republican fold, but after the AAA program they eagerly joined the Roosevelt coalition. And as late as 1948 it was clear that many were still there, for the farmers held the key to Harry Truman's unexpected victory that year. Numerous relief payments to workers, labor legislation, and the benevolent interest of the President himself succeeded in tying the working classes of the city more firmly and in greater numbers than ever before to the wheels of the Democratic chariot. Not until the election of 1956 was there any noticeable breach in the solid Democratic allegiance of the big cities. Even then what breaks appeared seemed to be attributable more to the charismatic effects of Ike than to any massive shift in party allegiance.

Perhaps the most unexpected result of the revolution was the transfer of the Negro vote from the Republicans, where it had lain for three generations, to the Democrats.

. . . .

What brought about this dramatic reversal? Part of the answer, of course, lies in the demographic facts of migration, but, as the Negro voting in 1932 demonstrates, the really operative force was the Roosevelt administration's recognition of the Negro. It is most interesting that very little of the Democratic appeal to the Negro before 1940 can be illustrated in pronouncements or even in particular pieces of legislation. Only rarely does one find in the literature of Franklin Roosevelt and his New Deal such self-conscious appeals to the Negro as, say, in Harry Truman's Fair Deal or Henry Wallace's Progressive party.

There are several reasons for this. Primary, of course, is the fact that these other two movements developed after the Roosevelt regime had already given the Negro a bigger and higher platform from which to articulate his demands. Moreover, because F. D. R., as a working politician, was always conscious of his party's southern wing, he would rarely antagonize the Southerners on the race issue alone. Furthermore, Roosevelt as a leader was only tangentially aware of the Negro as a special case, as a minority to be singled out for exceptional treatment or concern. It was Eleanor Roosevelt, not Franklin, who went out of her way to be racially democratic and to concern herself with minority problems.

Nonetheless, the Roosevelt administration in its relatively undramatic fashion did much for the Negro, and this too stemmed from both the character of Franklin Roosevelt and the underlying philosophy of his administration. Just as the federal government found a place for the artist, so its humane outlook could not exclude the Negro. Thus if white men were to be given relief work, so must Negroes; and if so, then why not on an equal basis? "We are going to make a country in which no one is left out," the President said in another connection. And there was nothing to suggest that he had any mental reservations about race when he said it. Besides, although F. D. R. would do little publicly to antagonize his southern allies on the race question, his political perspicacity told him that in the North his power was heavily dependent upon city machines, many of which could or did benefit from Negro votes.

From the very outset the Democratic regime in Washington accepted the black man. Negroes were sprinkled through almost all its agencies either as advisers or as employees in a lesser capacity. The administration consulted and bestowed office upon nonpolitical Negroes (the Republicans had generally used Negroes as political appointees) like William H. Hastie, later to be the first Negro federal judge; Robert C. Weaver, the economist; and Mrs. Mary Bethune, the educator. When low-cost housing went up, Negroes got their share; Negro youths were welcome in the CCC and the NYA just as the whites were, though in the former the races were segregated. Recreational centers, hospitals, and schools were built for Negroes with federal money. Evenhandedly distributed federal relief funds were a gift from heaven to the black man, who was traditionally "hired last and fired first." As one Negro newspaperman told Samuel Lubell, "The really important thing about WPA is that it is a guarantee of a living wage. It means Negroes don't have to work for anything people want to give them." In the votings conducted by the AAA among farmers and those supervised by the National Labor Relations Board among workers, Negroes were treated the same as white men, even though in the South these same black men were excluded from political elections. In short, the Roosevelt administration took a number of concrete steps toward accepting the Negro as a full citizen—a simple innovation of portentous consequences. It would be difficult hereafter for any party in power to do less.

All the credit for converting the Negro from his Republicanism, however, should not go to positive acts of the Democratic administration; the objective economic and social environment also deserves some. Negroes, for example, began to secure jobs in a greater variety of occupations than ever before; under the impact of the depression, some employers were willing to hire Negroes for the first time, if only because the black worker accepted lower wages. Moreover, the C.I.O. unions now began to organize Negro workers on an equal basis with whites. To accomplish this end, Negro organizers were sent among the steel, maritime, and auto workers, and, when the permanent Congress of Industrial Organizations was formed in 1938, a clause in the constitution prohibited any constituent union from discriminating on grounds of race. The startling improvement in the Negro's position in the thirties could not help but redound to the benefit of the party in power.

By 1940, the capturing of the Negro vote by the Democrats was an accomplished fact, and the party platform of that year, using the word "Negro" for the first time, boasted of its friendship for the black man. "Our Negro citizens," the platform proclaimed, "have participated actively in the economic and social advances launched by this Administration." It would not have been an exaggeration, for once in the history of political platforms, if it had been noted that this was about the first time since the 1870's that any party could truthfully say half as much.

The change wrought in the political affiliations of Negroes by the depression was as nothing compared with the catalytic and subversive effect it worked upon the labor movement. And, analogous to the change in the preference of the Negro voter, the alteration in the position and power of labor was indebted to the action of the Roosevelt administration, the Democratic Congress, and the new social atmosphere of the depression era.

During the prosperity of the twenties the labor movement had gone into a decline rare in the history of unionization. The usual tendency had been for membership to rise in prosperous times and to decline in bad. But whereas in 1920 organized labor could claim its largest membership to date —some five million workers—by 1929 barely three million could be counted. Thus labor entered the depression under the handicap of declining membership. But instead of killing off many unions, as depressions had done earlier, the depression of the thirties seemed to stimulate a new and aggressive organizing spirit among the workers. In the light of the later tremendous expansion of union membership, it might be said that the depression created a class consciousness among American workingmen for the first time sufficient to permit large-scale unionization.

. . . .

The enormous expansion of unionization in the last years of the depression was not solely attributable to the novel spirit among the unions and the workers. Much of the impetus came from the new attitude of the government. We have already seen the catalytic effect the NRA had on the rush toward unionization, and it would be difficult to exaggerate that effect. When that act was declared unconstitutional in 1935, its place was taken by the National Labor Relations Act (the Wagner Act), in itself perhaps the most revolutionary single measure in American labor history.

The Wagner Act started from the same premise as section 7a of the NRA—that is, that workers should be free to choose their own unions and employers must abstain from interfering in this choice. It also required that employers accept duly constituted unions as legitimate representatives of their employees and bargain with them. The act also set up a board—the National Labor Relations Board—whose duty it was to supervise elections for the certification of unions as representatives of a majority of the workers in a plant, and to hear complaints against employers for having interfered with union organizing. The Board was also empowered to hear complaints against employers for refusing to bargain with a certified union.

In two different ways, the act threw the enormous prestige and power of the government behind the drive for organizing workers. In the first place, it flatly declared unionization to be a desirable thing for the national economy, forbidding employers to interfere in the process of organization. Five so-called unfair labor practices were listed, all of them acts which only an employer could commit; the act listed no "unfair" practices of labor. (Actually, the courts had built up such a large body of common-law interpretations of unfair labor practices by unions that it was hardly necessary to add to them in the act.) Moreover, as an additional indication of its belief in the labor movement, the law virtually outlawed the company union—that is, the labor organization sponsored by the employer. In the second place, once a union was formed, and it had been certified by the Board as speaking for a majority of the workers, the employer, under the act, had no alternative but to recognize it as the representative of his employees. Though it is true that many employers refused to accept the constitutionality of the law—usually on the advice of their lawyers—until after the Supreme Court decision of 1937 in the Jones and Laughlin Steel case, this placing of the government on the side of unionization was of central importance in the success of many an organizational drive of the C.I.O., notably those against Ford and Little Steel.[7]

The passage of this controversial act marked, insofar as labor was concerned, an acceptance of governmental assistance which would have made old Sam Gompers apoplectic. All during his leadership of the A.F. of L., labor had consistently refused to accept (except for the war emergency) government intervention at the bargaining table of labor and business. But by accepting governmental assistance, the American labor movement not only departed from its own traditions, but from those of European labor as well. Although well aware of the benefits to be derived from such government support as the American movement received, labor in England and on the Continent has not abandoned its historic independence of the state. European labor unions have preferred to remain untouched by the quasi-governmental status in which the American labor movement has permitted itself to be clothed. Labor's bête noire, the Taft-Hartley Act, is an obvious

---

[7] Even before the Wagner Act had won the support of the Supreme Court, Presidential "pressure" and prestige helped the C.I.O. attain some of its most telling victories, like that over General Motors in February of 1937. The sensational exposure of union-busting tactics of employers by Senator Robert La Follette's investigating committee, beginning in 1936, was still another form of governmental assistance to the cause of labor.

confirmation of the truism that dependence on government is a knife which cuts both ways.

      . . . .

The Wagner Act broke new ground in labor law, going even beyond the epoch-making Norris-La Guardia Act of 1932. This latter act, passed after years of agitation and half a dozen tries on the part of labor and liberal congressmen and senators, severely restricted the use of antiunion injunctions issuing from federal courts in the course of labor disputes. So expertly was the act drawn that it overthrew in one stroke a mountain of legal obstacles to labor organization and activity which ingenious judges and lawyers had quarried out of the common law. In substance, though, the main achievement of the act could be summed up in the phrase "laissez faire in labor relations." Labor would now be free to use its full economic power, without judicial hamstringing, just as employers had always been free to use theirs. In no way, it should be emphasized, did the Norris-La Guardia Act compel, or even advise, employers to accept unions or to bargain with them.

      . . . .

Enormous as was the assistance which labor received from government in the form of the NLRA, there was still another piece of legislation which offered a boost to labor. This was the Wages and Hours Act of 1938, which set minimum wages and maximum hours for workers in industries engaged in interstate commerce. Since its example has been followed by several industrial states like New York, the principle of a legislative floor under wages and a ceiling on hours has been extended beyond the constitutional limits of the federal government's power. Because the minimum set by law was well below the going industrial wage, the act did not affect most workers, but it helped considerably to pull up wages in certain unorganized industries. Furthermore, it helped to narrow the wage differences between northern and southern industries. During the first two years of the act, nearly a million workers received increased wages under its provisions and over three million had their hours shortened. Subsequent to that time, the minimum wage has been progressively increased from the original 25 cents an hour to the present (1958) $1, thereby putting a rising floor under the nation's industrial wage scale. Furthermore, in abolishing child labor in all industries involved in interstate commerce, the act achieved a long-sought goal of the labor and liberal movements in the United States. And once again, it is worth noticing, it was accomplished through the powerful intervention of an active federal government.

Seen against a broader canvas, the depression, together with government support, profoundly altered the position of labor in American society. Girded with its new-found power and protections, Big Labor now took its place beside Big Business and Big Government to complete a triumvirate of economic power. And when it is recognized that through the so-called farm bloc in Congress agriculture also has attained a sort of veto power on the operations of the economic system, it is not difficult to appreciate the aptness of John Galbraith's description of modern American capitalism as a system of "countervailing power." Instead of competition being the regulator of the economic system, Professor Galbraith persuasively argues, we now have a system of economic checks and balances—Big Labor, Big Business, Big Agriculture, and so forth—no one of which is big enough or powerful enough to control the total economy. Though Galbraith's argument is not totally convincing, his conception of the American economy is much closer to reality than is the old competitive model. And insofar as Professor Galbraith's analysis is correct, it is clear that this system of countervailing power came into being during the depression, with the rise of Big Government, Organized Agriculture, and Big Labor.

· · · · ·

One of the most enduring monuments to the Great Depression was that congeries of contradictions, naïveté, humanitarianism, realistic politics, and economic horse sense called the New Deal of Franklin D. Roosevelt. As the governmental agent which recast American thinking on the responsibilities of government, the New Deal was clearly the offspring of the depression. As we have seen, it was also more than that: it was a revitalization of the Democratic party; it was the political manifestation of that new spirit of reform which was stirring among the ranks of labor and the Negro people.

In their own time and since, the New Deal and Franklin Roosevelt have had a polarizing effect upon Americans. Probably at no time before Roosevelt has the leader of a great democratic nation come to symbolize as he did the hopes and the fears of so many people.[8] Not even Jackson, in whom Roosevelt himself recognized a President of his own popularity- and hatred-producing caliber, could rival him. Over a decade after Roosevelt's death, the mention of his name still evokes emotions, betrayed by the wistful look in the eye or in the hard set of the jaw. The election of 1956, moreover, demonstrated once again that the Old Guard of the Republican party still fights the dead Roosevelt while the Democratic party wanders leaderless in his absence. This too is a measure of the political revolution he led.

For the Democratic party, Roosevelt was like a lightning rod, drawing to himself all venom and hatred of the opposition, only to discharge it harmlessly; nothing, it seemed, could weaken his personal hold on the affections of the majority of Americans. That something more was involved than sheer popularity is shown by the example of Dwight Eisenhower. Though

---

[8] According to Harold Ickes, Roosevelt was profoundly struck by the adoration which was bestowed upon him by his admirers. During the 1936 campaign, the President told Ickes "that there was something terrible about the crowds that lined the streets along which he passed. He went on to explain what he meant, which was exclamations from individuals in the crowd, such as 'He saved my home,' 'He gave me a job,' 'God bless you, Mr. President,' etc." In May, 1936, Marquis Childs published an article in *Harper's*, entitled "They Hate Roosevelt," in which he described and tried to account for the unreasoning hatred for the President on the part of what Childs called the upper 2 per cent of the population.

held in even greater popular esteem, Eisenhower has been unable to invest his party with his own vote-getting power; Republicans lose though Eisenhower wins. The difference between F. D. R. and Ike is that one stood for a program, a hope, and a future, while the other stands for himself as a good, well-intentioned man whom all instinctively trust and perhaps even admire. The one is a leader of a nation, the other a popular hero. Roosevelt is already a member of that tiny pantheon of great leaders of Americans in which Washington, Jackson, Lincoln, and Wilson are included; it is difficult to believe that Eisenhower will be included. His monument is more likely to be inscribed: "The best-liked man ever to be President."

In the thirties, as now, the place of the New Deal in the broad stream of American development has been a matter of controversy. Historians and commentators on the American scene have not yet reached a firm agreement —if they ever will—as to whether the New Deal was conservative or radical in character, though it does appear that the consensus now seems to lean toward calling it conservative and traditional.[9] Certainly if one searches the writings and utterances of Franklin Roosevelt, his own consciousness of conservative aims is quickly apparent. "The New Deal is an old deal—as old as the earliest aspirations of humanity for liberty and justice and the good life," he declared in 1934. "It was this administration," he told a Chicago audience in 1936, "which saved the system of private profit and free enterprise after it had been dragged to the brink of ruin. . . ."

But men making a revolution among a profoundly conservative people do not advertise their activity, and above all Franklin Roosevelt understood the temper of his people.[10] Nor should such a statement be interpreted as an insinuation of high conspiracy—far from it. Roosevelt was at heart a conservative, as his lifelong interest in history, among other things, suggests. But he was without dogma in his conservatism, which was heavily interlaced with genuine concern for people.[11] He did not shy away from new means and new approaches to problems when circumstances demanded it. His willingness to experiment, to listen to his university-bred Brains Trust, to accept a

---

[9] For example, one of the most recent short evaluations of the New Deal, by a most knowledgeable historian, Arthur Link, concludes as follows: "The chief significance of the reform legislation of the 1930's was its essentially conservative character and the fact that it stemmed from a half century or more of discussion and practical experience and from ideas proposed as well by Republicans as by Democrats." *American Epoch* (New York, 1955), p. 425.

[10] It is significant that only once during the 1932 campaign, according to Ernest K. Lindley, did Roosevelt call for "a revolution"; and then he promptly qualified it to "the right kind, the only kind of revolution this nation can stand for—a revolution at the ballot box."

[11] When an economist suggested to F. D. R. that the depression be permitted to run its course and that then the economic system would soon right itself—as Frances Perkins tells the story—the President's face took on a "gray look of horror" as he told the economist: "People aren't cattle you know!"

measure like the TVA, reveal the flexibility in his thought. Both his lack of theoretical presuppositions and his flexibility are to be seen in the way he came to support novel measures like social security and the Wagner Act. Response to popular demand was the major reason. "The Congress can't stand the pressure of the Townsend Plan unless we have a real old-age insurance system," he complained to Frances Perkins, "nor can I face the country without having . . . a solid plan which will give some assurance to old people of systematic assistance upon retirement." In like manner, the revolutionary NLRA was adopted as a part of his otherwise sketchy and rule-of-thumb philosophy of society. Though ultimately Roosevelt championed the Wagner bill in the House, it was a belated conversion dictated by the foreshadowed success of the measure and the recent invalidation of the NRA. In his pragmatic and common-sense reactions to the exigencies of the depression, Roosevelt, the easygoing conservative, ironically enough became the embodiment of a new era and a new social philosophy for the American people.

"This election," Herbert Hoover presciently said in 1932, "is not a mere shift from the ins to the outs. It means deciding the direction our nation will take over a century to come." The election of Franklin Roosevelt, he predicted, would result in "a radical departure from the foundations of 150 years which have made this the greatest nation in the world." Though Hoover may be charged with nothing more than campaign flourishing, it is nevertheless a fact that his speech was made just after Roosevelt's revealing Commonwealth Club address of September. Only in this single utterance, it should be remembered, did Roosevelt disclose in clear outline the philosophy and program which was later to be the New Deal. "Every man has a right to life," he had said, "and this means that he has also a right to make a comfortable living. . . . Our government, formal and informal, political and economic," he went on, "owes to everyone an avenue to possess himself of a portion of that plenty [from our industrial society] sufficient for his needs, through his own work." Here were the intimations of those new goals which the New Deal set for America.

Accent as heavily as one wishes the continuity between the reforms of the Progressive era and the New Deal, yet the wide difference between the goals of the two periods still remains. The Progressive impulse was narrowly reformist: it limited business, it assisted agriculture, it freed labor from some of the shackles imposed by the courts, but it continued to conceive of the state as policeman or judge and nothing more. The New Deal, on the other hand, was more than a regulator—though it was that too, as shown by the SEC and the reinvigoration of the antitrust division of the Justice Department. To the old goals for America set forth and fought for by the Jeffersonians and the Progressives the New Deal appended new ones. Its primary and general innovation was the guaranteeing of a minimum standard of welfare for the people of the nation. WPA and the whole series of relief agencies which were a part of it, wages and hours legislation, AAA, bank deposit insurance, and social security,[12] each illustrates this new conception of the federal government. A resolution offered by New Deal Senator Walsh in 1935 clearly enunciated the new obligations of government. The resolution took notice of the disastrous effects of the depression "upon the lives of young men and women . . ." and then went on to say that "it is the duty of the Federal Government to use every possible means of opening up opportunities" for the youth of the nation "so that they may be rehabilitated and restored to *a decent standard of living* and ensured proper development of their talents. . . ."

But the guarantor state as it developed under the New Deal was more active and positive than this. It was a vigorous and dynamic force in the society, energizing and, if necessary, supplanting private enterprise when the general welfare required it. With the Wagner Act, for example, the government served notice that it would actively participate in securing the unionization of the American worker; the state was no longer to be an impartial policeman merely keeping order; it now declared for the side of labor. When social and economic problems like the rehabilitation of the Valley of the Tennessee were ignored or shirked by private enterprise, then the federal government undertook to do the job. Did private enterprise fail to provide adequate and sufficient housing for a minimum standard of welfare for the people, then the government would build houses. As a result, boasted Nathan Straus, head of the U.S. Housing Authority, "for the first time in a hundred years the slums of America ceased growing and began to shrink."

Few areas of American life were beyond the touch of the experimenting fingers of the New Deal; even the once sacrosanct domain of prices and the valuation of money felt the tinkering. The devaluation of the dollar, the gold-purchase program, the departure from the gold standard—in short, the whole monetary policy undertaken by F. D. R. as a means to stimulate recovery through a price rise—constituted an unprecedented repudiation of orthodox public finance. To achieve that minimum standard of well-being which the depression had taught the American people to expect of their government, nothing was out of bounds.

But it is not the variety of change which stamps the New Deal as the creator of a new America; its significance lies in the permanence of its program. For, novel as the New Deal program was, it has, significantly, not been repudiated by the Eisenhower administration, the first Republican government since the reforms were instituted. Verbally, it is true, the Republican

---

[12] Social security is an excellent example of how, under the New Deal, reform measures, when they conflicted with recovery, were given priority. In siphoning millions of dollars of social security taxes from the purchasing power of the workers, social security was a deflationary measure, which must have seriously threatened the precariously based new economic recovery. For this reason and others, Abraham Epstein, the foremost authority in America on social security, denounced the act as a "sharing of poverty."

administration has had to minimize its actual commitments to the New Deal philosophy, and it tends to trust private business more than the New Dealers did—witness, for example, its elimination of the minor governmental manufacturing enterprises which competed with private firms. But despite this, the administration's firm commitment to the guaranteeing of prosperity and averting depression at all costs is an accurate reflection of the American people's agreement with the New Deal's diagnosis of the depression. Nor has the Republican party dared to repeal or even emasculate the legislation which made up the vitals of the New Deal: TVA, banking and currency, SEC, social security, the Wagner Act, and fair treatment of the Negro. The New Deal Revolution has become so much a part of the American Way that no political party which aspires to high office dares now to repudiate it.

It may or may not be significant in this regard (for apothegms are more slippery than precise) but it is nonetheless interesting that Roosevelt and Eisenhower have both been impressed with the same single sentence from Lincoln regarding the role of government. "The legitimate object of Government," wrote Lincoln, "is to do for a community of people whatever they need to have done but cannot do at all or cannot do so well for themselves in their separate or individual capacities." Twice, in 1934 and again in 1936, F. D. R. in public addresses used this expression to epitomize his own New Deal, and Robert Donovan in his officially inspired book on the Eisenhower administration writes that this same "fragment of Lincoln's writing . . . Eisenhower uses time and again in describing his own philosophy of government." Between Lincoln and Eisenhower there was no Republican President, except perhaps Theodore Roosevelt, who would have been willing to subscribe to such a freewheeling description of the federal power; in this can be measured the impact of the New Deal and the depression.

The conclusion seems inescapable that, traditional as the words may have been in which the New Deal expressed itself, in actuality it was a revolutionary response to a revolutionary situation. In its long history America has passed through two revolutions since the first one in 1776, but only the last two, the Civil War and the depression, were of such force as to change the direction of the relatively smooth flow of its progress. The Civil War rendered a final and irrevocable decision in the long debate over the nature of the Union and the position of the Negro in American society. From that revolutionary experience, America emerged a strong national state and dedicated by the words of its most hallowed document to the inclusion of the black man in a democratic culture. The searing ordeal of the Great Depression purged the American people of their belief in the limited powers of the federal government and convinced them of the necessity of the guarantor state. And as the Civil War constituted a watershed in American thought, so the depression and its New Deal marked the crossing of a divide from which, it would seem, there could be no turning back.

SUGGESTED READING

Mario Einaudi in *The Roosevelt Revolution* (Harcourt, Brace & World, 1959) shares Degler's conclusions about the New Deal. Walter Galenson's *The CIO Challenge to the AFL* (Harvard Univ. Press, 1960) and David Brody's "The Emergence of Mass Production Unionism," in Braeman *et al.*, eds., *Change and Continuity in Twentieth-Century America* ° (Ohio State Univ. Press, 1964) offer slightly different analyses of the rise of the CIO.

Sidney Fine's *The Automobile Under the Blue Eagle* (Univ. of Michigan Press, 1963) is a thorough study of the National Recovery Administration labor code in the automobile industry. Irving Bernstein's *The New Deal Collective Bargaining Policy* (Univ. of California Press, 1950) examines the legislative history of major labor bills during Roosevelt's first three years in office. There is still need for an analysis of the dynamics and "ideology" of the sit-down strikes, but Sidney Fine's, "The General Motors Sit-Down Strike: A Re-examination," *American Historical Review*, LXX (April, 1965), 691–713 is the best existing study. Jerold Auerbach in *Labor and Liberty: The La Follette Committee and the New Deal* (Bobbs-Merrill, 1967) stresses civil liberties and the difficulties confronted by organized labor; he views the achievement of the New Deal decade as a significant departure from the immediate past.

David Conrad's *The Forgotten Farmer: The Story of Share Croppers and the New Deal* (Univ. of Illinois Press, 1965); Jerold Auerbach's "Southern Tenant Farmers: Socialist Critics of the New Deal," *Labor History*, VII (Winter, 1966), 3–18; and M. S. Venkartaramani's "Norman Thomas, Arkansas Sharecroppers and the Roosevelt Agricultural Policies, 1933–1937," *Mississippi Valley Historical Review*, XLVII (Sept., 1960), 225–46, all present evidence critical of New Deal agricultural policies and, by implication, dispute Degler's view of "The Third American Revolution." Grant McConnell in *The Decline of Agrarian Democracy* (Univ. of California Press, 1959) examines the American Farm Bureau and its great power. Christiana M. Campbell's *The Farm Bureau and the New Deal* (Univ. of Illinois Press, 1962) provides a detailed study of the Bureau. Richard S. Kirkendall's *Social Scientists and Farm Politics in the Age of Roosevelt* (Univ. of Missouri Press, 1966) is a useful volume on a largely neglected topic. Sidney Baldwin's *Poverty and Politics: The Rise and Decline of the Farm Security Administration* (Univ. of North Carolina Press, 1967) and John Shover's *Cornbelt Rebellion: The Farmers' Holiday Association* (Univ. of Oklahoma Press, 1965) are important volumes for understanding farm discontent and the farm programs of the New Deal.

Among the more useful sources on the experience of unemployment are Mirra Komarovsky's, *The Unemployed Man and His Family* (Dryden Press, 1940); E. Wight Bakke's *Citizens Without Work* (Yale

Univ. Press, 1940) and *The Unemployed Worker* (Yale Univ. Press, 1940); R. C. Angell's *The Family Encounters the Depression* (Scribner, 1936); and Robert and Helen Lynd's *Middletown in Transition* ° (Harcourt, Brace & World, 1937), the most perceptive source. Unfortunately there is still no probing study of the American worker during the Depression.

The *Journal of Sociology*, XLVII (May, 1942) devoted a full issue to recent social changes. Oscar Handlin's *The American People in the Twentieth Century* ° (Harvard Univ. Press, 1954) is rich in insights about the 1930's.

LESLIE H. FISHEL, JR.

The Negro in the New Deal Era

INTRODUCTION

For the federal government during the New Deal years—as for most of white America—the plight of the nation's black citizens remained a peripheral concern. Confronted by economic crisis and struggling to repair the economy, the Government was never prepared to bestow much attention or to expend any political capital on the Negro. "Roosevelt's actual commitments to the American Negro were slim. He was more a symbol than an activist . . . ," concludes Leslie H. Fishel, Jr., a scholar of black-white relations.

The President, as Roy Wilkins noted years later, befriended the Negro "only insofar as he refused to exclude [him] from his general policies that applied to the whole country" (Columbia Univ. Oral History, "Memoir," 51). In most programs the number of Ne-

FROM Leslie H. Fishel, Jr., "The Negro in the New Deal Era." Copyright © 1967, by Scott, Foresman and Company and reprinted with their permission. The version reprinted here appeared in *Wisconsin Magazine of History*, XLVIII (Winter, 1964–65), pp. 111–21, and was published in 1967 in somewhat different form in *The Negro American: A Documentary History* by Leslie H. Fishel, Jr., and Benjamin Quarles.

groes that were involved fell well below their need and often even below their percentage of the population. Yet Roosevelt's Government, by its programs and occasional words of recognition, offered more than the Republicans and brought the black masses into the urban Democratic coalition. The midterm elections of 1934 revealed that Negroes were breaking free from their traditional loyalty to the Republican party, and in 1936 they constituted an important source of support in Roosevelt's landslide victory. When the Democratic coalition crumbled in later years, they still clung tenaciously to the party.

Part of Roosevelt's extraordinary success in winning black support can be attributed to the Republican party's failure to make a serious effort to retain the Negro vote. Because it was not in power, the GOP could not woo the Negro with federal relief. The party failed in general to support the mild civil rights legislation proposed by Negro organizations, for many Republican legislators felt that antilynching bills and the repeal of the poll tax threatened states rights. Moreover, members of the GOP were reluctant to abandon their hopes of breaking the solid Democratic South and were therefore unwilling to risk estranging prospective white allies by courting the Negro.

During the New Deal years, the National Association for the Advancement of Colored People lobbied in Washington for antilynching legislation that it knew would not pass. The NAACP apparently hoped to use this issue as a device to publicize the organization and to alert the nation to violence against Negroes. (Between 1932 and 1935 there were sixty-eight lynchings, but in the last five years of the decade the total dropped by nearly half.) In the 1930's the NAACP, still dominated largely by white liberals, was not seeking to assault segregation so much as to put an end to such unconstitutional practices as lynching and disfranchisement. Its efforts in the courts, however, constituted an oblique flanking attack on the then-constitutional doctrine of "separate but equal" at a time when most Americans still assumed that racial segregation was compatible with equality under the law.

Though American liberalism was slowly undergoing redefinition and would soon actually oppose segregation, the energies of only a few reformers in the 1930's were directed to racial problems. Social science, purged of its racism earlier in the twentieth century, was beginning to provide the theories and evidence challenging racial inequality that would later lead Americans to reconsider the racial order.

*T*he rhythm and the tone of the New Deal was set by the man in the White House, since Franklin D. Roosevelt was the spokesman and the master of his administration. His first public statement, the inaugural address of March 4, 1933, pierced the depression-fostered gloom and stabbed deftly and surely at the nation's physical and psychological ills. In stark contrast to his predecessor, Roosevelt recognized the prevailing despair, "the dark realities of the moment," and committed himself and his administration to a brighter future. He lashed out in Biblical terms against the profiteers and the selfish among the monied classes and laid down an emphasis which would characterize his administration more than he then realized: "The measure of the restoration lies in the extent to which we apply social values more noble than mere monetary profit." Identifying himself with the unemployed and underprivileged—"our greatest primary task is to put people to work"—he compared the depression to a war emergency and he warned that he was prepared to mobilize the resources of the federal government to fight it.[1]

Like so many of FDR's speeches, including his informal radio fireside chats, the written version of this one paled on paper. His voice exuded warmth and a personal inflection which brought him close to his listeners. His own physical affliction and the way he bore it earned him deserved admiration and gave encouragement to those who had afflictions of their own, even a darker skin. John Gunther testified to Roosevelt's attraction for people as "concrete and intimate. . . . He set up goals in human terms that the average man could grasp for."[2] The general public responded to his magnetism; one of his secretaries selected a list of salutations which were used on letters addressed to him, and they ran the gamut from "Dear humanitarian friend of the people" to "My Pal!" and "Dear Buddy."[3] Almost all of his callers remarked on his personal charm and persuasiveness.

These characteristics of FDR the man, taken with his consummate ability to personalize his understanding of human exploitation and underprivilege, made him the most attractive President, for Negro citizens, since the Civil War. Robert Vann, publisher of the Negro weekly Pittsburgh *Courier*, who was brought into the 1932 campaign by some of Roosevelt's lieutenants, advised his race to "go home and turn Lincoln's picture to the wall. The debt has been paid in full."[4] Yet, like Lincoln, Roosevelt's actual commitments to the American Negro were slim. He was more a symbol than an activist in his own right. His compassion, though real, was tempered by his own background, by the enormity of the decisions which came up to him, and by political considerations. An enthusiastic politician, he used political

---

[1] Franklin D. Roosevelt (ed.), *The Public Papers of Franklin D. Roosevelt* (New York, 1938) II: 11, 12, 13.

[2] John Gunther, *Roosevelt in Retrospect: A Profile in History* (New York, 1950), 37.

[3] Lela Stiles to FDR, April 25, 1940, in Elliott Roosevelt (ed.), *FDR: His Personal Letters* (New York, 1950), II: 1018–1019.

[4] Quoted in Arthur M. Schlesinger, Jr., *The Politics of Upheaval: The Age of Roosevelt* (Boston, 1960), III:430.

weights and measures on a political scale to judge the evidence, and the Negro was often found wanting. When Walter White, the executive secretary of the NAACP, obtained an audience through the good graces of Mrs. Eleanor Roosevelt to plead for the President's public support of the anti-lynching bill, FDR demurred because he needed Southern votes in Congress on other matters.

Nevertheless, the FDR image eventually became a favorable one; his picture hung in living rooms and infant sons carried his name. At first, though, Negroes waited to be shown. Their publications granted him the benefit of doubt when he spoke about justice and equality, in the hope that he was talking, too, to Negroes. He called lynching murder, remarked W. E. B. DuBois, and "these things give us hope." [5] His acknowledgment, through his Secretary of Labor, of the National Urban League's survey of economic conditions among Negroes was, in the words of an *Opportunity* editorial, "an evidence of his deep interest in the Negroes' welfare." [6] By midway through his first term, FDR had captured the admiration and affection of the Negro people and, with that, their votes. During the campaign of 1936, Negroes were outspoken in their support of the Democratic national ticket. Sixteen thousand Harlem residents traveled to Madison Square Garden in September of that year to attend a political rally, and sixty other cities held similar and simultaneous rallies. The New Yorkers mixed a rich fare of music and entertainment with leading New Dealers talking politics, but it was an African Methodist Episcopal Bishop, the Reverend C. Ransome, who symbolized the affair and its meaning by reading a "New Emancipation Proclamation." The vote in November was anticlimactic; the second Roosevelt had weaned the Negro away from the Republican party.

Roosevelt did not publicly associate himself with Negro projects or Negro leaders before 1935, but his programs and some of his associates were more aggressive. Early in 1933, he approved of a suggestion that someone in his administration assume the responsibility for fair treatment of the Negroes, and he asked Harold Ickes to make the appointment. A young white Georgian, Clark Foreman, came to Washington at Ickes' request to handle the task, and brought in as his assistant an even younger Negro of great promise, Robert C. Weaver. Foreman successfully made his way through the burgeoning maze of new agencies which were springing up and did a respectable job of calling to the attention of agency heads and their assistants an awareness of the special problems of Negroes. Along with Ickes, Daniel Roper, the Secretary of Commerce; Harry Hopkins, FDR's relief administrator; and Aubrey Williams, a Hopkins deputy, were sympathetic to committing the New Deal to work more generously with and for Negroes.

---

[5] *The Crisis*, XLI: 20 (January, 1934).

[6] *Opportunity*, XI: 167 (June, 1933).

From the first, the various New Deal agencies carried the major burden of this emphasis, since they translated words into bread and butter, shelter and schooling. For the Negro, the most significant were the Federal Employment Relief Administration (FERA), the National Recovery Administration (NRA), the Works Progress Administration, later called the Work Projects Administration (WPA), the Agricultural Adjustment Administration (AAA), the Tennessee Valley Authority (TVA), the National Youth Administration (NYA), the Civilian Conservation Corps (CCC), and the public housing efforts of several agencies. There were others in the alphabetical jungle which assisted Negroes, as whites, in more specialized ways, such as the Federal Writers' Project and the Office of Education studies. The very number of agencies added credence to the emergent fact that, for the first time, the federal government had engaged and was grappling with some of the fundamental barriers to race progress.

It was one thing to engage and grapple with a problem at the federal level, and another thing to implement it at lower levels. Most of the New Deal agency programs ran afoul of local laws and customs and most of them capitulated on very practical grounds. As a consequence, Negroes vigorously attacked the inequities, even while they appreciated the limited benefits. FERA, the first New Deal agency to work directly to alleviate the plight of the destitute, tried by locally administered dole and work-projects to pump more money into circulation. Until the end of 1935, when it was abolished, it administered most of the direct relief and work relief programs which the New Dealers initiated, distributing about four billion dollars. Its progress was dogged by racial discrimination, since the design of projects and allocation of funds remained in local hands. Jacksonville, Florida, Negro families on relief outnumbered white families three to one, but the money was divided according to proportions of the total city population. Thus 15,000 Negro families received 45 per cent of the funds and 5,000 white families got 55 per cent. Along the Mississippi River, from Natchez to New Orleans, Negroes were passed over for skilled jobs and frequently received less than the stipulated minimum wage. When the state of Georgia squeezed out of the FERA administrator the right to fix hourly wages for Negroes below thirty cents an hour, *Opportunity* mournfully questioned, "Does this presage the end of that heralded concern for the Forgotten Man?" [7]

If the relief program raised questions of discrimination, the NRA brought howls of indignation. In the words of a Negro labor specialist, the NRA administrator, General Hugh A. Johnson, was "a complete failure" for not properly recognizing the Negro.[8] The industrial codes established under NRA deferred to geographic wage and employment consideration so that the Negro worker generally earned less money for equal time and was frozen out

[7] *Ibid.*, XII: 360 (December, 1934).

[8] T. Arnold Hill in the *New York Times,* June 25, 1937, p. 7.

of skilled jobs. A young Negro lawyer, John P. Davis, organized the Joint Committee on National Recovery in the fall of 1933 to persuade federal authorities to rectify these policies. "It has filed briefs, made appearances at public hearings," he wrote, and "buttonholed administrative officers relative to the elimination of unfair clauses in the codes," but to little avail.[9] In self-defense, NRA officials explained the difficulty in bucking local customs, pointing out also that the NRA was responsible only for industrial workers. Agricultural laborers, domestic servants, and the service trades were not included, and most of the unskilled workers were exempted by statute from wage and hour minimums. "It is not fair," wrote an NRA administrator in a Negro journal, "to blame the NRA for not curing all these ills, if such they be, within a year." [10] Until the Supreme Court decreed its demise in the spring of 1935, the NRA was a favored whipping boy for Negroes, as well as for others. "The Blue Eagle," a Virginia newspaper observed, "may be [for Negroes] a predatory bird instead of a feathered messenger of happiness." [11]

The TVA and the AAA came under fire in the early years of the New Deal for similar reasons. Negro critics raged at the all-white model towns, such as Norris, Tennessee, which were established in conjunction with TVA. Homes for white workers on the project were substantial, while Negro workers lived in substandard temporary barracks. Skilled jobs went first to whites and most labor crews were segregated. TVA, it appeared to two observers in 1934, "aims to maintain the *status quo*." [12] A year later, the situation seemed little better. In one sample two-week period, Negroes were 11 per cent of the working force, receiving only 9.5 per cent of the payroll. Under AAA, Negro tenant farmers and sharecroppers, as the most dispensable laborers, suffered first from the crop-reduction policy and found themselves without employment. Concerned about the evolving discriminatory pattern, the NAACP in 1934 devoted a major share of its energy to trying to prevent white landlords from illegally depriving their Negro tenants of crop-reduction bonuses.

Two New Deal programs for young people operated with a minimum of discrimination: the CCC and the NYA. The CCC established segregated camps in the South and in some parts of the North; the great bulk of the integrated camps were in New England. By 1935, its peak year, CCC had over a half million boys in camp. In general, Negroes stayed in CCC camps longer than whites, were not moved up to administrative posts in camps as readily as whites, and were restricted to less than 10 per cent of the total enrollment. Since the proportion of young Negro men in need was substantively higher

---

[9] John P. Davis, "What Price National Recovery?," in *The Crisis*, XL: 272 (December, 1933).

[10] Gustav Peck, "The Negro Worker and the NRA," in *ibid.*, XLI: 262 (September, 1934).

[11] Quoted in the *New York Times*, August 19, 1933, p. 10.

[12] Charles H. Houston and John P. Davis, "TVA: Lily-White Construction," in *The Crisis*, XLI: 291 (October, 1934).

than this, the quota system was actually inequitable. The NYA, which Mary McLeod Bethune served as administrator of Negro affairs, was shaped to help young men and women in school and with schooling. It grew out of the university and college student relief program established under FERA, and by the end of its first six months, in late 1935, had distributed more than forty million dollars. Conforming to existing state and regional patterns, the NYA still managed to help a critical age group among Negroes.

The debit side of the New Deal's efforts to assist Negroes fell far short of its material and psychological credits. Never before had Negro leaders participated in government affairs as freely and as frequently. The Department of Commerce had E. K. Jones, on leave from the National Urban League; the NYA had Mrs. Bethune; Interior had William H. Hastie and Weaver; the Social Security Board had Ira DeA. Reid; Labor had Lawrence W. Oxley; the Office of Education had Ambrose Caliver, to mention a few. Never before had there been so great a stress on improving the education of Negroes. Many relief programs included elementary education and training classes as part of the regimen. Negro colleges and universities received funds for buildings. The Office of Education, along with other agencies, began an important study of the status of Negro education.

Professional opportunities opened up in government, although not at the rate at which Negroes were graduating from college. For the first time, Negroes were employed as architects, lawyers, engineers, economists, statisticians, interviewers, office managers, case aids, and librarians. Nonprofessional white-collar jobs, which had rarely been within reach of the race, now became available to trained stenographers, clerks, and secretaries. While many of these jobs centered around programs for Negroes within the government, such as Negro slum clearance projects, Negro NYA offices, and the like, they broke the dam which had hitherto kept Negroes out of these kinds of positions.

Harold Ickes, a former president of the Chicago chapter of the NAACP, was the first New Dealer to be recognized as a tried friend. He quickly ended discrimination in his department and set the example by placing professionally-trained Negroes in responsible positions. He first drew FDR's attention to Hastie as a candidate for the federal judge vacancy in the Virgin Islands, and Roosevelt made the appointment in 1937. Ickes appeared at predominantly Negro functions and in 1936, on the occasion of an address at Howard University, even went so far as to wear a University of Alabama hood with his cap and gown because "it seemed to have the best color effect. . . ." [13] While Ickes could not breach established segregation patterns in housing, one-eighth of the federal housing projects planned before the end

---

[13] Harold L. Ickes, *The First Thousand Days, 1933–1936: The Secret Diary of Harold L. Ickes* (New York, 1953), I: 541.

of 1935 were in mixed neighborhoods. Approximately one-half of them were in Negro slum areas and, thanks to the negotiating skill of Ickes' assistant, Robert C. Weaver, the contracts for a substantial portion of these called for the employment of both skilled and unskilled Negro workers.

Eleanor Roosevelt, the New Deal's conscience, made it her business to reaffirm by word and deed her faith in the equality of opportunity for all. She included Negro and mixed organizations on her itineraries, welcomed mixed groups of adults and children to the White House, and spoke up for the race at critical times. In 1936, as part of a long memo on political strategy in the presidential campaign, she urged party leaders to ask respected Negroes like Mrs. Bethune to participate among Negro groups. The penalty for her unflagging advocacy of the Negro's cause was abuse or occasionally embarrassing questions. As the European war spread after 1939, she confronted questions about the Negro's loyalty. "Rarely," she told a group of New Jersey college women in 1940, "do you come across a case where a Negro has failed to measure up to the standard of loyalty and devotion to his country." [14]

Eleanor Roosevelt was more than a symbol of the New Deal's conscience; she was a vehicle for approaching and influencing the President. She performed this service for Walter White when the antilynching bill was before Congress. When the DAR refused to allow Marian Anderson to sing in Constitution Hall, Mrs. Roosevelt was the intermediary who secured permission to use the Lincoln Memorial for the concert. It was useful for the President to have his wife serve in these varying capacities, absorbing some of the criticism, supplying him with information he could get from no other source, and sparking his conscience, when that was needed. This relieved the President from having to punctuate his speeches and press conferences with references to the Negro. Before 1935, these were almost nonexistent; after 1935, they increased in frequence and directness, but Roosevelt did not directly commit himself, as his wife did, until his famous Executive Order 8802 of June, 1941, established a Fair Employment Practice Committee to supervise all defense-contract industries.

In many ways, 1935 seemed to be a pivotal year for the President's public statements to and about the Negro. His annual message to Congress in January asserted that "in spite of our efforts and in spite of our talk, we have not weeded out the overprivileged and we have not effectively lifted up the underprivileged." Uplift and underprivilege were two words which Negroes understood, two words which footnoted their history; yet Roosevelt did not mention the Negro specifically. Shortly after that, he told WPA state administrators that "we cannot discriminate in any of the work we are conducting either because of race or religion or politics," and although he went on to speak of political pressures, the word "race" was there for Negroes to see. In two other public statements later in the year, FDR paid lip service to the

[14] *New York Times*, December 29, 1940, p. 12.

accomplishments of the race and by 1936, an election year, he proclaimed his policy that "among American citizens there should be no forgotten men and no forgotten races." [15] The transformation was more one of degree than of conviction; Roosevelt was beginning to speak to the Negro, however rarely, rather than to lump him without identification into massive generalizations. But his eye was ever on the balance of political forces and he never voluntarily came out foursquare for the Negro.

In perspective, Roosevelt's circumspection on some domestic issues was less significant than his New Deal legislative program. Labor unions received substantial encouragement from Section 7a of NRA and from the Wagner Act, although the White House maintained an equivocal position toward both labor and management. The jump in union memberships and the rise of the Committee on Industrial Organization, first within the AF of L and later as the independent Congress of Industrial Organizations (CIO), gained impetus from the newly established right to strike and the newly created federal board to mediate labor disputes. A strengthened labor movement confronted, as one of its problems, the question of Negro members. Older unions such as the United Mine Workers and the International Ladies Garment Workers Union welcomed Negroes without distinction. When the CIO broke from the AF of L, its nucleus of unions including the new and somewhat fragile organizations in the automobile, rubber, and steel industries accepted Negroes on an equal basis, except in those localities where race friction was high. The United Textile Workers attempted to do the same, but the existence of textile plants in southern states made this task more onerous. It was not enough for a union to resolve, as the CIO did, to accept members without regard to race, creed, or color, or even, as the UAW and the organizing committees of the steelworkers did, to offer Negro workers a chance to join up. Negroes still hung back, alternately tempted and frightened by management's offers and threats. The wave of the future was with the industrial unions, and *Opportunity's* declaration to Negro steelworkers that it would be "the apotheosis of stupidity" for them to stay out of the union battling for recognizance in 1937, was prophetic.[16] The success of the Brotherhood of Sleeping Car Porters, under the leadership of A. Philip Randolph, in gaining recognition as the bargaining agent with the Pullman Company after a twelve-year struggle, marked the beginning of the race's influence in national labor circles and on national labor policy. After his union was recognized, Randolph prodded the AF of L to grant it an international charter, making it an equal with other member unions, and he never eased up his fight to liberalize the AF of L's racial policies. Even though he was not persuasive enough to break down these craft and railway-union

---

[15] Roosevelt, *Public Papers*, IV: 16, 262; V: 538.

[16] *Opportunity*, XV: 133 (May, 1937).

prejudices, Randolph emerged before World War II as a dominant voice in Negro circles and a power to be reckoned with in American unionism.

Of the many voices which spoke out for and against the race, none was more deceptive than that of the Communists. Before 1935, their ideology committed their followers to support a separate state for Negroes, the so-called Black Republic, and insisted that they work independent of all other groups toward this end. When the NAACP unsuccessfully defended the Scottsboro boys—nine young Negroes accused of rape on an Alabama freight train in 1931—the Communists abusively blamed the NAACP for the failure. With shrill bravado, they muscled the NAACP out of the picture and took over the defense. They were unsuccessful in court, but they publicized the case all over the world as an example of capitalistic exploitation and milked the American public for uncounted (and unaccountable) thousands of dollars. In 1935, the Communist ideology swung over to a united-front tactic, and they abandoned their attacks on existing non-Communist organizations and held out the carrot of co-operation. Their purpose was to mix with these organizations and either subvert them directly or gain control behind the scenes. The National Urban League and the NAACP quickly recognized the move for what it was and co-operated at a chilly distance. The League had to dissolve some of its worker's Councils, established in northern cities, because the Communists took them over. The NAACP agreed to work with Communist support on the Scottsboro case, but continued to warn against close co-operation.

Failing to engage the two dominant Negro organizations, the Communists jumped at the chance to work with these and other Negro groups through the newly formed National Negro Congress. The brainchild of New Deal critic John P. Davis, it was organized under the co-sponsorship of almost forty Negro organizations and met in Chicago in 1936 with close to 900 delegates. The Communists stayed in the background—Davis was sympathetic—and the resolutions were non-Stalinist, but Davis was elected executive secretary and maintained close touch with Communist leaders. The 1937 Congress met in Philadelphia with even larger crowds. But soon after that the more conservative organizations and individuals withdrew their sponsorship and the Congress, handicapped by lack of funds, began to crumble. Some local councils established by the Congress were active in Western cities, but after 1937 the Congress as a national group dwindled into impotence and in 1940 became an openly controlled Communist organization. This take-over followed the Stalin-Hitler pact and signalized the 180-degree pivot which American Communists were forced to execute, exploding the united front movement. Organizations like the NAACP which had worked with Communists at a distance suddenly found themselves subject to vituperative and irrational attack, but the vast majority of Negroes merely continued to ignore Communism as a method of achieving their goals.

With the exception of the church, the major Negro organizations felt the sting of mass apathy. "We recognize our lack of skill at mass appeal," NAACP's Roy Wilkins admitted in 1941.[17] The national office of NAACP attracted men and women of an intellectual bent whose convictions on race matters had not changed with the seasons, since the organization was still dedicated to the abolition of segregation and discrimination. But the spark which had sent John Shillady, Walter White, and James Weldon Johnson into race-hatred areas, North and South, burned low. On the national level, the NAACP fought its battles in court, in Congress, and in the press, but not in communities where racism flourished. At local levels, it depended upon its branches, many of which were woefully weak in finances and leadership, to seek out and rectify racial problems of every description. Its base was too narrow for its superstructure, and its bones creaked from inaction at the community level; yet it thrived because it learned to speak the language of influence in political circles and because it chose wisely the cases of discrimination and segregation which it pursued through the courts. Indeed, the road to the 1954 desegregation decisions was charted, bulldozed, paved, and landscaped by the NAACP.

The National Urban League was tested during the depression and not found wanting. Its leadership was similar to that of the NAACP, except that to the extent that its goals were more specific, framed in terms of employment, family welfare, health, and education, it was accused of being more timid, dominated by white liberals, and hostile to trade unionism. Its chief executive, E. K. Jones, replied to these criticisms in a private memo in 1941. The League, he said, was not a Negro but "truly an interracial movement. . . . Any movement of this character which advocates understanding through conference and discussion must necessarily refrain from advocating mass action of one race calculated to force the other group to make concessions." Gunnar Myrdal, the Swedish sociologist whose monumental study of the Negro in America was published during World War II, found that the League worked actively with unions and held "the lead as a pro-union force among the Negro people." [18] Urban League branches were beginning to receive local support from Community Funds, which gave them greater strength and a source for independent leadership. Taken together, these two Negro organizations, in spite of their lack of popular support, moved together in harmony along parallel paths to the great good of the race.

The Negro's church maintained its grip on the masses during these years as it had for centuries, but its hold was loosening. Strong in numbers and appeal, the church had inherent weaknesses which gradually reduced its potency in modern America. It was not one church but many, from the strong

---

[17] Quoted in Gunnar Myrdal, *An American Dilemma* (New York, 1944), II: 836n.

[18] *Ibid.*, II: 840, 841.

African Methodist Episcopal (AME) and African Methodist Episcopal Zion (AMEZ) to the independent colored branches of the Baptist denomination. To these were added smaller denominations and sects and store-front evangelical churches which dissipated the religious energies of the race. The differences were more personal than ideological; in fact, except for the split between the liberal and the fundamentalist churches—a split matched in white denominations—there was no basic theological difference. The churches' hierarchies stood in the way of closer co-operation. The Negro church was all-Negro and proudly so, a self-perpetuating, segregated institution which made no effort to reach across race barriers, individually or institutionally. In the North, this would have been troublesome for white churches, whose precepts were in advance of practice. Negro preachers generally stayed in Negro pulpits. In the South this would have been almost impossible. The Northern Negro church bred isolation; the Southern Negro church fostered accommodation. Fettered by a strain of fundamentalism and emotionalism, and weakened by the diffusion of denominations, the Negro church had little appeal for the younger generation. In the 1930's and 1940's it struggled without success to find a vehicle for its latent power, but its leadership had lost touch with the material and moral issues of the day. It failed to see its obligation as a participant in the fight for equal rights. "We are the policemen of the Negroes," a Southern colored preacher observed in 1941. "If we did not keep down their ambitions and divert them into religion, there would be upheaval in the South." [19] For the second third of the twentieth century, this message was anachronistic.

It would be simplistic to suggest as have some recent novelists, such as James Baldwin in *Go Tell It on the Mountain,* that the church's withdrawal for fear of upheaval led directly to upheaval, but there is a trace of truth in it. When Harlem rioted in 1935, *The Crisis* explained that only the patience of the Negro had delayed it that long. Patience was not enough to counter the "sneers, impertinence, and personal opinions of smart-aleck investigators, supervisors and personnel directors." [20] Unemployment, rent gouging, and the belief that Harlem had not received its share of relief money snapped the uneasy calm; the riot erupted with a frenzied attack on whites and the purposeful looting of food and clothing stores. The prompt on-the-scene appearance of New York City's popular mayor, Fiorello H. La Guardia, helped restore rationality. When the United States entered World War II, Harlem still seethed from overcrowding, white insolence, and price gouging, and again rioting broke out, followed by riots in other cities, most notably Detroit. The hands of the clock had swung half circle and the Negro had learned from the white how to use violence and lawlessness when order and the law were not sufficient.

---

[19] *Ibid.,* II: 876n.

[20] *The Crisis,* XLII: 145 (May, 1935).

Toward the end of the 1930's the federal government turned more and more of its attention to the European conflict, the economy flourished as the industrial bastion of the embattled Allies, and the Negro had committed himself to the New Deal and to President Roosevelt. Polls in 1940 showed that Negro voters overwhelmingly supported Roosevelt for a third term, and the polls were right. The reason for this support was not difficult to surmise. Outside of what the Democratic Administration had tried to do directly and indirectly, the decade itself was marked with identifiable milestones of progress. In athletics, Jesse Owen was an Olympic champion, and Negro football players starred on many of the major college teams. Professional baseball still resisted, but its time was not far off. In interracial activities, conferences on a variety of subjects began to meet with overbearing regularity and, though self-consciously interracial, the pattern developed almost irrevocably. College students and adults met to talk about education, religion, economic matters, and, of course, civil rights. Even in the South, the indomitable Mrs. Bethune organized an interracial conference at the college she founded, and the white University of Florida tentatively sent delegates. In the deep South, interracial conferences were held on a segregated basis; Eleanor Roosevelt told of attending one in Birmingham and inadvertently sitting in the colored section. "At once the police appeared to remind us of the rules and regulations on segregation. . . . Rather than give in I asked that chairs be placed for us with the speakers facing the whole group." [21] White Southerners began to speak up for the Negro. They were still a small minority, but the mere fact that a white state supervisor of schools in Georgia would admit to the inequalities of segregated schools, or a white North Carolina legislator would question a decreased appropriation for a Negro college, was a sign of change. The rise of Huey Long in Louisiana brought a different attitude, one of ignoring race differences without changing race relationships. The all-white Mississippi Education Association established a committee in 1938 to recommend ways in which students might study Negro life, and several Northern newspapers in 1940 editorially acknowledged the importance of Negro History Week. The tide had turned, and Negroes credited the turning to the New Deal.

SUGGESTED READING

Historians have barely penetrated the problem of the New Deal and the Negro. Frank Freidel in *F. D. R. and the South* (Louisiana State Univ. Press, 1965) acknowledges the President's unwillingness to invest any political capital in obtaining Negro rights. Allan Morrison's "The Secret Papers of FDR," *Negro Digest,* IX (Jan., 1951), 3–13, is a superficial

---

[21] Eleanor Roosevelt, *This I Believe* (New York, 1949), 173–174.

but useful journalistic survey based on brief research in the Roosevelt papers at Hyde Park.

Robert Zangrando in "The NAACP and a Federal Anti-Lynching Bill, 1934–1940," *Journal of Negro History*, L (April, 1946), 106–17, notes the NAACP's tactics of dramatizing the Negro's plight. Wilson Record's *Race and Radicalism: The NAACP and the Communist Party in Conflict* ° (Cornell Univ. Press, 1964) and *The Negro and the Communist Party* (Univ. of North Carolina Press, 1951) are studies praising the Negro for his lack of receptivity to communism.

John Salmond's "The Civilian Conservation Corps and the Negro," *Journal of American History*, LII (June, 1965), 75–88, is a brief examination of one New Deal agency. E. L. Tatum's *Changed Political Thought of the Negro* (Exposition Press, 1951) is a flimsy study of an important and neglected subject.

Southern agriculture and the collapse of Southern farm tenancy constitute one of the few well-explored subjects in Negro history during the twenties and the New Deal years. Among the better studies published during the New Deal are Charles Johnson, Will Alexander, and Edward Embree's *The Collapse of Cotton Tenancy* ° (Univ. of North Carolina Press, 1935); Arthur Raper's *Preface to Peasantry* ° (Univ. of North Carolina Press, 1933); and Raper and Ira DeA. Reid's *Sharecroppers All* (Univ. of North Carolina Press, 1941). John Dollard in *Caste and Class in a Southern Town* ° (Yale Univ. Press, 1937) and Allison David, Burleigh Gardner, and Mary Gardner in *Deep South* (Univ. of Chicago Press, 1941) are classic studies of Southern race relations.

For the activities of participants in the struggle to advance Negro rights, see Tamara Hareven, *Eleanor Roosevelt: An American Conscience* (Quadrangle, 1968) and Walter White, *A Man Called White* (Viking Press, 1948).

ELLIS W. HAWLEY

The New Deal
and the Problem of Monopoly

INTRODUCTION

Though the aims of big business during the New Deal have never been systematically studied, Ellis W. Hawley has made a start in gathering considerable evidence on the subject. He concludes that business rhetoric championing laissez faire frequently cloaked an enthusiasm for industrial cooperation. Even after the Supreme Court declared the National Recovery Administration unconstitutional in 1935, "business supporters were in effect trying to maintain a private NRA." As late as 1937, the Business Advisory Council—composed of many of the nation's prominent businessmen—proposed the establishment within each industry of price and production controls, to be subject to federal approval. Though this program foundered, Hawley finds that most major industries

FROM Ellis W. Hawley, *The New Deal and the Problem of Monopoly*, Princeton University Press, 1966, pp. 472–90. Reprinted by permission of Princeton University Press.

were, nevertheless, able to eliminate price competition and achieve stability through private controls and informal arrangements.

Hawley's book *The New Deal and the Problem of Monopoly*, from which the following essay is taken, is more concerned with the actual business policies of the New Deal than with the aims of big business. He stresses Administration twists and turns in economic policy, from the NRA and federal support of cartels and business planning to antitrust activity and an assault on rigid prices. But he also discerns an underlying *political* "logic and consistency"— the need to balance antagonistic pressures and to make concessions both to those who wanted to increase competition and to those who wished to limit it. Roosevelt, responding to demands from antitrusters and critics of big business, condemned monopoly and attacked the "economic royalists." Yet, while making "proper obeisance to the antitrust tradition," the Administration also confronted demands for planning, control, and rationalization, and therefore allowed "industrial pressure groups to write their programs of market control into law, particularly in areas where they could come up with the necessary lobbies and symbols."

Although Hawley does not analyze the political power of business during the New Deal years, his study of the Government's shifting responses to the politically challenging problem of monopoly is, nevertheless, impressive.

Two souls dwell in the bosom of this Administration," wrote Dorothy Thompson in 1938, "as indeed, they do in the bosom of the American people. The one loves the Abundant Life, as expressed in the cheap and plentiful products of large-scale mass production and distribution. . . . The other soul yearns for former simplicities, for decentralization, for the interests of the 'little man,' revolts against high-pressure salesmanship, denounces 'monopoly' and 'economic empires,' and seeks means of breaking them up." "Our Administration," she continued, "manages a remarkable . . . stunt of being . . . in favor of organizing and regulating the Economic Empires to greater and greater efficiency, and of breaking them up as a tribute to perennial American populist feeling." [1]

Dorothy Thompson was a persistent critic of the Roosevelt Administration; yet her remarks did show considerable insight into the dilemma that confronted New Dealers, and indeed, the dilemma that confronted industrial America. The problem of reconciling liberty and order, individualism and collective organization, was admittedly an ancient one, but the creation of a highly integrated industrial system in a land that had long cherished its

---

[1] Dorothy Thompson, in *New York Herald Tribune*, Jan. 24, 1938.

liberal, democratic, and individualistic traditions presented the problem in a peculiarly acute form. Both the American people and their political leaders tended to view modern industrialism with mingled feelings of pride and regret. On one hand, they tended to associate large business units and economic organization with abundance, progress, and a rising standard of living. On the other, they associated them with a wide variety of economic abuses, which, because of past ideals and past standards, they felt to be injurious to society. Also, deep in their hearts, they retained a soft spot for the "little fellow." In moments of introspection, they looked upon the immense concentrations of economic power that they had created and accused them of destroying the good life, of destroying the independent businessman and the satisfactions that came from owning one's own business and working for oneself, of reducing Americans to a race of clerks and machine tenders, of creating an impersonal, mechanized world that destroyed man as an individual.[2]

The search in twentieth-century America, then, was for some solution that would reconcile the practical necessity with the individualistic ideal, some arrangement that would preserve the industrial order, necessarily based upon a high degree of collective organization, and yet would preserve America's democratic heritage at the same time. Americans wanted a stable, efficient industrial system, one that turned out a large quantity of material goods, insured full employment, and provided a relatively high degree of economic security. Yet at the same time they wanted a system as free as possible from centralized direction, one in which economic power was dispersed and economic opportunity was really open, one that preserved the dignity of the individual and adjusted itself automatically to market forces. And they were unwilling to renounce the hope of achieving both. In spite of periodic hurricanes of anti-big-business sentiment, they refused to follow the prophets that would destroy their industrial system and return to former simplicities. Nor did they pay much attention to those that would sacrifice democratic ideals and liberal traditions in order to create a more orderly and more rational system, one that promised greater security, greater stability, and possibly even greater material benefits.

There were times, of course, when this dilemma was virtually forgotten. During periods of economic prosperity, when Americans were imbued with a psychological sense of well-being and satiated with a steady outflow of material benefits, it was hard to convince them that their industrial organization was seriously out of step with their ideals. During such periods, the majority rallied to the support of the business system; so long as it continued to operate at a high level, they saw no need for any major reforms. So long as the competitive ideal was embodied in statutes and industrial and political lead-

---

[2] See Arthur R. Burns, in *AER*, June 1949, pp. 691–95; Burton R. Fisher and Stephen B. Withey, *Big Business as the People See It* (Ann Arbor: U. of Mich. Press, 1951), 21–22, 34–38; Rexford G. Tugwell, in *Western Political Quarterly*, Sept. 1950, pp. 392–400.

ers paid lip service to it, there was a general willingness to leave it at that. If there were troubled consciences left, these could be soothed by clothing collective organizations in the attributes of rugged individuals and by the assurances of economic experts that anything short of pure monopoly was "competition" and therefore assured the benefits that were supposed to flow from competition.

In a time of economic adversity, however, Americans became painfully aware of the gap between ideal and reality. Paradoxically, this awareness produced two conflicting and contradictory reactions. Some pointed to the gap, to the failure of business organizations to live by the competitive creed, and concluded that it was the cause of the economic debacle, that the breakdown of the industrial machine was the inevitable consequence of its failure to conform to competitive standards. Others pointed to the same gap and concluded that the ideal itself was at fault, that it had prevented the organization and conscious direction of a rational system that would provide stability and security. On one hand, the presence of depression conditions seemed to intensify anti-big-business sentiment and generate new demands for antitrust crusades. On the other, it inspired demands for planning, rationalization, and the creation of economic organizations that could weather deflationary forces. The first general effect grew directly out of the loss of confidence in business leadership, the conviction that industrial leaders had sinned against the economic creed, and the determination that they should be allowed to sin no more. The second grew out of the black fear of economic death, the urgent desire to stem the deflationary tide, and the mounting conviction that a policy of laissez-faire or real implementation of the competitive ideal would result in economic disaster.

During such a period, moreover, it would seem practically inevitable that the policy-making apparatus of a democracy should register both streams of sentiment. Regardless of their logical inconsistency, the two streams were so intermixed in the ideology of the average man that any administration, if it wished to retain political power, had to make concessions to both. It must move to check the deflationary spiral, to provide some sort of central direction, and to salvage economic groups through the erection of cartels and economic controls. Yet while it was doing this, it must make a proper show of maintaining competitive ideals. Its actions must be justified by an appeal to competitive traditions, by showing that they were designed to save the underdog, or if this was impossible, by an appeal to other arguments and other traditions that for the moment justified making an exception. Nor could antitrust action ever be much more than a matter of performing the proper rituals and manipulating the proper symbols. It might attack unusually privileged and widely hated groups, break up a few loose combinations, and set forth a general program that was presumably designed to make the competitive ideal a reality. But the limit of the program would, of necessity, be that point at which changes in business practice or business structures would cause serious economic dislocation. It could not risk the disruption of going concerns or a further shrinkage in employment and production, and it would not subject men to the logical working out of deflationary trends. To do so would amount to political suicide.

To condemn these policies for their inconsistency was to miss the point. From an economic standpoint, condemnation might very well be to the point. They were inconsistent. One line of action tended to cancel the other, with the result that little was accomplished. Yet from the political standpoint, this very inconsistency, so long as the dilemma persisted, was the safest method of retaining political power. President Roosevelt, it seems, never suffered politically from his reluctance to choose between planning and antitrust action. His mixed emotions so closely reflected the popular mind that they were a political asset rather than a liability.[3]

That New Deal policy was inconsistent, then, should occasion little surprise. Such inconsistency, in fact, was readily apparent in the National Industrial Recovery Act, the first major effort to deal with the problems of industrial organization. When Roosevelt took office in 1933, the depression had reached its most acute stage. Almost every economic group was crying for salvation through political means, for some sort of rationalization and planning, although they might differ as to just who was to do the planning and the type and amount of it that would be required. Pro-business planners, drawing upon the trade association ideology of the nineteen twenties and the precedent of the War Industries Board, envisioned a semi-cartelized business commonwealth in which industrial leaders would plan and the state would enforce the decisions. Other men, convinced that there was already too much planning by businessmen, hoped to create an order in which other economic groups would participate in the policy-making process. Even under these circumstances, however, the resulting legislation had to be clothed in competitive symbols. Proponents of the NRA advanced the theory that it would help small businessmen and industrial laborers by protecting them from predatory practices and monopolistic abuses. The devices used to erect monopolistic controls became "codes of fair competition." And each such device contained the proper incantation against monopoly.

Consequently, the NRA was not a single program with a single objective, but rather a series of programs with a series of objectives, some of which were in direct conflict with each other. In effect, the National Industrial Recovery Act provided a phraseology that could be used to urge almost any approach to the problem of economic organization and an administrative machine that each of the conflicting economic and ideological groups might

---

[3] See Adolf A. Berle, Jr., in *Virginia Quarterly Review*, Summer 1938, pp. 324–33; K. E. Boulding, in *QJE*, Aug. 1945, pp. 524, 529–42; Arthur M. Schlesinger, Jr., *The Politics of Upheaval* (Boston: Houghton Mifflin, 1960), 650–54.

possibly use for their own ends. Under the circumstances, a bitter clash over basic policies was probably inevitable.

For a short period these inconsistencies were glossed over by the summer boomlet of 1933 and by a massive propaganda campaign appealing to wartime precedents and attempting to create a new set of cooperative symbols. As the propaganda wore off, however, and the economic indices turned downward again, the inconsistencies inherent in the program moved to the forefront of the picture. In the code-writing process, organized business had emerged as the dominant economic group, and once this became apparent, criticism of the NRA began to mount. Agrarians, convinced that rising industrial prices were canceling out any gains from the farm program, demanded that businessmen live up to the competitive faith. Labor spokesmen, bitterly disillusioned when the program failed to guarantee union recognition and collective bargaining, charged that the Administration had sold out to management. Small businessmen, certain that the new code authorities were only devices to increase the power of their larger rivals, raised the ancient cry of monopolistic exploitation. Antitrusters, convinced that the talk about strengthening competition was sheer hypocrisy, demanded that this disastrous trust-building program come to a halt. Economic planners, alienated by a process in which the businessmen did the planning, charged that the government was only sanctioning private monopolistic arrangements. And the American public, disillusioned with rising prices and the failure of the program to bring economic recovery, listened to the criticisms and demanded that its competitive ideals be made good.

The rising tide of public resentment greatly strengthened the hand of those that viewed the NRA primarily as a device for raising the plane of competition and securing social justice for labor. Picking up support from discontented groups, from other governmental agencies, and from such investigations as that conducted by Clarence Darrow's National Recovery Review Board, this group within the NRA had soon launched a campaign to bring about a reorientation in policy. By June 1934 it had obtained a formal written policy embodying its views, one that committed the NRA to the competitive ideal, renounced the use of price and production controls, and promised to subject the code authorities to strict public supervision. By this time, however, most of the major codes had been written, and the market restorers were never able to apply their policy to codes already approved. The chief effect of their efforts to do so was to antagonize businessmen and to complicate the difficulties of enforcing code provisions that were out of line with announced policy.

The result was a deadlock that persisted for the remainder of the agency's life. Putting the announced policy into effect would have meant, in all probability, the complete alienation of business support and the collapse of the whole structure. Yet accepting and enforcing the codes for what they were would have resulted, again in all probability, in an outraged public and congressional opinion that would have swept away the whole edifice. Thus the NRA tended to reflect the whole dilemma confronting the New Deal. Admittedly, declared policy was inconsistent with practice. Admittedly, the NRA was accomplishing little. Yet from a political standpoint, if the agency were to continue at all, a deadlock of this sort seemed to be the only solution. If the Supreme Court had not taken a hand in the matter, the probable outcome would have been either the abolition of the agency or a continuation of the deadlock.

The practical effect of the NRA, then, was to allow the erection, extension, and fortification of private monopolistic arrangements, particularly for groups that already possessed a fairly high degree of integration and monopoly power. Once these arrangements had been approved and vested interests had developed, the Administration found it difficult to deal with them. It could not move against them without alienating powerful interest groups, producing new economic dislocations, and running the risk of setting off the whole process of deflation again. Yet, because of the competitive ideal, it could not lend much support to the arrangements or provide much in the way of public supervision. Only in areas where other arguments, other ideals, and political pressure justified making an exception, in such areas as agriculture, natural resources, transportation, and to a certain extent labor, could the government lend its open support and direction.

Moreover, the policy dilemma, coupled with the sheer complexity of the undertaking, made it impossible to provide much central direction. There was little planning of a broad, general nature, either by businessmen or by the state; there was merely the half-hearted acceptance of a series of legalized, but generally uncoordinated, monopolistic combinations. The result was not over-all direction, but a type of partial, piecemeal, pressure-group planning, a type of planning designed by specific economic groups to balance production with consumption regardless of the dislocations produced elsewhere in the economy.

There were, certainly, proposals for other types of planning. But under the circumstances, they were and remained politically unfeasible, both during the NRA period and after. The idea of a government-supported business commonwealth still persisted, and a few men still felt that if the NRA had really applied it, the depression would have been over. Yet in the political context of the time, the idea was thoroughly unrealistic. For one thing, there was the growing gap between businessmen and New Dealers, the conviction of one side that cooperation would lead to bureaucratic socialism, of the other that it would lead to fascism or economic oppression. Even if this quarrel had not existed, the Administration could not have secured a program that ran directly counter to the anti-big-business sentiment of the time. The monopolistic implications in such a program were too obvious, and there was little that could be done to disguise them. Most industrial leaders recognized the situation, and the majority of them came to the conclusion that a political program of this sort was no longer necessary. With the crisis past and the deflationary process checked, private controls and such governmental aids as tariffs, subsidies, and loans would be sufficient.

The idea of national economic planning also persisted. A number of New Dealers continued to advocate the transfer of monopoly power from businessmen to the state or to other organized economic groups. Each major economic group, they argued, should be organized and allowed to participate in the formulation of a central plan, one that would result in expanded production, increased employment, a more equitable distribution, and a better balance of prices. Yet this idea, too, was thoroughly impractical when judged in terms of existing political realities. It ran counter to competitive and individualistic traditions. It threatened important vested interests. It largely ignored the complexities of the planning process or the tendency of regulated interests to dominate their regulators. And it was regarded by the majority of Americans as being overly radical, socialistic, and un-American.

Consequently, the planning of the New Deal was essentially single-industry planning, partial, piecemeal, and opportunistic, planning that could circumvent the competitive ideal or could be based on other ideals that justified making an exception. After the NRA experience, organized business groups found it increasingly difficult to devise these justifications. Some business leaders, to be sure, continued to talk about a public agency with power to waive the antitrust laws and sanction private controls. Yet few of them were willing to accept government participation in the planning process, and few were willing to come before the public with proposals that were immediately vulnerable to charges of monopoly. It was preferable, they felt, to let the whole issue lie quiet, to rely upon unauthorized private controls, and to hope that these would be little disturbed by antitrust action. Only a few peculiarly depressed groups, like the cotton textile industry, continued to agitate for government-supported cartels, and most of these groups lacked the cohesion, power, and alternative symbols that would have been necessary to put their programs through.

In some areas, however, especially in areas where alternative symbols were present and where private controls had broken down or proven impractical, it was possible to secure a type of partial planning. Agriculture was able to avoid most of the agitation against monopoly, and while retaining to a large extent its individualistic operations, to find ways of using the state to fix prices, plan production, and regularize markets. Its ability to do so was attributable in part to the political power of the farmers, but it was also due to manipulation of certain symbols that effectively masked the monopolistic implications in the program. The ideal of the yeoman farmer—honest, independent, and morally upright—still had a strong appeal in America, and to many Americans it justified the salvation of farming as a "way of life," even at the cost of subsidies and the violation of competitive standards. Agriculture, moreover, was supposed to be the basic industry, the activity that supported all others. The country, so it was said, could not be prosperous unless its farmers were prosperous. Finally, there was the conservation argument, the great concern over conservation of the soil, which served to justify some degree of public planning and some type of production control.

Similar justifications were sometimes possible for other areas of the economy. Monopolistic arrangements in certain food-processing industries could be camouflaged as an essential part of the farm program. Departures from competitive standards in such natural resource industries as bituminous coal and crude oil production could be justified on the grounds of conservation. Public controls and economic cartelization in the fields of transportation and communication could be justified on the ground that these were "natural monopolies" in which the public had a vital interest. And in the distributive trades, it was possible to turn anti-big-business sentiment against the mass distributors, to brand them as "monopolies," and to obtain a series of essentially anti-competitive measures on the theory that they were designed to preserve competition by preserving small competitors. The small merchant, however, was never able to dodge the agitation against monopoly to the same extent that the farmer did. The supports granted him were weak to begin with, and to obtain them he had to make concessions to the competitive ideal, concessions that robbed his measures of much of their intended effectiveness.

In some ways, too, the Roosevelt Administration helped to create monopoly power for labor. Under the New Deal program, the government proceeded to absorb surplus labor and prescribe minimum labor standards; more important, it encouraged labor organization to the extent that it maintained a friendly attitude, required employer recognition of unions, and restrained certain practices that had been used to break unions in the past. For a time, the appeals to social justice, humanitarianism, and anti-big-business sentiment overrode the appeal of business spokesmen and classical economists to the competitive ideal and individualistic traditions. The doctrine that labor was not a commodity, that men who had worked and produced and kept their obligations to society were entitled to be taken care of, was widely accepted. Along with it went a growing belief that labor unions were necessary to maintain purchasing power and counterbalance big business. Consequently, even the New Dealers of an antitrust persuasion generally made a place in their program for social legislation and labor organization.

The general effect of this whole line of New Deal policy might be summed up in the word counterorganization, that is, the creation of monopoly power in areas previously unorganized. One can only conclude, however, that this did not happen according to any preconceived plan. Nor did it necessarily promote economic expansion or raise consumer purchasing power. Public support of monopolistic arrangements occurred in a piecemeal, haphazard fashion, in response to pressure from specific economic groups and as opportunities presented themselves. Since consumer organizations were weak and efforts to aid consumers made little progress, the benefits went primarily to producer groups interested in restricting production and raising prices. In the distributive trades, the efforts to help small merchants tended, insofar as they were successful, to impede technological changes, hamper mass distributors, and reduce consumer purchasing power. In the natural resource and transportation industries, most of the new legislation was designed to restrict production, reduce competition, and protect invested capital. And in the labor and agricultural fields, the strengthening of market controls was often at the expense of consumers and in conjunction with business groups. The whole tendency of interest-group planning, in fact, was toward the promotion of economic scarcity. Each group, it seemed, was trying to secure a larger piece from a pie that was steadily dwindling in size.

From an economic standpoint, then, the partial planning of the post-NRA type made little sense, and most economists, be they antitrusters, planners, or devotees of laissez-faire, felt that such an approach was doing more harm than good. It was understandable only in a political context, and as a political solution, it did possess obvious elements of strength. It retained the antitrust laws and avoided any direct attack upon the competitive ideal or competitive mythology. Yet by appealing to other goals and alternative ideals and by using these to justify special and presumably exceptional departures from competitive standards, it could make the necessary concessions to pressure groups interested in reducing competition and erecting government-sponsored cartels.[4] Such a program might be logically inconsistent and economically harmful. Perhaps, as one critic suggested at the time, it combined the worst features of both worlds, "an impairment of the efficiency of the competitive system without the compensating benefits of rationalized collective action." [5] But politically it was a going concern, and efforts to achieve theoretical consistency met with little success.

Perhaps the greatest defect in these limited planning measures was their tendency toward restriction, their failure to provide any incentive for expansion when an expanding economy was the crying need of the time. The easiest way to counteract this tendency, it seemed, was through government expenditures and deficit financing; in practice, this was essentially the path that the New Deal took. By 1938 Roosevelt seemed willing to accept the Keynesian arguments for a permanent spending program, and eventually, when war demands necessitated pump-priming on a gigantic scale, the spending solution worked. It overcame the restrictive tendencies in the economy, re-

---

[4] See Paul T. Homan, in AEA, *Readings in the Social Control of Industry* (Philadelphia: Blakiston, 1942), 242–46, 252–54; and in *Political Science Quarterly*, June 1936, pp. 169–72, 178–84; Berle, in *Virginia Quarterly Review*, Summer 1938, pp. 330–31; Ernest Griffith, *Impasse of Democracy* (N.Y.: Harrison-Hilton, 1939), 231.

[5] Homan, in *Political Science Quarterly*, June 1936, p. 181.

stored full employment, and brought rapid economic expansion. Drastic institutional reform, it seemed, was unnecessary. Limited, piecemeal, pressure-group planning could continue, and the spending weapon could be relied upon to stimulate expansion and maintain economic balance.

One major stream of New Deal policy, then, ran toward partial planning. Yet this stream was shaped and altered, at least in a negative sense, by its encounters with the antitrust tradition and the competitive ideal. In a time when Americans distrusted business leadership and blamed big business for the prevailing economic misery, it was only natural that an antitrust approach should have wide political appeal. Concessions had to be made to it, and these concessions meant that planning had to be limited, piecemeal, and disguised. There could be no over-all program of centralized controls. There could be no government-sponsored business commonwealth. And there could be only a minimum of government participation in the planning process.

In and of itself, however, the antitrust approach did not offer a politically workable alternative. The antitrusters might set forth their own vision of the good society. They might blame the depression upon the departure from competitive standards and suggest measures to make industrial organization correspond more closely to the competitive model. But they could never ignore or explain away the deflationary and disruptive implications of their program. Nor could they enlist much support from the important political and economic pressure groups. Consequently, the antitrust approach, like that of planning, had to be applied on a limited basis. Action could be taken only in special or exceptional areas, against unusually privileged groups that were actively hated and particularly vulnerable, in fields where one business group was fighting another, in cases where no one would get hurt, or against practices that violated common standards of decency and fairness.

This was particularly true during the period prior to 1938. The power trust, for example, was a special demon in the progressive faith, one that was actively hated by large numbers of people and one that had not only violated competitive standards but had also outraged accepted canons of honesty and tampered with democratic political ideals. For such an institution, nothing was too bad, not even a little competition; and the resulting battle, limited though its gains might be, did provide a suitable outlet for popular antitrust feeling. Much the same was also true of the other antitrust activities. Financial reform provided another outlet for antitrust sentiment, although its practical results were little more than regulation for the promotion of honesty and facilitation of the governmental spending program. The attacks upon such practices as collusive bidding, basing-point pricing, and block-booking benefited from a long history of past agitation. And the suits in the petroleum and auto-finance industries had the support of discontented business groups. The result of such activities, however, could hardly be more than marginal.

When the antitrusters reached for real weapons, when they tried, for example, to use the taxing power or make drastic changes in corporate law, they found that any thorough-going program was simply not within the realm of political possibilities.

Under the circumstances, it appeared, neither planning nor antitrust action could be applied in a thorough-going fashion. Neither approach could completely eclipse the other. Yet the political climate and situation did change; and, as a result of these changes, policy vacillated between the two extremes. One period might see more emphasis on planning, the next on antitrust action, and considerable changes might also take place in the nature, content, and scope of each program.

Superficially, the crisis of 1937 was much like that of 1933. Again there were new demands for antitrust action, and again these demands were blended with new proposals for planning, rationalization, and monopolistic controls. In some respects, too, the results were similar. There was more partial planning in unorganized areas, and eventually, this was accompanied by a resumption of large-scale federal spending. The big difference was in the greater emphasis on an antitrust approach, which could be attributed primarily to the difference in political circumstances. The alienation of the business community, memories of NRA experiences, and the growing influence of antimonopolists in the Roosevelt Administration made it difficult to work out any new scheme of business-government cooperation. These same factors, coupled with the direct appeal of New Dealers to the competitive ideal, made it difficult for business groups to secure public sanction for monopolistic arrangements. The political repercussions of the recession, the fact that the new setback had occurred while the New Deal was in power, made it necessary to appeal directly to anti-big-business sentiment and to use the administered price thesis to explain why the recession had occurred and why the New Deal had failed to achieve sustained recovery. Under the circumstances, the initiative passed to the anti-trusters, and larger concessions had to be made to their point of view.

One such concession was the creation of the Temporary National Economic Committee. Yet this was not so much a victory for the antitrusters as it was a way of avoiding the issue, a means of minimizing the policy conflict within the Administration and postponing any final decision. Essentially, the TNEC was a harmless device that could be used by each group to urge a specific line of action or no action at all. Antimonopolists hoped that it would generate the political sentiment necessary for a major breakthrough against concentrated economic power, but these hopes were never realized. In practice, the investigation became largely an ineffective duplicate of the frustrating debate that produced it, and by the time its report was filed, the circumstances had changed. Most of the steam had gone out of the monopoly issue, and antitrust sentiment was being replaced by war-induced patriotism.

The second major concession to antimonopoly sentiment was Thurman

Arnold's revival of antitrust prosecutions, a program that presumably was designed to restore a competitive system, one in which prices were flexible and competition would provide the incentive for expansion. Actually, the underlying assumptions behind such a program were of doubtful validity. Price flexibility, even if attainable, might do more harm than good. The Arnold approach had definite limitations, even assuming that the underlying theories were sound. It could and did break up a number of loose combinations; it could and did disrupt monopolistic arrangements that were no necessary part of modern industrialism. It could and, in some cases, did succeed in convincing businessmen that they should adopt practices that corresponded a bit more closely to the competitive model. But it made no real effort to rearrange the underlying industrial structure itself, no real attempt to dislodge vested interests, disrupt controls that were actual checks against deflation, or break up going concerns. And since the practices and policies complained of would appear in many cases to be the outgrowth of this underlying structure, the Arnold program had little success in achieving its avowed goals.

Even within these limits, moreover, Arnold's antitrust campaign ran into all sorts of difficulties. Often the combinations that he sought to break up were the very ones that the earlier New Deal had fostered. Often, even though the arrangements involved bore little relation to actual production, their sponsors claimed that they did, that their disruption would set the process of deflation in motion again and impair industrial efficiency. Arnold claimed that his activities enjoyed great popular support, and as a symbol and generality they probably did. But when they moved against specific arrangements, it was a different story. There they succeeded in alienating one political pressure group after another. Then, with the coming of the war, opposition became stronger than ever. As antitrust sentiment was replaced by wartime patriotism, it seemed indeed that the disruption of private controls would reduce efficiency and impair the war effort. Consequently, the Arnold program gradually faded from the scene.

It is doubtful, then, that the innovations of 1938 should be regarded as a basic reversal in economic policy. What actually happened was not the substitution of one set of policies for another, but rather a shift in emphasis between two sets of policies that had existed side by side throughout the entire period. Policies that attacked monopoly and those that fostered it, policies that reflected the underlying dilemma of industrial America, had long been inextricably intertwined in American history, and this basic inconsistency persisted in an acute form during the nineteen thirties. Policy might and did vacillate between the two extremes; but because of the limitations of the American political structure and of American economic ideology, it was virtually impossible for one set of policies to displace the other. The New Deal reform movement was forced to adjust to this basic fact. The practical outcome was an economy characterized by private controls, partial planning, compensatory governmental spending, and occasional gestures toward the competitive ideal.

SUGGESTED READING

George Wolfskill in *The Revolt of the Conservatives* (Houghton Mifflin, 1962) and Frederick Rudolph in "The American Liberty League, 1934–1940," *American Historical Review*, LVI (Oct., 1950), 19–33, focus on the Liberty League, a business group opposed to the New Deal, but fail to examine the business community in general and hence give inadequate analyses. Gene Gressley's "Thurman Arnold, Antitrust and the New Deal," *Business History Review*, XXXVIII (Summer, 1964), 214–31; and Ralph DeBedts' *The New Deal's SEC: The Formative Years* (Columbia Univ. Press, 1964) are worth consulting. William H. Wilson in "How the Chamber of Commerce Viewed the NRA: A Reexamination," *Mid-America*, XLIV (April, 1962), 95–108, seeks to correct Schlesinger's interpretation that the Chamber firmly supported the NRA.

There is still no volume that specifically treats the history of the NRA, but Hugh Johnson's *The Blue Eagle from Egg to Earth* (Doubleday, 1935) and Donald Richberg's *The Rainbow* (Doubleday, 1936) are useful works by two administrators of the agency. Other contemporary evaluations may be found in Leverett Lyon *et al.*, *The National Recovery Administration* (Brookings Institute, 1935) and Douglas V. Brown *et al.*, *The Economics of the Recovery Administration* (Brookings Institute, 1935).

James P. Johnson's "Drafting the NRA Code of Fair Competition for the Bituminous Coal Industry," *Journal of American History*, LIII (Dec., 1966), 521–41, is a useful source on the coal industry; Louis Galambos' *Competition and Cooperation* (Johns Hopkins Univ. Press, 1966) should be consulted for information regarding the cotton textile industry. Gerald Nash, in *United States Oil Policy, 1890–1964: Business and Government in Twentieth-Century America* (Univ. of Pittsburgh Press, 1968) discusses efforts to restrict competition during the New Deal years. Nash has also made a brief study of the relation between World War I mobilization and the NRA in "Experiments in Industrial Mobilization: WIB and NRA," *Mid-America*, XLV (July, 1963), 157–74.

Focusing on a few items of New Deal legislation and the apparent deemphasis on industrial cooperation, many historians, beginning with Basil Rauch in *A History of the New Deal* ° (Creative Age, 1944), have discovered in the 1934–35 period a shift from conservative programs, stressing recovery, to liberal programs, emphasizing reform. Arthur Schlesinger, Jr., in *The Politics of Upheaval*,° (Houghton Mifflin, 1960) reversed this analysis, claiming that there was at this time a significant shift from the liberalism of accepting corporate bigness to the ideas of the backward-looking neo-Brandeisians. William E. Leuchtenburg in *Franklin D. Roosevelt and the New Deal, 1932–1940* ° (Harper & Row, 1963) acknowledges that each view provides useful insights but finds the distinctions between the so-called First and Second New Deals overdrawn. William H. Wilson in "The Two New Deals: A Valid Concept?" *Historian*, XXVIII (Feb., 1966), 268–88, reassesses this thesis; and Otis L. Graham, Jr., in "Historians and the New Deals, 1944–1960," *Social Studies*, LIV (April, 1963) presents a sensitive analysis of the historical literature.

PAUL W. SCHROEDER

The Axis Alliance and Japanese-American Relations, 1941: An Appraisal of the American Policy

INTRODUCTION

In the last decade of the nineteenth century, both Japan and the United States began to manifest imperial urges toward China. However, as Secretary of State John Hay made clear in a series of notes to the great powers in 1899 and 1900, the United States desired not territory in China but trade; Hay expected the other interested powers to assist America's commercial domination of China by maintaining the Open Door policy and respecting China's territorial integrity. Japan, on the other hand, harbored a quite traditional, and thereby conflicting, notion of imperial grandeur. In time, Japan and the United States co-existed only unhappily as the great powers of the Pacific.

FROM Paul W. Schroeder, *The Axis Alliance and Japanese-American Relations, 1941,* pp. 200–16. Copyright© 1958 by American Historical Association. Reprinted by permission of the Cornell University Press.

In 1931, when the Japanese Army defied John Hay's famous principles and ended the fiction of Chinese sovereignty in Manchuria, Japanese-American relations entered a particularly bitter period. To express the Government's moral indignation at Japanese aggression in Manchuria, in January, 1932, Secretary of State Henry Stimson withheld recognition of Manchukuo, the puppet kingdom established by Japan to replace the Chinese province. Stimson's doctrine of nonrecognition made clear America's disapproval, but his gesture, unaccompanied as it was by sanctions, merely poisoned Japanese-American relations without rendering assistance to the Chinese.

When the Roosevelt Administration came to power in 1933, it also refused to recognize Manchukuo, but it refrained from further moralistic denunciations. Relations improved markedly thereafter until 1937, when an accidental clash in North China between Chinese and Japanese troops expanded into full-scale war. The United States then resumed its condemnation of Japan. As the war dragged on, American hostility to Japan intensified, and in 1939 the Administration began granting small loans to the Chinese Government. At the end of the year, the United States abrogated its commercial treaty with Japan to allow for a possible embargo later on.

When Hitler's stunning triumphs in Western Europe in May of 1940 revealed how vulnerable the Dutch, French, and even British empires in the Pacific were, Japan decided to extend her imperial sway southward. In June Japan forced the French colonial administration in Indo-China to permit the Japanese Army to occupy the northern half of Vietnam. And in September Japan concluded a military alliance with Germany and Italy to secure her position in world politics. These developments alarmed Roosevelt and led him to take a momentous step. He knew, of course, that exports of American oil and scrap metal were making Japanese war production possible; however, he feared that a total embargo might induce not moderation in Tokyo, but a Japanese invasion of the Dutch East Indies, whose natural resources could solve Japan's problems. On September 28, 1940, therefore, Roosevelt ended American shipments of scrap metal and iron to Japan, but he permitted the oil trade to continue.

After a brief, indecisive period in which she neither advanced nor retreated, Japan moved in July, 1941, into the south of Vietnam to complete the occupation of that country and to prepare an assault on the rest of Southeast Asia. Roosevelt moved at last on July 25 to cut off Japan's supply of American oil. His decision left Japan with only two courses of action: she would have to either negotiate a settlement with the United States or obtain her own source of oil in Southeast Asia. Shrinking from the prospect of war with the Western powers, Prime Minister Konoye in August of 1941 offered to meet with Roosevelt to work out the terms of settlement quickly at the highest level. But Roosevelt refused, acting on Secretary of

State Cordell Hull's advice that the President reject the meeting un-less the Prime Minister offered in advance to make specific com-mitments about China. Konoye refused, and as a result negotia-tions had to continue through normal diplomatic channels. Because Roosevelt's rebuff strengthened the argument of Japa-nese expansionists and because Konoye was unable to find suitable terms of settlement, the Cabinet was forced to resign in October. The Government was then turned over to the extremist General Hideki Tojo.

At the urging of the emperor, Tojo's Government made a last attempt at peace. On November 5, Japan offered the United States a general settlement (Plan A); if that was refused, a temporary truce (Plan B) would be presented. If no agreement was achieved by November 25, the Japanese war machine would roll. Because the Japanese diplomatic code had been broken, Washington knew the contents of Plans A and B in advance. Secretary of State Hull rejected Plan A out of hand: Its implementation, he believed, would mean a sell-out in China. In Plan B, which was subsequently of-fered, Japan promised, in effect, not to make new moves in South-east Asia and the South Pacific, to draw her forces back to northern Vietnam, and to abandon Vietnam entirely at the conclusion of a general peace. In return the United States was to resume exports of oil to Japan and agree to a vaguely worded statement (Point 5) concerning China.

Point 5 stated, "The Government of the United States under-takes to refrain from such measures and actions as will be prejudi-cial to the endeavors for restoration of general peace between Japan and China." Hopelessly bogged down in China and desper-ate for a compromise solution, Japan believed that American aid to China was the major obstacle to a settlement. Though the meaning of Point 5 has been variously interpreted, Hull assumed that it required the immediate abandonment of China; on No-vember 26, 1941, he rejected Plan B.

Hull was by now so outraged at Japan for her disregard of international law that he would not countenance even temporary compromise over China, and he chose to uphold principle even if that meant war. He did have a general idea of the consequences of his decision, for as Roosevelt and Hull were studying Plan B, an incoming cable from Tokyo to the Japanese Ambassador was being deciphered. It said, "If you can bring about the signing of the pertinent notes we will wait till November 29. . . . After that things are automatically going to happen." It was only on December 7, 1941, that Hull learned the particulars.

The Japanese attack on Pearl Harbor extinguished the doubts of those Americans who had wished their nation to stay out of the war; they firmly supported their President's request on De-cember 8 for a declaration of war against Japan. Three days later Hitler responded to Japan's request for a German declaration of war against the United States. When the President and Congress reciprocated, America entered the global conflict that would end with the defeat of Japan and Germany. Had Hull's inflexibility not provoked Japan's attack, it is at least possible, though not probable, that the United States might not have entered the European war and taken arms against Nazism, an ideology that was soon regarded by many Americans as a radical evil.

Paul Schroeder is perhaps the most effective critic of Hull's diplomacy. In *The Axis Alliance and Japanese-American Relations*, Schroeder indicts the general assumption of American policy, as well as the execution of it. About Plan B, for instance, he writes, "It is far from certain that Point 5 actually was a demand for immediate cessation of aid [to China] or that the Japanese would have insisted upon this as a *sine qua non* for agreement." In the following selection from his book, Schroeder sums up his case.

*I*n judging American policy toward Japan in 1941, it might be well to separate what is still controversial from what is not. There is no longer any real doubt that the war came about over China. Even an administration stalwart like Henry L. Stimson and a sympathetic critic like Herbert Feis concur in this.[1] Nor is it necessary to speculate any longer as to what could have induced Japan to launch such an incredible attack upon the United States and Great Britain as occurred at Pearl Harbor and in the south Pacific. One need not, as Winston Churchill did in wartime, characterize it as "an irrational act" incompatible "with prudence or even with sanity."[2] The Japanese were realistic about their position throughout; they did not suddenly go insane. The attack was an act of desperation, not madness. Japan fought only when she had her back to the wall as a result of America's diplomatic and economic offensive.

The main point still at issue is whether the United States was wise in maintaining a "hard" program of diplomatic and economic pressure on Japan from July 1941 on. Along with this issue go two subsidiary questions: the first, whether it was wise to make the liberation of China the central aim of Ameri-

---

[1] "If at any time the United States had been willing to concede Japan a free hand in China, there would have been no war in the Pacific" (Henry Stimson and McGeorge Bundy, *On Active Service* [New York: Harper & Row, 1948], 256). "Our full induction into this last World War followed our refusal to let China fend for itself. We had rejected all proposals which would have allowed Japan to remain in China and Manchuria. . . . Japan had struck—rather than accept frustration" (Herbert Feis, *The China Tangle* [Princeton: Princeton University Press, 1953], 3).

[2] Speech to U.S. Congress, Washington, Dec. 26, 1941, *War Speeches of Churchill*, II, 150.

can policy and the immediate evacuation of Japanese troops a requirement for agreement; the second, whether it was wise to decline Premier Konoye's invitation to a meeting of leaders in the Pacific. On all these points, the policy which the United States carried out still has distinguished defenders. The paramount issue between Japan and the United States, they contend, always was the China problem. In her China policy, Japan showed that she was determined to secure domination over a large area of East Asia by force. Apart from the legitimate American commercial interests which would be ruined or excluded by this Japanese action, the United States, for reasons of her own security and of world peace, had sufficient stake in Far Eastern questions to oppose such aggression. Finally, after ten years of Japanese expansion, it was only sensible and prudent for the United States to demand that it come to an end and that Japan retreat. In order to meet the Japanese threat, the United States had a perfect right to use the economic power she possessed in order to compel the Japanese to evacuate their conquered territory. If Japan chose to make this a cause for war, the United States could not be held responsible.

A similar defense is offered on the decision to turn down Konoye's Leaders' Conference. Historians may concede, as do Langer and Gleason, that Konoye was probably sincere in wanting peace and that he "envisaged making additional concessions to Washington, including concessions on the crucial issue of the withdrawal of Japanese troops from China." But, they point out, Konoye could never have carried the Army with him on any such concession.[3] If the United States was right in requiring Japan to abandon the Co-Prosperity Sphere, then her leaders were equally right in declining to meet with a Japanese Premier who, however conciliatory he might have been personally, was bound by his own promises and the exigencies of Japanese politics to maintain this national aim. In addition, there was the serious possiblity that much could be lost from such a meeting—the confidence of China, the cohesiveness of the coalition with Great Britain and Russia. In short, there was not enough prospect of gain to merit taking the chance.

This is a point of view which must be taken seriously. Any judgment on the wisdom or folly of the American policy, in fact, must be made with caution—there are no grounds for dogmatic certainty. The opinion here to be developed, nonetheless, is that the American policy from the end of July to December was a grave mistake. It should not be necessary to add that this does not make it treason. There is a "back door to war" theory, espoused in various forms by Charles A. Beard, George Morgenstern, Charles C. Tansill, and, most recently, Rear Admiral Robert A. Theobald, which holds that the President chose the Far East as a rear entrance to the war in Europe and to

---

[3] William L. Langer and S. Everett Gleason, *The Undeclared War, 1940–1941* (New York: Harper & Row, 1953), 706–707.

that end deliberately goaded the Japanese into an attack.[4] This theory is quite different and quite incredible. It is as impossible to accept as the idea that Japan attacked the United States in a spirit of overconfidence or that Hitler pushed the Japanese into war. Roosevelt's fault, if any, was not that of deliberately provoking the Japanese to attack, but of allowing Hull and others to talk him out of impulses and ideas which, had he pursued them, might have averted the conflict. Moreover, the mistake (assuming that it was a mistake) of a too hard and rigid policy with Japan was, as has been pointed out, a mistake shared by the whole nation, with causes that were deeply organic. Behind it was not sinister design or warlike intent, but a sincere and uncompromising adherence to moral principles and liberal doctrines.

This is going ahead too fast, however; one needs first of all to define the mistake with which American policy is charged. Briefly, it was this. In the attempt to gain everything at once, the United States lost her opportunity to secure immediately her essential requirements in the Far East and to continue to work toward her long-range goals. She succeeded instead only in making inevitable an unnecessary and avoidable war—an outcome which constitutes the ultimate failure of diplomacy. Until July 1941, as already demonstrated, the United States consistently sought to attain two limited objectives in the Far East, those of splitting the Axis and of stopping Japan's advance southward. Both aims were in accordance with America's broad strategic interests; both were reasonable, attainable goals. Through a combination of favorable circumstance and forceful American action, the United States reached the position where the achievement of these two goals was within sight. At this very moment, on the verge of a major diplomatic victory, the United States abandoned her original goals and concentrated on a third, the liberation of China. This last aim was not in accord with American strategic interests, was not a limited objective, and, most important, was completely incapable of being achieved by peaceful means and doubtful of attainment even by war. Through her single-minded pursuit of this unattainable goal, the United States forfeited the diplomatic victory which she had already virtually won. The unrelenting application of extreme economic pressure on Japan, instead of compelling the evacuation of China, rendered war inevitable, drove Japan back into the arms of Germany for better or for worse, and precipitated the wholesale plunge by Japan into the South Seas. As it ultimately turned out, the United States succeeded in liberating China only at great cost and when it was too late to do the cause of the Nationalist Chinese much real good.

This is not, of course, a new viewpoint. It is in the main simply that of

[4] Charles A. Beard, *President Roosevelt and the Coming of the War, 1941* (New Haven: Yale University Press, 1948); George E. Morgenstern, *Pearl Harbor: The Story of the Secret War* (New York: Devin-Adair, 1947); Charles C. Tansill, *Back Door to War* (Chicago: Regnery, 1952); Rear Admiral Robert A. Theobald, *The Final Secret of Pearl Harbor* (New York: Devin-Adair, 1954).

Ambassador Grew, who has held and defended it since 1941. The arguments he advances seem cogent and sensible in the light of present knowledge. Briefly summarized, they are the following: First is his insistence on the necessity of distinguishing between long-range and immediate goals in foreign policy and on the folly of demanding the immediate realization of both.[5] Second is his contention that governments are brought to abandon aggressive policies not by sudden conversion through moral lectures, but by the gradual recognition that the policy of aggression will not succeed. According to Grew, enough awareness of failure existed in the government of Japan in late 1941 to enable it to make a beginning in the process of reversal of policy—but not nearly enough to force Japan to a wholesale surrender of her conquests and aims.[6] Third was his conviction that what was needed on both sides was time—time in which the United States could grow stronger and in which the tide of war in Europe could be turned definitely against Germany, time in which the sense of failure could grow in Japan and in which moderates could gain better control of the situation. A victory in Europe, Grew observed, would either automatically solve the problem of Japan or make that problem, if necessary, much easier to solve by force.[7] Fourth was his belief that Japan would fight if backed to the wall (a view vindicated by events)[8] and that a war at this time with Japan could not possibly serve the interests of the United States. Even if one considered war as the only final answer to Japanese militarism, still, Grew would answer, the United States stood to gain nothing by seeking a decision in 1941. The time factor was entirely in America's favor. Japan could not hope to gain as much from a limited relaxation of the embargo as the United States could from time gained for mobilization; Roosevelt and the military strategists were in fact anxious to gain time by a *modus vivendi*.[9]

There is one real weakness in Grew's argument upon which his critics have always seized. This is his contention that Konoye, faced after July 26 with the two clear alternatives of war or a genuine peace move, which would

---

[5] Joseph Grew, *Turbulent Era*, edited by Walter Johnson (Boston: Houghton Mufflin, 1952), II, 1255.

[6] *Ibid.*, 1290.

[7] *Ibid.*, 1268–1269, 1286.

[8] The opposite belief, that Japan would give way, not only was inconsonant with the best available political and military intelligence, but was also a bad estimate of Japanese national psychology and of expansionist psychology in general. F. C. Jones rightly criticizes it as "the folly of supposing that the rulers of a powerful nation, having committed themselves to an expansionist policy, will abandon or reverse that policy when confronted by the threat of war. So long as they see, or think they see, any possibility of success, they will elect to fight rather than face the humiliation and probable internal revolt which submission to the demands of their opponents would entail" (F. C. Jones, *Japan's New Order in East Asia* [Toronto: Oxford University Press, 1954], 461).

[9] Grew, *Turbulent Era*, II, 1276–1277.

of necessity include a settlement with China, had chosen the latter course and could have carried through a policy of peace had he been given the time. "We believed," he writes, "that Prince Konoye was in a position to carry the country with him in a program of peace" and to make commitments to the United States which would "eventually, if not immediately" meet the conditions of Hull's Four Points.[10] The answer of critics is that, even if one credits Konoye's sincerity and takes his assurances at face value, there is still no reason to believe that he could have carried even his own cabinet, much less the whole nation, with him on any program approximating that of Hull. In particular, as events show, he could not have persuaded the Army to evacuate China.[11]

The objection is well taken; Grew was undoubtedly over-optimistic about Konoye's capacity to carry through a peaceful policy. This one objection, however, does not ruin Grew's case. He countered it later with the argument that a settlement with Japan which allowed Japanese garrisons to remain in China on a temporary basis would not have been a bad idea. Although far from an ideal solution, it would have been better, for China as well, than the policy the United States actually followed. It would have brought China what was all-important—a cessation of fighting—without involving the United States, as many contended, in either a sacrifice of principle or a betrayal of China. The United States, Grew points out, had never committed herself to guaranteeing China's integrity. Further, it would not have been necessary to agree to anything other than temporary garrisons in North China which, in more favorable times, the United States could work to have removed. The great mistake was to allow American policy to be guided by a sentimental attitude toward China which in the long run could do neither the United States nor China any good. As Grew puts it:

> Japan's advance to the south, including her occupation of portions of China, constituted for us a real danger, and it was definitely in our national interest that it be stopped, by peaceful means if possible, by force of arms if necessary. American aid to China should have been regarded, as we believe it was regarded by our Government, as an indirect means to this end, and not from a sentimental viewpoint. The President's letter of January 21, 1941, shows that he then sensed the important issues in the Far East, and that he did not include China, purely for China's sake, among them. . . . The failure of the Washington Administration to seize the opportunity presented in August and September, 1941, to halt the southward advance by peaceful means, together with the paramount importance attached to the China question during the conversations in Washington, gives rise to the belief that not our Government

---

[10] *Ibid.*, 1263–1264.

[11] Herbert Feis, *Road to Pearl Harbor* (Princeton: Princeton University Press, 1950), 275–277; Jones, *Japan's New Order*, 457–458.

but millions of quite understandably sympathetic but almost totally uninformed American citizens had assumed control of our Far Eastern policy.[12]

There remains the obvious objection that Grew's solution, however plausible it may now seem, was politically impracticable in 1941. No American government could then have treated China as expendable, just as no Japanese government could have written off the China Affair as a dead loss. This is in good measure true and goes a long way to explain, if not to justify, the hard American policy. Yet it is not entirely certain that no solution could have been found which would both have averted war and have been accepted by the American people, had a determined effort been made to find one. As F. C. Jones points out, the United States and Japan were not faced in July 1941 with an absolute dilemma of peace or war, of complete settlement or open conflict. Hull believed that they were, of course; but his all-or-nothing attitude constituted one of his major shortcomings as a diplomat. Between the two extremes existed the possibility of a *modus vivendi*, an agreement settling some issues and leaving others in abeyance. Had Roosevelt and Konoye met, Jones argues, they might have been able to agree on a relaxation of the embargo in exchange for satisfactory assurances on the Tripartite Pact and southward expansion, with the China issue laid aside. The United States would not have had to cease aid, nor Japan to remove her troops. The final settlement of the Far Eastern question, Jones concludes,

> would then have depended upon the issue of the struggle in Europe. If Germany prevailed, then the United States would be in no position to oppose Japanese ambitions in Asia; if Germany were defeated, Japan would be in no position to persist in those ambitions in the face of the United States, the USSR, and the British Commonwealth.[13]

Such an agreement, limited and temporary in nature, would have involved no sacrifice of principle for either nation, yet would have removed the immediate danger of war. As a temporary expedient and as an alternative to otherwise inevitable and useless conflict, it could have been sold by determined effort to the public on both sides. Nor would it have been impossible, in the writer's opinion, to have accompanied or followed such an agreement with a simple truce or standstill in the China conflict through American mediation.

This appraisal, to be sure, is one based on realism. Grew's criticism of Hull's policy and the alternative he offers to it are both characterized by fundamental attention to what is practical and expedient at a given time and to limited objectives within the scope of the national interest. In general, the writer agrees with this point of view, believing that, as William A. Orton

---

[12] Grew, *Turbulent Era*, II, 1367–1368.

[13] Jones, *Japan's New Order*, 459.

points out, it is foolish and disastrous to treat nations as morally responsible persons, "because their nature falls far short of personality," and that, as George F. Kennan contends, the right role for moral considerations in foreign affairs is not to determine policy, but rather to soften and ameliorate actions necessarily based on the realities of world politics.[14]

From this realistic standpoint, the policy of the State Department would seem to be open to other criticisms besides those of Grew. The criticisms, which may be briefly mentioned here, are those of inconsistency, blindness to reality, and futility. A notable example of the first would be the inconsistency of a strong no-compromise stand against Japan with the policy of broad accommodation to America's allies, especially Russia, both before and after the American entrance into the war.[15] The inconsistency may perhaps best be seen by comparing the American stand in 1941 on such questions as free trade, the Open Door in China, the territorial and administrative integrity of China, the maintenance of the prewar *status quo* in the Far East, and the sanctity of international agreements with the position taken on the same questions at the Yalta Conference in 1945.[16]

---

[14] William A. Orton, *The Liberal Tradition* (New Haven: Yale University Press, 1944), 239; George F. Kennan, *American Diplomacy, 1900–1950* (Chicago: University of Chicago Press, 1951), 95–103.

[15] One notes with interest, for example, a pre-Pearl Harbor statement by Senator Lister Hill of Alabama, a strong proponent of a radical anti-Japanese policy, as to America's attitude toward the Soviet Union: "It is not the business of this government to ask or to receive any assurance from Stalin about what he will do with regard to Finland after the war. . . . It is the business of this government to look out for and defend the vital interests of the United States" (*New York Times*, Nov. 5, 1941). If in the above quotation one reads "Tojo" for "Stalin" and "China" for "Finland," the result is a statement of the extreme isolationist position on the Far East which Hill and other supporters of the administration found so detestable.

[16] The writer has no desire to enter here into the controversy over the merits of the Yalta decisions, but only to draw a certain parallel. The standard defense for the Yalta policy on the Far East has been the contention that the United States conceded to Soviet Russia only what the U.S.S.R. could and would have seized without American leave, that the only alternative to aggreement would have been war with Russia, and that securing Russian entrance into the Far Eastern war was considered militarily necessary (George F. Lensen, "Yalta and the Far East," in John L. Snell, Forrest C. Pogue, Charles F. Delzell, and George F. Lensen, *The Meaning of Yalta: Big Three Diplomacy and the New Balance of Power* [Baton Rouge: Louisiana State University Press, 1956], 163–164). The argument may be quite sound, but surely it would serve equally well—indeed, much better, *mutatis mutandis*—to justify a policy of conciliation toward Japan in 1941. Applied to Japan, the argument would then read as follows: The United States would have conceded to Japan only the temporary possession of a part of what Japan had already seized without American leave; the only alternative to agreement would have been war with Japan; and preventing Japanese entrance into the European war was considered militarily necessary. The great difference between the two situations would seem to be that the concessions envisioned by Japan in 1941 were temporary and reversible; those gained by Russia in 1945 were not. The very necessity of pursuing the Yalta policy in 1945 casts doubt on the wisdom of the hard-and-fast stand of 1941. Felix Morley has put the parallel neatly: "To assert that the sudden and complete reversal of the long-established Far Eastern policy was justified was also to say, by implication, that the policy reversed was fundamentally

The blindness to reality may be seen in the apparent inability of American policy makers to take seriously into account the gravity of Japan's economic plight or the real exigencies of her military and strategic position, particularly as these factors would affect the United States over the long run.[17] Equally unrealistic and more fateful was the lack of appreciation on the part of many influential people and of wide sections of the public of the almost certain consequences to be expected from the pressure exerted on Japan—namely, American involvement in a war her military strategists considered highly undesirable. The attitude has been well termed by Robert Osgood, "this blind indifference toward the military and political consequences of a morally-inspired position."[18]

The charge of futility, finally, could be laid to the practice of insisting on a literal subscription to principles which, however noble, had no chance of general acceptance or practical application. The best example is the persistent demand that the Japanese pledge themselves to carrying out nineteenth-century principles of free trade and equal access to raw materials in a twentieth-century world where economic nationalism and autarchy, trade barriers and restrictions were everywhere the order of the day, and not the least in the United States under the New Deal. Not one of America's major allies would have subscribed whole heartedly to Hull's free-trade formula; what good it could have done to pin the Japanese down to it is hard to determine.[19]

---

faulty, that to fight a war with Japan in behalf of Chinese nationalism had been a dreadful mistake" (*The Foreign Policy of the United States* [New York: Alfred A. Knopf, 1951], 87–88). One may, as Morley does, reject both the above premise and the conclusion, or one may accept both; but it is difficult to see how one may affirm the premise and deny the conclusion. For those who believe that a vital moral difference existed between the two cases, the problem would seem to be how to show that it is morally unjustifiable to violate principle in order to keep a potential enemy out of a war, yet morally justifiable to sacrifice principle in order to get a potential ally into it. The dilemma appears insoluble.

[17] In his very interesting book, *America's Strategy in World Politics* (New York: Harcourt, Brace, 1942), Nicholas Spykman displays some of the insights which seem to have been lacking in the American policy of the time. He points out, for example, that Japan's economic and geographic position was essentially the same as that of Great Britain; that her position vis-à-vis the United States was also roughly equivalent to England's; that therefore it made little sense for America to aid Great Britain in maintaining a European balance of power, while at the same time trying to force Japan to give up all her buffer states in Asia; that the Japanese war potential could not compare to that of a revivified and unified China; and that one day (a striking prediction in 1942!) the United States would have to undertake to protect Japan from Soviet Russia and China (pp. 135–137, 469–470). Spykman saw then what is today so painfully evident—that without a Japanese foothold on the Asiatic mainland no real balance of power is possible in Asia.

[18] Robert E. Osgood, *Ideals and Self-Interest in America's Foreign Relations* (Chicago: University of Chicago Press, 1953), 361.

[19] A memorandum by the Chief of the State Department Division of Commercial Policy and Agreements (Hawkins) to Ballantine, Washington, Nov. 10, 1941, offers interesting comments on the extent and nature of the trade discriminations then being practiced against Japan by nations throughout the world, including the United States (*Foreign Relations, 1941*, IV, 576–577).

But these are all criticisms based on a realistic point of view, and to judge the American policy solely from this point of view is to judge it unfairly and by a standard inappropriate to it. The policy of the United States was avowedly not one of realism, but of principle. If then it is to be understood on its own grounds and judged by its own standards, the main question will be whether the policy was morally right—that is, in accord with principles of peace and international justice. Here, according to its defenders, the American policy stands vindicated. For any other policy, any settlement with Japan at the expense of China, would have meant a betrayal not only of China, but also of vital principles and of America's moral task in the world.

This, as we know, was the position of Hull and his co-workers. It has been stated more recently by Basil Rauch, who writes:

> No one but an absolute pacifist would argue that the danger of war is a greater evil than violation of principle. . . . The isolationist believes that appeasement of Japan without China's consent violated no principle worth a risk of war. The internationalist must believe that the principle did justify a risk of war.[20]

This is not an argument to be dismissed lightly. The contention that the United States had a duty to fulfill in 1941, and that this duty consisted in holding to justice and morality in a world given to international lawlessness and barbarism and in standing on principle against an unprincipled and ruthless aggressor, commands respect. It is not answered by dismissing it as unrealistic or by proscribing all moral considerations in foreign policy. An answer may be found, however, in a closer definition of America's moral duty in 1941. According to Hull, and apparently also Rauch, the task was primarily one of upholding principle. This is not the only possible definition. It may well be contended that the moral duty was rather one of doing the most practical good possible in a chaotic world situation and, further, that this was the main task President Roosevelt and the administration had in mind at least till the end of July 1941.

If the moral task of the United States in the Far East was to uphold a principle of absolute moral value, the principle of nonappeasement of aggressors, then the American policy was entirely successful in fulfilling it. The American diplomats proved that the United States was capable of holding to its position in disregard and even in defiance of national interests narrowly conceived. If, however, the task was one of doing concrete good and giving practical help where needed, especially to China, then the American policy falls fatally short. For it can easily be seen not only that the policy followed did not in practice help China, but also that it could not have been expected to. Although it was a pro-China and even a China-first policy in

---

[20] Basil Rauch, *Roosevelt, From Munich to Pearl Harbor* (Creative Age, 1950), 472.

principle, it was not in practical fact designed to give China the kind of help needed.

What China required above all by late 1941 was clearly an end to the fighting, a chance to recoup her strength. Her chaotic financial condition, a disastrous inflation, civil strife with the Communists, severe hunger and privation, and falling morale all enfeebled and endangered her further resistance. Chiang Kai-shek, who knew this, could hope only for an end to the war through the massive intervention of American forces and the consequent liberation of China. It was in this hope that he pleaded so strongly for a hard American policy toward Japan. Chiang's hopes, however, were wholly unrealistic. For though the United States was willing to risk war for China's sake, and finally did incur it over the China issue, the Washington government never intended in case of war to throw America's full weight against Japan in order to liberate China. The American strategy always was to concentrate on Europe first, fighting a defensive naval war in the Far East and aiding China, as before, in order to keep the Japanese bogged down. The possibility was faced and accepted that the Chinese might have to go on fighting for some years before eventual liberation through the defeat of Japan. The vehement Chinese protests over this policy were unavailing, and the bitter disillusionment suffered by the Chinese only helped to bring on in 1942 the virtual collapse of the Chinese war effort during the latter years of the war.[21]

As a realistic appraisal of America's military capabilities and of her world-wide strategic interests, the Europe-first policy has a great deal to recommend it. But the combination of this realistic strategy with a moralistic diplomacy led to the noteworthy paradox of a war incurred for the sake of China which could not then be fought for the sake of China and whose practical value for China at the time was, to say the least, dubious. The plain fact is that the United States in 1941 was not capable of forcing Japan out of China by means short of war and was neither willing nor, under existing circumstances, able to throw the Japanese out by war. The American government could conceivably have told the Chinese this and tried to work out the best possible program of help for China under these limitations. Instead, it yielded to Chinese importunities and followed a policy almost sure to eventuate in war, knowing that if the Japanese did attack, China and her deliverance would have to take a back seat. It is difficult to conceive of such a policy as a program of practical aid to China.

The main, though not the only, reason why this policy was followed is clearly the overwhelming importance of principle in American diplomacy,

---

[21] Werner Levi, *Modern China's Foreign Policy* (Minneapolis: University of Minnesota Press, 1953), 229–237. On the danger of internal collapse in China as early as 1940, see U.S. Department of State, *Foreign Relations of the United States: 1940*, vol. IV, *The Far East* (Washington: Government Printing Office, 1955), 672–677.

particularly the principle of nonappeasement of aggressors. Once most leaders in the administration and wide sections of the public became convinced that it was America's prime moral duty to stand hard and fast against aggressors, whatever the consequences, and once this conviction became decisive in the formulation of policy, the end result was almost inevitable: a policy designed to uphold principle and to punish the aggressor, but not to save the victim.[22]

It is this conviction as to America's moral duty, however sincere and understandable, which the writer believes constitutes a fundamental misreading of America's moral task. The policy it gave rise to was bad not simply because it was moralistic but because it was obsessed with the wrong kind of morality—with that abstract "Let justice be done though the heavens fall" kind which so often, when relentlessly pursued, does more harm than good. It would be interesting to investigate the role which this conception of America's moral task played in the formulation of the American war aims in the Far East, with their twin goals of unconditional surrender and the destruction of Japan as a major power, especially after the desire to vindicate American principles and to punish the aggressor was intensified a hundredfold by the attack on Pearl Harbor.[23] To pursue the later implications of this kind of morality in foreign policy, with its attendant legalistic and vindictive overtones, would, however, be a task for [a] volume.

In contrast, the different kind of policy which Grew advocated and toward which Roosevelt so long inclined need not really be considered immoral or unprincipled, however much it undoubtedly would have been

---

[22] It is Secretary of War Henry L. Stimson who gives evidence on how strong was the role of avenging justice in the prevailing picture of America's moral duty. He displays a striking anxiety to acquit the administration of the charge of being "soft" on Japan and to prove that the administration was always fully aware of the Japanese crimes and morally aroused by them. The nation's leaders, he insists in one place, were "as well aware as their critics of the wickedness of the Japanese." Avenging justice, too, plays an important role in the defense he makes of the postwar Nuremberg and Tokyo war crimes trials. These trials, he claims, fulfilled a vital moral task. The main trouble with the Kellogg Pact and the policy of nonrecognition and moral sanctions, according to Stimson, was that they named the international lawbreakers but failed to capture and punish them. The United States, along with other nations in the prewar world, had neglected "a duty to catch the criminal. . . . Our offense was thus that of the man who passed by on the other side." Now, this is a curious revision of the parable of the Good Samaritan, to which the Secretary here alludes. According to the Stimson version, the Good Samaritan should not have stopped to bind up the victim's wounds, put him on his beast of burden, and arranged for his care. Had he been cognizant of his real moral duty, he would rather have mounted his steed and rode off in hot pursuit of the robbers, to bring them to justice. This is only an illustration, but an apt one, of the prevailing concept of America's moral duty, with its emphasis on meting out justice rather than doing good (Stimson and Bundy, *On Active Service*, 384, 262).

[23] Admiral William D. Leahy (*I Was There* [New York: McGraw-Hill, 1950], 81) expresses his view of America's war aims in dubious Latin but with admirable forthrightness: "*Delenda est Japanico.*" He was, of course, not the only American leader to want to emulate Cato.

denounced as such. A limited *modus vivendi* agreement would not have required the United States in any way to sanction Japanese aggression or to abandon her stand on Chinese integrity and independence. It would have constituted only a recognition that the American government was not then in a position to enforce its principles, reserving for America full freedom of action at some later, more favorable time. Nor would it have meant the abandonment and betrayal of China. Rather it would have involved the frank recognition that the kind of help the Chinese wanted was impossible for the United States to give at that time. It would in no way have precluded giving China the best kind of help then possible—in the author's opinion, the offer of American mediation for a truce in the war and the grant of fuller economic aid to try to help the Chinese recover—and promising China greater assistance once the crucial European situation was settled. Only that kind of morality which sees every sort of dealing with an aggressor, every instance of accommodation or conciliation, as appeasement and therefore criminal would find the policy immoral.[24]

What the practical results of such a policy, if attempted, would have been is of course a matter for conjecture. It would be rash to claim that it would have saved China, either from her wartime collapse or from the final victory of communism. It may well be that already in 1941 the situation in China was out of control. Nor can one assert with confidence that, had this policy enabled her to keep out of war with Japan, the United States would have been able to bring greater forces to bear in Europe much earlier, thus shortening the war and saving more of Europe from communism. Since the major part of the American armed forces were always concentrated in Europe and since in any case a certain proportion would have had to stand guard in the Pacific, it is possible that the avoidance of war with Japan, however desirable in itself, would not have made a decisive difference in the duration of the European conflict. The writer does, however, permit himself the modest conclusions that the kind of policy advocated by Grew presented real possibilities of success entirely closed to the policy actually followed and that it was by no means so immoral and unprincipled that it could not have been pursued by the United States with decency and honor.

SUGGESTED READING

Francis Jones' *Japan's New Order in East Asia, Its Rise and Fall, 1937–45* (Oxford Univ. Press, 1954) is also critical of the Administration's policies in Asia, but it should be supplemented by James Crowley's *Japan's*

---

[24] See the introductory remarks on the possibilities of appeasement, under certain circumstances, as a useful diplomatic tool, along with an excellent case study in the wrong use of it, in J. W. Wheeler-Bennett, *Munich: Prologue to Tragedy* (London: Macmillan, 1948), 3–8.

Quest for Autonomy (Princeton Univ. Press, 1966). For the argument
that the Administration deliberately maneuvered the nation toward
war, see Charles A. Beard's *American Foreign Policy in the Making,
1932–1940* (Yale Univ. Press, 1946) and *President Roosevelt and the
Coming of the War, 1941* (Yale Univ. Press, 1948), which not only in-
dict Roosevelt's policies but also emphasize the danger of presidential
power in foreign relations and the Chief Executive's capacity to circumvent constitutional restraints.

Samuel Eliot Morison, who served as an official historian for the
Navy during the war, gives a savage reply to Beard in "Did Roosevelt
Start the War—History Through a Beard," *Atlantic Monthly,*
CLXXXII (Aug., 1949), 91–97. Another answer to Beard and early
"revisionism" is provided by William L. Langer and S. Everett Gleason
in *The Challenge to Isolation, 1937–1940* (Harper & Row, 1952) and
The Undeclared War, 1940–1941 (Harper & Row, 1953), histories
written on the basis of privileged access to restricted materials.

Dorothy Borg's *The United States and the Far Eastern Crisis of
1933–1938* (Harvard Univ. Press, 1964) should be examined on this
earlier period. William Appleman Williams in *The Tragedy of American Diplomacy,*° rev. ed. (World, 1962), and his student, Lloyd Gardner, in *Economic Aspects of New Deal Diplomacy* (Univ. of Wisconsin
Press, 1964) emphasize the role of American ideology, and its concern
for expanding markets, in interpreting responses to Japanese and German actions.

Recent studies of the relation between Germany and the United
States include James Compton's *The Swastika and The Eagle* (Houghton Mifflin, 1967) and Alton Frye's *Nazi Germany and the American
Hemisphere* (Yale Univ. Press, 1967). Though acknowledging that
there is no evidence of a German military plan to attack the United
States, both Compton and Frye believe that Germany imperiled American security. Compton's evidence, however, supports the view of A. J. P.
Taylor in *The Origins of the Second World War* ° (Atheneum, 1962)
that Hitler's ambitions were not global but continental (Europe) and
that he lacked a grand design for world conquest. Robert Dallek's
Democrat: The Life of William E. Dodd (Oxford Univ. Press, 1968), a
study of the American ambassador to Germany from 1933–1938, emphasizes Dodd's opposition to fascism and argues that Roosevelt was not
(privately) an isolationist between 1933 and 1937.

The best bibliographical survey is Wayne Cole's "American Entry into World War II: A Historiographical Appraisal," *Mississippi Valley Historical Review,* XLIII (March, 1957), 595–617. Surveys of the
period are found in Robert A. Divine's *The Reluctant Belligerent* °
(Wiley, 1965) and John Wiltz's *From Isolation to War, 1931–1941* °
(T. Y. Crowell, 1968).

HERBERT FEIS

War Came at Pearl Harbor: Suspicions Considered

INTRODUCTION

Herbert Feis, a former economic adviser in the State Department and special consultant to the Secretary of War, has written a distinguished series of books on the diplomatic history of World War II. *The Road to Pearl Harbor* (Princeton Univ. Press, 1950) is an invaluable account of American relations with Japan before the outbreak of war. As is usual in his writings, Feis sympathizes with American policy; in the following article he presents the case for Secretary Hull's policies before Pearl Harbor.

FROM Herbert Feis, "War Came at Pearl Harbor: Suspicions Considered," *The Yale Review*, XLV (March, 1956), pp. 378–90. Copyright 1956 by Yale University Press. Reprinted by permission.

*T*en years after victory, we look ruefully at the way the world has gone. It is right and natural to search out any errors of judgment or faults of character that have led us to our present pass. But such self-scrutiny can go awry if governed by a wish to revile rather than a wish to understand. Unless we are alert, that could happen as a result of the suspicions that have come to cluster around the way in which the United States became engaged in the Second World War—torch-lit by the Pearl Harbor disaster.

The more recently available sources have added but little to our knowledge of the events that led to our entry into the war. The books of memoirs written by Japanese witnesses have told us something more, especially about the struggle within the Japanese Government. But in my reading, while they may improve our knowledge of details, they do not change the fundamental view of this experience or its main features. In American and British records still kept secret there may be information or explanations that would do so. But even this I doubt. With no new great revealing facts to display, and no great new insights to impart, the most useful service would seem to be to act as caretaker of what is known, and in particular to deal with certain warped comments and inferences that seasonally must feel the straightening edge of evidence.

Of all the accusations made, the one most shocking to me is that Roosevelt and his chief advisers deliberately left the Pacific Fleet and base at Pearl Harbor exposed as a lure to bring about a direct Japanese attack upon us.

This has been diffused in the face of the fact that the Japanese High Military Command conference before the Imperial Throne on September 6, 1941, resolved that "If by the early part of October there is no reasonable hope of having our demands agreed to in the diplomatic negotiations mentioned above, we will immediately make up our minds to get ready for war against America (and England and Holland)." This is September 6. The plan for the attack on Pearl Harbor was not approved and adopted until October; and Secret Operation Order #1, the execution of the plan, was not issued until November 5. The presence of the Pacific Fleet at Pearl Harbor was not a lure but an obstacle.

The literature of accusation ignores or rejects the real reasons why the Pacific Fleet was kept in Hawaii. It must do so, since one of the main reasons was the hope that its presence there would deter the Japanese from making so threatening a move south or north that American armed forces might have to join in the war. It scorns the fact that the American military plans—to be executed in the event that we became engaged in war—assigned vital tasks to this Pacific Fleet. A mind must indeed be distracted if it can believe that the American Government could, at one and the same time, use the Pacific Fleet as a target and count on having it as part of its main defending force.

A variant of this accusation, which at least does not require such a willingness to believe the worst, might also be noted—that despite ample knowledge that Pearl Harbor was about to be attacked, the American Government purposefully left it exposed and allowed the event to happen.

Those who do not find such an idea at odds with their view of the sense of duty and regard for human life of President Roosevelt and his chief advisers can find striking points about the occurrence that may be construed to correspond with this conception. How they glare out of the record in hindsight: Ambassador Grew's warnings; Secretary Hull's acute gleam put into words at least three times in Cabinet Councils in November that the Japanese attack might come "at any moment, anywhere"; the intercepted Japanese messages telling of the Japanese effort to secure minute information as to the location of the ships of our Pacific Fleet in the Harbor; carelessness in checking up on the protective measures taken by the local commanders; failure to use the chance to give an effective last-minute warning to Hawaii. How else, it is asked, can these be explained except in terms of secret and conscious purpose?

However, just as hindsight makes the failure of perception plain, so it also makes it understandable—but only by bringing back to mind the total circumstances. That can be done here only in the barest way. Up to then Japanese strategy had been wary, one small creeping step after another, from Manchuria to North China into China and down into Indo-China. American military circles came to take it for granted that it would go on that way. Then there was the fact that Japan's basic objectives lay to the south and southeast; there and there only it could get what it needed—raw materials, oil, and island bases to withstand the attack from the West. Expectation already set in that direction was kept there by impressive and accurate intelligence reports of movements under way. Against this flow of preconception, the signs pointing to Pearl Harbor were not heeded.

Such features of contemporary thinking within the American Government explain, though they do not excuse, the failure to discern that Pearl Harbor was going to be attacked. To think the contrary is to believe that the President and the heads of the American Army, Navy, and Air Force were given to deep deception, and in order to have us enter the war were ready to sacrifice not only the Pacific Fleet but the whole war plan for the Pacific. This, I think, is the difference between history and police court history.

I have taken note of these accusations that have been built about the disaster at Pearl Harbor because they appeal to the sense of the sinister which is so lively in our times. But I am glad to turn to ideas and interpretations of broader historical import.

The first of these is that Roosevelt and the Joint Chiefs of Staff were obligated by secret agreements with Churchill and their British colleagues to enter the war at some time or other, in one way or other. Therefore, it is further supposed, the American authors of this agreement had to cause either Germany or Japan, or both, to attack us.

This view derives encouragement from the fact that the American Government *did* enter into a secret agreement about strategy with the British. The accord, known as ABC-1 Staff Agreement, adopted at Washington in March, 1941, set down the respective missions of the British and American elements in the event that the United States should be at war with Germany or Japan, or both; and subsequently the American basic joint war plan, Rainbow-5, was adjusted to fit this combined plan of operations. An attempt was made at a similar conference in Singapore soon after to work out a more detailed United States–British–Dutch operating plan for the Pacific. This attempt failed; but the discussion that took place there left a lasting mark on American official thinking, for the conferees defined the limits on land and sea beyond which Japanese forces could not be permitted to go without great risk to the defenders.

The ABC-1 agreement did not place the Roosevelt Administration under *political* obligation to enter the war against either Germany or Japan, not even if Japan attacked British or Dutch areas in the Far East. Nor did Roosevelt give a promise to this effect to Churchill when they met at Newfoundland in August, 1941. Up to the very eve of the Japanese assault the President refused to tell the British or Dutch what we would do. In short, the Government kept itself officially free from any obligation to enter the war, certainly free of any obligation to thrust itself into the war.

But I do think this accord conveyed responsibilities of a moral sort. After ABC-1 was adopted, production of weapons in the United States and the British Commonwealth took it into account; and the allocation of weapons, troops, ships, and planes as between threatened areas was based on the expectation that the United States would carry out the assignments set down in the plan.

Thus, it may be fairly thought, Roosevelt and his administration were obligated to try to gain the consent of Congress and the American people to play the part designated in the joint plans if Japanese assaults crossed the land and sea boundaries of resistance that were defined at these joint staff conferences. In the last November weeks when the end of the diplomatic talks with Japan came into sight, and General Marshall and Admiral Stark were asked what measures should be taken in face of the threatened Japanese advances, they advised the President to declare the limits defined at Singapore, and to warn the Japanese that we would fight if these were crossed. There is much reason to think this would have been done even had the Japanese not struck at Pearl Harbor and the Philippines, and this boundary would have been the line between peace and war. But this reaffirmation was made not as a measure required to carry out a secret accord, but because it was believed to be the best course.

A variant explanation of the way we dealt with Japan runs somewhat as follows: that Roosevelt was determined to to get into the war against Germany; that he had to find a release from his public promises that the United States would not enter "foreign wars" unless attacked; that his efforts to do so by unneutral aid to Britain and the Soviet Union had failed because Hitler had refused to accept the challenge; and so he sought another door into war, a back door, by inviting or compelling the Japanese attack.

This interpretation, with its kick at the end, twists the record around its own preconception. The actions taken did not flow from a settled wish to get us into war. They trailed along the rim of necessity of the true purpose—which was to sustain resistance against the Axis. How many times the American Government refused to do what the British, French, Chinese, Russians, Dutch asked it to do, because it might involve us in actual combat!

This slant of reasoning about American action passes by the course of Japanese conduct which aroused our fears and stimulated our opposition: the way in which, despite all our pleas and warnings, Japan pressed on. By not recognizing that these Japanese actions called for American counteraction, it excuses them. Thus our resistance is made to appear as nothing else but a deceitful plot to plunge us into war. Furthermore, it dismisses as insincere the patient attempt to calm Japan by diplomatic talks, by offers to join in safeguarding its security.

There were influential individuals in the Roosevelt Administration who wanted to get into the war and indifferent as to how we got into it. Of these, Secretary of the Interior Ickes was, I believe, the most candid, at any rate in his diary entries. Secretary of the Treasury Morgenthau and his staff also had a positive wish that we should engage in war—but against Germany, not against Japan, for that might have brought a diversion of forces to the Pacific. Secretary of War Stimson thought that it would not be possible for Great Britain to sustain the fight unless we entered it; but toward the very end, particularly as it was becoming plain that the Soviet Union was going to survive the Nazi assault, he began to wish for delay. However, time and time again the memoirs and diaries record the impatience of these officials, and those who thought like them, with Hull's caution and Roosevelt's watchful indirection.

The most genuine point made by those who dissent, one that merits thorough analysis, is that the American Government, in conjunction with the British and Dutch, refused to continue to supply Japan with machines and materials vital to it—especially oil. It is contended that they thereby compelled Japan to resort to war, or at least fixed a time period in which Japan was faced with the need of deciding to yield to our terms or go to war.

In reflecting upon this action, the reasons for it must not be confused with the Japanese response to it. Japan showed no signs of curbing its aggressive course. It paid no heed to repeated and friendly warnings that unless it did, the threatened countries would have to take counter-measures. As when on February 14, 1941, while the Lend-Lease Act was being argued in Congress, Dooman, Counsellor of the American Embassy in Japan and known to be a firm and straightforward friend of that country, carried back from Washington the message for the Vice-Minister for Foreign Affairs: that the American people were determined to support Britain even at the risk of war; that if Japan or any other country menaced that effort "it would have to expect to come in conflict with the United States"; and that the United States had abstained from an oil embargo in order not to impel Japan to create a situation that could only lead to the most serious outcome. Japan's answer over the following months had been to force its way further into Indo-China and threaten the Dutch East Indies.

This sustained proof that Japan was going on with its effort to dominate Asia, and the alliance pledging it to stand by Germany if that country got into war with the United States, made a continuation of trade with Japan an act of meekness on our part. Japan was concentrating its foreign purchases on products needed for war, while reducing civilian use by every means, and was thus accumulating great reserve stocks. These were enabling it to maintain its invasion of China without much strain, while continuing to expand its war-making power. Had *effective* restraints—note that I do not say *total* restraints—not been imposed, the American Government would have been in the strange position of having declared an unlimited national emergency, of calling upon the American people to strengthen their army, navy, and air force in great urgency, while at the same time nourishing the opponent that might have to be met in battle. This was a grave, if not intolerable, responsibility.

It is hard to tell how squarely the American and British Governments faced the possible consequence of their restrictive measures. My impression is that they knew the danger of war with Japan was being increased; that Japan might try to get by force the means denied it. The Japanese Government served plain warnings that this game of thrust and counterthrust might so end. These were soberly regarded, but did not weaken the will that Japan was not to have its way by threat.

Mingled with the anxiety lest these restrictive measures would make war more likely, there was a real hope that they might be a deterrent to war. Conceivably they would bring home to the Japanese people that if it came to war, they might soon run out of the means for combat, while the rapid growth of American military strength would make it clear that they could not in the end win. And, as evidence of these probabilities became plain, the conciliatory elements in the Japanese Government would prevail over the more militant ones.

This almost happened. But the reckless ones, those who would rather court fatality than accept frustration, managed to retain control of Japanese decision. The pressure applied by us did not prevent war, and may have brought the time of decision for war closer. The valid question, however, is not whether the American Government resorted to these restrictions *in order* to drive Japan to attack; it is whether the American Government failed to grasp a real chance, after the restraints had begun to leave their mark in Japanese official circles, to arrive at a satisfactory understanding that would have averted war. Twice, in the opinion of some qualified students of the subject, such a chance emerged, or at least appeared on the horizon of diplomacy. Were they real opportunities or merely mirages or decoys?

The first of these was the occasion when in the autumn of 1941, the Japanese Prime Minister, Prince Konoye, sought a personal meeting with the President. It is averred that the President's failure to respond lost a chance to avert the war without yielding any American principle or purpose. Some think the reason was that American diplomacy was inflexible, dull in its insight, and too soaked in mistrust. Others, more accusatory, explain the decision by a lack of desire for an agreement that would have thwarted the design for war.

Since there is no conclusive evidence of what Konoye intended to propose or could have achieved, comment on this subject must enter into "the boggy ground of what-might-have-been." Some observers, including Ambassador Grew, believe that Konoye could have made a real, and an irreversible, start toward meeting American terms. It will always be possible to think that this is so. But to the Americans in authority, the chance seemed small. Konoye was a man who in every past crisis had allowed himself to flounder between criss-crossed promises; hence there was good reason to fear an attempt at deception. Such glimpses as we have of what he might have proposed do not support the view that he could have offered a suspension or end of the fight against China. His freedom to negotiate would have been subject to the conditions stated by those who had controlled Japan's course up to then—their price for allowing him to go to meet the President.

Even so, to repeat, it is possible that skilled and more daring American diplomacy might have handled the meeting so as to get a satisfactory accord; or, failing that—and this is the more likely chance—to bring about so deep a division within the Japanese circle of decision as to have prevented warlike action. These alluring historical queries will continue to roam in the land of might-have-been.

But the risks were great. The echoes of Munich and its aftermath were still loud. The American Government might have found itself forced to make a miserable choice: either to accept an accord which would have left Japan free to complete its conquest of China and menace the rest of Asia, or to face a deep division among the American people. Any understanding with Japan that was not clear and decisive would have had unpredictable consequences. The Chinese Government might have felt justified in making a deal following our own. The Soviet Union, at this time just managing with the greatest effort and agony to prevent German victory, might also have chosen to compromise with Hitler rather than to fight it out. Speculations such as these must leave the subject unsettled. But in any case I think it clear that the American decision was one of judgment, not of secret intent. Konoye was not told that the President would not meet with him; he was told that he would not do so until more progress had been made toward defining what the Japanese Government was prepared to propose.

The same basic question had to be faced in the final crisis of negotiation in November, 1941: whether to relax restraints on Japan and leave it in a position to keep on trying to control much of Asia in return for a promise not to press on farther for the time being.

The opinion that the Japanese truce offer made at this last juncture accepted the main purposes and principles for which the American Government had been standing may be summarily dismissed. It was ambiguously worded, it was silent about the alliance with Germany, and it would have required the American Government to end its support of China—for the last of its numbered five points read: "The Government of the United States undertakes to refrain from such measures and actions as will be prejudicial to the endeavors for the restoration of general peace between Japan and China." This scant and unclear proposal was at once deemed "entirely unacceptable." Furthermore, there seemed little use and much possible damage in making a counter truce-offer of the same variety. The intercepted Japanese messages stated flatly that this was Japan's last and best offer. They told of the swift dismissal of a much more nearly acceptable one that Nomura and Kurusu asked their superiors in Tokyo to consider. A deadline had been set. Thus it was all but sure that the reduced counter-offer which had been patched together in Washington would be unheeded. But it might shake the coalition to which by then the opponents of the Axis had pledged their lives and national destinies.

This seems to have been the thought uppermost in Hull's mind in recommending to the President that the counter truce-offer be withheld. As set down in his historic memo of November 26, he had been led to this conclusion by the opposition of the Chinese, the half-hearted support or actual opposition of the British, Dutch, and Australian governments, and the further excited opposition to be expected because of lack of appreciation of the importance and value of a truce. This I believe to have been the true determining reason for a decision reluctantly taken. Even if by then Japan was genuinely ready for reform, the repentance had come too late. The situation had grown too entangled by then for minor measures, its momentum too great. Germany-Italy-Japan had forced the creation of a defensive coalition more vast than the empire of the Pacific for which Japan plotted. This was not now to be quieted or endangered by a temporary halt along the fringe of the Japanese advance.

Even though these reasons for dropping the idea of a truce may seem sufficient, they leave the question why the American Government could not have given a softer and less declaratory answer. Why had it to give one so "bleakly uncompromising"? It could have said simply that the Japanese offer did not convey the assurances that would warrant us and the alliance for which we spoke to resume the shipment of war materials to Japan and end our aid to China. Why was it deemed advisable or essential at this juncture to state fully and forcibly our maximum terms for a settlement in the Pacific? Was it foreseen that, scanned with mistrust as it would almost surely be, this would be construed as a demand for the swift abandonment of Japan's whole program? Was it done, as the accusation runs, with the deliberate intent of banning any last chance for an accord? Of propelling the Japanese attack?

That this was not the reason I am as sure as anyone can be on a matter of this sort; but I can offer only conjecture as to what the inspiring purposes were. Perhaps to vindicate past actions and decisions. Perhaps a wish to use the dramatic chance to put in the record a statement of the aims for which the risk of war was being accepted, and of the basis on which the Americans would found the peace when the time came. Such an idea was in accord with the usual mode of thought of the men in charge of the Executive Branch of the Government and of most of the American people. It gave vent to the propensity exemplified in Hull to find a base in general principles meant to be at once political standards and moral ideals. After long caution, it appealed as a defiant contradiction of the Axis program. All this, however, is surmise rather than evidenced history.

But I think it is well within the realm of evidenced history that the memo of November 26 was not in any usual sense of the word an ultimatum. It did not threaten the Japanese with war or any other form of forceful punishment if our terms were not accepted. It simply left them in the state of distress in which they were, with the prospect that they might later have to submit to our requirements. The Japanese Government could have, as Konoye and Nomura pleaded with it to do, allowed the situation to drag along, with or without resuming talks with the American Government. Its power to make war would have been depleted, but neither quickly nor crucially. The armed forces and even the position in China could have been maintained.

Notably, the final Japanese answer which ended negotiations on December 7, 1941, does not accuse the American Government of confronting it with an ultimatum, but only of thwarting the larger Japanese aims. Part 14—the clinching part of this note—reads: "Obviously it is the intention of the American Government to conspire with Great Britain and other countries to obstruct Japan's efforts toward the establishment of peace through the creation of a New Order in East Asia, and especially to preserve Anglo-American rights and interests by keeping Japan and China at war. This intention has been revealed clearly during the course of the present negotiations. Thus, the earnest hope of the Japanese Government to adjust Japanese-American relations and to preserve and promote the peace of the Pacific through coöperation with the American Government has finally been lost."

This is a more nearly accurate description of the purposes of the American Government under Roosevelt than those attributed to it by hostile and suspicious American critics. Our Government did obstruct Japanese efforts, believing them to be unjust, cruel, and a threat to our national security, especially after Japan became a partner with Hitler's Germany and Mussolini's Italy and bent its efforts toward bringing the world under their combined control.

This determination stood on the proposition that it was better to take the risks of having to share in the suffering of the war than of finding ourselves moved or compelled to fight a more desperate battle against the Axis later on. The American Government, I believe, knew how serious a risk of war was being taken. But in its addresses to the American people it chose to put in the forefront the perils we would face if the Axis won, and to leave in the background, even to camouflage, the risks of finding ourselves plunged into wars which during the election campaign it had promised would not occur. Whether any large number of Americans were fooled by this, or whether most of them, in reality, were content to have the prospect presented that way rather than in a more blunt and candid way, I do not know.

This essay in interpretation has compelled me to recall and stress the aggressive Japanese assault—though I should have been glad to let that slip into the past. The passage of time does not alter facts, but it can bring a fuller and calmer understanding of them. It frees the mind for fairer appreciation of the causes and circumstances which impelled Japan along its tragic course and which impelled us to resist it. For both countries there are many common lessons. One of them is that continued friendliness requires mutual effort to relieve the other, to the extent it can, of deep cause for anxiety—the Japanese people of their anxiety over the means of living decently, the American people of anxiety about their security and power to defend the free world. Another is that they must both feel, speak, and act so honestly and steadily that their view of each other will be cleared of mistrust, and brightened by trust.

SUGGESTED READING

Dexter Perkins in "Was Roosevelt Wrong?" *Virginia Quarterly Review,* XXX (Summer, 1954), 355–72, expresses views similar to those of Feis. Robert Ferrell's "Pearl Harbor and the Revisionists," *Historian,* XVII (Spring, 1955), 215–33, is a critical view of the revisionists, especially those who argue that Roosevelt maneuvered the nation into war and even sacrificed the fleet at Pearl Harbor as part of his larger strategy.

Roberta Wohlstetter in *Pearl Harbor: Warning and Decision* ° (Stanford Univ. Press, 1962) concludes that defects in the system of gathering and assessing intelligence data were chiefly responsible for the surprise at Pearl Harbor. Others who should be consulted on

Japanese-American relations are Cordell Hull, *The Memoirs of Cordell Hull* (Macmillan, 1948, 2 vols.); Joseph Grew, *Ten Years in Japan* (Simon & Schuster, 1944); Waldo Heinrichs, *American Ambassador: Joseph C. Grew and the Development of the United States Diplomatic Tradition* (Little, Brown, 1966); Julius Pratt, *Cordell Hull* (Cooper Square, 1964, 2 vols.); Robert Sherwood, *Roosevelt and Hopkins* ° (Harper & Row, 1948); Henry Stimson and McGeorge Bundy, *On Active Service in Peace and War* (Harper & Row, 1948); Elting E. Morison, *Turmoil and Tradition: A Study of the Life and Times of Henry L. Stimson* ° (Houghton Mifflin, 1960); and John M. Blum, *From the Morgenthau Diaries* (Houghton Mifflin, 1959–67, 3 vols.).

IV

The Era of the Cold War

Until the Vietnam War, the American people in the era of the Cold War were united by common perceptions of the world in which they lived. In the belief that communism was expansionary and that it could be contained abroad only by American military power, the nation accepted the necessity for a large permanent army, established worldwide military alliances, fought the Korean War, and expended huge sums for foreign aid and intercontinental ballistic missiles. At home Americans looked with satisfaction on the apparent disappearance of poverty, the equitable distribution of national wealth, and the benign character of the modern business corporation. Thankful that a half-century of reform had established social justice, most Americans were content to leave the institutions just as they were.

Before the Vietnam War only two movements of dissent against this consensus attained mass proportions. In the years immediately following the end of World War II, Henry A. Wallace, Roosevelt's Vice President in his third term, rallied left-wing Americans to fight for expansion of the New Deal and rejection of Truman's anti-communist foreign policy. By the time of his crushing defeat in 1948 as a third party presidential candidate, Wallace's crusade was already disintegrating. The other movement of dissent rallied those on the American right. Fighting for fiscal orthodoxy and individual liberty, Senator Robert A. Taft, Republican of Ohio, led a losing effort to curb not only the federal bureaucracy but also such internationalist policies as foreign aid and entangling alliances, policies that Taft feared would create trouble rather than security for his country. By 1950 reverses in Southeast Asia and evidence of communist subversion at home broadened the discontent with the Democratic Administration. At this point Senator Joseph R. McCarthy, Republican of Wisconsin, assumed command of the right wing and appealed mainly to Taft's earlier constituency as he led a movement against communist influence inside America. Although McCarthy succeeded for a time in disrupting the nation's political life, his efforts ultimately proved ephemeral, and organized right-wing power declined rapidly after 1955. A right-wing minority in the Republican party succeeded in nominating Barry Goldwater for President in 1964, but his disastrous showing merely demonstrated the impotence of the right in national politics.

Intellectuals in the early Cold War era played an important role in shaping the national consensus, for their writings reinforced the general public's tendency to praise American life. Some intellectuals initially had reservations about the waging of a Cold War, but the brutal Communist coup in Czechoslovakia in 1948 and the Berlin Blockade of the same year convinced the skeptical that Soviet Communism was no less malevolent than Nazism and just as expansionary in its intentions. Liberal intellectuals became, in fact, among the most strident advocates of a large military establishment and nuclear deterrents. When Senator Joseph McCarthy assaulted the established institutions, intellectuals rallied to defend America with explicitly conservative justifications of the existing social order. The vogue of the "new conservatism" in the mid-1950's reflected not merely revulsion against the so-called radical right but also the genuine belief that American society was amply providing freedom and justice for its citizens. Theorists of countervailing power and pluralism in the social order (for example, John K. Galbraith, Seymour M. Lipset, and Daniel Bell) recognized the existing distribution of power as the best way of protecting the separate interests composing American society. Since McCarthyism had seemed a popular uprising, many intellectuals became distrustful of the masses and sympathetic to leadership by the élite.

Liberal intellectuals conceded that the second-class citizenship of the Negro was a regrettable exception to their optimistic analysis but noted approvingly that the civil rights victories of the mid-1950's and early 1960's were establishing legal equality for black men. (Curiously, the poverty and serious unemployment in the Negro community remained largely unnoticed until the ghetto revolt of the mid-1960's). Intellectuals had reservations only about the quality of national culture and the tastes of the public. Why should the common man, seemingly emancipated at last from drudgery, still prefer football and cowboys to Kafka and Kant?

During the liberal Administration of John F. Kennedy, the intellectuals received recognition and even some power. With their help, the Government sought to mobilize the energy, enthusiasm, and humanitarianism of youth in the establishment of the Peace Corps. More significantly, the Government strengthened the military, implemented the concept of counterinsurgency and applied force to keep communism out of the Caribbean and Southeast Asia, and created the Alliance for Progress to promote economic growth and counteract revolution in Latin America. At home the New Frontier saw as its main task the maintenance of consumer demand to advance prosperity and to keep private corporations productive and profitable. To the Kennedy circle, reform meant technical adjustments in the American economy. The Kennedy liberals proposed no basic alteration in the social order.

But in the years of the Johnson Administration the consensus broke down. The continuing conflict in Vietnam alarmed the intellectuals and provoked a reassessment of the Cold War, causing some liberals to re-examine their nation's foreign policy since World War II and to question the morality and wisdom of that policy. Rampaging ghetto Negroes made a mockery of the exercises in social apology by liberals. The resulting ferment revived the dormant Old Left, created a "New Left," produced the movement of Eugene Mc-Carthy and the third party of George Wallace, and unleashed a powerful criticism against American society. By the end of the Johnson Administration, the celebration of American life was over and the nation was convulsed by internal struggles more severe than anything known in this country since the Civil War.

SUGGESTED READING

There are no scholarly volumes that examine in depth American history from 1940 or 1945 well into the 1960's. Dewey Grantham in *The United States Since 1945* (Service Center for Teachers pamphlet, 1967) surveys some of the major literature on parts of this period. Gaddis Smith's *American Diplomacy During the Second World War, 1941–1945* * (Wiley, 1965) is a fine brief study of the war years. John Spanier's *American Foreign Policy Since World War II* * (Praeger, 1968, 2nd rev. ed.) is a thoughtful volume from a "realist" perspective, as is Norman Graebner's perceptive *Cold War Diplomacy, 1945–1960* * (Van Nostrand, 1961). John Lukacs' *A New History of the Cold War* * (Doubleday, 1962, rev. ed.) is worth consulting, as is Paul Y. Hammond's *American Foreign Policy Since 1945* (Harcourt, Brace & World, 1969). *The Cold War: Ideological Conflict or Power Struggle* (D. C. Heath, 1963), edited by Norman Graebner, is a collection of useful essays and excerpts from books on the Cold War.

William Appleman Williams' *The Tragedy of American Diplomacy* * (World, 1962, rev. ed.) is a major "revisionist" interpretation of American foreign policy through 1962. Williams stresses the quest for the "open door," locating in American policy most of the responsibility for the Cold War. Denna Frank Fleming's *The Cold War and Its Origins* (Doubleday, 1961, 2 vols.) is a "revisionist" interpretation that shifts from Wilsonianism to Williams; it is now being revised and extended past 1960. David Horowitz in *The Free World Colossus* * (Hill & Wang, 1965) follows Fleming but reaches into the early Johnson years. Walter La Feber explicitly continues the Williams analysis in *America, Russia, and the Cold War, 1945–1966* * (Wiley, 1967), the best general "revisionist" analysis of the Cold War. Richard Barnet's *Intervention and Revolution* (World, 1968) is harshly critical of America's postwar foreign policy.

Tang T'sou's *America's Failure in China* * (Univ. of Chicago Press, 1963) and Herbert Feis's *The China Tangle* * (Princeton Univ. Press, 1953) are the best analyses of America's Chinese policy. *Vietnam: Documents and Opinions on a Major World Crisis* * edited by Marvin Gettleman (Fawcett, 1966), and *Vietnam Reader,* * edited by Richard Barnet and Bernard Fall (Grove, 1966), are the most useful collections on Vietnam.

Eric Goldman's *The Crucial Decade and After, 1945–1960* * (Knopf, 1961) is a breezy survey criticizing the tone and style of much of postwar domestic politics but respectful of the early foreign policy of containment. Ernest May, editor of *Anxiety and Affluence: America, 1945–1965* * (McGraw-Hill, 1966), and Richard Watson, editor of *The United States in the Contemporary World, 1945–1962* * (Free Press, 1965), provide collections of useful documents on domestic and foreign affairs. Oscar Handlin's *The American People in the Twentieth Century* * (Harvard Univ. Press, 1964) includes two chapters on social history after 1939. In *Wealth and Power in America* * (Praeger, 1962), Gabriel Kolko argues that wealth and power have remained concentrated within certain groups since before the New Deal. Walter Johnson in *1600 Pennsylvania Avenue* * (Little, Brown, 1963) analyzes the politics of the years 1929–1960 from a liberal perspective.

Cabell Phillips' superficial *The Truman Presidency* (Macmillan, 1966) unfortunately remains the best volume on the subject. *The Truman Period as a Research Field,* edited by Richard Kirkendall (Univ. of Missouri Press, 1967), contains five historiographical essays on the war and postwar years. Barton J. Bernstein and Allen J. Matusow, editors of *The Truman Administration: A Documentary History* * (Harper & Row, 1966), include reprints of some manuscript materials in their survey of the period. Richard Neustadt's *Presidential Power: The Politics of Leadership* * (Wiley, 1960), a perceptive essay based on events in the Truman and Eisenhower years, emphasizes the subtle restraints on the President's exercise of his formal powers.

Eisenhower as President, * edited by Dean Albertson (Hill & Wang, 1963), is a fine collection of essays and portions of books that assess the Administration. Arthur M. Schlesinger, Jr.'s *A Thousand Days* * (Houghton Mifflin, 1965) and Theodore Sorenson's *Kennedy* * (Harper & Row, 1965) are flattering descriptions by two former aides to the President. Aida Di-Pace Donald, editor of *John F. Kennedy and the New Frontier* * (Hill & Wang, 1967), has compiled useful appraisals of Kennedy. Edward Flash in *Economic Advice and Presidential Leadership* (Columbia Univ. Press, 1965) covers the activities of the Council of Economic Advisers through the Kennedy years. Bert G. Hickman's *Growth and Stability of the Postwar Economy* (Brookings Institute, 1960) examines factors of the economy up to 1958, and Harold Vatter's *The U. S. Economy in the Fifties* * (Norton, 1963) surveys the economic trends of that decade.

Rowland Evans and Robert Novak in *Lyndon B. Johnson: The Exercise of power* * (New American Library, 1966) concentrate on Johnson's Senate career and are occasionally critical of his tactics, although they endorse his policies in the Dominican Republic and Vietnam. Marvin Gettleman and David Mermelstein, editors of *The Great Society Reader* * (Random House, 1967), include statements by the Administration as well as harsh assessments of contemporary liberalism.

James Gilbert's *Writers and Partisans* (Wiley, 1968), focusing on *Partisan Review*, traces some of the literary radicals into 1948. Christopher Lasch's *The New Radicalism in America* * (Knopf, 1965) analyzes a selected group of intellectuals in the postwar period, and his "Cultural Cold War," in Bernstein, ed., *Towards a New Past* * (Pantheon, 1968), severely criticizes the Congress for Cultural Freedom for its anti-communism. Philip Green in "Science, Government, and the Case of RAND: A Singular Pluralism," *World Politics*, XX (Jan., 1968), 300—26, emphasizes the shortcomings of "defense intellectuals." Ronald Berman's *America in the Sixties* (Free Press, 1968) is harshly critical of the liberal and radical intellectual currents of the decade.

John Higham in "The Cult of the Consensus," *Commentary*, XXXVII (Feb., 1959), 93—100, criticizes the dominant American historiography of the postwar years, and Irwin Unger in "The 'New Left' and American History: Some Recent Trends in United States Historiography," *American Historical Review*, LXXII (June, 1967), 1237—63, analyzes and attacks several so-called New Left historians.

Analyses of contemporary developments in the civil rights movement and in the black communities abound since the early sixties. C. Eric Lincoln's *The Black Muslims in America* * (Beacon, 1961) and E. U. Essien-Udom's *Black Nationalism: A Search for an Identity in America* * (Harvard Univ. Press, 1962) are the best studies of the Black Muslims. Anthony Lewis and the *New York Times* in *Portrait of a Decade* * (Random House, 1964) summarize the ten years of civil rights since *Brown v. Board of Education*. Harold Cruse's *The Crisis of the Negro Intellectual* (Morrow, 1967) is a black Marxist's analysis of the conflict between racial nationalism and integration. Arthur Ross and Herbert Hill, editors of *Employment, Race, and Poverty* * (Harcourt, Brace & World, 1967) analyze the economic problems of blacks. V. O. Key's *Southern Politics* * (Knopf, 1949) is a brilliant study of the subject up to the late forties. "American South, 1950—1970," *Journal of Politics*, XXVI (Feb., 1964), analyzes the contemporary South.

The literature on the contemporary student protest movements is already vast. The Berkeley movement of 1964 is discussed in *The Berkeley Student Revolt,* * edited by Seymour M. Lipset and Sheldon Wolin (Anchor, 1965); and in *Revolution at Berkeley,* * edited by Michael Miller and Susan Gilmore (Dell, 1965). Events at Columbia in 1968 are analyzed in the study prepared by Jerry Alvorn and other members of the Columbia *Spectator*, *Up Against the Ivy Wall* * (Atheneum, 1968); and in *Crisis at Columbia: Report of the Fact-Finding Commission Appointed to Investigate the Disturbances at Columbia* * (Vintage, 1968).

BARTON J. BERNSTEIN

America in War and Peace:
The Test of Liberalism

INTRODUCTION

In *Towards A New Past: Dissenting Essays in American History*
(Pantheon, 1968) a group of young historians, considered members
of the so-called New Left, present essays critical of the American
liberal tradition. Generally unwilling to view the crisis of the 1960's
as a historical aberration, many of them sought to locate in the
American past and "ideology" the sources of contemporary poverty, racism, and war.

Barton J. Bernstein, the editor of *Towards A New Past*,
argues in the following essay from that volume that the liberal administrations of the 1940's and early 1950's were guided by a limited social vision. They had only a shallow commitment to racial

FROM Barton J. Bernstein, "America in War and Peace: The Test of Liberalism," in Bernstein, ed., *Towards a New Past*, pp. 289–321.© Copyright 1967, 1968 by Random House,
Inc. Reprinted by permission of the publisher.

equality, they accepted the power of corporate enterprise, and the Truman Administration unintentionally contributed to McCarthyism by the use of anti-communist rhetoric.

Unfortunately, Bernstein does not define liberalism in this essay, and he is sometimes unclear about whether the principles of liberalism were defective or whether the commitment to these principles was weak.

*T*he domestic events of the war and postwar years have failed to attract as much scholarly effort as have the few years of the New Deal. The reforms of the thirties and the struggle against depression have captured the enthusiasm of many liberal historians and have constituted the major themes shaping their interpretations. Compared with the excitement of the New Deal years, the events at home during the next decade seem less interesting, certainly less dramatic.

The issues of these years also seem less clear, perhaps because the period lacks the restrictive unity imposed upon the New Deal. Despite the fragmentary scholarship, however, the major issues are definable: economic policies,[1] civil rights, civil liberties,[2] and social welfare policies.[3] The continued dominance by big business, the consolidation of other groups within the economy, the challenge of racial inequality—these are the themes of the wartime Roosevelt administration. Toward the end of Roosevelt's years, they are joined by another concern, the quest for social reform, and in Truman's years by such themes as economic readjustment, the renewed struggle against inflation, and the fear of disloyalty and communism. These problems are largely the legacy of the New Deal: the extension of its limited achievements, the response to its shortcomings, the criticism of its liberalism.

It was during the war years that the nation climbed out of depression, that big business regained admiration and increased its power, and that other interests became effective partners in the political economy of large-scale corporate capitalism. While the major interests focused on foreign policy and on domestic economic problems—on mobilization and stabilization, later on reconversion and inflation—liberal democracy was revealing serious weaknesses. Opposing fascism abroad as a threat to democratic

---

[1] See Bernstein, "The Economic Policies of the Truman Administration: A Bibliographic Essay," in Richard Kirkendall, ed., *The Truman Period as a Research Field* (Columbia, Mo., 1967).

[2] Also see William Berman, "Civil Rights and Civil Liberties in the Truman Administration," in *ibid.*

[3] Also see Richard O. Davies, "Harry S. Truman and the Social Service State," in *ibid.*

values, the nation remained generally insensitive to the plight of its citizens who suffered indignity or injury because of their color. Violating liberal values in the process of saving American democracy, Roosevelt's government, swept along by a wave of racism, victimized Japanese-Americans. Uncommitted to advancing the Negroes' cause, the war government resisted their demands for full participation in democracy and prosperity, and grudgingly extended to them only limited rights.

Though the New Deal had gone intellectually bankrupt long before Pearl Harbor and reform energies were submerged during most of the war, they reappeared in the last years of the conflict. Reviving the reform spirit in 1944, Roosevelt called for an "Economic Bill of Rights" for postwar America. In his last year, however, he was unable to achieve his goals, and Truman's efforts were usually too weak to overcome the conservative coalition blocking his expanded reform program. Mobilized by apprehension, liberals wrongly believed that the conservative bloc wished to destroy unions, to reorganize the corporate economy, and to leave the nation without protection from depression. But as unions endured and the economy grew, the fears and energies of liberals waned. Exaggerating the accomplishments of past reforms and believing that widespread prosperity had been achieved, they lost much of their social vision: they came to praise big business, to celebrate pluralism, to ignore poverty. Yet to their surprise they fell under vigorous attack from the right, in a new assault on civil liberties. In viewing McCarthyism as an attack upon the reform tradition, however, liberals failed to understand that they and the Democratic administration, as zealous anticommunists, also shared responsibility for the "red scare."

During the war and postwar years, big business regained national admiration and received lavish praise for contributing to victory over fascism. Yet few realized that business had not initially been an enthusiastic participant in the "arsenal of democracy." Such firms as Standard Oil of New Jersey, Dow Chemical, United States Steel, Dupont, General Motors, and the Aluminum Company of America had assisted the growth of Nazi industry and delayed America's preparation for war. Even after most Americans had come to condemn fascism, these corporations had collaborated with German business, sharing patents and often blocking production of defense materials in America.[4] The general ideology of these firms was probably best expressed by Alfred Sloan, Jr., the chairman of the General Motors board, when he replied to a stockholder: ". . . an international business operating throughout the world should conduct its operations in strictly business terms without

---

[4] Gabriel Kolko, "American Business and Germany, 1930–1941," *Western Political Quarterly*, XV (December 1962), 713–28; cf. Roland Stromberg, "American Business and the Approach of War, 1935–1941," *Journal of Economic History*, XIII (Winter 1953), 58–78.

regard to the political beliefs in its management, or the political beliefs of the country in which it is operating." [5]

In the two years before Pearl Harbor, major industries were also reluctant to prepare for defense. Though the aircraft industry ended its "sit-down" strike after the government had relaxed profit restrictions and improved terms for amortization,[6] other industries continued to resist expansion and production for defense. Sharing the common opinion that American intervention was unlikely, and painfully recalling the glutted markets of the depression decade, the steel industry and the aluminum monopoly (Alcoa) opposed growth, which might endanger profits. Nor were the automobile makers and larger producers of consumer durables willing to take defense contracts which would convert assembly lines from profitable, peacetime goods to preparation for a war that many believed, and President Roosevelt seemed to promise, America would never enter.[7]

Fearful of bad publicity, the leaders of these industries never challenged the administration nor demanded a clear statement of their responsibility. They avoided a dialogue on the basic issues. Still suffering from the opprobrium of the depression, industrialists would not deny corporate responsibility to the nation. Though privately concerned about the welfare of their companies, industrialists never argued that they owed primary responsibility to their stockholders. Fearful of jeopardizing their firms' well-being, company officials did not publicly express their doubts. Yet they could have objected publicly to executive suasion and contended that the issues were so grave that a Congressional mandate was necessary. Instead, they publicly accepted their obligation to risk profits for American defense, but in practice they continued to avoid such risks. Often they made promises they did not fulfill, and when they resisted administration policy, they took refuge in evasion. They restricted the dialogue to matters of feasibility and tactics—that expansion in steel and aluminum was unnecessary, that partial conversion was impossible, and that available tools could not produce defense goods.

The government also avoided opening the dialogue. The prewar mobilization agencies, administered largely by dollar-a-year men, did not seek to embarrass or coerce recalcitrant industries. Protecting business from public censure, the directors of mobilization—such men as William Knudsen of General Motors and Edward Stettinius of United States Steel—resisted the

---

[5] Quoted in Corwin Edwards, *Economic and Political Aspects of International Cartels,* A Study for the Subcommittee on War Mobilization of the Senate Committee on Military Affairs, 78th Cong., 2nd Sess., pp. 43–44.

[6] House Committee on Ways and Means and Senate Committee on Finance, 76th Cong., 3rd Sess., *Joint Hearings on Excess Profits Taxation,* p. 22; *New York Times,* July 26, August 9, 1940; *Wall Street Journal,* July 15, 1940.

[7] The next four paragraphs draw upon Bernstein, "The Automobile Industry and the Coming of the Second World War," *Southwestern Social Science Quarterly,* XLVII (June 1966), 24–33.

efforts of other government officials to force prompt expansion and conversion. In effect, Knudsen, Stettinius, and their cohorts acted as protectors of "business as usual." Despite the protests of the service secretaries, Roosevelt permitted the businessmen in government to move slowly. Though he encouraged some assistants to prod business, and occasionally spurred the dollar-a-year men, he avoided exerting direct pressure on big business.

The President was following the strategy of caution. reluctant to encourage public criticism of, or even debate on, his foreign policy, he maneuvered to avoid conflict or challenge. Because the nation respected big businessmen, he chose them to direct mobilization. He too had faith in their ability, and he hoped to win cooperation from the suspicious business community by selecting its leaders as his agents.

While many liberals criticized Roosevelt's reliance upon big business, the most direct, public challenge to business power came from Walter Reuther, vice-president of the recently formed United Automobile Workers, and from Philip Murray, president of the CIO and the United Steel Workers.[8] Criticizing "business as usual" policies, they proposed a labor-management council to guide industry during war. The plan shocked industrialists. It was radicalism, an invasion of management's prerogatives, a threat to private enterprise, asserted business leaders.[9] They would not share power or sanction a redefinition of private property. Having grudgingly recognized industrial unions shortly before the war, they remained suspicious of organized labor and were unwilling to invite its leaders into the industrial councils of decision making.[10]

Despite these suspicions, the administration called upon labor leaders and their organizations for cooperation in the war effort. Needing their support, Roosevelt appointed union chiefs to positions in the stabilization and mobilization agencies, and thus bestowed prestige upon organized labor. Calling for a labor-management partnership, he secured a wartime no-strike pledge.[11] As junior partners in the controlled economy, labor leaders generally kept the pledge.[12] Cooperating with business leaders in the defense effort, union representatives, by their actions, convinced many businessmen

---

[8] Walter Reuther, 500 *Planes a Day* (1940); *CIO News*, December, 1940.

[9] Bruce Catton to Robert Horton, Policy Documentation File 631.0423, War Production Board Records, RG 179, National Archives.

[10] Richard Wilcock, "Industrial Management's Policies Towards Unionism," in Milton Derber and Edwin Young, *Labor and the New Deal* (Madison, Wis., 1957), pp. 305–8.

[11] Joel Seidman, *American Labor from Defense to Reconversion* (Chicago, 1953), pp. 41–87.

[12] *Ibid.*, pp. 131–51. It was in response to the coal strikes led by John Lewis that Congress passed the Smith-Connally Act.

that organized labor did not threaten large-scale corporate capitalism.[13] By encouraging labor-management cooperation, the war years, then, provided a necessary respite between the industrial violence of the thirties and sustained collective bargaining, and speeded the consolidation of the new organization of the American economy.

It was within a government-controlled economy (dominated by business) that the major interests struggled for economic advantages. Farmers, rescued from the depression by enlarged demand, initially battled price controls but soon acceded to them and tried simply to use political power to increase their benefits. Also reaping the gains of war, workers received higher incomes but bitterly criticized the tight restraints on hourly wage increases. Business, also recovering from the depression, complained about price controls, which indirectly limited profits. Though all interests chafed under the restraints, none disputed in principle the need for government-imposed restraints on wages and prices: all agreed that a free price system during war, when civilian demand greatly outstripped consumer goods, would have created inequity and chaos.[14]

Despite price restrictions and the excess-profits tax, the major corporations prospered, benefitting from cost-plus contracts and the five-year amortization plan (which made the new plants partial gifts from the government).[15] As dollar-a-year men poured into Washington, big firms gained influence and contracts. Smaller businessmen, unable to match the influence and mistrusted by procurement officers, declined in importance. In a nation that prized the large corporation, few had confidence in small business. Even the creation of a government agency to protect small business failed to increase significantly its share in the war economy.[16]

The interests of big business were defended and advanced by the dollar-a-year men, and particularly by those on the War Production Board (WPB), the agency controlling resources. In many wartime Washington agencies, and especially on the WPB, the leaders of big business and the military served together and learned to cooperate. Burying earlier differences

---

[13] "With few exceptions, throughout the war years labor, not management, made the sacrifices when sacrifices were necessary," concludes Paul A. C. Koistinen, "The Hammer and the Sword: Labor, the Military, and Industrial Mobilization" (unpublished Ph.D. dissertation, University of California at Berkeley, 1965), p. 143.

[14] Bernstein, "The Truman Administration and the Politics of Inflation" (unpublished Ph.D. dissertation, Harvard University, 1963), Ch. 2.

[15] Senate Special Committee to Study Problems of American Small Business, 79th Cong., 2nd Sess., Senate Document 208, *Economic Concentration and World War II*, pp. 42–64. On concentration, see *ibid., passim;* cf. M. A. Adelman, "The Measurement of Industrial Concentration," *Review of Economics and Statistics*, XXXIII (November 1951), 269–96.

[16] *Economic Concentration and World War II*, pp. 22–39.

about preparation for war, they developed similar views of the national interest and identified it with the goals of their own groups. The reconversion controversy of 1944, which C. Wright Mills views as the beginning of the military-industrial alliance,[17] is the outstanding example of this coalition of interests.

In early 1944, big business was experiencing large military cutbacks and withdrawing subcontracts from smaller firms, often leaving them idle. Temporarily proponents of strong controls, most of the WPB executives from industry and finance would not allow these smaller firms to return to consumer goods. They collaborated with representatives of the military to block the reconversion program. Desiring control of the wartime economy, such military leaders as Robert P. Patterson, Under Secretary of War, James Forrestal, Under Secretary of the Navy, and Major General Lucius Clay, Assistant Chief of Staff for Matériel, feared that reconversion would siphon off scarce labor and disrupt vital production. Joining them were such WPB executives as Charles E. Wilson, president of General Electric, Lemuel Boulware, a Celotex executive and later a General Electric vice-president, and financiers Arthur H. Bunker of Lehman Brothers and Sidney Weinberg of Goldman, Sachs. Sympathetic to military demands, they were also afraid that the earlier return of small producers to consumer markets would injure big business. While some may have acted to protect their own companies, most were simply operating in a value system that could not accept a policy which seemed to threaten big business. Through cunning maneuvering, these military and industrial leaders acted to protect the prewar oligopolistic structure of the American economy.[18]

The war, while creating the limited prosperity that the New Deal had failed to create, did not disrupt the economic distribution of power. Nor did the extension of the wartime income tax significantly reallocate income and wealth, for the Congress even rebuffed Roosevelt's effort to limit the war incomes of the wealthy. Though the wartime measures and not the New Deal increased the tax burden on the upper-income groups, "the major weight," emphasizes Gabriel Kolko, "fell on income groups that had never before been subjected to the income tax." [19]

---

[17] C. Wright Mills, *The Power Elite* (New York, 1956), p. 273.

[18] This paragraph is based on Bernstein, "Industrial Reconversion: The Protection of Oligopoly and Military Control of the War Economy," *American Journal of Economics and Sociology*, XXVI (April 1967), 159–72. Cf. Jack Peltason, *The Reconversion Controversy* (Washington, 1950).

[19] Gabriel Kolko, *Wealth and Power in America* (New York, 1962), pp. 9–45; quotation from p. 31. Also see U.S. Bureau of the Census, *Income Distribution of the United States* (Washington, 1966), pp. 2–27; and Simon Kuznets, *Shares of Upper Income Groups in Income and Savings* (New York, 1953).

Failing to limit business power or to reallocate wealth, the wartime government was more active in other areas. Yielding to pressures, Roosevelt slightly advanced the welfare of the Negro, but the President also bowed to illiberal pressures and dealt a terrible blow to civil liberties when he authorized the forced evacuation of 110,000 loyal Americans of Japanese descent.

It was the "worst single wholesale violation of civil rights" in American history, judged the American Civil Liberties Union.[20] Succumbing to the anti-Japanese hysteria of Westerners (including the pleas of California Attorney-General Earl Warren and the Pacific coast congressional delegation under Senator Hiram Johnson) and the demands of the military commander on the coast, the President empowered the Army to remove the Japanese-Americans.[21] ("He was never theoretical about things. What must be done to defend the country must be done," Roosevelt believed, later wrote Francis Biddle, his Attorney-General.[22]) "Japanese raids on the west coast seemed not only possible but probable in the first months of war, and it was quite impossible to be sure that the raiders would not receive important help from individuals of Japanese origin," was the explanation later endorsed by Secretary of War Henry Stimson.[23]

Privately Stimson called the episode a "tragedy," but he supported it as War Department policy.[24] Opposing the decision, Biddle could not weaken the resolve of Roosevelt. Though liberals protested the action, the Supreme Court later upheld Roosevelt and the War Department.[25] "The meaning of the decision," concludes Arthur Link, "was clear and foreboding: in future emergencies no American citizen would have any rights that the President and the army were bound to respect when, *in their judgment,* the emergency justified drastic denial of civil rights." [26]

Though anti-Japanese feeling was most virulent on the Pacific coast, racism was not restricted to any part of America. In most of America, Negroes

---

[20] Quoted from Francis Biddle, *In Brief Authority* (Garden City, N.Y., 1962), p. 213.

[21] Stetson Conn *et al., Guarding the United States and Its Outposts,* in *United States Army in World War II: The Western Hemisphere* (Washington, 1964), pp. 115–49. The Canadian government also moved Japanese away from the coast.

[22] Biddle, *In Brief Authority,* p. 219.

[23] Quoted from Henry L. Stimson and McGeorge Bundy, *On Active Service* (New York, 1948), p. 406. The prose is presumably Bundy's, but Stimson apparently endorsed the thought (p. xi). Also see War Department, *Final Report: Japanese Evacuation from the West Coast* (Washington, 1943), pp. 9–10.

[24] Quoted from Biddle, *In Brief Authority,* p. 219.

[25] *Korematsu* v. *U.S.,* 323 US 214, at 219. The Court split and Justice Black wrote the opinion. Justices Roberts, Murphy and Jackson dissented. Also see *Hirabayshi* v. *U.S.,* 320 US 81.

[26] *American Epoch* (New York, 1955), p. 528 (italics in original).

had long been the victims of hatred. Frequently lacking effective legal protection in the South, Negroes also encountered prejudice, fear, and hatred in the North. During the war there were racial clashes in Northern cities. New York narrowly averted a major riot. In Los Angeles whites attacked Negroes and Mexicans, and in Detroit whites invaded the Negro sector and pillaged and killed.[27]

Despite the evidence of deep racism, liberal historians have usually avoided focusing upon the hatred in white America and the resort to violence.[28] Curiously, though emphasizing the disorganization of the Negro community, they have also neglected the scattered protests by organized Negroes—boycotts of white-owned stores in Negro areas of Memphis and Houston when they would not hire Negroes, a sit-in in a public library in Alexandria, Virginia, a Harlem boycott of a bus line to compel the hiring of Negro drivers.[29]

Condemned to inferiority in nearly all sectors of American life, Negroes did not share in the benefits of the early defense economy.[30] Denied jobs in many industries, they also met discrimination by the military. The Air Corps barred them, the Navy segregated them to the mess corps, and the Army held them to a small quota, generally restricting them to menial tasks.[31] During the 1940 campaign, Negro leaders attacked the administration for permitting segregation and discrimination, and demanded the broadening of opportunity in the military. It is not "a fight merely to wear a uniform," explained *Crisis* (the NAACP publication). "This is a struggle for status, a struggle to take democracy off a parchment and give it life." [32]

Negroes gained admission to the Air Corps when it yielded under

---

[27] Apparently Roosevelt refused to condemn the riots. Vito Marcantonio to Roosevelt, June 16, 1943, and reply, July 14, 1943, Vito Marcantonio Papers, New York Public Library. Also see Roosevelt's Proclamation No. 2588, in Samuel Rosenman, ed., *The Public Papers of Franklin D. Roosevelt* (13 vols.; New York, 1938–50), XII, 258–59.

[28] "This was the dark side of an otherwise bright picture," concludes Link, *American Epoch*, p. 529. Also see Frank Freidel, *America in the Twentieth Century* (New York, 1960), p. 405. Oscar Handlin, *The American People in the Twentieth Century* (Cambridge, Mass., 1954), p. 215; Everett C. Hughes, "Race Relations and the Sociological Imagination," *American Sociological Review*, XXVIII (December 1963), 879–90.

[29] *Pittsburgh Courier*, July 15, September 2, 9, November 11, 1939; March 2, 9, 1940; April 26, 1941; cited in Richard Dalfiume, "Desegregation of the United States Armed Forces, 1939–1953" (unpublished Ph.D. dissertation, University of Missouri, 1966), pp. ix–x. For other protests, see *Pittsburgh Courier*, September 16, 30, 1939, November 23, and December 7, 1940.

[30] *Amsterdam News*, May 10, 1940; Louis Ruchams, *Race, Jobs, and Politics* (New York, 1953), pp. 11–17.

[31] Ulysses Lee, *The Employment of Negro Troops*, in *United States Army in World War II: Special Studies* (Washington, 1966), pp. 35–52.

[32] Quoted from "For Manhood in National Defense," *Crisis*, XLVII (December 1940), 375. Also see Lee, *Employment of Negro Troops*, pp. 62–65.

White House pressure, but they failed to gain congressional support for wider participation in the military. At Roosevelt's direction the War Department did raise its quota of Negroes—to their proportion in the population. But the Army remained segregated. Though unwilling to challenge segregation, the administration still courted Negro leaders and the black vote. Rather than bestowing benefits upon the masses, Roosevelt maintained their allegiance by offering symbolic recognition: Colonel Benjamin O. Davis, the Army's highest ranking Negro, was promoted to Brigadier General, and some prominent Negroes were appointed as advisers to the Secretary of War and the Director of Selective Service.[33] ("We asked Mr. Roosevelt to change the rules of the game and he countered by giving us some new uniforms," complained the editors of the *Baltimore Afro-American*. "That is what it amounts to and we have called it appeasement." [34])

As the nation headed toward war, Negroes struggled to wring other concessions from a president who never enlisted in their cause and would not risk antagonizing powerful Southerners. Discriminated against by federal agencies during the depression and denied an equal share of defense prosperity, Negroes were unwilling to acquiesce before continued injustice. In some industrial areas the NAACP and *ad hoc* groups organized local protests. After numerous unsuccessful appeals to the President, Negro leaders planned more dramatic action—a march on Washington.[35]

Demanding "the right to work and fight for our country," the leaders of the March on Washington Movement—A. Philip Randolph, head of the Brotherhood of Sleeping Car Porters, Walter White, executive secretary of the NAACP, and Lester Granger, executive secretary of the Urban League —publicly requested executive orders ending racial discrimination in federal agencies, the military and defense employment.[36] In private correspondence with the President they sought more: the end of segregation in these areas. So bold were their goals that some still have not been enforced by the government, and it is unlikely that Negro leaders expected to secure them.[37]

Refusing to give up the march for the promise of negotiations, Negro leaders escaped the politics of accommodation. Though white liberals urged

---

[33] Lee, *ibid.*, pp. 69–84.

[34] Dalfiume, "Desegregation of the Armed Forces," p. 57, is the source of this quotation from the *Baltimore Afro-American*, November 2, 1940. Cf. *Pittsburgh Courier*, November 2, 1940.

[35] Herbert Garfinkel, *When Negroes March* (Glencoe, Ill., 1959), pp. 37–38.

[36] Quoted from the *Pittsburgh Courier*, January 25, 1941, and from the *Black Worker*, May 1941.

[37] "Proposals of the Negro March-on-Washington Committee" (undated), OF 391, Roosevelt Library. This was called to my attention by Dalfiume, "Desegregation of the Armed Forces," pp. 172–73.

Randolph and his cohorts to call off the march, they would not yield.[38] Applying pressure on an uncomfortable administration, they ultimately settled for
less than they had requested (and perhaps less than they had anticipated [39])
—an executive order barring discrimination in defense work and creating a
Federal Employment Practices Committee (FEPC). Meager as the order
was, it was the greatest achievement in American history for organized Negro action.[40]

FEPC did not contribute significantly to the wartime advancement of
the Negro. His gains were less the results of federal efforts than of the labor
shortage. Undoubtedly, the committee would have been more effective if
Roosevelt had provided it with a larger budget, but the Negro's cause never
commanded the President's enthusiasm. Yet he did protect FEPC from its
enemies, and by maintaining the agency, stressed its symbolic importance.[41]

It affirmed the rights of Negroes to jobs and focused attention on the
power of the federal government to advance the interests of its black citizens.
It did not smash the walls of prejudices; it only removed a few bricks. FEPC,
concludes Louis Ruchames, "brought hope and a new confidence into their
[Negro] lives. It gave them cause to believe in democracy and in America. It
made them feel that in answering the call to their country's colors, they were
defending, not the oppression and degradation, to which they were accustomed, but democracy, equality of opportunity, and a better world for themselves and their children." [42]

Still relegated to second-class citizenship, Negroes had found new dignity and new opportunity during the war. Loyal followers of Roosevelt, lov-
ing him for the few benefits his government had extended, black Americans
had become important members of the shifting Democratic coalition. By
their presence in Northern cities, they would also become a new
political force.[43] For the Democratic party and the nation, their
expectations and needs would constitute a moral and political challenge. By
its response, white America would test the promise of liberal democracy.

---

[38] Edwin Watson to Roosevelt, June 14, 1941; A. Philip Randolph to Roosevelt, June 16,
1941; both in OF 391, Roosevelt Library; Garfinkel, *When Negroes March*, pp. 60–61.

[39] Dalfiume, "Desegregation of the Armed Forces," pp. 173–76, concludes that the Negro leaders may have met defeat. Cf. "The Negro's War," *Fortune*, XXV (April 1942),
76–80ff.; *Amsterdam News*, July 5, 1941; *Chicago Defender*, July 5, 1941; Randolph,
"Why and How the March Was Postponed" (mimeo, n.d.), Schomburg Collection, New
York Public Library.

[40] For the notion that the events of the war years constitute the beginnings of the civil
rights revolution, see Dalfiume, "Desegregation of the Armed Forces," pp. 177–89.

[41] Ruchames, *Race, Jobs & Politics*, pp. 162–64.

[42] *Ibid.*, p. 164.

[43] Samuel Lubell, *The Future of American Politics* (New York, 1952), *passim*.

When the nation joined the Allies, Roosevelt had explained that "Dr. Win-the-War" was taking over from "Dr. New Deal," and there were few liberal legislative achievements during the war years. Those benefits that disadvantaged groups did receive were usually a direct result of the labor shortage and the flourishing economy, not of liberal politics. By 1944, however, Roosevelt was prepared to revive the reform spirit, and he revealed his liberal vision for the postwar years. Announcing an "Economic Bill of Rights," he outlined "a new basis for security and prosperity": the right to a job, adequate food, clothing, and recreation, a decent home, a good education, adequate medical care, and protection against sickness and unemployment.[44]

Noble as was his vision of the future society, Roosevelt was still unprepared to move far beyond rhetoric, and the Congress was unsympathetic to his program.[45] While approving the GI Bill of Rights,[46] including educational benefits and extended unemployment pay, Congress resisted most liberal programs during the war. Asserting its independence of the executive, the war Congress also thwarted Roosevelt in other ways—by rejecting a large tax bill designed to spread the cost of war and to reduce inflationary pressures [47] and by liquidating the National Resources Planning Board, which had originated the "second bill of rights" and also studied postwar economic planning.[48]

By its opposition to planning and social reform, Congress increased the anxieties of labor and liberals about the postwar years and left the new Truman administration poorly prepared for the difficult transition to a peacetime economy when the war suddenly ended.[49] Fearing the depression that most economists forecast, the administration did, however, propose a tax cut of $5 billion. While removing many low-income recipients from the tax rolls, the law was also of great benefit to large corporations. Charging

---

[44] Message on the State of the Union, January 11, 1944, in Rosenman, ed., *Public Papers of Roosevelt*, XIII, p. 41. For some evidence that Roosevelt was at least talking about a new alignment of politics, see Samuel Rosenman, *Working with Roosevelt* (London, 1952), pp. 423–29. Probably this was a tactical maneuver.

[45] Mary Hinchey, "The Frustration of the New Deal Revival, 1944–1946" (Unpublished Ph.D. dissertation, University of Missouri, 1965), Chs. 1–2.

[46] President's statement on signing the GI Bill of Rights, June 22, 1944, in Rosenman, ed., *Public Papers of Roosevelt*, XIII, 180–82, and Rosenman's notes, pp. 183–84. The GI Bill has generally been neglected as an antidepression measure.

[47] President's veto of the tax bill, February 22, 1944, in Rosenman, ed., *Public Papers of Roosevelt*, XIII, 80–84.

[48] Charles Merriam, "The National Resources Planning Board: A Chapter in American Planning Experience," *American Political Science Review*, XXXVIII (December 1944), 1075–88.

[49] Bernstein, "The Truman Administration and the Politics of Inflation," Chs. 3–4.

inequity, organized labor found little support in Congress or the executive, for the government was relying upon business activity, rather than on consumer purchasing power, to soften the economic decline. Significantly, despite the anticipated $30 billion deficit (plus the $5 billion tax), no congressman expressed any fear of an unbalanced budget. Clearly, fiscal orthodoxy did not occupy a very high place in the scale of values of congressional conservatives, and they accepted in practice the necessity of an unbalanced budget.[50]

Before the tax bill passed, the wartime harmony of the major interest groups had crumbled: each struggled to consolidate its gains and advance its welfare before the anticipated economic collapse. Chafing under the no-strike pledge and restrictions on wage raises, organized labor compelled the administration to relax its policy and free unions to bargain collectively.[51] Farmers, fearful of depression, demanded the withdrawal of subsidies which artificially depressed prices.[52] Big business, despite anticipated shortages, secured the removal of most controls on the allocation of resources.[53]

As the economic forecasts shifted in late autumn, the administration discovered belatedly that inflation, not depression, was the immediate economic danger. The President acted sporadically to restrain inflationary pressures, but his efforts were too occasional, often misguided, and too weak to resist the demands of interest groups and the actions of his own subordinates.[54]

Beset by factionalism and staffed often by men of limited ability, Truman's early government floundered. By adopting the practice of cabinet responsibility and delegating excessive authority to department chiefs, Truman created a structure that left him uninformed: problems frequently developed unnoticed until they had swelled to crises, and the choice then was often between undesirable alternatives. Operating in a new politics, in

---

[50] Bernstein, "Charting a Course Between Inflation and Deflation: Secretary Fred Vinson and the Truman Administration's Tax Bill," scheduled for *Register of the Kentucky Historical Society.*

[51] Bernstein, "The Truman Administration and Its Reconversion Wage Policy," *Labor History,* VI (Fall 1965), 214–31.

[52] Bernstein, "Clash of Interests: The Postwar Battle Between the Office of Price Administration and the Department of Agriculture," *Agricultural History,* XL (January 1967), 45–57; Allen J. Matusow, "Food and Farm Policies During the First Truman Administration, 1945–1948" (unpublished Ph.D. dissertation, Harvard University, 1963), Chs. 1–3.

[53] Bernstein, "The Removal of War Production Board Controls on Business, 1944–1946," *Business History Review,* XXXIX (Summer 1965), 243–60.

[54] Bernstein, "The Truman Administration and the Steel Strike of 1946," *Journal of American History,* LII (March 1966), 791–803; "Walter Reuther and the General Motors Strike of 1945–1946," *Michigan History,* IL (September 1965), 260–77; "The Postwar Famine and Price Control, 1946," *Agricultural History,* XXXIX (October 1964), 235–40; and Matusow, "Food and Farm Policies," Chs. 1–3.

the politics of inflation, he confronted problems requiring greater tactical skill than those Roosevelt had confronted. Seeking to maintain economic controls, and compelled to deny the rising expectations of major interest groups, his administration found it difficult to avoid antagonizing the rival groups. In the politics of depression, the Roosevelt administration could frequently maintain political support by bestowing specific advantages on groups, but in the politics of inflation the major interest groups came to seek freedom from restrictive federal controls.[55]

So difficult were the problems facing Truman that even a more experienced and skilled president would have encountered great difficulty. Inheriting the hostile Congress that had resisted occasional wartime attempts at social reform, Truman lacked the skill or leverage to guide a legislature seeking to assert its independence of the executive. Unable to halt fragmentation of the Democratic coalition, and incapable of ending dissension in his government, he also found that conservative subordinates undercut his occasional liberalism. Though he had gone on record early in endorsing a reform program [56] ("a declaration of independence" from congressional conservatives, he called it),[57] he had been unsuccessful in securing most of the legislation—a higher minimum wage, public housing, expanded unemployment benefits, and FEPC. Even the employment act was little more, as one congressman said, than a license to look for a job.[58] The President, through ineptitude or lack of commitment, often chose not to struggle for his program. Unable to dramatize the issues or to command enthusiasm, he was an ineffectual leader.[59]

So unsuccessful was his government that voters began jibing, "To err is Truman." Despairing of a resurgence of liberalism under Truman, New Dealers left the government in droves. By the fall of 1946, none of Roosevelt's associates was left in a prominent position. So disgruntled were many liberals

---

[55] Bernstein, "The Presidency Under Truman," IV (Fall 1964), 8ff.

[56] Truman's message to Congress, September 6, 1945, in *Public Papers of the Presidents of the United States* (8 vols.; Washington, 1961–66), pp. 263–309 (1948).

[57] Quoted in Jonathan Daniels, *The Man of Independence* (Philadelphia, 1950), p. 288. For evidence that Truman was trying to head off a bolt by liberals, see *New York Times*, August 12, 1945; Harold Smith Daily Record, August 13, 1945, Bureau of the Budget Library, Washington, D.C.

[58] Harold Stein, "Twenty Years of the Employment Act" (unpublished ms., 1965, copy in my possession), p. 2. Also see Stephen K. Bailey, *Congress Makes a Law: The Story Behind the Employment Act of 1946* (New York, 1950).

[59] Lubell, *The Future of American Politics*, pp. 8–27, while emphasizing the continuation of the prewar executive-legislative stalemate and the strength of conservative forces in the postwar years, has also been critical of Truman. "All his skills and energies . . . were directed to standing still. . . . When he took vigorous action in one direction it was axiomatic that he would contrive soon afterward to move in the conflicting direction" (p. 10). Cf. Richard Neustadt, "Congress and the Fair Deal: A Legislative Balance Sheet," in Carl Friedrich and John Galbraith, eds., *Public Policy*, V, 351–81.

about Truman and his advisers, about his unwillingness to fight for price controls, housing, benefits for labor, and civil rights, that some turned briefly to serious consideration of a new party.[60]

Achieving few reforms during his White House years, Truman, with the notable exception of civil rights, never moved significantly beyond Roosevelt. The Fair Deal was largely an extension of earlier Democratic liberalism,[61] but Truman's new vigor and fierce partisanship ultimately made him more attractive to liberals who despairingly watched the GOP-dominated Eightieth Congress and feared a repeal of the New Deal.

Their fears were unwarranted, as was their enthusiasm for the Fair Deal program. In practice it proved very limited—the housing program only provided for 810,000 units in six years of which only 60,000 were constructed;[62] social security benefits were extended to ten million[63] and increased by about 75 percent, and the minimum wage was increased to 75 cents, but coverage was reduced by nearly a million.[64] But even had all of the Fair Deal been enacted, liberal reform would have left many millions beyond the benefits of government. The very poor, the marginal men, those neglected but acknowledged by the New Deal, went ultimately unnoticed by the Fair Deal.[65]

---

[60] Curtis MacDougall, *Gideon's Army* (3 vols.; New York, 1965–66), I, 102–27. The National Educational Committee for a New Party, which would be explicitly anticommunist, included John Dewey, A. Philip Randolph, Daniel Bell, and Lewis Corey.

[61] On the continuity, see Mario Einaudi, *The Roosevelt Revolution* (New York, 1959), pp. 125, 334; Neustadt, "Congress and the Fair Deal"; Eric Goldman, *Rendezvous with Destiny* (New York, 1952), pp. 314–15; and Goldman, *The Crucial Decade and After, America 1945–1960* (New York, 1960).

[62] Richard O. Davis, *Housing Reform during the Truman Administration* (Columbia, Mo.), p. 136. The original measure aimed for 1,050,000 units in seven years, at a time when the nation needed more than 12,000,000 units to replace inadequate housing. During the Truman years, the government constructed 60,000 units of public housing (pp. 105–38). Rather than creating programs to keep pace with urban needs, the government in these years fell further behind. In contrast, private industry was more active, and it was assisted by noncontroversial federal aid. Under Truman's government, then, the greatest achievement in housing was that private capital, protected by the government, built houses for the higher-income market.

[63] Under the old law, the maximum benefit for families was $85 a month and the minimum was $15, depending on prior earnings. The new minimum was $25 and the maximum $150. (*Social Security Bulletin*, September 1950, p. 3.) Unless couples also had other sources of income, even maximum benefits ($1,800 a year) placed them $616 under the BLS "maintenance" standard of living and $109 above the WPA-based "emergency" standard of living—the poverty level. (Calculations based on Kolko, *Wealth and Power*, pp. 96–98.) Since the payments were based on earnings, lower-income groups would receive even fewer benefits. They were the people generally without substantial savings or significant supplementary sources of income, and therefore they needed even more, not less, assistance.

[64] *Congressional Quarterly Almanac*, V (1949), 434–35.

[65] Bernstein, "Economic Policies of the Truman Administration." Truman had achieved very little: improved unemployment benefits, some public power and conservation projects,

While liberals frequently chafed under Truman's leadership and questioned his commitment, they failed generally to recognize how shallow were his reforms. As the nation escaped a postwar depression, American liberals gained new faith in the American economy. Expressing their enthusiasm, they came to extoll big business for its contributions. Believing firmly in the success of progressive taxation, they exaggerated its effects, and congratulated themselves on the redistribution of income and the virtual abolition of poverty. Praising the economic system, they accepted big agriculture and big labor as evidence of healthy pluralism that protected freedom and guaranteed an equitable distribution of resources.[66]

Despite the haggling over details and the liberals' occasional dismay at Truman's style, he expressed many of their values. Like Roosevelt, Truman never challenged big business, never endangered large-scale capitalism. Indeed, his efforts as well as theirs were directed largely to maintaining and adjusting the powers of the major economic groups.

Fearing that organized labor was threatened with destruction, Truman, along with the liberals, had been sincerely frightened by the postwar rancor toward labor.[67] What they failed to understand was that most Americans had accepted unions as part of the political economy. Certainly most major industrialists had accepted organized labor, though smaller businessmen were often hostile.[68] Despite the overwrought rhetoric of debates, Congress did not actually menace labor. It was not seeking to destroy labor, only to restrict its power.

Many Americans did believe that the Wagner Act had unduly favored labor and was creating unions indifferent to the public welfare and hostile to corporate power. Capitalizing on this exaggerated fear of excessive union power, and the resentment from the postwar strikes, businessmen secured the Taft-Hartley Act.[69] Designed to weaken organized labor, it tried but failed to protect the membership from leaders; it did not effectively chal-

---

agricultural assistance, and a National Science Foundation. He failed to secure the ill-conceived Brannan Plan and two programs suggested by Roosevelt: federal aid to education and health insurance. For his health insurance programs, see his messages of November 19, 1945, in *Public Papers of Truman* (1945), pp. 485–90, and of May 19, 1947, in *ibid.* (1947), pp. 250–52. In 1951, when the BLS calculated that a family of four needed $4,166 to reach the "maintenance" level, 55.6 percent of the nation's families had incomes beneath that level (Bureau of the Census, *Income Distribution in the United States*, p. 16.).

[66] Bernstein, "Economic Policies of the Truman Administration."

[67] Truman to William Green, September 13, 1952, PPF 85, Truman Papers, Truman Library.

[68] Wilcock, "Industrial Management's Policies Toward Unionism," pp. 305–11; "Public Opinion on the Case Bill," OF 407B, Truman Papers, Truman Library; Robert Brady, *Business as a System of Power* (New York, 1943), pp. 210–15; Harry Millis and Emily Clark Brown, *From the Wagner Act to Taft-Hartley* (Chicago, 1950), pp. 286–98.

[69] R. Alton Lee, *Truman and Taft-Hartley: A Question of Mandate* (Lexington, Ky., 1966), pp. 22–71.

lenge the power of established unions. However, labor chiefs, recalling the bitter industrial warfare of the thirties, were still uneasy in their new positions. Condemning the legislation as a "slave-labor" act, they responded with fear, assailed the Congress, and declared that Taft-Hartley was the major political issue.[70]

Within a few years, when unions discovered that they were safe, Taft-Hartley faded as an issue. But in 1948 it served Truman well by establishing the GOP's hostility to labor and casting it back into the Democratic ranks. Both the President and union chiefs conveniently neglected his own kindling of antilabor passions (as when he had tried to draft strikers).[71] Exploiting Taft-Hartley as part of his strategy of patching the tattered Democratic coalition, Truman tied repeal of the "slave-labor" law to price controls, farm benefits, anticommunism, and civil rights in the campaign which won his election in his own right.

In courting the Negro the Truman administration in 1948 made greater promises to black citizens than had any previous federal government in American history. Yet, like many Americans, Truman as a senator had regarded the Negro's plight as peripheral to his interests, and with many of his generation he believed that equality was compatible with segregation.[72] As President, however, he found himself slowly prodded by conscience and pushed by politics. He moved cautiously at first and endorsed only measures affirming legal equality and protecting Negroes from violence.

Reluctant to fragment the crumbling Democratic coalition, Truman, in his first year, had seemed to avoid taking positions on civil rights which might upset the delicate balance between Northern and Southern Democrats. While he endorsed legislation for a statutory FEPC that the Congress would not grant, his efforts on behalf of the temporary FEPC (created by Roosevelt's executive order) were weaker. Having already weakened the power of the temporary agency, he also acquiesced in the legislative decision to kill it.[73] Despite the fears of Negro leaders that the death of FEPC would leave Negroes virtually unprotected from discrimination in the postwar job market, Truman would not even issue an order requiring nondiscrimination in the federal service and by government contractors.[74]

---

[70] Lee, *Truman and Taft-Hartley*, pp. 79–130.

[71] Truman's message to Congress, May 25, 1946, in *Public Papers of Truman* (1946), pp. 277–80.

[72] Truman's address of July 14, 1940, reprinted in *Congressional Record*, 76th Cong., 3rd Sess., 5367–69.

[73] Ruchames, *Race, Jobs & Politics*, pp. 130–36. This section relies upon Bernstein, "The Ambiguous Legacy: The Truman Administration and Civil Rights" (paper given at the AHA, December 1966; copy at the Truman Library).

[74] Truman to David Niles, July 22, 1946, and drafts (undated) of an order on nondiscrimination; and Philleo Nash to Niles (undated), Nash Files, Truman Library.

Though Truman was unwilling to use the prestige or power of his great office significantly on behalf of Negroes, he did assist their cause. While sidestepping political conflict, he occasionally supported FEPC and abolition of the poll tax. When Negroes were attacked, he did condemn the racial violence.[75] Though generally reluctant to move beyond rhetoric during his early years, Truman, shortly before the 1946 election, found conscience and politics demanding more. So distressed was he by racial violence that when Walter White of the NAACP and a group of white liberals urged him to assist the Negro, he promised to create a committee to study civil rights.[76]

The promise of a committee could have been a device to resist pressures, to delay the matter until after the election. And Truman could have appointed a group of politically safe men of limited reputation—men he could control. But instead, after the election, perhaps in an effort to mobilize the liberals for 1948, he appointed a committee of prominent men sympathetic to civil rights. They were men he could not control and did not seek to control.[77]

The committee's report, undoubtedly far bolder than Truman's expectations,[78] confirmed charges that America treated its Negroes as second-class citizens. It called for FEPC, an antilynching law, an anti-poll tax measure, abolition of segregation in interstate transportation, and the end of discrimination and segregation in federal agencies and the military. By attacking Jim Crow, the committee had moved to a redefinition of equality and interpreted segregation as incompatible with equality.[79]

Forced by the report to take a position, he no longer could easily remain an ally of Southern Democrats and maintain the wary allegiance of Negro leaders and urban liberals. Compelled earlier to yield to demands for advancement of the Negro, pressures which he did not wish fully to resist, Truman had encouraged these forces and they were moving beyond his control. On his decision, his political future might precariously rest. Threatened by Henry Wallace's candidacy on a third-party ticket, Truman had to take a bold position on civil rights or risk losing the important votes of urban Negroes. Though he might antagonize Southern voters, he foresaw no risk of losing Southern Democrats, no possibility of a bolt by dissidents, and the mild Southern response to the Civil Rights Report seemed to confirm this judgment.[80]

---

[75] Truman to Walter White, June 11, 1946, PPF 393, Truman Papers, Truman Library.

[76] Walter White, *A Man Called White* (New York, 1948), pp. 331–32.

[77] Robert Carr to Bernstein, August 11, 1966.

[78] Interview with Philleo Nash, September 19, 1966.

[79] President's Committee on Civil Rights, *To Secure These Rights* (Washington, 1947), pp. 1–95.

[80] Clark Clifford, "Memorandum for the President," November 17, 1947, Clifford Papers (his possession), Washington, D.C.

On February 2, 1948, Truman asked the Congress to enact most of the recommendations of his Civil Rights Committee (except most of those attacking segregation). Rather than using his executive powers, as the committee had urged, to end segregation in federal employment or to abolish segregation and discrimination in the military, he *promised* only to issue orders ending discrimination (but not specifying segregation) in the military and in federal agencies.[81] Retreating to moderation, the administration did not submit any of the legislation, nor did Truman issue the promised executive orders. "The strategy," an assistant later explained, "was to start with a bold measure and then temporize to pick up the right-wing forces. Simply stated, backtrack after the bang."[82]

Truman sought to ease Southern doubts by inserting in the 1948 platform the party's moderate 1944 plank on civil rights. Most Negro leaders, fearing the taint of Wallace and unwilling to return to the GOP, appeared stuck with Truman and they praised him. Though they desired a stronger plank, they would not abandon him at the convention, for his advocacy of rights for Negroes was unmatched by any twentieth-century president. To turn their backs on him in this time of need, most Negroes feared, would be injuring their own cause. But others were prepared to struggle for a stronger plank. Urban bosses, persuaded that Truman would lose, hoped to save their local tickets, and prominent white liberals sought power and principle. Triumphing at the convention, they secured a stronger plank, but it did not promise social equality. By promising equality when it was still regarded as compatible with segregation, they were offering far less than the "walk forthrightly into the bright sunshine of human rights," which Hubert Humphrey, then mayor of Minneapolis, had pledged in leading the liberal effort.[83]

When some of the Southerners bolted and formed the States Rights party, Truman was freed of any need for tender courtship of the South. He had to capture the Northern vote. Quickly he issued the long-delayed executive orders, which established a federal antidiscrimination board, declared a policy of equal opportunity in the armed forces, and established a committee to end military discrimination and segregation. (In doing so, Truman courted Negro voters and halted the efforts of A. Philip Randolph to lead a Negro revolt against the draft unless the military was integrated.[84]) Playing politics carefully during the campaign, Truman generally stayed away from civil rights and concentrated on inflation, public housing, and Taft-Hartley.

---

[81] Truman's message to Congress, February 2, 1948, in *Public Papers of Truman* (1948), pp. 117–26.

[82] Interview with Nash.

[83] On the struggle, see Clifton Brock, *Americans for Democratic Action: Its Role in National Politics* (Washington, 1962), pp. 94–99; quotation at p. 98.

[84] Grant Reynolds, "A Triumph for Civil Disobedience," *Nation*, CLXVI (August 28, 1948), pp. 228–29.

In the new Democratic Congress Truman could not secure the civil rights program, and a coalition of Southern Democrats and Northern Republicans blocked his efforts. Though liberals were unhappy with his leadership, they did not question his proposed legislation. All agreed on the emphasis on social change through legislation and judicial decisions. The liberal way was the legal way, and it seldom acknowledged the depth of American racism or even considered the possibility of bold new tactics. Only occasionally—in the threatened March on Washington in 1941, in some ride-ins in 1947,[85] and in the campaign of civil disobedience against the draft in 1948—had there been bolder means. In each case Negroes had devised and carried out these tactics. But generally they relied upon more traditional means: they expected white America to yield to political pressure and subscribe to the dictates of American democracy. By relying upon legal change, however, and by emphasizing measures to restore a *modicum* of human dignity, Negroes and whites did not confront the deeper problems of race relations which they failed to understand.[86]

Struggling for moderate institutional changes, liberals were disappointed by Truman's frequent unwillingness to use his executive powers in behalf of the cause he claimed to espouse. Only after considerable pressure did he create a FEPC-type agency during the Korean War.[87] His loyalty-and-security program, in its operation, discriminated against Negroes, and federal investigators, despite protests to Truman, apparently continued to inquire into attitudes of inter-racial sympathy as evidence relevant to a determination of disloyalty.[88] He was also slow to require the Federal Housing Administration to stop issuing mortgages on property with restrictive covenants, and it continued, by its policies, to protect residential segregation.[89]

Yet his government was not without significant achievements in civil rights. His special committee had quietly acted to integrate the armed

[85] George Houser and Bayard Rustin, "Journey of Reconciliation" (mimeo, n.d., probably 1947), Core Files, Schomburg Collection, New York Public Library.

[86] There was no urging of special programs to assist Negroes left unemployed (at roughly double the white rate) in the mild recession of 1949–1950, nor was there open acknowledgement of race hatred.

[87] National Council of Negro Women to Truman, November 18, 1950, Nash Files, Truman Library; Senator William Benton to Truman, October 21, 1951, OF 526B, Truman Library.

[88] Carl Murphy to Truman, April 10, 1950, OF 93 misc.; Walter White to Truman, November 26, 1948, OF 252K; both in Truman Library.

[89] NAACP press release, February 4, 1949, Schomburg Collection, New York Public Library; Hortense Gabel to Raymond Foley, February 26, 1953, Foley Papers, Truman Library; Housing and Home Finance Agency, *Fifth Annual Report* (Washington, 1952), p. 413.

forces,[90] and even the recalcitrant Army had abolished racial quotas when the President secretly promised their restoration if the racial imbalance became severe.[91] And the Department of Justice, despite Truman's apparent indifference,[92] had been an active warrior in the battle against Jim Crow. Entering cases as an *amicus curiae*, Justice had submitted briefs arguing the unconstitutionality of enforcing restrictive covenants and of requiring separate-but-equal facilities in interstate transportation and in higher education.[93] During the summer of 1952, the Solicitor-General's Office even won the administration's approval for a brief directly challenging segregated primary education.[94]

The accomplishments of the Truman years were moderate, and the shortcomings left the nation with a great burden of unresolved problems. Viewed from the perspective of today, Truman's own views seem unduly mild and his government excessively cautious; viewed even by his own time he was a reluctant liberal, troubled by terror and eager to establish limited equality. He was ahead of public opinion in his legislative requests, but not usually in his actions. By his occasional advocacy, he educated the nation and held high the promise of equality. By kindling hope, he also may have prevented rebellion and restrained or delayed impulses to work outside of the system. But he also unleashed expectations he could not foresee, and forces which future governments would not be able to restrain.

Never as committed to civil rights as he was opposed to communism at home and abroad, Truman ultimately became a victim of his own loyalty-and-security policies. Mildly criticized in 1945 and 1946 for being "soft on communism," the administration belatedly responded after the disastrous election of 1946.[95] Truman appointed a committee to investigate loyalty and security, promptly accepted its standard of judgment ("reasonable grounds of belief in disloyalty"), and created a system of loyalty boards.[96]

---

[90] President's Committee on Equality of Treatment and Opportunity in the Armed Forces, *Freedom to Serve* (Washington 1950); Dalfiume, "Desegregation of the Armed Forces."

[91] Gordon Gray to Truman, March 1, 1950, OF 1285B, Truman Library.

[92] Interview with Philip Elman, December 21, 1966.

[93] *Shelley* v. *Kraemer*, 334 US 1; *Henderson* v. *United States* 339 US 816; *McLaurin* v. *Board of Regents*, 339 US 641.

[94] Interview with Elman; *Brown* v. *Board of Education*, 347 US 483.

[95] "The Report of the President's Temporary Commission on Employee Loyalty," Appendix III, Charles Murphy Papers, Truman Library; Rep. Jennings Bryan to Truman, July 25, 1946, OF 2521, and Stephen Spingarn, "Notes on Meeting of Subcommittee of February 5, 1947," Spingarn Papers, Truman Library.

[96] E.O. 9806, 11 Fed. Reg. 13863; "The Report of the President's Temporary Commission on Employee Loyalty," quotation at 3; E.O. 9835, 12 F.R. 1935. On earlier programs, see Eleanor Bontecou, *The Federal Loyalty-Security Program* (Ithaca, N.Y., 1953), pp. 1–19.

Outraging many liberals, his loyalty program provoked vigorous criticisms—for its secret investigations, for the failure to guarantee the accused the right to know the identity of and cross-examine the accuser, for its loose standards of proof, for its attempt to anticipate disloyal behavior by inquiring into attitudes.[97] In seeking to protect the nation, the government seemed to be searching for all who *might* be disloyal—"potential subversives," Truman called them.[98]

Dangerously confusing the problems of loyalty and security, the administration, in what might seem a burst of democratic enthusiasm, decided to apply the same standards to diplomats and gardeners. Disloyalty at any level of government would endanger the nation. "The presence within the government of any disloyal or subversive persons constitutes a threat to democratic processes," asserted Truman in launching the program.[99] Anxious to remove communism in government as a possible issue, Truman had exaggerated the dangers to the nation. And by assuming that disloyalty could be determined and subversives discovered, Truman seemed also to be promising *absolute* internal security.[100]

Shocked by earlier lax security procedures and unwilling to rely exclusively upon counterintelligence to uncover spies, the administration had responded without proper concern for civil liberties. So extreme was the program that it should have removed loyalty and security as a political issue. But by failing to distinguish between radical political activity and disloyalty, the administration endangered dissent and liberal politics: it made present or past membership in organizations on the Attorney-General's list evidence of possible disloyalty. Thus, in justifying investigations of political activity, it also legitimized occasional right-wing attacks on the liberal past and encouraged emphasis on the radicalism of a few New Dealers as evidence of earlier subversion.[101]

---

[97] Letter by Zechariah Chafee, Jr., Erwin Griswold, Milton Katz, and Austin Scott, in *New York Times*, April 13, 1947; L. A. Nikoloric, "The Government Loyalty Program," *American Scholar*, XIX (Summer 1950), 285–98; Bontecou, *Federal Loyalty-Security Program*, pp. 30–34.

[98] Quoted from Bontecou, *Federal Loyalty-Security Program*, p. 32, who suggests that Truman may have really meant Communists who might be subject to future orders by the party. Also see Truman's statement of November 14, 1947, in *Public Papers of Truman* (1947), pp. 489–91.

[99] Quoted from E.O. 9835, 12 Fed. Reg. 1935.

[100] Much of the analysis of this program and its contribution to the rise of McCarthyism is indebted to Athan Theoharis, "The Rhetoric of Politics: Foreign Policy, Internal Security and Domestic Politics in the Truman Era, 1945–1950" (paper delivered at the Southern Historical Association, November 1966). Cf. Daniel Bell, ed., *The New American Right* (New York, 1955). On the need for absolute security, see Tom Clark to A. Devitt Vanech, February 14, 1947, OF 2521, Truman Library; "Report of the President's Temporary Commission on Employee Loyalty"; Theoharis, "Rhetoric of Politics," pp. 26–32.

[101] Theoharis, "Rhetoric of Politics," pp. 29–31.

In their own activities, many liberals were busy combatting domestic communism. Taking up the cudgels, the liberal Americans for Democratic Action (ADA) came often to define its purpose by its anticommunism. As an enemy of those liberals who would not renounce association with Communists, and, hence, as vigorous foes of the Progressive party, the ADA was prepared to do battle. Following Truman's strategy, ADA members assailed Wallace and his supporters as Communists, dupes of the Communists, and fellow travelers. To publicize its case the ADA even relied upon the tactic of guilt by association and paid for advertisements listing the Progressive party's major donors and the organizations on the Attorney-General's list with which they were or had been affiliated.[102] (Truman himself also red-baited. "I do not want and will not accept the political support of Henry Wallace and his Communists. . . . These are days of high prices for everything, but any price for Wallace and his Communists is too much for me to pay.") [103] In the labor movement liberals like the Reuther brothers led anticommunist crusades, and the CIO ultimately expelled its Communist-led unions. ("Granting the desirability of eliminating Communist influence from the trade union movement," later wrote Irving Howe and Louis Coser, "one might still have argued that mass expulsions were not only a poor way of achieving this end but constituted a threat to democratic values and procedures.") [104]

Expressing the administration's position, Attorney-General J. Howard McGrath proclaimed a "struggle against pagan communist philosophies that seek to enslave the world." "There are today many Communists in America," he warned. "They are everywhere—in factories, offices, butcher stores, on street corners, in private business. And each carries in himself the death of our society." [105] ("I don't think anybody ought to be employed as instructors [sic] for the young people of this country who believes in the destruction of our form of government," declared Truman.) [106]

---

[102] Karl M. Schmidt, *Henry A. Wallace: Quixotic Crusade, 1948* (Syracuse, N.Y., 1960), pp. 159–60, 252–53, 261–62. On the strategy of letting the liberal intellectuals attack Wallace, see Clifford, "Memorandum for the President," November 17, 1947. On the split in liberal ranks on cooperation with Communists, see Curtis MacDougall, *Gideon's Army,* I, 122–25.

[103] Truman's address of March 17, 1948, in *Public Papers of Truman* (1948), p. 189.

[104] Howe and Coser, *The American Communist Party,* 2nd ed. (New York, 1962), p. 468; see pp. 457–68 for the activity of labor.

[105] McGrath's address of April 8, 1949, McGrath Papers, Truman Library, which was called to my attention by Theoharis. Also see Theoharis, "Rhetoric of Politics," n. 37.

[106] Quoted from transcript of President's News Conference of June 9, 1949, Truman Library. Also see Sidney Hook, "Academic Integrity and Academic Freedom," *Commentary,* VIII (October 1949), cf., Alexander Meiklejohn, *New York Times Magazine,* March 27, 1949, pp. 10ff. In his veto of the McCarran Act, Truman failed to defend civil liberties effectively and instead emphasized that the act would impair the government's anticommunist efforts. Veto message of September 22, 1950, *Public Papers of Truman* (1950), pp. 645–53.

Calling for a crusade against evil, viewing communism as a virulent poison, the administration continued to emphasize the need for *absolute* protection, for *absolute* security. By creating such high standards and considering their fulfillment easy, by making success evidence of will and resolution, the administration risked assaults if its loyalty-and-security program was proved imperfect. To discredit the administration, all that was needed was the discovery of some red "spies," and after 1948 the evidence seemed abundant—Alger Hiss, William Remington, Judith Coplon, Julius and Ethel Rosenberg.[107]

In foreign policy, too, Truman, though emphasizing the danger of communism, had promised success. Containment could stop the spread of communism: military expansion could be restrained and revolutions prevented. Since revolutions, by liberal definition, were imposed on innocent people by a small minority, a vigilant American government could block them. By his rhetoric, he encouraged American innocence and left many citizens little choice but to believe in their own government's failure when America could not thwart revolution—when the Chinese Communists triumphed. If only resolute will was necessary, as the administration suggested, then what could citizens believe about America's failure? Was it simply bungling? Or treason and betrayal? [108]

By his rhetoric and action, Truman had contributed to the loss of public confidence, and set the scene in which Joseph McCarthy could flourish. Rather than resisting the early movement of anticommunism, he had acted energetically to become a leader, and ultimately contributed to its transformation into a crusade which threatened his administration. But the President could never understand his own responsibility, and his failure handicapped him. Because he had a record of vigorous anticommunism, Truman was ill-prepared to respond to McCarthy's charges. At first the President could not foresee any danger and tried to dispense with McCarthy as "the greatest asset the Kremlin has." [109] And later, as the Senator terrorized the government, Truman was so puzzled and pained that he retreated from the conflict and sought to starve McCarthy without publicity. Rather than responding directly to charges, the President tried instead to tighten his program. But he could not understand that such efforts (for example, revising the loyalty standard to "reasonable doubt as to the loyalty of the individual") [110] could not protect the administration from charges of being soft on

---

[107] Theoharis, "Rhetoric of Politics," pp. 32–38.

[108] See Truman's addresses of March 17, 1948, in *Public Papers of Truman* (1948), pp. 182–86; and of June 7, 1949, in *ibid.* (1949), pp. 277–80. See Theoharis, "Rhetoric of Politics," pp. 17–27.

[109] Quoted from transcript of President's News Conference, March 30, 1950, Truman Library.

[110] E.O. 10241, 16 Fed. Reg. 9795.

communism. He only encouraged these charges by seeming to yield to criticism, admitting that the earlier program was unnecessarily lax.

The President was a victim of his own policies and tactics. But bristling anticommunism was not simply Truman's way, but often the liberal way.[111] And the use of guilt by association, the discrediting of dissent, the intemperate rhetoric—these, too, were not simply the tactics of the Truman administration. The rancor and wrath of these years were not new to American politics, nor to liberals.[112] Indeed, the style of passionate charges and impugning opponents' motives may be endemic to American democratic politics. Submerging the issues in passion, using labels as substitutes for thought, questioning motives, these tactics characterized much of the foreign policy debate of the prewar and postwar years as well—a debate in which the liberals frequently triumphed. Developing a more extreme form of this rancorous style, relying upon even wilder charges and more flagrant use of guilt by association, McCarthy and his cohorts flailed the liberals and the Democratic administration.

In looking at the war and postwar years, liberal scholars have emphasized the achievements of democratic reform, the extension of prosperity, the movements to greater economic and social equality. Confident that big business had become socially responsible and that economic security was widespread, they have celebrated the triumph of democratic liberalism. In charting the course of national progress, they frequently neglected or minimized major problems, or they interpreted them as temporary aberrations, or blamed them on conservative forces.[113]

Yet the developments of the sixties—the rediscovery of poverty and racism—suggest that the emphasis has been misplaced in interpreting these earlier years. In the forties and fifties white racism did not greatly yield to the dictates of American democracy, and the failure was not only the South's. The achievements of democratic liberalism were more limited than its advocates believed, and its reforms left many Americans still without adequate assistance. Though many liberal programs were blocked or diluted by conservative opposition, the liberal vision itself was dim. Liberalism in practice was defective, and its defects contributed to the temporary success of Mc-

---

[111] On liberal confusion about this period, see Joseph Rauh, "The Way to Fight Communism," *Future*, January 1962. For the argument that liberal naiveté about Stalinism had led to McCarthyism, see Irving Kristol, "Civil Liberties, 1952—A Study in Confusion," *Commentary*, XIII (March 1952), 228–36.

[112] For earlier antitotalitarianism, see Freda Kirchway, "Curb the Fascist Press," *Nation*, CLIV (March 28, 1942), 357–58.

[113] Although there are no thorough, scholarly histories of these years, there are many texts that embody these characteristics. In addition, much of the monographic literature by other social scientists conforms to the pattern described in this paragraph. For a discussion, see Bernstein, "Economic Policies of the Truman Administration."

Carthyism. Curiously, though liberalism was scrutinized by some sympathizers [114] who attacked its faith in progress and by others who sought to trace McCarthyism to the reform impulses of earlier generations,[115] most liberals failed to understand their own responsibility for the assault upon civil liberties or to respond to the needs of an "other America" which they but dimly perceived.

SUGGESTED READING

Scholars are just beginning to explore the history of domestic America during the war and early postwar years. Roland Young's *Congressional Politics in the Second World War* (Columbia Univ. Press, 1956) and Joel Seidman's *American Labor from Defense to Reconversion* (Univ. of Chicago Press, 1953) are useful surveys of their subjects. Richard M. Dalfiume in "The 'Forgotten Years' of the Negro Revolution," *Journal of American History*, LV (June, 1968), 90–106, finds the sources of the Negro "revolution" in the war years. *America at War,*° edited by Richard Polenberg (Prentice-Hall, 1968), provides important documents on the war years.

A forthcoming volume, *The Politics and Policies of the Truman Administration,* edited by Barton J. Bernstein (Quadrangle, 1969), includes essays critical of the Administration's policies in civil rights and civil liberties. Eleanor Bontecou in *The Federal Loyalty-Security Program* (Cornell Univ. Press, 1953) also evaluates that program; and Earl Latham in *The Communist Controversy in Washington* (Harvard Univ. Press, 1966) concludes that significant communist espionage in the Federal government did exist.

Irwin Ross's *The Loneliest Campaign* (New American Library, 1968) is a superficial account of the 1948 election. Samuel Lubell's *The Future of American Politics* ° (Doubleday, 1956, rev. ed.) is a fine analysis of ethnic groups, politics, and the Truman Administration.

Richard Neustadt, former assistant to both Truman and Kennedy, has published a sympathetic assessment of the Truman Administration in "Congress and the Fair Deal: A Legislative Balance Sheet," in Carl Friedrich and John K. Galbraith, eds., *Public Policy,* V (1954), 351–81.

---

[114] In particular see the works of Reinhold Niebuhr and the new realism that he has influenced: Niebuhr, *Moral Man and Immoral Society* (New York, 1932); *The Children of Light and the Children of Darkness* (New York, 1944); Arthur Schlesinger, Jr., *The Vital Center* (Cambridge, Mass., 1947). What is needed is a critical study of wartime and postwar liberalism, an explanation for many on "Where We Came Out" (to use the title of Granville Hicks's volume). See Jason Epstein, "The CIA and the Intellectuals," *New York Review of Books,* VII (April 20, 1967), 16–21.

[115] See Bell, ed., *The New American Right,* and the tendency to trace McCarthyism back to earlier reform movements and often to Populism. The volume, interestingly, is dedicated to the managing editor of the *New Leader.* For a former radical's attempt to reappraise the liberal past, see Richard Hofstadter, *The Age of Reform* (New York, 1956).

Allen J. Matusow in *Farm Politics and Policies of the Truman Years* (Harvard Univ. Press, 1967) is critical of the Administration, but Richard C. Davies in *Housing Reform During the Truman Administration* (Univ. of Missouri Press, 1966) is more favorable.

Jonathan Daniels' *The Man of Independence* (Lippincott, 1950) is a flattering study by one of Truman's early assistants. Richard Rovere's "President Harry," *Harper's*, CXCVII (July, 1948), 27–35, and "Truman After Seven Years," *ibid.*, CCIV (May, 1952), 27–33, are contemporary evaluations. The President's own memoirs, *Year of Decisions* ° (Doubleday, 1955) and *Years of Trial and Hope* ° (Doubleday, 1956), are rich but—like most partly ghostwritten recollections—not always reliable.

GAR ALPEROVITZ

Why We Dropped the Bomb

INTRODUCTION

In the decade after Hiroshima, very few Americans were troubled by their nation's use of atomic weapons against Japan, and those who expressed doubts usually confined them to moral considerations. Most citizens seemed content to agree with President Harry S Truman that the bomb "saved millions of lives," meaning principally the American soldiers who might otherwise have been lost in the invasion of Japan.

Though Truman's explanation may have allayed creeping doubts for some at that time, it also glosses over important facts and obscures chronology. In July and August of 1945, the means by

FROM Gar Alperovitz, "Why We Dropped the Bomb," *The Progressive* (August, 1965), pp. 11–14. Another version of this essay appears in *Atomic Diplomacy: Hiroshima and Potsdam;* copyright © 1965 by Gar Alperovitz. Reprinted by permission of Simon & Schuster, Inc.

377

which to defeat Japan were not simply the atomic bomb or imminent invasion. There were also the possibilities of pursuing peace feelers from the Japanese or awaiting Russian entry into the Pacific war, which might have induced the Japanese to surrender. And the invasion of Japan, in which MacArthur anticipated only "light casualties," was planned not for August but for early November. (The large-scale invasion, which Truman cited as justification for using the bomb, was not scheduled until the following spring.) Thus Truman never confronted what now seems to be the relevant question: Why did the United States *rush* to use the bomb without first testing other ways to end the war?

In 1948, P. M. S. Blackett, British Nobel Laureate in physics, contended that "the dropping of the atomic bombs was not so much the last military act of the second World War, as the first major operation of the cold diplomatic war with Russia. . . ." (*Fear, War, and the Bomb* [Whittsley, 1948]). He argued that the bomb had been unnecessary to end the Japanese war, and he emphasized that American policy-makers had not pursued other paths to peace. Blackett concluded that the Administration was precipitous in using the bomb because it wanted to end the war before Russian armies could gain a toehold in Manchuria and to prevent the Soviet Union from demanding an equal voice in the postwar occupation of Japan.

Critics rightly pointed out that much of Blackett's argument rested on conjecture, that it imposed on complex decisions a rationality rarely present, and that it conflicted with published recollections by the decision-makers, especially with the influential article by former Secretary of War Henry L. Stimson in *Harper's,* "The Decision to Use the Atomic Bomb" (CLCIV, Feb., 1947, 97–107). Only later did manuscript material supporting Blackett's view become available. For instance, in his diary on July 28, 1945, Secretary of the Navy James Forrestal reported that Secretary of State James F. Byrnes "said he was most anxious to get the Japanese affair over with before the Russians got in, with particular reference to Dairen and Port Arthur. Once in there, he felt, it would not be easy to get them out. . . ." (Walter Millis, ed., *The Forrestal Diaries* [Viking, 1956]). Another rich source of evidence revealing that relations with Russia affected the A-bomb decision is the collection of Stimson's papers, now at Yale University.

It was the Stimson papers that Gar Alperovitz heavily relied on in the early 1960's when he wrote his important book *Atomic Diplomacy* (Simon & Schuster, 1965), from which the article reprinted below was adapted. Rather than focus directly in his book on why the bomb was used, Alperovitz concentrates on a more subtle problem: Did the bomb influence the formation of American policy during the months between Truman's assumption of office and the explosions at Hiroshima and Nagasaki? Ascribing to Truman a mastery of details and skill as a diplomatic strategist that some other "revisionist" historians would deny, Alperovitz finds in the seemingly convoluted policies of the Administration an underlying pattern of intelligence. Truman, he argues, delayed a meeting of the Big Three and even a confrontation with Stalin over Poland because he wanted first to ascertain the success of the bomb, in which case he expected that the Russians would become more tractable.

Alperovitz's subtle thesis has frequently been misunderstood by unfriendly critics, but more sympathetic scholars have also raised some problems. Much of the evidence about the Administration's strategy rests on the Stimson papers, but it is not clear whether they constitute a thoroughly reliable source of information on Truman's intentions. Evidence exists indicating that the President, who greatly respected Stimson, often deferred to the Secretary in his presence but did not necessarily follow his counsel. Indeed, at Potsdam, where, according to Alperovitz, the bomb shaped Truman's responses, Stimson tagged along with Truman's retinue and was shunted to the sidelines. Furthermore, much of Alperovitz's additional evidence comes not from documents contemporaneous with the events but from articles and books written after the Cold War had hardened and that are perhaps influenced by the events after 1945—for example, Truman's *Memoirs* (Doubleday, 1955), Byrnes' *Speaking Frankly* (Harper & Row, 1947), the speech of Leo Szilard, "A Personal History of the Atomic Bomb," University of Chicago *Roundtable*, No. 601 (Sept. 25, 1949), 10–15.

But even those who would reject many of the details of Alperovitz's argument must now acknowledge on the basis of his evidence that the bomb did influence American foreign policy before Potsdam. And there are additional materials in manuscript collections—such as the papers of Joseph Davies, former ambassador to Russia—that Alperovitz did not exploit but that support some of his contentions. For example, on May 21, 1945, Truman confided to Davies that he was postponing the Potsdam conference until July, when he expected to know whether the atomic bomb worked. And there is ample evidence on the state of mind of Secretary of State James F. Byrnes—more so than on that of Truman. At Potsdam, for example, on July 29, 1945, Davies recorded, "Byrnes suggested that the New Mexico situation [the bomb] had given us great power, and that in the last analysis, it would control."

Dear Mr. President,

I think it is very important that I should have a talk with you as soon as possible on a highly secret matter. I mentioned it to you shortly after you took office, but have not urged it since on account of the pressure you have been under. It, however, has such a bearing on our present foreign relations and

*has such an important effect upon all my thinking in this field that I think you
ought to know about it without much further delay.*

— Secretary of War Henry L.
Stimson to President Truman,
April 24, 1945

*T*his note was written twelve days after Franklin Delano
Roosevelt's death and two weeks before World War II ended in Europe. The
following day Secretary Stimson advised President Truman that the "highly
secret matter" would have a "decisive" effect upon America's postwar foreign policy. Stimson then outlined the role the atomic bomb would play in
America's relations with other countries. In diplomacy, he confided to his
diary, the weapon would be a "master card."

In the spring of 1945, postwar problems unfolded as rapidly as the
Allied armies converged in Central Europe. During the fighting which preceded Nazi surrender the Red Army conquered a great belt of territory
bordering the Soviet Union. Debating the consequences of this fact, American policy-makers defined a series of interrelated problems: What political
and economic pattern was likely to emerge in Eastern and Central Europe?
Would Soviet influence predominate? Most important, what power—if any
—did the United States have to effect the ultimate settlement on the very
borders of Russia?

Roosevelt, Churchill, and Stalin had attempted to resolve these issues
of East-West influence at the February, 1945, Yalta Conference. With the
Red Army clearly in control of Eastern Europe, the West was in a weak bargaining position. It was important to reach an understanding with Stalin before American troops began their planned withdrawal from the European
continent. Poland, the first major country intensely discussed by the Big
Three, took on unusual significance; the balance of influence struck between
Soviet-oriented and Western-oriented politicians in the government of this
one country could set a pattern for big-power relationships in the rest of
Eastern Europe.

Although the Yalta Conference ended with a signed accord covering
Poland, within a few weeks it was clear that Allied understanding was more
apparent than real. None of the heads of government interpreted the somewhat vague agreement in the same way. Churchill began to press for more
Western influence; Stalin urged less. True to his well-known policy of cooperation and conciliation, Roosevelt attempted to achieve a more definite
understanding for Poland and a pattern for East-West relations in Europe.
Caught for much of the last of his life between the determination of Churchill
and the stubbornness of Stalin, Roosevelt at times fired off angry cables to
Moscow, and at others warned London against an "attempt to evade the fact
that we placed, as clearly shown in the agreement, somewhat more emphasis
. . . [on Soviet-oriented Polish politicians in the government]."

President Roosevelt died on April 12, 1945, only two months after

Yalta. When President Truman met with Secretary Stimson to discuss the "bearing" of the atomic bomb upon foreign relations, the powers were deeply ensnarled in a tense public struggle over the meaning of the Yalta agreement. Poland had come to symbolize *all* East-West relations. Truman was forced to pick up the tangled threads of policy with little knowledge of the broader, more complex issues involved.

Herbert Feis, a noted expert on the period, has written that "Truman made up his mind that he would not depart from Roosevelt's course or renounce his ways." Others have argued that "we tried to work out the problems of the peace in close cooperation with the Russians." It is often believed that American policy followed a conciliatory course, changing—in reaction to Soviet intransigence—only in 1947 with the Truman Doctrine and the Marshall Plan. My own belief is somewhat different. It derives from the comment of Mr. Truman's Secretary of State, James F. Byrnes, that by early autumn of 1945 it was "understandable" that Soviet leaders should feel American policy had shifted radically after Roosevelt's death: It is now evident that, far from following his predecessor's policy of cooperation, shortly after taking office President Truman launched a powerful foreign policy initiative aimed at reducing or eliminating Soviet influence in Europe.

The ultimate point of this study is not, however, that America's approach to Russia changed after Roosevelt. Rather it is that the atomic bomb played a role in the formulation of policy, particularly in connection with President Truman's only meeting with Stalin, the Potsdam Conference of late July and early August, 1945. Again, my judgment differs from Feis's conclusion that "the light of the explosion 'brighter than a thousand suns' filtered into the conference rooms at Potsdam only as a distant gleam." I believe new evidence proves not only that the atomic bomb influenced diplomacy, but that it determined much of Mr. Truman's shift to a tough policy aimed at forcing Soviet acquiescence to American plans for Eastern and Central Europe.

The weapon "gave him an entirely new feeling of confidence," the President told his Secretary of War, Henry L. Stimson. By the time of Potsdam, Mr. Truman had been advised on the role of the atomic bomb by both Secretary Stimson and Secretary of State Byrnes. Though the two men differed as to tactics, each urged a tough line. Part of my study attempts to define how closely Truman followed a subtle policy outlined by Stimson, and to what extent he followed the straightforward advice of Byrnes that the bomb (in Mr. Truman's words) "put us in a position to dictate our own terms at the end of the war."

Stalin's approach seems to have been cautiously moderate during the brief few months here described. It is perhaps symbolized by the Soviet-sponsored free elections which routed the Communist Party in Hungary in the autumn of 1945. I do not attempt to interpret this moderation, nor to explain how or why Soviet policy changed to the harsh totalitarian controls characteristic of the period after 1946.

The judgment that Truman radically altered Roosevelt's policy in mid-1945 nevertheless obviously suggests a new point of departure for interpretations of the cold war. In late 1945, General Dwight D. Eisenhower observed in Moscow that "before the atom bomb was used, I would have said, yes, I was sure we could keep the peace with Russia. Now I don't know . . . People are frightened and disturbed all over. Everyone feels insecure again." To what extent did postwar Soviet policies derive from insecurity based upon a fear of America's atom bomb and changed policy? I stop short of this fundamental question, concluding that further research is needed to test Secretary Stimson's judgment that "the problem of our satisfactory relations with Russia [was] not merely connected with but [was] virtually dominated by the problem of the atomic bomb."

Similarly, I believe more research and more information are needed to reach a conclusive understanding of why the atomic bomb was used. The common belief is that the question is closed, and that President Truman's explanation is correct: "The dropping of the bombs stopped the war, saved millions of lives." My own view is that available evidence shows the atomic bomb was not needed to end the war or to save lives—and that this was understood by American leaders at the time.

General Eisenhower recently recalled that in mid-1945 he expressed a similar opinion to the Secretary of War: "I told him I was against it on two counts. First, the Japanese were ready to surrender and it wasn't necessary to hit them with that awful thing. Second, I hated to see our country be the first to use such a weapon . . ." To go beyond the limited conclusion that the bomb was unnecessary is not possible at present.

Perhaps the most remarkable aspect of the decision to use the atomic bomb is that the President and his senior political advisers do not seem ever to have shared Eisenhower's "grave misgivings." They simply assumed that they would use the bomb, never really giving serious consideration to not using it. Hence, to state in a precise way the question, "Why was the atomic bomb used?" is to ask why senior political officials did *not* seriously question its use, as General Eisenhower did.

The first point to note is that the decision to use the weapon did not derive from overriding military considerations. Despite Mr. Truman's subsequent statement that the weapon "saved millions of lives," Eisenhower's judgment that it was "completely unnecessary" as a measure to save lives was almost certainly correct. This is not a matter of hindsight; *before the atomic bomb was dropped each of the joint Chiefs of Staff advised that it was highly likely that Japan could be forced to surrender "unconditionally," without use of the bomb and without an invasion.* Indeed, this characterization of the position taken by the senior military advisers is a conservative one.

General George C. Marshall's June 18 appraisal was the most cautiously phrased advice offered by any of the Joint Chiefs: "The impact of Russian entry on the already hopeless Japanese may well be the decisive action levering them into capitulation. . . ." Admiral William D. Leahy was absolutely certain there was no need for the bombing to obviate the necessity of an invasion. His judgment after the fact was the same as his view before the bombing: "It is my opinion that the use of this barbarous weapon at Hiroshima and Nagasaki was of no material assistance in our war against Japan. The Japanese were already defeated and ready to surrender. . . ." Similarly, through most of 1945, Admiral Ernest J. King believed the bomb unnecessary, and Generals Henry H. Arnold and Curtis E. LeMay defined the official Air Force position in this way: Whether or not the atomic bomb should be dropped was not for the Air Force to decide, but explosion of the bomb was not necessary to win the war or make an invasion unnecessary.

Similar views prevailed in Britain long before the bombs were used. General Hastings Ismay recalls that by the time of Potsdam, "for some time past it had been firmly fixed in my mind that the Japanese were tottering." Ismay's reaction to the suggestion of the bombing was, like Eisenhower's and Leahy's, one of "revulsion." And Churchill, who as early as September, 1944, felt that Russian entry into the war with Japan was likely to force capitulation, has written: "It would be a mistake to suppose that the fate of Japan was settled by the atomic bomb. Her defeat was certain before the first bomb fell. . . ."

The military appraisals made before the weapons were used have been confirmed by numerous post-surrender studies. The best known is that of the United States Strategic Bombing Survey. The Survey's conclusion is unequivocal: "Japan would have surrendered even if the atomic bombs had not been dropped, even if Russia had not entered the war, and even if no invasion had been planned or contemplated."

That military considerations were not decisive is confirmed—and illuminated—by the fact that the President did not even ask the opinion of the military adviser most directly concerned. General Douglas MacArthur, Supreme Commander of Allied Forces in the Pacific, was simply informed of the weapon shortly before it was used at Hiroshima. Before his death he stated on numerous occasions that, like Eisenhower, he believed the atomic bomb was completely unnecessary from a military point of view.

Although military considerations were not primary, unquestionably political considerations related to Russia played a major role in the decision; from at least mid-May in 1945, American policy-makers hoped to end the hostilities before the Red Army entered Manchuria. For this reason they had no wish to test whether Russian entry into the war would force capitulation—as most thought likely—long before the scheduled November Allied invasion of Japan. Indeed, they actively attempted to delay Stalin's declaration of war.

Nevertheless, it would be wrong to conclude that the atomic bomb was used simply to keep the Red Army out of Manchuria. Given the desperate efforts of the Japanese to surrender, and President Truman's willingness to offer assurances to the Emperor, it is entirely possible that the war could have been ended by negotiation before the Red Army had begun its attack. But after history's first atomic explosion at Alamogordo neither the President nor his senior political advisers were interested in exploring this possibility.

One reason may have been their fear that if time-consuming negotiations were once initiated, the Red Army might attack in order to seize Manchurian objectives. But, if this explanation is accepted, once more one must conclude that the bomb was used primarily because it was felt to be politically important to prevent Soviet domination of the area.

Such a conclusion is difficult to accept, for American interests in Manchuria, although historically important to the State Department, were not of great significance. The further question therefore arises: Were there other political reasons for using the atomic bomb? In approaching this question, it is important to note that most of the men involved at the time who since have made their views public always mention *two* considerations which dominated discussions. The first was the desire to end the Japanese war quickly, which was not primarily a military consideration, but a political one. The second is always referred to indirectly.

In June, for example, a leading member of President Truman's Advisory Interim Committee's scientific panel, A. H. Compton, advised against the Franck report's suggestion of a technical demonstration of the new weapon: Not only was there a possibility that this might not end the war promptly, but failure to make a combat demonstration would mean the "loss of the opportunity to impress the world with the national sacrifices that enduring security demanded." The general phrasing that the bomb was needed "to impress the world" has been made more specific by J. Robert Oppenheimer. Testifying on this matter some years later he stated that the second of the two "overriding considerations" in discussions regarding the bomb was "the effect of our actions on the stability, on our strength, and the stability of the postwar world." And the problem of postwar stability was inevitably the problem of Russia. Oppenheimer has put it this way: "Much of the discussion revolved around the question raised by Secretary Stimson as to whether there was any hope at all of using this development to get less barbarous relations with the Russians."

Vannevar Bush, Stimson's chief aide for atomic matters, has been quite explicit: "That bomb was developed on time. . . ." Not only did it mean a quick end to the Japanese war, but "it was also delivered on time so that there was no necessity for any concessions to Russia at the end of the war."

In essence, the second of the two overriding considerations seems to have been that a combat demonstration was needed to convince the Russians to accept the American plan for a stable peace. And the crucial point of this effort was the need to force agreement on the main questions in dispute: the American proposals for Central and Eastern Europe. President Truman may well have expressed the key consideration in October, 1945; publicly urging the necessity of a more conventional form of military power (his proposal for universal military training), in a personal appearance before Congress, the President declared: "It is only by strength that we can impress the fact upon possible future aggressors that we will tolerate no threat to peace. . . ."

If indeed the "second consideration" involved in the bombing of Hiroshima and Nagasaki was the desire to impress the Russians, it might explain the strangely ambiguous statement by Mr. Truman that not only did the bomb end the war, but it gave the world "a chance to face the facts." It would also accord with Stimson's private advice to Assistant Secretary of War John J. McCloy: "We have got to regain the lead and perhaps do it in a pretty rough and realistic way. . . . We have coming into action a weapon which will be unique. Now the thing [to do is] . . . let our actions speak for themselves."

Again, it would accord with Stimson's statement to Mr. Truman that the "greatest complication" would occur if the President negotiated with Stalin before the bomb had been "laid on Japan." It would tie in with the fact that from mid-May, strategy toward all major diplomatic problems was based upon the assumption the bomb would be demonstrated. Finally, it might explain why none of the highest civilian officials seriously questioned the use of the bomb as Eisenhower did; for, having reversed the basic direction of diplomatic strategy *because* of the atomic bomb, it would have been difficult indeed for anyone subsequently to challenge an idea which had come to dominate all calculations of high policy.

It might also explain why the sober and self-controlled Stimson reacted so strongly when General Eisenhower objected to the bombing: "The Secretary was deeply perturbed by my attitude, almost angrily refuting the reasons I gave. . . ." Stimson's post-Hiroshima reversal, and his repeated references to the gravity of the moral issues raised by the new weapon, are evidence of his own doubts. General Eisenhower's searching criticism may well have touched upon a tender point—namely, Stimson's undoubted awareness that Hiroshima and Nagasaki were to be sacrificed primarily for political, not military, reasons.

At present no final conclusion can be reached on this question. But the problem can be defined with some precision: Why did the American government refuse to attempt to exploit Japanese efforts to surrender? Or, alternatively, why did it refuse to test whether a Russian declaration of war would force capitulation? Were Hiroshima and Nagasaki bombed primarily to impress the world with the need to accept America's plan for a stable and lasting peace—that is, primarily, America's plan for Europe? The evidence strongly suggests that the view which the President's personal representative offered to one of the atomic scientists in May, 1945, was an accurate statement of policy: "Mr. Byrnes did not argue that it was necessary to use the bomb against the cities of Japan in order to win the war. . . . Mr. Byrnes's . . . view [was] that our possessing and demonstrating the bomb would make Russia more manageable in Europe. . . ."

SUGGESTED READING

Norman Cousins and Thomas Finletter in "A Beginning of Sanity," *Saturday Review of Literature*, XXIX (June 5, 1946), 5 ff., first suggested that the bomb was used to end the war before the Russians could intervene. Blackett's analysis, mentioned in the Introduction, may be found in *Fear, War and the Bomb* (Whittsley, 1948). Louis Morton's "The Decision to Use the Atomic Bomb," *Foreign Affairs*, XXXV (Jan., 1957), 334–53, is an essay by a military historian who disagrees with the Cousins-Finletter suggestion and Blackett's analysis. Rudolph Winnacker, also a military historian, defends the realistic morality behind the decision to drop the bomb in "The Debate About Hiroshima," *Military Affairs*, XI (Spring, 1947), 25–30.

Herbert Feis's *Japan Subdued: The Atomic Bomb and the End of the War in the Pacific* (Princeton Univ. Press, 1961), for a time considered the definitive volume on the A-bomb decision, concludes that "the impelling reason for the decision to use [the bomb] was military." Feis unaccountably either failed to use the Stimson papers or to acknowledge the evidence in these papers of intense concern before and during Potsdam about the bomb and Russia. In his first edition there is only a paragraph of conjecture about this theme, but in a revised edition, *The Atomic Bomb and the End of World War II* (Princeton Univ. Press, 1966), presumably provoked by Alperovitz, Feis treats the issue at greater length, although still without confronting the important questions directly. Gar Alperovitz's "The Trump Card," *New York Review of Books* (June 15, 1967), 7–13, is a harsh critical review of Feis's revised volume.

Gabriel Kolko in *The Politics of War* (Random House 1969) and Barton J. Bernstein in Bernstein, ed., *The Politics and Policies of the Truman Administration* (Quadrangle, 1969) dissent from Alperovitz's analysis of the bomb's great influence on American policy before Hiroshima. For reviews of Alperovitz's book, see Michael Amrine, "The Day the Sun Rose Twice," *Book Week* (July 18, 1965) and Athan Theoharis in *New University Thought*, V (May–June, 1967), 12 ff. Alperovitz responded in that same issue to the criticisms by Theoharis.

Alice K. Smith in *A Peril and a Hope: The Scientists' Movement in America, 1945–47* (Univ. of Chicago Press, 1965) and Richard Hewlett and Oscar Anderson, Jr., in *The New World*, Vol. I of *A History of the United States Atomic Energy Commission* (Pennsylvania State Univ. Press, 1962), provide important background on the A-bomb decision; Hewlett and Anderson's book contains information on Byrnes' postwar design for the bomb. Henry Stimson and McGeorge Bundy's *On Active Service* (Harper & Row, 1948), an "autobiography" of Stimson, includes the article from *Harper's* but, strangely, excludes nearly all the evidence in the manuscript diaries showing that Stimson stressed to Truman before Hiroshima the impact of the bomb on future Russian relations. Elting E. Morison in *Turmoil and Tradition* ° (Houghton Mifflin, 1960), a biography of Stimson, notes *some* of this evidence. *The Atomic Bomb: The Great Decision,*° edited by Paul Baker (Holt, Rinehart & Winston, 1968), and *Hiroshima: The Decision to Use the A-Bomb,* edited by Edwin Fogelman (Scribner, 1964), are useful collections of essays and excerpts from books about the bomb.

GAR ALPEROVITZ

How Did the Cold War Begin?

INTRODUCTION

Using a review of Martin F. Herz's *Beginnings of the Cold War* (Indiana Univ. Press, 1966) as a springboard for his own views on the subject, Gar Alperovitz explains in the following essay why he believes that the United States was largely responsible for the Cold War. First, he argues that President Truman regrettably reversed Roosevelt's policy of accepting spheres of influence in Eastern Europe. By attempting instead to impose Western notions of democracy on the entire area, Truman forced the Russians to give up hope for a *modus vivendi.* Second, Alperovitz believes that American policy-makers must bear much of the blame for the division of Germany. America's refusal to grant the U.S.S.R. a loan for post-

FROM Gar Alperovitz, "How Did the Cold War Begin?," *New York Review of Books,* VIII (March 23, 1967), pp. 6, 8, 9, 11, 12. Reprinted by permission of the author. This essay also appears in Gar Alperovitz, *Cold War Essays,* Doubleday & Company, Inc., 1969.

war reconstruction left the Russians economically dependent on reparations from their zone in Germany. Although the American Government apparently hoped that its atomic monopoly would make its views impossible to resist, the American position on reparations was so contrary to Russian interests that early attempts to negotiate the German question broke down, and the division of Germany began to harden.

At numerous points Alperovitz's analysis conflicts with the views of other historians. First of all, defenders of American policy dispute his view of Stalin, arguing that the dictator's apparent moderation in 1945 and 1946 merely cloaked malicious intentions. Second, some historians deny that Roosevelt ever accepted even temporary, much less permanent, spheres of influence. Among this group are revisionists Gabriel Kolko (*The Politics of War* [Random House, 1969]) and Lloyd Gardner (*Economic Aspects of New Deal Diplomacy* [Univ. of Wisconsin Press, 1964]), who contend that Roosevelt never accepted permanent spheres of influence because he, like Truman, saw foreign policy as an instrument for opening both the British and Soviet empires to American economic penetration.

A third issue is the role that the atomic bomb played in shaping American foreign policy in 1945 and 1946. Minimizing the scattered evidence in the Potsdam papers (Department of State, *The Conference of Berlin* [*Potsdam*], 1955, 2 vols.) and in other collections, most American historians of the early Cold War years disagree with Alperovitz and conclude that there is no direct evidence of the bomb's influence on such crucial policies as the American position on reparations at Potsdam. Yet, to cite one piece of evidence, Joseph Davies, former ambassador to the Soviet Union, wrote in his diary at Potsdam on July 28, 1945: "Had a talk this morning with Jim Byrnes. He was still having a hard time over reparations. The details as to the success of the Atomic Bomb, which he had just received, gave him confidence that the Soviets would agree as to these difficulties."

As for the Russian loan, nonrevisionists take at face value the State Department's false claims that a six-month delay in replying to the Russian request for aid was the result not of economic coercion but of a misplaced document. It now seems, however, that the United States did try to use economic leverage against the Soviet Union, as for example when on May 12, 1945, lend-lease shipments to the Russians were temporarily cut off. In his *Memoirs* Truman states that the order terminating lend-lease originated as a routine document, which he signed without reading, but it now appears that the Government was acting on the recommendation of W. Averell Harriman, American ambassador to the Soviet Union, who had counseled a display of economic power to make the Russians tractable (Joseph Grew diary, May 11, 1945). It is evidence such as this that has led Alperovitz in the following essay to reject the no-

tion that Russian ill will alone was responsible for the deterioration
of the Grand Alliance.

*W*riting as "Mr. X," George Kennan suggested twenty years
ago that the mechanism of Soviet diplomacy "moves inexorably along the
prescribed path, like a persistent toy automobile wound up and headed in
a given direction, stopping only when it meets with some unanswerable
force." [1] A generation of Americans quickly embraced Kennan's view as an
explanation of the tension, danger, and waste of the Cold War. But was his
theory of inexorable Soviet expansion—and its matching recommendation of
"containment"—correct? A cautious but important book, *Beginnings of the
Cold War*, suggests we might well have been more critical of so mechanistic
an idea of the way Great Powers act and how the Cold War began.

Martin F. Herz is currently a United States diplomat serving in
Teheran. His book is mainly concerned with the few months between the
1945 Yalta and Potsdam Conferences. It is well-documented and contains no
polemic; indeed, as he says, "the author expresses few views of his own . . ."
The book begins by recapitulating the main issues in dispute when Truman
became President: Poland, German reparations, lend-lease aid. It moves
from the Polish issue to a broader discussion of spheres of influence, and from
reparations and lend-lease to a general analysis of aid to Russia and its relation to other diplomatic considerations. The two issues are integrated in a
brief concluding discussion of how the "die was cast" in 1945, and the Cold
War began.

Any examination of the very earliest postwar period forces us to think
about developments *before* 1947 when it was decided to contain the Soviet
Union by "unanswerable force." Herz's study is important because it makes
two serious judgments about this period: first, that in 1945 Soviet policy was
by no means inexorably prescribed and expansionist; second, that mistakes
made by American officials just after the war may well have prevented the
kind of compromise and accommodation which is just beginning to emerge in
Europe today.

These suggestions recall Walter Lippmann's *The Cold War*, published
in 1947, which also argued—with greater candor and less detail—that the
Russians might have been willing to accept a negotiated settlement in 1945
and 1946, but that US policy ignored opportunities to meet them halfway.
Lippmann's now little-remembered book offered a powerful critique of Kennan's theory of Soviet expansion and American containment. If Herz's view is
correct, accepted interpretations of American Russian relations are called

---

[1] *Foreign Affairs*, July, 1947.

into question. And if Lippmann was right in saying that American policy helped to prevent an accommodation in 1945 and 1946, the Cold War itself must be regarded, at least in part, as the result of fundamental errors of American diplomacy. These are startling conclusions, but anyone willing to bring an open mind to Herz's book or to Lippmann's will find that they have exposed many weaknesses in the usual explanations of early events in the Cold War.

No one, of course, can be certain of "what might have been." But Herz refutes at least one accepted myth. Contrary to current historical reconstructions, there is abundant evidence that American leaders in 1945 were not much worried about the expansion of communism into *Western* Europe. That worry came later. In the days just after the war, most Communists in Italy, France, and elsewhere were cooperating with bourgeois governments. At Potsdam, in 1945, Truman regarded the Russians' desires for concessions beyond their area of occupation as largely bluff. The major issues in dispute were all in Eastern Europe, deep within the zone of Soviet military occupation. The real expansion of Soviet power, we are reminded, took place in Poland, Hungary, Bulgaria, Rumania, Czechoslovakia, and the eastern regions of Germany and Austria.

The US in 1945 wanted Russia to give up the control and influence the Red Army had gained in the battle against Hitler. American demands may have been motivated by an idealistic desire to foster democracy, but Herz's main point is that in countries like Rumania and Bulgaria they were about as realistic as would be Soviet demands for changes in, say, Mexico. Any such parallel has obvious limits, the most significant of which is not that democracy and communism cannot so easily be compared, but that Eastern Europe is of far greater importance to Soviet security than is Mexico to American security: from the time of Napoleon—and twice in the lifetime of millions of presentday Russians—bloody invasions have swept through the area to their "Middle West."

In the early Spring of 1945, negotiations concerning one border state—Poland—brought the main issue into the open. At Yalta and immediately thereafter, the US had mainly mediated between Stalin and Churchill on Poland; Roosevelt had warned Churchill that to make extreme demands would doom the negotiations. A month later, in the faltering last days of Roosevelt's life, the US itself adopted a new tough line, demanding that pro-Western and openly anti-Russian Polish politicians be given more influence in negotiations to set up a new government for Poland. As was predicted, the Russians balked at the idea of such an expansion of anti-Soviet influence in a country so important to their security, and the negotiations ground to a halt.[2]

---

[2] The details of this history are often greatly misunderstood. Herz also vacillates in describing Roosevelt's Polish policy. See Appendix I of my *Atomic Diplomacy: Hiroshima and Potsdam* for a discussion of this question. Documentation for other facts and quotations not specifically given in this review can also be found here.

Moreover, at this precise moment, Russian suspicions about the West deep-
ened with Allen Dulles's concurrent but unrelated secret negotiations with
Nazi generals in Switzerland.[3] The result was a violent quarrel which shook
the entire structure of American-Soviet relations. But this was only the beginning. The demands on the Polish question reflected the ideas of the men
who were to surround the new President; led by Joseph Grew and James F.
Byrnes, they soon convinced Truman to attempt to make stronger demands
elsewhere in Eastern Europe.

For most of the year Roosevelt had been highly ambivalent toward
such matters. By late 1944, however, (in spite of wavering on the politically
sensitive Polish issue in his dying days) Roosevelt concluded it would be a
fundamental error to put too much pressure on Russia over other regions
vital to her security. In September and October 1944, and in early January
1945, he gave form to his conclusion by entering into armistice agreements
with Britain and Russia, which gave the Soviet military almost complete control of internal politics in each Eastern European ex-Nazi satellite. It was understood, for instance, that the Soviets would have authority to issue orders
to the Rumanian government, and that, specifically, the Allied Control Commission would be "under the general direction of the Allied (Soviet) High
Command acting on behalf of the Allied Powers." The Rumanian accords,
and the similar but slightly less severe Bulgarian and Hungarian armistice
agreements, served to formalize the famous Churchill-Stalin spheres-of-
influence arrangement which, without FDR's agreement, had previously
given the Russians "90 per cent" influence in Rumania, "80 per cent" influence in Bulgaria, and "75 per cent" influence in Hungary, in exchange for "90
per cent" British influence in Greece and a "50-50" split of influence in Yugo-
slavia. The armistice accords were also modeled after a previous understanding which had contained Soviet endorsement of dominant American-British
influence in Italy. The Eastern European armistice agreements have been
available to the public for years, but have been successfully buried, or
avoided by most scholars. Herz has exhumed them, and he shows that they
contain American endorsement of dominant Soviet influence in the ex-Nazi
satellites.

At Yalta, in early February, 1945, Roosevelt pasted over these specific
texts the vague and idealistic rhetoric of the famous Declaration on Liberated Europe. The President apparently wished to use the Declaration mainly

---

[3] See *The New York Review*, October 8, 1965. The only important new information in
Cornelius Ryan's popularized history, *The Last Battle* (Simon and Schuster, 1966, 571 pp.,
$7.50) suggests that Stalin was so aroused by Dulles's negotiations (and the West's blatant
denial they were taking place) that he suspiciously concluded other Western statements at
this time were also lies. According to Ryan, when Eisenhower informed Stalin he did not
intend to capture Berlin, Stalin thought this was another Western attempt to deceive him.
On this basis he, in turn, lied to Eisenhower, misleading him about the timing of the Red
Army's own thrust to take the city.

to appease certain politically important ethnic groups in America; he devoted only a few minutes to the matter at the Yalta Conference, and the familiar rhetoric promising democracy was almost devoid of practical meaning. For example, who was to decide in given instances between the American and Soviet definitions of common but vague terms like "democratic"? Much more important, as Herz shows, in the broad language of the Declaration the Allies agreed merely to "consult" about matters within the liberated countries, not to "act," and they authorized consultations only when all parties agreed they were necessary. Thus the United States itself confirmed the Russians' right to refuse to talk about the ex-Nazi satellites. The State Department knew this and, in fact, had tried to insert operative clauses into the Declaration. But Roosevelt, having just signed the armistice agreements, rejected this unrealistic proposal. Moreover, when the Soviets after Yalta crudely tossed out a Rumanian government they did not like, the President, though unhappy that he had not been consulted, reaffirmed his basic position by refusing to intervene.

Ironically, Herz's book lends credence to the old Republican charge that Roosevelt accepted a compromise at Yalta which bolstered Stalin's position in Eastern Europe. The charge, while correct in essentials, was silly in assuming that much else, short of war, could have been done while the Red Army occupied the area. The Republican politicians also ignored the fact that at Yalta Roosevelt could not expect a continued American military presence in Europe for very long after the war. This not only deprived him of leverage, it made an accommodation with Russia much more desirable for another reason: Red Army help became essential as a guarantee that Germany would not rise from defeat to start yet a third World War. Stalin also needed American help, as he too made clear, to hold down the Germans. Hence, underlying the American-Soviet plans for peace at Yalta was not "faith" but a common interest—the German threat—which had cemented the World War II alliance. From this 1945 perspective the crucial portion of the Yalta agreement was not the Declaration on Liberated Europe, nor even the provisions on Poland, but rather the understanding that the United States and Russia (with Britain and France as minor partners) would work together to control Germany. This meant, among other things, joint action to reduce Germany's physical power by extracting reparations from German industry.

Although Herz tends to play down the German issue, he does take up important economic matters that relate to it. He understands that Moscow was in a cruel dilemma which, had the US been shrewd enough, might have been resolved to the benefit of both American diplomacy and the economic health of Europe. The Russians were greatly in need of aid for their huge postwar reconstruction program. Importing industrial equipment from Eastern Europe was a possible solution, though a doubtful one, for taking this equipment would inevitably cause political problems. Reparations from Germany were another, but the key industrial sectors were in American hands. Finally, the United States itself was a potential source. Herz argues (as did Ambassadors Harriman and Winant at the time) that a US reconstruction loan for Russia would have been wise; it would have given US diplomacy strong leverage in a variety of negotiations. (Without other sources of aid for reconstruction the Russians were almost inevitably reduced to extracting industrial goods from either Germany or Eastern Europe.) American officials seriously considered such a loan, but, as Herz shows, they did not actively pursue it with the Russians—though one or two crude attempts were made to use a loan as a bludgeon in negotiations. With a future US troop commitment unlikely, and a large loan ruled out, the United States had no real bargaining power. Hence its attempts at intervention in Eastern Europe amounted to little more than bluster.

The State Department wanted to have it both ways: it wanted to hold the Russians to the vague promises of the Yalta Declaration; it also wanted to avoid the specific texts of the armistice agreements. But the Republicans, and even Secretary Byrnes in his later writings, understood the weakness of this position. The Republicans, for their part, also wanted to have it both ways. They wanted to argue both that Roosevelt gave the Russians all the authority they needed for their actions *and* that the Russians broke their agreements.

The Republican attack on Yalta came late in the Cold War, and was combined with a new demand that the US "roll back" Soviet influence. Few now realize how unoriginal the demand was, for a "roll back" effort—without its latter-day label—was, in fact, at the center of Harry Truman's first postwar policy. The President, we now know, made this effort in a spurt of confidence derived from the new atomic bomb. But the policy failed in its continuing attempt to reduce Soviet control by expanding Western influence in Poland. It also failed in its bold follow-up effort to force the Russians to change the Bulgarian and Rumanian governments. Nevertheless, these opening moves of the postwar period helped to set the tone of the new Administration's attitude toward Russia. Truman, although publicly proclaiming his adherence to Roosevelt's policy of cooperation, seems to have understood that his approach differed fundamentally from his predecessor's. (In private, as Secretary of State Stettinius has written, he complained that the intervention in Poland rested on rather shaky diplomatic ground.) Indeed, by September 1945, the basic change in US policy was so clearly defined that, as Secretary of State Byrnes later wrote, the Russian complaint that Roosevelt's policy had been abandoned was "understandable." [4]

What was the result? Like Herz, John Foster Dulles (who assisted Byrnes at the time) also believed that the Cold War began in 1945. Dulles emphasized in his book *War or Peace* (1950) that a new tough line of US policy was adopted at this time over dimly remembered issues deep within

[4] *Speaking Frankly*, Harper, 1947.

the Soviet-controlled Balkans. Herz prints almost the full text of the crucial 1945 Hopkins-Stalin talks, which reveal the equally important point that, in Russia, the change in American policy produced what Stalin termed "a certain alarm." A few thoughtful US officials recognized the significance of these developments. Secretary of War Henry L. Stimson, for example, tried to block the campaign to engage American prestige in Eastern Europe. In White House discussions he argued, first, that the demand for more Western influence in Poland was a mistake: "The Russians perhaps were being more realistic than we were in regard to their own security. . . ." He then tried to cut short efforts to intervene elsewhere, reminding Truman, as Stimson's diary shows, that "we have made up our minds on the broad policy that it was not wise to get into the Balkan mess even if the thing seemed to be disruptive of policies which the State Department thought were wise." Stimson pointed out that "we have taken that policy right from the beginning, Mr. Roosevelt having done it himself or having been a party to it himself."

When Stimson failed in his conservative effort to limit American objectives, the stage was set for one of the great tragedies of the Cold War. As Stimson understood, the Russians, though extremely touchy about the buffer area, were not impossible to deal with. Had their security requirements been met, there is evidence that their domination of Eastern Europe might have been much different from what it turned out to be. Churchill, too, thought the Russians were approachable. Obviously, conditions in Eastern Europe would not meet Western ideals; but Churchill judged, in late 1944 and early 1945, that Moscow was convinced it would be much easier to secure its objectives through moderate policies. In Greece at this time, as Churchill was to stress in *Triumph and Tragedy,* Stalin was "strictly and faithfully" holding to his agreement *not* to aid the Greek Communists. Even in much of the border area the Russians seemed willing to accept substantial capitalism and some form of democracy—with the crucial proviso that the Eastern European governments had to be "friendly" to Russia in defense and foreign policies. Finland serves as a rough model of a successful border state. Here, too, the armistice made the Soviets supreme, giving rights parallel to the Bulgarian and Rumanian accords plus the right to maintain Soviet military installations. However, the US made no independent effort to intervene; Finland maintained a foreign policy "friendly" to Russia; and the Russians were—as they still seem to be—prepared to accept a moderate government.

Although it is often forgotten, a modified application of the Finnish formula seemed to be shaping up elsewhere in 1945 and much of 1946. In Hungary, Soviet-sponsored free elections routed the Communist Party in 1945. In Bulgaria, a country with rather weak democratic traditions, the 1945 elections were complicated by competition for Great Power support among the various internal factions. Certainly the results were not perfect, but most Western observers (except the State Department) felt they should have been accepted. In Austria, the Communists were swamped in Soviet-run free elections in their zone in 1945, and, after a hesitant start, a free democratic government emerged for the entire country. In Czechoslovakia, from which the Red Army withdrew in December of 1945, democracy was so clearly acceptable to Soviet policy that the US had little to protest at the time.[5]

Almost all of this was to change, of course. The freedoms in Hungary were to end in 1947. The initial pattern in Czechoslovakia was to be reversed in 1948. But writers who focus only on the brutal period of totalitarian control after 1947 and 1948 often ignore what happened earlier. The few who try to account for the known facts of the 1945–46 interlude usually do so in passing, either to suggest that the democratic governments "must have been" mere smokescreens, formed while Moscow waited for the US to leave the Continent; or that the Russians "must have been" secretly planning to take full control, but were methodically using the early period to prepare the groundwork for what came later. (Communists, too, like to ignore the 1945–46 period, for it suggests the possibility that Soviet Russia was more interested in an old-fashioned *modus vivendi* with the capitalists than in spreading World Communism. This was the essence of Tito's bitter complaint that Stalin tried to turn back the Yugoslav revolution.)

The Russians have displayed so much duplicity, brutality, and intransigence that it is easy to imagine the 1945–46 interlude as a mere smokescreen. But they also have a long history of protecting "socialism in one country" in a rather conservative, nationalistic way: the moderation of the 1945–46 interlude can be viewed as a logical extension of this tradition. That at least two quite different interpretations of their 1945–46 policy are conceivable is now rarely admitted, and the relative merits of each have not been seriously examined. Herz's study calls for a careful reappraisal of early postwar Soviet objectives.[6] If the Russians were secretly harboring plans for an ultimate take over, they certainly were preparing a lot of trouble for themselves by sponsoring free politics, by pulling out the Red Army (it is not particularly shrewd to have to *re*-introduce foreign troops), by ripping up the Red Army's main rail connections across Poland—as they did in the fall of 1945. As well informed an observer as Averell Harriman believed, as he once

---

[5] W. H. McNeill's *America, Britain and Russia* provides a good general survey of this period. Note that early in 1946 the Red Army also withdrew from control of two other border areas: Northern Iran and Manchuria.

[6] Today most writers simply take the mechanistic theory of Soviet expansion for granted. An example of what this can lead to is John Toland's *The Last 100 Days* (Random House, 1965), an account of the closing months of World War II which assumes that the Russians were inevitably evil and expansionistic, and that therefore the "good" Germans had to be used to help contain them. Toland dwells on details of the Western Front. He devotes much less attention to the Eastern Front, taking much of his material from German sources. Accordingly, the book popularizes a one-sided caricature of Russians as pillaging sadists and irrepressible rapists. (As for the Germans, it is only the rare Nazi camp guard who is a brutal exception to the rule of "the other guards, who generally treated the prisoners well"!)

testified to Congress, that Soviet policy in 1945 was ambivalent, that it could have become either more moderate within a framework of security and understanding with the West, or that it could have become hard-line and totalitarian, within the framework of insecurity and conflict. Harriman, though puzzled by the ultimate Russian decision in favor of the iron-fisted policy, clearly saw that Soviet expansion was neither inexorable nor inevitable.

At least one reason for Russia's shift to a tough line may be traced to mistakes made by US officials. As Stimson argued—and as history later showed—the demand for more influence in Soviet-controlled areas was almost certainly doomed from the start. This basic miscalculation stemmed, finally, from an attempt to overextend *American* diplomatic sway. Lippmann was, I believe correct in seeing that the other error was the failure of US policy makers to turn their energies to an early solution of the crucial German problem. Bolstered by the atomic bomb, which eliminated the threat that had been Roosevelt's central concern, American leaders dallied over Germany. Moreover, by refusing to hold to Roosevelt's agreement that a specific target for German reparations would be set (July, 1945), by permitting France to hamstring the German Control Commission (Fall, 1945), by halting German reparations shipments (Spring, 1946)—US policy suggested the very prospect Russia feared most: the abandonment of economic and political controls and the possibility that a new and powerful Germany would rise from the ashes of Nazism to become the bastion of Western capitalistic aggression in Europe. The United States had no such aggressive intent. Nonetheless, the US chose not to negotiate seriously on Germany until a full year-and-a-half after the war's end. Especially after Secretary Byrnes's tough speech in Stuttgart in the Fall of 1946, American policy was shortsighted enough to suggest a threat to Russia at the very time it was attempting to weaken Soviet control in the vital area which lay—protectively or threateningly—between German power and the Russian heartland. The Russians, who had no nuclear weapons, were far less casual about the question of security; their grip seemed to tighten in the buffer area month by month, as their worst fears about Germany seemed to come true.

The Russians were not easy to deal with, either in Germany or elsewhere. Nevertheless, if the hypothesis suggested by Lippmann's book is correct—and Herz's study indirectly supports it—there are reasons to believe that US policy itself may have to share responsibility for the imposition of totalitarian control in Eastern Europe, and possibly also for the subsequent expanding Communist agitation in Western Europe. The *addition* of increased insecurity to known Soviet paranoid tendencies may explain the rigidity which Soviet leaders displayed in their satellite policy after 1946. The first pattern seemed crudely similar to the Finnish or Austrian models. Would it have been reversed had the US seriously tried from the first to resolve the European security problem—as Lippmann urged? That Soviet actions may have been in part reactions to their judgments of American intentions may also help to explain why sustained Communist opposition developed in the West only *after* the clear breakdown of German control arrangements. It was not in 1945, but late in 1946 and in 1947 that the Italian and French Communists began to reverse their initial policy of cooperation with bourgeois governments. Was the changed focus of Communist politics part of the inexorable plan? Or was it primarily a rather shortsighted response to American policy itself?

Once the Communists became active in Western Europe, of course, the United States was faced with quite another set of issues. Disputes with Russia moved out of the border regions. The threat some officials had anticipated while reading Marx and listening to Communist propaganda began to become a political reality. In 1947, those who proposed a mechanical theory of Soviet expansion had to deal with expanding Communist political activity in the West. And it was in July of that year, precisely two years after Truman faced Stalin in his first Potsdam showdown over Eastern Europe, that Kennan's containment recommendation was publicly offered.

We do not yet have answers to all the questions about postwar American-Russian relations, but we know enough to consider afresh whether either of the Great Powers ever really did move inexorably, like a wound-up toy automobile, as "Mr. X" argued. Herz's sturdy little book suggests they did not, and is at least the beginning of a more subtle explanation of the complex sequence of interacting events which produced the Cold War.

SUGGESTED READING

William McNeill's *America, Britain, and Russia* (Oxford Univ. Press, 1953) is a valuable book on wartime relations that is generally overlooked by historians. *The Meaning of Yalta: Big Three Diplomacy and the New Balance of Power,*° edited by John Snell (Louisiana State Univ. Press, 1955), defends Roosevelt from charges that he "sold out" American interests. Isaac Deutscher's *Stalin* ° (Oxford Univ. Press, 1949) is a harsh criticism of the Soviet leader by a Marxist who emphasizes the conservatism of Stalin's foreign policy in the early postwar period. Herbert Feis had privileged access to classified materials in writing *Churchill, Roosevelt, Stalin* ° (Princeton Univ. Press, 1957) and *Between War and Peace: The Potsdam Conference* ° (Princeton Univ. Press, 1960), which depart from Alperovitz's views. Most historians uncritically accepted these volumes by Feis until the past few years.

William Appleman Williams' *American-Russian Relations, 1781–1947* (Holt, Rinehart & Winston, 1952) is the first significant "revisionist" interpretation of the Cold War by a scholar and includes a thoughtful critique of containment. Geoffrey Warner in "From Teheran to Yalta: Reflections on F.D.R.'s Foreign Policy," *International Affairs*, XLIII (July, 1967), 530–36, follows Alperovitz on spheres of influence

in 1944–1945. *Containment and Revolution,*° edited by David Horo-
witz (Beacon Press, 1967), is a volume of "revisionist" essays on the
Cold War and includes a fine essay by John Bagguley called "The
World War and the Cold War."

Christopher Lasch's "The Cold War, Revisited and Re-visioned,"
New York Times Magazine (Jan. 14, 1968), is a good summary of "revisionism." "Origins of the Post-war Crisis," *Journal of Contemporary
History*, III (April, 1968), 217–52, is a loose-knit symposium generally
critical of recent "revisionism." Henry Pachter's "Revisionist Historians
and the Cold War," *Dissent* (Nov.–Dec., 1968), 505–18, is an intemperate and flawed attack on "revisionism."

On economic policy, Herbert Feis's "Political Aspects of Foreign
Loans," *Foreign Affairs*, XXIII (July, 1945), 609–19, and his "The
Conflict over Trade Ideologies," *ibid.*, XXV (Jan., 1947), 217–28, are
important analyses. E. F. Penrose's *Economic Planning for the Peace*
(Princeton Univ. Press, 1953) is a thoughtful study by a State Department adviser. George Herring in "Lendlease to Russia and the Origins
of the Cold War," *Journal of American History* (a forthcoming issue in
1969), having had privileged access to restricted materials, argues that
the brief termination of lendlease to Russia in May was not intended to
coerce the Russians but that it occurred for legal reasons. According to
Herring, the order was misunderstood by some officials who took more
extreme action than was desired by the President and his close advisers.
In disagreement, Thomas G. Paterson in "The Abortive Russian Loan,"
Journal of American History (a forthcoming issue in 1969), writing
without benefit of the restricted sources, concludes that the loan was
used to coerce the Russians and that lendlease was halted in May for the
same reason.

Manuel Gottlieb, a former economic adviser who had access to
valuable and generally unused sources, provides a study of American
policy in Germany in *The German Peace Settlement and the Berlin
Crisis* (Paine-Whitman, 1960). John Snell in *Wartime Origins of the
East-West Dilemma over Germany* (Louisiana State Univ. Press, 1959)
presents an interpretation close to Schlesinger's views of Soviet policies
(as presented in the next essay). Klaus Epstein's "The German Problem,
1945–50," *World Politics*, XX (Jan., 1968), 300–26, is an excellent
review-essay on important recent literature.

George Kennan's "The Sources of Soviet Conduct," *Foreign Affairs*, XXXV (July, 1947), 566–82, is the first explicit *public* statement
of containment. The text of the telegram of February, 1946, on which
Kennan's article is based, is reprinted in his *Memoirs, 1925–1950* (Little, Brown, 1967); Kennan struggles—somewhat unconvincingly—in
this volume to retreat from the military implications of containment.
Walter Lippmann's *The Cold War* (Harper & Row, 1947), based on a
series of newspaper columns, is a penetrating contemporary criticism of
what containment seemed to mean then.

ARTHUR SCHLESINGER, JR.

Origins of the Cold War

INTRODUCTION

Because he is dedicated to the liberalism of the "vital center," Arthur Schlesinger, Jr. celebrates moderate, nonideological reform; he has found much to praise in the efforts of the liberal Roosevelt and Kennedy Administrations. An historian who has been active in the political world, Schlesinger was a founding member of the Americans for Democratic Action, wrote campaign speeches for Adlai E. Stevenson and John F. Kennedy, and served the latter as a special assistant during the thousand days. For nearly half a year after Kennedy's death, Schlesinger stayed with the Johnson Administration and at first defended its policy in Vietnam. Not until late in 1966 did he publicly dissent from the continued escalation of the war. He attributes the error in America's

FROM Arthur Schlesinger, Jr., "Origins of the Cold War," *Foreign Affairs*, XLVI (October, 1967), pp. 22–52. Copyright © 1967 by the Council on Foreign Relations, Inc., New York. Reprinted by special permission.

Vietnam policy not to American ideology but simply to a number of petty mistakes that had led policy-makers astray.

In the past few years Schlesinger has become distressed by the "revisionist" analyses of the early Cold War. In an outburst in 1966, which he later good-naturedly labeled intemperate, he wanted to "blow the whistle" (letter to *The New York Review of Books,* Oct. 20, 1966) on "revisionism," and in 1967 he offered his own vigorous counter-argument. Though the essay that follows was intended as a reply to the "revisionists," the first half does not differ markedly from the moderate "revisionist" case advanced by Staughton Lynd in 1960 ("How the Cold War Began," *Commentary,* XXX [Nov., 1960], 370–89). The United States, Schlesinger concedes, made mistakes that contributed to the Cold War, and Soviet policies were indeed cautious and directed at creating a security zone. "In other words," writes Schlesinger of Stalin, "his initial objectives were very probably not world conquest but Russian security." But Schlesinger abruptly retreats from his incipient "revisionism." He shifts ground and undermines much of his earlier analysis by explaining Stalin's actions in terms of his paranoia. He concludes that even different American policies could not have avoided the Cold War and achieved an accommodation with the Soviet Union.

William Appleman Williams, one of the heroes of revisionism, wrote a brief reply to Schlesinger ("The Cold-War Revisionists," *Nation,* CCV [Nov. 13, 1967], 492–95) in which he questions Schlesinger's psychiatric judgments. Williams points out that "no major American policy maker between 1943 and 1948 defined and dealt with the Soviet Union in those [psychiatric] terms." Why invoke paranoia to explain Stalin's reactions when there is ample evidence of American hostility? asks Williams. He criticizes Schlesinger for overlooking the American antibolshevik attitudes that had been operating since 1917 and for neglecting to admit that American "universalism" (that is, Wilsonianism) was implicitly anticommunist. Rather than paranoiac or rigidly ideological, Stalin's attempts to create a security zone as protection against the West were reasonable, Williams concludes, in view of earlier capitalist hostility.

As evidence of Soviet hostility toward the West and the impossibility of accommodation in April of 1945, Schlesinger points to the public letter of that month by Jacques Duclos, who had been the Comintern official responsible for Western Communist parties. Schlesinger interprets the letter as a militant call for subversion and preparation for revolution. But it can also be understood as a call for independent electoral politics in the West, as Gar Alperovitz argues (*New York Review,* Oct. 20, 1966). In view of the participation of the French and Italian Communist parties in coalition governments until 1947, the latter interpretation seems more consistent with the evidence.

Schlesinger overlooks the fact that American policy-makers in 1945 did not fear imminent Russian military expansion into Western Europe. In addition, he skirts the issue of the atomic bomb, accepts the official American claims about the lost Russian request for a loan and termination of lend-lease, and disregards the manuscript collections that would have compelled a more direct confrontation with the "revisionist" arguments.

The Cold War in its original form was a presumably mortal antagonism, arising in the wake of the Second World War, between two rigidly hostile blocs, one led by the Soviet Union, the other by the United States. For nearly two somber and dangerous decades this antagonism dominated the fears of mankind; it may even, on occasion, have come close to blowing up the planet. In recent years, however, the once implacable struggle has lost its familiar clarity of outline. With the passing of old issues and the emergence of new conflicts and contestants, there is a natural tendency, especially on the part of the generation which grew up during the Cold War, to take a fresh look at the causes of the great contention between Russia and America.

Some exercises in reappraisal have merely elaborated the orthodoxies promulgated in Washington or Moscow during the boom years of the Cold War. But others, especially in the United States (there are no signs, alas, of this in the Soviet Union), represent what American historians call "revisionism"—that is, a readiness to challenge official explanations. No one should be surprised by this phenomenon. Every war in American history has been followed in due course by skeptical reassessments of supposedly sacred assumptions. So the War of 1812, fought at the time for the freedom of the seas, was in later years ascribed to the expansionist ambitions of Congressional war hawks; so the Mexican War became a slaveholders' conspiracy. So the Civil War has been pronounced a "needless war," and Lincoln has even been accused of manœuvring the rebel attack on Fort Sumter. So too the Spanish-American War and the First and Second World Wars have, each in its turn, undergone revisionist critiques. It is not to be supposed that the Cold War would remain exempt.

In the case of the Cold War, special factors reinforce the predictable historiographical rhythm. The outburst of polycentrism in the communist empire has made people wonder whether communism was ever so monolithic as official theories of the Cold War supposed. A generation with no vivid memories of Stalinism may see the Russia of the forties in the image of the relatively mild, seedy and irresolute Russia of the sixties. And for this same generation the American course of widening the war in Viet Nam—which even non-revisionists can easily regard as folly—has unquestionably stirred doubts about the wisdom of American foreign policy in the sixties which younger historians may have begun to read back into the forties.

It is useful to remember that, on the whole, past exercises in revisionism have failed to stick. Few historians today believe that the war hawks caused the War of 1812 or the slaveholders the Mexican War, or that the Civil War was needless, or that the House of Morgan brought America into the First World War or that Franklin Roosevelt schemed to produce the attack on Pearl Harbor. But this does not mean that one should deplore the rise of Cold War revisionism.[1] For revisionism is an essential part of the process by which history, through the posing of new problems and the investigation of new possibilities, enlarges its perspectives and enriches its insights.

More than this, in the present context, revisionism expresses a deep, legitimate and tragic apprehension. As the Cold War has begun to lose its purity of definition, as the moral absolutes of the fifties become the moralistic clichés of the sixties, some have begun to ask whether the appalling risks which humanity ran during the Cold War were, after all, necessary and inevitable; whether more restrained and rational policies might not have guided the energies of man from the perils of conflict into the potentialities of collaboration. The fact that such questions are in their nature unanswerable does not mean that it is not right and useful to raise them. Nor does it mean that our sons and daughters are not entitled to an accounting from the generation of Russians and Americans who produced the Cold War.

The orthodox American view, as originally set forth by the American government and as reaffirmed until recently by most American scholars, has been that the Cold War was the brave and essential response of free men to communist aggression. Some have gone back well before the Second World War to lay open the sources of Russian expansionism. Geopoliticians traced the Cold War to imperial Russian strategic ambitions which in the nineteenth century led to the Crimean War, to Russian penetration of the Balkans and the Middle East and to Russian pressure on Britain's "lifeline" to India. Ideologists traced it to the Communist Manifesto of 1848 ("the violent overthrow of the bourgeoisie lays the foundation for the sway of the proletariat"). Thoughtful observers (a phrase meant to exclude those who speak in Dullese about the unlimited evil of godless, atheistic, militant communism) concluded that classical Russian imperialism and Pan-Slavism, compounded after 1917 by Leninist messianism, confronted the West at the end of the Second World War with an inexorable drive for domination.[2]

---

[1] As this writer somewhat intemperately did in a letter to *The New York Review of Books*, October 20, 1966.

[2] Every student of the Cold War must acknowledge his debt to W. H. McNeill's remarkable account, *America, Britain and Russia: Their Cooperation and Conflict, 1941–1946* (New York, 1953) and to the brilliant and indispensable series by Herbert Feis: *Churchill, Roosevelt, Stalin: The War They Waged and the Peace They Sought* (Princeton, 1957);

The revisionist thesis is very different.[3] In its extreme form, it is that, after the death of Franklin Roosevelt and the end of the Second World War, the United States deliberately abandoned the wartime policy of collaboration and, exhilarated by the possession of the atomic bomb, undertook a course of aggression of its own designed to expel all Russian influence from Eastern Europe and to establish democratic-capitalist states on the very border of the Soviet Union. As the revisionists see it, this radically new American policy—or rather this resumption by Truman of the pre-Roosevelt policy of insensate anti-communism—left Moscow no alternative but to take measures in defense of its own borders. The result was the Cold War.

These two views, of course, could not be more starkly contrasting. It is therefore not unreasonable to look again at the half-dozen critical years between June 22, 1941, when Hitler attacked Russia, and July 2, 1947, when the

---

Between War and Peace: The Potsdam Conference (Princeton, 1960); and *The Atomic Bomb and the End of World War II* (Princeton, 1966). Useful recent analyses include André Fontaine, *Histoire de la Guerre Froide* (2 v., Paris, 1965, 1967); N. A. Graebner, *Cold War Diplomacy, 1945–1960* (Princeton, 1962); L. J. Halle, *The Cold War as History* (London, 1967); M. F. Herz, *Beginnings of the Cold War* (Bloomington, 1966) and W. L. Neumann, *After Victory: Churchill, Roosevelt, Stalin and the Making of the Peace* (New York, 1967).

[3] The fullest statement of this case is to be found in D. F. Fleming's voluminous *The Cold War and Its Origins* (New York, 1961). For a shorter version of this argument, see David Horowitz, *The Free World Colossus* (New York, 1965); the most subtle and ingenious statements come in W. A. Williams' *The Tragedy of American Diplomacy* (rev. ed., New York, 1962) and in Gar Alperowitz's *Atomic Diplomacy: Hiroshima and Potsdam* (New York, 1965) and in subsequent articles and reviews by Mr. Alperowitz in *The New York Review of Books*. The fact that in some aspects the revisionist thesis parallels the official Soviet argument must not, of course, prevent consideration of the case on its merits, nor raise questions about the motives of the writers, all of whom, so far as I know, are independent-minded scholars.

I might further add that all these books, in spite of their ostentatious display of scholarly apparatus, must be used with caution. Professor Fleming, for example, relies heavily on newspaper articles and even columnists. While Mr. Alperowitz bases his case on official documents or authoritative reminiscences, he sometimes twists his material in a most unscholarly way. For example, in describing Ambassador Harriman's talk with President Truman on April 20, 1945, Mr. Alperowitz writes, "He argued that a reconsideration of Roosevelt's policy was necessary" (p. 22, repeated on p. 24). The citation is to p. 70–72 in President Truman's *Years of Decision*. What President Truman reported Harriman as saying was the exact opposite: "Before leaving, Harriman took me aside and said, 'Frankly, one of the reasons that made me rush back to Washington was the fear that you did not understand, as I had seen Roosevelt understand, that Stalin is breaking his agreements.'" Similarly, in an appendix (p. 271) Mr. Alperowitz writes that the Hopkins and Davies missions of May 1945 "were opposed by the 'firm' advisers." Actually the Hopkins mission was proposed by Harriman and Charles E. Bohlen, who Mr. Alperowitz elsewhere suggests were the firmest of the firm—and was proposed by them precisely to impress on Stalin the continuity of American policy from Roosevelt to Truman. While the idea that Truman reversed Roosevelt's policy is tempting dramatically, it is a myth. See, for example, the testimony of Anna Rosenberg Hoffman, who lunched with Roosevelt on March 24, 1945, the last day he spent in Washington. After luncheon, Roosevelt was handed a cable. "He read it and became quite angry. He banged his fists on the arms of his wheelchair and said, 'Averell is right; we can't do business with Stalin. He has broken every one of the promises he made at Yalta.' He was very upset and continued in the same vein on the subject."

Russians walked out of the Marshall Plan meeting in Paris. Several things should be borne in mind as this reëxamination is made. For one thing, we have thought a great deal more in recent years, in part because of writers like Roberta Wohlstetter and T. C. Schelling, about the problems of communication in diplomacy—the signals which one nation, by word or by deed, gives, inadvertently or intentionally, to another. Any honest reappraisal of the origins of the Cold War requires the imaginative leap—which should in any case be as instinctive for the historian as it is prudent for the statesman— into the adversary's viewpoint. We must strive to see how, given Soviet perspectives, the Russians might conceivably have misread our signals, as we must reconsider how intelligently we read theirs.

For another, the historian must not overindulge the man of power in the illusion cherished by those in office that high position carries with it the easy ability to shape history. Violating the statesman's creed, Lincoln once blurted out the truth in his letter of 1864 to A. G. Hodges: "I claim not to have controlled events, but confess plainly that events have controlled me." He was not asserting Tolstoyan fatalism but rather suggesting how greatly events limit the capacity of the statesman to bend history to his will. The physical course of the Second World War—the military operations undertaken, the position of the respective armies at the war's end, the momentum generated by victory and the vacuums created by defeat—all these determined the future as much as the character of individual leaders and the substance of national ideology and purpose.

Nor can the historian forget the conditions under which decisions are made, especially in a time like the Second World War. These were tired, overworked, aging men: in 1945, Churchill was 71 years old, Stalin had governed his country for 17 exacting years, Roosevelt his for 12 years nearly as exacting. During the war, moreover, the importunities of military operations had shoved postwar questions to the margins of their minds. All—even Stalin, behind his screen of ideology—had became addicts of improvisation, relying on authority and virtuosity to conceal the fact that they were constantly surprised by developments. Like Eliza, they leaped from one cake of ice to the next in the effort to reach the other side of the river. None showed great tactical consistency, or cared much about it; all employed a certain ambiguity to preserve their power to decide big issues; and it is hard to know how to interpret anything any one of them said on any specific occasion. This was partly because, like all princes, they designed their expressions to have particular effects on particular audiences; partly because the entirely genuine intellectual difficulty of the questions they faced made a degree of vacillation and mind-changing eminently reasonable. If historians cannot solve their problems in retrospect, who are they to blame Roosevelt, Stalin and Churchill for not having solved them at the time?

Peacemaking after the Second World War was not so much a tapestry as it was a hopelessly raveled and knotted mess of yarn. Yet, for purposes of clarity, it is essential to follow certain threads. One theme indispensable to an understanding of the Cold War is the contrast between two clashing views of world order: the "universalist" view, by which all nations shared a common interest in all the affairs of the world, and the "sphere-of-influence" view, by which each great power would be assured by the other great powers of an acknowledged predominance in its own area of special interest. The universalist view assumed that national security would be guaranteed by an international organization. The sphere-of-interest view assumed that national security would be guaranteed by the balance of power. While in practice these views have by no means been incompatible (indeed, our shaky peace has been based on a combination of the two), in the abstract they involved sharp contradictions.

The tradition of American thought in these matters was universalist—*i.e.* Wilsonian. Roosevelt had been a member of Wilson's subcabinet; in 1920, as candidate for Vice President, he had campaigned for the League of Nations. It is true that, within Roosevelt's infinitely complex mind, Wilsonianism warred with the perception of vital strategic interests he had imbibed from Mahan. Morever, his temperamental inclination to settle things with fellow princes around the conference table led him to regard the Big Three —or Four—as trustees for the rest of the world. On occasion, as this narrative will show, he was beguiled into flirtation with the sphere-of-influence heresy. But in principle he believed in joint action and remained a Wilsonian. His hope for Yalta, as he told the Congress on his return, was that it would "spell the end of the system of unilateral action, the exclusive alliances, the spheres of influence, the balances of power, and all the other expedients that have been tried for centuries—and have always failed."

Whenever Roosevelt backslid, he had at his side that Wilsonian fundamentalist, Secretary of State Cordell Hull, to recall him to the pure faith. After his visit to Moscow in 1943, Hull characteristically said that, with the Declaration of Four Nations on General Security (in which America, Russia, Britain and China pledged "united action . . . for the organization and maintenance of peace and security"), "there will no longer be need for spheres of influence, for alliances, for balance of power, or any other of the special arrangements through which, in the unhappy past, the nations strove to safeguard their security or to promote their interests."

Remembering the corruption of the Wilsonian vision by the secret treaties of the First World War, Hull was determined to prevent any sphere-of-influence nonsense after the Second World War. He therefore fought all proposals to settle border questions while the war was still on and, excluded as he largely was from wartime diplomacy, poured his not inconsiderable moral energy and frustration into the promulgation of virtuous and spacious general principles.

In adopting the universalist view, Roosevelt and Hull were not indulging personal hobbies. Sumner Welles, Adolf Berle, Averell Harriman,

Charles Bohlen—all, if with a variety of nuances, opposed the sphere-of-influence approach. And here the State Department was expressing what seems clearly to have been the predominant mood of the American people, so long mistrustful of European power politics. The Republicans shared the true faith. John Foster Dulles argued that the great threat to peace after the war would lie in the revival of sphere-of-influence thinking. The United States, he said, must not permit Britain and Russia to revert to these bad old ways; it must therefore insist on American participation in all policy decisions for all territories in the world. Dulles wrote pessimistically in January 1945, "The three great powers which at Moscow agreed upon the 'closest coöperation' about European questions have shifted to a practice of separate, regional responsibility."

It is true that critics, and even friends, of the United States sometimes noted a discrepancy between the American passion for universalism when it applied to territory far from American shores and the preëminence the United States accorded its own interests nearer home. Churchill, seeking Washington's blessing for a sphere-of-influence initiative in Eastern Europe, could not forbear reminding the Americans, "We follow the lead of the United States in South America;" nor did any universalist of record propose the abolition of the Monroe Doctrine. But a convenient myopia prevented such inconsistencies from qualifying the ardency of the universalist faith.

There seem only to have been three officials in the United States Government who dissented. One was the Secretary of War, Henry L. Stimson, a classical balance-of-power man, who in 1944 opposed the creation of a vacuum in Central Europe by the pastoralization of Germany and in 1945 urged "the settlement of all territorial acquisitions in the shape of defense posts which each of these four powers may deem to be necessary for their own safety" in advance of any effort to establish a peacetime United Nations. Stimson considered the claim of Russia to a preferred position in Eastern Europe as not unreasonable: as he told President Truman, "he thought the Russians perhaps were being more realistic than we were in regard to their own security." Such a position for Russia seemed to him comparable to the preferred American position in Latin America; he even spoke of "our respective orbits." Stimson was therefore skeptical of what he regarded as the prevailing tendency "to hang on to exaggerated views of the Monroe Doctrine and at the same time butt into every question that comes up in Central Europe." Acceptance of spheres of influence seemed to him the way to avoid "a head-on collision."

A second official opponent of universalism was George Kennan, an eloquent advocate from the American Embassy in Moscow of "a prompt and clear recognition of the division of Europe into spheres of influence and of a policy based on the fact of such division." Kennan argued that nothing we could do would possibly alter the course of events in Eastern Europe; that we were deceiving ourselves by supposing that these countries had any future

but Russian domination; that we should therefore relinquish Eastern Europe
to the Soviet Union and avoid anything which would make things easier for
the Russians by giving them economic assistance or by sharing moral responsibility for their actions.

A third voice within the government against universalism was (at least
after the war) Henry A. Wallace. As Secretary of Commerce, he stated the
sphere-of-influence case with trenchancy in the famous Madison Square
Garden speech of September 1946 which led to his dismissal by President
Truman:

> On our part, we should recognize that we have no more business in the *politi-
> cal* affairs of Eastern Europe than Russian has in the *political* affairs of Latin
> America, Western Europe, and the United States. . . . . Whether we like it
> or not, the Russians will try to socialize their sphere of influence just as we try
> to democratize our sphere of influence. . . . The Russians have no more
> business stirring up native Communists to political activity in Western Eu-
> rope, Latin America, and the United States than we have in interfering with
> the politics of Eastern Europe and Russia.

Stimson, Kennan and Wallace seem to have been alone in the government, however, in taking these views. They were very much minority voices.
Meanwhile universalism, rooted in the American legal and moral tradition,
overwhelmingly backed by contemporary opinion, received successive en-
shrinements in the Atlantic Charter of 1941, in the Declaration of the United
Nations in 1942 and in the Moscow Declaration of 1943.

The Kremlin, on the other hand, thought *only* of spheres of interest;
above all, the Russians were determined to protect their frontiers, and especially their border to the west, crossed so often and so bloodily in the dark
course of their history. These western frontiers lacked natural means of defense—no great oceans, rugged mountains, steaming swamps or impenetra-
ble jungles. The history of Russia had been the history of invasion, the last of
which was by now horribly killing up to twenty million of its people. The
protocol of Russia therefore meant the enlargement of the area of Russian
influence. Kennan himself wrote (in May 1944), "Behind Russia's stubborn
expansion lies only the age-old sense of insecurity of a sedentary people
reared on an exposed plain in the neighborhood of fierce nomadic peoples,"
and he called this "urge" a "permanent feature of Russian psychology."

In earlier times the "urge" had produced the tsarist search for buffer
states and maritime outlets. In 1939 the Soviet-Nazi pact and its secret protocol had enabled Russia to begin to satisfy in the Baltic states, Karelian Finland and Poland, part of what it conceived as its security requirements in
Eastern Europe. But the "urge" persisted, causing the friction between Russia and Germany in 1940 as each jostled for position in the area which separated them. Later it led to Molotov's new demands on Hitler in November

1940—a free hand in Finland, Soviet predominance in Rumania and Bulgaria, bases in the Dardanelles—the demands which convinced Hitler that he had no choice but to attack Russia. Now Stalin hoped to gain from the West what Hitler, a closer neighbor, had not dared yield him.

It is true that, so long as Russian survival appeared to require a second front to relieve the Nazi pressure, Moscow's demand for Eastern Europe was a little muffled. Thus the Soviet government adhered to the Atlantic Charter (though with a significant if obscure reservation about adapting its principles to "the circumstances, needs, and historic peculiarities of particular countries"). Thus it also adhered to the Moscow Declaration of 1943, and Molotov then, with his easy mendacity, even denied that Russia had any desire to divide Europe into spheres of influence. But this was guff, which the Russians were perfectly willing to ladle out if it would keep the Americans, and especially Secretary Hull (who made a strong personal impression at the Moscow conference) happy. "A declaration," as Stalin once observed to Eden, "I regard as algebra, but an agreement as practical arithmetic. I do not wish to decry algebra, but I prefer practical arithmetic."

The more consistent Russian purpose was revealed when Stalin offered the British a straight sphere-of-influence deal at the end of 1941. Britain, he suggested, should recognize the Russian absorption of the Baltic states, part of Finland, eastern Poland and Bessarabia; in return, Russia would support any special British need for bases or security arrangements in Western Europe. There was nothing specifically communist about these ambitions. If Stalin achieved them, he would be fulfilling an age-old dream of the tsars. The British reaction was mixed. "Soviet policy is amoral," as Anthony Eden noted at the time; "United States policy is exaggeratedly moral, at least where non-American interests are concerned." If Roosevelt was a universalist with occasional leanings toward spheres of influence and Stalin was a sphere-of-influence man with occasional gestures toward universalism, Churchill seemed evenly poised between the familiar realism of the balance of power, which he had so long recorded as an historian and manipulated as a statesman, and the hope that there must be some better way of doing things. His 1943 proposal of a world organization divided into regional councils represented an effort to blend universalist and sphere-of-interest conceptions. His initial rejection of Stalin's proposal in December 1941 as "directly contrary to the first, second and third articles of the Atlantic Charter" thus did not spring entirely from a desire to propitiate the United States. On the other hand, he had himself already reinterpreted the Atlantic Charter as applying only to Europe (and thus not to the British Empire), and he was, above all, an empiricist who never believed in sacrificing reality on the altar of doctrine.

So in April 1942 he wrote Roosevelt that "the increasing gravity of the war" had led him to feel that the Charter "ought not to be construed so as to deny Russia the frontiers she occupied when Germany attacked her." Hull, however, remained fiercely hostile to the inclusion of territorial provisions in the Anglo-Russian treaty; the American position, Eden noted, "chilled me with Wilsonian memories." Though Stalin complained that it looked "as if the Atlantic Charter was directed against the U.S.S.R.," it was the Russian season of military adversity in the spring of 1942, and he dropped his demands.

He did not, however, change his intentions. A year later Ambassador Standley could cable Washington from Moscow: "In 1918 Western Europe attempted to set up a *cordon sanitaire* to protect it from the influence of bolshevism. Might not now the Kremlin envisage the formation of a belt of pro-Soviet states to protect it from the influences of the West?" It well might; and that purpose became increasingly clear as the war approached its end. Indeed, it derived sustenance from Western policy in the first area of liberation.

The unconditional surrender of Italy in July 1943 created the first major test of the Western devotion to universalism. America and Britain, having won the Italian war, handled the capitulation, keeping Moscow informed at a distance. Stalin complained:

> The United States and Great Britain made agreements but the Soviet Union received information about the results . . . just as a passive third observer. I have to tell you that it is impossible to tolerate the situation any longer. I propose that the [tripartite military-political commission] be established and that Sicily be assigned . . . as its place of residence.

Roosevelt, who had no intention of sharing the control of Italy with the Russians, suavely replied with the suggestion that Stalin send an officer "to General Eisenhower's headquarters in connection with the commission." Unimpressed, Stalin continued to press for a tripartite body; but his Western allies were adamant in keeping the Soviet Union off the Control Commission for Italy, and the Russians in the end had to be satisfied with a seat, along with minor Allied states, on a meaningless Inter-Allied Advisory Council. Their acquiescence in this was doubtless not unconnected with a desire to establish precedents for Eastern Europe.

Teheran in December 1943 marked the high point of three-power collaboration. Still, when Churchill asked about Russian territorial interests, Stalin replied a little ominously, "There is no need to speak at the present time about any Soviet desires, but when the time comes we will speak." In the next weeks, there were increasing indications of a Soviet determination to deal unilaterally with Eastern Europe—so much so that in early February 1944 Hull cabled Harriman in Moscow:

> Matters are rapidly approaching the point where the Soviet Government will have to choose between the development and extension of the foundation of international cooperation as the guiding principle of the postwar world as against the continuance of a unilateral and arbitrary method of dealing with its special problems even though these problems are admittedly of more direct interest to the Soviet Union than to other great powers.

As against this approach, however, Churchill, more tolerant of sphere-of-influence deviations, soon proposed that, with the impending liberation of the Balkans, Russia should run things in Rumania and Britain in Greece. Hull strongly opposed this suggestion but made the mistake of leaving Washington for a few days; and Roosevelt, momentarily free from his Wilsonian conscience, yielded to Churchill's plea for a three-months' trial. Hull resumed the fight on his return, and Churchill postponed the matter.

The Red Army continued its advance into Eastern Europe. In August the Polish Home Army, urged on by Polish-language broadcasts from Moscow, rose up against the Nazis in Warsaw. For 63 terrible days, the Poles fought valiantly on, while the Red Army halted on the banks of the Vistula a few miles away, and in Moscow Stalin for more than half this time declined to coöperate with the Western effort to drop supplies to the Warsaw Resistance. It appeared a calculated Soviet decision to let the Nazis slaughter the anti-Soviet Polish underground; and, indeed, the result was to destroy any substantial alternative to a Soviet solution in Poland. The agony of Warsaw caused the most deep and genuine moral shock in Britain and America and provoked dark forebodings about Soviet postwar purposes.

Again history enjoins the imaginative leap in order to see things for a moment from Moscow's viewpoint. The Polish question, Churchill would say at Yalta, was for Britain a question of honor. "It is not only a question of honor for Russia," Stalin replied, "but one of life and death. . . . Throughout history Poland had been the corridor for attack on Russia." A top postwar priority for any Russian régime must be to close that corridor. The Home Army was led by anti-communists. It clearly hoped by its action to forestall the Soviet occupation of Warsaw and, in Russian eyes, to prepare the way for an anti-Russian Poland. In addition, the uprising from a strictly operational viewpoint was premature. The Russians, it is evident in retrospect, had real military problems at the Vistula. The Soviet attempt in September to send Polish units from the Red Army across the river to join forces with the Home Army was a disaster. Heavy German shelling thereafter prevented the ferrying of tanks necessary for an assault on the German position. The Red Army itself did not take Warsaw for another three months. None the less, Stalin's indifference to the human tragedy, his effort to blackmail the London Poles during the ordeal, his sanctimonious opposition during five precious weeks to aerial resupply, the invariable coldness of his explanations ("the Soviet command has come to the conclusion that it must dissociate itself from the Warsaw adventure") and the obvious political benefit to the Soviet Union from the destruction of the Home Army—all these had the effect of suddenly dropping the mask of wartime comradeship and displaying to the West the hard face of Soviet policy. In now pursuing what he grimly regarded as the minimal requirements for the postwar security of his country, Stalin was inadvertently showing the irreconcilability of both his means and his ends with the Anglo-American conception of the peace.

Meanwhile Eastern Europe presented the Alliance with still another crisis that same September. Bulgaria, which was not at war with Russia, decided to surrender to the Western Allies while it still could; and the English and Americans at Cairo began to discuss armistice terms with Bulgarian envoys. Moscow, challenged by what it plainly saw as a Western intrusion into its own zone of vital interest, promptly declared war on Bulgaria, took over the surrender negotiations and, invoking the Italian precedent, denied its Western Allies any role in the Bulgarian Control Commission. In a long and thoughtful cable, Ambassador Harriman meditated on the problems of communication with the Soviet Union. "Words," he reflected, "have a different connotation to the Soviets than they have to us. When they speak of insisting on 'friendly governments' in their neighboring countries, they have in mind something quite different from what we would mean." The Russians, he surmised, really believed that Washington accepted "their position that although they would keep us informed they had the right to settle their problems with their western neighbors unilaterally." But the Soviet position was still in flux: "the Soviet Government is not one mind." The problem, as Harriman had earlier told Harry Hopkins, was "to strengthen the hands of those around Stalin who want to play the game along our lines." The way to do this, he now told Hull, was to

> be understanding of their sensitivity, meet them much more than half way, encourage them and support them wherever we can, and yet oppose them promptly with the greatest of firmness where we see them going wrong. . . . The only way we can eventually come to an understanding with the Soviet Union on the question of non-interference in the internal affairs of other countries is for us to take a definite interest in the solution of the problems of each individual country as they arise.

As against Harriman's sophisticated universalist strategy, however, Churchill, increasingly fearful of the consequences of unrestrained competition in Eastern Europe, decided in early October to carry his sphere-of-influence proposal directly to Moscow. Roosevelt was at first content to have Churchill speak for him too and even prepared a cable to that effect. But Hopkins, a more rigorous universalist, took it upon himself to stop the cable and warn Roosevelt of its possible implications. Eventually Roosevelt sent a message to Harriman in Moscow emphasizing that he expected to "retain complete freedom of action after this conference is over." It was now that Churchill quickly proposed—and Stalin as quickly accepted—the celebrated division of southeastern Europe: ending (after further haggling between Eden and Molotov) with 90 percent Soviet predominance in Rumania, 80 percent in Bulgaria and Hungary, fifty-fifty in Jugoslavia, 90 percent British predominance in Greece.

Churchill in discussing this with Harriman used the phrase "spheres of influence." But he insisted that these were only "immediate wartime arrangements" and received a highly general blessing from Roosevelt. Yet, whatever Churchill intended, there is reason to believe that Stalin construed the percentages as an agreement, not a declaration; as practical arithmetic, not algebra. For Stalin, it should be understood, the sphere-of-influence idea did not mean that he would abandon all efforts to spread communism in some other nation's sphere; it did mean that, if he tried this and the other side cracked down, he could not feel he had serious cause for complaint. As Kennan wrote to Harriman at the end of 1944:

> As far as border states are concerned the Soviet government has never ceased to think in terms of spheres of interest. They expect us to support them in whatever action they wish to take in those regions, regardless of whether that action seems to us or to the rest of the world to be right or wrong. . . . I have no doubt that this position is honestly maintained on their part, and that they would be equally prepared to reserve moral judgment on any actions which we might wish to carry out, i.e., in the Caribbean area.

In any case, the matter was already under test a good deal closer to Moscow than the Caribbean. The communist-dominated resistance movement in Greece was in open revolt against the effort of the Papandreou government to disarm and disband the guerrillas (the same Papandreou whom the Greek colonels have recently arrested on the claim that he is a tool of the communists). Churchill now called in British Army units to crush the insurrection. This action produced a storm of criticism in his own country and in the United States; the American Government even publicly dissociated itself from the intervention, thereby emphasizing its detachment from the sphere-of-influence deal. But Stalin, Churchill later claimed, "adhered strictly and faithfully to our agreement of October, and during all the long weeks of fighting the Communists in the streets of Athens not one word of reproach came from *Pravda* or *Izvestia*," though there is no evidence that he tried to call off the Greek communists. Still, when the communist rebellion later broke out again in Greece, Stalin told Kardelj and Djilas of Jugoslavia in 1948, "The uprising in Greece must be stopped, and as quickly as possible."

No one, of course, can know what really was in the minds of the Russian leaders. The Kremlin archives are locked; of the primary actors, only Molotov survives, and he has not yet indicated any desire to collaborate with the Columbia Oral History Project. We do know that Stalin did not wholly surrender to sentimental illusion about his new friends. In June 1944, on the night before the landings in Normandy, he told Djilas that the English "find nothing sweeter than to trick their allies. . . . And Churchill? Churchill is the kind who, if you don't watch him, will slip a kopeck out of your pocket. Yes, a kopeck out of your pocket! . . . Roosevelt is not like that. He dips in his hand only for bigger coins." But whatever his views of his colleagues it is not unreasonable to suppose that Stalin would have been satisfied at the end of the war to secure what Kennan has called "a protective glacis along Russia's western border," and that, in exchange for a free hand in Eastern Europe, he was prepared to give the British and Americans equally free hands in their zones of vital interest, including in nations as close to Russia as Greece (for the British) and, very probably—or at least so the Jugoslavs believe—China (for the United States). In other words, his initial objectives were very probably not world conquest but Russian security.

It is now pertinent to inquire why the United States rejected the idea of stabilizing the world by division into spheres of influence and insisted on an East European strategy. One should warn against rushing to the conclusion that it was all a row between hard-nosed, balance-of-power realists and starry-eyed Wilsonians. Roosevelt, Hopkins, Welles, Harriman, Bohlen, Berle, Dulles and other universalists were tough and serious men. Why then did they rebuff the sphere-of-influence solution?

The first reason is that they regarded this solution as containing within itself the seeds of a third world war. The balance-of-power idea seemed inherently unstable. It had always broken down in the past. It held out to each power the permanent temptation to try to alter the balance in its own favor, and it built this temptation into the international order. It would turn the great powers of 1945 away from the objective of concerting common policies toward competition for postwar advantage. As Hopkins told Molotov at Teheran, "The President feels it essential to world peace that Russia, Great Britain and the United States work out this control question in a manner which will not start each of the three powers arming against the others." "The greatest likelihood of eventual conflict," said the Joint Chiefs of Staff in 1944 (the only conflict which the J.C.S., in its wisdom, could then glimpse "in the foreseeable future" was between Britain and Russia), ". . . would seem to grow out of either nation initiating attempts to build up its strength, by seeking to attach to herself parts of Europe to the disadvantage and possible danger of her potential adversary." The Americans were perfectly ready to acknowledge that Russia was entitled to convincing assurance of her national security—but not this way. "I could sympathize fully with Stalin's desire to protect his western borders from future attack," as Hull put it. "But I felt that this security could best be obtained through a strong postwar peace organization."

Hull's remark suggests the second objection: that the sphere-of-influence approach would, in the words of the State Department in 1945, "militate against the establishment and effective functioning of a broader system of general security in which all countries will have their part." The United Nations, in short, was seen as the alternative to the balance of power. Nor did the universalists see any necessary incompatibility between the Russian desire for "friendly governments" on its frontier and the American desire for self-determination in Eastern Europe. Before Yalta the State Department judged the general mood of Europe as "to the left and strongly in favor of far-reaching economic and social reforms, but not, however, in favor of a left-wing totalitarian regime to achieve these reforms." Governments in Eastern Europe could be sufficiently to the left "to allay Soviet suspicions" but sufficiently representative "of the center and *petit bourgeois* elements" not to seem a prelude to communist dictatorship. The American criteria were therefore that the government "should be dedicated to the preservation of civil liberties" and "should favor social and economic reforms." A string of New Deal states—of Finlands and Czechoslovakias—seemed a reasonable compromise solution.

Third, the universalists feared that the sphere-of-interest approach would be what Hull termed "a haven for the isolationists," who would advocate America's participation in Western Hemisphere affairs on condition that it did not participate in European or Asian affairs. Hull also feared that spheres of interest would lead to "closed trade areas or discriminatory systems" and thus defeat his cherished dream of a low-tariff, freely trading world.

Fourth, the sphere-of-interest solution meant the betrayal of the principles for which the Second World War was being fought—the Atlantic Charter, the Four Freedoms, the Declaration of the United Nations. Poland summed up the problem. Britain, having gone to war to defend the independence of Poland from the Germans, could not easily conclude the war by surrendering the independence of Poland to the Russians. Thus, as Hopkins told Stalin after Roosevelt's death in 1945, Poland had "become the symbol of our ability to work out problems with the Soviet Union." Nor could American liberals in general watch with equanimity while the police state spread into countries which, if they had mostly not been real democracies, had mostly not been tyrannies either. The execution in 1943 of Ehrlich and Alter, the Polish socialist trade union leaders, excited deep concern. "I have particularly in mind," Harriman cabled in 1944, "objection to the institution of secret police who may become involved in the persecution of persons of truly democratic convictions who may not be willing to conform to Soviet methods."

Fifth, the sphere-of-influence solution would create difficult domestic problems in American politics. Roosevelt was aware of the six million or more Polish votes in the 1944 election; even more acutely, he was aware of the broader and deeper attack which would follow if, after going to war to stop the Nazi conquest of Europe, he permitted the war to end with the communist conquest of Eastern Europe. As Archibald MacLeish, then Assistant Secretary of State for Public Affairs, warned in January 1945, "The wave of disillusionment which has distressed us in the last several weeks will be increased if the impression is permitted to get abroad that potentially totalitarian provisional governments are to be set up without adequate safeguards as to the holding of free elections and the realization of the principles of the Atlantic Charter." Roosevelt believed that no administration could survive which did not try everything short of war to save Eastern Europe, and he was the supreme American politician of the century.

Sixth, if the Russians were allowed to overrun Eastern Europe without argument, would that satisfy them? Even Kennan, in a dispatch of May 1944, admitted that the "urge" had dreadful potentialities: "If initially successful, will it know where to stop? Will it not be inexorably carried forward, by its very nature, in a struggle to reach the whole—to attain complete mastery of the shores of the Atlantic and the Pacific?" His own answer was that there were inherent limits to the Russian capacity to expand—"that Russia will not have an easy time in maintaining the power which it has seized over other people in Eastern and Central Europe, unless it receives both moral and material assistance from the West." Subsequent developments have vindicated Kennan's argument. By the late forties, Jugoslavia and Albania, the two East European states farthest from the Soviet Union and the two in which communism was imposed from within rather than from without, had declared their independence of Moscow. But, given Russia's success in maintaining centralized control over the international communist movement for a quarter of a century, who in 1944 could have had much confidence in the idea of communist revolts against Moscow?

Most of those involved therefore rejected Kennan's answer and stayed with his question. If the West turned its back on Eastern Europe, the higher probability, in their view, was that the Russians would use their security zone, not just for defensive purposes, but as a springboard from which to mount an attack on Western Europe, now shattered by war, a vacuum of power awaiting its master. "If the policy is accepted that the Soviet Union has a right to penetrate her immediate neighbors for security," Harriman said in 1944, "penetration of the next immediate neighbors becomes at a certain time equally logical." If a row with Russia were inevitable, every consideration of prudence dictated that it should take place in Eastern rather than Western Europe.

Thus idealism and realism joined in opposition to the sphere-of-influence solution. The consequence was a determination to assert an American interest in the postwar destiny of all nations, including those of Eastern Europe. In the message which Roosevelt and Hopkins drafted after Hopkins had stopped Roosevelt's initial cable authorizing Churchill to speak for the United States at the Moscow meeting of October 1944, Roosevelt now said, "There is in this global war literally no question, either military or political, in which the United States is not interested." After Roosevelt's death Hopkins repeated the point to Stalin: "The cardinal basis of President Roosevelt's policy which the American people had fully supported had been the concept that the interests of the U.S. were worldwide and not confined to North and South America and the Pacific Ocean."

For better or worse, this was the American position. It is now necessary to attempt the imaginative leap and consider the impact of this position on the leaders of the Soviet Union who, also for better or for worse, had reached the bitter conclusion that the survival of their country depended on their unchallenged control of the corridors through which enemies had so often invaded their homeland. They could claim to have been keeping their own side of the sphere-of-influence bargain. Of course, they were working to capture the resistance movements of Western Europe; indeed, with the appointment of Oumansky as Ambassador to Mexico they were even beginning to enlarge underground operations in the Western Hemisphere. But, from their viewpoint, if the West permitted this, the more fools they; and, if the West stopped it, it was within their right to do so. In overt political matters the Russians were scrupulously playing the game. They had watched in silence while the British shot down communists in Greece. In Jugoslavia Stalin was urging Tito (as Djilas later revealed) to keep King Peter. They had not only acknowledged Western preëminence in Italy but had recognized the Badoglio régime; the Italian Communists had even voted (against the Socialists and the Liberals) for the renewal of the Lateran Pacts.

They would not regard anti-communist action in a Western zone as a *casus belli*; and they expected reciprocal license to assert their own authority in the East. But the principle of self-determination was carrying the United States into a deeper entanglement in Eastern Europe than the Soviet Union claimed as a right (whatever it was doing underground) in the affairs of Italy, Greece or China. When the Russians now exercised in Eastern Europe the same brutal control they were prepared to have Washington exercise in the American sphere of influence, the American protests, given the paranoia produced alike by Russian history and Leninist ideology, no doubt seemed not only an act of hypocrisy but a threat to security. To the Russians, a stroll into the neighborhood easily became a plot to burn down the house: when, for example, damaged American planes made emergency landings in Poland and Hungary, Moscow took this as attempts to organize the local resistance. It is not unusual to suspect one's adversary of doing what one is already doing oneself. At the same time, the cruelty with which the Russians executed their idea of spheres of influence—in a sense, perhaps, an unwitting cruelty, since Stalin treated the East Europeans no worse than he had treated the Russians in the thirties—discouraged the West from accepting the equation (for example, Italy = Rumania) which seemed so self-evident to the Kremlin.

So Moscow very probably, and not unnaturally, perceived the emphasis on self-determination as a systematic and deliberate pressure on Russia's western frontiers. Moreover, the restoration of capitalism to countries freed at frightful cost by the Red Army no doubt struck the Russians as the betrayal of the principles for which *they* were fighting. "That they, the victors," Isaac Deutscher has suggested, "should now preserve an order from which they had experienced nothing but hostility, and could expect nothing but hostility . . . would have been the most miserable anti-climax to their great 'war of liberation.'" By 1944 Poland was the critical issue; Harriman later said that "under instructions from President Roosevelt, I talked about Poland with Stalin more frequently than any other subject." While the West saw the point of Stalin's demand for a "friendly government" in Warsaw, the American insistence on the sovereign virtues of free elections (ironically in the spirit of the 1917 Bolshevik decree of peace, which affirmed "the right" of a nation "to decide the forms of its state existence by a free vote, taken after the complete evacuation of the incorporating or, generally, of the stronger nation") created an insoluble problem in those countries, like Poland (and Rumania) where free elections would almost certainly produce anti-Soviet governments.

The Russians thus may well have estimated the Western pressures as calculated to encourage their enemies in Eastern Europe and to defeat their own minimum objective of a protective glacis. Everything still hung, however, on the course of military operations. The wartime collaboration had been created by one thing, and one thing alone: the threat of Nazi victory. So long as this threat was real, so was the collaboration. In late December 1944, von Rundstedt launched his counter-offensive in the Ardennes. A few weeks later, when Roosevelt, Churchill and Stalin gathered in the Crimea, it was in the shadow of this last considerable explosion of German power. The meeting at Yalta was still dominated by the mood of war.

Yalta remains something of an historical perplexity—less, from the perspective of 1967, because of a mythical American deference to the sphere-of-influence thesis than because of the documentable Russian deference to the universalist thesis. Why should Stalin in 1945 have accepted the Declaration on Liberated Europe and an agreement on Poland pledging that "the three governments will jointly" act to assure "free elections of governments responsive to the will of the people"? There are several probable answers: that the war was not over and the Russians still wanted the Americans to intensify their military effort in the West; that one clause in the Declaration premised action on "the opinion of the three governments" and thus implied a Soviet veto, though the Polish agreement was more definite; most of all that the universalist algebra of the Declaration was plainly in Stalin's mind to be construed in terms of the practical arithmetic of his sphere-of-influence agreement with Churchill the previous October. Stalin's assurance to Churchill at Yalta that a proposed Russian amendment to the Declaration would not apply to Greece makes it clear that Roosevelt's pieties did not, in Stalin's mind, nullify Churchill's percentages. He could well have been strengthened in this supposition by the fact that *after* Yalta, Churchill himself repeatedly reasserted the terms of the October agreement as if he regarded it, despite Yalta, as controlling.

Harriman still had the feeling before Yalta that the Kremlin had "two approaches to their postwar policies" and that Stalin himself was "of two minds." One approach emphasized the internal reconstruction and development of Russia; the other its external expansion. But in the meantime the fact which dominated all political decisions—that is, the war against Germany —was moving into its final phase. In the weeks after Yalta, the military situation changed with great rapidity. As the Nazi threat declined, so too did the need for coöperation. The Soviet Union, feeling itself menaced by the American idea of self-determination and the borderlands diplomacy to which it was leading, skeptical whether the United Nations would protect its frontiers as reliably as its own domination in Eastern Europe, began to fulfill its security requirements unilaterally.

In March Stalin expressed his evaluation of the United Nations by rejecting Roosevelt's plea that Molotov come to the San Francisco conference, if only for the opening sessions. In the next weeks the Russians emphatically and crudely worked their will in Eastern Europe, above all in the test country of Poland. They were ignoring the Declaration on Liberated Europe, ignoring the Atlantic Charter, self-determination, human freedom and everything else the Americans considered essential for a stable peace. "We must clearly recognize," Harriman wired Washington a few days before Roosevelt's death, "that the Soviet program is the establishment of totalitarianism, ending personal liberty and democracy as we know and respect it."

At the same time, the Russians also began to mobilize communist resources in the United States itself to block American universalism. In April 1945 Jacques Duclos, who had been the Comintern official responsible for the Western communist parties, launched in *Cahiers du Communisme* an uncompromising attack on the policy of the American Communist Party. Duclos sharply condemned the revisionism of Earl Browder, the American Communist leader, as "expressed in the concept of a long-term class peace in the United States, of the possibility of the suppression of the class struggle in the postwar period and of establishment of harmony between labor and capital." Browder was specifically rebuked for favoring the "self-determination" of Europe "west of the Soviet Union" on a bourgeois-democratic basis. The excommunication of Browderism was plainly the Politburo's considered reaction to the impending defeat of Germany; it was a signal to the communist parties of the West that they should recover their identity; it was Moscow's alert to communists everywhere that they should prepare for new policies in the postwar world.

The Duclos piece obviously could not have been planned and written much later than the Yalta conference—that is, well before a number of events which revisionists now cite in order to demonstrate American responsibility for the Cold War: before Allen Dulles, for example, began to negotiate the surrender of the German armies in Italy (the episode which provoked Stalin to charge Roosevelt with seeking a separate peace and provoked Roosevelt to denounce the "vile misrepresentations" of Stalin's informants); well before Roosevelt died; many months before the testing of the atomic bomb; even more months before Truman ordered that the bomb be dropped on Japan. William Z. Foster, who soon replaced Browder as the leader of the

American Communist Party and embodied the new Moscow line, later boasted of having said in January 1944, "A post-war Roosevelt administration would continue to be, as it is now, an imperialist government." With ancient suspicions revived by the American insistence on universalism, this was no doubt the conclusion which the Russians were reaching at the same time. The Soviet canonization of Roosevelt (like their present-day canonization of Kennedy) took place after the American President's death.

The atmosphere of mutual suspicion was beginning to rise. In January 1945 Molotov formally proposed that the United States grant Russia a $6 billion credit for postwar reconstruction. With characteristic tact he explained that he was doing this as a favor to save America from a postwar depression. The proposal seems to have been diffidently made and diffidently received. Roosevelt requested that the matter "not be pressed further" on the American side until he had a chance to talk with Stalin; but the Russians did not follow it up either at Yalta in February (save for a single glancing reference) or during the Stalin-Hopkins talks in May or at Potsdam. Finally the proposal was renewed in the very different political atmosphere of August. This time Washington inexplicably mislaid the request during the transfer of the records of the Foreign Economic Administration to the State Department. It did not turn up again until March 1946. Of course this was impossible for the Russians to believe; it is hard enough even for those acquainted with the capacity of the American government for incompetence to believe; and it only strengthened Soviet suspicions of American purposes.

The American credit was one conceivable form of Western contribution to Russian reconstruction. Another was lend-lease, and the possibility of reconstruction aid under the lend-lease protocol had already been discussed in 1944. But in May 1945 Russia, like Britain, suffered from Truman's abrupt termination of lend-lease shipments—"unfortunate and even brutal," Stalin told Hopkins, adding that, if it was "designed as pressure on the Russians in order to soften them up, then it was a fundamental mistake." A third form was German reparations. Here Stalin in demanding $10 billion in reparations for the Soviet Union made his strongest fight at Yalta. Roosevelt, while agreeing essentially with Churchill's opposition, tried to postpone the matter by accepting the Soviet figure as a "basis for discussion"—a formula which led to future misunderstanding. In short, the Russian hope for major Western assistance in postwar reconstruction foundered on three events which the Kremlin could well have interpreted respectively as deliberate sabotage (the loan request), blackmail (lend-lease cancellation) and pro-Germanism (reparations).

Actually the American attempt to settle the fourth lend-lease protocol was generous and the Russians for their own reasons declined to come to an agreement. It is not clear, though, that satisfying Moscow on any of these financial scores would have made much essential difference. It might have persuaded some doves in the Kremlin that the U.S. government was genuinely friendly; it might have persuaded some hawks that the American anxiety for Soviet friendship was such that Moscow could do as it wished without inviting challenge from the United States. It would, in short, merely have reinforced both sides of the Kremlin debate; it would hardly have reversed deeper tendencies toward the deterioration of political relationships. Economic deals were surely subordinate to the quality of mutual political confidence; and here, in the months after Yalta, the decay was steady.

The Cold War had now begun. It was the product not of a decision but of a dilemma. Each side felt compelled to adopt policies which the other could not but regard as a threat to the principles of the peace. Each then felt compelled to undertake defensive measures. Thus the Russians saw no choice but to consolidate their security in Eastern Europe. The Americans, regarding Eastern Europe as the first step toward Western Europe, responded by asserting their interest in the zone the Russians deemed vital to their security. The Russians concluded that the West was resuming its old course of capitalist encirclement; that it was purposefully laying the foundation for anti-Soviet régimes in the area defined by the blood of centuries as crucial to Russian survival. Each side believed with passion that future international stability depended on the success of its own conception of world order. Each side, in pursuing its own clearly indicated and deeply cherished principles, was only confirming the fear of the other that it was bent on aggression.

Very soon the process began to acquire a cumulative momentum. The impending collapse of Germany thus provoked new troubles: the Russians, for example, sincerely feared that the West was planning a separate surrender of the German armies in Italy in a way which would release troops for Hitler's eastern front, as they subsequently feared that the Nazis might succeed in surrendering Berlin to the West. This was the context in which the atomic bomb now appeared. Though the revisionist argument that Truman dropped the bomb less to defeat Japan than to intimidate Russia is not convincing, this thought unquestionably appealed to some in Washington as at least an advantageous side-effect of Hiroshima.

So the machinery of suspicion and counter-suspicion, action and counter-action, was set in motion. But, given relations among traditional national states, there was still no reason, even with all the postwar jostling, why this should not have remained a manageable situation. What made it unmanageable, what caused the rapid escalation of the Cold War and in another two years completed the division of Europe, was a set of considerations which this account has thus far excluded.

Up to this point, the discussion has considered the schism within the wartime coalition as if it were entirely the result of disagreements among national states. Assuming this framework, there was unquestionably a failure of communication between America and Russia, a misperception of signals and, as time went on, a mounting tendency to ascribe ominous motives to the other side. It seems hard, for example, to deny that American postwar policy created genuine difficulties for the Russians and even assumed a threatening aspect for them. All this the revisionists have rightly and usefully emphasized.

But the great omission of the revisionists—and also the fundamental explanation of the speed with which the Cold War escalated—lies precisely in the fact that the Soviet Union was *not* a traditional national state.[4] This is where the "mirror image," invoked by some psychologists, falls down. For the Soviet Union was a phenomenon very different from America or Britain: it was a totalitarian state, endowed with an all-explanatory, all-consuming ideology, committed to the infallibility of government and party, still in a somewhat messianic mood, equating dissent with treason, and ruled by a dictator who, for all his quite extraordinary abilities, had his paranoid moments.

Marxism-Leninism gave the Russian leaders a view of the world according to which all societies were inexorably destined to proceed along appointed roads by appointed stages until they achieved the classless nirvana. Moreover, given the resistance of the capitalists to this development, the existence of any non-communist state was *by definition* a threat to the Soviet Union. "As long as capitalism and socialism exist," Lenin wrote, "we cannot live in peace: in the end, one or the other will triumph—a funeral dirge will be sung either over the Soviet Republic or over world capitalism."

Stalin and his associates, whatever Roosevelt or Truman did or failed to do, were bound to regard the United States as the enemy, not because of this deed or that, but because of the primordial fact that America was the leading capitalist power and thus, by Leninist syllogism, unappeasably hostile, driven by the logic of its system to oppose, encircle and destroy Soviet Russia. Nothing the United States could have done in 1944–45 would have abolished this mistrust, required and sanctified as it was by Marxist gospel—nothing short of the conversion of the United States into a Stalinist despotism; and even this would not have sufficed, as the experience of Jugoslavia and China soon showed, unless it were accompanied by total subservience to Moscow. So long as the United States remained a capitalist democracy, no American policy, given Moscow's theology, could hope to win basic Soviet confidence, and every American action was poisoned from the source. So long as the Soviet Union remained a messianic state, ideology compelled a steady expansion of communist power.

---

[4] This is the classical revisionist fallacy—the assumption of the rationality, or at least of the traditionalism, of states where ideology and social organization have created a different range of motives. So the Second World War revisionists omit the totalitarian dynamism of Nazism and the fanaticism of Hitler, as the Civil War revisionists omit the fact that the slavery system was producing a doctrinaire closed society in the American South. For a consideration of some of these issues, see "The Causes of the Civil War: A Note on Historical Sentimentalism" in my *The Politics of Hope* (Boston, 1963).

It is easy, of course, to exaggerate the capacity of ideology to control events. The tension of acting according to revolutionary abstractions is too much for most nations to sustain over a long period: that is why Mao Tse-tung has launched his Cultural Revolution, hoping thereby to create a permanent revolutionary mood and save Chinese communism from the degeneration which, in his view, has overtaken Russian communism. Still, as any revolution grows older, normal human and social motives will increasingly reassert themselves. In due course, we can be sure, Leninism will be about as effective in governing the daily lives of Russians as Christianity is in governing the daily lives of Americans. Like the Ten Commandments and the Sermon on the Mount, the Leninist verities will increasingly become platitudes for ritual observance, not guides to secular decision. There can be no worse fallacy (even if respectable people practiced it diligently for a season in the United States) than that of drawing from a nation's ideology permanent conclusions about its behavior.

A temporary recession of ideology was already taking place during the Second World War when Stalin, to rally his people against the invader, had to replace the appeal of Marxism by that of nationalism. ("We are under no illusions that they are fighting for us," Stalin once said to Harriman. "They are fighting for Mother Russia.") But this was still taking place within the strictest limitations. The Soviet Union remained as much a police state as ever; the régime was as infallible as ever; foreigners and their ideas were as suspect as ever. "Never, except possibly during my later experience as ambassador in Moscow," Kennan has written, "did the insistence of the Soviet authorities on isolation of the diplomatic corps weigh more heavily on me . . . than in these first weeks following my return to Russia in the final months of the war. . . . [We were] treated as though we were the bearers of some species of the plague"—which, of course, from the Soviet viewpoint, they were: the plague of skepticism.

Paradoxically, of the forces capable of bringing about a modification of ideology, the most practical and effective was the Soviet dictatorship itself. If Stalin was an ideologist, he was also a pragmatist. If he saw everything through the lenses of Marxism-Leninism, he also, as the infallible expositor of the faith, could reinterpret Marxism-Leninism to justify anything he wanted to do at any given moment. No doubt Roosevelt's ignorance of Marxism-Leninism was inexcusable and led to grievous miscalculations. But Roosevelt's efforts to work on and through Stalin were not so hopelessly naïve as it used to be fashionable to think. With the extraordinary instinct of a great political leader, Roosevelt intuitively understood that Stalin was the *only* lever available to the West against the Leninist ideology and the Soviet system. If Stalin could be reached, then alone was there a chance of getting the Russians to act contrary to the prescriptions of their faith. The best evidence is that Roosevelt retained a certain capacity to influence Stalin to the end; the nominal Soviet acquiescence in American universalism as late as Yalta was perhaps an indication of that. It is in this way that the death of Roosevelt was crucial—not in the vulgar sense that his policy was then reversed by his successor, which did not happen, but in the sense that no other American could hope to have the restraining impact on Stalin which Roosevelt might for a while have had.

Stalin alone could have made any difference. Yet Stalin, in spite of the impression of sobriety and realism he made on Westerners who saw him during the Second World War, was plainly a man of deep and morbid obsessions and compulsions. When he was still a young man, Lenin had criticized his rude and arbitrary ways. A reasonably authoritative observer (N. S. Khrushchev) later commented, "These negative characteristics of his developed steadily and during the last years acquired an absolutely insufferable character." His paranoia, probably set off by the suicide of his wife in 1932, led to the terrible purges of the mid-thirties and the wanton murder of thousands of his Bolshevik commrades. "Everywhere and in everything," Khrushchev says of this period, "he saw 'enemies,' 'double-dealers' and 'spies.'" The crisis of war evidently steadied him in some way, though Khrushchev speaks of his "nervousness and hysteria . . . even after the war began." The madness, so rigidly controlled for a time, burst out with new and shocking intensity in the postwar years. "After the war," Khrushchev testifies,

> the situation became even more complicated. Stalin became even more capricious, irritable and brutal; in particular, his suspicion grew. His persecution mania reached unbelievable dimensions. . . . He decided everything, without any consideration for anyone or anything.
>
> Stalin's wilfulness showed itself . . . also in the international relations of the Soviet Union. . . . He had completely lost a sense of reality; he demonstrated his suspicion and haughtiness not only in relation to individuals in the USSR, but in relation to whole parties and nations.

A revisionist fallacy has been to treat Stalin as just another Realpolitik statesman, as Second World War revisionists see Hitler as just another Stresemann or Bismarck. But the record makes it clear that in the end nothing could satisfy Stalin's paranoia. His own associates failed. Why does anyone suppose that any conceivable American policy would have succeeded?

An analysis of the origins of the Cold War which leaves out these factors—the intransigence of Leninist ideology, the sinister dynamics of a totalitarian society and the madness of Stalin—is obviously incomplete. It was these factors which made it hard for the West to accept the thesis that Russia was moved only by a desire to protect its security and would be satisfied by the control of Eastern Europe; it was these factors which charged the debate between universalism and spheres of influence with apocalyptic potentiality.

Leninism and totalitarianism created a structure of thought and behavior which made postwar collaboration between Russia and America—in any normal sense of civilized intercourse between national states—inherently impossible. The Soviet dictatorship of 1945 simply could not have survived such a collaboration. Indeed, nearly a quarter-century later, the Soviet régime, though it has meanwhile moved a good distance, could still hardly survive it without risking the release inside Russia of energies profoundly opposed to communist despotism. As for Stalin, he may have represented the only force in 1945 capable of overcoming Stalinism, but the very traits which enabled him to win absolute power expressed terrifying instabilities of mind and temperament and hardly offered a solid foundation for a peaceful world.

The difference between America and Russia in 1945 was that some Americans fundamentally believed that, over a long run, a modus vivendi with Russia was possible; while the Russians, so far as one can tell, believed in no more than a short-run modus vivendi with the United States.

Harriman and Kennan, this narrative has made clear, took the lead in warning Washington about the difficulties of short-run dealings with the Soviet Union. But both argued that, if the United States developed a rational policy and stuck to it, there would be, after long and rough passages, the prospect of eventual clearing. "I am, as you know," Harriman cabled Washington in early April, "a most earnest advocate of the closest possible understanding with the Soviet Union so that what I am saying relates only to how best to attain such understanding." Kennan has similarly made it clear that the function of his containment policy was "to tide us over a difficult time and bring us to the point where we could discuss effectively with the Russians the dangers and drawbacks this status quo involved, and to arrange with them for its peaceful replacement by a better and sounder one." The subsequent careers of both men attest to the honesty of these statements.

There is no corresponding evidence on the Russian side that anyone seriously sought a modus vivendi in these terms. Stalin's choice was whether his long-term ideological and national interests would be better served by a short-run truce with the West or by an immediate resumption of pressure. In October 1945 Stalin indicated to Harriman at Sochi that he planned to adopt the second course—that the Soviet Union was going isolationist. No doubt the succession of problems with the United States contributed to this decision, but the basic causes most probably lay elsewhere: in the developing situations in Eastern Europe, in Western Europe and in the United States.

In Eastern Europe, Stalin was still for a moment experimenting with techniques of control. But he must by now have begun to conclude that he had underestimated the hostility of the people to Russian dominion. The Hungarian elections in November would finally convince him that the Yalta formula was a road to anti-Soviet governments. At the same time, he was feeling more strongly than ever a sense of his opportunities in Western Europe. The other half of the Continent lay unexpectedly before him, politically demoralized, economically prostrate, militarily defenseless. The hunting would be better and safer than he had anticipated. As for the United States, the alacrity of postwar demobilization must have recalled Roosevelt's offhand remark at Yalta that "two years would be the limit" for keeping American troops in Europe. And, despite Dr. Eugene Varga's doubts about the immi-. nence of American economic breakdown, Marxist theology assured Stalin that the United States was heading into a bitter postwar depression and would be consumed with its own problems. If the condition of Eastern Europe made unilateral action seem essential in the interests of Russian security, the condition of Western Europe and the United States offered new temptations for communist expansion. The Cold War was now in full swing.

It still had its year of modulations and accommodations. Secretary Byrnes conducted his long and fruitless campaign to persuade the Russians that America only sought governments in Eastern Europe "both friendly to the Soviet Union and representative of all the democratic elements of the country." Crises were surmounted in Trieste and Iran. Secretary Marshall evidently did not give up hope of a modus vivendi until the Moscow conference of foreign secretaries of March 1947. Even then, the Soviet Union was invited to participate in the Marshall Plan.

The point of no return came on July 2, 1947, when Molotov, after bringing 89 technical specialists with him to Paris and evincing initial interest in the project for European reconstruction, received the hot flash from the Kremlin, denounced the whole idea and walked out of the conference. For the next fifteen years the Cold War raged unabated, passing out of historical ambiguity into the realm of good versus evil and breeding on both sides simplifications, stereotypes and self-serving absolutes, often couched in interchangeable phrases. Under the pressure even America, for a deplorable decade, forsook its pragmatic and pluralist traditions, posed as God's appointed messenger to ignorant and sinful man and followed the Soviet example in looking to a world remade in its own image.

In retrospect, if it is impossible to see the Cold War as a case of American aggression and Russian response, it is also hard to see it as a pure case of Russian aggression and American response. "In what is truly tragic," wrote Hegel, "there must be valid moral powers on both the sides which come into collision. . . . Both suffer loss and yet both are mutually justified." In this sense, the Cold War had its tragic elements. The question remains whether it was an instance of Greek tragedy—as Auden has called it, "the tragedy of necessity," where the feeling aroused in the spectator is "What a pity it had to be this way"—or of Christian tragedy, "the tragedy of possibility," where the feeling aroused is "What a pity it was this way when it might have been otherwise."

Once something has happened, the historian is tempted to assume that it had to happen; but this may often be a highly unphilosophical assumption. The Cold War could have been avoided only if the Soviet Union had not been possessed by convictions both of the infallibility of the communist word and of the inevitability of a communist world. These convictions transformed an impasse between national states into a religious war, a tragedy of possibility into one of necessity. One might wish that America had preserved the poise and proportion of the first years of the Cold War and had not in time succumbed to its own forms of self-righteousness. But the most rational of American policies could hardly have averted the Cold War. Only today, as Russia begins to recede from its messianic mission and to accept, in practice if not yet in principle, the permanence of the world of diversity, only now can the hope flicker that this long, dreary, costly contest may at last be taking on forms less dramatic, less obsessive and less dangerous to the future of mankind.

SUGGESTED READING

George Kennan's *Memoirs, 1925–1950* (Little, Brown, 1967) is a beautifully literate, often personal statement about the early Cold War; it reveals how unsuccessful the author was in freeing himself from the very moralism that he has decried in his call for a foreign policy based on the national interest. In *The Cold War as History* (Harper & Row, 1967), Louis Halle, a member of the Policy Planning Staff in Truman's State Department, wavers in his judgments on the Cold War between historical inevitability (and Olympian perspective) and uneasy moralism.

Walt W. Rostow's *The United States in the World Arena* (Harper & Row, 1960) is a representative view of the early Cold War by a Kennedy liberal writing during the Eisenhower years. Philip Mosely's *The Kremlin and World Politics: Studies in Soviet Policy & Action* ° (Random House, 1960) and Marshall Shulman's *Stalin's Foreign Policy Reappraised* ° (Harvard Univ. Press, 1963) are analyses by two former State Department advisers. John Snell's "The Cold War: Four Contemporary Appraisals," *American Historical Review*, LXVIII (Oct., 1962), 69–75, includes a vigorous attack on D. F. Fleming's *The Cold War and Its Origins* and on *From Yalta to Disarmament: Cold War Debate*, edited by J. P. Morray (Monthly Review Press, 1952).

In "Henry A. Wallace, the Liberals, and Soviet-American Relations," *Review of Politics*, XXX (April, 1968), 153–69, Alonzo Hamby is close to Schlesinger's position. For Schlesinger's thought, see *The Vital Center* ° (Houghton Mifflin, 1949), a passionate defense of liberalism and anticommunism; *The Age of Roosevelt* ° (Houghton Mifflin, 1957–1960, 3 vols.), which views the New Deal as the triumph of the middle way; *A Thousand Days* ° (Houghton Mifflin, 1965), which emphasizes the value of tough liberalism; *The Bitter Heritage* ° (Houghton Mifflin, 1966), a brief volume critical of Administration policies in Vietnam; and "Vietnam and the End of the Age of the Superpowers," *Harper's* (May, 1969), which blames the "tragedy of Vietnam" partly on a "warrior class" and explains the tragedy as "the catastrophic overextension . . . of valid principles."

RICHARD HOFSTADTER

The Pseudo-Conservative Revolt—1954

INTRODUCTION

In the years 1950 to 1955 the excesses of McCarthyism deeply shocked the American intellectual community. Regardless of how wild their charges of Communist subversion, Red-hunters in Congress apparently could count on the support of millions of "patriots" no less willing than themselves to trample on civil liberties. The intellectuals, who often were victims of McCarthy's rage, brooded over his seemingly wide popularity and became estranged from the masses they had romanticized in the 1930's. Historians and social scientists, disturbed by the contemporary uprising on the right, searched for the causes of the periodic eruptions of popular hysteria in America, of which McCarthyism seemed only the

FROM Richard Hofstadter, "The Pseudo-Conservative Revolt—1954," in *The Paranoid Style in American Politics and Other Essays*, pp. 41–65. Copyright 1954 by Richard Hofstadter. Reprinted by permission of Alfred A. Knopf, Inc., and Jonathan Cape Ltd.

most recent example. The most important contribution by a historian was Richard Hofstadter's *Age of Reform* (Knopf, 1955).

In this book Hofstadter argues that "elements of illiberalism . . . frequently seem to be an indissoluble part of popular movements." He finds, for example, that Populism, an uprising of discontented farmers in the 1890's, "was not an unambiguous forerunner of modern authoritarian movements," and that it "has survived in our own time, partly as an undercurrent of provincial resentments, popular and 'democratic' rebelliousness and suspiciousness, and nativism." As exemplified in the Populist hatred of the "money power," grassroots Americans, Hofstadter argues, tend to blame complex problems on conspiratorial forces such as big business, the Catholic Church, or the Communist party. Since observers of McCarthyism believed support for the movement was particularly strong in the rural Midwest, Hofstadter had apparently uncovered in the region's fading tradition of agrarian radicalism a major cause for its irrational behavior in the early 1950's.

The McCarthy phenomenon prompted the publication of a collection of essays edited by Daniel Bell and entitled *The New American Right* (published by Criterion in 1955 and reissued and revised in 1964 under the Doubleday imprint as *The Radical Right*). The contributions to this book analyze and try to account for the right-wing position; in the process they apply the *theory of pluralism*. Pluralists believe that mass movements threaten the rights of individuals, that power should be divided among competing interest groups and the responsible élite to prevent its concentration, that power in the postwar years was ordinarily sufficiently fragmented to assure preservation of liberty, and therefore that institutions had to be protected from popular uprisings like McCarthyism (a mass movement), which challenged the polity.

Hofstadter contributed to Bell's *The New American Right* an essay in which he relied quite heavily on "social-psychological" categories to explain the "pseudo-conservative" revolt of which McCarthyism was a part. Hofstadter's hypothesis is built on the concept of status anxiety, which the other contributors (including David Riesman, Talcott Parsons, Seymour M. Lipset, Daniel Bell, and Peter Viereck) also find at work among McCarthy's supporters. According to this hypothesis, old-stock Americans who are losing status and Americans of recent-immigrant origin who are on the way up suffer social strain that they relieve by safe but irrational attacks against liberals, left-wing intellectuals, and "subversives."

Since the late 1950's, Hofstadter's work, particularly *The Age of Reform* and the essay mentioned above, both based on his concept of status politics, has been the object of heavy criticism. On empirical grounds historians and political scientists have disputed his indictment of Populism and his contention that McCarthyism (or pseudo-conservatism) was peculiarly virulent in the rural Midwest and among the children of immigrants. But even within itself, Hofstadter's discussion of pseudo-conservatism presents problems. Changing status is a constant phenomenon of American life and affects too many groups of varying political persuasions to serve as a convincing explanation of McCarthyism. What of the substantial number of Irish-Americans, for instance, whose alleged status insecurity did not result in McCarthyism?

Eleven years after writing his essay on pseudo-conservatism, Hofstadter reprinted it in a collection of his work, *The Paranoid Style in American Politics* (Knopf, 1965). Acknowledging that "on some counts" he no longer accepted what he had originally written, he explained that "it proved impossible to take adequate account of [its] limitations merely by revising it; and since it serves as a record of how things looked to some of us in 1954 and as a useful way of opening up a dialogue between the present and recent past, it still seemed desirable to include it." As a result, he made only a "few minor textual changes and a few monitory footnotes." The essay as it appears in *The Paranoid Style in American Politics* is reprinted below.

*T*wenty years ago the dynamic force in American political life came from the side of liberal dissent, from the impulse to reform the inequities of our economic and social system and to change our ways of doing things, to the end that the sufferings of the Great Depression would never be repeated. Today the dynamic force in our political life no longer comes from the liberals who made the New Deal possible. By 1952 the liberals had had at least the trappings of power for twenty years. They could look back to a brief, exciting period in the mid-1930's when they had held power itself and had been able to transform the economic and administrative life of the nation. After twenty years the New Deal liberals have quite unconsciously taken on the psychology of those who have entered into possession. Moreover, a large part of the New Deal public, the jobless, distracted, and bewildered men of 1933, have in the course of the years found substantial places in society for themselves, have become homeowners, suburbanites, and solid citizens. Many of them still have the emotional commitments to the liberal dissent with which they grew up politically, but their social position is one of solid comfort. Among them the dominant tone has become one of satisfaction, even of a kind of conservatism. Insofar as Adlai Stevenson stirred their enthusiasm in 1952, it was not in spite of but in part because of the air of poised and reliable conservatism that he brought to the Democratic convention. By comparison, Harry Truman's impassioned rhetoric, with its occasional thrusts at "Wall Street," seemed passé and rather embarrassing. The change did not escape Stevenson himself. "The strange alchemy of time," he said in a speech at Columbus, "has somehow converted the Democrats into the truly conservative party of this country—the party dedicated to conserving all that is best, and building solidly and safely on these foundations." What most liberals now hope for is not to carry on with some ambitious new program, but simply to defend as much as possible of the old achievements and to try to keep traditional liberties of expression that are threatened.

There is, however, a dynamic of dissent in America today. Representing no more than a modest fraction of the electorate, it is not so powerful as the liberal dissent of the New Deal era, but it is powerful enough to set the tone of our political life and to establish throughout the country a kind of punitive reaction. The new dissent is certainly not radical—there are hardly any radicals of any sort left—nor is it precisely conservative. Unlike most of the liberal dissent of the past, the new dissent not only has no respect for nonconformism, but is based upon a relentless demand for conformity. It can most accurately be called pseudo-conservative—I borrow the term from *The Authoritarian Personality,* published in 1950 by Theodore W. Adorno and his associates—because its exponents, although they believe themselves to be conservatives and usually employ the rhetoric of conservatism, show signs of a serious and restless dissatisfaction with American life, traditions, and institutions. They have little in common with the temperate and compromising spirit of true conservatism in the classical sense of the word, and they are far from pleased with the dominant practical conservatism of the moment as it is represented by the Eisenhower administration. Their political reactions express rather a profound if largely unconscious hatred of our society and its ways—a hatred which one would hesitate to impute to them if one did not have suggestive evidence both from clinical techniques and from their own modes of expression.

From clinical interviews and thematic apperception tests, Adorno and his co-workers found that their pseudo-conservative subjects, although given to a form of political expression that combines a curious mixture of largely conservative with occasional radical notions, succeed in concealing from themselves impulsive tendencies that, if released in action, would be very far from conservative. The pseudo-conservative, Adorno writes, shows "conventionality and authoritarian submissiveness" in his conscious thinking and "violence, anarchic impulses, and chaotic destructiveness in the unconscious sphere. . . . The pseudo-conservative is a man who, in the name of upholding traditional American values and institutions and defending them against more or less fictitious dangers, consciously or unconsciously aims at their abolition." [1]

---

[1] Theodore W. Adorno et al.: *The Authoritarian Personality* (New York, 1950), pp. 675–6. While I have drawn heavily upon this enlightening study, I have some reservations about its methods and conclusions. For a critical review, see Richard Christie and Marie Jahoda (eds.): *Studies in the Scope and Method of "The Authoritarian Personality"* (Glencoe, Ill., 1954), particularly the penetrating comments by Edward Shils.

Who is the pseudo-conservative, and what does he want? It is impossible to identify him by social class, for the pseudo-conservative impulse can be found in practically all classes in society, although its power probably rests largely upon its appeal to the less-educated members of the middle classes. The ideology of pseudo-conservatism can be characterized but not defined, because the pseudo-conservative tends to be more than ordinarily incoherent about politics. The lady who, when General Eisenhower's victory over Senator Taft had finally become official in 1952, stalked out of the Hilton Hotel declaiming: "This means eight more years of socialism," was probably a fairly good representative of the pseudo-conservative mentality. So also were the gentleman who, at the Freedom Congress held at Omaha over a year ago by some "patriotic" organizations, objected to Earl Warren's appointment to the Supreme Court with the assertion: "Middle-of-the-road thinking can and will destroy us"; the general who spoke to the same group, demanding "an Air Force capable of wiping out the Russian Air Force and industry in one sweep," but also "a material reduction in military expenditures";[2] the people who a few years ago believed simultaneously that we had no business to be fighting communism in Korea and that the war should immediately be extended to an Asia-wide crusade against communism; and the most ardent supporters of the Bricker Amendment. Many of the most zealous followers of Senator McCarthy are also pseudo-conservatives, although his appeal clearly embraces a wider public.

The restlessness, suspicion, and fear shown in various phases of the pseudo-conservative revolt give evidence of the anguish which the pseudo-conservative experiences in his capacity as a citizen. He believes himself to be living in a world in which he is spied upon, plotted against, betrayed, and very likely destined for total ruin. He feels that his liberties have been arbitrarily and outrageously invaded. He is opposed to almost everything that has happened in American politics in the past twenty years. He hates the very thought of Franklin D. Roosevelt. He is disturbed deeply by American participation in the United Nations, which he can see only as a sinister organization. He sees his own country as being so weak that it is constantly about to fall victim to subversion; and yet he feels that it is so all-powerful that any failure it may experience in getting its way in the world—for instance, in the Orient—cannot possibly be due to its limitations but must be attributed to its having been betrayed.[3] He is the most bitter of all our citizens about our involvement in the wars of the past, but seems the least concerned about avoiding the next one. While he naturally does not like Soviet communism, what distinguishes him from the rest of us who also dislike it is that he shows

---

[2] On the Omaha Freedom Congress, see Leonard Boasberg: "Radical Reactionaries," *The Progressive*, December 1953.

[3] See the comments of D. W. Brogan in "The Illusion of American Omnipotence," *Harper's Magazine*, December 1952, pp. 21–8.

little interest in, is often indeed bitterly hostile to, such realistic measures as might actually strengthen the United States vis-à-vis Russia. He would much rather concern himself with the domestic scene, where communism is weak, than with those areas of the world where it is really strong and threatening. He wants to have nothing to do with the democratic nations of Western Europe, which seem to draw more of his ire than the Soviet Communists, and he is opposed to all "giveaway programs" designed to aid and strengthen these nations. Indeed, he is likely to be antagonistic to most of the operations of our federal government except congressional investigations, and to almost all its expenditures. Not always, however, does he go so far as the speaker at the Freedom Congress who attributed the greater part of our national difficulties to "this nasty, stinking 16th [income tax] Amendment."

A great deal of pseudo-conservative thinking takes the form of trying to devise means of absolute protection against that betrayal by our own officialdom which the pseudo-conservative feels is always imminent. The Bricker Amendment, indeed, might be taken as one of the primary symptoms of pseudo-conservatism. Every dissenting movement brings its demand for constitutional changes; and the pseudo-conservative revolt, far from being an exception to this principle, seems to specialize in constitutional revision, at least as a speculative enterprise. The widespread latent hostility toward American institutions takes the form, among other things, of a flood of proposals to write drastic changes into the body of our fundamental law. In June 1954, Richard Rovere pointed out in a characteristically astute piece that Constitution-amending had become almost a major diversion in the Eighty-third Congress.[4] About a hundred amendments were introduced and referred to committee. Several of these called for the repeal of the income tax. Several embodied formulas of various kinds to limit non-military expenditures to some fixed portion of the national income. One proposed to bar all federal expenditures on "the general welfare"; another, to prohibit American troops from serving in any foreign country except on the soil of the potential enemy; another, to redefine treason to embrace not only persons trying to overthrow the government but also those trying to "weaken" it, even by peaceful means. The last proposal might bring the pseudo-conservative rebels themselves under the ban of treason: for the sum total of these amendments could easily serve to send the whole structure of American society crashing to the ground.

As Mr. Rovere points out, it is not unusual for a large number of constitutional amendments to be lying about somewhere in the congressional hoppers. What is unusual is the readiness the Senate has shown to give them respectful consideration, and the peculiar populistic arguments some of its leading members have used to justify referring them to the state legislatures.

---

[4] Richard Rovere: "Letter from Washington," *The New Yorker*, June 19, 1954, pp. 67–72.

While the ordinary Congress hardly ever has occasion to consider more than one amendment, the Eighty-third Congress saw six constitutional amendments brought to the floor of the Senate, all summoning simple majorities, and four winning the two-thirds majority necessary before they can be sent to the House and ultimately to the state legislatures. It must be added that, with the possible exception of the Bricker Amendment itself, none of the six amendments so honored can be classed with the most extreme proposals. But the pliability of the senators, the eagerness of some of them to pass the buck and defer to "the people of the country," suggests how strong they feel the pressure to be for some kind of change that will give expression to the vague desire to repudiate the past which underlies the pseudo-conservative revolt.

One of the most urgent questions we can ask about the United States in our time is: Where did all this sentiment arise? The readiest answer is that the new pseudo-conservatism is simply the old ultra-conservatism and the old isolationism heightened by the extraordinary pressures of the contemporary world. This answer, true though it may be, gives a deceptive sense of familiarity without much deepening our understanding, for the particular patterns of American isolationism and extreme right-wing thinking have themselves not been very satisfactorily explored. It will not do, to take but one example, to say that some people want the income-tax amendment repealed because taxes have become very heavy in the past twenty years: for this will not explain why, of three people in the same tax bracket, one will grin and bear it and continue to support social-welfare legislation as well as an adequate military establishment, while another responds by supporting in a matter-of-fact way the practical conservative leadership of the moment, and the third finds his feelings satisfied only by the angry accusations of conspiracy and extreme demands of the pseudo-conservative.

No doubt the circumstances determining the political style of any individual are complex. Although I am concerned here to discuss some of the neglected social-psychological elements in pseudo-conservatism, I do not wish to appear to deny the presence of important economic and political causes. I am aware, for instance, that wealthy reactionaries try to use pseudo-conservative organizers, spokesmen, and groups to propagate their notions of public policy, and that some organizers of pseudo-conservative and "patriotic" groups often find in this work a means of making a living—thus turning a tendency toward paranoia into a vocational asset, probably one of the most perverse forms of occupational therapy known to man. A number of other circumstances—the drastic inflation and heavy taxes of our time, the imbalance in our party system, the deterioration of American urban life, considerations of partisan political expediency—also play a part. But none of these things seems to explain the broad appeal of pseudo-conservatism, its emotional intensity, its dense and massive irrationality, or some of the peculiar ideas it generates. Nor will they explain why those who profit by the organized movements find such a ready following among a large number of people, and why the rank-and-file janizaries of pseudo-conservatism are so eager to hurl accusations, write letters to congressmen and editors, and expend so much emotional energy and crusading idealism upon causes that plainly bring them no material reward.

Elmer Davis, seeking to account for such sentiment in his recent book *But We Were Born Free*, ventures a psychological hypothesis. He concludes, if I understand him correctly, that the genuine difficulties of our situation in the face of the power of international communism have inspired a widespread feeling of fear and frustration, and that those who cannot face these problems in a more rational way "take it out on their less influential neighbors, in the mood of a man who, being afraid to stand up to his wife in a domestic argument, relieves his feelings by kicking the cat." [5] This suggestion has the merit of both simplicity and plausibility, and it may begin to account for a portion of the pseudo-conservative public. But while we may dismiss our curiosity about the man who kicks the cat by remarking that some idiosyncrasy in his personal development has brought him to this pass, we can hardly help but wonder whether there are not, in the backgrounds of the hundreds of thousands of persons who are moved by the pseudo-conservative impulse, some commonly shared circumstances that will help to account for their all kicking the cat in unison.

All of us have reason to fear the power of international communism, and all our lives are profoundly affected by it. Why do some Americans try to face this threat for what it is, a problem that exists in a world-wide theater of action, while others try to reduce it largely to a matter of domestic conformity? Why do some of us prefer to look for allies in the democratic world, while others seem to prefer authoritarian allies or none at all? Why do the pseudo-conservatives express such a persistent fear and suspicion of *their own government*, whether its leadership rests in the hands of Roosevelt, Truman, or Eisenhower? Why is the pseudo-conservative impelled to go beyond the more or less routine partisan argument that we have been the victims of considerable misgovernment during the past twenty years to the disquieting accusation that we have actually been the victims of persistent conspiracy and betrayal—"twenty years of treason"? Is it not true, moreover, that political types very similar to the pseudo-conservative have had a long history in the United States, and that this history goes back to a time when the Soviet power did not loom nearly so large on our mental horizons? Was the Ku Klux Klan, for instance, which was responsibly estimated to have had a membership of from 4,000,000 to 4,500,000 persons at its peak in the 1920's, a phenomenon totally dissimilar to the pseudo-conservative revolt?

What I wish to suggest—and I do so in the spirit of one setting forth nothing more than a speculative hypothesis—is that pseudo-conservatism is

---

[5] Elmer Davis: *But We Were Born Free* (New York, 1954), pp. 35–6; cf. pp. 21–2 and passim.

in good part a product of the rootlessness and heterogeneity of American life and, above all, of its peculiar scramble for status and its peculiar search for secure identity. Normally there is a world of difference between one's sense of national identity or cultural belonging and one's social status. However, in American historical development, these two things, so easily distinguishable in analysis, have been jumbled together in reality, and it is precisely this that has given such a special poignancy and urgency to our status strivings. In this country a person's status—that is, his relative place in the prestige hierarchy of his community—and his rudimentary sense of belonging to the community—that is, what we call his "Americanism"—have been intimately joined. Because, as a people extremely democratic in our social institutions, we have had no clear, consistent, and recognizable system of status, our personal status problems have an unusual intensity. Because we no longer have the relative ethnic homogeneity we had up to about eighty years ago, our sense of belonging has long had about it a high degree of uncertainty. We boast of "the melting pot," but we are not quite sure what it is that will remain when we have been melted down.

We have always been proud of the high degree of occupational mobility in our country—of the greater readiness, as compared with other countries, with which a person starting in a very humble place in our social structure could rise to a position of moderate wealth and status, and with which a person starting with a middling position could rise to great eminence. We have looked upon this as laudable in principle, for it is democratic, and as pragmatically desirable, for it has served many a man as a stimulus to effort and has, no doubt, a great deal to do with the energetic and effectual tone of our economic life. The American pattern of occupational mobility, while often much exaggerated, as in the Horatio Alger stories and a great deal of the rest of our mythology, may properly be credited with many of the virtues and beneficial effects that are usually attributed to it. But this occupational and social mobility, compounded by our extraordinary mobility from place to place, has also had its less frequently recognized drawbacks. Not the least of them is that this has become a country in which so many people do not know who they are or what they are or what they belong to or what belongs to them. It is a country of people whose status expectations are random and uncertain, and yet whose status aspirations have been whipped up to a high pitch by our democratic ethos and our rags-to-riches mythology.[6]

In a country where physical needs have been, by the scale of the world's living standards, on the whole well met, the luxury of questing after

---

[6] Cf. in this respect the observation of Tocqueville: "It cannot be denied that democratic institutions strongly tend to promote the feeling of envy in the human heart; not so much because they afford to everyone the means of rising to the same level with others as because these means perpetually disappoint the persons who employ them. Democratic institutions awaken and foster a passion for equality which they can never entirely satisfy." Alexis de Tocqueville: *Democracy in America*, ed. by Phillips Bradley (New York, 1945), I, 201.

status has assumed an unusually prominent place in our civic consciousness. Political life is not simply an arena in which the conflicting interests of various social groups in concrete material gains are fought out; it is also an arena into which status aspirations and frustrations are, as the psychologists would say, projected. It is at this point that the issues of politics, or the pretended issues of politics, become interwoven with and dependent upon the personal problems of individuals. We have, at all times, two kinds of processes going on in inextricable connection with each other: *interest politics,* the clash of material aims and needs among various groups and blocs; and *status politics,* the clash of various projective rationalizations arising from status aspirations and other personal motives. In times of depression and economic discontent—and by and large in times of acute national emergency—politics is more clearly a matter of interests, although of course status considerations are still present. In times of prosperity and general well-being on the material plane, status considerations among the masses can become much more influential in our politics. The two periods in our recent history in which status politics has been particularly prominent, the present era and the 1920's, have both been periods of prosperity.

During depressions, the dominant motif in dissent takes expression in proposals for reform or in panaceas. Dissent then tends to be highly programmatic—that is, it gets itself embodied in many kinds of concrete legislative proposals. It is also future-oriented and forward-looking, in the sense that it looks to a time when the adoption of this or that program will materially alleviate or eliminate certain discontents. In prosperity, however, when status politics becomes relatively more important, there is a tendency to embody discontent not so much in legislative proposals as in grousing. For the basic aspirations that underlie status discontent are only partially conscious; and, even so far as they are conscious, it is difficult to give them a programmatic expression. It is more difficult for the old lady who belongs to the D.A.R. and who sees her ancestral home swamped by new working-class dwellings to express her animus in concrete proposals of any degree of reality than it is, say, for the jobless worker during a slump to rally to a relief program. Therefore, it is the tendency of status politics to be expressed more in vindictiveness, in sour memories, in the search for scapegoats, than in realistic proposals for positive action.[7]

---

[7] Cf. Samuel Lubell's characterization of isolationism as a vengeful memory. *The Future of American Politics* (New York, 1952), Ch. 7. See also the comments of Leo Lowenthal and Norbert Gutterman on the right-wing agitator: "The agitator seems to steer clear of the area of material needs on which liberal and democratic movements concentrate; his main concern is a sphere of frustration that is usually ignored in traditional politics. The programs that concentrate on material needs seem to overlook that area of moral uncertainties and emotional frustrations that are the immediate manifestations of malaise. It may therefore be conjectured that his followers find the agitator's statements attractive not because he occasionally promises to 'maintain the American standard of living' or to provide a job for everyone,' but because he intimates that he will give them the emotional satisfactions that are denied them in the contemporary social and economic set-up. He offers attitudes, not bread." *Prophets of Deceit* (New York, 1949), pp. 91–2.

Paradoxically the intense status concerns of present-day politics are shared by two types of persons who arrive at them from opposite directions. The first are found among some types of old-family, Anglo-Saxon Protestants, and the second are found among many types of immigrant families, most notably among the Germans and Irish, who are very frequently Catholic. The Anglo-Saxons are most disposed toward pseudo-conservatism when they are losing caste, the immigrants when they are gaining.[8]

Consider first the old-family Americans. These people, whose stocks were once far more unequivocally dominant in America than they are today, feel that their ancestors made and settled and fought for this country. They have a certain inherited sense of proprietorship in it. Since America has always accorded a certain special deference to old families—so many of our families are *new*—these people have considerable claims to status by descent, which they celebrate by membership in such organizations as the D.A.R. and the S.A.R. But large numbers of them are actually losing their other claims to status. For there are among them a considerable number of the shabby genteel, of those who for one reason or another have lost their old objective positions in the life of business and politics and the professions, and who therefore cling with exceptional desperation to such remnants of their prestige as they can muster from their ancestors. These people, although very often quite well-to-do, feel that they have been pushed out of their rightful place in American life, even out of their neighborhoods. Most of them have been traditional Republicans by family inheritance, and they have felt themselves edged aside by the immigrants, the trade unions, and the urban machines in the past thirty years. When the immigrants were weak, these native elements used to indulge themselves in ethnic and religious snobberies at their expense.[9] Now the immigrant groups have developed ample means, po-

---

[8] Every ethnic group has its own peculiar status history, and I am well aware that my remarks in the text slur over many important differences. The status history of the older immigrant groups like the Germans and the Irish is quite different from that of ethnic elements like the Italians, Poles, and Czechs, who have more recently arrived at the point at which they are bidding for wide acceptance in the professional and white-collar classes, or at least for the middle-class standards of housing and consumption enjoyed by these classes. The case of the Irish is of special interest, because the Irish, with their long-standing prominence in municipal politics, qualified as it has been by their relative non-acceptance in many other spheres, have an unusually ambiguous status. In many ways they have gained, while in others, particularly insofar as their municipal power has recently been challenged by other groups, especially the Italians, they have lost some status and power. The election of 1928, with its religious bigotry and social snobbery, inflicted upon them a status trauma from which they have never fully recovered, for it was a symbol of the Protestant majority's rejection of their ablest leadership on grounds quite irrelevant to merit. This feeling was kept alive by the breach between Al Smith and F.D.R., followed by the rejection of Jim Farley from the New Deal succession. A study of the Germans would perhaps emphasize the effects of uneasiness over national loyalties arising from the Hitler era and the Second World War, but extending back even to the First World War.

[9] One of the noteworthy features of the current situation is that fundamentalist Protestants and fundamentalist Catholics have so commonly subordinated their old feuds (and for the first time in our history) to unite in opposition to what they usually describe as "godless" elements.

litical and economic, of self-defense, and the second and third generations have become considerably more capable of looking out for themselves. Some of the old-family Americans have turned to find new objects for their resentment among liberals, left-wingers, intellectuals, and the like—for in true pseudo-conservative fashion they relish weak victims and shrink from asserting themselves against the strong.

New-family Americans have had their own peculiar status problem. From 1881 to 1900 over 8,800,000 immigrants came here, and during the next twenty years another 14,500,000. These immigrants, together with their descendants, constitute such a large portion of the population that Margaret Mead, in a stimulating analysis of our national character, has persuasively argued that the characteristic American outlook is now a third-generation point of view.[10] In their search for new lives and new nationality, these immigrants have suffered much, and they have been rebuffed and made to feel inferior by the "native stock," commonly being excluded from the better occupations and even from what has bitterly been called "first-class citizenship." Insecurity over social status has thus been mixed with insecurity over one's very identity and sense of belonging. Achieving a better type of job or a better social status and becoming "more American" have been practically synonymous, and the passions that ordinarily attach to social position have been vastly heightened by being associated with the need to belong.[11]

The problems raised by the tasks of keeping the family together, disciplining children for the American race for success, trying to conform to unfamiliar standards, protecting economic and social status won at the cost of much sacrifice, holding the respect of children who grow American more rapidly than their parents, have thrown heavy burdens on the internal relationships of many new American families. Both new and old American families have been troubled by the changes of the past thirty years—the new because of their striving for middle-class respectability and American identity, the old because of their efforts to maintain an inherited social position and to realize under increasingly unfavorable social conditions imperatives of character and personal conduct deriving from nineteenth-century Yankee-Protestant-rural backgrounds. The relations between generations, being cast in no stable mold, have been disordered, and the status anxieties of parents have been inflicted upon children.[12] Often parents entertain status aspira-

---

[10] Margaret Mead: *And Keep Your Powder Dry* (New York, 1942), Ch. 3.

[11] Addendum, 1965: Much of the following paragraph now seems to me to be gratuitously speculative, and I think the emphasis on authoritarianism in immigrant as opposed to native families questionable. That the pseudo-conservative mentality is characterized by a disorder in relation to authority, however, still seems to me to be a central point.

[12] See Else Frenkel-Brunswik's "Parents and Childhood as Seen Through the Interviews," in Adorno: op. cit., Ch. 10. The author remarks (pp. 387–8) concerning subjects who were relatively *free* from ethnic prejudice that in their families "less obedience is expected of the children. Parents are less status-ridden and thus show less anxiety with respect to conformity and are less intolerant toward manifestations of socially unaccepted behavior.

tions that they are unable to gratify, or that they can gratify only at exceptional psychic cost. Their children are expected to relieve their frustrations and redeem their lives. They become objects to be manipulated to that end. An extraordinarily high level of achievement is expected of them, and along with it a tremendous effort to conform and be respectable. From the standpoint of the children these expectations often appear in the form of an exorbitantly demanding authority that one dare not question or defy. Resistance and hostility, finding no moderate outlet in give-and-take, have to be suppressed, and reappear in the form of an internal destructive rage. An enormous hostility to authority, which cannot be admitted to consciousness, calls forth a massive overcompensation which is manifest in the form of extravagant submissiveness to strong power. Among those found by Adorno and his colleagues to have strong ethnic prejudices and pseudo-conservative tendencies, there is a high proportion of persons who have been unable to develop the capacity to criticize justly and in moderation the failings of parents and who are profoundly intolerant of the ambiguities of thought and feeling that one is so likely to find in real-life situations. For pseudo-conservatism is among other things a disorder in relation to authority, characterized by an inability to find other modes for human relationship than those of more or less complete domination or submission. The pseudo-conservative always imagines himself to be dominated and imposed upon because he feels that he is not dominant, and knows of no other way of interpreting his position. He imagines that his own government and his own leaders are engaged in a more or less continuous conspiracy against him because he has come to think of authority only as something that aims to manipulate and deprive him. It is for this reason, among others, that he enjoys seeing outstanding generals, distinguished Secretaries of State, and prominent scholars browbeaten.

Status problems take on a special importance in American life because a very large part of the population suffers from one of the most troublesome of all status questions: unable to enjoy the simple luxury of assuming their own nationality as a natural event, they are tormented by a nagging doubt as to whether they are really and truly and fully American. Since their forebears voluntarily left one country and embraced another, they cannot, as people do elsewhere, think of nationality as something that comes with birth; for them it is a matter of *choice*, and an object of striving. This is one reason why problems of "loyalty" arouse such an emotional response in many Americans and why it is so hard in the American climate of opinion to make any clear distinction between the problem of national security and the question of personal loyalty. Of course, there is no real reason to doubt the loyalty to Amer-

---

. . . Comparatively less pronounced status-concern often goes hand in hand with greater richness and liberation of emotional life. There is, on the whole, more affection, or more unconditional affection, in the families of unprejudiced subjects. There is less surrender to conventional rules."

ica of the immigrants and their descendants, or their willingness to serve the
country as fully as if their ancestors had lived here for three centuries. Nonetheless, they have been thrown on the defensive by those who have in the
past cast doubts upon the fullness of their Americanism. Possibly they are
also, consciously or unconsciously, troubled by the thought that since their
forebears have already abandoned one country, one allegiance, their own national allegiance might be considered fickle. For this I believe there is some
evidence in our national practices. What other country finds it so necessary
to create institutional rituals for the sole purpose of guaranteeing to its
people the genuineness of their nationality? Does the Frenchman or the
Englishman or the Italian find it necessary to speak of himself as "one
hundred per cent" English, French, or Italian? Do they find it necessary to
have their equivalents of "I Am an American Day"? When they disagree with
one another over national policies, do they find it necessary to call one another un-English, un-French, or un-Italian? No doubt they too are troubled
by subversive activities and espionage, but are their countermeasures taken
under the name of committees on un-English, un-French, or un-Italian activities?

The primary value that patriotic societies and anti-subversive ideologies have for their exponents can be found here. They provide additional and
continued reassurance both to those who are of old-American ancestry and
have other status grievances and to those who are of recent American ancestry and therefore feel in need of reassurance about their nationality. Veterans' organizations offer the same satisfaction—what better evidence can
there be of the genuineness of nationality and *earned* citizenship than military service under the flag of one's country? Of course, such organizations,
once they exist, are liable to exploitation by vested interests that can use
them as pressure groups on behalf of particular measures and interests. (Veterans' groups, since they lobby for the concrete interests of veterans, have a
double role in this respect.) But the cement that holds them together is the
status motivation and the desire for an identity.

Sociological studies have shown that there is a close relation between
social mobility and ethnic prejudice. Persons moving downward in the social
scale, and even upward under many circumstances, tend to show greater
prejudice against such ethnic minorities as the Jews and Negroes than commonly prevails in the social strata they have left or are entering.[13] While the
existing studies in this field have been focused upon prejudice rather than
the kind of hyper-patriotism and hyper-conformism that I am most concerned with, I believe that the typical prejudiced person and the typical

---

13 Cf. Joseph Greenblum and Leonard I. Pearlin: "Vertical Mobility and Prejudice," in
Reinhard Bendix and Seymour M. Lipset (eds.): *Class, Status and Power* (Glencoe, Ill.,
1953), pp. 480–91; Bruno Bettelheim and Morris Janowitz: "Ethnic Tolerance: A Function of Personal and Social Control," *American Journal of Sociology*, IV (1949), 137–45.

pseudo-conservative dissenter are usually the same person, that the mechanisms at work in both complexes are quite the same,[14] and that it is merely the expediencies and the strategy of the situation today that cause groups that once stressed racial discrimination to find other scapegoats. Both the displaced old-American type and the new ethnic elements that are so desperately eager for reassurance of their fundamental Americanism can conveniently converge upon liberals, critics, and nonconformists of various sorts, as well as Communists and suspected Communists. To proclaim themselves vigilant in the pursuit of those who are even so much as accused of "disloyalty" to the United States is a way not only of reasserting but of advertising their own loyalty—and one of the chief characteristics of American super-patriotism is its constant inner urge toward self-advertisement. One notable quality in this new wave of conformism is that its advocates are much happier to have as their objects of hatred the Anglo-Saxon, Eastern, Ivy League intellectual gentlemen than they are to have such bedraggled souls as, say, Julius and Ethel Rosenberg. The reason, I believe, is that in the minds of the status-driven it is no special virtue to be more American than the Rosenbergs, but it is really something to be more American than Dean Acheson or John Foster Dulles—or Franklin Delano Roosevelt.[15] The status aspirations of some of the ethnic groups are actually higher than they were twenty years ago—which suggests one reason (there are others) why, in the ideology of the authoritarian right wing, anti-Semitism and other blatant forms of prejudice have recently been soft-pedaled. Anti-Semitism, it has been said, is the poor man's snobbery. We Americans are always trying to raise the standard of living, and the same principle now seems to apply to standards of hating. So during the past fifteen years or so, the authoritarians have moved on from anti-Negroism and anti-Semitism to anti-Achesonianism, anti-intellectualism, anti-nonconformism, and other variants of the same idea, much in the same way as the average American, if he can manage it, will move on from a Ford to a Buick.

Such status strivings may help us to understand some of the otherwise unintelligible figments of the pseudo-conservative ideology—the incredibly bitter feeling against the United Nations, for instance. Is it not understandable that such a feeling might be, paradoxically, shared at one and the same time by an old Yankee-Protestant American, who feels that his social position is not what it ought to be and that these foreigners are crowding in on his country and diluting its sovereignty just as "foreigners" have crowded into

---

[14] The similarity is also posited by Adorno: op. cit., pp. 152 ff., and by others (see the studies cited by him, p. 152).

[15] I refer to such men to make the point that this animosity extends to those who are guilty of no wrongdoing. Of course, a person like Alger Hiss, who has been guilty, suits much better. Hiss is the hostage the pseudo-conservatives hold from the New Deal generation. He is a heaven-sent gift. If he did not exist, the pseudo-conservatives would not have been able to invent him.

his neighborhood, and by a second- or third-generation immigrant who has been trying so hard to de-Europeanize himself, to get Europe out of his personal heritage, and who finds his own government mocking him by its complicity in these Old World schemes?

Similarly, is it not status aspiration that in good part spurs the pseudo-conservative on toward his demand for conformity in a wide variety of spheres of life? Conformity is a way of guaranteeing and manifesting respectability among those who are not sure that they are respectable enough. The nonconformity of others appears to such persons as a frivolous challenge to the whole order of things they are trying so hard to become part of. Naturally it is resented, and the demand for conformity in public becomes at once an expression of such resentment and a means of displaying one's own soundness. This habit has a tendency to spread from politics into intellectual and social spheres, where it can be made to challenge almost anyone whose pattern of life is different and who is imagined to enjoy a superior social position —notably, as one agitator put it, those in the "parlors of the sophisticated, the intellectuals, the so-called academic minds."

Why has this tide of pseudo-conservative dissent risen to such heights in our time? To a considerable degree, we must remember, it is a response, however unrealistic, to realities. We do live in a disordered world, threatened by a great power and a powerful ideology, a world of enormous potential violence, which has already shown us the ugliest capacities of the human spirit. In our own country there has indeed been espionage, and laxity over security has in fact allowed some spies to reach high places. There is just enough reality at most points along the line to give a touch of credibility to the melodramatics of the pseudo-conservative imagination.

However, a number of developments in our recent history make this pseudo-conservative uprising more intelligible. For two hundred years and more, various conditions of American development—the process of settling the continent, the continuous establishment of new status patterns in new areas, the arrival of continuous waves of new immigrants, each pushing the preceding waves upward in the ethnic hierarchy—made it possible to satisfy a remarkably large part of the extravagant status aspirations that were aroused. There was a sort of automatic built-in status elevator in the American social edifice. Today that elevator no longer operates automatically, or at least no longer operates in the same way.[16]

Second, the growth of the mass media of communication and their use in politics have brought politics closer to the people than ever before and have made politics a form of entertainment in which the spectators feel themselves involved. Thus it has become, more than ever before, an arena into

---

[16] Addendum, 1965: The substantive point may still be a good one, but it occurs to me that this paragraph might be taken to mean that social mobility in the United States has been decreasing; the evidence points to the contrary.

which private emotions and personal problems can be readily projected. Mass communications have made it possible to keep the mass man in an almost constant state of political mobilization.

Third, the long tenure in power of the liberal elements to which the pseudo-conservatives are most opposed and the wide variety of changes that have been introduced into our social, economic, and administrative life have intensified the sense of powerlessness and victimization among the opponents of these changes and have widened the area of social issues over which they feel discontent. There has been, among other things, the emergence of a wholly new struggle: the conflict between businessmen of certain types and the New Deal bureaucracy, which has spilled over into a resentment of intellectuals and experts.

Finally, unlike our previous postwar periods, ours has been a period of continued crisis, from which the future promises no relief. In no foreign war of our history did we fight so long or make such sacrifices as in the Second World War. When it was over, instead of being able to resume our peacetime preoccupations, we were very promptly confronted with another war. It is hard for a certain type of American, who does not think much about the world outside and does not want to have to do so, to understand why we must become involved in such an unremitting struggle. It will be the fate of those in power for a long time to come to have to conduct the delicate diplomacy of the cold peace without the sympathy or understanding of a large part of their own people. From bitter experience, Eisenhower and Dulles are learning today what Truman and Acheson learned yesterday.

These considerations suggest that the pseudo-conservative political style, while it may already have passed the peak of its influence, is one of the long waves of twentieth-century American history and not a momentary mood. I do not share the widespread foreboding among liberals that this form of dissent will grow until it overwhelms our liberties altogether and plunges us into a totalitarian nightmare. Indeed, the idea that it is purely and simply fascist or totalitarian, as we have known these things in recent European history, is to my mind a false conception, based upon the failure to read American developments in terms of our peculiar American constellation of political realities. (It reminds me of the people who, because they found several close parallels between the N.R.A. and Mussolini's corporate state, were once deeply troubled at the thought that the N.R.A. was the beginning of American fascism.) However, in a populistic culture like ours, which seems to lack a responsible elite with political and moral autonomy, and in which it is possible to exploit the wildest currents of public sentiment for private purposes, it is at least conceivable that a highly organized, vocal, active, and well-financed minority could create a political climate in which the rational pursuit of our well-being and safety would become impossible.

SUGGESTED READING

C. Vann Woodward's "The Populist Heritage and the Intellectual," *American Scholar,* XXVIII (Winter, 1959–1960), 55–72, generally criticizes Hofstadter's analysis of Populism in *The Age of Reform,*° pointing to the existence of sour impulses elsewhere in late nineteenth-century American society and emphasizing on behalf of the Populists their brief Negro-white alliance. William Appleman Williams in "The Age of Re-Forming History," *Nation,* CLXXXII (June 30, 1956), 554, criticizes *The Age of Reform* from a radical perspective. David Shannon's "Was McCarthy a Political Heir of La Follette?" *Wisconsin Magazine of History,* XLV (Autumn, 1961), 3–10, fails to find a connection between La Follette's constituency and that of McCarthy in Wisconsin.

The most penetrating study of the relationship between McCarthyism and agrarian radical constituencies is Michael Rogin's *The Intellectuals and McCarthy* (M.I.T. Press, 1967). As a result of analyzing the voting returns in three Midwestern states for over half a century, he discovers that the main source of McCarthyism in that area was not agrarian radicals but regular Republicans, who had usually opposed movements of farmer protest. Though he defends rural radicals against charges of a linkage with McCarthyism, he does not deal with urban ethnic groups; the possibility thus remains that McCarthyism had some basis in a mass social neurosis. Nevertheless, his book is the finest theoretical critique of the pluralistic social theory advanced by Hofstadter, Lipset, Bell, and other contributors to *The New American Right* and brings into serious question their use of the concepts *mass movements* and *group politics.*

Norman Pollack in "Hofstadter on Populism: A Critique of *The Age of Reform,*" *Journal of Southern History,* XXVII (Nov., 1960), 478–500, and in *The Populist Response to Industrial America* ° (Harvard Univ. Press, 1962) assails Hofstadter's analysis, arguing that the Populists were radical critics of the capitalist system. In his "Fear of Man: Populism, Authoritarianism, and the Historian," *Agricultural History,* XXXIX (April, 1965), 59–67, Pollack attributes authoritarian tendencies to some of the pluralists who dealt with Populism. Williams, interestingly, in "The Vicious Circle of American Imperialism," *New Politics,* IV (Fall, 1965), 48–55, moves the Populists back into a "realistic" capitalist consensus, intent on the need to expand overseas markets.

In *The Paranoid Style in American Politics* ° Hofstadter answers some of the criticisms of his original essay on the pseudo-conservative revolt in *The American Scholar,* XXIV (Winter, 1954–55), 9–27; he addresses himself in particular to Martin Trow's "Small Businessmen, Political Tolerance and Support for McCarthy," *American Journal of Sociology,* LXIV (Nov., 1958), 270–81; and Nelson W. Polsby's "Towards an Explanation of McCarthyism," *Political Studies,* VIII (1960), 250–71. In the same volume, Hofstadter includes a postscript on the John Birch Society and extends his theory to account for the Goldwater movement, a theory challenged by the earlier work of Raymond Wolfinger *et al.* in "America's Radical Right: Politics and Ideology," in David Apter, ed., *Ideology and Discontent* (Free Press, 1964). When *The Radical Right* was issued in 1963, Hofstadter added a brief note, "Pseudo-Conservatism Revisited: A Postscript," in which he explained that the term "status politics" had been unduly narrow and that it required supplementation by what might be called "cultural politics," which would explain political clashes over such (cultural) issues as prohibition.

  The Meaning of McCarthyism,° edited by Earl Latham (Heath, 1965), is a useful collection of essays and excerpts from books and includes the articles by Polsby and Trow as well as parts of Richard Rovere's *Senator Joe McCarthy* (Harcourt, Brace & World, 1959), an indictment of the Senator, and William F. Buckley, Jr., and L. Brent Bozell's *McCarthy and His Enemies* ° (Regnery, 1954), a spirited defense of the McCarthy crusade and an attack on the Senator's critics.

NORMAN A. GRAEBNER

Eisenhower's Popular Leadership

INTRODUCTION

During the Eisenhower years liberal intellectuals were fond of chiding Americans for the blandness of their culture and their President for his addiction to golf and Westerns. They deplored Eisenhower's mangled syntax, his homilies and platitudes, and his distrust of intellectuals. They also lamented his popularity and warned that history would not confirm the choice of the voters who confused the President's good will with leadership and his private virtue with wisdom.

In the following essay, written during the 1960 presidential campaign, Norman Graebner reflects many of the liberal judgments of the 1950's in his assessment of the Eisenhower Presi-

FROM Norman A. Graebner, "Eisenhower's Popular Leadership," *Current History*, XXXVI (October, 1960), pp. 230–36, 244. Reprinted by permission of Current History, Inc., and the author.

dency. Although he acknowledges that the Administration consolidated the gains of the Democratic past and adapted that legacy to the 1950's, he believes that it failed to resolve the dilemmas of the time or to prepare the nation "for the cataclysm that is sure to come." In substance, according to Graebner, Eisenhower's achievements fell too far short of the national need to justify his popularity, and that popularity was no measure of his success.

Graebner's essay, however, does not always specify the precise nature of the Administration's failures nor the programs that should have been tried but were not—in civil rights, in the economy, and particularly in foreign policy. As did Kennedy in the 1960 campaign, Graebner emphasizes that Eisenhower sacrificed military strength and flexibility (in the form of non-nuclear deterrent weapons) to fiscal orthodoxy, and squandered American prestige. Moreover, Eisenhower even failed to bring articulated goals in foreign policy into line with the limit of American power.

This last theme—the limitations of American power—is central to the foreign policy criticisms of the realists—George Kennan (to whom Graebner dedicated his *Cold War Diplomacy, 1945–1960* [Van Nostrand, 1961]), Hans Morgenthau, and Walter Lippmann. Graebner, along with many other intellectuals of that time, criticized the Eisenhower Administration for a rhetoric that overreached its power and for words that promised more than the Government could or would deliver. The promise of liberation of communist satellites was fraudulent and massive retaliation ("more bang for the buck") was dangerous and impractical. These critics lamented the fact that the Administration never educated the American public to the realities of the Cold War, to the impossibility of clear-cut victories, and to the termination of American omnipotence.

Although Graebner is ambiguous about whether negotiations with the Russians after Stalin's death could have relaxed the tensions of the Cold War, other realists have attacked the Administration for avoiding meaningful private negotiations and for moralistic rhetoric and inflexible policies. For example, Secretary of State John Foster Dulles told the Senate Foreign Relations Committee in January of 1953 that Soviet Communism "believes human beings are nothing more than somewhat superior animals . . . and that the best kind of a world is that world which is organized as a well-managed farm. . . . I do not see how, as long as Soviet Communism holds those views . . . there can be any permanent reconciliation. . . . This is an irreconcilable conflict." (Quoted in Walter LaFeber, *America, Russia, and The Cold War, 1945–1966* [Wiley, 1967].)

Despite the realists' criticisms of the Administration's simple moralisms and their attacks on Dulles' strident platitudes, there is a more favorable way than Graebner suggests of viewing much of the Eisenhower Administration's foreign policy and of interpreting the discrepancy between self-righteous rhetoric and generally cautious (but not pacific) actions. Moralistic rhetoric satisfied the demands of many on the right who accepted words as substitutes for action. The relative moderation of the Administration was often disguised by this rhetoric; because Eisenhower refused to move very far beyond self-righteous platitudes, much American bloodshed was avoided.

It would be a mistake, however, to accept uncritically Graebner's characterization of the Administration's *actions* in foreign policy as flaccid. Caution did not mean inaction. During the Eisenhower Administration, the CIA overthrew the Government of Guatemala in 1954 and marines were landed in Lebanon in 1958. Even the Bay of Pigs invasion of 1961 was conceived by the CIA during the Eisenhower years. In an action that was endorsed by the liberals, the State Department, guided by Dulles, set up a new government in South Vietnam to prevent the reunification of the country under Ho Chi Minh. These very small-scale interventions—in Guatemala, Lebanon, and Vietnam—were usually limited, however, by Eisenhower's overall desire to avoid war. Even in the case of Vietnam in April, 1954, when he was considering armed intervention to stop the revolution against French rule, the President was cautious, pulling back after England refused to join the proposed coalition and after General Matthew Ridgway, his Army Chief of Staff, counseled against military actions.

In conclusion, it seems that Eisenhower, who has been rightly accused of allowing the nation to be without adequate forces for limited war, was not *in practice* restricted to the alternatives of taking no military action or of moving to nuclear war. Ultimately, then, new analyses of Eisenhower's Presidency may depart from Graebner's assessment and emphasize the Government's cautious deployment of very limited resources to expand the nation's influence in a Cold War that had the support of most Americans. And the self-imposed restraints on action meant the practical recognition of the limits of American power—an understanding that Graebner contends the Eisenhower Administration lacked. Whatever the subtle losses in national prestige, perhaps they do not outweigh the success of Eisenhower's Government, unlike its Democratic predecessors and successors, in keeping America out of war.

*A*fter almost eight years in the White House, Dwight D. Eisenhower remains the most enigmatic phenomenon in the history of the American presidency. Never has a popular leader who dominated so completely the national political scene affected so negligibly the essential historic processes of his time. Never has a President so renowned for his humanitarian instincts avoided so assiduously all the direct challenges to the status of individual civil rights. Promoted in 1952 as the man best qualified to deal with the Russians, he has resolved or mitigated none of the cold war conflicts which existed when he assumed office. Elected with an unshakable reputation in military affairs, he has met expanding criticism from military experts for his primary decisions on national defense. Heralded as a man of peace, he has entered his last months in office with the United States subjected to humiliating and unprecedented abuse in many areas of the free world.

This evident dichotomy between the popular image of the President and the net gains of his leadership is a simple and disturbing expression of that traditional American philosophy which denies politics a distinct and honorable place in national affairs. American society has long admired personality more than political wisdom, technique more than substance, honesty more than judgment. In a nation where private virtues have become the measure for public as well as private action, the President's transparent goodness and integrity alone have permitted him to escape direct responsibility for the nation's performance at home and abroad.

But Eisenhower as a political phenomenon has also been the product of his times, for he has fit the 1950's like a glove. Prosperity, by 1953, had eliminated most of the direct economic and social challenges of the past and with them the hard contest of power which characterizes politics in periods of stress. This absence of pervading strife has contributed to the nation's complacency and sustained the illusion that good will is sufficient for successful leadership. When the President has failed to achieve what was expected of him, the country has excused the failure as either inconsequential or the product of perversity in others.

For Republican leaders, therefore, the task of maintaining Eisenhower's popularity has consisted largely in keeping the American people mindful of his personal attributes. Republican editors, whether motivated by the President's obvious good intentions or by the knowledge that for a minority party he has been the greatest asset in over a generation, have given him the most adulatory press coverage in American history. The principle that right intent is of the essence has permitted White House officials to isolate Eisenhower from his policies. Indeed, even those Democratic leaders in Congress who have lampooned most things that the administration has done have been careful not to blame the President directly.

That Eisenhower's personality would become the dominant fact of American politics in the 1950's was apparent even before his nomination. As a purely military figure he was clearly one of the most "available" candidates in the nation's experience. His widely publicized and genuine personal charm, added to an illustrious military reputation at a time when such a reputation had some relevance to the requirements for successful leadership, made his selection by the Republican convention synonymous with his election to the White House.

Beyond Eisenhower's personal popularity nothing in the 1952 election was clear. The Republican candidate was not offered to the nation as the exponent of any specific economic faith. His personal "creed" had been published in the New York *Herald Tribune* prior to his nomination; it avowed a fundamental economic conservatism in which he warned that too much federal intervention would turn "the American dream into an American nightmare." But such views were not publicized, and Republican campaigning avoided any open clash with established Democratic economic dogma.

In electing Eisenhower, the nation demanded nothing more than a kind of independent leadership from a great personality who could rise above the strife of party. It was this quality in him that brought millions of stay-at-homes to the polls to produce a landslide victory. Eisenhower had not shattered the Democratic party. Adlai Stevenson, his Democratic opponent, received 3,000,000 more votes than did Harry Truman in 1948.

Dominating the new administration in January, 1953, were representatives of the managerial class—the highly-paid men hired to manage the great industrial and commercial enterprises of the country. This new class had thrown its corporate power behind Eisenhower in 1952; now it provided two-thirds of his original appointments to cabinet and key administrative posts. This group interpreted the election as a clarion call to effect a conservative revolution.

Whatever the composition and intent of the new leadership, it could not ignore the twin legacies of the past—the New Deal and the cold war. Republican leaders might speak the rhetoric of free enterprise, but in the essential areas of national action they deviated scarcely from the Truman tradition. Secretary Humphrey could neither dismantle the budget nor halt the continuing inflation. Nor could Secretary Benson return the American farmer to free enterprise. Eventually he would hand out more in agricultural subsidies than any of his Democratic predecessors.

The "New Look" in military policy spelled out the administration's effort to fulfill its promise of tax reduction without endangering the nation. The President made it clear that he was tailoring military power to budgetary considerations. In May, 1953, he suggested a budget cut of $8 billion to achieve "maximum military strength within economic capacities." A healthy and functioning economy, he said, was inseparable from true defense.

Eventually the New Look resulted in the burgeoning emphasis on nuclear weapons, for with such weapons the nation could achieve maximum destructiveness at minimum cost. Military experts warned that the concentration on such weapons limited the nation's strategic flexibility and, in the event of aggression, narrowed the American response to inaction or the mushroom cloud. The President held his own simply by throwing his personal prestige behind the administration's basic military decisions.

Necessity had taken its toll of Republican ambitions. Occasional legislation like Tidelands Oil or the Dixon-Yates contract caught the old spirit, but most bills resembled the remnants of the New Deal. Never had a national leadership been forced to operate so completely outside its established philosophy. This, in essence, spelled out the Republican dilemma. With its deep allegiance to American business, the administration refused to modify or restate its neo-Hooverian beliefs. It talked the language of Main Street, but Main Street does not control elections.

What remained in the Republican arsenal were the alleged failures in Truman foreign policy that had been exploited effectively in the 1952 campaign. For the Taftites in Congress, foreign policy had become the pawn in the conservative revolution with American failures in the Far East attributed to Democratic subversion and even New Dealism itself. Through congressional investigation the Republican leadership in Congress proceeded to delve into everything from past treason and corruption to the decisions of the Korean War.

Eisenhower did nothing to prevent this continuing Republican assault on the Democratic past although Democratic support was essential for the success of his program in Congress. His administration quickly came to terms with Senator Joseph McCarthy of Wisconsin as the price of party unity. In exchange for administration silence the Wisconsin Senator agreed to attack nothing that occurred after January 20, 1953. Eventually the administration itself became implicated in offering the diet of "warmed-over spy" when Herbert Brownell, the Attorney General, resurrected the Harry Dexter White case in 1953. As the administration, under Executive Order 10450, relieved hundreds from the federal payroll, it never made clear the nature of the charges.

Democratic leaders never forced the President to pay the political price for silencing his own right wing for their support in Congress. The foreign aid bill of 1953, for example, passed an almost equally divided House with 160 Democratic and 119 Republican votes. On critical matters of foreign affairs it was the Democratic party that carried the administration's program. These Democratic votes, for which nothing was required, permitted Eisenhower to escape the internal warfare of his party.

Sharp Republican reverses in November, 1953, demonstrated that the party leadership had not found a satisfactory formula. Republican chairman Leonard W. Hall admitted, "There is no question about it—as of today we are in trouble politically." To liberal Republicans there was an answer. The party required essentially a restatement of its philosophy that would form a better compromise between the past and present. Jacob K. Javits of New

York suggested that liberal Republicanism contained the balance that would meet the challenge of American politics. "Republican progressives," he wrote in *The New York Times Magazine Section* of November 15, 1953,

> subscribe whole-heartedly to the principle of individual freedom and to the idea of an economic system of competitive, private enterprise functioning with government help and cooperation rather than under government domination. But they also hold that belief in free enterprise does not eliminate a wide area of activities in which government can and should provide the individual's welfare by providing him with greater opportunities for social improvement than he could otherwise obtain.

Eisenhower grasped at the new formula. The government, he explained, believed in a program that was liberal with respect to public needs but conservative in matters of finance. In his message of January, 1954, he promised the business community that it would be expected to meet the basic need of an expanding economy. But the government, he added, would face the issues of welfare, social security, health, education and housing. "Banishing of destitution and cushioning the shock of personal disaster on the individual," he said, "are proper concerns of all levels of government, including the federal government."

Republican writers such as Arthur Larson, author of *A Republican Looks at his Party*, accepted the challenge of giving the new consensus the stature of a philosophy which was neither old Republicanism or New Dealism. They insisted that Eisenhower had become the architect and embodiment of a coherent political movement which had an entity of its own and which would continue after him. In a sense the new Republicanism reflected the President's amorphous vision of the general good which could best be achieved with moderation in everything. To describe his program, the President applied the terms "moderate progressivism" and "progressive moderation."

Essentially the new middle represented Republican conservatism which had made its bargain with the New Deal. As such it was an apt expression of the times, not a new philosophy of government. It simply reflected the conviction that policies of moderation are most suitable for times of prosperity. Efficiency and decentralization are natural goals in any post-crisis period.

Eventually the new Republicanism was reduced to an effort to explain the nation's high prosperity in terms of expanded economic freedom under the new Republican hegemony. At times it even identified prosperity with American virtues—a strong devotion to the family, the urge to work and save, the ambition to excel. Nowhere did Republican faith harbor the slightest doubt that the new balance had cured the business cycle. Assuming the persistence of prosperity, it contained no body of thought to guide the nation when things went wrong. It was not concerned with innovation or foreign affairs.

Actually the nation had long been moving toward what has been called the Eisenhower equilibrium. But the movement was prompted more by the mood of complacency and the conviction that enough had been done than by the attraction of any new economic doctrine. At the heart of the new center stood the conservative Democrats who after 1954 managed the affairs of Congress. With them were the Eisenhower Republicans of 1952 strengthened by the increasing conversion of Old Guard Republicans through political, economic and diplomatic necessity. Both groups agreed that the economy was basically sound and that the United States could not escape its challenges abroad. In the new consensus was an almost unprecedented feeling of interparty comradeship which blurred party distinctions. It left little room for the extremes in national political affairs. But the new center would last only as long as the nation's prosperity. Any serious cracking of the economy would again send politicians and the public scurrying to the edges of the political spectrum in search of answers and action.

Eisenhower's concept of his office was humble, even deferential, when compared to that of successful Presidents of the past. He had little taste for politics—the struggle for power among rival interests. Claiming no constitutional prerogatives for the executive branch, he pledged himself to restore confidence between the President and Congress so that both branches might work "with patience and good will to insure that the government is not divided against itself."

Eisenhower viewed his role as that of a presiding officer who exhorted and proposed, but who refused to enforce party discipline. Congressmen, he has said repeatedly, have a right to vote their own consciences.

Eisenhower was by training and habit a man of action, not of ideas. Abstractions never meant so much to him as things. For that reason the White House organization was designed to keep intellectual conflict within the administration to a minimum. Sherman Adams, White House Chief of Staff, controlled the information coming into the White House. James C. Hagerty, White House Press Secretary, controlled the information that came out. Together they managed to keep the President almost completely isolated. The President had never acquired the habit of reading the newspapers when he was in the Army; nor did he develop the habit after he entered the White House. He secured his news largely through the Army system of being "briefed" by spokesmen of Central Intelligence, the Pentagon, the State Department, or the White House staff.

Nor had the President any greater interest in other outside sources of information. Washington officials complained that they could not reach the President. Occasionally he conferred with Republican leaders in formal meetings, with White House aides sitting in.

Eisenhower once explained why he refused to become involved in details. "I do not believe," he informed a press conference, "that any individual . . . can do the best job just sitting at a desk and putting his face in a bunch of papers." It was his purpose, he added, "to keep his mind free of inconsequential details" so that he could make "clearer and better judgments." The President constructed his White House staff to eliminate the burden of detail.

Some writers have become ecstatic over Eisenhower's concept and use of his cabinet. They have prophesied that this organization, with its regularly scheduled meetings and carefully prepared agenda, will remain an integral part of the American governmental system. Perhaps the uniqueness of the system, relying on papers prepared by the executive departments, rests in the fact that it is admirably designed to achieve a broad consensus on administrative decisions. Eisenhower has viewed his administrative machine as partially a military staff, partially a board of directors.

The cohesion and loyalty of the White House team was a controlling factor in the President's willingness to run for a second term. "It's taken four years to get this outfit into top working shape," he told a friend. "It would be a shame to wash it out just as they are reaching their peak efficiency." If the staff system has secured the President's objectives of consensus and efficiency, it has also led to a diffusion of responsibility, illustrated most clearly in the U-2 incident of May, 1960.

Eisenhower has refused to permit his official duties to interfere with hunting, golfing and bridge. He has sought relaxation at every opportunity away from Washington, usually at his Gettysburg farm or at the Augusta National Golf Club. Occasionally he has taken a vacation in the West or New England. He once explained to a Washington press conference that recreation was essential to maintain the fitness necessary to meet the demands of the presidency. Hagerty has made it clear that when the President is absent from Washington a courier plane brings official papers every other day. In addition, the President often confers with officials in Washington by telephone, although more than once he has revealed extreme impatience at being disturbed by official calls from the capital.

Most Presidents have sought relief from the burdens of office. It was to the President's critics simply a matter of balance, and many believed that too often golf took precedence over matters of state. Edward P. Morgan of A.B.C. quipped characteristically in April, 1960: "President Eisenhower had hoped to helicopter to Gettysburg to cast his ballot today but found his schedule too tight. At the last minute, however, he did manage to squeeze in a round of golf."

Undoubtedly Eisenhower's concern for things material has had its effect on the intellectual climate of Washington. Many of the experts who drifted into Washington as economic and foreign policy advisers soon left. In every area of public policy the most impressive writers and thinkers are not only outside the government service but also almost totally ignored by those who make policy. Noting the absence of intellect in the nation's capital, James Reston of *The New York Times* Washington staff, complained in December, 1957:

> We are in a race with the pace of history. We are in a time when brain power is more important than fire power, but in the last five years, the President has gradually drifted apart from the intellectual opinion of the country, filled up his social hours with bantering locker-room cronies, and denied himself the mental stimulus that is always available to any President.

Whatever the nature of Eisenhower's leadership, his personality remained the unquestioned phenomenon in presidential politics. His image was that of a well-meaning man standing at the center of American life. Never was its impact clearer than at the San Francisco convention of 1956. Eisenhower was the convention; he was the party. He was beyond challenge. Much of the President's power, ironically, resulted from his party's decline during his first term.

This commanding position was also the product of the President's new look. Under Hagerty's coaching Eisenhower had learned to dominate the Washington press conference—an exceedingly important method of shaping the public impression of the President. By 1954, he was completely at ease, often bantering with reporters. He was increasingly better informed. He had learned to dodge questions for which he had no ready answer, avoiding the "bloopers" of his early months. Republican professionals now called him the greatest instinctive politician since F.D.R.

Eisenhower's television style, assiduously cultivated by professionals, had become technically perfect. Television, in fact, provided party managers with the perfect medium for maintaining the Eisenhower image, for what mattered was not the intellectual content of his speeches, but the sincerity and warmth which he communicated to the public.

The Eisenhower personality overshadowed the presidency itself. The traditional duties and obligations of office appeared inconsequential when contrasted with the warm and easy smile, the beaming face, the informal, simple and unpretentious manner that captured the imagination of people everywhere. Even the most popular Presidents of the past had begun to lose much of their lustre long before they left the White House. But Eisenhower's stature continued to grow.

With the new look the President revealed more determination in office, more familiarity with issues. He spoke less of cooperation with Congress and more about defending the prerogatives of the executive. But energy and action are not the sole criteria for effective leadership. With his increased interest in the exercise of his powers the President demonstrated no new awareness of the great political forces in the world, no new evidence that he had any greater interest in ideas. Often he seemed to be placing his new leadership in the service of drift, providing, in the words of Richard H. Rovere, "the spectacle, novel in the history of the Presidency, of a man strenuously in motion yet doing essentially nothing—traveling all the time yet going nowhere."

The difficulty was not the President's firmness; it was the nature of his policies. It was less the decisiveness than the decisions themselves. Despite the energy behind them, Eisenhower's actions still suggested that there were no problems that good intentions would not cure.

Sustaining the Eisenhower image did little for the Republican organization. Party managers sought to exploit the President's personality. They succeeded merely in assuring the American people that whatever happened, the President, not the party, would assume the burdens of leadership. This accounts for the strange dichotomy between the President's growing popularity and the persistent decline in Republican strength. Republican Governor Theodore R. McKeldin of Maryland reminded a Republican audience in February, 1957, that the party "hasn't a thing that the country wants" except Eisenhower. Nowhere had the Republican party succeeded in turning the President's image into any genuine political gains.

What has characterized the Eisenhower foreign policies has been the substitution of principle and personality for the traditional ingredients of diplomacy. In large measure this approach was dictated by the successful Republican campaigning of 1952. For when the Republican leadership, with its rhetoric of liberation, promised no less than the dismantling of both the Iron and Bamboo curtains, it denied itself the freedom to create future policy compatible with limited American power. Only when that leadership had disposed of its political symbols of Democratic iniquity and admitted publicly that it could not achieve what its key spokesmen, including the President, continued to promise during the months of party consolidation, could it formulate policy goals that had some relationship to the means at its disposal.

So completely had party objectives abroad over-reached American interest that the President's noteworthy achievements lay in *not* doing what members of his party demanded. His stature in the area of foreign affairs rested in his *refusal* to engage in war against mainland China, to become involved in the Indochinese civil war, to employ massive retaliation against Chinese cities.

It was the contribution of Secretary of State John Foster Dulles to translate American demands on Moscow and Peking, anchored to domestic political requirements, to the high realm of principle. If politics and principle converged, it was because both sought the retreat of the Soviet bloc. To that extent Dulles' principles appeared to square with American security interests, and the fact that through six years they exceeded what this nation's power could achieve and prevented the settlement of every outstanding issue in the cold war seemed to make no difference. If United States leadership could not secure what it wanted of others, it could at least take comfort in its ideals.

Unfortunately this reduced Mr. Dulles' diplomacy to rhetoric, for nothing else remained. As Hans J. Morgenthau wrote in December, 1956:

> When we heard spokesmen for the government propound the legal and moral platitudes which had passed for foreign policy in the interwar period, we thought that this was the way in which the government—as all governments must—tried to make the stark facts of foreign policy palatable to the people. . . . We were mistaken. Those platitudes *are* the foreign policy of the United States. . . .

If Dulles settled nothing, he also gave nothing away. The result of his tenure as Secretary of State was stalemate—a stalemate in which the cold war shifted to intense military and economic competition. Here Dulles' leadership could not prevent sharp reverses in Western power and prestige.

With Dulles' death in 1959 American policy became equated with the personality of the President. The rhetoric of liberation, now anchored to such homilies as "peace under freedom" or "peace with justice," continued, but even more important in the new diplomacy was the very person of the President. State visits abroad would give him the opportunity to demonstrate his good will before the world. Thereafter his success was measured not by diplomatic settlement but by the size and enthusiasm of the crowds that lined the thoroughfares of the cities of Europe, Asia and Latin America when he visited. These pressing throngs gave the impression that this nation was at last winning the cold war.

Unfortunately there was always the marked dichotomy between the cheers of the crowds and the lack of diplomatic progress in the chancelleries. Eisenhower's world travels were continuing expressions of American good intent, but they encompassed no action, commitments, or positive ideas to give permanent meaning to the tours. What remained after the experience was the evidence of personality and the absence of concrete achievement.

It was ironic that the President's good will tour of the Orient should be marred by Tokyo mobs, for the new diplomacy had been directed toward mobs. The President had been warned by writers, editors and even members of Congress, after the collapse of the Paris summit conference of May, 1960, not to run the risk of a trip around the fringes of the Communist world in the Far East. But to men who equated large crowds with diplomatic success here was the easiest method available to prove that the United States had lost nothing at Paris. What the cheers at Taipei and Tokyo might achieve was not clear. Had the President managed his trip to Japan he would have measured the triumph by the shouts of the people, for there was little to be gained in the quiet of the Japanese Foreign Office.

In a sense, Eisenhower's world tours comprised a final effort to create the illusion of peace when all genuine diplomacy had ceased to exist. What seemed to matter was the President's ability to draw larger and more enthusiastic crowds than Premier Khrushchev. But the visit of a president or premier to another land has no function other than to expose the visiting dignitary to the people that jam the thoroughfares. It is a mutual demonstration of good will, but nothing more. For if actual diplomacy were the objective, that could be pursued more cheaply and effectively via normal diplomatic channels. Nothing better illustrates the ephemeral nature of state visits than Khrushchev's conviction that he had won over the support of the American public during his remarkable visit of September, 1959. In retrospect, the visit had no effect on Russian-American relations at all.

Eisenhower responded to his failures in Paris and Tokyo with an air of injured innocence. His own dignity amid the collapse of the summit created the impression that whatever went wrong he was not at fault. He continued to detach himself from personal responsibility or the opinion of the free world. For the loss of American prestige in the Far East he blamed the Communists, not the deep and reasonable doubts created by missiles and Soviet threats. He continued to identify world peace with his personal diplomacy, repeating this conviction after his return from the Orient in July, 1960:

> No consideration of personal fatigue or inconvenience, no threat or argument would deter me from once again setting out on a course that has meant much for our country, for her friends, and for the cause of freedom—and peace with justice in the world.

Always the sacrifice was to the person, not to the nation in the form of added strength or reduced ambitions. In equating the cause of peace with the enthusiasm he received abroad, the President forgot that it is this nation's relations with the governments at Moscow and Peking, not with the crowds of New Delhi, Paris, or Taipei, that matter. In denying any error in judgment or policy, the President permitted no official review of his record. This solved no problems, but merely swept them under the rug.

Eisenhower's leadership has given rise to a curious standard of appraisal. For almost eight years his adherents have measured his success by popularity, not achievement. As George E. Allen concluded in his *Saturday Evening Post* article on Eisenhower in April, 1960:

> The man who took office mistrusting politics and politicians will leave office having proved himself one of the most successful politicians ever to occupy the Presidency. He will leave the White House more popular than when he moved in, and this will be an unprecedented feat—a political feat.

By such standards of personal popularity Harding and Coolidge would rank among the most successful of American presidents; Washington, John Adams, Polk, Lincoln, and Wilson among the failures.

What matters far more in presidential success are, first, the intellectual
alertness necessary to penetrate contemporary movements and, second, the
political craftsmanship required to translate victory into political action
which meets the challenge of the times. Measured by its adaptation of the
Democratic past to the conditions of the 1950's, the Eisenhower leadership
had been a success, indeed an historical necessity. But the permanent judgment of that leadership will hinge on the President's achievement in influencing, within the limits of his power, the fundamental trends of this age toward the protection of this nation's well-being.

The recent past is interlude. The dilemmas of the 1950's await their
disposal in some future time. Only in that future will men be permitted to
judge finally whether the present leadership has prepared the nation men-
tally and physically for the cataclysm that is sure to come.

SUGGESTED READING

The papers of the Eisenhower Administration have been open to scholars for just a few years, and so far practically no research on that Government's domestic activities exists. As a result, the bulk of the available
literature is composed of journalistic accounts written during those
years or memoirs recorded at the end of the Administration.

Samuel Lubell's *The Revolt of the Moderates* (Harper & Row,
1956) is an analysis of the "new politics" and is often critical of Eisenhower. Richard Rovere in *Affairs of State: The Eisenhower Years* (Far-
rar, Straus & Giroux, 1956), and Marquis Childs in *Eisenhower: Captive
Hero* (Harcourt, Brace & World, 1958) express the unhappiness of
liberals with the tone, style, and accomplishments of the man and his
Administration. William V. Shannon's "Eisenhower as President,"
Commentary, XXVI (Nov., 1958), 390–98, offers similar judgments
and emphasizes the shortcomings of the Administration's irresolute foreign
policy.

Robert J. Donovan's *Eisenhower: The Inside Story* (Harper &
Row, 1956) is a generally flattering account based on privileged acess to
private papers. The disillusionment expressed in *Ordeal of Power*
(Atheneum, 1963) by speech-writer and liberal Republican Emmet
John Hughes contrasts sharply with the portrait presented in *Firsthand
Report* (Harper & Row, 1961) by Sherman Adams, Eisenhower's "exec-
utive secretary," who was dismissed for unethical business dealings.

Dwight Eisenhower's *The White House Years: Mandate for
Change, 1953–1956* ° (Doubleday, 1963) and *The White House
Years: Waging Peace* ° (Doubleday, 1965) have predictable biases but
also contain considerable information for an assessment of his Presidency. Other reminiscences by members of Eisenhower's Administration include Ezra Taft Benson's *Cross Fire: The Eight Years with
Eisenhower* (Doubleday, 1962), Allen Dulles' *The Craft of Intelli-*

gence ° (Harper & Row, 1963), Richard Nixon's *Six Crises* ° (Doubleday, 1962), and Lewis Strauss' *Men and Decisions* (Doubleday, 1962).

Herman Finer's *Dulles Over Suez* (Quadrangle, 1964) is a savage indictment of the Secretary's policies. Louis Gerson's *John Foster Dulles* (Cooper Square, 1967) offers more moderate judgments.

On Vietnam, Chalmers Roberts' "The Day We Didn't Go to War," *Reporter*, XI (Sept., 1954), 31–35, seems generally reliable. Involvement in Vietnam is traced in *Vietnam: Documents and Opinions on a Major World Crisis,*° edited by Marvin Gettleman (Fawcett, 1966), and in *The Vietnam Reader,*° rev. ed., edited by Marcus Raskin and Bernard Fall (Vintage, 1967). The foreign policy of right wing Republicans, the so-called isolationists, has never been sympathetically analyzed. Henry Berger's "A Conservative Critique of Containment: Senator Taft on the Early Cold War Program," in *Containment and Revolution,* edited by David Horowitz (Beacon Press, 1967), argues that the most prominent of the early "isolationists" offered in 1945–47 a substantial critique of the dangers of overextending American power. Norman Graebner's *The New Isolationism* (Ronald Press, 1956) emphasizes their pro-Asian orientation and their ambivalence about withdrawing the United States from foreign involvements or using additional (usually military) power to triumph in disputes abroad.

Robert Scheer and Maurice Zeitlin in *Cuba: Tragedy in Our Hemisphere* ° (Grove Press, 1963) detail the efforts by the American ambassador to stop Castro from reaching power. George Kennan in *Russia, the Atom and the West* ° (Harper & Row, 1958) presents the argument for disengagement, whereas Dean Acheson's "The Illusion of Disengagement," *Foreign Affairs*, XXXVI (April, 1958), 371–82, is a vigorous critique.

GEORGE KATEB

Kennedy As Statesman

INTRODUCTION

Since John F. Kennedy's tragic death in November of 1963, liberal politicians have vied with one another to wear his mantle, and his name has become a symbol of hope and vitality, of toughness and idealism, of compassion and wisdom. Beginning with his presidential campaign in 1960, Kennedy demonstrated the power to excite the public and mobilize the energies of the young. He capitalized on vague discontents in promising the nation renewed purpose, economic growth, a stronger and more flexible military defense, and a restoration of prestige in the Cold War—in short, a New Frontier.

During the campaign, Kennedy had pledged vigorous domestic reform, but his slim plurality over Richard Nixon forced him to

FROM George Kateb, "Kennedy as Statesman," *Commentary*, XLIV (June, 1966), pp. 54–60. Copyright © 1966 by the American Jewish Committee. Reprinted from *Commentary*, by permission.

take a more cautious approach when in office. Even so, he could neither coerce nor cajole Congress to do his bidding in domestic affairs, particularly in regard to civil rights legislation and the tax cut. It was not Kennedy but his successor who would see enacted many of the programs that the departed President had initiated during his brief period in office. His contemporaries, however, believe that Kennedy left his mark not in domestic policy, but in foreign policy. The "disasters" of the first year—the Bay of Pigs invasion and the Berlin Wall crisis—were followed by "triumphs"—the Cuban missile crisis, the nuclear test ban treaty, and the détente with the Soviet Union.

It is Kennedy's foreign policy that the political theorist George Kateb critically examines in the following essay, written in 1966, when the Vietnam conflict had begun to drain American dollars and lives at an alarming rate. Kateb, unlike many of Kennedy's liberal admirers, stresses the defects and questionable achievements of Kennedy's foreign policy. He points out that the Kennedy Administration unwisely reversed Eisenhower's decision and implemented counter-insurgency, thus making possible large-scale American intervention in Vietnam.

Citing Kennedy's own words, Kateb also raises serious questions about whether the President's response to the presence of Russian missiles was necessary, since the balance of military power was not actually threatened. In defense of Kennedy, it can be pointed out that the missiles in Cuba trapped him in the cruel dilemma inherent in the theory of nuclear deterrence. This theory claims that deterrence is effective only if the enemy believes that a nation possesses the necessary weapons and means of delivery and, just as important, that it has the will to resort to nuclear warfare. It was Kennedy's will, his credibility, that seemed threatened by the installation of Soviet missiles in Cuba. To preserve credibility in order to prevent war, a nation may actually have to run a serious risk of war. There is another dimension to the missile crisis that Kateb overlooks. How candid in spirit and words was President Kennedy in his talk to the nation on the evening of October 22, 1962, when he reported that the Soviet Union had surreptitiously overturned the balance of power and planted "offensive" weapons ninety miles from Florida? If the danger was not as imminent as he suggested, did he not mislead the nation?

The missile crisis, the Bay of Pigs, and the armed intervention in Vietnam raise profound questions about the nature of and restraints on presidential power. The conduct of American foreign policy leaves to the President great discretion that allows him to bypass constitutional requirements. Without formal congressional approval, he can plunge the nation into armed conflict—as Truman did in Korea and Kennedy and Johnson did in Vietnam. The dangers of expanded presidential authority in the Cold War have come to seem so serious in recent years that historians are beginning to reappraise their criteria for measuring the success of Presidents, and some have recently expressed doubts that vigorous action in foreign affairs necessarily constitutes evidence of greatness. Kateb, though never explicitly raising these issues, seems to share these doubts.

*T*he dream of the political outsider is to know why men of state are doing what they do. There are, of course, some resources available to the diligent student: he can rely on the New York *Times* for an accumulation of indispensable detail, he can infer motive on the basis of a general theory of political behavior, he can immerse himself in the reading of history for the sake of plucking rough analogies from the inexhaustible record of the crimes and follies of mankind. But a nagging sense of insufficiency is always there. Detail, inference, analogy do not quite add up to the real thing. How can the student be sure that he is not catching at shadows, that he is not lost in the maze of his own imaginings, that he does not see a plot where there is only confusion or an impulse where there is in fact calculation? To be sure, his occupational hazard is paranoid suspicion, dirty-mindedness, motive-mongering; and his self-administered therapy is to take refuge in the epilogues to *War and Peace,* or in a desperate skepticism, or finally in an acceptance of things at face value. The lust to know what really is happening, however, cannot be checked. The voices of consolation or derision will inevitably be drowned out. The truth must be pursued. He will cling to the belief—perhaps it is a delusion—that secrecy is the one great obstacle between him and his goal, which is to perceive the time in which he lives.

So it is with enormous expectations that one opens the pages of the two recent books on John F. Kennedy by Theodore Sorensen [*Kennedy* (Harper & Row, 1966)] and Arthur Schlesinger, Jr. [*A Thousand Days* (Houghton Mifflin, 1966)]. Obviously, the whole truth will not be contained in them. Allowance must be made for tact and for national security. No single chronicler can have at his disposal more than a small amount of the raw ingredients of countless Presidential and bureaucratic decisions. For all that, both Sorensen and Schlesinger were close to the center; both would want to fill in the picture; Schlesinger especially could be expected to befriend the academic inquirer by letting him in on the daily actuality of the Kennedy administration. The events covered are not yet cold: we are now locked in their ramifications. Surely the intimate truth about the years 1961–1963 will make the immediate present more intelligible?

Neither book disappoints; each deepens our understanding of the Kennedy years. It would not be correct to say that any startling revelations are made; it may even be that a few vain readers will come away from these books (especially Sorensen's) with the feeling that there is nothing at all new in them, and that what the *Times* and a few journals had not already reported and disclosed, political shrewdness could supply. So be it. The fact remains that, at the very least, *Kennedy* and *A Thousand Days* put a great many things together, and by their very inclusiveness, permit a more definite sense of the recent past to emerge.

Truly, the sense that emerges is not the sense intended. The aim of both writers is naturally to praise—not indiscriminately, but for one main trait: newness. In the eyes of Sorensen and Schlesinger, Kennedy stood for a break with the past, and a break that was all to the good. He injected vitality into a stagnant nation, while striving to direct that vitality away from cold-war bellicosity, toward the deepest problems of the age, toward hunger, backwardness, and the craving for peace. Who can doubt that if it were only a question of Kennedy's abstract intention, this description of him would be perfectly accurate? What is so awful is that in case after case, as these two narratives (in spite of themselves) make clear, Kennedy's abstract intention gave way before pressures of one sort or another. Even more, Kennedy's initiative, in the absence of immediate pressures, was sometimes in direct contradiction to his abstract intention. To put the matter briefly: the break that Kennedy effected with the past resulted in an intensification of cold-war bellicosity, not in its lessening. Sometimes he acted deliberately; sometimes he acted as he did because he thought he could not act in any other way. The tendency of his actions, however, was to change the direction of Eisenhower's policy, and prepare the way for Johnson's activism. A good part of the story is found in these two books.

The story begins with the adoption of the so-called "McNamara strategy." This was a deliberate act of policy on the part of the Kennedy administration; a free choice, so to speak. It is certain that if Rockefeller had been President, the same strategy would have been adopted.[1] It is probable that if Nixon had been elected, he would have moved in the same direction as Kennedy. It is likely that only Stevenson, among the leading Democrats, would at least have tried, as President, to resist the adoption of the "McNamara strategy." Among the Republicans it had been, in fact, none other than Eisenhower who prevented its earlier acceptance, thereby causing the resignations of Ridgway, Gavin, and Maxwell Taylor. Which is to say that Kennedy's position represented no new departure in principle, but rather was faithful to widespread assumptions—assumptions shared by men wanting a more vigorous and extended American involvement in the struggle against Communism. From the very start of his administration, then, Kennedy was

---

[1] Sorensen says that in mid-1961, when McNamara's views were assuming final shape, Kennedy thought that Rockefeller was the most likely Republican opponent in 1964. "Nor was [Kennedy] unmindful of the fact that . . . Rockefeller . . . was criticizing the administration's complacency on civil defense in much the same terms Kennedy had applied to the 'missile gap' in earlier years."

determined to make American capacities more powerful because more re-
fined, even though he sincerely believed, and had believed for a long time,
that the affairs of the world perhaps needed an altogether different approach.

The McNamara strategy was meant to repeal the principal military
theory of the Eisenhower administration, the doctrine of massive retaliation.
Under this doctrine, the Soviet Union was to be held directly responsible for
any Leninist coup or insurrection anywhere in the world, and would stand to
suffer an overwhelming nuclear attack as punishment for its imputed responsibility. Furthermore, the response to any Soviet conventional military move
would also be an overwhelming nuclear attack. The doctrine needs only to
be stated to be convicted of monstrous absurdity; but there were doubtless
numerous officials who accepted it in its full absurdity. It is impossible, however, to believe that either Eisenhower or Dulles ever took their own theory
literally. It may even be possible to believe that by talking about massive
retaliation, Eisenhower was indirectly saying two things. First, American
opposition to coups and insurrections would have to take essentially non-
military forms, like bribery, good works, economic pressure, and backstage
conspiracy. Second, the old cold war was over, and no overt Russian military move was foreseen. In any case, the development of American anti-
guerrilla forces and, more important, the buildup of conventional forces, in
the name of open American engagement, were ruled out. The costs were
prohibitive; the effort provocative; the consequences treacherously uncertain. Schlesinger says half in humor, "Eisenhower could never find the use
of local aggression to which nuclear warfare seemed a sensible response."
But the joke is now on Schlesinger.

Kennedy initiated the abandonment of that policy. He embraced, as
Schlesinger neatly puts it, ". . . the strong view taken by the service whose
mission, money and traditions were most threatened by the . . . doctrine
[of massive retaliation]—the Army." In his first months, he added six billion
dollars to the last Eisenhower military budget. A large fraction went to the
nuclear deterrent: McNamara was, and is, a firm believer in something called
"flexible response": nuclear weapons must be so diverse and sophisticated as
to permit selectivity and gradation in their use. This is another phantom, and
I need not chase it now. The important point is that great sums were allo-
cated to the buildup of anti-guerrilla and conventional forces. Sorensen gives
the rationale: ". . . if this country was to be able to confine a limited challenge to the local and non-nuclear level, without permitting a Communist
victory—then it was necessary to build our own non-nuclear forces to the
point where any aggressor would be confronted with the same poor choice
Kennedy wanted to avoid: humiliation or escalation. A limited Communist
conventional action, in short, could best be deterred by a capacity to respond
effectively in kind." The only trouble with this rationale, in regard to Russia,
is that the buildup of conventional forces was much more a provocation than
a deterrence. Who could take seriously the possibility that Russia would in-

vade Western Europe or the Near East—who except the army and its intellectuals? What was there to deter? The trouble with this rationale, in regard to revolutionary movements, is that the inability of conventional and anti-guerrilla forces to deter would soon become apparent, and America would be tempted to use its strength to destroy what it could not deter. The counter-revolutionary career would be launched in earnest, with no end in sight. A task more huge, more hopeless, could not be conceived. The view of Communism as a monolithic force was retained from the old theory of massive retaliation; but now the ambition of meeting it in all its forms became entirely serious. Containment became a universal and undiscriminating principle of foreign policy. The threats to American security were seen as infinite.

Kennedy's vision of the world comes out most clearly in his conversations with Khrushchev at Vienna in June 1961. Schlesinger's report is fuller than Sorensen's, though Sorensen's is also quite valuable. Tension over Berlin, the Laotian crisis, and the Bay of Pigs episode were the background to the conference. But the great theme was the balance of power throughout the world, and the relation of "wars of national liberation" to that balance. Delicately but insistently, Kennedy tried to get Khrushchev to see the world as he saw it. War between the two great powers was out of the question; the use of nuclear weapons was too terrible to contemplate. But each great power had vital interests which had to be respected; let there be no miscalculation concerning the determination of either side to protect its vital interests. The effort to impose Communism by force of arms in any country would obviously imperil the balance of power in the world. The United States and the Soviet Union would compete peacefully, and allow the uncommitted world to choose freely its way of life.

Obviously, Khrushchev did not accept the responsibility that Kennedy seemed to wish to thrust on him. Sorensen paraphrases his reply: "Was the President saying that Communism should exist only in Communist countries, that its development elsewhere would be regarded by the U.S. as a hostile act by the Soviet Union? The United States wants the U.S.S.R., he said, to sit like a schoolboy with hands on the table, but there is no immunization against ideas. . . . [Khrushchev] returned time and again to the thesis that the Soviet Union could not be held responsible for every spontaneous uprising or Communist trend. . . . Castro was not a Communist but U.S. policy could make him one. . . ."

It is apparent from the reports that Khrushchev alternated between two responses. Either the Soviet Union could not be held responsible for the surge of revolutionary discontent throughout the world, or the Soviet Union could not be expected to withhold aid, when asked, to insurgent movements and new regimes. It is hard to see what else Khrushchev could have said: he was, in effect, describing the role of the Soviet Union in world affairs analogously to that of the United States. He nowhere said that the Soviet Union would export revolution in the old Trotskyist sense: not by Soviet arms, or by Soviet instigation in an otherwise tranquil situation. That there would be uncontrolled revolutionary movements could not be denied; but Soviet responsibility could not possibly extend to them.

Kennedy's words at Vienna, and the policies he followed, show that he accepted the view that all insurgencies in which Communists take part are inspired by and directed from Moscow. In turn, the triumph of any such insurgency represents a shift in the balance of power between the great power-blocs, a defeat for the West, a serious impairment of its security. As Sorensen says, "The extent of U.S. commitment and of Communist power involvement differed from one to the other, but the dilemma facing John Kennedy in each one was essentially the same: how to disengage the Russians from the 'liberation' movement and prevent a Communist military conquest without precipitating a major Soviet-American military confrontation." The way out of the seeming dilemma was to increase the American anti-guerrilla and conventional capacity.

Sooner or later that capacity would be used. Political moves are determined by the means on hand as much as by anything else: men do all they can. One would like to praise Kennedy unreservedly for apparently limiting American military involvement in the Laotian crisis of 1961–62 to dramatic but empty gestures, despite intense pressure put on him by his military advisers to land American troops in Laos. (Sorensen says his "posture . . . combined bluff with real determination in proportions he made known to *no one*. . . .) But the praise must be qualified. First, Kennedy was strongly inclined to intervene: he saw the Laotian crisis as a manifestation of the world Communist conspiracy rather than as the product of local antagonisms, in which local Communists played a part; and he thought that a Communist victory in Laos would imperil the security of the United States and its major allies.[2] Second, the reason for staying out of Laos was, in part, the Bay of Pigs affair. " 'Thank God the Bay of Pigs happened when it did,' he would say to me [Sorensen] in September. . . . 'Otherwise we'd be in Laos by now—and that would be a hundred times worse.' " Kennedy told Schlesinger the same thing. It took one fiasco to prevent another. As it turned out, the Pathet Lao stopped short of total victory: Khrushchev, appalled at the prospect of American military intervention, managed to police an insurgency he had no part in starting and little part in sustaining. By acting as he did, Khrushchev must have lent credibility to the view that all insurgencies were his to turn on and off. The nature of his act was not seen for what it was.

---

[2] There was also a political consideration. Schlesinger says, "Kennedy told Rostow that Eisenhower could stand the political consequences of Dien Bien Phu and the expulsion of the West from Vietnam in 1954 because the blame fell on the French; 'I can't take a 1954 defeat today.' "

The stage was set for a reversal of Eisenhower's policy in Vietnam. In May 1961, Vice-President Johnson reported to Kennedy, according to Schlesinger, ". . . the basic decision in Southeast Asia is here. We must decide whether to help these countries to the best of our ability or throw in the towel in the area and pull back our defenses to San Francisco and a 'Fortress America' concept." In October, General Maxwell Taylor made a three-week visit to Vietnam and urged positive action on Kennedy. Once again, Kennedy was induced to see a local struggle as an element in a greater struggle. Schlesinger says, ". . . given the truculence of Moscow, the Berlin crisis and the resumption of nuclear testing, the President unquestionably felt that an American retreat in Asia might upset the whole world balance." Sorensen says, "What was needed, Kennedy agreed with his advisers, was a major counterinsurgency effort—the first ever mounted by this country. . . . Formally, Kennedy never made a final negative decision on troops. In typical Kennedy fashion, he made it difficult for any of the pro-intervention advocates to charge him privately with weakness." Gradually, almost insensibly, the American commitment grew and became irreversible. This is not to say that Kennedy would necessarily have permitted the expansion of American force which Johnson has permitted. It is impossible to speculate; one must simply acknowledge that by the end of 1963 "only" 15,500 American soldiers were in Vietnam. Nevertheless, it is hard to imagine Johnson's commitment having been made without Kennedy's prior one, and without the wholehearted support Kennedy gave to the development of American non-nuclear capability—to the McNamara strategy. When anti-guerrilla activity fails (as it must in conditions like those in Vietnam), a next step can be taken. There will be many to say that it must be taken. Guerrilla warfare will be changed into conventional warfare, so that American technical superiority can be brought into play.

The idea that the power of the West and the Communist bloc were in a balance that required constant vigilance to be preserved drove Kennedy not only to look on insurgencies as suitable for American military involvement, but also led him to invest every direct Soviet-American problem with a high degree of passion. The passion was of a special sort: an intense desire to avoid giving the impression of weakness. Let it be noted that this desire is not the same as the desire to give the impression of overbearing strength. No one could ever accuse Kennedy of enjoying the role of bully. The matter is more sad, more complicated. In his early book, *Why England Slept,* he expressed the belief that democracies were inherently pacific and self-absorbed, and that they had to have "shocks" to keep them alert to the dangers surrounding them. Being alert, they would not give the appearance of weakness; they would thereby dissuade aggressors from rashness. In line with this aim, Kennedy wanted to raise taxes in 1961 in order to enhance a sense of sacrifice and impress on Americans the gravity of world affairs. His ill-considered support of fallout shelters was part of the same purpose. More than that, all one can briefly say is that Kennedy seems to have had a naturally agonistic conception of world politics. He did not look for fights; rather he thought that they were inevitable, that crisis was the normality of international relations, even in the nuclear age. (He shocked Stevenson by referring to disarmament proposals as "propaganda.") Beyond the conflict of aims that always exists between nations, Kennedy saw a contest of wills, an almost formal antagonism in which the prize was pride at least as much as any substantive outcome. In discussing Dean Acheson's advice during the Berlin crisis of 1961, Schlesinger says, "[Khrushchev's] object, as Acheson saw it, was not to rectify a local situation but to test the general American will to resist; his hope was that, by making us back down on a sacred commitment, he could shatter our world power and influence. This was a simple conflict of wills, and, until it was resolved, any effort to negotiate the Berlin issue per se would be fatal. . . . For Acheson the test of will seemed almost an end in itself rather than a means to a political end." Schlesinger and Sorensen both make it clear that the tone of Kennedy's military advisers was practically identical to Acheson's. What is so troubling is that Kennedy's reasons for policy, on numerous occasions, were similar. They prominently included the wish to appear to be accepting a challenge. He was inclined to define the world as the "realists" defined it, though possessed of a self-doubt and a magnanimity foreign to them. Fortunately, one could probably say that the United States under Kennedy never yielded in a contest of wills, was never bested. But the precedents perhaps established, the opportunities perhaps missed, are not easily dismissed.

It would be heavy-handed to make much of the Bay of Pigs affair. Kennedy regretted the failure; he may even have regretted the effort. (The one time Sorensen raises his voice in censure of Kennedy is when he is reporting this event.) But the analysis made by Sorensen of Kennedy's mood before he allowed the expedition to get under way is fairly depressing: "He did not regard Castro as a direct threat to the United States, but neither did he see why he should 'protect' Castro from Cubans embittered by the fact that their revolution had been sold out to the Communists. Cancellation of the plan at that stage, he feared, would be interpreted as an admission that Castro ruled with popular support and would be around to harass Latin America for many years to come. His campaign pledges to aid anti-Castro rebels had not forced his hand, as some suspected, but he did feel that his disapproval of the plan would be a show of weakness inconsistent with his general stance." Anxiety was piled on anxiety, but the sharpest of them all was the fear of having himself or his country thought weak. Appearances were accorded great weight; the United States was constantly having to prove itself. But why? Who was in a position to put this country on trial, who doubted its resolve, who was ignorant of its strength, who, indeed, was not terrified of its strength (the Soviet Union and China included)?

Again, in the case of the Berlin crisis in 1961, the same anxieties are disclosed. After a while, it becomes hard to keep on worrying about Berlin; any problem loses some of its reality through continuous exposure. One does not mean to be callous; but is a mutually satisfactory settlement out of the reach of human wit? Or is the problem useful to all parties as a source of manipulable tension? Before the U-2 incident, it seemed as if Eisenhower and Khrushchev were about to reach some accord. No accord, of course, was reached. Kennedy inherited Khrushchev's dissatisfaction, and the rigid incompetence of the imbecile East German regime. Schlesinger informs us that Kennedy "used to wonder later what had gone wrong in the spring of 1961. He thought at times that the March and May messages calling for an increased American defense effort might have sounded too threatening." The intended deterrence to crisis had helped bring one about. What, now, to do? Kennedy's advisers, led by Acheson, as we have already seen, refused to countenance any negotiations: the possibility that Khrushchev had perhaps a troublesome situation on his hands was not granted. The exact status-quo had to be maintained; some alternative to staying put on the old terms or getting out in a humiliating way was disregarded. Kennedy was determined, Sorensen says, ". . . to make [the Berlin crisis] not only a question of West Berlin's rights—on which U.S., British, French, and West German policies were not always in accord [3]—but a question of direct Soviet-American confrontation over a shift in the balance of power." The bondage to the cold war could not be relinquished. The result was, once more, dramatic gesture: ". . . draft calls were doubled, tripled, enlistments were extended and the Congress promptly and unanimously authorized the mobilization of up to 250,000 men. . . ." The Wall was built, the crisis faded. Only the people of East Berlin had lost, securely imprisoned as they were now to become. It will not do to place, as Sorensen does, the full responsibility for the stiffness of American policy on the inertia or philo-Germanism of the State Department. Kennedy had other sources of opinion—for example, Sorensen and Schlesinger. In reflecting on the crisis, Sorensen cannot forbear from remarking, ". . . no one knew when either side, convinced that the other would back down, might precipitate a situation from which neither could back down." Only flexibility, only an avoidance of seeing one's total position implicated in every situation, only a willingness to give up the ideology of confrontation, could help to insure that intolerable situations would not emerge. The Berlin crisis uselessly impaired Soviet-American relations, and prevented (temporarily, to be sure) certain kinds of cooperation with the Soviets.

The American decision of March 1962 to resume atmospheric testing of nuclear weapons is yet another example of the politics of appearances. Russia had itself resumed testing in September 1961, and had made, Sorensen says,

---

[3] How sly Sorensen sometimes is!—G.K.

"important weapons progress." That is, at the time they resumed, they must have felt that the nuclear buildup implemented by McNamara had weakened their security; the arms race had taken another leap forward. As both Sorensen and Schlesinger make clear, Kennedy's decision to resume derived primarily from considerations having little to do with American military needs. Sorensen says, "Nearly all the principal advisers involved favored resuming atmospheric tests (though a few days before the tests began, McNamara startled Rusk and Bundy at lunch by suggesting that they were not really necessary)." Schlesinger says, "Jerome Wiesner maintained in December that it remained basically a political question: 'While these tests would certainly contribute to our military strength, they are not critical or even very important to our over-all military posture.'" Schlesinger indicates that Kennedy agreed more or less. Sorensen says that Kennedy ". . . still had doubts about the value of his test series (although not about the necessity of his decision). . . . Privately he speculated that fears of Soviet nuclear test progress might have been akin to previous fears of a Soviet 'bomber gap' and 'missile gap.' . . ." But still the order to resume was given. In reply to Harold Macmillan's impassioned plea to avoid resumption, Kennedy said (in Sorensen's paraphrase) that the Soviets ". . . would be more likely to attribute such a decision to weakness rather than goodwill. . . ." To Adlai Stevenson, he was equally emphatic: "What choice did we have? . . . [Khrushchev] has had a succession of apparent victories—space, Cuba, [the Berlin Wall]. . . . He wants to give out the feeling that he has us on the run. . . ." Feeling challenged, fearing to be thought fearful, Kennedy decided to do what he hated to do, and had little faith in. He could not escape the tyranny of appearances.

The Cuban missile crisis, the greatest of all crises in the Kennedy years, also contained this same obsession. Kennedy's most desperate anguish came at a moment when he felt that appearances were not to be endured; his most stunning victory came at a moment when he succeeded in altering appearances. It would be foolish to reduce the crisis to this single element of appearances; but to ignore its possibly *preponderant* role would also be foolish.

In a wonderfully lucid exposition, Sorensen describes the several theories suggested by the President's advisers to explain Khrushchev's move. (One of the most fascinating small aspects of this affair was the response of the Chinese, who accused Khrushchev of "adventurism" in trying to place missiles in Cuba—and of cowardice for removing them.) The theories mentioned by Sorensen are (1) that Khrushchev was testing the will of the United States, and hoped to make the United States look weak, irresolute, and faithless to its sworn commitments; (2) that Khrushchev hoped to induce us to invade Cuba in order to disgrace us in the eyes of the world; (3) that Khrushchev was genuinely concerned for Cuba's security,[4] (4) that Khrushchev

---

[4] Sorensen says, "It should be noted that the Soviet Union stuck throughout to this position. Mikoyan claimed in a conversation with the President weeks after it was all over that the weapons were purely defensive, that they had been justified by threats of invasion

was bargaining, and hoped to trade off the Cuban bases for a Berlin settlement or American bases overseas; and (5) that Khrushchev was desirous of improving his strategic nuclear position. Sorensen says that Kennedy's own analysis ". . . regarded the third and fifth theories as offering likely but insufficient motives and he leaned most strongly to the first." That is, Kennedy interpreted the move as primarily an affront to the United States, a calculated probe of weakness, a contest of wills. He increasingly insisted to his advisers that the entire matter be defined as a Soviet-American confrontation. Irrespective of interpretation, however, Kennedy insisted that the missiles "would have to be removed by the Soviets in response to direct American action." In a television interview on December 16, 1962, to which Sorensen makes only a brief allusion, Kennedy gave a splendidly candid account of his reasons for taking any risk to prevail. He said, ". . . [the Russians] were planning in November to open to the world the fact that they had these missiles so close to the United States; not that they were intending to fire them, because if they were going to get into a nuclear struggle, they have their own missiles in the Soviet Union. But it would have politically changed the balance of power. It would have appeared to, and appearances contribute to reality."

Harold Macmillan could wonder "what all the fuss was about"; after all, Europe was used to living under the nuclear threat. He seems to have missed the point, namely that there was no military threat but instead a threat to America's reputation as a world power. Largely for the sake of great-power reputation (though other reasons, including the reputation of the Democratic party, figured), the world was brought close to a terrible event. (One assumes that this is so, but *The Penkovskiy Papers* say that Kennedy knew the Soviet nuclear capacity to be unready for action, and that Kennedy was therefore quite free to be as tough as he wanted and not incur grave risks.) Appearances do contribute to reality: reputation for power is a source of power: you are if they think you are. But was America's reputation so fragile? The irony is that America's very strength permitted Kennedy to act out of fear of being thought weak. Its very strength, however, should have permitted him to mitigate this fear. He did not carry his consciousness of American power far enough—as far as Eisenhower, before him, had carried it. And a relentless pursuit of right appearances can be catastrophic. In this instance, the pursuit was not catastrophic, but what guarantee was there? Kennedy later told Sorensen that "The odds that the Soviets would go all the way to war seemed to him then 'somewhere between one out of three and even.'" A nuclear war to eliminate a nuclear installation—can such thoughts be entertained?

_____

voiced by Richard Nixon and Pentagon generals, and that the Soviets intended to inform the United States of these weapons immediately after the elections to prevent the matter from affecting the American political campaign." Sorensen acknowledges that the administration in 1962 had been ". . . readying a plan of military action in the knowledge that an internal revolt, a Berlin grab or some other action might someday require it. . . ."

474   George Kateb

The alternative was not mortified acceptance, but negotiation before the crisis escaped control. Stevenson, according to Schlesinger, proposed the removal of the missiles in exchange for a UN presence in Cuba, an American non-invasion guarantee, and relinquishment of the base at Guantanamo. This program struck Kennedy as premature, and some of his advisers ". . . felt strongly that the thought of negotiations at this point would be taken as an admission of the moral weakness of our case and the military weakness of our posture." The blockade was declared; unless Khrushchev backed down, ". . . the United States would have had no real choice but to take action against Cuba the next week." The implications of invasion were understood: Kennedy said that "If we had invaded Cuba . . . I am sure the Soviets would have acted. They would have to, just as we would have to. I think there are certain compulsions on any major power." Khrushchev did back down, and was freely granted a guarantee against the invasion of Cuba. But he did back down; he refused to breach the blockade; he agreed to withdraw the missiles. How is his decision to be assessed? Was it cowardice or was it sanity? Did he not also win a victory of sorts in the realm of appearances by emerging as a champion of rationality? As such, did not his reputation improve, and indirectly with it, the power of the Soviet Union?

Redefinition of radical revolution as Muscovite conspiracy, redefinition of every problem as a great-power confrontation affecting the global balance of power, the adoption of the McNamara strategy in order to have the means to act on the basis of these redefinitions—can this be all that Kennedy bequeathed us in foreign policy? The answer is, of course, no. Who can repress nostalgia for those days in late 1962 and early 1963, when Kennedy, abetted by Pope John and Khrushchev, seemed to recapture the spirit of his inaugural address and of many of his earlier speeches? Surely this was the real Kennedy who, hitherto distracted from his mission and victimized by the foreign-policy establishment, had finally struggled free. The Cuban missile crisis may have petrified Khrushchev; it seems to have altered Kennedy. The very next morning after Khrushchev's capitulation, Kennedy told Schlesinger that ". . . he was afraid that people would conclude from this experience that all we had to do in dealing with the Russians was to be tough and they would collapse." After a shrewd analysis of the affair, he went on to say, "They were in the wrong and knew it. So, when we stood firm, they had to back down. But this doesn't mean at all that they would back down when they felt that they were in the right and had vital interests involved." But these words do not capture the full transformation. After the Cuban crisis, Schlesinger says, Kennedy's feelings ". . . underwent a qualitative change . . . a world in which nations threatened each other with nuclear weapons now seemed to him not just an irrational but an intolerable and impossible world." The proof of this sentiment came in the form of strenuous negotiation to produce the Nuclear Test Ban Treaty. The fact is that much of the strenuousness was spent on Kennedy's own military advisers. Once again, the passion for right appearances was exhibited by the Chiefs of Staff. Maxwell Taylor told the Senate Foreign Relations Committee that "the most serious reservations of the military had to do with the fear of a euphoria in the West which will eventually reduce our vigilance." Only this time Kennedy, after making some concessions to the military, rejected the logic of appearances and went ahead with the treaty.

The real victory that Kennedy won in Cuba was over his own advisers. Some would like to say that he had softened up Khrushchev: that a show of strength and determination, on such a scale and under such trying conditions, had so demoralized the Russian leader that he had no choice but to feign moderation and accept Kennedy's overtures of peace. It would be equally plausible to say that Kennedy's show of strength and determination had (for the time being) won him so much prestige and brought him so much self-confidence that he could at last prevail even over his bellicose aides, and pursue a policy that he (and Khrushchev) wanted from the beginning. Not out of a good heart, but out of cold prudence, out of dread of American power, Khrushchev had been straining to be compliant. Success in Cuba accidentally made it possible for Kennedy to take advantage of Khrushchev's wishes. Kennedy's sense of reality shone through. If he had lived, would he have imposed that sense on the men around him? One wants to believe that he would.

SUGGESTED READING

Roger Hilsman, Kennedy's Assistant Secretary of State for Far Eastern Affairs, wrote a sympathetic but sometimes critical assessment of Kennedy's foreign policy in *To Move A Nation* ° (Doubleday, 1967). The book is sharply reviewed by John MacDermott in "Crisis Manager," *New York Review*, IX (Sept. 14, 1967). Robert McNamara in *The Essence of Security* (Harper & Row, 1968) has written a brief account of his years as Secretary of Defense under Kennedy and Johnson. An excellent source for a left-liberal criticism of the Administration's foreign policy is *Council for Correspondence Newsletter* (1961–65, becoming *The Correspondent* in 1963). *John F. Kennedy and the New Frontier*,° edited by Aida DePace Donald (Hill & Wang, 1967), is a useful collection of appraisals of the former President, although the range of political positions of the contributors (with one exception) is remarkably narrow. In "Kennedy in the Presidency: A Premature Appraisal," *Political Science Quarterly*, LXXIX (Sept., 1964), 321–34, Richard E. Neustadt, a former assistant to Kennedy, finds much to praise in Kennedy's style of handling foreign affairs. Walt W. Rostow, foreign-policy adviser to Kennedy (and later to Johnson), presents in *View from the Seventh Floor* (Harper & Row, 1964) his analysis of foreign policy and his thoughts about Kennedy's policies.

William G. Carleton in "Kennedy in History: An Early Appraisal," *Antioch Review*, XXVII (Fall, 1964), 277–99, is critical of Kennedy's foreign policy and concludes that in his first two years he "needlessly fanned the flames of the Cold War." In "The Kennedy Administration: The Early Months," *American Scholar*, XLII (Autumn, 1961), William V. Shannon emphasizes the "cult of toughness" in the Kennedy Administration and laments that the President and his advisers, continuing the policies of Dean Acheson, regarded the basic issues of the Cold War as unnegotiable.

Nuclear strategy is analyzed in Robert Levine's *The Arms Debate* (Harvard Univ. Press, 1963) and in William Kaufmann's *The McNamara Strategy* (Harper & Row, 1964). Arthur Dean's *The Test Ban and Disarmament* (Harper & Row, 1966) is a discussion by a key participant in the negotiations.

Roger Hagan and Barton Bernstein in "Military Value of Missiles in Cuba," *Bulletin of the Atomic Scientists*, XIX (Feb., 1963), 8–12; Leslie Dewart in "The Cuban Crisis Revisited," *Studies on the Left*, V (Spring, 1965), 15–40; and the *Council for Correspondence Newsletter* (Nov., 1962) all criticize Kennedy's role in the Cuban crisis and speculate about Soviet policy. Arnold Horelick's "Cuban Missile Crisis: An Analysis of Soviet Calculations and Behavior," *World Politics*, XVI (April, 1964), 363–89, is part of a larger RAND Corporation study of the crisis by the same title (memorandum RM–3779–PR). Henry Pachter in *Collision Course* ° (Praeger, 1963) offers an ambivalent and confusing interpretation. Elie Abel in *The Missile Crisis* (Lippincott, 1966) summarizes the events of the crisis. Robert Kennedy's *Thirteen Days* (Norton, 1969), a fragmentary memoir of the missile crisis, published posthumously, presents information about decision-making and disputes within the inner circle of the government that corrects the sensational journalistic accounts that appeared in the months after the crisis. Ronald Steel, in "Endgame," a review-essay of Kennedy's book, in the *New York Review of Books*, XII (March 13, 1969), 15–22, distills the evidence and some of the theories about the responses of the Russian and American governments.

American policy toward Cuba is severely criticized by Robert Scheer and Maurice Zeitlin in *Cuba: Tragedy in our Hemisphere* ° (Grove, 1963) and defended, despite occasional disclaimers, by Theodore Draper in *Castro's Revolution, Myths and Realities* ° (Praeger, 1962) and in *Castroism, Theory and Practice* ° (Praeger, 1965). Haynes Johnson in *The Bay of Pigs; The Leaders' Story* (Norton, 1964), and Karl E. Meyer and Tad Szulc in *The Cuban Invasion* ° (Praeger, 1962) cover the events of the Bay of Pigs.

Hobart Rowen in *The Free Enterprisers* (Putnam, 1964) and James Heath in *The Kennedy Administration and the Business Community* (Univ. of Chicago Press, 1969) discuss the economic policies of the Kennedy Government. *New Dimensions of Political Economy* ° (Harvard Univ. Press, 1966) is an important volume by Walter Heller, the chairman of Kennedy's first Council of Economic Advisers.

THEODORE DRAPER

Vietnam: From Kennedy to Johnson

INTRODUCTION

In his early Presidency Lyndon Johnson knew only triumphs: the tactful succession, his salvation of Kennedy's program, the landslide victory over Barry Goldwater. In 1965 Johnson's legislative record fulfilled the hopes of his liberal supporters, and he was admired throughout the land as a political genius. But even as he savored these victories, Johnson was preparing the way for his own downfall. The worsening course of the war in Vietnam began to absorb his energies and undermine his commitment to domestic reform and reconciliation. His pride—that of person and that of nation—drove him to expend ever more resources to force a settlement in Vietnam on American terms. But the expenditure of money and men grew beyond reason and, instead of peace,

FROM *The Abuse of Power* by Theodore Draper, pp. 61–87. Copyright © 1966, 1967 by Theodore Draper. All rights reserved. Reprinted by permission of The Viking Press, Inc.

brought only a discontent at home that destroyed his hopes for a popular Presidency.

Johnson, of course, could not know in advance the tragic consequences of escalating the struggle; the nation's experience with the prolonged war in Korea a decade earlier was an ambiguous guide at best. When he faced his first war crisis in mid-1964, Johnson was already convinced that the United States had committed too much to accept anything less than a non-communist government in South Vietnam. Undeterred by fear of failure, he was prepared to take whatever steps were necessary to attain that objective. Consequently, when in September 1964 U Thant, Secretary General of the United Nations, privately informed the United States that North Vietnam was ready for secret negotiations, the American Government showed no interest and on January 30, 1965, politely rejected Thant's efforts. The feeling then was that negotiations at a time of weakness might overturn the Saigon government; moreover they could succeed only if the issues at stake were compromised.

It was to avoid compromise with communism that the United States had already decided to change the nature of its contribution to the war effort. In early February 1965 American bombers began their raids on North Vietnam, and some months later, the United States sent its first acknowledged combat troops. In the next three years the number of American soldiers there increased, the death rate for military personnel and civilians mounted, and the opposition at home spread from disaffected students and radicals to liberal Democrats and eventually to Americans of nearly every ideological persuasion. But President Johnson did not begin to lose confidence in a military solution until the Viet Cong offensive during the Tet holiday in February 1968.

In the following essay, taken from his book *The Abuse of Power,* Theodore Draper discusses the momentous events culminating in the escalation of 1965.

*O*nce more, a deceptive temporary improvement seemed to take place after the November 1963 *coup.* First a government dominated by General Duong Van Minh, better known as "Big Minh," came in, and then, in January 1964, it was overthrown by a military junta headed by General Nguyen Khanh. By this time, the agony of making the final American decisions had been handed on to Lyndon B. Johnson.

The leading American officials had especially "high hopes" for General Khanh, as Secretary McNamara expressed it in one of his most illuminating and ill-fated speeches, on March 26 of that year. General Khanh, said Secretary McNamara, was just the man to defeat the Communists. McNamara credited Khanh with a demonstrated grasp of the basic political, economic, and psychological elements needed to assure victory.

Five months later, in August, the State and Defense Departments issued a pamphlet which discounted the use of American combat units in a guerrilla war of the Vietnamese type "in which knowledge of terrain, language, and local customs is especially important." The pamphlet also warned that American combat units would provide "ammunition for Communist propaganda which falsely proclaims that the United States is conducting a 'white man's war' against Asians." [1]

At this late date, then, American policy was still ostensibly anchored to the Eisenhower-Kennedy principle of limited commitment and limited liability. All the right things were said on the eve of doing just the opposite.

What caused this abrupt and seemingly unanticipated change of policy at the beginning of 1965 in favor of sending massive American combat units to wage an increasingly "white man's war"?

The official American explanation is that a "foreign aggression" on the part of North Vietnam took place at the end of 1964. The foreign aggressor was North Vietnam. Its victim was South Vietnam. This did not mean that North Vietnam had previously watched the struggle in the South with folded arms; Southern cadres were undoubtedly trained and equipped in the North before the end of 1964.

But at that time, according to the official American thesis, a qualitative change occurred in the war. It came about because North Vietnam had allegedly exhausted its reserves of Southerners, who had moved to the North in the exchange of populations arranged ten years earlier, and had been forced to resort to its own regular troops to prosecute the war in the South. After the United States began to bomb North Vietnam regularly at the beginning of 1965, the appearance of a North Vietnamese regular division in the South was given as the crucial reason.

Of all the turning points in the war, this one was the most fateful because it increasingly changed the character of the conflict. Under Presidents Eisenhower and Kennedy, the main antagonists were still South Vietnamese, even if one side owed its training and equipment to the United States and the other side to North Vietnam. But the bombing of the North introduced a new factor—the direct confrontation between the United States and North Vietnam. The introduction of almost 200,000 American troops in 1965 was justified on the ground that the North Vietnamese were feeding their own regular army into the southern theater of the war.

This new stage of the war was additionally significant because it made an early compromise settlement infinitely more difficult. Later, the United

---

[1] *Viet Nam: The Struggle for Freedom* (Washington, D.C.: Government Printing Office, 1964), p. 21.

States seemed to take the position that the war could be ended with ease and without delay if only the North Vietnamese agreed to withdraw their forces from the South. On the other hand, the North Vietnamese demanded the unconditional cessation of the bombing of their territory as a prior condition for any peace negotiations.

As a result, if there is one phase of the war that bears the closest and most critical examination, it is that which led to the American decision to bomb North Vietnam. The American change of course in this period is seemingly infected with contradictions and confusions because of the peculiar circumstances in which it took place.

The Vietnam issue occupied a prominent, if not the foremost place, in the 1964 Presidential campaign. To the average American voter, the choice seemed to be between a Democratic candidate, Lyndon B. Johnson, who opposed bombing North Vietnam or sending American troops to South Vietnam, and a Republican candidate, Barry Goldwater, who spoke as if he might conceivably decide to use nuclear weapons or permit the military to make such a decision. Throughout the campaign, Mr. Johnson pushed this issue to the utmost, and the peculiar convolutions of his Vietnamese policy after the election can be understood only in terms of the "commitments" he made in the course of winning the Presidency.

The first American bombing of North Vietnam came in August 1964 in the midst of the presidential campaign. On August 2, according to the United States, three North Vietnamese torpedo boats fired torpedoes and machine guns at the United States destroyer *Maddox*, one of the most heavily armored and armed in the fleet, about 30 miles from the mainland of North Vietnam in the Gulf of Tonkin. In the exchange, two enemy boats were damaged at no cost to the American side. On August 4, enemy torpedo boats again allegedly fired at the *Maddox* and another destroyer, *C. Turner Joy*, this time 65 miles from the North Vietnamese shore. The score this time was reported to be two North Vietnamese boats sunk, no American losses.

Despite the one-sidedness of the engagement, Mr. Johnson chose to interpret the incidents as evidence of "open aggression on the high seas against the United States of America." On August 4 he ordered retaliatory air attacks on the North Vietnamese torpedo-boat bases and their oil-storage depots. This action constituted the first American air attacks on North Vietnamese soil.[2] The President also called for a Congressional resolution to give him authority to use whatever armed force he deemed necessary in Vietnam. On August 7, by a vote of 88 to 2, with only Democratic Senators Wayne Morse of

[2] Two well-informed correspondents have gone so far as to write: "President Johnson, after the Gulf of Tonkin incidents, felt he had to prove his mettle even though, in retrospect, it now seems doubtful whether the second Gulf of Tonkin incident, on the basis of which the first retaliatory bombing of North Vietnam had been ordered, was actually caused by enemy action" (Eward Weintal and Charles Bartlett, *Facing the Brink* [New York: Scribner's, 1967], p. 207).

Oregon and Ernest Gruening of Alaska opposed, the Senate authorized the President "to take all necessary measures to repel any armed attack against the forces of the United States and to prevent further aggression." The House of Representatives passed the resolution 416 to 0. The resolution was so loosely worded that it later enabled the President to claim, despite Senatorial protests to the contrary, that the Congress had given him a "blank check" in Vietnam.[3]

Later information on the Gulf of Tonkin incident seemed to present it in a somewhat different light. The Senate Foreign Relations Committee held hearings on the resolution on August 6, 1964, but the text of these hearings was not released until November 24, 1966, and then in a highly truncated form, especially in those sections devoted to the Tonkin Gulf incident itself. However, some members of the Senate Committee who participated in the debate on the resolution on August 5 and 6, 1964, had listened to the full testimony, and one of them, Senator Morse, referred to some of the secret testimony.

But first it should be noted that a Saigon newspaper had already reported a sharp stepping-up of *South* Vietnamese commando raids on Northern territory, beginning on July 10, 1964, more than three weeks before the first torpedo boat attack.[4] On July 31, 1964, *South* Vietnamese torpedo boats, obtained from the United States through the aid program, had bombarded two North Vietnamese islands, approximately 3 and 5 miles from the North Vietnamese coast. Senator Morse asserted that American authorities "knew that the bombing was going to take place." American destroyers, which had been patrolling the waters of the Gulf of Tonkin for about a year and a half, moved within the 12-mile "limit" (claimed by North Vietnam but not recognized by the United States) of the North Vietnamese shore on July 31. Then, evidently as a result of some intelligence information which Senator Morse did not feel privileged to reveal in detail, the *Maddox* hastened away from the scene of the South Vietnamese attacks, and the alleged engagement with

---

[3] Ironically, Senator Fulbright served as floor leader in support of this resolution. The following exchange took place between Democratic Senator Daniel B. Brewster of Maryland and Senator Fulbright:

MR. BREWSTER: I would look with great dismay on a situation involving the landing of large land armies on the continent of Asia. So my question is whether there is anything in the resolution which would authorize or recommend or approve the landing of large American armies in Vietnam or in China.

MR. FULBRIGHT: There is nothing in the resolution, as I read it, that contemplates it. I agree with the Senator that that is the last thing we would want to do. However, the language of the resolution would not prevent it. It would authorize whatever the Commander in Chief feels is necessary. It does not restrain the Executive from doing it. . . . Speaking for my own committee, everyone I have heard has said that the last thing we want to do is to become involved in a land war in Asia . . . (*Congressional Record*, Senate, August 5, 1964, p. 18403).

[4] *Saigon Post*, July 23, 1964 (cited in full in *I. F. Stone's Weekly*, September 12, 1966, p. 3).

the pursuing North Vietnamese torpedo boats took place approximately 65 miles from the North Vietnamese shore.[5]

In any event, the North Vietnamese "aggression," which the torpedo boats' audacity supposedly heralded, failed to materialize. Despite the severe American reaction, North Vietnam licked its wounds and at that time made no effort to hit back. Senator Morse took the position that the American ships were entirely justified in returning the North Vietnamese torpedo boats' fire but that President Johnson's subsequent order to bomb North Vietnamese naval facilities in retaliation constituted a serious violation of international law and "a major escalation of this war." As Morse predicted about the resolution, "Senators who vote for it will live to regret it." One of those Senators who voted for it and lived to regret it most was J. William Fulbright.

President Johnson's "sense of timing" in obtaining this wide-open authorization from the Senate, which was filled with doubters about the wisdom of our Vietnam policy, struck journalistic observers as little less than "awe-inspiring." Tom Wicker, head of *The New York Times* Washington bureau, later wrote: "Usually the timing is precisely his own—as when he presented his Vietnam resolution to Congress the day after the Gulf of Tonkin crisis. He had been carrying it around in his pocket for weeks waiting for the moment." [6]

Nevertheless, the Gulf of Tonkin incident did not seem to portend any American enlargement or intensification of the war. In fact, Presidential candidate Johnson accused his opponents of harboring just such designs, and his campaign speeches were pervaded with protestations of innocence and remonstration.

On August 12, 1964, Mr. Johnson said in New York:

> Some others are eager to enlarge the conflict. They call upon us to supply American boys to do the job that Asian boys should do. They ask us to take reckless action which might risk the lives of millions and engulf much of Asia and certainly threaten the peace of the entire world. Moreover, such action would offer no solution at all to the real problem of Vietnam.

As the campaign warmed up, he spoke up directly on the subject of bombing North Vietnam. On August 29, 1964, he declared in Texas:

> I have had advice to load our planes with bombs and to drop them on certain areas that I think would enlarge the war and escalate the war, and result in our committing a good many American boys to fighting a war that I think ought to be fought by the boys of Asia to help protect their own land. And for that reason, I haven't chosen to enlarge the war.

---

[5] *Congressional Record*, Senate, August 6, 1964, pp. 18423–25.

[6] Tom Wicker, "Lyndon Johnson vs. the Ghost of Jack Kennedy," *Esquire*, November 1965, p. 152.

His most extended statement in this vein was made on September 28, 1964, in Manchester, New Hampshire:

> Some of our people—Mr. Nixon, Mr. Rockefeller, Mr. Scranton, and Mr. Goldwater—have all, at some time or other, suggested the possible wisdom of going north in Vietnam. Well, now, before you start attacking someone and you launch a big offensive, you better give some consideration to how you are going to protect what you have. And when a brigadier general can walk down the streets of Saigon as they did the other day, and take over the police station, the radio station, and the government without firing a shot, I don't know how much offensive we are prepared to launch. As far as I am concerned, I want to be very cautious and careful, and use it only as a last resort, when I start dropping bombs around that are likely to involve American boys in a war in Asia with 700 million Chinese.
>
> So just for the moment I have not thought that we were ready for American boys to do the fighting for Asian boys. What I have been trying to do, with the situation that I found, was to get the boys in Vietnam to do their own fighting with our advice and with our equipment. That is the course we are following. So we are not going north and drop bombs at this stage of the game, and we are not going south and run out and leave it for the Communists to take over. Now we have lost 190 American lives, and to each one of those 190 families this is a major war. We lost that many in Texas on the Fourth of July in wrecks. But I often wake up in the night and think about how many I could lose if I made a misstep. When we retaliated in the Tonkin Gulf, we dropped bombs on their nests where they had their PT boats housed, and we dropped them within 35 miles of the Chinese border. I don't know what you would think if they started dropping them 35 miles from your border, but I think that that is something you have to take into consideration.
>
> So we are not going north and we are not going south; we are going to continue to try to get them to save their own freedom with their own men, with our leadership and our officer direction, and such equipment as we can furnish them. We think that losing 190 lives in the period that we have been out there is bad. But it is not like 190,000 that we might lose the first month if we escalated that war. So we are trying somehow to evolve a way, as we have in some other places, where the North Vietnamese and the Chinese Communists finally, after getting worn down, conclude that they will leave their neighbors alone. And if they do, we will come home tomorrow.

Thus Mr. Johnson succeeded in demonstrating that he could be as tough as anyone else in the Gulf of Tonkin; he extorted a seemingly indeterminate, all-inclusive war resolution from Congress on the basis of a local, limited incident for which the responsibility was far from clear; and he successfully presented himself as the candidate who could be trusted to prevent the enlargement of the war.

But other things were happening at the same time. In retrospect, they suggest that the bombing of North Vietnam was not as far away as President Johnson's campaign speeches seemed to imply.

In Saigon, the South Vietnamese regime headed by General Nguyen Khanh began to show familiar signs of disintegration in the summer of 1964. To bolster his regime, it was reported in early August, he called for an extension of the war to the North. This was not, from the American point of view, the right thing to say at that time, and the American Ambassador, General Taylor, was reported to have told him so.[7] Almost two years later, however, an editorial in *The New York Times* stated flatly: "In the summer of 1964 Premier Khanh was promised a bombing offensive against the North, presumably on Presidential authority, to extract pledges from Saigon of governmental stability and efficacity." [8] Inasmuch as the editorial gave no source or further details, the entire incident is still obscure, except that it seems clear that Premier Khanh, if not Mr. Johnson's Republican opponents, was just then demanding "going north in Vietnam." That pressure for such a move was coming from the South Vietnamese was also intimated later by one of the reasons given for the bombing—that it was intended to bolster their morale.

At least two hints of what was to come or what was tentatively being considered in the State Department came from Assistant Secretary for Far Eastern Affairs William P. Bundy in August and September 1964, before any incidents took place to provide possible justification for American bombing of North Vietnam or large-scale American troop movements to South Vietnam.[9]

On August 15, 1964, Mr. Bundy was asked whether the United States might decide to interdict supply routes in North Vietnam. First he replied that "we want no wider war." Then he added, still sticking close to the old line but not excluding a new one: "We have made it clear that we cannot exclude the possibility that wider action against the North might become necessary, and we have carefully studied what might be involved, and all the rest, but I think it is clear enough that anything in the nature of attacks on North Vietnam of a systematic character by the South Vietnamese or by our-

---

[7] Seymour Topping, "Khanh, Warned of Plots, Seeks to Bolster Regime," *The New York Times*, August 5, 1964.

[8] *The New York Times*, May 20, 1966.

[9] Edward Weintal and Charles Bartlett have provided background which, if verified, goes far to explain Mr. Bundy's intimations. "It was not publicly known at the time that, since March of 1964, the government had a plan for 'measured pressure' against North Vietnam. The plan had been thrashed out by an inter-agency task force and was to become the blueprint for escalation. This was planning of a bold and thorough variety—the assumptions and anticipations which were an integral part of the thick loose-leaf volume prepared for the President have been proved by time to be valid. The planners recognized that little short of direct U.S. intervention would be likely to deter the Viet Cong more than momentarily and that the Viet Cong threat could not be dissipated even by subversion of the support coming from North Vietnam. They accepted the likelihood that Hanoi would respond to an American escalation by escalating its own role in the war, and warned that a major Communist escalation would be successfully met only by the introduction of 'several U.S. divisions.'" (*Facing the Brink*, op. cit., p. 73.)

selves would involve very grave issues and we would, therefore, prefer to pursue the policy we are now pursuing of maximum assistance in South Vietnam." [10]

On September 29, 1964, he delivered a major address in Tokyo in which he again obliquely referred to the possible expansion of the war:

> Expansion of the war outside South Vietnam, while not a course we want to seek, could be forced upon us by the increased pressures of the Communists, including a rising scale of infiltration.[11]

This and similar official views, privately expressed, apparently aroused the suspicions of James Reston, the noted Washington commentator of *The New York Times*. On October 2, 1964, he reported that

> it is difficult to understand why prominent officials, a few weeks before a national election, should be talking so openly about expanding the war, and not only advocating it but almost lobbying for such a course of action.
>
> It is even possible now to hear officials of this Government talking casually about how easy it would be to "provoke an incident" in the Gulf of Tonkin that would justify an attack on North Vietnam, and thus, according to this thesis, enable the United States to bring strong military pressure on the Communists there to let up on their pressure on South Vietnam.

Another well-known Washington correspondent, Charles Roberts of *Newsweek*, made October 1964 even more significant. "As a matter of fact," Roberts later wrote, "he [Johnson] had made the momentous *decision* to bomb North Vietnam nearly four months earlier. That decision was made, it can now be revealed, in October, 1964, at the height of the Presidential election campaign." According to Roberts, the President had personally told him "he had made the decision to bomb four months before Pleiku." [12]

Whether or not the President made a personal decision in October, before the election, the official decision was reported to have been made in December, after the election. The last half of 1964 was an especially exasperating period for the American ambassador in Saigon, General Taylor, whose travails with one South Vietnamese government after another forced him to return to Washington for consultation with unusual frequency. These visits seemed to coincide with important American decisions. On December 1, 1964, during one of the ambassador's sojourns in Washington, the attendance at a top-level meeting in the White House indicated that it was rather less routine than usual. Those present were President Johnson, Ambassador

[10] *Department of State Bulletin*, September 7, 1964, p. 336.

[11] Ibid., October 19, 1964, p. 538.

[12] Charles Roberts, *L.B.J.'s Inner Circle* (New York: Delacorte Press, 1965), pp. 20–21.

Taylor, Secretary of State Rusk, Secretary of Defense McNamara, Director of Central Intelligence John A. McCone, and the Chairman of the Joint Chiefs of Staff, General Earle G. Wheeler.[13] Later, John W. Finney of *The New York Times* reported that the Johnson Administration had adopted a new strategy for the war during Ambassador Taylor's visit to Washington in December 1964. This strategy, according to Mr. Finney, called for, among other things, "air strikes against the north to persuade the Hanoi regime to stop its support of the insurgents and to seek a negotiated settlement." [14]

Richard N. Goodwin, then an Assistant to President Johnson, has given a somewhat later date for the crucial decision. According to Goodwin,

> early in 1965, the President was advised that morale in South Vietnam could be revived only if we bombed military targets in North Vietnam. This would assure Saigon of our determination to stay the course, and perhaps, if we were lucky, would so weaken Hanoi's will to fight that we could avoid the unpleasant, looming need to send in large numbers of combat troops. Thus the most fateful decision of all was made. The war went North.[15]

Mr. Goodwin's version raises some questions that only a complete disclosure of the record may answer. Pressure on the President to bomb North Vietnam to buck up South Vietnamese morale undoubtedly antedated 1965. Indeed, news of such demands began to appear in the American press by the summer of 1964. The advice the President received early in 1965 may have been particularly urgent or persuasive, but it did not start that train of thought. It is also hard to understand how anyone could have believed that the bombing might somehow save us from sending in troops, though Goodwin may be perfectly right about the existence of such an official delusion. Unless Hanoi's will was expected to weaken almost immediately, the decision to send in troops followed the decision to bomb with so little delay that the bombing was given very little time to work its wonders. Whatever the time sequence may be, however, Goodwin's main point further suggests that there was a predisposition to bomb North Vietnam before there occurred any "incident" on which to pin it.

Finally, on February 2, 1965, a high State Department official told Philip L. Geyelin of the *Wall Street Journal:* "We could hang on there for ten years. But as a practical matter, patience is wearing thin, in Congress, in the Administration, in the country, and a decision to change the rules of the game, one way or another, seems probable before very long." [16] General Taylor has

---

[13] *Department of State Bulletin*, December 21, 1954, p. 869.

[14] *The New York Times*, April 3, 1966.

[15] Richard N. Goodwin, *Triumph or Tragedy: Reflections on Vietnam* (New York: Random House, Vintage Books, 1966), p. 31.

[16] Philip L. Geyelin, *Lyndon B. Johnson and the World* (New York: Praeger, 1966), p. 216.

also offered some evidence for the view that the bombing of North Vietnamese military targets was no sudden impulse brought about by the incident
at Pleiku. "I do not know," he has written, "of any element in the Vietnamese
situation which caused longer debate, longer discussions," dating at least as
far back as 1961.[17]

Yet Mr. Johnson's campaign oratory had made it awkward for him to
change "the rules of the game." Only a month after he was inaugurated, and
four days after the tip to Geyelin, another "incident" came providentially to
the President's rescue.

On February 7, 1965 (Saigon time), Vietcong guerrillas carried out
three attacks, including one against an American installation at Pleiku, about
250 miles north of Saigon. Seven American soldiers were killed and 109 were
wounded, 76 of them seriously. When the news reached the White House,
President Johnson reacted explosively. In retaliation, he ordered the United
States Air Force to attack barrack areas and staging areas in the southern
portion of North Vietnam. At first, the bombing of the North was made to
seem a perhaps over-forceful reaction to the Pleiku incident, which implied
that the bombing might be short-lived if the Vietcong did not manage to
catch an American camp off guard again. But on February 28, President
Johnson announced a policy of continuous air strikes against Northern military targets to force the enemy into a "negotiated settlement." And this step
was soon followed by another, even more far-reaching decision—to send
thousands of American combat troops to South Vietnam.

These measures were so extreme that they could not possibly be accounted for as mere reprisals for the Pleiku incident, though they were psychologically related to it in the public mind. The entire sequence of events
was apparently another "awe-inspiring" example of Mr. Johnson's "sense of
timing."

The decision to commit American combat troops on a large scale was
also made early in 1965, though the exact time has not yet been established.

In any event, we have been told by General Taylor that the introduction of American ground forces was a "very difficult, long-debated decision." [18] It had, in fact, been debated for at least eleven years, the first time
in 1954, ever since Generals Ridgway and Gavin had successfully argued
against it. The reluctance of Presidents Eisenhower and Kennedy was not
based on what the North Vietnam Communists were doing; both presidents were rather motivated by what they thought the United States
should not be doing—fighting another land war against Asians on Asian soil.

Once President Johnson decided to rid himself of this inhibition, however, a different kind of justification was needed. It was expressed no less

---

[17] General Maxwell D. Taylor, *Responsibility and Response* (New York: Harper & Row,
1967), pp. 25–26.

[18] Ibid., p. 25.

than three times by Secretary of State Rusk at the Senate Foreign Relations Committee's hearings in January and February 1966.

The first time came on January 28, 1966, in an exchange with Democratic Senator Albert Gore of Tennessee:

> SECRETARY RUSK: From November of 1964 until January of 1965 they moved the 325th Division of the North Vietnamese Army down to South Vietnam. There was no bombing going on at that time. Now, this is an aggression by means of an armed attack.
>
> SENATOR GORE: Was that before or after we moved forces into South Vietnam?
>
> SECRETARY RUSK: Well, the division moved after we had put—had reinforced our own forces there.

The second time came on February 18, 1966, again in a reply to Senator Gore:

> At no stage have we ourselves wanted to escalate this war, as the expression goes. At no stage have we wanted a larger war. But it was in November, December, January, over the turn of the year 1964–65, that North Vietnam moved the 325th Division of the regular North Vietnamese Army from North Vietnam to South Vietnam to up the ante. That was before the bombing started. That wasn't in response to an escalation by the United States. It seemed to be the result of a decision on their part that, well, "the United States says it doesn't want a big war, maybe we can have a big one without undue risk."

The third time occurred the same day in a discussion with Democratic Senator Claiborne Pell of Rhode Island. At this point, Secretary Rusk merely reiterated that the North Vietnamese infiltration had "included a division of the regular North Vietnamese Army, before there was any bombing." The 325th was obviously Secretary Rusk's trump card, and he played it for all it was worth without arousing any suspicion on the part of his senatorial questioners that he might have overplayed his hand.

From all this, one might gather that North Vietnam, with a total population of about 18,500,000, had deliberately decided to pit its military manpower against the United States, with a population of almost 195,000,000. The usually cautious Ho Chi Minh, according to Secretary Rusk, had tried to get away with a one-sided "big war," and the United States had merely called his bluff. In terms of the main consideration which had weighed on Presidents Eisenhower and Kennedy, even the presence of an entire North Vietnamese division in the South might not have swayed them from the principle of avoiding an American land war in Asia against Asians, even Asian Communists. In any event, the role played by the 325th North Vietnamese Division in Secretary Rusk's rationale for the new line made it the crucial causative factor in the massive increase of American military manpower which took place in 1965 and 1966.

What we know of this division comes wholly from American sources. The least that might be expected from these sources is that they should tell the same story. Peculiarly, the Secretary of State did not seem to be speaking of the same war as the Secretary of Defense.

According to the former, the 325th, *as a division,* had moved from North to South Vietnam by January 1965.[19] At the end of the following month, however, the State Department issued its second White Paper entitled *Aggression from the North: The Record of North Viet-Nam's Campaign to Conquer South Viet-Nam.* This publication, one imagines, would have emphasized or at least mentioned the momentous 325th. But, no, it never appears in its pages at all. In one section, this White Paper states that one captured Private First Class of the 2nd Battalion of the North Vietnamese 9th Regiment said that his entire battalion had infiltrated into the South between February and May 1964; another captured Private First Class of the North Vietnamese 324th Division told of 90 North Vietnamese draftees who had infiltrated in May 1964; and a third prisoner gave information that one Vietcong battalion had received 80 North Vietnamese replacements in February 1964. One incident referred to in the document took place as late as February 16, 1965, only eleven days before it was issued. That the entire 325th Division should have been in the South by January 1965 without getting some publicity in this White Paper would seem to require some kind of explanation.

Other information in this White Paper, however, gives some idea of the order of magnitude of the alleged North Vietnamese infiltration. At least 4400 and possibly as many as 7400 "men" were said to have come in from the North in the entire year of 1964. In the six years from 1959 to 1964, "nearly 20,000 VC [Vietcong] officers, soldiers, and technicians" were ordered to enter the South from Hanoi, and an "estimated 17,000 infiltrators" were also dispatched southward in the same period. At this rate, even if these figures can be trusted, the North sent annually only about 6000 men southward, many if not most of them native Southerners. If we exclude the "estimated 17,000 infiltrators" as too vague a classification to merit being included in what is supposed to have been a full-fledged military "invasion," the annual rate must be reduced to less than 3500.[20] One suspects that the United States would not have needed to send hundreds of thousands of its own troops to South Vietnam if the rate of Northern infiltration could have been kept down to some such figure in 1965 and 1966.

But we are not finished with the memorable 325th.

---

[19] That the 325th moved in "as a division" was emphasized by Secretary Rusk on a later occasion (*Department of State Bulletin,* September 19, 1966, p. 423). Assistant Secretary William P. Bundy said that the first "organized units" of the North Vietnamese army, presumably from the same 325th Division, first entered the South in December 1964 (ibid., June 20, 1966, p. 967).

[20] *Aggression from the North: The Record of North Viet-Nam's Campaign to Conquer South Viet-Nam,* op. cit., p. 3.

The first official mention of it seems to have been made on April 27, 1965, three months after its alleged appearance, by Secretary of Defense Mc-Namara. He said that "evidence accumulated within the last month," that is, since late March 1965, had confirmed the presence in the northwest sector of South Vietnam "of the 2nd Battalion of the 325th Division of the regular North Vietnamese Army." Then Secretary McNamara went on to estimate the size of the battalion "on the order of 400 to 500 men." [21]

In June 1965, a special subcommittee of the House Committee on Armed Services, headed by Democratic Representative Otis G. Pike of New York, visited South Vietnam, six months after the 325th had allegedly transformed the character of the war. Its report did not even mention North Vietnamese units or their military action in the South; it was written wholly in terms of what was still referred to as a "guerrilla war." [22] By August 1965, however, the 325th's battalion had allegedly grown to a regiment. In that month, General Earle G. Wheeler, Chairman of the Joint Chiefs of Staff, claimed evidence of the infiltration of "at least one regiment of about 1200 to 1400 men, I would think, of the 325th North Vietnamese Division." [23] Since the 325th's movement south was supposed to have started in November 1964, according to Secretary Rusk, it must have, even on this account, taken the North Vietnamese nine months to get only about a single regiment into the fighting zone. But the late Bernard B. Fall, that indefatigable student who refused to be hoodwinked by either side, happened to visit South Vietnam in late 1965. "As of the time I left a few days ago," he wrote in an article published in October, "no Intelligence officer was ready to swear that the 325th as a unit had joined the battle in South Vietnam." [24] A bipartisan group of the Senate Committee on Foreign Relations, headed by Senator Mike Mansfield, visited South Vietnam at the end of 1965. It reported that North Vietnamese regular soldiers made up only 14,000 of the estimated 230,000-man enemy force in December 1965, a year after the celebrated incursion of the Northern 325th Division. This report accepted the official version that North Vietnam regular army troops had begun to enter the South about the end of 1964, but it did not mention this division at all and, in any case, the numbers cited put the whole matter in a different perspective.[25]

---

[21] *Department of State Bulletin,* May 17, 1965, pp. 750 and 753.

[22] *Report of Special Subcommittee to South Vietnam* of the Committee on Armed Services, House of Representatives, June 10–21, 1965, committee reprint, p. 3248.

[23] CBS television Special Report, August 16, 1965 (text in *Congressional Record,* Senate, August 24, 1965, p. 20653).

[24] Bernard B. Fall, "Vietnam Blitz," in *The New Republic,* October 9, 1965, p. 17.

[25] "The Vietnam Conflict: The Substance and the Shadow," Report of Senators Mike Mansfield (Dem., Montana), Edmund S. Muskie (Dem., Maine), Daniel K. Inouye (Dem., Hawaii), George D. Aiken (Rep., Vermont), and J. Caleb Boggs (Rep., Delaware) in the *Congressional Record,* Senate, January 24, 1966, p. 908.

But Secretary Rusk would not be satisfied with anything less than a division. At a press conference on November 5, 1965, he again called attention to the 325th Division which, he said, had been "brought down" late last year and early this year.[26] At the Senate Foreign Relations Committee hearings in January-February, 1966, as we have seen, he referred to the division at least three times. On April 27, 1966, in a television interview, he tried to prove that "Hanoi, encouraged and backed by Peiping," had escalated the war by giving as an example "the 325th Division of the North Vietnamese Regular Army" which had been moved "from North Vietnam into South Vietnam, before we started bombing North Vietnam." [27] Again on May 17, 1966, Secretary Rusk told a press conference: "The 325th North Vietnamese Division came from North Vietnam into South Vietnam before we started the bombing of North Vietnam." [28]

This was apparently too much for Senator Mike Mansfield, the Democratic Majority Leader. On June 16, 1966, he delivered an address at Yeshiva University in which he saw fit to make the following observation: "When the sharp increase in the American military effort began in early 1965, it was estimated that only about 400 North Vietnamese soldiers were among the enemy forces in the South which totaled 140,000 at that time." [29] Since the same estimate had previously been made by Secretary of Defense McNamara, Senator Mansfield was not revealing anything new or risking an official denial from the Pentagon, which was presumably in a better position than the Department of State to determine enemy forces. By this time, however, Secretary McNamara's original reference to the size of the 325th's battalion almost fourteen months earlier had been forgotten, and Ted Knap, a Scripps-Howard staff writer, went to the Department of Defense to inquire about Senator Mansfield's startlingly low figure. "Mansfield's office said the 400 figure came from the Pentagon and was for March 1965," Knap reported. "An official in the office of Defense Secretary Robert McNamara confirmed giving it to Mansfield's office and said it is 'essentially correct.' " The Defense Department spokesman also said: "The figures attributed to Senator Mansfield are accurate and reflect the confirmed North Vietnamese force presence in the South at that time." The spokesman added that "he is aware of the wide difference between the Pentagon's 'confirmed' figures and others' estimates." [30] The "others" were, of course, the military experts of the State Department. Unfortunately, Senator Mansfield's figure was not widely reported

26 *Department of State Bulletin*, November 29, 1965, p. 855.

27 Ibid., May 16, 1966, p. 773.

28 Ibid., June 6, 1966, p. 886.

29 Mike Mansfield, address at Yeshiva University, June 16, 1966 (text in *Congressional Record*, Senate, June 16, 1966, pp. 12856–58).

30 Ted Knap in Washington *Daily News*, June 23, 1966 and other Scripps-Howard papers.

in the press, and he himself delicately refrained from suggesting that there might be any incongruity between his figure and the State Department's thesis.[31]

Still, this was not the end of the 325th's strange career as recorded by American officialdom. On May 30, 1966, less than three weeks before Senator Mansfield's address at Yeshiva University, President Johnson delivered a Memorial Day speech in which he tried to explain how confusing the war was:

> The conflict in South Vietnam is confusing for many of our people.
> The aggression there does not take the form of organized divisions marching brazenly and openly across frontiers.

On July 12, 1966, Secretary Rusk also discouraged the idea that any significant change had taken place in the character of the war:

> Well, we have not seen organized forces on a large scale who have tried to maintain themselves in sustained combat. . . . The primary problem still is to find the other fellow, to locate these units. . . . So the general technique is still basically that of the guerrilla tactic, the hit-and-run, the hide-and-seek, and not that of a sustained fixed engagement.

This seemed to put the war back where it had always been, despite the alleged presence of an entire North Vietnamese division or more in the South.[32] The previous emphasis on the divisional nature of the northern "invasion" had strongly implied that the North Vietnamese command had gone over to the so-called "third stage" of Mao Tse-tung's famous formula, which called for a large-scale counter-offensive by the main armed forces. But Secretary Rusk explicitly denied that the Vietcong or the North Vietnamese regular troops had ever tried to move into this stage.

At this point, it might have seemed more important to stress the num-

---

[31] Both *The New York Times* and the Washington *Post* of June 17, 1966, reported the speech but omitted mention of this passage. A letter in *The New York Times* of November 15, 1966, by William L. Standard and Joseph Crown of the Lawyers Committee on American Policy Towards Vietnam quoted the relevant sentence.

[32] A constant reader of the State Department's official publication might also wonder whether its highest officials bother to read each other's speeches and statements. On March 14, 1966, Deputy Under Secretary for Political Affairs U. Alexis Johnson assured an audience in Montreal: "Today we have every reason to believe that *nine* regiments of regular North Vietnamese forces are *fighting in organized units* in South Vietnam" (*Department of State Bulletin*, April 4, 1966, p. 531. My italics, T.D.). On July 7, 1966, Secretary of State Rusk assured a news conference in Tokyo: "There are more than *four* regiments of the official North Vietnamese army now present in South Vietnam" (ibid., August 1, 1966, p. 182. My italics, T.D.). Nine is, of course, more than four, but it does seem odd that Secretary Rusk might not have gone up at least to five or more almost four months after Alexis Johnson had escalated the North Vietnamese regiments to as many as nine.

bers rather than the organized units of the North Vietnamese incursion. But, no, Secretary Rusk soon went back to his favorite division. This occasion, on August 25, 1966, was all the more curious inasmuch as it took the form of a joint interview with Secretary McNamara, who was still talking in terms of the gradual infiltration of northern regiments while the Secretary of State was still determined to put an entire North Vietnam division into the south as early as the beginning of 1965.

> Q. From what point do you date "on the basis of intelligence" we have the decision to send a full division across?
>
> SECRETARY MC NAMARA: They began by sending regiments. So you should talk about formal military units across. I would think that decision was probably made sometime in 1964.
>
> SECRETARY RUSK: It was the end of 1964, the beginning of 1965, one of their divisions as a division moved from North Vietnam to South Vietnam. That was the end of 1964, the beginning of 1965, before the bombing started, by the way, if you are thinking about escalation.[33]

Unfortunately, no one reminded Secretary McNamara that on April 27, 1965, almost sixteen months earlier, he had "confirmed" the presence in South Vietnam only of a battalion of the 325th Division numbering 400 to 500 men, and that this figure had been repeated by Senator Mansfield on June 16, 1966, and again confirmed by the Pentagon. Since it is safe to assume that the State Department received its military information from the Department of Defense, the vicissitudes of the 325th North Vietnamese Regular Division, as far as we know them from American sources, probably tell us less about the division than about the sources.

Clearly we cannot be sure whether a battalion or a regiment or all of the 325th Division crossed into South Vietnam by January 1965 or at any other time. We could not be sure even if Secretaries Rusk and McNamara agreed, and their disagreement adds a dash of farce to what was otherwise one of the most grievous moments of the war. The most we can conclude from the available evidence is that it was extraordinarily necessary for the Secretary of State to have an "invasion" of South Vietnam by a North Vietnamese organized military unit at least as large as a division before the United States began its systematic bombing of the North in February 1965. The point is not that the North Vietnamese were incapable of making such a move; it may simply not have suited their interests to give the United States the pretext which American officials had been unmistakably hinting would bring on large-scale intervention. If Secretary McNamara is right and they sent in 400 to 500 regular troops, the number is too small for one to imagine that this was Ho Chi Minh's way of signifying that he was willing to take the risk of a "big war" against overwhelming odds.

---

[33] *Department of State Bulletin*, September 19, 1966, p. 423.

We may still not know much about the elusive 325th, but we can know a great deal about how it was bandied to and fro by high American officials who could not even convince each other. The overwhelming impression one gets from studying the record is that this was an incredibly bumbling diplomatic operation. One almost yearns for the days of John Foster Dulles and his elegant casuistries. Perhaps the most perplexing problem raised by this and other episodes of the Vietnamese war is not whether the United States is right or wrong but rather whether it has the traditions, the ideology, and the bureaucracy to carry off such operations in Asia with the necessary finesse and dispatch. Those who fear the encroachments of "American imperialism" might take some comfort in the thought that it has come too late into the world to develop the men and the methods for doing a good job of it.

It would have been a sorry moment in American history if so few North Vietnamese troops could have panicked Washington into making such a far-reaching change of course. The truth was bad enough, but not that bad. The Mansfield report came much closer by putting the emphasis where it belonged—on South Vietnamese weakness rather than North Vietnamese strength. "In short," the report stated grimly, "a total collapse of the Saigon government's authority appeared imminent in the early months of 1965." And it linked the need for large-scale American combat forces to this threatened collapse, which it did not attribute to the infiltration of a few hundred North Vietnamese regulars. Later, Secretary McNamara revealed how menacing the outlook had been in the first half of 1965. The United States, he said, had put over 100,000 men into the South in about 120 days to prevent a "disaster" to the South Vietnamese armed forces. The latter, according to him, were being overpowered and destroyed by the Vietcong and Northern Army infiltrators in the summer of 1965. The United States intervened in force, he declared, because the enemy had been "approaching possible victory." [34]

The decision to bomb North Vietnamese military targets was made in February 1965. The decision to commit American combat troops on a large scale was also made in 1965, though different periods of the year have been given by different officials. At the end of 1964, the American combat forces in Vietnam numbered 23,000.[35] The first wave of the vastly enlarged force landed on March 6, 1965. By May 1965, according to the Mansfield report, the number had increased to 34,000 but it was still "basically an advisory organization." The report added that the logistic system to support the vastly expanded United States effort had started "almost from scratch in May of 1965." By July, the United States forces had jumped to 75,000, and on July 28

[34] Robert S. McNamara, News Conference, Johnson City, Texas, November 5, 1966 (*The New York Times*, November 6, 1966).

[35] *Congressional Record*, Senate, October 10, 1966, p. 24855.

President Johnson announced that they would go up to 125,000 "almost immediately." [36] By November 20, 1965, the figure was 165,000.[37]

General William Westmoreland, the United States Commander in Vietnam, later revealed: "Early in 1965 we knew that the enemy hoped to deliver the *coup de grâce* by launching a major summer offensive to cut the Republic of Vietnam in two with a drive across the central highlands to the sea. I had to make a decision, and did. I chose a rapid build-up of combat forces, in the full knowledge that we should not have a fully developed logistic base to support those forces." [38] When the former American Ambassador, General Maxwell D. Taylor, was asked when the commitment was made for active American participation in the military operations, he replied: "We, insofar as the use of our combat forces are concerned, that took place, of course, only in the spring of 1965. In the air, we had been participating more actively over two or three years." [39] Ambassador Lodge once dated the "turning point" as July 28, 1965, when the President formally announced the decision to commit American troops on a large scale.[40] According to another source, President Johnson sent Secretary McNamara to Saigon on July 14, 1965, to determine exactly what manpower General Westmoreland needed. McNamara, it is said, returned with the recommendation that the American forces should be quadrupled within a year from the 70,000 troops already there, with another 50,000 sent as soon as possible. Mr. Johnson started the last week of intensive studies leading to his "grave decision" on July 21, and made it public a week later.[41] From this version one gathers that a considerable build-up took place between March and July 1965, but that the "open-ended" decision was actually made between July 21 and 28.[42]

This background shows that incidents such as the Tonkin Gulf and Pleiku could not possibly account for the decisions in early 1965 to bomb North Vietnam and to introduce thousands more American combat forces into South Vietnam. They were occasioned by a far more endemic and fun-

---

[36] Lyndon B. Johnson, speech of July 28, 1965.

[37] *Congressional Record*, Senate, October 10, 1966, p. 248–55.

[38] *U.S. News & World Report*, November 28, 1966, p. 49.

[39] General Maxwell D. Taylor, testimony before Senate Foreign Relations Committee, February 17, 1966.

[40] *U.S. News & World Report*, November 21, 1966, p. 67.

[41] Rowland Evans and Robert Novak, *Lyndon B. Johnson: The Exercise of Power* (New York: New American Library, 1966), p. 548.

[42] General Earle G. Wheeler also specified the summer of 1965 as the time of decision. "By the late spring of that year, due to a combination of causes, the Viet Cong/North Vietnamese Army was threatening to overwhelm the armed forces of South Vietnam. That summer, at the request of the South Vietnamese, the United States made a decision to commit major forces to halt aggression" (*Department of State Bulletin*, February 6, 1967, p. 187).

damental factor—the progressive deterioration toward the end of 1964 of General Nguyen Khanh's South Vietnamese regime and the subsequent near-breakdown of the South Vietnamese armed forces. South Vietnamese regimes could, by their very weakness, exert an influence akin to political blackmail on American policy. If one of them threatened to disintegrate, and demanded some American action to prevent it from committing suicide, that action was likely to be forthcoming sooner or later, even if the President and Secretary of State were just then protesting that they had no intention of doing any such thing. The American decisions in early 1965 were basically intended to bolster the morale of the South Vietnam government and to seek some way out of the military cul-de-sac in the South by extending the war to North Vietnam. The Gulf of Tonkin and Pleiku incidents were no more than extenuating circumstances enabling the President to obscure the real signifi-cance and ease the shock for the benefit of American public opinion.

The crisis in 1965 in South Vietnam was far more intimately related to South Vietnamese disintegration than to North Vietnamese infiltration. Gen-eral Khanh, whom Secretary McNamara had praised so highly in March 1964, turned out to be another illusion. At the Senate Committee hearings, General Taylor, the American Ambassador in Saigon from June 1964 to July 1965, the very period leading to the vast American build-up, was asked whether the present regime of Air Vice Marshal Nguyen Cao Ky was more stable than its predecessors had been. Taylor replied: "Almost anything would be an improvement over what I saw while I was Ambassador." [43] John Mecklin explained the South Vietnamese "malaise" of 1965 in these terms: "The nation was desperately weary of war, its people verging on such despair that they would soon accept anything to get it over with." [44] Bernard B. Fall attributed the trouble to the fact that Diem's successors evolved a policy which he called "Diemism without Diem." [45] Premier Nguyen Cao Ky de-scribed his predecessors in these terms: "Every Prime Minister or even Min-ister said: 'I'm here for two months, so money, money, and if necessary I'll go abroad.' " [46] He explained his own accession to power in June 1965 as the result of the shortcomings of the South Vietnamese "politicians," who, he said, "were unable to find appropriate measures to solve their differences." [47]

In effect, the South Vietnamese crisis of 1965 was essentially a reprise of the 1968 crisis, not a totally new phenomenon as argued by the State Depart-ment. The qualitative change came *after* the American decision to bomb

[43] *The Vietnam Hearings*, op. cit., p. 183.

[44] Mecklin, op. cit., p. 290.

[45] Bernard B. Fall, "The Year of the Hawks," in *The New York Times Magazine*, Decem-ber 12, 1965, p. 48.

[46] *The New York Times*, December 3, 1966.

[47] Nguyen Cao Ky, speech of October 1, 1965 (*Congressional Record*, Senate, October 22, 1965, p. 27368).

North Vietnam and pour troops into South Vietnam. The American combat forces increased from 23,000 at the end of 1964 to 165,700 on November 20, 1965.[48] According to the Mansfield report, the best available estimates in December 1965 placed the total Vietcong strength in South Vietnam at 230,000 men, of which the North Vietnamese regulars allegedly numbered only 14,000.[49] As in the case of the Dominican Republic, where the State Department tried to play the numbers game with its lists of Dominican Communists, the numbers game of North Vietnamese Army regulars also backfired, thanks mainly to Secretary McNamara and ⌐enator Mansfield, who may or may not have intended to bring about this result.

Again it may be well to note that the decisions of 1965 to bomb North Vietnam and to send thousands of American troops to South Vietnam are not merely or mainly of historical interest. They overshadowed the entire future course of the war and the problem of bringing it to an end. The bombing was intended to reduce the flow of men and materials from the North or to make it more costly and difficult for the North Vietnamese to send them southward. It appears to have been far less successful in the first respect than in the second.

But another question arises: Would it have been so necessary to reduce the flow of men and material to the south if the United States had not made such fateful decisions two years earlier? The figures given by official American sources themselves raise this question. In the summer of 1964, Secretary of State Rusk gave the total enemy force as consisting of 30,000 "hard-core" Vietcong and 60,000 "sort of part-time help or casual help." [50] The Vietcong was doing very well at the time with this limited force. The State Department's White Paper of February 1965 estimated that the "so-called hard-core forces" of the Vietcong numbered 35,000, with another 60,000 to 80,000 of "local forces." [51] This was not a striking increase in over six months. At that point, the bombing started. The Northern troops began to come down, and the more we bombed, the more they came. On August 25, 1966, Secretary McNamara claimed that about 40,000 Northern troops had infiltrated southward during the first eight months of 1966, twice the rate of 1965.[52] In February 1967, General Earle G. Wheeler estimated the enemy force as consisting of about 235,000 Vietcong, both in main-force and guerrilla units, and somewhere between 45,000 and 48,000 North Vietnamese regulars.[53] One wonders

---

[48] *Congressional Record*, Senate, October 10, 1966, p. 24855.

[49] Ibid., January 13, 1966, p. 141.

[50] *Department of State Bulletin*, August 17, 1964, p. 235. The statement was made on July 26, 1964.

[51] *Aggression from the North*, op. cit., p. 3.

[52] *Department of State Bulletin*, September 19, 1966, p. 418.

[53] *U.S. News & World Report*, February 27, 1967, p. 41.

how much more the enemy forces would have increased if we had bombed
even more to reduce them.

SUGGESTED READING

Joseph Buttinger's *The Smaller Dragon: A Political History of Vietnam*
(Praeger, 1958) surveys Vietnamese history from ancient times to 1900;
Buttinger's *Vietnam: A Dragon Embattled* (Praeger, 1967, 2 vols.) takes
the history from 1900 to the end of the Diem regime. Ellen Hammer's
The Struggle for Indochina, 1940–1955 ° (Stanford Univ. Press,
1956) is useful on French policies from 1946 to 1953. John Mecklin's
Mission in Torment (Doubleday, 1966) is a colorful account by a United
States official of the Diem family in its last years of power.

The most respected scholar of the Vietnamese war was Bernard
Fall, a writer whose views on crucial questions underwent constant revision. His books include *The Two Viet-Nams: A Political and Military
History*, 5th rev. ed. (Praeger, 1965), an encyclopedic compendium of
useful information that is, unfortunately, extremely difficult to read;
Street Without Joy, 4th rev. ed. (Stackpole, 1964), on the French war
against the Vietminh; *Hell in a Very Small Place* ° (Lippincott, 1966),
on the fall of Dien Bien Phu; *Viet-Nam Witness, 1953–66* ° (Praeger,
1966), a fine collection of some of Fall's articles; and *Last Reflections on
War* (Doubleday, 1967), a collection of articles and interviews published after his tragic death in Vietnam.

Jean Lacouture in *Vietnam Between Two Truces* ° (Random
House, 1966) emphasizes the indigenous and independent nature of the
guerrilla movement. Douglas Pike's *Viet Cong* ° (M.I.T. Press, 1966)
is a sometimes inconsistent account by a USIA employee asserting the
primacy of Hanoi in the rebellion.

Victor Bator's *Vietnam: A Diplomatic Tragedy* (Oceana, 1965)
contains a critical analysis of Dulles' diplomacy. George Kahin and John
Lewis in *The United States in Vietnam* (Dial Press, 1965) are critical of
American policies. Three books by American newspapermen critical of
American political and military tactics but not of the basic commitment
are Malcolm Browne's *The New Face of War* (Bobbs-Merrill, 1965);
David Halberstam's *The Making of a Quagmire* (Random House, 1965);
and Robert Shaplen's *The Lost Revolution* ° (Harper & Row, 1965).

A critique summarizing the views of most liberal opponents of
the war can be found in Arthur Schlesinger, Jr.'s *The Bitter Heritage* °
(Fawcett, 1967). Franz Schurman *et al.* in *The Politics of Escalation in
Vietnam* ° (Beacon, 1966) conclude that the Johnson Administration
avoided negotiations and rebuffed peace feelers while escalating the
war. *Viet-Report*, a special magazine established in 1965 by critics of
Administration policy, and *I. F. Stone's Weekly* (later a bi-weekly) are
publications deeply hostile to American policy in Southeast Asia. The
State Department presents its case in *Aggression from the North: The*

Record of North Vietnam's Campaign to Conquer South Vietnam (Government Printing Office, 1965). Frank Trager in *Why Viet Nam?* (Praeger, 1966) supports the views of the Government. *Can We Win in Vietnam?* (1968), a publication in the Hudson Institute Series on National Security and International Order, presents the views of five essayists, three of whom believe that the United States can and should win the war. The wisdom of the American commitment is both defended and attacked in *The Vietnam Hearings* (Random House, 1966), a volume containing the complete statements before the Senate Committee on Foreign Relations by Dean Rusk, James M. Gavin, George Kennan, and Maxwell Taylor. Gabriel Kolko's *The Roots of American Foreign Policy* (Beacon Press, 1969) includes a substantial chapter on American intervention in Vietnam, which the author first prepared as a paper for the international war crimes tribunal headed by Bertrand Russell in 1967.

Because of the emphasis on Vietnam, scholars have unfortunately neglected other aspects of Johnson's foreign policy. On the Dominican intervention see *Overtaken by Events: The Dominican Crisis From the Fall of Trujillo to the Civil War* (Doubleday, 1966) by John Bartlow Martin, the American ambassador to the Dominican Republic; and *The Unfinished Experiment: Democracy in the Dominican Republic* (Praeger, 1966) by Juan Bosch, the President who was ousted by American intervention. Phillip Geyelin's *Lyndon B. Johnson and the World* (Praeger, 1966) is the best general volume on Johnson and foreign policy. Eric Goldman, a former White House adviser, laments in his book *The Tragedy of Lyndon Johnson* (Knopf, 1969) that Johnson was overly sensitive to criticism and rigid in his policies.

DWIGHT MACDONALD

Our Invisible Poor

INTRODUCTION

Through the efforts of a few concerned writers, whose work Dwight
Macdonald summarizes below in his essay, Americans in 1962 re-
discovered poverty. As ghetto rioting became a commonplace occurrence in the national life of the succeeding years, attempts to
draw a statistical picture of the poor took on critical relevance.
Subsequent researchers sustained Macdonald's indictment of the
American welfare state, but in some ways his essay is already
dated.

For instance, at the time Macdonald wrote, the concept of a
"culture of poverty," now the focus of intense debate, was only beginning to enter into popular discussions of poverty. Oscar Lewis
in *The Children of Sanchez* (Random House, 1961) had already

FROM Dwight Macdonald, "Our Invisible Poor," *The New Yorker*, XXXVIII (January 19,
1963), pp. 82–132. © 1963 The New Yorker Magazine, Inc.; reprinted by permission.

suggested that poverty was more than just economic deprivation; it was, he said, a way of life with "a structure, a rationale, and defense mechanisms" that pass from generation to generation. If poverty is indeed a culture, as Lewis argued, it cannot be eradicated merely by better welfare programs or more money, and its causes lie partly within the poor community itself. But presumably Macdonald would side with those who reject Lewis' view, for in suggesting subsidies for the poor as the solution to their problem, he implies that low income is the main cause of poverty and that the power to end poverty rests with society as a whole.

Since 1963, when Macdonald wrote his essay, statistical analyses of poverty have profited from refinements and corrections. Macdonald noted estimates of the poor varying from thirty-five to fifty million people, with Gabriel Kolko in *Wealth and Power in America* (Praeger, 1962) claiming that half of America, or ninety million people, lacked a "maintenance standard of living." These estimates, some later writers have argued, resulted from unsophisticated methods of measurement and are exaggerated. Thus, in *This U.S.A.* (Doubleday, 1965) Ben J. Wattenberg and Richard M. Scammon (Director of the Census from 1961 to 1965) assert: "We are *not* a nation with huge numbers of seething, shuffling poor people who invisibly tramp through our streets with neither hope nor health. There is hard-core poverty in the United States, but it does not involve 40% of our population—nor 20% of our population." They believe that definitions of poverty relying on arbitrary income levels —such as Leon Keyserling's $4,000 per family or $2,000 for unattached individuals—"are virtually meaningless because they are so very grand and cannot therefore take into account the immense variations in household size, region, residence and race."

Students and hospital interns, young couples, retired persons with homes paid for and money in the bank, are among those millions who fall below Keyserling's income line but who are not actually poor. According to Wattenberg and Scammon, poverty must be defined not by income but by failure to possess adequate food, clothing, and shelter. The authors do not attack the problem of how to measure such inadequacy; they imply that only 10 percent or less of the American people are poor. Even so, the optimistic authors of *This U.S.A.* regard nearly twenty million poor people as an intolerably large number.

A writer gifted at clarifying statistical problems is Herman Miller, special assistant to the Director of the Census. Although Miller is also unhappy with arbitrary income definitions of poverty, he attempted to make a precise numerical estimate of those below subsistence income levels. The result of Miller's research appeared in a collection called *Poverty As a Public Issue,* edited by Ben Seligman (Free Press, 1965). Miller noted that to administer welfare programs in accordance with the Social Security Act of 1935, each state must determine what constitutes minimum subsistence incomes for families of varying sizes within its jurisdiction. Miller found that 23.5 million Americans (13 percent) have incomes below the subsistence level established by the states they reside in and therefore can be considered poor. Though he recognized that wide variations in state standards posed a problem for his method, he made no consequent adjustments in his figures; thus it is possible that in the South, for instance, in terms of adequate food, clothing, and shelter, there is more poverty than his figures indicate. Nevertheless Miller, along with Wattenberg and Scammon, has at least made a convincing case against the inflated figures of other writers.

In his essay, Macdonald disputes Kolko's contention that distribution of wealth "is essentially the same as in 1939, or even in 1910"; to prove his case, Macdonald cites figures showing that the very rich have lost ground since 1929. (Actually his figures are not much different from Kolko's, but Kolko argues that all such estimates are unreliable because they take no account of the billions of dollars in hidden and undeclared income belonging to the rich.) Macdonald does concede, however, that poor people did not gain from whatever redistribution took place. In *Income Distribution in the United States* (Government Printing Office, 1966) and elsewhere, Herman Miller offers figures that support Macdonald's general position. Between 1929 and 1944, according to Miller, the share of the national income (before taxes) going to the richest Americans decreased—for the upper 5 percent, from 30 percent to 21 percent; for the upper 20 percent, from 54 percent to 46 percent. As for the poorest fifth of the population, its share rose from 4 percent during the Depression to 5 percent in 1962. According to Miller, "These figures hardly support the view held by many Americans that incomes in our society are becoming more evenly distributed." After they paid their income taxes, the top 5 percent in recent years saw their share decline from 20 percent to 18 percent. But as Miller points out, the income tax accounted for only 37 percent of all local, state, and federal taxes in 1962. Since most of the other taxes are regressive, the total effect of taxation on wealth distribution is, at best, marginal. These figures suggest that one way to fight poverty might be to redistribute wealth and, more debatably, that the unwillingness of society to redistribute significantly has caused the poor to remain poor.

Another subject that has received useful statistical attention since Macdonald's article is Negro poverty. Depending on the definition of poverty, the black poor constitute only one-fifth to one-third of all the poor in America, but the crisis of our time is in large measure indicated by the far higher incidence of poverty among blacks than among whites. In such studies as Herman Miller's *Rich Man, Poor Man* (New American Library, 1964) and Rashi Fein's "An Economic and Social Profile of the Negro American" (*Daedalus*, XCIV [Fall, 1965]), the disadvantages of being a black man in America are made depressingly clear. Of 3.6 million Negro men employed in 1960, 40 percent were either laborers or service trade workers like elevator operators or janitors. Negro factory hands earned 32 percent less than did white factory workers, and in service trades Negroes made 29 percent less. Only 10 percent of Negro men worked as craftsmen, and they made 35 percent less than did white craftsmen. Of the 113,000 Negro men who had professional and technical employment, 40 percent were concentrated in the two lowest-paying professions—teaching and the ministry.

In part, the economic plight of the Negro stems from educational deficiencies: in 1960 the average white had 2.7 more years of school than the average black. But as Rashi Fein notes, "The Negro who has attended (but not completed) college earns less than the whites with only eight years of elementary school; the Negro college graduate earns but slightly more than does the white high school graduate." Not surprisingly, average Negro income was 52 percent of white income in 1959 (compared to 53 percent in 1945); 7.7 percent of Negro families earned less than $1,000 in 1964 compared to 2.7 percent of white families, and in that year, 21 percent of the unemployed were blacks while blacks were only 11 percent of the whole labor force.

In 1960 the American Negro could expect to live six years less than the Caucasian. He had three chances in ten of living in a dwelling unit without showers or bathtubs compared to one in eight for whites. And he had a far greater chance of dying from tuberculosis or losing his children in infancy. This catalogue of disparity is, unfortunately, by no means complete.

In spite of advances in knowledge of the poor since 1963, Macdonald's article remains one of the best discussions of the problem of poverty. Widely read at the time of its publication, it even had an impact in the White House. But as we now know, recognition and description of a problem cannot by themselves serve as its solution.

*I*n his significantly titled *The Affluent Society* (1958) Professor J. K. Galbraith states that poverty in this country is no longer "a massive affliction [but] more nearly an afterthought." Dr. Galbraith is a humane critic of the American capitalist system, and he is generously indignant about the continued existence of even this nonmassive and afterthoughtish poverty. But the interesting thing about his pronouncement, aside from the fact that it is inaccurate, is that it was generally accepted as obvious. For a long time now, almost everybody has assumed that, because of the New Deal's social legislation and—more important—the prosperity we have enjoyed since 1940, mass poverty no longer exists in this country.

Dr. Galbraith states that our poor have dwindled to two hard-core categories. One is the "insular poverty" of those who live in the rural South or in depressed areas like West Virginia. The other category is "case poverty," which he says is "commonly and properly related to [such] characteristics of the individuals so afflicted [as] mental deficiency, bad health, inability to adapt to the discipline of modern economic life, excessive procreation, alcohol, insufficient education." He reasons that such poverty must be due to individual defects, since "nearly everyone else has mastered his environment; this proves that it is not intractable." Without pressing the similarity of this concept to the "Social Darwinism" whose fallacies Dr. Galbraith easily disposes of elsewhere in his book, one may observe that most of these characteristics are as much the result of poverty as its cause.

Dr. Galbraith's error is understandable, and common. Last April the newspapers reported some exhilarating statistics in a Department of Commerce study: the average family income increased from $2,340 in 1929 to $7,020 in 1961. (These figures are calculated in current dollars, as are all the others I shall cite.) But the papers did not report the fine type, so to speak, which showed that almost all the recent gain was made by families with incomes of over $7,500, and that the rate at which poverty is being eliminated has slowed down alarmingly since 1953. Only the specialists and the statisticians read the fine type, which is why illusions continue to exist about American poverty.

Now Michael Harrington, an alumnus of the *Catholic Worker* and the Fund for the Republic who is at present a contributing editor of *Dissent* and the chief editor of the Socialist Party biweekly, *New America,* has written *The Other America: Poverty in the United States* (Macmillan). In the admirably short space of under two hundred pages, he outlines the problem, describes in imaginative detail what it means to be poor in this country today, summarizes the findings of recent studies by economists and sociologists, and analyzes the reasons for the persistence of mass poverty in the midst of general prosperity. It is an excellent book—and a most important one.

My only serious criticism is that Mr. Harrington has popularized the treatment a bit too much. Not in the writing, which is on a decent level, but in a certain vagueness. There are no index, no bibliography, no reference footnotes. In our overspecialized culture, books like this tend to fall into two categories: Popular (no scholarly "apparatus") and Academic (too much). I favor something intermediate—why should the academics have *all* the footnotes? The lack of references means that the book is of limited use to future researchers and writers. A pity, since the author has brought together a great range of material.

I must also object that Mr. Harrington's treatment of statistics is more than a little impressionistic. His appendix, which he calls a coming to grips with the professional material, doesn't live up to its billing. "If my interpretation is bleak and grim," he writes, "and even if it overstates the case slightly, that is intentional. My moral point of departure is a sense of outrage. . . . In such a discussion it is inevitable that one gets mixed up with dry, graceless, technical matters. That should not conceal the crucial fact that these numbers represent people and that any tendency toward understatement is an intellectual way of acquiescing in suffering." But a fact is a fact, and Mr. Harrington confuses the issue when he writes that "these numbers represent people." They do—and one virtue of his book is that he never forgets it— but in dealing with statistics, this truism must be firmly repressed lest one begin to think from the heart rather than from the head, as he seems to do when he charges those statisticians who "understate" the numbers of the poor with having found "an intellectual way of acquiescing in suffering." This is moral bullying, and it reminds me, *toutes proportions gardées*, of the habitual confusion in Communist thinking between facts and political inferences from them. "A sense of outrage" is proper for a "moral point of departure," but statistics are the appropriate *factual* point of departure, as in the writings of Marx and Engels on the agony of the nineteenth-century English working class—writings that are by no means lacking in a sense of moral outrage, either.

These objections, however, do not affect Mr. Harrington's two main contentions: that mass poverty still exists in the United States, and that it is disappearing more slowly than is commonly thought. Two recent dry, graceless, and technical reports bear him out. One is that Commerce Department study, already mentioned. More important is *Poverty and Deprivation in the U.S.*, a bulky pamphlet issued by the Conference on Economic Progress, in Washington, whose national committee includes Thurman Arnold, Leon H. Keyserling (said to be the principal author of the pamphlet), and Walter P. Reuther.

In the last year we seem to have suddenly awakened, rubbing our eyes like Rip van Winkle, to the fact that mass poverty persists, and that it is one of our two gravest social problems. (The other is related: While only eleven per cent of our population is non-white, twenty-five per cent of our poor are.) Two other current books confirm Mr. Harrington's thesis: *Wealth and Power in America* (Praeger), by Dr. Gabriel Kolko, a social historian who has recently been at Harvard and the University of Melbourne, Australia, and *Income and Welfare in the United States* (McGraw-Hill), compiled by an imposing battery of four socio-economists headed by Dr. James N. Morgan, who rejoices in the title of Program Director of the Survey Research Center of the Institute for Social Research at the University of Michigan.

Dr. Kolko's book resembles Mr. Harrington's in several ways: It is short, it is based on earlier studies, and it is liberally inclined. It is less readable, because it is written in an academic jargon that is merely a vehicle for the clinching Statistic. Although it is impossible to write seriously about poverty without a copious use of statistics—as this review will demonstrate —it *is* possible to bring thought and feeling.to bear on such raw material. Mr. Harrington does this more successfully than Dr. Kolko, whose prose is afflicted not only with academic blight but also with creeping ideology. Dr. Kolko leans so far to the socialist side that he sometimes falls on his nose, as when he clinches the inequality of wealth in the United States with a statistic: "In 1959, 23% of those earning less than $1,000 [a year] owned a car, compared to 95% of those earning more than $10,000." The real point is just the opposite, as any citizen of Iran, Ghana, Yemen, or the U.S.S.R. would appreciate—not that the rich have cars but that almost a quarter of the extremely poor do. Similarly, although Dr. Kolko has two chapters on poverty that confirm Mr. Harrington's argument, his main point is a different and more vulnerable one: "The basic distribution of income and wealth in the United States is essentially the same now as it was in 1939, or even 1910." This is a half fact. The rich are almost as rich as ever and the poor are even poorer, in the percentage of the national income they receive. Yet, as will become apparent later, there have been major changes in the distribution of wealth, and there has been a general improvement in living standards, so that the poor are much fewer today than they were in 1939. "Most low-income groups live substantially better today," Dr. Kolko admits. "But even though their real wages have mounted, their percentage of the national income has not changed." That in the last half century the rich have kept their riches and the poor their poverty is indeed a scandal. But it is theoretically possible, assuming enough general increase in wealth, that the relatively poor might by now have achieved a decent standard of living, no matter how inferior to that of the rich. As the books under consideration show, however, this theoretical possibility has not been realized.

Inequality of wealth is not necessarily a major social problem per se. Poverty is. The late French philosopher Charles Péguy remarks, in his classic essay on poverty, "The duty of tearing the destitute from their destitution and the duty of distributing goods equitably are not of the same order. The first is an urgent duty, the second is a duty of convenience. . . . When all men are provided with the necessities . . . what do we care about the distribution of luxury?" What indeed? Envy and emulation are the motives— and not very good ones—for the equalization of wealth. The problem of poverty goes much deeper.

Income and Welfare in the United States differs from the other works reviewed here in length (531 big pages) and in being the result of original research; 2,800 families were interviewed "in depth." I must confess that, aside from a few interesting bits of data, I got almost nothing out of it. I assume the authors think poverty is still an important social problem, else why would they have gone to all this labor, but I'm not at all sure what their general conclusions are; maybe there aren't supposed to be any, in the best tradition of American scholarship. Their book is one of those behemoths of collective research financed by a foundation (in this case, largely by Ford) that daunt the stoutest-hearted lay reader (in this case, me). Based on "a multi-stage area probability sample that gives equal chance of selection to all non-institutional dwelling units in the conterminous United States [and that] was clustered geographically at each stage and stratified with interlaced controls," it is a specimen of what Charles Lamb called *biblia abiblia* —things that have the outward appearance of books but are not books, since they cannot be read. Methodologically, it employs something called the "multivariate analysis," which is explained in Appendix E. Typographically, Appendix E looks like language, but it turns out to be strewn with booby traps, all doubtless well known in the trade, like "dummy variables," "F ratios," "regression coefficients," "beta coefficients" (and "partial beta coefficients"), and two kinds of "standard deviations"—"of explanatory variable A" and "of the dependent variable."

My experience with such works may be summarized as follows: (alpha) the coefficient of comprehensibility decreases in direct ratio to the increase in length, or the longer the incomprehensibler, a notion that is illustrated here by the fact that Dr. Kolko's short work is more understandable than Dr. Morgan et al.'s long one; (beta) the standard deviation from truism is inversely related to the magnitude of the generalization, or the bigger the statement the more obvious. (Beta) is illustrated by the authors' five general proposals for action ("Implications for Public Policy"). The second of these is: "Fuller employment and the elimination of discrimination based on prejudice would contribute greatly to the independence of non-white persons, women, teenagers, and some of the aged." That is, if Negroes and the rest had jobs and were not discriminated against, they would be better off— a point that doesn't need to be argued or, for that matter, stated. The authors have achieved such a mastery of truism that they sometimes achieve the same monumental effect even in non-magnitudinous statements, as: "Table 28-1 shows that the proportion of parents who indicated that their children will attend private colleges is approximately twice as large for those with incomes over $10,000 as for those with incomes under $3,000." Could be.

What is "poverty"? It is a historically relative concept, first of all. "There are new definitions [in America] of what man can achieve, of what a human standard of life should be," Mr. Harrington writes. "Those who suffer levels of life well below those that are possible, even though they live better than medieval knights or Asian peasants, are poor. . . . Poverty should be defined in terms of those who are denied the minimal levels of health, housing, food, and education that our present stage of scientific knowledge specifies as necessary for life as it is now lived in the United States." His dividing line follows that proposed in recent studies by the United States Bureau of Labor Statistics: $4,000 a year for a family of four and $2,000 for an individual living alone. (All kinds of income are included, such as food grown and consumed on farms.) This is the cutoff line generally drawn today.

Mr. Harrington estimates that between forty and fifty million Americans, or about a fourth of the population, are now living in poverty. Not just below the level of comfortable living, but real poverty, in the old-fashioned sense of the word—that they are hard put to it to get the mere necessities, beginning with enough to eat. This is difficult to believe in the United States of 1963, but one has to make the effort, and it is now being made. The extent of our poverty has suddenly become visible. The same thing has happened in England, where working-class gains as a result of the Labour Party's post-1945 welfare state blinded almost everybody to the continued existence of mass poverty. It was not until Professor Richard M. Titmuss, of the London School of Economics, published a series of articles in the *New Statesman* last fall, based on his new book, *Income Distribution and Social Change* (Allen & Unwin), that even the liberal public in England became aware that the problem still persists on a scale that is "statistically significant," as the economists put it.

Statistics on poverty are even trickier than most. For example, age and geography make a difference. There is a distinction, which cannot be rendered arithmetically, between poverty and low income. A childless young couple with $3,000 a year is not poor in the way an elderly couple might be with the same income. The young couple's statistical poverty may be a temporary inconvenience; if the husband is a graduate student or a skilled worker, there are prospects of later affluence or at least comfort. But the old couple can look forward only to diminishing earnings and increasing medical expenses. So also geographically: A family of four in a small town with $4,000 a year may be better off than a like family in a city—lower rent, no bus fares to get to work, fewer occasions (or temptations) to spend money. Even more so with a rural family. Although allowance is made for the value of the vegetables they may raise to feed themselves, it is impossible to calculate how much money they *don't* spend on clothes, say, or furniture, because they don't have to keep up with the Joneses. Lurking in the crevices of a city, like piranha fish in a Brazilian stream, are numerous tempting opportunities for expenditure, small but voracious, which can strip a budget to its bones in a surprisingly short time. The subtlety and complexity of poverty statistics may be discovered by a look at Dr. Kolko's statement that in 1959 "23% of those earning less than $1,000 owned a car." Does this include college students, or are they included in their families' statistics? If the first is true, then Dr. Kolko's figure loses much of its meaning. If the second is, then it is almost *too* meaningful, since it says that one-fourth of those earning less than twenty dollars a week are able to afford a car. Which it is, deponent sayeth not.

It is not, therefore, surprising to find that there is some disagreement about just how many millions of Americans are poor. The point is that all these recent studies agree that American poverty is still a mass phenomenon. One of the lowest estimates appears in the University of Michigan's *Income and Welfare*, which states, "Poor families comprise one-fifth of the nation's families." The authors do not develop this large and crucial statement, or even give sources for it, despite their meticulous pedantry in all unimportant matters. So one can only murmur that the other experts put the number of poor much higher. (Though even a fifth is still over 35,000,000 people.) The lowness of the Michigan estimate is especially puzzling since its cutoff figure for poverty is $4,330, which is slightly higher than the commonly accepted one. The tendentious Dr. Kolko is also unconvincing, in the opposite direction. "Since 1947," he writes, "one-half of the nation's families and unattached individuals have had an income too small to provide them with a maintenance standard of living," which he sets at $4,500 a year for a family. He does give a table, with a long supporting footnote that failed to make clear to me how he could have possibly decided that 90,000,000 Americans are now living on less than $4,500 a year; I suspect some confusion between a "maintenance" and a "minimum-comfort" budget.

More persuasive estimates appear in the Conference on Economic Progress pamphlet, *Poverty and Deprivation*. Using the $4,000 cutoff, the authors conclude that 38,000,000 persons are now living in poverty, which is slightly less than Mr. Harrington's lowest estimate. One reason may be that the pamphlet discriminates, as most studies don't, between "multiple-person families" and "unattached individuals," rating the latter as poor only if they have less than $2,000 a year. But there is more to it than that, including a few things I don't feel competent to judge. Income statistics are never compiled on exactly the same bases and there are all kinds of refinements, which vary from one study to another. Thus the Commerce Department's April report estimates there are 17,500,000 families *and* "unattached individuals" with incomes of less than $4,000. How many of the latter are there? *Poverty and Deprivation* puts the number of single persons with under $2,000 at 4,000,000. Let us say that in the 17,500,000 under $4,000 there are 6,500,000 single persons—the proportion of unattached individuals tends to go down as income rises. This homemade estimate gives us 11,000,000 families with incomes of under $4,000. Figuring the average American family at three and a half persons—which it is—this makes 38,500,000 individuals in families, or a grand total, if we add in the 4,000,000 "unattached individuals" with under $2,000 a year, of 42,500,000 Americans now living in poverty, which is close to a fourth of the total population.

The reason Dr. Galbraith was able to see poverty as no longer "a massive affliction" is that he used a cutoff of $1,000, which even in 1949, when it was adopted in a Congressional study, was probably too low (the C.I.O. argued for $2,000) and in 1958, when *The Affluent Society* appeared, was simply fantastic.

The model postwar budgets drawn up in 1951 by the Bureau of Labor Statistics to "maintain a level of adequate living" give a concrete idea of what poverty means in this country—or would mean if poor families lived within

their income and spent it wisely, which they don't. Dr. Kolko summarizes the
kind of living these budgets provide:

> Three members of the family see a movie once every three weeks, and one
> member sees a movie once every two weeks. There is no telephone in the
> house, but the family makes three pay calls a week. They buy one book a year
> and write one letter a week.
>   The father buys one heavy wool suit every two years and a light wool suit
> every three years; the wife, one suit every ten years or one skirt every five
> years. Every three or four years, depending on the distance and time in-
> volved, the family takes a vacation outside their own city. In 1950, the family
> spent a total of $80 to $90 on all types of home furnishings, electrical appli-
> ances, and laundry equipment. . . . The family eats cheaper cuts of meat
> several times a week, but has more expensive cuts on holidays. The entire
> family consumes a total of two five-cent ice cream cones, one five-cent candy
> bar, two bottles of soda, and one bottle of beer a week. The family owes no
> money, but has no savings except for a small insurance policy.

One other item is included in the B.L.S. "maintenance" budget: a new
car every twelve to eighteen years.
     This is an ideal picture, drawn up by social workers, of how a poor fam-
ily *should* spend its money. But the poor are much less provident—installment debts take up a lot of their cash, and only a statistician could expect an
actual live woman, however poor, to buy new clothes at intervals of five or
ten years. Also, one suspects that a lot more movies are seen and ice-cream
cones and bottles of beer are consumed than in the Spartan ideal. But these
necessary luxuries are had only at the cost of displacing other items—necessary necessities, so to speak—in the B.L.S. budget.

     The Conference on Economic Progress's *Poverty and Deprivation*
deals not only with the poor but also with another large section of the "underprivileged," which is an American euphemism almost as good as "senior
citizen;" namely, the 37,000,000 persons whose family income is between
$4,000 and $5,999 and the 2,000,000 singles who have from $2,000 to $2,999.
The authors define "deprivation" as "above poverty but short of minimum
requirements for a modestly comfortable level of living." They claim that
77,000,000 Americans, or *almost half the population,* live in poverty or
deprivation. One recalls the furor Roosevelt aroused with his "one-third of a
nation—ill-housed, ill-clad, ill-nourished." But the political climate was different then.
     The distinction between a family income of $3,500 ("poverty") and
$4,500 ("deprivation") is not vivid to those who run things—the 31 per cent
whose incomes are between $7,500 and $14,999 and the 7 per cent of the top-

most top dogs, who get $15,000 or more. These two minorities, sizable enough to feel they *are* the nation, have been as unaware of the continued existence of mass poverty as this reviewer was until he read Mr. Harrington's book. They are businessmen, congressmen, judges, government officials, politicians, lawyers, doctors, engineers, scientists, editors, journalists, and administrators in colleges, churches, and foundations. Since their education, income, and social status are superior, they, if anybody, might be expected to accept responsibility for what the Constitution calls "the general welfare." They have not done so in the case of the poor. And they have a good excuse. It is becoming harder and harder simply to *see* the one-fourth of our fellow-citizens who live below the poverty line.

> The poor are increasingly slipping out of the very experience and consciousness of the nation [Mr. Harrington writes]. If the middle class never did like ugliness and poverty, it was at least aware of them. "Across the tracks" was not a very long way to go. . . . Now the American city has been transformed. The poor still inhabit the miserable housing in the central area, but they are increasingly isolated from contact with, or sight of, anybody else. . . . Living out in the suburbs, it is easy to assume that ours is, indeed, an affluent society. . . .
>
> Clothes make the poor invisible too: America has the best-dressed poverty the world has ever known. . . . It is much easier in the United States to be decently dressed than it is to be decently housed, fed, or doctored. . . .
>
> Many of the poor are the wrong age to be seen. A good number of them are sixty-five years of age or better; an even larger number are under eighteen. . . .
>
> And finally, the poor are politically invisible. . . . They are without lobbies of their own; they put forward no legislative program. As a group, they are atomized. They have no face; they have no voice. . . . Only the social agencies have a really direct involvement with the other America, and they are without any great political power. . . .
>
> Forty to fifty million people are becoming increasingly invisible.

These invisible people fall mostly into the following categories, some of them overlapping: poor farmers, who operate 40 per cent of the farms and get 7 per cent of the farm cash income; migratory farm workers; unskilled, unorganized workers in offices, hotels, restaurants, hospitals, laundries, and other service jobs; inhabitants of areas where poverty is either endemic ("peculiar to a people or district"), as in the rural South, or epidemic ("prevalent among a community at a special time and produced by some special causes"), as in West Virginia, where the special cause was the closing of coal mines and steel plants; Negroes and Puerto Ricans, who are a fourth of the total poor; the alcoholic derelicts in the big-city skid rows; the hillbillies from Kentucky,

Tennessee, and Oklahoma who have migrated to Midwestern cities in search of better jobs. And, finally, almost half our "senior citizens."

The only pages in *Poverty and Deprivation* that can be read are the statistical tables. The rest is a jungle of inchoate data that seems deliberately to eschew, like other collective research projects, such human qualities as reason (the reader has to do most of the work of ordering the material) and feeling (if Mr. Harrington sometimes has too much, it is a venial sin compared to the bleakness of this prose). My hypothesis is that *Poverty and Deprivation* was composed on that TX-0 "electronic brain" at M.I.T. This would account both for the vitality of the tables and for the deadness of the text.

And what shall one say about the University of Michigan's *Income and Welfare in the United States?* Even its *tables* are not readable. And its text makes *Poverty and Deprivation* look like the Federalist Papers. On the first page, the authors unloose a generalization of stupefying generality: "The United States has arrived at the point where poverty could be abolished easily and simply by a stroke of the pen. [Where have we heard *that* before?] To raise every individual and family in the nation now below a subsistence income to the subsistence level would cost about $10 billion a year. This is less than 2 per cent of the gross national product. It is less than 10 per cent of tax revenues. [They mean, but forgot to say so, *federal* taxes, since if state and local taxes were added, the total would be much higher than $100 billion.] It is about one-fifth of the cost of national defense." (They might have added that it is slightly more than three times the $3 billion Americans spend on their dogs and cats and canaries every year.) This got big headlines in the press, as must have been expected: " 'STROKE OF PEN' COULD ELIMINATE POVERTY IN U.S., 4 SCIENTISTS SAY." But the authors, having dropped the $10 billion figure on the first page, never explain its meaning—is it a seedbed operation or a permanent dole? They are not clear even on how they arrived at it. At their own estimate of 35,000,000 poor, $10 billion would work out to slightly less than $300 per person. This seems too little to abolish poverty "easily and simply by a stroke of the pen."

There are other vaguenesses: "A careful analysis of the characteristics of families whose incomes are inadequate reveals that they should earn considerably more than they do on the basis of their education and other characteristics. The multivariate analysis . . . indicates that heads of poor families should average $2,204 in earnings. In fact heads of poor families earned an average of only $932 in 1959." I have already confessed my inability to understand the multivariate analysis, but the compilers seem to be saying that according to the variables in their study (race, age, sex, education, physical disabilities, and locale), heads of poor families should now be making twice as much as they are. And why don't they? "The discrepancy may arise from psychological dependency, lack of motivation, lack of intelligence, and a variety of other factors that were not studied." One wonders why they were not studied—and what those "other factors" were, exactly. Also, whether such a discrepancy—the earnings the researchers expected to find were actually less than half those they *did* find—may not indicate some ghastly flaw in that "multivariate analysis." There is, of course, no suggestion in the book that Dr. Morgan and his team are in any way worried.

The most obvious citizens of the Other America are those whose skins are the wrong color. The folk slogans are realistic: "Last to be hired, first to be fired" and "If you're black, stay back." There has been some progress. In 1939, the non-white worker's wage averaged 41.4 per cent of the white worker's; by 1958 it had climbed to 58 per cent. A famous victory, but the non-whites still average only slightly more than half as much as the whites. Even this modest gain was due not to any Rooseveltian or Trumanian social reform but merely to the fact that for some years there was a war on and workers were in demand, whether black, white, or violet. By 1947, the non-whites had achieved most of their advance—to 54 per cent of white earnings, which means they have gained, in the last fifteen years, just 4 per cent.

The least obvious poverty affects our "senior citizens"—those over sixty-five. Mr. Harrington estimates that half of them—8,000,000—live in poverty, and he thinks they are even more atomized and politically helpless than the rest of the Other America. He estimates that one-fourth of the "unrelated individuals" among them, or a million persons, have less than $580 a year, which is about what is allotted *for food alone* in the Department of Agriculture's minimum-subsistence budget. (The average American family now spends only 20 per cent of its income for food—an indication of the remarkable prosperity we are all enjoying, except for one-quarter of us.) One can imagine, or perhaps one can't, what it would be like to live on $580 a year, or $11 a week. It is only fair to note that most of our senior citizens do better: The average per-capita income of those over sixty-five is now estimated to be slightly over $20 a week. That is, about $1,000 a year.

The aged poor have two sources of income besides their earnings or savings. One is contributions by relatives. A 1961 White House Conference Report put this at 10 per cent of income, which works out to $8 a week for an income of $4,000—and the 8,000,000 aged poor all have less than that. The other is Social Security, whose benefits in 1959 averaged $18 a week. Even this modest sum is more than any of the under-$4,000 got, since payments are proportionate to earnings and the poor, of course, earned less than the rest. A quarter of them, and those in general the neediest, are not covered by Social Security. The last resort is relief, and Mr. Harrington describes most vividly the humiliations the poor often have to put up with to get that.

The problem of the aged poor is aggravated by the fact that, unlike the Italians or the English, we seem to have little respect for or interest in our "senior citizens," beyond giving them that honorific title, and we don't include them in family life. If we can afford it, we are likely to send them to nursing homes—"a storage-bin philosophy," a Senate report calls it—and if we can't, which is the case with the poor, they must make do with the resources noted above. The Michigan study has a depressing chapter on "The Economics of Living with Relatives." Nearly two-thirds of the heads of families queried were opposed to having their aged parents live with their children. "The old do not understand the young, and the young do not understand the old or the young," observed one respondent, who must have had a sense of humor. Other replies were "Old people are pretty hard to get along with" and "The parents and the children try to boss each other and when they live with you there's always fighting." The minority in favor gave practical reasons, like "It's a good thing to have them with you so you can see after them" and "The old folks might get a pension or something, so they could help you out." Hardly anyone expressed any particular respect for the old, or a feeling that their experience might enrich family life. The most depressing finding was "People most able to provide for relatives are most opposed to it. Older people with some college education are eleven to one against it." The most favorable toward including older people in the home were Negroes, and even they were mostly against it.

The whole problem of poverty and the aged is especially serious today because Americans are living longer. In the first half of this century, life expectancy increased 17.6 years for men and 20.3 years for women. And between 1950 and 1960 the over-sixty-five group increased twice as fast as the population as a whole.

The worst part of being old and poor in this country is the loneliness. Mr. Harrington notes that we have not only racial ghettos but geriatric ones, in the cheap rooming-house districts of large cities. He gives one peculiarly disturbing statistic: "One-third of the aged in the United States, some 5,000,-000 or more human beings, have no phone in their place of residence. They are literally cut off from the rest of America."

Ernest Hemingway's celebrated deflation of Scott Fitzgerald's romantic notion that the rich are "different" somehow—"Yes, they have money"—doesn't apply to the poor. They are different in more important ways than their lack of money, as Mr. Harrington demonstrates:

> Emotional upset is one of the main forms of the vicious circle of impoverishment. The structure of the society is hostile to these people. The poor tend to become pessimistic and depressed; they seek immediate gratification instead of saving; they act out.
>
> Once this mood, this unarticulated philosophy becomes a fact, society can change, the recession can end, and yet there is no motive for movement. The depression has become internalized. The middle class looks upon this process and sees "lazy" people who "just don't want to get ahead." People who are much too sensitive to demand of cripples that they run races ask of the poor that they get up and act just like everyone else in the society.

> The poor are not like everyone else. . . . They think and feel differently;
> they look upon a different America than the middle class looks upon.

The poor are also different in a physical sense: they are much less healthy. According to *Poverty and Deprivation,* the proportion of those "disabled or limited in their major activity by chronic ill health" rises sharply as income sinks. In reasonably well-off families ($7,000 and up), 4.3 per cent are so disabled; in reasonably poor families ($2,000 to $3,999), the proportion doubles, to 8 per cent; and in unreasonably poor families (under $2,000), it doubles again, to 16.5 per cent. An obvious cause, among others, for the very poor being four times as much disabled by "chronic ill health" as the well-to-do is that they have much less money to spend for medical care—in fact, almost nothing. This weighs with special heaviness on the aged poor. During the fifties, Mr. Harrington notes, "all costs on the Consumer Price Index went up by 12 per cent. But medical costs, that terrible staple of the aged, went up by 36 per cent, hospitalization rose by 65 per cent, and group hospitalization costs (Blue Cross premiums) were up by 83 per cent."

This last figure is particularly interesting, since Blue Cross and such plans are the A.M.A.'s alternative to socialized medicine, or, rather, to the timid fumblings toward it that even our most liberal politicians have dared to propose. Such figures throw an unpleasant light on the Senate's rejection of Medicare. The defeat was all the more bitter because, in the usual effort to appease the conservatives (with the usual lack of success—only five Republicans and only four Southern Democrats voted pro), the bill was watered down in advance. Not until he had spent $90 of his own money—which is 10 per cent of the annual income of some 3,000,000 aged poor—would a patient have been eligible. And the original program included only people already covered by Social Security or Railroad Retirement pensions and excluded the neediest of all—the 2,500,000 aged poor who are left out of both these systems. These untouchables were finally included in order to placate five liberal Republican senators, led by Javits of New York. They did vote for Medicare, but they were the only Republicans who did.

Mental as well as physical illness is much greater among the poor, even though our complacent cliché is that nervous breakdowns are a prerogative of the rich because the poor "can't afford" them. (They can't, but they have them anyway.) This bit of middle-class folklore should be laid to rest by a study made in New Haven: *Social Class and Mental Illness,* by August B. Hollingshead and Frederick C. Redlich (Wiley). They found that the rate of "treated psychiatric illness" is about the same from the rich down through decently paid workers—an average of 573 per 100,000. But in the bottom fifth it shoots up to 1,659 per 100,000. There is an even more striking difference in the *kind* of mental illness. Of those in the four top income groups who had undergone psychiatric treatment, 65 per cent had been treated for neurotic problems and 35 per cent for psychotic disturbances. In the bottom fifth, the treated illnesses were almost all psychotic (90 per cent). This shows there

is something to the notion that the poor "can't afford" nervous breakdowns
—the milder kind, that is—since the reason the proportion of *treated*
neuroses among the poor is only 10 per cent is that a neurotic can keep going,
after a fashion. But the argument cuts deeper the other way. The poor go to a
psychiatrist (or, more commonly, are committed to a mental institution) only
when they are completely unable to function because of psychotic symptoms.
Therefore, even that nearly threefold increase in mental disorders among the
poor is probably an underestimate.

The poor are different, then, both physically and psychologically. During the fifties, a team of psychiatrists from Cornell studied "Midtown," a residential area in this city that contained 170,000 people, of all social classes.
The area was 99 per cent white, so the findings may be presumed to understate the problem of poverty. The description of the poor—the "low social
economic status individual"—is blunt: "[They are] rigid, suspicious, and
have a fatalistic outlook on life. They do not plan ahead. . . . They are
prone to depression, have feelings of futility, lack of belongingness, friendliness, and a lack of trust in others." Only a Dr. Pangloss would expect anything else. As Mr. Harrington points out, such characteristics are "a realistic
adaptation to a socially perverse situation."

As for the isolation that is the lot of the American poor, that is a point on
which Mr. Harrington is very good:

> America has a self-image of itself as a nation of joiners and doers. There are
> social clubs, charities, community drives, and the like. [One might add organ-
> izations like the Elks and Masons, Rotary and Kiwanis, cultural groups like
> our women's clubs, also alumni associations and professional organizations.]
> And yet this entire structure is a phenomenon of the middle class. Some time
> ago, a study in Franklin, Indiana [this vagueness of reference is all too typical
> of *The Other America*], reported that the percentage of people in the bottom
> class who were without affiliations of any kind was eight times as great as the
> percentage in the high-income class.
>
> Paradoxically, one of the factors that intensifies the social isolation of the
> poor is that America thinks of itself as a nation without social classes. As a
> result, there are few social or civic organizations that are separated on the
> basis of income and class. The "working-class culture" that sociologists have
> described in a country like England does not exist here. . . . The poor per-
> son who might want to join an organization is afraid. Because he or she will
> have less education, less money, less competence to articulate ideas than any-
> one else in the group, they stay away.

One reason our society is a comparatively violent one is that the French
and Italian and British poor have a communal life and culture that the American poor lack. As one reads *The Other America*, one wonders why there is
not even more violence than there is.

The richest city of all, New York, has been steadily growing poorer, if one looks beyond Park Avenue and Wall Street. Of its 2,080,000 families, just under half (49 per cent) had incomes in 1959 of less than $6,000; for the city's non-white families, the percentage was 71. And a fourth of all New York families in 1959 were below the poverty line of $4,000. These percentages are at present slightly higher than the national average—an ominous reversal of the city's earlier position. In 1932, the average national weekly wage was only 67 per cent of the New York City average. In 1960, it was 108 per cent. The city's manufacturing workers in 1946 earned $11 more a week than the national average; in 1960 they earned $6.55 a week less. The two chief reasons are probably the postwar influx of Puerto Ricans and the exodus to the suburbs of the well-to-do. But whatever the reasons, the city seems to be turning into an economically backward area, like Arkansas or New Hampshire. Even the bankers—the "non-supervisory" ones, that is— are modestly paid: 54 per cent of the males and 78 per cent of the females make less than $80 a week. All these statistics come from John O'Rourke, president of Joint Council 16, International Brotherhood of Teamsters, which has 168,000 members in the area. Mr. O'Rourke has been campaigning to persuade Mayor Wagner to raise the city's minimum hourly wage to $1.50. (The Mayor has gone as far as $1.25.) The New York teamsters are motivated by enlightened self-interest: the more other wages stagnate, the harder it will be to maintain their own comparatively high level of pay. They complain especially about the low wages in the highly organized garment trade, to which Mr. Dubinsky's International Ladies' Garment Workers' Union replies that if it presses for higher wages the manufacturers will simply move to low-wage, non-union areas, mostly in the South, as the New England textile manufacturers did many years ago—a riposte that is as realistic as it is uncheering. However, Mr. O'Rourke has an enterprising research staff, plenty of persistence, and a sharp tongue. "New Yorkers," he says, "are accustomed to thinking of themselves as pacesetters in an allegedly affluent society [but] at the rate we are going, we will soon qualify for the title 'Sweatshop Capital of the Nation.'"

The main reason the American poor have become invisible is that since 1936 their numbers have been reduced by two-thirds. Astounding as it may seem, the fact is that President Roosevelt's "one-third of a nation" was a considerable understatement; over two-thirds of us then lived below the poverty line, as is shown by the tables that follow. But today the poor are a minority, and minorities can be ignored if they are so heterogeneous that they cannot be organized. When the poor were a majority, they simply could not be overlooked. Poverty is also hard to see today because the middle class ($6,000 to $14,999) has vastly increased—from 13 per cent of all families in 1936 to a near-majority (47 per cent) today. That mass poverty can persist despite this rise to affluence is hard to believe, or see, especially if one is among those who have risen.

Two tables in *Poverty and Deprivation* summarize what has been happening in the last thirty years. They cover only multiple-person families; all figures are converted to 1960 dollars; and the income is before taxes. I have omitted, for clarity, all fractions.

The first table is the percentage of families with a given income:

	1935-6	1947	1953	1960
Under $ 4,000	68%	37%	28%	23%
$4,000 to $ 5,999	17	29	28	23
$6,000 to $ 7,499	6	12	17	16
$7,500 to $14,999	7	17	23	31
Over $15,000	2	4	5	7

The second table is the share each group had in the family income of the nation:

	1935-6	1947	1953	1960
Under $ 4,000	35%	16%	11%	7%
$4,000 to $ 5,999	21	24	21	15
$6,000 to $ 7,499	10	14	17	14
$7,500 to $14,999	16	28	33	40
Over $15,000	18	18	19	24

Several interesting conclusions can be drawn from these tables:

(1) The New Deal didn't do anything about poverty: The under-$4,000 families in 1936 were 68 per cent of the total population, which was slightly *more* than the 1929 figure of 65 per cent.

(2) The war economy (hot and cold) did do something about poverty: Between 1936 and 1960 the proportion of all families who were poor was reduced from 68 per cent to 23 per cent.

(3) If the percentage of under-$4,000 families decreased by two-thirds between 1936 and 1960, their share of the national income dropped a great deal more—from 35 per cent to 7 per cent. .

(4) The well-to-do ($7,500 to $14,999) have enormously increased, from 7 per cent of all families in 1936 to 31 per cent today. The rich ($15,000 and over) have also multiplied—from 2 to 7 per cent. But it should be noted that the very rich, according to another new study, *The Share of Top Wealth-Holders in National Wealth, 1922–1956*, by Robert J. Lampman (Princeton), have experienced a decline. He finds that the top 1 per cent of wealth-holders owned 38 per cent of the national wealth in 1929 and own only 28 per cent today. (Though let's not get sentimental over that "only.") Thus, *pace* Dr. Kolko, there has in fact been a redistribution of wealth—in favor of the well-to-do and the rich at the expense of the poor and the very rich.

(5) The reduction of poverty has slowed down. In the six years 1947–53, the number of poor families declined 9 per cent, but in the following seven years only 5 per cent. The economic stasis that set in with Eisenhower and that still persists under Kennedy was responsible. (This stagnation, however, did not affect the over-$7,500 families, who increased from 28 per cent to 38 per cent between 1953 and 1960.) In the New York *Times Magazine* for last November 11th, Herman P. Miller, of the Bureau of the Census, wrote, "During the forties, the lower-paid occupations made the greatest relative gains in average income. Laborers and service workers . . . had increases of about 180% . . . and professional and managerial workers, the highest paid workers of all, had the lowest relative gains—96%." But in the last decade the trend has been reversed; laborers and service workers have gained 39% while professional-managerial workers have gained 68%. This is because in the wartime forties the unskilled were in great demand, while now they are being replaced by machines. Automation is today the same kind of menace to the unskilled—that is, the poor—that the enclosure movement was to the British agricultural population centuries ago. "The facts show that our 'social revolution' ended nearly twenty years ago," Mr. Miller concludes, "yet important segments of the American public, many of them highly placed Government officials and prominent educators, think and act as though it were a continuing process."

"A reduction of about 19% [in the under-$6,000 families] in more than thirty years, or at a rate of about 0.7% per year, is no ground for complacency," the authors of *Poverty and Deprivation* justly observe. There is even less ground for complacency in the recent figures on *extreme* poverty. The authors estimate the number of families in 1929 with incomes of under $2,000 (in current dollars) at 7,500,000. By 1947 there were less than 4,000,000, not because of any philanthropic effort by their more prosperous fellow-citizens but entirely because of those first glorious years of a war economy. Six years later, in 1953, when the economy had begun to slow down, there were still 3,300,000 of these families with incomes of less than $2,000, and seven years later, in 1960, "there had been no further reduction." Thus in the last fifteen years the bottom dogs have remained on the bottom, sharing hardly at all in the advances that the income groups above them have made in an ascending scale that is exquisitely adjusted, by the automatic workings of capitalism, so that it is inversely proportionate to need.

There are, finally, the bottomest bottom dogs; i.e., *families* with incomes of *under $1,000*. I apologize for the italics, but some facts insist on them. According to *Poverty and Deprivation*, the numbers of these families "appear to have risen slightly" of late (1953–60), from 800,000 to about 1,000,-000. It is only fair, and patriotic, to add that according to the Commerce Department study, about 10,000,000 of our families and unattached individuals now enjoy incomes of $10,000 a year and up. So while some 3,500,000 Americans are in under-$1,000 families, ten times as many are in over-$10,000 families. Not bad at all—in a way.

The post-1940 decrease in poverty was not due to the policies or actions of those who are not poor, those in positions of power and responsibility. The war economy needed workers, wages went up, and the poor became less poor. When economic stasis set in, the rate of decrease in poverty slowed down proportionately, and it is still slow. Kennedy's efforts to "get the country moving again" have been unsuccessful, possibly because he has, despite the suggestions of many of his economic advisers, not yet advocated the one big step that might push the economy off dead center: a massive increase in government spending. This would be politically courageous, perhaps even dangerous, because of the superstitious fear of "deficit spending" and an "unbalanced" federal budget. American folklore insists that a government's budget must be arranged like a private family's. Walter Lippmann wrote, after the collapse of the stock market last spring:

> There is mounting evidence that those economists were right who told the Administration last winter that it was making the mistake of trying to balance the budget too soon. It will be said that the budget is not balanced: it shows a deficit in fiscal 1962 of $7 billion. . . . But . . . the budget that matters is the Department of Commerce's income and product accounts budget. Nobody looks at it except the economists [but] while the Administrative budget is necessary for administration and is like a man's checkbook, the income budget tells the real story. . . .
> [It] shows that at the end of 1962 the outgo and ingo accounts will be virtually in balance, with a deficit of only about half a billion dollars. Thus, in reality, the Kennedy administration is no longer stimulating the economy, and the economy is stagnating for lack of stimulation. We have one of the lowest rates of growth among the advanced industrial nations of the world.

One shouldn't be hard on the President. Franklin Roosevelt, a more daring and experimental politician, at least in his domestic policy, listened to the American disciples of J. M. Keynes in the early New Deal years and unbalanced his budgets, with splendid results. But by 1936 he had lost his nerve. He cut back government spending and there ensued the 1937 recession, from which the economy recovered only when war orders began to make up for the deficiency in domestic buying power. *Poverty and Deprivation* estimates that between 1953 and 1961 the annual growth rate of our economy was "only 2.5 per cent per annum contrasted with an estimated 4.2 per cent required to maintain utilization of manpower and other productive resources." The poor, who always experience the worst the first, understand quite personally the meaning of that dry statistic, as they understand Kipling's "The toad beneath the harrow knows/Exactly where each tooth-point goes." They are also most intimately acquainted with another set of statistics: the steady postwar rise in the unemployment rate, from 3.1 per cent in 1949 to 4.3 per cent in 1954 to 5.1 per cent in 1958 to over 7 per cent in 1961. (The Tory Government is worried because British unemployment is now at its highest point for the last three years. This point is 2.1 per cent, which is less than our lowest rate in the last fifteen years.)

Some of the post-1940 gains of the poor have been their own doing. "Moonlighting"—or holding two or more jobs at once—was practiced by about 3 per cent of the employed in 1950; today this percentage has almost doubled. Far more important is what might be called "wife-flitting": Between 1940 and 1957, the percentage of wives with jobs outside the home doubled, from 15 per cent to 30 per cent. The head of the United States Children's Bureau, Mrs. Katherine B. Oettinger, announced last summer, not at all triumphantly, that there are now two-thirds more working mothers than there were ten years ago and that these mothers have about 15,000,000 children under eighteen—of whom 4,000,000 are under six. This kind of economic enterprise ought to impress Senator Goldwater and the ideologues of the *National Review*, whose reaction to the poor, when they think about such an uninspiring subject, is "Why don't they *do* something about it?" The poor have done something about it and the family pay check is bigger and the statistics on poverty look better. But the effects on family life and on those 4,000,000 pre-school children is something else. Mrs. Oettinger quoted a roadside sign, "IRONING, DAY CARE AND WORMS FOR FISHING BAIT," and mentioned a baby-sitter who pacified her charge with sleeping pills and another who met the problem of a cold apartment by putting the baby in the oven. "The situation has become a 'national disgrace,' with many unfortunate conditions that do not come to public attention until a crisis arises," the *Times* summed up her conclusion. This crisis has finally penetrated to public attention. The President recently signed a law that might be called Day-care. It provides $5,000,000 for such facilities this fiscal year, which works out to $1.25 for each of the 4,000,000 under-six children with working mothers. Next year, the program will provide all of $2.50 per child. This is a free, democratic society's notion of an adequate response. Almost a century ago, Bismarck instituted in Germany state-financed social benefits far beyond anything we have yet ventured. Granted that he did it merely to take the play away from the Social Democratic Party founded by Marx and Engels. Still, one imagines that Count Bismarck must be amused—in the circle of Hell reserved for reactionaries—by that $2.50 a child.

It's not that Public Opinion doesn't become Aroused every now and then. But the arousement never leads to much. It was aroused twenty-four years ago when John Steinbeck published "The Grapes of Wrath," but Mr. Harrington reports that things in the Imperial Valley are still much the same: low wages, bad housing, no effective union. Public Opinion is too public—that is, too general; of its very nature, it can have no sustained interest in

California agriculture. The only groups with such a continuing interest are the workers and the farmers who hire them. Once Public Opinion ceased to be Aroused, the battle was again between the two antagonists with a real, personal stake in the outcome, and there was no question about which was stronger. So with the rural poor in general. In the late fifties, the average annual wage for white male American farm workers was slightly over $1,000; women, children, Negroes, and Mexicans got less. One recalls Edward R. Murrow's celebrated television program about these people, "Harvest of Shame." Once more everybody was shocked, but the harvest is still shameful. One also recalls that Mr. Murrow, after President Kennedy had appointed him head of the United States Information Agency, tried to persuade the B.B.C. not to show "Harvest of Shame." His argument was that it would give an undesirable "image" of America to foreign audiences.

There is a monotony about the injustices suffered by the poor that perhaps accounts for the lack of interest the rest of society shows in them. Everything seems to go wrong with them. They never win. It's just boring.

Public housing turns out not to be for them. The 1949 Housing Act authorized 810,000 new units of low-cost housing in the following four years. Twelve years later, in 1961, the A.F.L.-C.I.O. proposed 400,000 units to complete the lagging 1949 program. The Kennedy administration ventured to recommend 100,000 to Congress. Thus, instead of 810,000 low-cost units by 1953, the poor will get, if they are lucky, 500,000 by 1963. And they are more likely to be injured than helped by slum clearance, since the new projects usually have higher rents than the displaced slum-dwellers can afford. (There has been no dearth of government-financed *middle*-income housing since 1949.) These refugees from the bulldozers for the most part simply emigrate to other slums. They also become invisible; Mr. Harrington notes that half of them are recorded as "address unknown." Several years ago, Charles Abrams, who was New York State Rent Administrator under Harriman and who is now president of the National Committee Against Discrimination in Housing, summed up what he had learned in two decades in public housing: "Once social reforms have won tonal appeal in the public mind, their slogans and goal-symbols may degenerate into tools of the dominant class for beleaguering the minority and often for defeating the very aims which the original sponsors had intended for their reforms." Mr. Abrams was probably thinking, in part, of the Title I adventures of Robert Moses in dealing with New York housing. There is a Moses or two in every American city, determined to lead us away from the promised land.

And this is not the end of tribulation. The poor, who can least afford to lose pay because of ill health, lose the most. A National Health Survey, made a few years ago, found that workers earning under $2,000 a year had twice as many "restricted-activity days" as those earning over $4,000.

The poor are even fatter than the rich. (The cartoonists will have to revise their clichés.) "Obesity is seven times more frequent among women of the lowest socio-economic level than it is among those of the highest level," state Drs. Moore, Stunkard, and Srole in a recent issue of the *Journal of the American Medical Association.* (The proportion is almost the same for men.) They also found that overweight associated with poverty is related to mental disease. Fatness used to be a sign of wealth, as it still is in some parts of Africa, but in more advanced societies it is now a stigma of poverty, since it means too many cheap carbohydrates and too little exercise—which has changed from a necessity for the poor into a luxury for the rich, as may be confirmed by a glance at the models in any fashion magazine.

Although they are the most in need of hospital insurance, the poor have the least, since they can't afford the premiums; only 40 per cent of poor families have it, as against 63 per cent of all families. (It should be noted, however, that the poor who are war veterans can get free treatment, at government expense, in Veterans Administration Hospitals.)

The poor actually pay more taxes, in proportion to their income, than the rich. A recent study by the Tax Foundation estimates that 28 per cent of incomes under $2,000 goes for taxes, as against 24 per cent of the incomes of families earning five to seven times as much. Sales and other excise taxes are largely responsible for this curious statistic. It is true that such taxes fall impartially on all, like the blessed rain from heaven, but it is a form of egalitarianism that perhaps only Senator Goldwater can fully appreciate.

The final irony is that the Welfare State, which Roosevelt erected and which Eisenhower, no matter how strongly he felt about it, didn't attempt to pull down, is not for the poor, either. Agricultural workers are not covered by Social Security, nor are many of the desperately poor among the aged, such as "unrelated individuals" with incomes of less than $1,000, of whom only 37 per cent are covered, which is just half the percentage of coverage among the aged in general. Of the Welfare State, Mr. Harrington says, "Its creation had been stimulated by mass impoverishment and misery, yet it helped the poor least of all. Laws like unemployment compensation, the Wagner Act, the various farm programs, all these were designed for the middle third in the cities, for the organized workers, and for the . . . big market farmers. . . . [It] benefits those least who need help most." The industrial workers, led by John L. Lewis, mobilized enough political force to put through Section 7 (a) of the National Industrial Recovery Act, which, with the Wagner Act, made the C.I.O. possible. The big farmers put enough pressure on Henry Wallace, Roosevelt's first Secretary of Agriculture—who talked a good fight for liberal principles but was a Hamlet when it came to action—to establish the two basic propositions of Welfare State agriculture: subsidies that now cost $3 billion a year and that chiefly benefit the big farmers; and the exclusion of sharecroppers, tenant farmers, and migratory workers from the protection of minimum-wage and Social Security laws.

No doubt the Kennedy administration would like to do more for the poor than it has, but it is hampered by the cabal of Republicans and Southern Democrats in Congress. The 1961 revision of the Fair Labor Standards Act, which raised the national minimum wage to the not exorbitant figure of $1.15 an hour, was a slight improvement over the previous act. For instance, it increased coverage of retail-trade workers from 3 per cent to 33 per cent. (But one-fourth of the retail workers still excluded earn less than $1 an hour.) There was also a considerable amount of shadowboxing involved: Of the 3,600,000 workers newly covered, only 663,000 were making less than $1 an hour. And there was the exclusion of a particularly ill-paid group of workers. Nobody had anything against the laundry workers *personally*. It was just that they were weak, unorganized, and politically expendable. To appease the conservatives in Congress, whose votes were needed to get the revision through, they were therefore expended. The result is that of the 500,000 workers in the laundry, dry-cleaning, and dyeing industries, just 17,000 are now protected by the Fair Labor Standards Act.

In short, one reaches the unstartling conclusion that rewards in class societies, including Communist ones, are according to power rather than need. A recent illustration is the campaign of an obscure organization called Veterans of World War I of the U.S.A. to get a bill through Congress for pensions of about $25 a week. It was formed by older men who think other veterans' organizations (such as the American Legion, which claims 2,500,000 members to their 200,000) are dominated by the relatively young. It asks for pensions for veterans of the First World War with incomes of under $2,400 (if single) or $3,600 (if married)—that is, only for *poor* veterans. The editorials have been violent: "STOP THIS VETERANS' GRAB," implored the *Herald Tribune;* "WORLD WAR I PENSION GRAB," echoed the *Saturday Evening Post.* Their objection was, in part, that many of the beneficiaries would not be bona fide poor, since pensions, annuities, and Social Security benefits were excluded from the maximum income needed to qualify. Considering that the average Social Security payment is about $1,000 a year, this would not put any potential beneficiary into the rich or even the comfortably-off class, even if one assumes another $1,000, which is surely too high, from annuities and pensions. It's all very confusing. The one clear aspect is that the minuscule Veterans of World War I of the U.S.A. came very near to bringing it off. Although their bill was opposed by both the White House and by the chairman of the House Committee on Veterans' Affairs, two hundred and one members of the House signed a petition to bring the measure to a vote, only eighteen less than needed "to accomplish this unusual parliamentary strategy," as the *Times* put it. These congressmen were motivated by politics rather than charity, one may assume. Many were up for reëlection last November, and the two hundred thousand Veterans of World War I had two advantages over the fifty million poor: They were organized, and they had a patriotic appeal only a wink away from the demagogic. Their "unusual parliamentary strategy" failed by eighteen votes in the Congress. But there will be another Congress.

It seems likely that mass poverty will continue in this country for a long time. The more it is reduced, the harder it is to keep on reducing it. The poor, having dwindled from two-thirds of the population in 1936 to one-quarter today, no longer are a significant political force, as is shown by the Senate's rejection of Medicare and by the Democrats' dropping it as an issue in the elections last year. Also, as poverty decreases, those left behind tend more and more to be the ones who have for so long accepted poverty as their destiny that they need outside help to climb out of it. This new minority mass poverty, so much more isolated and hopeless than the old majority poverty, shows signs of becoming chronic. "The permanence of low incomes is inferred from a variety of findings," write the authors of the Michigan survey. "In many poor families the head has never earned enough to cover the family's present needs." They give a vignette of what the statistics mean in human terms:

> For most families, however, the problem of chronic poverty is serious. One such family is headed by a thirty-two-year-old man who is employed as a dishwasher. Though he works steadily and more than full time, he earned slightly over $2,000 in 1959. His wife earned $300 more, but their combined incomes are not enough to support themselves and their three children. Although the head of the family is only thirty-two, he feels that he has no chance of advancement partly because he finished only seven grades of school. . . . The possibility of such families leaving the ranks of the poor is not high.

Children born into poor families today have less chance of "improving themselves" than the children of the pre-1940 poor. Rags to riches is now more likely to be rags to rags. "Indeed," the Michigan surveyors conclude, "it appears that a number of the heads of poor families have moved into less skilled jobs than their fathers had." Over a third of the children of the poor, according to the survey, don't go beyond the eighth grade and "will probably perpetuate the poverty of their parents." There are a great many of these children. In an important study of poverty, made for a Congressional committee in 1959, Dr. Robert J. Lampman estimated that eleven million of the poor were under eighteen. "A considerable number of younger persons are starting life in a condition of 'inherited poverty,'" he observed. To which Mr. Harrington adds, "The character of poverty has changed, and it has become more deadly for the young. It is no longer associated with immigrant groups with high aspirations; it is now identified with those whose social existence makes it more and more difficult to break out into the larger society." Even when children from poor families show intellectual promise, there is nothing in the values of their friends or families to encourage them to make use of it. Dr. Kolko, citing impressive sources, states that of the top 16 per cent of high-school students—those scoring 120 and over in I.Q. tests—only half go on to college. The explanation for this amazing—and alarming—situation is as much cultural as economic. The children of the poor now tend to lack what the sociologists call "motivation." At least one foundation is working on the problem of why so many bright children from poor families don't ever try to go beyond high school.

Mr. Raymond M. Hilliard, at present director of the Cook County (i.e., Chicago) Department of Public Aid and formerly Commissioner of Welfare for New York City, recently directed a "representative-sample" investigation, which showed that more than half of the 225,000 able-bodied Cook County residents who were on relief were "functionally illiterate." One reason Cook County has to spend $16,500,000 a month on relief is "the lack of basic educational skills of relief recipients which are essential to compete in our modern society." An interesting footnote, apropos of recent happenings at "Ole Miss," is that the illiteracy rate of the relief recipients who were educated in Chicago is 33 per cent, while among those who were educated in Mississippi and later moved to Chicago it is 77 per cent.

The problem of educating the poor has changed since 1900. Then it was the language and cultural difficulties of immigrants from foreign countries; now it is the subtler but more intractable problems of internal migration from backward regions, mostly in the South. The old immigrants wanted to Better Themselves and to Get Ahead. The new migrants are less ambitious, and they come into a less ambitious atmosphere. "When they arrive in the city," wrote Christopher Jencks in an excellent two-part survey, "Slums and Schools," in the *New Republic* last fall, "they join others equally unprepared for urban life in the slums—a milieu which is in many ways utterly dissociated from the rest of America. Often this milieu is self-perpetuating. I have been unable to find any statistics on how many of these migrants' children and grandchildren have become middle-class, but it is probably not too inaccurate to estimate that about 30,000,000 people live in urban slums, and that about half are second-generation residents." The immigrants of 1890–1910 also arrived in a milieu that was "in many ways utterly dissociated from the rest of America," yet they had a vision—a rather materialistic one, but still a vision—of what life in America could be if they worked hard enough; and they did work, and they did aspire to something more than they had; and they did get out of the slums. The disturbing thing about the poor today is that so many of them seem to lack any such vision. Mr. Jencks remarks:

> While the economy is changing in a way which makes the eventual liquidation of the slums at least conceivable, young people are not seizing the opportunities this change presents. Too many are dropping out of school before graduation (more than half in many slums); too few are going to college. . . . As a result there are serious shortages of teachers, nurses, doctors, technicians, and scientifically trained executives, but 4,500,000 unemployables.

"Poverty is the parent of revolution and crime," Aristotle wrote. This is now a half truth—the last half. Our poor are alienated; they don't consider themselves part of society. But precisely because they don't they are not politically dangerous. It is people with "a stake in the country" who make revolutions. The best—though by no means the only—reason for worrying about the Other America is that its existence should make us feel uncomfortable.

The federal government is the only purposeful force—I assume wars are not purposeful—that can reduce the numbers of the poor and make their lives more bearable. The authors of *Poverty and Deprivation* take a dim view of the Kennedy administration's efforts to date:

> The Federal Budget is the most important single instrument available to us as a free people to induce satisfactory economic performance, and to reduce poverty and deprivation. . . .
> Projected Federal outlays in the fiscal 1963 Budget are too small. The items in this Budget covering programs directly related to human improvement and the reduction of mass poverty and deprivation allocate far too small a portion of our total national production to these great purposes.

The effect of government policy on poverty has two quite distinct aspects. One is the indirect effect of the stimulation of the economy by federal spending. Such stimulation—though by war-time demands rather than government policy—has in the past produced a prosperity that did cut down American poverty by almost two-thirds. But I am inclined to agree with Dr. Galbraith that it would not have a comparable effect on present-day poverty:

> It is assumed that with increasing output poverty must disappear [he writes]. Increased output eliminated the general poverty of all who worked. Accordingly it must, sooner or later, eliminate the special poverty that still remains. . . . Yet just as the arithmetic of modern politics makes it tempting to overlook the very poor, so the supposition that increasing output will remedy their case has made it easy to do so too.

He underestimates the massiveness of American poverty, but he is right when he says there is now a hard core of the specially disadvantaged—because of age, race, environment, physical or mental defects, etc.—that would not be significantly reduced by general prosperity. (Although I think the majority of our present poor *would* benefit, if only by a reduction in the present high rate of unemployment.)

To do something about this hard core, a second line of government policy would be required; namely, direct intervention to help the poor. We have had this since the New Deal, but it has always been grudging and miserly, and we have never accepted the principle that every citizen should be provided, at state expense, with a reasonable minimum standard of living regardless of any other considerations. It should not depend on earnings, as does Social Security, which continues the inequalities and inequities and so tends to keep the poor forever poor. Nor should it exclude millions of our poorest citizens because they lack the political pressure to force their way into the Welfare State. The governmental obligation to provide, out of taxes, such a minimum living standard for all who need it should be taken as much for granted as free public schools have always been in our history.

It may be objected that the economy cannot bear the cost, and certainly costs must be calculated. But the point is not the calculation but the principle. Statistics—and especially statistical forecasts—can be pushed one way or the other. Who can determine in advance to what extent the extra expense of giving our 40,000,000 poor enough income to rise above the poverty line would be offset by the lift to the economy from their increased purchasing power? We really don't know. Nor did we know what the budgetary effects would be when we established the principle of free public education. The rationale then was that all citizens should have an equal chance of competing for a better status. The rationale now is different: that every citizen has a right to become or remain part of our society because if this right is denied, as it is in the case of at least one-fourth of our citizens, it impoverishes us all. Since 1932, "the government"—local, state, and federal—has recognized a responsibility to provide its citizens with a subsistence living. Apples will never again be sold on the street by jobless accountants, it seems safe to predict, nor will any serious political leader ever again suggest that share-the-work and local charity can solve the problem of unemployment. "Nobody starves" in this country any more, but, like every social statistic, this is a tricky business. Nobody starves, but who can measure the starvation, not to be calculated by daily intake of proteins and calories, that reduces life for many of our poor to a long vestibule to death? Nobody starves, but every fourth citizen rubs along on a standard of living that is below what Mr. Harrington defines as "the minimal levels of health, housing, food, and education that our present stage of scientific knowledge specifies as necessary for life as it is now lived in the United States." Nobody starves, but a fourth of us are excluded from the common social existence. Not to be able to afford a movie or a glass of beer is a kind of starvation—if everybody else can.

The problem is obvious: the persistence of mass poverty in a prosperous country. The solution is also obvious: to provide, out of taxes, the kind of subsidies that have always been given to the public schools (not to mention the police and fire departments and the post office)—subsidies that would raise incomes above the poverty level, so that every citizen could feel he is indeed such. "Civis Romanus sum!" cried St. Paul when he was threatened with flogging—and he was not flogged. Until our poor can be proud to say "Civis Americanus sum!," until the act of justice that would make this possible has been performed by the three-quarters of Americans who are not poor—until then the shame of the Other America will continue.

SUGGESTED READING

David Potter's *People of Plenty* ° (Univ. of Chicago Press, 1954) is a very perceptive book, arguing that abundance has shaped American character. Though Potter does not recognize the vast number of America's poor, his emphasis on the nation's abundance compared to the rest of the world places American poverty in international perspective, and his conclusions about American character may explain why deprivation in America is such a bitter experience. Robert Bremner's essay in John Braeman *et al.*, eds., *Change and Continuity in Twentieth-Century America* ° (Ohio State Univ. Press, 1964) sketches the periodic rediscovery of poverty.

Poverty As a Public Issue,° edited by Ben Seligman (Free Press, 1965), is an uneven collection that analyzes poverty among various groups and criticizes early antipoverty programs. *Permanent Poverty: An American Syndrome,* also edited by Seligman (Quadrangle, 1968), is a collection of rather pessimistic essays. Stephan Thernstrom in "Is There Really a New Poor," *Dissent,* XV (Jan.–Feb., 1968), concludes that the country is "[not] now threatened by a mass of 'new poor' whose objective situations, especially their opportunities to rise out of poverty, are much worse than those of earlier generations." Jeremy Larner and Irving Howe, two editors of *Dissent,* have edited *Poverty; Views from the Left* ° (Morrow, 1968).

Harry Caudill's *Night Comes to the Cumberlands* ° (Little Press, 1963) is a sympathetic discussion of rural poverty among native whites. Oscar Lewis' *La Vida: A Puerto Rican Family in the Culture of Poverty —San Juan and New York* ° (Random House, 1966) applies the author's concepts of the culture of poverty (properly a "subculture of poverty," as he acknowledges). Elizabeth Herzog in "Some Assumptions About the Poor," *Social Service Review,* XXXVII (Dec., 1963), 389–402, briefly discusses the "culture of poverty." Charles Valentine in *Culture and Poverty* (Univ. of Chicago Press, 1968) criticizes Lewis and others who the author concludes place much of the responsibility for poverty on the poor. Valentine's indictment of Lewis is weakened by his misuse of quotes.

Daniel P. Moynihan's *The Negro Family: The Case for National Action* (Government Printing Office, 1965) is the famous Moynihan Report that provoked attacks from those who charged its author with blaming the Negro and the breakdown of his family structure for his plight. Lee Rainwater and W. L. Yancey, editors of *The Moynihan Report and the Politics of Controversy* ° (M.I.T. Press, 1967), reprint there many of the criticisms of the study. "The Negro American" is the subject of two volumes of *Daedalus,* XCIV (Fall, 1965) and XCV (Winter, 1966). *Poverty in Affluence,* edited by Robert E. Will and Harold G. Vatter (Harcourt, Brace & World, 1965), is a useful anthology of materials relating to the social, political, and economic aspects of poverty in twentieth-century America.

Daniel Moynihan's *Maximum Feasible Misunderstanding* (Free Press, 1968), offered as a biopsy of the Community Action Projects, devices for the "maximum feasible participation" of the poor, concludes that the Government "did not know what it was doing," that the program was mismanaged, and that the conception was for the most part untested. Frank Riessman's *Strategies Against Poverty* (Random House, 1968) assaults the ideas of Saul Alinsky and the efforts to destroy existing welfare systems, proposes opening new jobs for the poor, and calls for a study of middle-class America, which he holds largely responsible for poverty.

ALLEN J. MATUSOW

From Civil Rights to Black Power: The Case of SNCC, 1960–1966

INTRODUCTION

In 1954 when the Supreme Court declared laws requiring racial segregation in public schools to be unconstitutional, American liberals rejoiced and looked forward to the achievement of racial integration. They believed that the major struggles would be waged in the South, and they rested their hopes on the willingness of the federal executive and judiciary to compel compliance with the law of the land. Although the slowness of school desegregation in the late 1950's dampened their expectations for quick success, the liberals still clung comfortably to the heady principles that destruction of legal segregation and increased mingling between blacks and whites would solve America's racial problems.

Martin Luther King symbolized their hopes. His courage and philosophy inspired respect, and his tactics seemed to hold the

---

This essay was written especially for this volume.

promise of ultimate success. Preaching and practicing nonviolence, he offered love to his enemies and relied on the coercive power of local black economic boycotts and outraged liberal sentiment beyond the South to force changes in Dixie.

The black civil rights movement of 1960, beginning with the sit-ins at Woolworth counters, self-consciously adhered to the tactics of King and shared the liberal faith in the desirability and likelihood of establishing racial equality in America. The Student Nonviolent Coordinating Committee (SNCC) was formed from the 1960 sit-in movement and dedicated its energies to gaining for black Americans in the South a place in white middle-class life. Yet within a few years the betrayals of civil rights by white liberals and the freshly uncovered depths of racial misunderstanding and mistrust dramatically challenged earlier optimistic liberal assumptions and compelled healthy introspection among whites and blacks who toiled for civil rights in the South. (In SNCC, unlike in King's Southern Christian Leadership Conference, the fears and attractions of interracial sex also rose to the surface, indicating that the gap between the races had been narrowed but that a chasm still separated them.) Blacks and even some whites in SNCC were deciding by 1966 that black power offered a more appropriate strategy and philosophy for "liberating the blacks from white oppression." The history of SNCC, concludes Allen J. Matusow, discloses the roots of black power and charts "the sad fate of the whole civil rights movement."

Matusow considers the black man's recognition of racism and paternalism among whites to be healthy, but he is critical of the doctrine of black power as expressed by Stokely Carmichael, its first prominent spokesman. Emphasizing that Carmichael seeks a radical reconstruction of American society, Matusow challenges his claim that black power is largely traditional ethnic-bloc politics practiced by a new group. "Its greatest weakness," Matusow further argues, "is its failure to propose adequate solutions," for he regards as unrealistic the hopes of a socialist alliance of poor whites and poor blacks. He sees as more realistic the liberal-labor-civil rights coalition proposed by Bayard Rustin, a former aide of King. This coalition has been eagerly endorsed by some white liberals who view it as a way of redeeming American society for racial integration and equality and saving the society from continued violence.

What Matusow does not directly confront, his critics would contend, is whether this alliance and its program of $100 billion for social justice are possible, or whether the earlier liberal betrayals and the continued power of Southern conservatives in Congress can be taken as evidence that the political system cannot become truly responsive to the aspirations and needs of the blacks and other disadvantaged Americans.

The transformation of black protest in the 1960's from civil rights to black power has seemed in retrospect an inevitable development. When the inherent limitations of the civil rights movement finally became apparent and when the expectations that the movement created met frustration, some kind of militant reaction in the black community seemed certain. However predictable this development may have been, it tells little about the concrete events that led to the abandonment of the civil rights program and to the adoption of a doctrine that is in many ways its opposite. For black power was not plucked whole from impersonal historical forces; nor was its content the only possible expression of rising black militancy. Rather, black power both as a slogan and a doctrine was in large measure the creation of a small group of civil rights workers who in the early 1960's manned the barricades of black protest in the Deep South. The group was called the Student Nonviolent Coordinating Committee (SNCC). Through its spokesman, Stokely Carmichael, SNCC first proclaimed black power and then became its foremost theoretician. Others would offer glosses on black power that differed from SNCC's concept, but because SNCC had contributed so much to the civil rights movement, no other group could speak with so much authority or command a comparable audience. Although SNCC borrowed freely from many sources to fashion black power into a doctrine, the elements of that doctrine were in the main the results of SNCC's own history. An examination of that history reveals not only the roots of black power but also the sad fate of the whole civil rights movement.

Founded in 1960, SNCC was an outgrowth of the historic sit-in movement, which began in Greensboro, North Carolina, on February 1 of that year. Four freshmen from a local Negro college attempted to desegregate the lunch counter at a Woolworth's five and ten store. The example of these four sent shock waves through the black colleges of the South and created overnight a base for a campaign of massive civil disobedience. The new generation of black students seemed suddenly unwilling to wait any longer for emancipation at the hands of the federal courts and in the next months supplied most of the recruits for the nonviolent army of 50,000 that rose spontaneously and integrated public facilities in 140 Southern cities. For the students on the picket lines, the prophet of the sit-in movement was Dr. Martin Luther King, the leader of the successful Montgomery bus boycott of 1955–56. The students found in King's nonviolent philosophy a ready-made ethic, a tactic, and a conviction of righteousness strong enough to sustain them on a sometimes hazardous mission.[1] It was King's organization, the

---

[1] For accounts of the sit-ins see Howard Zinn, SNCC: The New Abolitionists (Beacon, 1965), Chapter 2; Jack Newfield, A Prophetic Minority (Signet, 1966), Chapter 3; August

Southern Christian Leadership Conference (SCLC), that first suggested the need for some central direction of the sit-in movement. At the invitation of SCLC's executive secretary, some 300 activist students from throughout the South met in Raleigh, North Carolina, in April 1960, to discuss their problems. The students agreed to form a coordinating body, which became SNCC, and in May 1960, hired a secretary and opened an office in Atlanta. In October the organization decided to become a permanent one, and 235 delegates approved a founding statement inspired by King's philosophy:

> We affirm the philosophical or religious ideal of nonviolence as the foundation of our purpose, the presupposition of our belief, and the manner of our action. . . . Through nonviolence, courage displaces fear. Love transcends hate. Acceptance dissipates prejudice; hope ends despair. Faith reconciles doubt. Peace dominates war. Mutual regards cancel enmity. Justice for all overwhelms injustice. The redemptive community supersedes immoral social systems.[2]

In truth, the Christian rhetoric of SNCC's founding statement was not appropriate. The author of the statement was James Lawson, a young minister who never actually belonged to SNCC.[3] Most of the students who rallied to the sit-ins in 1960 accepted King's teachings more out of convenience than conviction and respected his courage more than his philosophy. For while King believed that Christian love was an end in itself and that Negro nonviolence would redeem American society, the students preferred to participate in America rather than to transform it. Sociologists who examined the attitudes of protesters in the black colleges found not alienation from American middle-class values but a desire to share fully in middle-class life.[4] In a perceptive piece written for *Dissent*, Michael Walzer supported these findings from his own first-hand impressions of the sit-ins. Walzer concluded that the students were materialistic as well as moral, were "willing to take risks in the name of both prosperity and virtue," and had as their goal "assimilation into American society." As for nonviolence, Walzer wrote, "I

Meier, "The Successful Sit-Ins in a Border City: A Study in Social Causation," *The Journal of Intergroup Relations*, II (Summer, 1961), 230–37; Charles U. Smith, "The Sit-Ins and the New Negro Student," *ibid.*, 223–29; James Peck, *Freedom Ride* (Simon & Schuster, 1962), Chapter 6.

[2] Quoted in Newfield, *A Prophetic Minority*, p. 47.

[3] Emily Schottenfeld Stoper, "The Student Nonviolent Coordinating Committee: The Growth of Radicalism in a Civil Rights Organization," unpublished dissertation, Harvard University, 1968, pp. 35–36.

[4] Ruth Searles and J. Allen Williams, Jr., "Negro College Students' Participation in Sit-Ins," *Social Forces*, (Dec., 1966), 215–20.

was told often that 'when one side has all the guns, then the other side is non-violent.' " [5]

In the beginning, the philosophical inconsistencies of the sit-ins did not trouble SNCC, for it stood at the forefront of a movement whose ultimate triumph seemed not far distant. But within months, as mysteriously as it began, the sit-in movement vanished. By the spring of 1961 the black campuses had lapsed into their customary quiescence, their contribution to the civil rights movement at an end. As for SNCC, since October 1960, the student representatives from each Southern state had been meeting monthly to squander their energies trying to coordinate a movement that was first too amorphous and then suddenly moribund. SNCC's attempts in early 1961 to raise up new hosts of students proved ineffectual, and lacking followers, the organization seemed without a future.[6] Then in May 1961, the Freedom Rides restored a sense of urgency to the civil rights movement and gave SNCC a second life.

On May 14, 1961, members of the Congress of Racial Equality (CORE) began the Freedom Rides to test a Supreme Court decision outlawing segregation in transportation terminals. On May 20, after one of CORE's integrated buses was bombed near Anniston, Alabama, and another was mobbed in Birmingham, CORE decided to call off its rides. But amid sensational publicity, students from Nashville and Atlanta, many associated with SNCC, rushed to Birmingham to continue the journey to New Orleans. After mobs assaulted this second wave of riders, the Federal Government stepped in to protect them, and they were permitted to go as far as Jackson, where local authorities put them in jail for defying segregation ordinances. Throughout the summer of 1961 some 300 citizens from all over America took Freedom Rides that brought them to the jails of Jackson.[7] For SNCC the Freedom Rides provided a temporary outlet for activism and, more important, inspired radical changes in the structure and purpose of the organization.

Perhaps the most important result of the Freedom Rides for SNCC was to focus its attention on the Deep South. Most of the sit-ins had occurred in the cities and larger towns of the Upper South, and the victories there had come with relative ease. Now the magnitude of the task confronting the civil

---

[5] Michael Walzer, "The Politics of the New Negro," *Dissent,* VII (Summer, 1960), 235–43.

[6] Anne Braden, "The Southern Freedom Movement in Perspective," *Monthly Review,* XVII (July–Aug., 1965), 31–32; also James Howard Laue, "Direct Action and Desegregation: Toward a Theory of the Rationalization of Protest," unpublished dissertation, Harvard University, 1965, p. 128.

[7] For accounts of the Freedom Rides, see Zinn, *SNCC,* Chapter 3; and Peck, *Freedom Ride,* Chapters 8 and 9.

rights movement became clearer. As some in SNCC had already perceived, sit-ins to desegregate public places offered no meaningful benefits to poverty-stricken tenant farmers in, say, Mississippi. In order to mobilize the black communities in the Deep South to fight for their rights, sporadic student demonstrations would be less useful than sustained efforts by full time field workers.[8] In the summer of 1961, as SNCC was beginning to grope toward the concept of community action, the Federal Government stepped in with an attractive suggestion.

Embarrassed by the Freedom Rides, Attorney General Robert F. Kennedy moved to direct the civil rights movement into paths that, in his view, were more constructive. Kennedy suggested that the civil rights organizations jointly sponsor a campaign to register Southern black voters. Such a drive, its proponents argued, would be difficult for even extreme segregationists to oppose and eventually might liberalize the Southern delegation in Congress. When the Justice Department seemed to offer federal protection for registration workers and when white liberals outside the Administration procured foundation money to finance anticipated costs, the civil rights groups agreed to undertake the project.[9] Within SNCC, advocates of direct action fought acceptance of the project, but the issue was compromised and a threatened split was averted. SNCC's decision to mobilize black communities behind efforts to secure political rights decisively changed the character of the organization. It thereafter ceased to be an extracurricular activity of student leaders and became instead the vocation of dedicated young men and women who temporarily abandoned their careers to become full time paid workers (or "field secretaries") in the movement. Moreover, as SNCC workers drifted away from the black campuses and began living among Deep South blacks, they cast aside the middle-class goals that had motivated the sit-ins of 1960 and put on the overalls of the poor. Begun as middle-class protest, SNCC was developing revolutionary potential.[10]

In Mississippi the major civil rights groups (NAACP, SCLC, CORE, and SNCC) ostensibly joined together to form the Council of Federated Organizations (COFO) to register black voters. But in reality, except for one Mississippi congressional district where CORE had a project of its own, COFO was manned almost entirely by SNCC people. The director of COFO was SNCC's now legendary Robert Moses, a product of Harlem with a Masters degree in philosophy from Harvard, whose courage and humanity made him the most respected figure in the organization. Moses had entered Pike

[8] Laue, "Direct Action and Desegregation," pp. 154, 160, 167–68.

[9] On origins of the voter registration drive, see Pat Watters and Reece Cleghorn, *Climbing Jacob's Ladder* (Harcourt, Brace & World, 1967), pp. 44–59; and Louis Lomax, *The Negro Revolt* (Signet, 1963), pp. 246–50.

[10] Braden, "Southern Freedom Movement," p. 36; Laue, "Direct Action and Desegregation," p. 171; Stoper, "The Student Nonviolent Coordinating Committee," pp. 6 and 8.

County, Mississippi, alone in 1961, stayed on in spite of a beating and a jail term, and in the spring of 1962 became COFO's director in charge of voting projects in Vicksburg, Cleveland, Greenwood, and a few other Mississippi towns.[11] Although SNCC also had registration projects in Arkansas, Alabama, and Georgia, it concentrated on Mississippi, where the obstacles were greatest.

Throughout 1962 and into 1963 SNCC workers endured assaults, offered brave challenges to local power structures, and exhorted local blacks to shake off fear and stand up for freedom. But SNCC scored no breakthroughs to sustain morale, and while its goals remained outwardly unchanged, its mood was turning bitter. To SNCC the hostility of local racists was not nearly so infuriating as the apparent betrayal that it suffered at the hands of the Justice Department. SNCC believed that in 1961 the Kennedy Administration had guaranteed protection to registration workers, but in Mississippi in 1962 and 1963, SNCC's only contact with federal authority consisted of the FBI agents who stood by taking notes while local policemen beat up SNCC members. SNCC and its supporters insisted that existing law empowered the Federal Government to intervene, but the Justice Department contended that it was in fact powerless. SNCC doubted the sincerity of the Government's arguments and became convinced that the Kennedys had broken a solemn promise for political reasons.[12] Thus by 1963 SNCC was already becoming estranged from established authority and suspicious of liberal politicians.

SNCC's growing sense of alienation cut it off even from other civil rights organizations and most importantly from Dr. King, who by 1963 had become a fallen idol for SNCC workers. They believed that King was too willing to compromise, wielded too much power, and too successfully monopolized the funds of the movement. Doubts about King had arisen as early as the Freedom Rides, when students turned to him for advice and leadership and received what they considered only vague sympathy. In fact, after CORE called off the first ride, King privately supported Robert Kennedy's plea for a "cooling-off" period. But much to SNCC's annoyance, when militant voices prevailed and the rides continued, the press gave King all the credit.[13] In Albany, Georgia, in December 1961, after SNCC aroused the black population to pack the local jails for freedom, King came to town, got arrested, monopolized the headlines, and almost stole the leadership of the Albany campaign from SNCC.[14] In SNCC's view, dependence on King's

---

[11] For an account of Moses in Mississippi, see Zinn, SNCC, Chapter 4.

[12] See ibid., Chapter 10; and Watters and Cleghorn, Climbing Jacob's Ladder, p. 58.

[13] Laue, "Direct Action and Desegregation," pp. 179, 338.

[14] Stoper, "The Student Nonviolent Coordinating Committee," p. 104; New York Times (Dec. 24, 1961), section IV, 5.

charisma actually weakened the civil rights movement, for it discouraged development of leadership at the grass-roots level. Why, SNCC asked, did King use his huge share of civil rights money to maintain a large staff in Atlanta, and why did he never account for the funds that he so skillfully collected? [15] As King lost influence on SNCC, dissenting attitudes about nonviolence, implicit since 1960, came to be frankly articulated. When Robert Penn Warren asked Robert Moses what he thought of King's philosophy, Moses replied,

> We don't agree with it, in a sense. The majority of the students are not sympathetic to the idea that they have to love the white people that they are struggling against. . . . For most of the members, it is tactical, it's a question of being able to have a method of attack rather than to be always on the defensive.[16]

During the March on Washington in August 1963, the nation almost caught a glimpse of SNCC's growing anger. John Lewis, the chairman of SNCC and one of the scheduled speakers, threatened to disrupt the harmony of that happy occasion by saying what he really thought. Only with difficulty did moderates persuade Lewis to delete the harshest passages of his address. So the nation did not know that SNCC scorned Kennedy's civil rights bill as "too little and too late." Lewis had intended to ask the 250,000 people gathered at the Lincoln Memorial,

> What is there in this bill to insure the equality of a maid who earns $5 a week in the home of a family whose income is $100,000 a year? . . . This nation is still a place of cheap political leaders who build their careers on immoral compromises and ally themselves with open forms of political, economic, and social exploitation. . . . The party of Kennedy is also the party of Eastland. The party of Javits is also the party of Goldwater. Where is *our* party? . . . We cannot depend on any political party, for the Democrats and the Republicans have betrayed the basic principles of the Declaration of Independence.

In those remarks that he never delivered, Lewis used both the language of Christian protest and images alive with the rage of SNCC field workers. "In the struggle we must seek more than mere civil rights; we must work for the community of love, peace, and true brotherhood." And,

> the time will come when we will not confine our marching to Washington. We will march through the South, through the heart of Dixie, the way Sherman did. We shall pursue our "scorched earth" policy and burn Jim Crow to

---

[15] "Integration: Hotter Fires," *Newsweek*, LXII (July 1, 1963), 19–21.

[16] Robert Penn Warren, *Who Speaks for the Negro* (Random House, 1965), p. 91.

the ground—nonviolently. We shall fragment the South into a thousand pieces and put them back together in the image of democracy.[17]

The crucial milestone of SNCC's road to radicalism was the Freedom Summer of 1964. Freedom Summer grew out of a remarkable mock election sponsored by SNCC in the autumn of 1963. Because the mass of Mississippi's black population could not legally participate in choosing the state's governor that year, Robert Moses conceived a freedom election to protest mass disfranchisement and to educate Mississippi's blacks to the mechanics of the political process. COFO organized a new party called the Mississippi Freedom Democrats, printed its own ballots, and in October conducted its own poll. Overwhelming the regular party candidates, Aaron Henry, head of the state NAACP and Freedom Democratic nominee for governor, received 70,000 votes, a tremendous protest against the denial of equal political rights. One reason for the success of the project was the presence in the state of 100 Yale and Stanford students, who worked for two weeks with SNCC on the election. SNCC was sufficiently impressed by the student contribution to consider inviting hundreds more to spend an entire summer in Mississippi. Sponsors of this plan hoped not only for workers but for publicity that might at last focus national attention on Mississippi.[18] By the winter of 1963–64, however, rising militancy in SNCC had begun to take on the overtones of black nationalism, and some of the membership resisted the summer project on the grounds that most of the volunteers would be white.

Present from the beginning, by mid-1964 whites made up one-fifth of SNCC's approximately 150 full time field secretaries. Though whites had suffered their fair share of beatings, some blacks in SNCC were expressing doubts about the role of white men in a movement for black freedom. At a staff meeting at Greenville, Mississippi, in November 1963, a debate on the proposed Freedom Summer brought the issue of white-black relations into the open. In his book *SNCC: The New Abolitionists*, Howard Zinn, who attended this meeting, summarizes the views of the militants:

> Four or five of the Negro staff members now urged that the role of whites be limited. For whites to talk to Mississippi Negroes about voter registration, they said, only reinforced the Southern Negro's tendency to believe that whites were superior. Whites tended to take over leadership roles in the movement, thus preventing Southern Negroes from being trained to lead. Why didn't whites just work in the white Southern community? One man noted that in Africa the new nations were training black Africans to take over all important government positions. Another told of meeting a Black Muslim

---

[17] Quoted in Watters and Cleghorn, *Climbing Jacob's Ladder*, pp. xiv–xv.

[18] On freedom ballot, see Len Holt, *The Summer That Didn't End* (William Morrow, 1965), pp. 35–36, 152–53.

in Atlanta who warned him that whites were taking over the movement. "I had the feeling inside. I felt what he said was true."

But Fannie Lou Hamer disagreed. Mrs. Hamer had been a time-keeper on a cotton plantation and was one of the local Mississippi blacks whom SNCC discovered and elevated to leadership. Speaking for the majority of the meeting, she said, "If we're trying to break down this barrier of segregation, we can't segregate ourselves." Thus in February 1964, SNCC sent an invitation to Northern college students to spend their summer vacation in Mississippi.[19]

In retrospect, the summer of 1964 was a turning point in the civil rights movement. When the summer began, SNCC was still operating within the framework of liberal America, still committed to integration and equal political rights for all citizens. But by the end of the summer of 1964, the fraying cords that bound SNCC to liberal goals and values finally snapped. In a sense, much of later black power thought was merely a postscript to SNCC's ill-fated summer project.

In June 1964, more than 700 selected students, judged by a staff psychiatrist at MIT to be "an extraordinarily healthy bunch of kids," [20] came to Oxford, Ohio, for two week-long orientation sessions conducted by veteran SNCC workers. The atmosphere in Oxford, tense from the outset, became on June 22 pervaded with gloom. Robert Moses quietly told the volunteers that three workers had gone into Neshoba county in Mississippi the day before and had not been heard from since. One was Michael Schwerner, a CORE staff member; the second was James Chaney, a black SNCC worker from Mississippi; and the third was Andrew Goodman, a student volunteer who had finished his orientation in Ohio a few days before.[21] (In August the bodies of these three were discovered in their shallow graves near Philadelphia, Mississippi.)

The volunteers in Ohio had to face not only their own fear but also unanticipated hostility from the SNCC workers whom they had come to assist. Tensions between black workers and white volunteers seethed under the surface for some days and then finally erupted. One night SNCC showed a film of a grotesque voting registrar turning away black applicants. When the student audience laughed at the scene, six SNCC people walked out, enraged at what they considered an insensitive response. There followed an exchange between the workers and the volunteers, in which the students

---

[19] Zinn, SNCC, pp. 8–9, 186–88; see also Calvin Trillin, "Letter from Jackson," New Yorker, XL (Aug. 29, 1964), 80–105.

[20] Quoted in James Atwater, "If We Can Crack Mississippi . . . ," Saturday Evening Post, CCXXXVII (July 25, 1964), 16.

[21] Sally Belfrage, Freedom Summer (Viking, 1965), p. 11.

complained that the staff was distant, uncommunicative, and "looked down on us for not having been through what they had." A SNCC worker replied,

> If you get mad at us for walking out, just wait until they break your head in, and see if you don't have something to get mad about. Ask Jimmy Travis over there what he thinks about the project. What does he think about Mississippi? He has six slugs in him, man, and the last one went right through the back of his neck when he was driving a car outside Greenwood. Ask Jesse here—he has been beaten so that we wouldn't recognize him time and time and time and time again. If you don't get scared, pack up and get the hell out of here because we don't need any favors of people who don't know what they are doing here in the first place.

The bitter words seemed to have a cathartic effect, and the meeting culminated in emotional singing. Said one volunteer a bit too optimistically, "The crisis is past, I think." [22]

From one perspective the story of the two months that followed is one of the human spirit triumphant. Though three more people were killed, eighty others were beaten, thirty-five churches were burned, and thirty other buildings bombed, few turned back; black and white together, the civil rights workers in Mississippi worked for racial justice.[23] The student volunteers taught in Freedom Schools, where 3,000 children were given their first glimpse of a world beyond Mississippi. They organized the disfranchised to march on county courthouses to face unyielding registrars. Most importantly, they walked the roads of Mississippi for the Freedom Democratic Party (FDP). Denying the legitimacy of the segregated Democratic party, COFO opened the FDP to members of all races and declared the party's loyalty to Lyndon Johnson. The goal of the FDP in the summer of 1964 was to send a delegation to the Democratic convention in Atlantic City to challenge the credentials of the regular Democrats and cast the state's vote for the party's nominees. To mount this challenge against the racist Democrats of Mississippi, COFO enrolled 60,000 members in the FDP and then organized precinct, county, and state conventions to choose 68 integrated delegates to go north. The FDP, in which tens of thousands of black Mississippi citizens invested tremendous hopes, was a true grass-roots political movement and the greatest achievement of Freedom Summer.[24]

Although the FDP brought to Atlantic City little more than a sense of moral outrage, it nevertheless managed to transform its challenge of the Mississippi regulars into a major threat to the peace of the national party. Mrs.

---

[22] Elizabeth Sutherland, ed., *Letters from Mississippi* (McGraw-Hill, 1965), pp. 5–6.

[23] Watters and Cleghorn, *Climbing Jacob's Ladder*, p. 139.

[24] Holt, *The Summer That Didn't End*, Chapter 8; Zinn, *SNCC*, p. 251.

Hamer helped make this feat possible by her electrifying (and televised) testimony before the credentials committee on how Mississippi policemen had beaten her up for trying to register to vote. As Northern liberals began rallying to the FDP, the managers of the convention sought a compromise that would satisfy the liberals and at the same time keep the bulk of the Southern delegations in the convention. President Johnson favored a proposal to seat all the Mississippi regulars who pledged their loyalty to the party, to deny any voting rights to the FDP delegates, but to permit them to sit on the floor of the convention. In addition, he proposed that at future conventions no state delegations chosen by racially discriminatory procedures would be accredited. But because this compromise denied the FDP's claims of legitimacy, the FDP and many liberals declared it unacceptable and threatened to take their case to the floor of the convention, a prospect that greatly displeased the President. Johnson then sent Senator Hubert Humphrey to Atlantic City to act as his agent in settling the controversy. Unsubstantiated rumors had it that if Humphrey's mission failed, the President would deny the Senator the party's vice-presidential nomination. In close touch with both the White House and the credentials committee, Humphrey proposed altering the original compromise by permitting two FDP delegates to sit in the convention as delegates at large with full voting rights. This was as far as Johnson would go, and at the time it seemed far enough. Though the Mississippi white regulars walked out, no Southern delegations followed them, and, at the same time, most liberals felt that the Administration had made a genuine concession. Black leaders, including Dr. King, pleaded with the FDP to accept Humphrey's compromise. But the FDP denied that the compromise was in any sense a victory.[25] Angered at Humphrey's insistence that he alone choose the two at-large delegates, the FDP announced that it had not come to Atlantic City "begging for crumbs." [26] Mrs. Hamer, by now a minor national celebrity, said of Humphrey's efforts, "It's a token of rights on the back row that we get in Mississippi. We didn't come all this way for that mess again." [27]

To the general public the FDP appeared to be a band of moral zealots hostile to reasonable compromise and ungrateful for the real concession that the party had offered. The true story was more complicated. Aware that total victory was impossible, the FDP had in fact been quite willing to accept any proposal that recognized its legitimacy. At the beginning of the controversy Oregon's Congresswoman Edith Green offered a compromise that the FDP found entirely acceptable. Mrs. Green proposed that the convention seat

[25] Holt, *The Summer That Didn't End*, pp. 16–17; Watters and Cleghorn, *Climbing Jacob's Ladder*, pp. 290–92; *New York Times* (Aug. 25, 1964), 23.

[26] William McCord, *Mississippi: The Long Hot Summer* (Norton, 1965), p. 117.

[27] Mrs. Hamer is quoted in Holt, *The Summer That Didn't End*, p. 174.

every member of both delegations who signed a pledge of loyalty and that Mississippi's vote be divided between the two groups according to the number of seated delegates in each. Since only eleven members of the credentials committee (10 percent of the total) had to sign a minority report to dislodge the Green compromise from committee, the FDP seemed assured that its case would reach the convention floor, where many believed that the Green compromise would prevail over Johnson's original proposal. FDP's hopes for a minority report rested chiefly on Joseph Rauh, a member of the credentials committee, leader of the Democratic party in the District of Columbia, veteran of innumerable liberal crusades, and, happily, adviser and legal counsel of the FDP. But Rauh was also a friend of Hubert Humphrey and an attorney for Humphrey's strong supporter, Walter Reuther. After Humphrey came on the scene with his compromise, Rauh backed away from the minority report.

In his semi-official history of the Mississippi Summer Project, *The Summer That Didn't End,* Len Holt presents the FDP and SNCC interpretation of what happened. Presumably pressured by his powerful friends, Rauh broke a promise to the FDP and would not support the Green compromise. One by one the FDP's other allies on the committee backed away—some to protect jobs, others to keep alive hopes for federal judgeships, and one because he feared the loss of a local antipoverty program. In the end the FDP failed to collect the needed signatures, and there was no minority report. The angry rhetoric that the FDP delegates let loose in Atlantic City was in reality inspired less by Humphrey's compromise than by what the FDP regarded as its betrayal at the hands of the white liberals on the credentials committee. By the end of the Democratic convention SNCC was convinced that membership in the Democratic coalition held little hope for Southern blacks and that, lacking power, they would always be sold out by the liberals. In Atlantic City the phrase "white power structure" took on concrete meaning. Freedom Summer, which began with SNCC fighting for entrance into the American political system, ended with the radical conviction that that system was beyond redemption.[28]

In the end the Freedom Summer Project of 1964 not only destroyed SNCC's faith in the American political system; it also undermined its commitment to integration. Within the project racial tensions between white and black workers were never successfully resolved. Though many white volunteers established warm relationships with the local black families that housed them,[29] healthy communication between students and veteran SNCC workers proved difficult at best. Staff members resented the officious

---

[28] *New York Times* (Aug. 25, 1964), 23; Holt, *The Summer That Didn't End,* pp. 171–78; see also Zinn, *SNCC,* pp. 251–56; and Stoper, "The Student Nonviolent Coordinating Committee," pp. 74, 77–79, 81.

[29] See, for instance, Sutherland, *Letters from Mississippi,* p. 48.

manner of better-educated volunteers and feared that the white students were taking over the movement. "Several times," one volunteer wrote, "I've had to completely re-do press statements or letters written by one of them." [30] Said a SNCC worker, "Look at those fly-by-night freedom fighters bossing everybody around." [31] SNCC people found it hard to respect the efforts of volunteers who they knew would retreat at the end of the summer to their safe middle-class world. One sensitive white female volunteer wrote that SNCC workers "were automatically suspicious of us, the white volunteers; throughout the summer they put us to the test, and few, if any, could pass. . . . It humbled, if not humiliated, one to realize that *finally they will never accept me.*" [32] By the end of the summer a spirit akin to black nationalism was rising inside the SNCC organization.

The overall failure of Freedom Summer administered a blow to SNCC's morale from which the organization almost did not recover. In November 1964, Robert Coles, a psychiatrist who had worked closely with SNCC, wrote about the tendency of veteran workers to develop battle fatigue. Even heroic temperaments, he said, could not escape the depression that inevitably results from long periods of unremitting dangers and disappointments. But by the fall of 1964 battle fatigue was no longer just the problem of individual SNCC members; it was pervading the entire organization. One patient told Coles,

> I'm tired, but so is the whole movement. We're busy worrying about our position or our finances, so we don't do anything. . . . We're becoming lifeless, just like all revolutions when they lose their first momentum and become more interested in preserving what they've won than going on to new challenges. . . . Only with us we haven't won that much, and we're either holding to the little we have as an organization, or we get bitter, and want to create a new revolution. . . . You know, one like the Muslims want which is the opposite of what we say we're for. It's as if we completely reverse ourselves because we can't get what we want.[33]

Uncertain of their purpose, SNCC workers in the winter of 1964–65 grew introspective. Months were consumed in discussing the future of whites in the movement and the proper structure of the organization. Fresh from a trip to Africa where he met the black nationalist Malcolm X, John Lewis, Chairman of SNCC, spoke for the majority in early 1965 when he demanded

---

[30] Quoted in *ibid.*, p. 202.

[31] Quoted in Pat Watters, *Encounter with the Future* (Southern Regional Council, May, 1965), p. 32.

[32] Belfrage, *Freedom Summer*, p. 80.

[33] Robert Coles, "Social Struggle and Awareness," *Psychiatry*, XXVII (Nov., 1964), 305 15.

that blacks lead their own movement.[34] At the same time, quarrels over organization almost tore SNCC apart. Some workers became "high on freedom" and advocated a romantic anarchism that rejected bureaucratic structure and leadership. Robert Moses, for instance, believed that SNCC workers should "go where the spirit say go, and do what the spirit say do." Moses was so disturbed by his own prestige in the movement that he changed his name, drifted into Alabama, and thereafter was only vaguely connected with SNCC. Meanwhile SNCC's field work tended to fall into neglect.[35]

In the summer of 1965 SNCC brought 300 white volunteers into Mississippi for its second and last summer project. The result was a shambles. Racial tensions caused some projects to break up and prevented serious work in others. Problems only dimly perceived a year before assumed stark clarity, and SNCC's resentment of the volunteers became overt and unambiguous. At staff meetings blacks would silence white students with such remarks as "How long have you been here?" and "How do you know what it's like being black?" and "if you don't like the way we do it, get the hell out of the state." [36] Not all the blame for the final breakdown of race relations in SNCC, however, belonged to the black staff. The questionable motivation of some of the white students led Alvin Poussaint, a black psychiatrist close to SNCC, to add a new neurosis to medical terminology—the white African Queen or Tarzan complex. The victim of this neurosis harbored repressed delusions of himself as an "intelligent, brave, and handsome white man or woman, leading the poor down-trodden and oppressed black men to freedom and salvation." [37]

But the most serious obstacle to healthy race relations inside SNCC was sex, and in this dimension, as really in all others, the villain was neither black worker nor white student, but rather the sad and twisted history of race relations in America. The white girl who came South to help SNCC found herself, according to Dr. Poussaint, "at the center of an emotionally shattering crossfire of racial tensions that have been nurtured for centuries." [38] In the summer of 1965 a veteran black civil rights worker in SCLC tried to warn

---

[34] Watters, *Encounter with the Future*, pp. 29–31; see also Lerone Bennett, Jr., "SNCC, Rebels with a Cause," *Ebony*, XX (July, 1965), 146–53.

[35] For the Moses quote, see Gene Roberts, "From Freedom High to 'Black Power,'" *New York Times Magazine* (Sept. 25, 1966), 21; see also Bruce Payne, "The Student Nonviolent Coordinating Committee: An Overview Two Years Later," *The Activist* (Nov., 1965), 6–7; and Stoper, "Student Nonviolent Coordinating Committee," pp. 126–27.

[36] These quotations are from transcripts of informal taped interviews conducted in the South in 1965 by students of Stanford University. The tapes are stored at Stanford.

[37] Alvin F. Poussaint, "Problems of White Civil Rights Workers in the South," *Psychiatric Opinion*, III (Dec., 1966), 21.

[38] Alvin F. Poussaint, "The Stresses of the White Female Worker in the Civil Rights Movement in the South," *American Journal of Psychiatry*, CXXIII (Oct., 1966), 401.

white girls of the perils that awaited them in their dealings with black men in the movement:

> What you have here is a man who had no possible way of being a man in the society in which he lives, save one. And that's the problem. The only way or place a Negro man has been able to express his manhood is sexually and so you find a tremendous sexual aggressiveness. And I say quite frankly, don't get carried away by it and don't get afraid of it either. I mean, don't think it's because you're so beautiful and so ravishing that this man is so enamoured of you. It's not that at all. He's just trying to find his manhood and he goes especially to the places that have robbed him of it. . . . And so, in a sense, what passes itself as desire is probably a combination of hostility and resentment— because he resents what the society has done to him and he wants to take it out on somebody who symbolizes the establishment of society.[39]

At the end of the summer a white girl spoke of her experiences:

> Well, I think that the white female should be very well prepared before she comes down here to be bombarded. And she also has to be well prepared to tell them to go to hell and be prepared to have them not give up. . . . I've never met such forward men as I have in Mississippi.[40]

The problem was complicated by the jealousy of black girls toward their white rivals, and by neurotic whites who sought to ease their guilt by permitting blacks to exploit them sexually and financially.[41] On leaving their projects to go home, a few white girls told Poussaint, "I hate Negroes." [42] By the end of the summer of 1965 no one could any longer doubt that the blacks reciprocated the feeling.

The year 1965 was a lost one for SNCC. For the first time since its founding, it was no longer on the frontier of protest, no longer the keeper of the nation's conscience, no longer the driving force of a moral revolution. The civil rights acts of 1964 and 1965 brought the civil rights movement, for which SNCC had suffered so much, to a triumphant conclusion, but SNCC had lost interest in integrated public accommodations and equal political rights. SNCC seemed to be losing its sense of mission and after years of providing heroes for the black protest movement, it now needed a hero of its own. Significantly it chose Malcolm X, the black nationalist who had been assassinated by Muslim rivals in February 1965.[43] Only a few years before,

---

[39] Taped by Stanford students in 1965.

[40] *Ibid.*

[41] Poussaint, "Problems of White Civil Rights Workers in the South," 20–21.

[42] Pousaint, "Stresses of the White Female Worker," 404.

[43] On influence of Malcolm X on SNCC, see Stoper, "The Student Nonviolent Coordinating Committee," p. 181.

SNCC and Malcolm X had seemed to occupy opposite poles of black protest. Thus while SNCC's John Lewis was toning down his speech at the March on Washington, Malcolm X was saying,

> Who ever heard of angry revolutionists all harmonizing "We Shall Overcome . . . Suum Day . . ." while tripping and swaying along arm-in-arm with the very people they were supposed to be angrily revolting against? Who ever heard of angry revolutionists swinging their bare feet together with their oppressors in lily-pad park pools, with gospels and guitars and "I Have a Dream" speeches? [44]

While policemen were clubbing SNCC workers in Mississippi, Malcolm X was saying, "If someone puts a hand on you, send him to the cemetery." [45] While SNCC was pondering the meaning of Atlantic City, Malcolm X was saying, "We *need* a Mau Mau. If they don't want to deal with the Mississippi Freedom Democratic Party, then we'll give them something else to deal with." While black nationalists were still a minority in SNCC, Malcolm X was calling for black control of black politicians in black communities, black ownership of ghetto businesses, and black unity "to lift the level of our community, to make our society beautiful so that we will be satisfied in our own social circles and won't be running around here trying to knock our way into a social circle where we're not wanted." [46] This was the language that had made Malcolm X the hero of the urban ghetto, and it was the language appropriate in 1965 to SNCC's militant mood. In a certain sense Malcolm X was the link that connected SNCC with the black radicalism that was arising in the North.

Unlike SNCC, the ghetto masses never had to disabuse themselves of the colorblind assumptions of the civil rights movement. Trapped permanently in their neighborhoods, the poor blacks of the North have always been painfully conscious of their racial separateness. As Essien-Udom, a historian of black nationalism, has written, blackness "is the stuff of their lives and an omnipresent, harsh reality. For this reason the Negro masses are instinctively 'race men.'" [47] But the civil rights movement nevertheless had its consequences in the ghetto. The spectacle of Southern blacks defying their white tormentors apparently inspired among Northern blacks race pride and resurgent outrage at the gap between American ideals and black realities. Thus the civil rights movement had the ironic effect of feeding the nationalist tendency in the ghetto to turn inward, to separate, and to identify the white

---

[44] *The Autobiography of Malcolm X* (Grove Press, 1966), pp. 280–81.

[45] *Malcolm X Speaks: Selected Speeches and Statements* (Merit, 1965), p. 12.

[46] *Ibid.*, 38–39.

[47] E. U. Essien-Udom, *Black Nationalism* (Univ. of Chicago Press, 1962), p. 3.

men outside as the enemy. SNCC's frustrations exploded intellectually in the formulation of black power doctrines, but ghetto rage took the form of riot.

The riot of August 1965, in Watts (the sprawling ghetto of Los Angeles) dwarfed the violent outbursts of the previous year and awakened America to the race crisis in her big cities. A social trauma of the first order, the Watts riot resulted in 35 deaths, 600 burned and looted buildings, and 4,000 persons arrested.[48] Above all it revealed the dangerous racial hatred that had been accumulating unnoticed in the nation's black ghettos. The official autopsy of Watts denied by implication that it was a revolt against white oppression. The McCone Commission (after its chairman, John McCone), appointed by California's Governor Pat Brown to investigate the riot, estimated that only 10,000 Watts residents, or 2 percent of the population in the riot area, had actually been on the streets during the uprising. This minor fraction, the Commission contended, was not protesting specific grievances, which admittedly existed in abundance, but was engaged in an "insensate rage of destruction" that was "formless, quite senseless."[49] Critics of the McCone report have ably challenged these findings. (For example, Robert Fogelson points out that "to claim that only 10,000 Negroes rioted when about 4,000 were arrested is to presume that the police apprehended fully 40 percent of the rioters.")[50] In reality, a rather large minority of the riot-age population in Watts was on the streets during the riot, and as one of the Commission's own staff reports revealed, the riot had significant support inside the ghetto, especially in the worst slum areas.[51]

On the crucial question of the riot's causes, observers on the scene agreed that the rioters were animated by a common anger against whites.[52] Robert Blauner, a staff member for the McCone Commission and its severest ciritic, has written,

> Most of the actions of the rioters appear to have been informed by the desire to clear out an alien presence, white men, rather than to kill them. . . . It was primarily an attack on property, particularly white-owned businesses. . . .

---

[48] A Report by the Governor's Commission on the Los Angeles Riot, *Violence in the City —An End or a Beginning?* (Dec. 2, 1965), pp. 1–2. (Referred to heareafter as the Mc-Cone Report.)

[49] McCone Report, pp. 1, 4–5.

[50] Robert M. Fogelson, "White on Black: A Critique of the McCone Commission Report on the Los Angeles Riots," *Political Science Quarterly*, LXXXII (Sept., 1967), 345.

[51] E. Edward Ransford, *Attitudes and Other Characteristics of Negroes in Watts, South Central, and Crenshaw Areas of Los Angeles* (a staff study prepared for the McCone Commission), p. 2.

[52] See, for instance, Robert Conot, *Rivers of Blood, Years of Darkness* (Bantam Books, 1967), p. 204.

The spirit of the Watts rioters appears similar to that of anti-colonial crowds demonstrating against foreign masters.[53]

Said Bayard Rustin, a moderate black intellectual who was in Watts during the riot, "The whole point of the outburst in Watts was that it marked the first major rebellion of Negroes against their masochism and was carried on with the express purpose of asserting that they would no longer quietly submit to the deprivation of slum life." [54] Thus in 1965, for different reasons, both the ghetto masses and the members of SNCC were seized by militant anti-white feelings, and it was this congruence of mood that would shortly permit SNCC to appeal to a nation-wide black audience.

After a year on the periphery of the black protest movement, SNCC in 1966 moved again to the forefront. In May 1966, at a time when the organization was apparently disintegrating, 135 staff members (25 of them white) met in Nashville to thrash out their future. Early in the emotional conference, by a vote of 60 to 22, John Lewis, the gentle advocate of nonviolence, retained the chairmanship of SNCC by defeating the challenge of the militant Stokely Carmichael. But as the conference went on, the arguments of the militants began to prevail. When the staff voted to boycott the coming White House conference on civil rights, Lewis announced that he would attend anyway, and the question of the chairmanship was then reopened. This time SNCC workers chose Carmichael as their new leader by a vote of 60 to 12. The conference next issued a statement calling, among other things, for "black Americans to begin building independent political, economic, and cultural institutions that they will control and use as instruments of social change in this country." [55]

A few weeks later the full meaning of Carmichael's election became clear to the whole nation. The occasion was the famous Meredith march through Mississippi in June of 1966. James Meredith, the man who integrated the University of Mississippi in 1962 with the help of the United States Army, embarked on a 200-mile walk from Memphis to Jackson to show the black people of Mississippi that they could walk to the voting booths without fear. On June 6, 28 miles out of Memphis, a white man felled Meredith with buckshot. Erroneously believing that Meredith had been killed, civil rights leaders immediately flew to Mississippi to continue his walk against fear. So it was that arm in arm, Martin Luther King of SCLC, Floyd McKissick of

---

[53] Quoted in Robert Blauner, "Whitewash over Watts: The Failure of the McCone Commission Report," *Transaction*, III (March–April, 1966), 9.

[54] Bayard Rustin, "The Watts 'Manifesto' and the McCone Report," *Commentary*, XLI (March, 1966), 30.

[55] This account of Carmichael's election and the quotations from SNCC's statement are from Newfield, *A Prophetic Minority*, pp. 75–77.

CORE, and Stokely Carmichael of SNCC marched down U.S. Highway 51.

Early efforts of the three leaders to maintain surface unity rapidly broke down. Significantly, the first issue that divided them was the role of white people in the Meredith march. King's workers publicly thanked Northern whites for joining the procession. McKissick also thanked the Northerners but announced that black men must now lead the civil rights movement. And Carmichael mused aloud that maybe the whites should go home. As the column moved onto the back roads and Southern white hostility increased, the leadership of the march failed to agree on how to respond to violence. In Philadelphia, Mississippi, Dr. King conducted a memorial service for Goodman, Chaney, and Schwerner and told a crowd of 300 jeering whites that the murderers of the three men were no doubt "somewhere around me at this moment." Declaring that "I am not afraid of any man," King then delivered a Christian sermon. But after the service was over and local whites got rough, the marchers returned punch for punch.

The real spokesman for the march, it soon developed, was not King but Stokely Carmichael. In one town, after spending a few hours in jail, Carmichael told a crowd, "I ain't going to jail no more. I ain't going to jail no more," and he announced, "Every courthouse in Mississippi ought to be burned down to get rid of the dirt." Carmichael then issued the cry that would make him famous. Five times he shouted "Black Power!" and, the *New York Times* reported, "each time the younger members of the audience shouted back, 'Black Power.' " Informed of this new slogan, Dr. King expressed disapproval, and SCLC workers exhorted crowds to call not for black power but for "freedom now." Nevertheless, by the end of the Meredith march, black power had become a force to reckon with.[56]

At its inception in June, 1966, black power was not a systematic doctrine but a cry of rage. In an article in the *New York Times Magazine*, Dr. Poussaint tried to explain the psychological origin of the anger expressed in the new slogan:

> I remember treating Negro workers after they had been beaten viciously by white toughs or policemen while conducting civil rights demonstrations. I would frequently comment, "You must feel pretty angry getting beaten up like that by those bigots." Often I received a reply such as: "No, I don't hate those white men, I love them because they must really be suffering with all that hatred in their souls. Dr. King says the only way we can win our freedom is through love. Anger and hatred has never solved anything."
>
> I used to sit there and wonder, "Now, what do they really do with their rage?"

---

[56] For the Meredith march, see *New York Times,* June 7, 1966, p. 1; June 8, pp. 1 and 26; June 9, p. 1; June 12, pp. 1 and 82; June 17, p. 1; June 21, p. 30; June 22, p. 25.

Poussaint reported that after a while these workers vented their mounting rage against each other.

> While they were talking about being nonviolent and "loving" the sheriff that just hit them over the head, they rampaged around the project houses beating up each other. I frequently had to calm Negro civil rights workers with large doses of tranquilizers for what I can describe clinically only as acute attacks of rage.

In time the civil rights workers began to direct their anger against white racists, the Federal Government, and finally white people in the movement. Said Poussaint:

> This rage was at a fever pitch for many months, before it became crystallized in the "Black Power" slogan. The workers who shouted it the loudest were those with the oldest battle scars from the terror, demoralization, and castration which they experienced through continual direct confrontation with Southern white racists. Furthermore, some of the most bellicose chanters of the slogan had been, just a few years before, examples of nonviolent, loving passive resistance in their struggle against white supremacy. These workers appeared to be seeking a sense of inner psychological emancipation from racists through self-assertion and release of aggressive angry feelings.[57]

In the months following the Meredith march, SNCC found itself at the center of a bitter national controversy and spokesman for an enlarged constituency. The anger implicit in the slogan "black power" assured SNCC a following in the ghettos of the North and ended its regional confinement. Through its leader, Stokely Carmichael, SNCC labored through 1966 and into 1967 to give intellectual substance to the black power slogan, seeking especially to frame an analysis that would be relevant to black Americans of all sections. Although his speeches were often inflammatory, Carmichael in his writing attempted serious, even restrained, argument suitable for an educated audience. But the elements of black power were not, in truth, derived from rational reflection but from wretched experience—from the beatings, jailhouses, and abortive crusades that SNCC veterans had endured for six years. SNCC had tried nonviolence and found it psychologically destructive. (The "days of the free head-whipping are over," Carmichael and his collaborator Charles Hamilton wrote. "Black people should and must fight back." [58]) SNCC, for example, had believed in integration and tried it within its own organization, but black and white together had not worked. (In-

---

[57] Alvin F. Poussaint, "A Negro Psychiatrist Explains the Negro Psyche," *New York Times Magazine* (Aug. 20, 1967), 55 ff.

[58] Stokely Carmichael and Charles V. Hamilton, *Black Power: The Politics of Liberation* (Vintage, 1967), p. 52.

tegration, said Carmichael, "is a subterfuge for the maintenance of white supremacy" and "reinforces, among both black and white, the idea that 'white' is automatically better and 'black' is by definition inferior."[59]) SNCC had allied with white liberals in the Democratic party and had come away convinced that it had been betrayed. (In dealing with blacks, Carmichael said, white liberals "perpetuate a paternalistic, colonial relationship."[60]) SNCC had struggled for equal political rights but concluded finally that political inequality was less oppressive than economic exploitation. In 1966 SNCC felt it was necessary to go beyond the assertion of these hard conclusions and to attempt to impose on them systematic form. So it was that after years of activism divorced from ideology, SNCC began to reduce its field work and concentrate on fashioning an intellectual rationale for its new militancy. At a time when the black protest movement was floundering and its future direction was uncertain, SNCC stepped forward to contribute the doctrines of black power, which were really the culmination of its career. No history of SNCC would be complete, therefore, without some consideration of those doctrines.

According to Stokely Carmichael, the black masses suffer from two different but reinforcing forms of oppression: class exploitation and white racism. To illustrate this point, he relies on an analogy apparently inspired by Franz Fanon's *Wretched of the Earth*, a book with considerable influence in black power circles. The black communities of contemporary America, Carmichael says, share many of the characteristics of African colonies under European rule. Thus as Africa once enriched its imperialist masters by exporting valuable raw materials to Europe, so now do the American ghettos "export" their labor for the profit of American capitalists. In both Africa and America, white men own local businesses and use them to drain away any wealth somehow possessed by the subject population. As in Africa, there exists in the ghetto a white power structure that is no abstraction, but is a visible and concrete presence—the white landlords, for instance, who collect rent and ignore needed repairs, the city agencies and school systems that systematically neglect black people, the policemen who abuse black citizens and collect payoffs from white racketeers. By far the most insidious method devised by the white imperialists for perpetuating class exploitation has been the use of race as a badge of inferiority. Colonial masters, says Carmichael, "purposely, maliciously, and with reckless abandon relegated the black man to a subordinated, inferior status in society. . . . White America's School of Slavery and Segregation, like the School of Colonialism, has taught the subject to hate himself and deny his humanity." As the colonies of Africa have done, black Americans must undergo "political

---

[59] Stokely Carmichael, "What We Want," *New York Review of Books* (Sept. 22, 1966), 6.

[60] Carmichael and Hamilton, *Black Power*, p. 65.

modernization," liberate their communities, and achieve self-determination. And like Africa, the ghetto must win the struggle by its own effort.[61]

For Carmichael, liberation begins with eradication of the effects of white racism. To overcome the shame of race bred in them by white men, blacks must develop a cultural identity, rediscover the rich African civilization from which they originally came, and learn from their history that they are a "vibrant, valiant people."[62] Freed of their damaging self-image, they can begin to challenge the capitalist values that have enslaved them as a class. The white middle class, says Carmichael, has fostered esteem for "material aggrandizement," is "without a viable conscience as regards humanity," and constitutes "the backbone of institutional reason in this country." Black men, however, will develop values emphasizing "the dignity of man, not . . . the sanctity of property," "free people," not "free enterpise."[63] "The society we seek to build among black people, then, is not a capitalist one. It is a society in which the spirit of community and humanistic love prevail."[64] To complete the process of liberation, black men will have to purge the ghetto of exploiting institutions and develop structures that conform to their new values.

The reconstruction of the black community, Carmichael contends, should be in the hands of black people in order to "convey the revolutionary idea . . . that black people are able to do things themselves." Among other acts of liberation that they can perform, ghetto blacks should conduct rent strikes against slum landlords and boycotts against the ghetto merchant who refuses to "'invest' say forty to fifty percent of his net profit in the indigenous community." Governmental structures that have violated the humanity of blacks will have to be either eliminated from the ghetto or made responsive to their black constituency. The school system must be taken from professionals, most of whom have demonstrated "insensitivity to the needs and problems of the black child" and given to black parents, who will control personnel and curriculum. The indifference of the existing political parties to black people necessitates formation of separate (parallel) black organizations, both in the 110 Southern counties with black majorities and in the ghettos of the North.[65] According to Carmichael, it is simply naive to think that poor and powerless blacks have anything in common with the other components of the Democratic coalition. White liberals inevitably fall under the "overpowering influence" of their racist environment, and their demands for civil

---

[61] For the colonial analogy, see *ibid.*, Chapter 1.

[62] *Ibid.*, pp. 37–39.

[63] *Ibid.*, pp. 40–4 .

[64] Carmichael, "What We Want," 7.

[65] Carmichael and Hamilton, *Black Power*, Chapter 8 and p. 166.

rights are "doing for blacks." Labor unions accept the existing order and, in the case of the AFL, even discriminate against black workers. Black political parties, Carmichael believes, will alone be devoted to real change and will in fact make possible emancipation from dominant American values and power centers.[66]

Carmichael professes to believe that black power is not really a departure from American practice. "Traditionally," he writes, "for each new ethnic group, the route to social and political integration into America's pluralistic society has been through the organization of their own institutions with which to represent their communal needs within the larger society." [67] Once in possession of power, blacks then could reenter the old coalitions for specific goals. But "let any ghetto group contemplating coalition be so tightly organized, so strong, that . . . it is an 'undigestible body' which cannot be absorbed or swallowed up." Given Carmichael's scheme for a radical reconstruction of American society, it is not surprising that the only group that he someday hopes to make his ally is the poor whites.[68]

As several critics have pointed out,[69] Carmichael's version of black power is hardly more than a collection of fragments, often lacking in clarity, consistency, and conviction. Thus, for example, Carmichael talks about the need for parallel institutions but offers only one example—black political organizations. He claims that these organizations can regenerate the entire political system but typically neglects to explain concretely how this regeneration is to be achieved. He calls for radical rejection of American values and institutions but at the same time portrays the black community as merely another ethnic group turning temporarily inward to prepare for later integration into American society. According to Carmichael, ghetto blacks are an exploited proletariat kept in bondage to enrich America's capitalist class; yet black workers seem more like a *lumpenproletariat* threatened with loss of economic function and forced to the margin of the American economy. Carmichael fails to reveal the mechanisms by which big business keeps the black man exploited, and indeed it seems doubtful that big business especially profits from the depressed condition of such a large group of potential consumers. But the real criticism of black power is not that as a body of thought it lacks coherence and sustained argument. Its greatest weakness is its failure to propose adequate solutions.

---

[66] *Ibid.*, pp. 60–66.

[67] Stokely Carmichael, "Toward Black Liberation," *The Massachusetts Review*, VII (Autumn, 1966), 642.

[68] Carmichael and Hamilton, *Black Power*, pp. 80, 82.

[69] For critiques of black power, see, for instance, Paul Feldman, "The Pathos of 'Black Power,'" *Dissent* (Jan.–Feb., 1967), 69–79; Bayard Rustin, "'Black Power' and Coalition Politics," *Commentary*, XLII (Sept., 1966), 35–40; Christopher Lasch, "The Trouble with Black Power," *New York Review of Books*, X (Feb. 29, 1968), 4 ff.

Carmichael began his argument by maintaining that black men suffer from two separate but related forms of discrimination—racial and economic. When Carmichael proposes ways for black men to undo the effects of racism, he makes good sense. Certainly black men should uncover their cultural roots and take pride in what has been of worth in their heritage. Certainly liberal paternalism is now anachronistic and black men should lead their own organizations. Nonviolence probably *was* psychologically damaging to many who practiced it, and integration into a hostile white society is not only an unrealistic goal but demeaning to a self-respecting people. Furthermore, some middle-class values, as Carmichael maintains, are less than ennobling, and elements of the black man's life style do have intrinsic merit. But it is doubtful whether black self-respect can ever be achieved without a solution of the second problem confronting ghetto blacks, and it is here that Carmichael's version of black power is most deficient.

Concerned primarily with humanizing social and governmental structures inside the ghetto, Carmichael has little to say about ending poverty in black America. Although more responsive policemen and schoolteachers and less dishonest slum lords and merchants will no doubt be a great step forward, these aspects of ghetto life are of less consequence than unemployment or poverty wages. Within the ghetto the resources for economic reconstruction are simply not available, and since Carmichael rejects coalitions outside the ghetto, he is barred from offering a realistic economic strategy. It is this weakness that led the black intellectual and long-time civil rights leader Bayard Rustin to oppose black power. Pointing to the futility of separatist politics in a society in which the black man is a minority, Rustin calls for "a liberal-labor-civil rights coalition which would work to make the Democratic party truly responsive to the aspirations of the poor, and which would develop support for programs (specifically those outlined in A. Philip Randolph's $100 billion Freedom Budget) aimed at the reconstruction of American society in the interest of greater social justice." [70] Rustin's goals are considerably less apocalyptic than Carmichael's, but they are far more realistic. Carmichael's radical ruminations about a socialist alliance of poor whites and poor blacks seem fantasies irrelevant to American social realities. Although Carmichael's vision holds out hope for some distant time, it offers no meaningful proposals for the present.

The true significance of black power lies not in the doctrines into which it evolved but in the historical circumstances that gave it birth. The real message of black power is that after years of struggle to make America an open and just society, an important group of civil rights workers, instructed by the brute facts of its own history, gave up the fight. Black power was a cry of rage directed against white bigots who overcame righteous men by force, a cry of bitterness against white liberals who had only a stunted comprehen-

---

[70] Bayard Rustin, " 'Black Power' and Coalition Politics," 36.

sion of the plight of the black poor, and a cry of frustration against gains that seemed meager when compared to needs. It is possible, however, that even rage can perform a useful function, and if the black power slogan brings about a constructive catharsis and helps rouse the black masses from apathy, then the intellectual shortcomings of black power doctrines may seem of little consequence, and what began as a cry of despair may yet play a creative role in the black protest movement. Therefore, whether the history of SNCC in this decade will be considered triumph or tragedy depends on events yet to occur.

SUGGESTED READING

Though much of the literature on the black protest movement of recent years has been more journalistic than scholarly, a few books have proved of value. Useful surveys include Arthur I. Waskow's *From Race Riot to Sit-In* (Doubleday, 1966), which begins its story in 1919, and Anthony Lewis' *Portrait of a Decade* (Random House, 1964), a study of the fight against segregation from 1954 to 1964. An excellent statement of the race problem as of the mid-1960's is Charles E. Silberman's *Crisis in Black and White* (Random House, 1964), which is remarkable for its sensitivity to developing trends. For an illuminating public opinion survey containing material on the initial impact of black power, see William Brink and Louis Harris, *Black and White* (Simon & Schuster, 1966). Especially valuable for its statistical information is the *Report of the National Advisory Commission on Civil Disorders* ° (Bantam Books, 1968).

Studies with important implications for the student of black power are Charles Eric Lincoln's *The Black Muslims in America* (Beacon Press, 1961); Lee Rainwater and William Yancey's *The Moynihan Report and the Politics of Controversy* (M.I.T. Press, 1967), which reprints Moynihan's famous study of the Negro family and many of the reactions that the study provoked; Eldridge Cleaver's *Soul on Ice* (McGraw-Hill, 1968); William H. Grier and Price M. Cobbs' *Black Rage* (Basic Books, 1968), a study by two psychiatrists that is too impressionistic to be convincing; and Jerry Cohen and William S. Murphy's *Burn, Baby, Burn* ° (Avon, 1966), which comments on the Watts riot.

For a Marxist's defense of black power, see Eugene Genovese, *The Legacy of Slavery and the Roots of Black Nationalism* (Southern Student Organization Committee, Nashville, Tennessee, no date); for a negative reaction on the white Left, see Christopher Lasch, "The Trouble with Black Power," *New York Review of Books*, X (Feb. 29, 1968), 4 ff.; and for a study of the problems that black power poses for the white liberal, see Hugh D. Graham, "The Storm over Black Power," *Virginia*

Quarterly Review, XLIII (Autumn, 1967), 545–65. Martin Duberman in "Black Power in America," *Partisan Review*, XXXV (Winter, 1968), 34–48, finds parallels between the development of black power and both abolitionism and anarchism. *The Black Power Revolt*,° edited by Floyd Barbour (Porter Sargent, 1968), is a useful collection of documents. Gary Marx's *Protest and Prejudice* ° (Harper & Row, 1968) is a sociological study of beliefs in the black community.

JOHN KENNETH GALBRAITH

The New Industrial State:
The Role of the State

INTRODUCTION

For decades American radicals have decried the political and economic power of the major corporations and their alliance with or
control of the state. Marxist and non-Marxist radicals alike have
pointed out that political power is not broadly distributed. They
have often emphasized the easy movement from corporate leadership to federal positions and argued that the occupants of these
high offices represent the same class and interests.

Traditionally the liberals have assailed this analysis, charg-
ing its proponents with gross over-simplification, ideological distortion—even blindness. The liberals generally have viewed the
central state as an independent force—a likely restraint on private power, although they too have in the past worried about indus-

FROM John Kenneth Galbraith, "The New Industrial State: The Role of the State," *The
Listener*, LXXVI (December 8, 1966), pp. 841–43, 853. Reprinted by permission of the
author.

trial concentration and the power of large corporations. By the early 1950's, however, even liberals came to extol the benefits of large-scale corporate enterprise and were little concerned about restricting its power.

Among those undisturbed by oligopoly was the economist John Kenneth Galbraith. In *American Capitalism: The Theory of Countervailing Power* (Houghton Mifflin, 1952; revised, 1956) he acknowledged economic concentration but he identified a self-regulating mechanism (countervailing power) that restrains powerful corporations and protects consumers. Even though much of the economy was dominated by oligopolies, which normally avoid price competition, Galbraith found that the struggle between large buyers and large sellers (in noninflationary periods) would restrain the power of both. United States Steel, for example, cannot economically coerce General Motors because the automobile company may always turn to another steel producer. On the basis of this sanguine theory, he concluded that the Government should use its antitrust powers sparingly. Galbraith also viewed labor unions as countervailing powers: they represent and protect the interests of workers, thus providing a counterweight to corporate powers.

Professional economists have pointed out many defects in Galbraith's theory: it relied unwarrantedly on competition at the retail level, neglected the control that vertical integration has bestowed on major corporations (consider, for example, the power of automobile producers over dealers), disregarded interlocking directorates, and failed to explain adequately the steady or rising administered prices during recent recessions. Even Galbraith acknowledged that countervailing power will not operate effectively in demand inflation, when there is little incentive for buyers to resist the demands of sellers (of materials or labor), since additional costs can be passed on to the consumer. Despite these criticisms, the theory of countervailing power in the economy won wide popularity in the 1950's, supporting as it did the pluralists' description of American society—that political power was broadly distributed, that interest groups competed for limited benefits and comfortably participated in the healthy American consensus.

Another volume by Galbraith, *The Affluent Society** (Houghton Mifflin, 1958), expresses the thinking of liberal intellectuals of the late 1950's and early 1960's. Like David Riesman and other pluralists, Galbraith assumed that America is a middle-class society and that the problems of the business cycle and poverty have been largely solved. (He acknowledged that there were some "pockets" of poverty—for example, Appalachia—and some "case" poverty—for example, the aged and infirm.) Lamenting the unwarranted emphasis on production for its own sake, he urged in his book a shift in spending from the private to the public sector. To improve the quality of American life (devalued, as he saw it, by advertising and symbolized by the tail fins that were then popular on Cadillacs) he recommended greater public expenditures on education, health, and recreation. Though Galbraith's volume largely avoided the problem of power, it implicitly embraced pluralism.

Yet, in *The Industrial State* (presented in part on the BBC in 1966 as the Reith lectures, the fourth of which is reprinted below, and then published by Houghton Mifflin in 1967), which stands in relation to *The Affluent Society* "as a house to a window," Galbraith presents a theory of modern capitalism that is close to the analysis of the radicals. Departing from his earlier pluralism, he argues that the five hundred or so largest corporations share personnel and common values with the state and possess dominant political and economic power. Subscribing to the Berle-Means thesis that management was divorced from ownership and emphasizing the corporation's dependence on planning and technology, he concludes that power in the modern corporation is diffused among directors, technicians, and experts. This "Technostructure" aims not to maximize profits but to advance its own security through corporate expansion, technological development, and control of its own capital and consumer markets. For control of the larger economic environment, the corporations call on the Government to provide what they cannot guarantee: a necessary level of aggregate demand and support for expensive technology. (Labor, he finds, generally acquiesces in this system and provides added stability, at the price of demands for higher wages.) The overall result is policies formulated and implemented by a ruling group: the corporate and state managers.

In some ways Galbraith's analysis is not far from recent Marxist interpretations, but he usually stops short of Marxist conclusions. He acknowledges, for example, that the interests and ideology of large corporations dominate foreign policy and admits that corporations depend on expanding markets, but he believes that the state does not have to find such markets abroad and that it can and *will* create them at home by expanding consumer demand. Like the Marxists, he also admits that defense spending has been an important source of postwar prosperity, but he is convinced that these expenditures can be transferred to road construction or the space program, *provided* they expand technological knowledge as well as aggregate demand. Unlike many Marxists, he assumes that the modern industrial system must be directed by an élite. He hopes that a new élite, composed of the educational and scientific estate, will replace the old élite and will use technology and economic power to achieve the goals outlined in *The Affluent Society* —intellectual and esthetic development and social welfare. The better society of Galbraith's vision, managed by a liberal élite, is the same society that the New Left finds a nightmare.

His analysis of the economic system seems flawed in some respects. Recent studies have questioned whether the separation of management and ownership is very great; they conclude that corporations are still interested in maximization of profits. In addition, these critics note that long-run maximization of profits does not necessarily differ in practice from the quest for growth and security. Professional economists have also questioned whether the modern American economy can be adequately understood as the major corporations writ large, and whether mature corporations have established the control over the market that Galbraith attributes to them. His theory of what he calls the "revised sequence" —that the corporation through advertising frees itself from *responding to* the consumer's desires and instead *creates* predictable wants for its product—is too simple.

Despite these criticisms, Galbraith's book offers an important interpretation of modern American capitalism. As an occasional economic adviser to John F. Kennedy during his pre-presidential years, as ambassador to India during the early Kennedy Administration, and as the Chairman of the Americans for Democratic Action, Galbraith by his political efforts and writings has commanded a wide audience, and his insights, while often fragmentary and exaggerated, are not unrepresentative of contemporary views of the modern American political economy.

I have undertaken to show in these lectures that the modern industrial society, or that part of it which is composed of the large corporations, is in major essentials a planned economy. By that I mean that production decisions are taken not in response to consumer demand as expressed in the market; rather they are taken by producers. These decisions are reflected in the prices that are set in the markets and in the further steps that are taken to insure that people will buy what is produced and sold at those prices. The ultimate influence is authority.

The role of such planning authority is also manifested in the prices that are set for the things that business enterprises buy. It is reflected in the further steps that insure that the requisite materials and components for production will be forthcoming at these prices; and it is manifested in the decisions to withhold earnings for reinvestment and thus for the expansion of the firms and ultimately the economy.

I am not arguing that market influences are entirely excluded from effect on these decisions. Economics, as it exists rather than as it is sometimes taught, has very few pure cases. It is a cocktail, a compote. But the notion that the consumer is the sovereign influence in the economy—that all decision begins with him—is a pure case that will not do. Or it will serve only for those who wish to believe in fairy tales. The important decisions in the modern economy are made by producing organizations in the service of their own goals. And, in one way or another, public behaviour is accommodated to these decisions. Thus, the planning.

In the non-socialist economy, the modern large corporation is the basic planning unit. For some planning tasks it is exceedingly competent. I have just now mentioned the more important. The large corporation can effectively fix minimum prices. It can manage consumer wants. In conjunction with other corporations, it can control prices of production requirements and arrange supplies at these prices. And it can extract from revenues the savings it needs for growth and expansion. But some things it cannot do. Though the modern corporation can set and maintain minimum prices, it cannot set maximum prices and wages. It cannot, in other words, prevent wages from forcing up prices and prices from forcing up wages in the familiar inflation spiral. And while it can manage the demand for individual products, it cannot control total demands—it cannot insure that total purchasing power in the economy will be equal, or approximately equal, to the supply of goods that can be produced by the current working force.

There are two other planning tasks that the large corporation cannot perform. It cannot supply the specialized manpower that modern technology, and organization and planning, require. It can train but it cannot educate. And it cannot absorb the risks and costs that are associated with very advanced forms of scientific and technical development—with the development of atomic power or supersonic air transport or anti-missile defences or weapons systems or other such requirements of modern civilized living.

I come now to a conclusion of some importance. The shortcomings of the large corporation, as a planning instrument, define the role of the modern state in economic policy. Wherever the private corporation cannot do the job, the state comes in and performs the required function. Wherever the private firm can do the job—as in setting minimum prices or managing consumer demand—the state is required to remain out. The private firm cannot fix maximum prices, so we have the state setting what in the United States we call wage and price guideposts and what here in Britain is called a pay and wage freeze. The private firm cannot regulate aggregate demand so the state comes in to manipulate taxes, public spending, and bank lending— to implement what we call modern Keynesian policy. The private firm cannot supply specialized manpower so we have a great expansion in publicly supported education. Private firms cannot afford to underwrite the Concord or what we call the SST. So governments—British, French, or American— come in to underwrite that job.

Our attitudes on the proper role of the state are firmly fixed by what private firms can or cannot do. A private corporation is perfectly capable of setting minimum prices for cigarettes; of persuading people to buy a new and totally implausible detergent; or of developing a new and more drastic kind of laxative. This being so, this planning is naturally held to be sacred to private enterprise.

The planning functions of the state are less sacred as public tasks. Most

of them are assumed to serve some special function. Or they have an improvised or *ad hoc* aspect. They are not yet seen as part of an overall structure of
planning that dovetails with private planning. Thus, ceilings on wages and
prices are perpetual emergency actions; Keynesian regulation of aggregate
demand is thought to have been occasioned by the particular imperatives of
full employment and growth; the expansion of education is regarded as the
result of a new enlightenment following the second world war; the underwriting of especially expensive technology is a pragmatic response to the
urgent social need for faster travel, emigration to the moon, bigger explosions, and, of course, competition with the Soviet Union.

So to regard matters is to fail to see the nature of modern planning. It is
also to assume that it is purely an accident that the state comes in to perform
the planning tasks that are beyond private reach. There are many reasons for
trying so to avert our eyes. Economists have a deeply vested interest in the
market. It is our intellectual stock-in-trade. In the United States, where faith
in free enterprise is deep, it is painful for us to concede that we have gradu-
ated into a directed or planned economy. And in Britain it is equally repug-
nant to socialists to realize that planning, which was supposed to originate
with the state, has come into existence very largely under private auspices.
Perhaps, with so many people finding the truth so unpleasant, it would contribute to general contentment were it just suppressed. But this is not practical. You cannot depend on people to leave an unpleasant truth alone. The
planning functions of the state are not *ad hoc* or separate developments.
They are a closely articulated set of functions which supplement and fill the
gaps in the planning of the modern large firm. Together these provide a comprehensive planning apparatus. It decides what people should have and then
arranges that they will get it and that they will want it. Not the least of its
achievements is in leaving them with the impression that the controlling decisions are theirs.

I would like now to examine in slightly more detail these planning
functions of the modern state.

On the fixing of maximum wages and prices, the guideposts or wage
and price freeze, I have only a word or two to add. It stands very much in
relation to modern economic policy as does prostitution to the theory of business management. Both are widely recognized to exist and to serve a function. But no one wants to admit of their permanent need. They are not
aspects of the good society. And certainly no one wishes to study them in
order to see how they could be made more efficient, or more serviceable to
the general public. It would be well were we to recognize that wage and
price fixing, at least, is indispensable in the planned economy. The next step
would be to learn how this wage and price fixing could be made more effective and more equitable. Even the universities might, in time, desert the fic-
tions of the free market for the modern reality of regulation and control. That,

however, may be optimistic. Thorstein Veblen once observed: "It has generally held true that the accredited learned class and the seminaries of the higher learning have looked askance at all innovation."

The Keynesian regulation of aggregate demand also requires only a word. It is a thoroughly well-established feature of modern industrial planning, although economists have pictured it *not* as a necessary aspect of planning but as a way of improving the market economy. The need for it follows in fact directly from modern industrial planning. As we have seen, corporations decide authoritatively what they will reserve from earnings for reinvestment and expansion. This planned corporate withholding is overwhelmingly important as a source of savings in the non-Soviet countries, as planned withholding by the state is the overwhelmingly important source of savings in the socialist economies. But in the non-Soviet economies there is no mechanism which insures that the amounts so withheld for investment will be matched in the economy as a whole by what is invested. That is to say there is no mechanism outside the state. So there must be direct action by the state to equate the two. And this the state does, primarily by manipulating spending and taxation. The need to equate the planned savings and the planned investment of the large corporations is not of course the only reason for such action. Saving and investment elsewhere in the economy must also be matched. But corporate savings and investment are by far the largest and most important in the total.

The successful regulation of demand requires that the quantitative role of the state in the modern economy be relatively large. Demand is regulated by increasing or decreasing the expenditures of the state or decreasing or increasing the taxes the state collects. Only when the state is large and its revenues substantial will these changes be large enough to serve. One effective way of insuring the requisite size is to have the state underwrite modern technology, which is admirably expensive. Such is the case with modern weaponry, space exploration, even highway and airport design. Technology . . . is a prime instrument in destroying the effectiveness of the market. But it does help make possible the planning that replaces the market.

The next function of the state is to provide the specialized and trained manpower which the industrial system cannot supply to itself. This has led in our time to a very great expansion in education, and especially in higher education, and this has been true in all of the advanced countries. In 1900 there were 24,000 teachers in colleges and universities in the United States; in 1920 there were 49,000; by 1970, three years hence, there will be 480,000. This is rarely pictured as an aspect of modern economic development; it is the vanity of educators like myself that we have the initiating power in this new enlightenment. But it is significant that when industry required for its purposes millions of unlettered proletarians, that is what the educational system supplied. As industry has come to need engineers, sales executives, copywriters, computer programmers, personnel managers, information retrieval specialists, product planners, and executive panjandrums, that is what the educational system has come to provide. I might say that anyone who listens to lectures should on occasion ask for some proof that is related to his common experience. And all who lecture should welcome this test. It arrests the mandarinism which is the principal occupational hazard of lecturers.

For proof of the point I have just made on specialized manpower you have only to turn to your Sunday, or even your daily, newspaper. Here you will find that every kind of esoteric and arcane specialism is being sought. Electronic engineers, senior systems programmers, instrument engineers, minerals dressing engineers, work study engineers, lady assistant training officers, and technically oriented personnel for an Embodiment Selling Team are my culling from a single London newspaper.

Once the ability to obtain capital was decisive for the firm that was seeking to expand. Now it is the supply of such manpower. Once in the industrially advanced world the community—or the nation—that wanted more industry gave first thought to its capital supply, and how to reassure the bankers. Now it gives first thought to its educational system: how to obtain the required specialists.

Nor can we be altogether happy about education that is so motivated. There is danger that it will be excessively vocational. We shall have a race of men who are strong on telemetry and space communications but who cannot read anything but a blueprint or write anything but a computer programme. When we realize that our new concern for education is the result not of a new enlightenment but a response to the needs of industrial planning, we shall begin to worry, I think, a good deal about the future of liberal and humane education. In the end college and university rectors, presidents and vice-chancellors may even make speeches about it, believing, as so many of these excellent men do, that a thoughtful speech is an effective substitute for serious action.

Much the most interesting of the planning functions of the state is the underwriting of expensive technology. Few changes in economic life have ever proceeded with such explosive rapidity. Few have so undermined conventional concepts of public and private enterprise. This activity includes . . . the direct financing of research and development; this is something on which the United States Government in 1962 spent an estimated $10.6 billions. This was more than its total dollar outlays for the United States Government for all purposes, military or civilian, before the second world war.

But this activity also involves the provision of a guaranteed market for a large number of highly technical products from aircraft to missiles to electronic gear to space vehicles. Nearly all of this expenditure—some 80–85 per cent.—goes to the large corporation, which is to say that it is in the planned sector of the American economy with which these lectures are concerned.[1] This activity brings the modern large corporation into the most inti-

[1] About 100 corporations and their subsidiaries accounted for 73.4 per cent of total Federal procurement in 1964. (H. L. Nieburg, *In The Name of Science*. Chicago Quadrangle Press, 1966, p. 192.)

mate association with the state; in the case of public agencies such as the United States Atomic Energy Commission or the United States Air Force, it is no longer easy to say where the public sector ends and the private sector begins. The private sector becomes, in effect, an extended arm of the public bureaucracy. I might add that no one flaunts the banner of private enterprise so aggressively as the firm that does 75 per cent. of its business with the government and yearns to have more.

In the past, it has been argued by good Keynesians that there is nothing very special about a particular kind of government business. Replying to standard Marxian charges that capitalism depends excessively on armaments, Keynesians have pointed out that spending for housing, concert halls and theatres, for more automobiles to drive into central London and for more highways to allow more automobiles to drive into central London, and for more radios to amuse people while they are sitting in the resulting traffic jams, and for other of the attributes of modern gracious living would serve just as well as spending on armaments. But this is not so certain. It is not that the Marxians are right; it is one of the rules of discourse that this must never be conceded. It is rather that the simple Keynesian view is incomplete.

The expenditures I have just mentioned for concert halls and highways would not serve to underwrite technology as do present expenditures of the state. And this underwriting is a function . . . that is beyond the reach of private planning. Replacement of military spending, with its emphasis on underwriting advanced technology, would have to be therefore by other equally technical outlays if it was to serve the same purpose. Otherwise, technology would have to be curtailed to that level where corporate planning units could underwrite it on their own. And this curtailment under present circumstances would be very, very drastic.

I find myself, in consequence of this analysis, a considerable supporter of the space race. It is not that I think that exploring the Moon, Mars, or even Saturn—which has always seemed to me the most original of the lot—is of high social urgency. And pleasant as it would be to select the passengers for the first flights, especially if they promise to be one-way, I imagine that President Johnson will want to do this himself. But the space race allows an extensive underwriting of advanced technology. And it does this in a field of activity where spending is large and where, in contrast with weapons and weapons systems, competition with the Soviets is comparatively safe and comparatively benign. So the turning of technological knowledge to this particular competition does not seem to me to be something we can entirely regret.

We see the modern corporation, in the technological aspects of its activities, moving into a very close association with the state. The state is the principal customer for such technology and the underwriter of major risk. In the planning of tasks and missions, the mapping of development work and the execution of contracts, there is nowadays a daily and intimate association between the bureaucracy and the large so-called private firm. But one thing, you will say, keeps them apart. You will say the state after all is in pursuit of broad national goals, whatever these may be. And the private firm is there to make money—in the more solemn language of economics it is there to maximise profits. This difference in goals, you will say, will always sufficiently differentiate the state from private enterprise.

But here again we find that the reality supplies that indispensable thread of consistency. For power, as we have seen, has passed from the owners of the corporation to the managers, and to the scientists and technicians. They now exercise full and autonomous power and, not surprisingly, they exercise it in their own interest. And this interest differs from that of the owners. For the managers and technicians security of return is more important than the level of total earnings. It is only when earnings fail that the power of the managers is threatened. And growth is more important to the managers than maximum earnings. That is because those in charge do not get the profits—or anyhow not much of them. But they—the scientists and technicians—do get the promotions, enlarged opportunities, higher salaries and prestige which go with growth of the firm. I might say here that for clarifying these matters I have been greatly indebted to the brilliant Cambridge economist Robin Marris, who has written very lucidly and very wisely on this question.

So here, following this line of thought, we encounter a remarkable fact. For economic security and growth as we reflect on it are also prime goals of the modern state. Nothing has been more emphasized in modern economic policy than the prevention of depression or recession. It is something that politicians promise automatically and without any perceptible thought. And no test of social achievement is so completely and totally accepted as the rate of economic growth. It is the common measure of accomplishment of all the economic systems. Transcending political faith, religion, occupation, or all except eccentric philosophical persuasion, the value of economic growth is something on which Americans, Russians, Englishmen, Frenchmen, Germans, Italians, and Yugoslavs all agree. I gather that not even the modern Irish dissent.

So there is in fact no conflict between essential goals and the goals of the leaders in the modern firms. On the contrary, there is a large symmetry. Both seek security. Both value growth. We have seen that, as an aspect of its planning, the modern industrial enterprise accommodates the behavior and beliefs of the individual consumer to its needs. It is reasonable to assume that it has also accommodated our social objectives and associated beliefs to what it needs. In any case, we may assume that there has been an interaction between state and firm which has brought the two to a unity of view.

A very sombre thought will occur to many of you here. We have seen that the state is necessary for underwriting the technology of modern industrial enterprise. Much of this it does within the framework of its military expenditure. In the consumer's goods economy, the wants and beliefs of the consumer, including his conviction that happiness is associated with the consumption of goods, these are all accommodated, in greater or less measure, to what producers need and want to produce. Is this true also of the state? Does it respond in its military procurement to what the supplying firms need to sell, and the technology that they wish to have underwritten? Are images of foreign policy in the planned industrial communities—in the United States, the Soviet Union, great industrial countries of western Europe—shaped by industrial need? Do we have an image of conflict because that serves technological and therewith planning need?

We cannot exclude that possibility; on the contrary, it is most plausible. We should also recall that it is a conclusion that was reached rather more intuitively by President Eisenhower while he was President of the United States. In President Eisenhower's now famous valedictory he warned of the influence of the "conjunction of an immense military establishment and a large arms industry." Our image is of a foreign policy which prescribes what will be required in responding armaments. This again will do for those for whom the mind is an instrument for evading reality. All others will see the possibility here of a two-way flow of influence. The image of the foreign policy affects the demand of the state on industry. But the needs of economic planning may affect the view of the state on foreign policy. And there can be few matters where it will be safer to be guided by reality. It will also be observed that I am not confining my argument here to any particular planned economy, west or east. We had better, at least in the beginning, worry lest it might be true of all.

SUGGESTED READING

Kenneth Boulding in *Book Week* (July 16, 1967) presents a penetrating critical review of Galbraith's *The New Industrial State*. George C. Allen's "Economic Fact and Fantasy: A Rejoinder to Galbraith's Reith Lectures" (Institute of Economic Affairs, 1967, Occasional Paper 14) also challenges Galbraith's theory of market control. Robert Solow's review, "The New Industrial State: Son of Affluence," in *The Public Interest*, No. 9 (Fall, 1967), 100–08, led to a further discussion in that issue and in *ibid.*, No. 11 (Spring, 1968), with Robin Morris's "Galbraith, Solow, and the Truth about Corporations," which supported Galbraith, thereby provoking a rejoinder from Solow in the same issue. Gabriel Kolko in *Wealth and Power in America* ° and Don Villarejo in "Stock Ownership and Control of Corporations," *New University Thought*, II (Autumn, 1961), 33–37, (Winter, 1962), 47–62, dispute the Berle-Means thesis about the divorce of managers and owners.

Arnold Rose's *The Power Structure* ° (Oxford Univ. Press, 1967) is a defense of pluralist theories. Disagreeing with the pluralists, C. Wright Mills in *The Power Élite* ° (Oxford Univ. Press, 1956) attributes power to the leaders of industry, the military, and the executive branch of government. G. William Domhoff, editor of *C. Wright Mills and the Power Élite* ° (Beacon Press, 1968), provides a collection of essays on Mills's theory and book. Talcott Parsons' "The Distribution of Power in American Society," *World Politics*, X (Oct., 1957), 123–43, is a temperate and challenging analysis of Mills's theories. Unfortunately, the Mills thesis—almost exclusively restricted to foreign policy—has not been explicitly tested by empirical investigations. Gabriel Kolko's *The Roots of American Foreign Policy* (Beacon Press, 1969), dissenting from Mills's theory, denies that military leaders have achieved "ascendancy" over political leaders and concludes that businessmen retain dominant power in government, which they use to assist their particular interests and to advance their class interests. Whereas Mills's volume lacked any theory of imperialism, Kolko contends that powerful business forces use the Government to protect and advance economic expansion abroad, which requires opposition to revolutions from the left.

Paul Baran and Paul Sweezy's *Monopoly Capital: The American Economic and Social Order* ° (Monthly Review Press, 1966) is a radical analysis by two leading Marxist scholars. David Bazelon's *The Paper Economy* ° (Random House, 1963); Michael Reagan's *The Managed Economy* ° (Oxford Univ. Press, 1963); and Richard Barber's "The New Partnership: Big Business and Big Government," *New Republic*, CLV (Aug. 13, 1966), 17–22, are analyses similar to Galbraith's. Richard Barber in *The Politics of Research* (Public Affairs Press, 1966) analyzes the dependence of corporations and scientists on the Federal Government. G. William Domhoff's *Who Rules America?* ° (Prentice-Hall, 1967) assaults pluralist conclusions about power in American society, and should be supplemented by Vernon K. Dibble's critical review in *Nation*, CCVII (Nov. 4, 1968), 469–74.

A 9
B 0
C 1
D 2
E 3
F 4
G 5
H 6
I 7
J 8

VERMONT COLLEGE
MONTPELIER, VERMONT